Practical Research

Planning and Design

EIGHTH EDITION

Paul D. Leedy
Late of American University

Jeanne Ellis Ormrod
University of Northern Colorado (Emerita)

University of New Hampshire

PEARSON

Merrill
Prentice Hall

Upper Saddle River, New Jersey
Columbus, Ohio

Library of Congress Cataloging in Publication Data
Leedy, Paul D.
    Practical research: planning and design--8th ed. / Paul D. Leedy and Jeanne Ellis Ormrod.
        p. cm.
    Includes bibliographical references and index.
    ISBN 0-13-110895-6
    1. Research--Methodology. I. Ormrod, Jeanne Ellis. II. Title

Q180.55.M4L43 2005
001.4--dc22   2003066035

Vice President and Executive Publisher: Jeffery W. Johnston
Publisher: Kevin M. Davis
Development Editor: Julie Peters, Autumn Crisp Benson
Editorial Assistant: Amanda King
Production Editor: Mary Harlan
Production Coordinator: Lea Baranowski, Carlisle Publishers Services
Design Coordinator: Diane C. Lorenzo
Text Design and Illustrations: Carlisle Publishers Services
Cover Design: Terry Rohrbach
Cover Image: Corbis
Production Manager: Laura Messerly
Director of Marketing: Ann Castel Davis
Marketing Manager: Autumn Purdy
Marketing Coordinator: Tyra Poole

This book was set in Garamond 3 by Carlisle Communications, Ltd. It was printed and bound by Courier Kendallville, Inc. The cover was printed by The Lehigh Press, Inc.

Pearson Education Ltd.
Pearson Education Singapore Pte. Ltd.
Pearson Education Canada, Ltd.
Pearson Education–Japan

Pearson Education Australia Pty. Limited
Pearson Education North Asia Ltd.
Pearson Educación de Mexico, S.A. de C.V.
Pearson Education Malaysia Pte. Ltd.

10 9 8 7 6 5 4 3 2 1
ISBN: 0-13-110895-6

PAUL D. LEEDY
1908–2002

I first met Paul Leedy in the pages of *Practical Research.* Merrill was beginning preparations for work on the fifth edition, and opening the book, I was surprised to find the acknowledgments section on the very first page of the text. One usually finds the acknowledgments tucked at the end of a preface or embedded in a foreword. I was even more surprised to find the section start with lines written over four hundred years ago by John Donne.

> *No man is an Iland, entire of it selfe; every man*
> *Is a peece of the continent, a part of the maine. . .*

A strange beginning for a research textbook, but I liked it. I liked its elegance, its humility. As I read on, I liked the book more and more and started, in fact, to like its author. I liked him because he wrote well, because his prose had something that is relatively rare in textbooks—a voice. Moreover, he not only spoke to his readers, but he also understood what his readers did and did not know. And what was perhaps even more important, in addition to understanding how to conduct research, Leedy also understood how to teach someone how to do research. A few days after my initial reading of *Practical Research,* I spoke with Paul on the phone to discuss a revision plan for the upcoming edition. The Paul Leedy I had met in the pages of his book was the same person I met on the phone that day. Over the decade we worked together, I came to know him as a man with an unwavering commitment to his readers' needs.

When Paul's son called me in August of 2002 to let me know that Paul had died, I remembered my first experience reading Paul's book, and I felt how true Donne's words were. Indeed, no man is an island. Paul lived those words in how he collaborated with publishing people, students, and professors to make his book better. Though, as Paul generously points out, over the years many people contributed to *Practical Research,* Paul's was the largest part in making the book. It was Paul's idea to do a practical, straightforward, hands-on text that would teach people how to do research regardless of their field of study. It was Paul who wrote the first six editions of the text. Each editor who worked with Paul, each of the hundreds of thousands of students who have used his book to help them in their first attempts at research, and each of the instructors who have used the book to help them teach owes Paul, as Paul gives to them in his acknowledgments, "acknowledgment and appreciation." I know I owe him at least that. There is another line in the Donne meditation quoted in *Practical Research.* I am sure that Paul knew this line too—"any man's death diminishes me." If this is true, it must also hold that any person's life enriches me. I learned a good deal from working with Paul, and I am grateful for it. And although I can still find him in the pages of his book, I know his legacy stretches well beyond the boundary of the covers of this text.

Kevin M. Davis
Publisher

ACKNOWLEDGMENTS

*No man is an Iland, entire of it selfe; every man
is a peece of the Continent, a part of the maine. . . .*

So wrote John Donne, the great Dean of St. Paul's Cathedral in the seventeenth century. And so write we at the beginning of the twenty-first.

Those who have had a part in the making of this book, known and unknown, friends and colleagues, gentle critics and able editors—all—are far too many to salute individually. Those of you who have written in journals and textbooks about research methods and strategies, the generations of graduates and undergraduates whom we have taught and who have also taught *us*, the kindly letters and e-mails that so many of you have written to tell us how this book has helped you in your own research endeavors—to all of you, we extend our acknowledgment and appreciation wherever you may be. You have had the greater part in bringing this book through its previous seven editions. To the reviewers who counseled us and piloted this eighth edition into safe harbor, we are especially grateful: Elizabeth Easter, University of Kentucky; H. Michael Johnson, Webster University; Rena Lewis, San Diego State University; Richard Paxton, University of Wisconsin–Oshkosh; and Sudipto Roy, Indiana State University. Their thorough scrutiny of the previous edition and creative suggestions for additions and modifications have enhanced this book considerably.

We are also indebted to the students whose doctoral dissertations and master's theses have enabled us to illustrate many of the research and writing strategies described in the book. In particular, we extend gratitude to Rosenna Bakari, Arthur Benton, Kay Corbett, Dinah Jackson, Ginny Kinnick, Peter Leavenworth, Matthew McKenzie, Kimberly Mitchell, Richard Ormrod, Luis Ramirez, Janie Shaklee, Nancy Thrailkill, and Debby Zambo. Peter Leavenworth and Matt McKenzie gave us their time as well as their research reports, and their recommendations for the chapter on historical research were superb.

No author is an island, entire of itself. Every author has had many hands guiding his or her pen and many minds adding richness and depth to his or her own thoughts. All of you have been exceedingly helpful, all of you have been "a peece of the continent, a part of the maine." For that, we offer our humble and hearty thanks.

Jeanne Ellis Ormrod

DISCOVER THE COMPANION WEBSITE ACCOMPANYING THIS BOOK

THE PRENTICE HALL COMPANION WEBSITE: A VIRTUAL LEARNING ENVIRONMENT

Technology is a constantly growing and changing aspect of our field that is creating a need for content and resources. To address this emerging need, Prentice Hall has developed an online learning environment for students and professors alike—Companion Websites—to support our textbooks.

In creating a Companion Website, our goal is to build on and enhance what the textbook already offers. For this reason, the content for each user-friendly website is organized by chapter and provides the professor and student with a variety of meaningful resources.

FOR THE PROFESSOR

Every Companion Website integrates **Syllabus Manager**™, an online syllabus creation and management utility.

- **Syllabus Manager**™ provides you, the instructor, with an easy, step-by-step process to create and revise syllabi, with direct links into Companion Website and other online content without having to learn HTML.
- Students may logon to your syllabus during any study session. All they need to know is the web address for the Companion Website and the password you've assigned to your syllabus.
- After you have created a syllabus using **Syllabus Manager**™, students may enter the syllabus for their course section from any point in the Companion Website.
- Clicking on a date, the student is shown the list of activities for the assignment. The activities for each assignment are linked directly to actual content, saving time for students
- Adding assignments consists of clicking on the desired due date, then filling in the details of the assignment—name of the assignment, instructions, and whether it is a one-time or repeating assignment.
- In addition, links to other activities can be created easily. If the activity is online, a URL can be entered in the space provided, and it will be linked automatically in the final syllabus.
- Your completed syllabus is hosted on our servers, allowing convenient updates from any computer on the Internet. Changes you make to your syllabus are immediately available to your students at their next logon.

FOR THE STUDENT

Companion Website features for students include:

- **Chapter Objectives**—Outline key concepts from the text.
- **Projects**—Allow students to become familiar with conducting research on the Web. Self-assessment quizzes are often linked to chapter projects and text applications or guidelines.
- **Interactive Self-quizzes**—Complete with hints and automatic grading that provide immediate feedback for students. After students submit their answers for the interactive self-quizzes, the Companion Website **Results Reporter** computes a percentage grade, provides a graphic representation of how many questions were answered correctly and incorrectly, and gives a question-by-question analysis of the quiz. Students are given the option to send their quiz to up to four email addresses (professor, teaching assistant, study partner, etc.).
- **Net Searches**—Offer links by key terms from each chapter to related Internet content.
- **Web Destinations**—Link to www sites that relate to chapter content.
- **Message Board**—Serves as a virtual bulletin board to post or respond to questions or comments from a national audience.

To take advantage of the many available resources, please visit the *Practical Research: Planning and Design*, Eighth Edition, Companion Website at

www.prenhall.com/leedy

RESEARCH NAVIGATOR: RESEARCH MADE SIMPLE!

www.ResearchNavigator.com

Merrill Education is pleased to introduce Research Navigator—a one-stop research solution for students that simplifies and streamlines the entire research process. At www.researchnavigator .com, students will find extensive resources to enhance their understanding of the research process so they can effectively complete research assignments. In addition, Research Navigator has three exclusive databases of credible and reliable source content to help students focus their research efforts and begin the research process.

HOW WILL RESEARCH NAVIGATOR ENHANCE YOUR COURSE?

- Extensive content on understanding the research process, including writing, Internet research, and citing sources
- Step-by-step tutorial guides students through the entire research process from selecting a topic to revising a rough draft
- Research Writing in the Disciplines section details the differences in research across disciplines
- Three exclusive databases—EBSCO's ContentSelect Academic Journal Database, *The New York Times* Search by Subject Archive, and "Best of the Web" Link Library—allow students to easily find journal articles and sources

WHAT'S THE COST?

A subscription to Research Navigator is $7.50 but is **free** when used in conjunction with this textbook. To obtain free passcodes for your students, simply contact your local Merril/Prentice Hall sales representative, and your representative will send you the Evaluating Online Resource Guide which contains the code to access Research Navigator as well as tips on how to use Research Navigator and how to evaluate research. To preview the value of this Web site to your students, please go to www.educatorlearningcenter.com and use the Login Name "Research" and the password "Demo."

BRIEF CONTENTS

CONTENTS

PART II   FOCUSING YOUR RESEARCH EFFORTS

CHAPTER 3

THE PROBLEM: THE HEART OF THE RESEARCH PROCESS   . . .43

CHAPTER 4

REVIEW OF THE RELATED LITERATURE 64

CHAPTER 5

PLANNING YOUR RESEARCH PROJECT 85

PART III   QUALITATIVE RESEARCH METHODOLOGIES

CHAPTER 7

QUALITATIVE RESEARCH 133

Contents   xix

Appendix   Using SPSS

NOTE: Every effort has been made to provide accurate and current Internet information in this book. However, the Internet and information posted on it are constantly changing, so it is inevitable that some of the Internet addresses listed in this textbook will change.

INTRODUCTION

THE PURPOSE OF THIS BOOK

Practical Research: Planning and Design is a broad-spectrum book suitable for all courses in basic research methodology. Unlike many texts, *Practical Research* was not written for any particular course or discipline. Many basic concepts and strategies in research transcend the boundaries of specific academic areas, and such concepts and strategies are at the heart of this book. To some degree, research methods vary from one subject area to another: The biologist gathers data by way of the microscope, the sociologist by using a questionnaire or interview, and the psychologist perhaps through tests or observations of behavior. Otherwise, the basic approach to research is the same. Regardless of the discipline, the researcher analyzes the obtained data, interprets it, and reaches conclusions that the data seem to warrant.

Students in education, the social sciences, the natural sciences, business administration, landscape architecture, nursing, and related academic disciplines have used this text as a guide to the successful completion of their research projects. *Practical Research* guides students from problem selection to completed research report with practical suggestions based on a solid theoretical framework and sound pedagogical devices. Students come to understand that research needs planning and design, and they discover how their own research projects can be executed effectively and professionally. Essentially, this is a do-it-yourself, understand-it-yourself manual. From that standpoint, it can be a guide for students who are left largely to their own resources in carrying out their research projects. The book, supplemented by occasional counseling by an academic advisor, can guide the student to the completion of a successful research report.

LEARNING ABOUT RESEARCH SHOULD BEGIN EARLY

Many students have found that *Practical Research* has helped them both to understand the nature of the research process and to complete their research projects. Its simplification of research concepts and its readability make it especially suitable for those undergraduate and graduate situations where students are introduced, perhaps for the first time, to genuine research methodology.

All too often, students labor under the assumption that merely transferring facts from one place to another and incorporating them into an extended, footnoted paper is a genuine research endeavor. They reach the threshold of a master's thesis or doctoral dissertation only to learn that simply assembling previously known facts is insufficient and unacceptable. Instead, they must do something that is entirely foreign to them: They must answer a question that has never been answered before and, in the process, discover something that no one else has ever discovered.

Something has gone tragically wrong in the education of students who have, for so many years of their schooling, entirely misunderstood the true nature of research.

Research has one end: the ultimate discovery of truth. Its purpose is to learn what has never been known before; to ask a significant question for which no conclusive answer has previously been found; and, by collecting and interpreting relevant data, to find an answer to that question.

Research Is More Than an Academic Requirement

Learning about and doing research are of value far beyond that of merely satisfying a program requirement. Research methods and their applications to the solution of problem situations are skills that will serve you for the rest of your life. Rightly considered, they should give you an opportunity to look beyond the classroom to the world of authentic research activity. And what you will see there is incredibly exciting.

The real world is alive with problems and, consequently, with research activity! Research is everywhere. The media are replete with fascinating reports of life-saving discoveries, of wonders on the earth, and of discoveries in the vastness of the universe—all the results of research. Research is not an academic banality; it is a vital and dynamic force that is indispensable to modern progress. Ultimately, perhaps, research may be the key to the continuing existence of the human species on this planet.

More immediate, however, is the need to apply research methodology to those lesser daily problems that nonetheless demand a thoughtful resolution. Those who have learned how to analyze problems systematically and dispassionately will live with more self-assurance and less panic than those who have shortsightedly dismissed research as nothing more than a necessary hurdle on the way to a degree. Given the advantages that a researcher's viewpoint provides, considering an academic research requirement as annoying and irrelevant to one's education is simply untenable.

KEY FEATURES OF THIS EDITION

The overall organization of this edition is generally the same as that of the preceding edition, although a few topics have migrated from one chapter to another. We have updated, streamlined, reorganized, and/or expanded our discussions of numerous topics, and we have added sections on several others.

New Topics

Key among the new, expanded, and significant revised topics in this edition are the following:

- Basic versus applied research (Chapter 1)
- Error in measurement (Chapter 2)
- Collaboration with other researchers (Chapter 2)
- Suggestions for effective use of a word processor (Chapter 2)
- Online databases (Chapters 2 and 8)
- Sampling in qualitative research (Chapter 7)
- Oral histories (Chapter 8)
- Conducting research on the Internet (Chapters 9 and 10)
- Within-subjects, single-group, single-subject, and multiple baseline designs (Chapter 10)
- Meta-analysis (Chapters 10 and 11)
- Computing standard scores (Chapter 11)
- Correlation of determination (Chapter 11)
- Structural equation modeling (Chapter 11)
- Referencing sources obtained on the Internet (Chapter 12)
- Using SPSS to conduct simple descriptive and inferential data analyses (Appendix)

In addition, we have added three new "sample dissertations" near the ends of Chapters 8, 9, and 11.

Support for Developing a Research Project

To some degree, this text is expressly written for students who are conducting a research project as part of an academic degree program and for novice researchers who are writing proposals for research grants. To help these individuals, we have included several key features throughout the book.

PRACTICAL APPLICATIONS. Each chapter has one or more "Practical Application" sections in which readers apply principles presented in the chapter. Some of these are in the form of exercises relevant to chapter content. Others are **guidelines** that provide helpful hints for executing an aspect of the research process more effectively. Still others are **checklists** that enable readers to apply evaluative criteria to their research proposals, projects, and reports. Taken together, these practical applications help readers do precisely what the title of this book suggests: *plan* and *design* a research project.

USING TECHNOLOGY. Basic computer literacy is an *absolute must* for the 21st-century researcher. Throughout the book, we have included many suggestions for how our readers might use computer technology to make the research process more efficient, and we have marked such discussions with "using technology" icons in the margins. From online literature searches to word processing programs, from questionnaire scanners to statistical software packages, computer hardware and software provide tools for the researcher that we could never have anticipated three or four decades ago.

RESOURCES ON THE WORLD WIDE WEB. With each passing day, the World Wide Web is becoming an increasingly valuable resource for researchers in all academic disciplines. Throughout the book, we identify Websites that readers might find useful, with a particular eye on those sites that have been around for a while and are likely to remain in place throughout the life of this edition.

SAMPLE PROPOSALS AND DISSERTATIONS. Students can learn a great deal from seeing how their peers have handled various topics in research proposals and final dissertations. Eight of the 12 chapters in this edition have lengthy excerpts from either doctoral dissertation proposals (Chapters 3, 4, and 6) or completed dissertations (Chapters 7, 8, 9, 10, and 11). These excerpts come from a variety of subject areas, including child development, education, history, nursing, human resources, psychology, and sociology. Shorter excerpts from additional dissertations are embedded throughout the book to illustrate particular methods and writing strategies.

AND SO . . . BON VOYAGE!

Now you have seen the philosophy and rationale that underlie this text. We have shared with you our reasons for writing the text and, we hope, convinced you that research methodology is not a temporary hurdle on the way to a degree but, instead, an unparalleled opportunity to learn how you might better tackle any problem for which you do not have a ready solution. In a few years you will undoubtedly look back on your course in research methodology as one of the most rewarding and practical courses in your entire educational experience. We have found it so in our own experience, and scores of our students have expressed a similar opinion.

Part I

The Fundamentals

1

What Is Research?

In virtually every subject area, our knowledge is incomplete and problems are waiting to be solved. We can address the holes in our knowledge and those unresolved problems by asking relevant questions and then seeking answers through systematic research.

The word *research* as it is used in everyday speech has a broad range of meanings, making it a decidedly confusing term for students, especially graduate students, who must learn to use the word in a narrower, more precise sense. From elementary school to college, students hear the word *research* used in the context of a variety of activities. In some situations, the word connotes finding an item of information or making notes and then writing a documented paper. In other situations, it refers to the act of informing oneself about what one does not know, perhaps by rummaging through available sources to retrieve a bit of information. Merchandisers sometimes use the word to suggest the discovery of a revolutionary product when, in reality, an existing product has been slightly modified to enhance the product's sales appeal. All these activities have been called research but are more appropriately called other names: information gathering, library skills, documentation, self-enlightenment, or an attention-getting sales pitch.

The word *research* has a certain mystique about it. To many people, it suggests an activity that is somehow exclusive and removed from everyday life. Researchers are sometimes regarded as aloof individuals who seclude themselves in laboratories, scholarly libraries, or the ivory towers of large universities. The public is often unaware of what researchers do on a day-to-day basis or of how their work contributes to people's overall quality of life and general welfare.

The purpose of this chapter is to dispel such myths and misconceptions about research. In the next few pages, we describe what research *is not* and then what it *is*.

WHAT RESEARCH IS NOT

We have suggested that the word *research* has been so loosely employed in everyday speech that few people have any idea of its real meaning. Following are several statements that describe what research is not. Accompanying each statement is an example that illustrates a common misconception about research.

1. *Research is not mere information gathering.* A fourth-grade student comes home from school with this announcement: "Mom, the teacher sent us to the library today to do research, and I

learned a lot about native Americans." This child has been given the idea that research means going to the library to get information or to glean a few facts. This may be *information discovery;* it may be learning *reference skills;* but it certainly is not, as the teacher labeled it, research.

2. *Research is not mere transportation of facts from one location to another.*   A student completes a "research paper" on the Dark Lady in the sonnets of William Shakespeare. Although the student did, indeed, go through certain activities associated with formal research—collecting data, assembling a bibliography, referencing statements properly—these activities still do not add up to a true research paper. The student missed the essence of research: the interpretation of data. Nowhere in the paper did the student say, in effect, "These facts that I have gathered seem to indicate *this* about the Dark Lady." Nowhere did the student draw conclusions or interpret the facts themselves. This student is approaching genuine research; however, the mere compilation of facts, presented with reference citations and arranged in a series—no matter how polished and appealing the format— misses genuine research by a hair. A little farther, and this student would have traveled from one world to another: from the world of mere transportation of fact to the world of interpretation of fact. The difference between the two worlds is the distinction between transference of information and genuine research, a distinction that is critical for novice researchers to understand.

Unfortunately, many students think that looking up a few facts and presenting them in a written paper with benefit of references constitutes research. Such activity is, of course, more realistically called *fact discovery*, *fact transportation*, and/or *fact transcription*.

3. *Research is not merely rummaging for information.*   The house across the street is for sale. You consider buying it, and so you call your realtor to find out for how much your present home would sell. "I'll have to do some research to determine the fair market value of your property," the realtor tells you. What the realtor calls doing "some research" means, of course, reviewing information about recent sales of properties comparable to yours; this information will help the realtor zero in on a reasonable asking price for your current home. Such an activity involves little more than rummaging through files to discover what the realtor previously did not know. Rummaging, whether through one's personal records or at the public or college library, is not research. It is more accurately called an *exercise in self-enlightenment*.

4. *Research is not a catchword used to get attention.*   The morning mail arrives. You open an envelope and pull out its contents. A statement in colorful type commands attention:

> Years of Research Have Produced a New Car Wash!
> Give Your Car a Miracle Shine with Soapy Suds!

The phrase "years of research" catches your attention. The product must be good, you reason, because years of research have been spent on developing it. You order the product, and what do you get? Dishwashing detergent! No research, merely the clever use of a catchword that, indeed, fulfilled its purpose: to catch your attention. "Years of research"—what an attention-getting phrase, yet how misleading!

As we define the term, research is entirely different from any of the activities listed previously. We describe its essential nature and characteristics in the following section.

WHAT RESEARCH IS

Research is a systematic process of collecting, analyzing, and interpreting information (data) in order to increase our understanding of the phenomenon about which we are interested or concerned. People often use a systematic approach when they collect and interpret information to solve the small problems of daily living. Here, however, we focus on *formal research,* research in which we intentionally set out to enhance our understanding of a phenomenon and expect to communicate what we discover to the larger scientific community.

Although research projects vary in complexity and duration, research typically has eight distinct characteristics:

1. Research originates with a question or problem.
2. Research requires clear articulation of a goal.

3. Research requires a specific plan for proceeding.
4. Research usually divides the principal problem into more manageable subproblems.
5. Research is guided by the specific research problem, question, or hypothesis.
6. Research accepts certain critical assumptions.
7. Research requires the collection and interpretation of data in an attempt to resolve the problem that initiated the research.
8. Research is, by its nature, cyclical or, more exactly, helical.

Each of these characteristics is discussed in turn so that you can appreciate more fully the nature of formal research.

1. *Research originates with a question or problem.*   The world is filled with unanswered questions and unresolved problems. Everywhere we look, we see things that cause us to wonder, to speculate, to ask questions. And by asking questions, we strike the first spark igniting a chain reaction that leads to the research process. An inquisitive mind is the beginning of research; as one popular tabloid puts it, "Inquiring minds want to know!"

Look around you. Consider the unresolved situations that evoke these questions: What is such-and-such a situation like? Why does such-and-such a phenomenon occur? What does it all mean? These are everyday questions. With questions like these, research begins.

In Chapter 3, we will discuss the research problem at greater length. The problem and its statement are important because they are the point of origin of formal research.

2. *Research requires clear articulation of a goal.*   A clear, unambiguous statement of the problem is critical. This statement is an exercise in intellectual honesty: The ultimate goal of the research must be set forth clearly and precisely in a grammatically complete sentence. The statement answers the question, "What problem do you intend to solve?" It is essential for the success of any research undertaking; without it, the research is on very shaky ground.

3. *Research requires a specific plan for proceeding.*   Research is not a blind excursion into the unknown, with the hope that the data necessary to answer the question at hand will somehow fortuitously turn up. It is, instead, a carefully planned attack, a search-and-discover mission explicitly outlined in advance. Consider the title of this text: *Practical Research: Planning and Design.* The last three words are the important ones. Researchers plan their overall research design and specific research methods in a purposeful way so that they can acquire data relevant to their research problem. Depending on the research question, different designs and methods will be more or less appropriate.

Therefore, in addition to identifying the specific goal of your research, you must also identify how you propose to reach your goal. You cannot wait until you're chin deep in the project to plan and design your strategy. In the formative stages of a research project, much can be decided: Where are the data? Do any existing data address themselves to the research problem? If the data exist, are you likely to have access to them? And if you have access to the data, what will you do with them after they are in your possession? We might go on and on. These questions merely hint at the fact that planning and design cannot be postponed. Each of the questions just listed must have an answer early in the research process.[1]

4. *Research usually divides the principal problem into more manageable subproblems.*   From a design standpoint, it is often helpful to break a main research problem into several subproblems that, when solved, will resolve the main problem.

Breaking down principal problems into small, easily solvable subproblems is a strategy we use in everyday living. For example, suppose you want to get from your hometown to a town 50 miles away. Your principal goal is to get from one location to the other as expeditiously as possible. You soon realize, however, that the problem involves several subproblems:

Main problem: How do I get from Town A to Town B?
Subproblems: 1. What is the most direct route?
                  2. How far do I travel on the highway?
                  3. Which exit should I take to leave the highway?

---

[1] It should be apparent from the questions in this paragraph that we are using the word *data* as a plural noun (For instance, we ask "Where *are* the data?" rather than "Where *is* the data?"). Contrary to popular belief, *data,* which was originally a Latin word, refers to more than one piece of information. A single piece of information is known as a *datum,* or sometimes as a *data point.*

What seems like a single question can be divided into at least three smaller questions that must be addressed before the principal question can be resolved.

So it is with most research problems. By closely inspecting the principal problem, the researcher often uncovers important subproblems. By addressing each of the subproblems, the researcher can more easily address the main problem. If researchers don't take the time or trouble to isolate the lesser problems within the major problem, their research projects can become cumbersome and unwieldy.

5. *Research is guided by the specific research problem, question, or hypothesis.*   Having stated the problem and its attendant subproblems, the researcher usually forms one or more hypotheses about what he or she may discover. A **hypothesis** is a logical supposition, a reasonable guess, an educated conjecture. It provides a tentative explanation for a phenomenon under investigation. It may direct your thinking to possible sources of information that will aid in resolving one or more subproblems and, in the process, the principal research problem.

Hypotheses are not unique to research. They are constant, recurring features of everyday life. They represent the natural working of the human mind. Something happens. Immediately you attempt to account for the cause of the event by making a series of reasonable guesses. In so doing, you are hypothesizing. As an example, let's take a commonplace event: You come home after dark, open the front door, and reach inside for the switch that turns on a nearby table lamp. Your fingers find the switch. You flip it. No light. At this point, you begin to construct a series of reasonable guesses—hypotheses—to explain the lamp's failure:

1. The bulb has burned out.
2. The lamp is not plugged into the wall outlet.
3. A late afternoon thunderstorm interrupted the electrical service.
4. The wire from the lamp to the wall outlet is defective.
5. You forgot to pay your electric bill.

Each of these hypotheses provides a direction to proceed in order to acquire information that may resolve the problem of the malfunctioning lamp. Now you go in search of information to determine which hypothesis is correct. In other words, you look for data that will support one of your hypotheses and enable you to reject others.

1. You go out to your car, get a flashlight, find a new bulb, and insert the new bulb. The lamp fails to light. (Hypothesis 1 is rejected.)
2. You glance down at the wall outlet and see that the lamp is plugged into it. (Hypothesis 2 is rejected.)
3. You look at your neighbors' homes. Everyone has electrical power. (Hypothesis 3 is rejected.)
4. You go back into your house and lift the cord that connects the lamp to the wall outlet. The lamp lights briefly and then goes out. You lift the cord again. Again, the lamp lights briefly. The connecting cord is defective. (Hypothesis 4 is supported.)
5. Fortunately, hypothesis 4 solved the problem, and by repairing or replacing the cord, you can count on adequate light in the near future.

In research, hypotheses are rarely proved or disproved; instead, they are either supported or not supported by the data. When the data run contrary to a particular hypothesis, the researcher *rejects* that hypothesis and turns to others as being more likely explanations of the phenomenon in question.

Over time, as particular hypotheses are supported by a growing body of data, they evolve into theories. A **theory** is an organized body of concepts and principles intended to explain a particular phenomenon. Like hypotheses, theories are tentative explanations that new data either support or do not support; to the extent that new data contradict a particular theory, a researcher will either modify it to better account for the data or reject the theory altogether in favor of an alternative explanation.

One common way of testing a theory is to make a prediction (hypothesis) about what should occur *if the theory is a viable explanation of the phenomenon under study*. As an example, let's consider Albert Einstein's theory of relativity, first proposed in 1915. Within the context of his theory, Einstein hypothesized that light passes through space as photons—tiny masses of spectral energy. If light has mass, Einstein reasoned, then it should be subject to the pull of a gravitational field.

A year later, K. Schwarzschild predicted that, based on Einstein's reasoning, the gravitational field of the sun should bend light rays considerably more than Isaac Newton had predicted many years earlier. In May 1919, a group of English astronomers traveled to Brazil and North Africa to observe how the sun's gravity distorted the light of a distant star now visible due to an eclipse of the sun. After the data were analyzed and interpreted, the results clearly supported the Einstein-Schwarzschild hypothesis and, thus, Einstein's theory of relativity.

At this point, we should return to a point made earlier, this time emphasizing a particular word: The researcher *usually* forms one or more hypotheses about what he or she may discover. Hypotheses—predictions—are an essential ingredient in certain kinds of research, especially experimental research (see Chapter 10). To a lesser degree, they guide most other forms of research as well, but they are intentionally *not* identified in the early stages of some kinds of qualitative research (e.g., see the discussion of grounded theory research in Chapter 7). Yet regardless of whether researchers form specific hypotheses in advance, they must, at a minimum, use their research problem or question to focus their efforts.

6. *Research accepts certain critical assumptions.*   In research, assumptions are equivalent to axioms in geometry—self-evident truths, the *sine qua non* of research. The assumptions must be valid or else the research is meaningless. For this reason, careful researchers—certainly those conducting research in an academic environment—set forth a statement of their assumptions as the bedrock upon which their study must rest. In your own research, it is essential that others know what you assume to be true with respect to your project. If one is to judge the quality of your study, then the knowledge of what you assume as basic to the very existence of your study is vitally important.

An example may clarify the point. Suppose your problem is to investigate whether students learn the unique grammatical structures of a language more quickly by studying only one foreign language at a time or by studying two foreign languages concurrently. What assumptions would underlie such a problem? At a minimum, the researcher must assume that

- The teachers used in the study are competent to teach the language or languages in question and have mastered the grammatical structures of the language(s) they are teaching.
- The students taking part in the research are capable of mastering the unique grammatical structures of any language(s) they are studying.
- The languages selected for the study have sufficiently different grammatical structures that students could learn to distinguish between them.

Whereas a hypothesis involves a prediction that may or may not be born out in the data, an **assumption** is a condition that is taken for granted, without which the research project would be pointless. In the Einstein example presented earlier, we assume that the astronomers who went to observe the star's light were competent to do so and that their instruments were sensitive enough to measure the slight aberration caused by the sun's gravitational pull.

Assumptions are usually so self-evident that a researcher may consider it unnecessary to mention them. For instance, two assumptions underlie almost all research:

- The phenomenon under investigation is somewhat lawful and predictable; it is *not* comprised of completely random events.
- Certain cause-effect relationships can account for the patterns observed in the phenomenon.

Aside from such basic ideas as these, careful researchers state their assumptions, so that others inspecting the research project may evaluate it in accordance with their *own* assumptions. For the beginning researcher, it is better to be overly explicit than to take too much for granted.

7. *Research requires the collection and interpretation of data in an attempt to resolve the problem that initiated the research.*   After a researcher has isolated the problem, divided it into appropriate subproblems, posited reasonable questions or hypotheses, and identified the assumptions that are basic to the entire effort, the next step is to collect whatever data seem appropriate and to organize them in meaningful ways so that they can be interpreted.

Data, events, and observations are, in and of themselves, *only* data, events, and observations—nothing more. The significance of the data depends on how the researcher extracts *meaning* from them. In research, data uninterpreted by the human mind are worthless: They can never help us answer the questions we have posed.

Yet researchers must recognize and come to terms with the subjective and dynamic nature of interpretation. Consider the myriad of books written on the assassination of U.S. President John F. Kennedy. Different historians have studied the same events: One may interpret them one way, and another may arrive at an entirely different conclusion. Which one is right? Perhaps they both are; perhaps neither is. Both may have merely posed new problems for other historians to try to resolve. Different minds often find different meanings in the same set of facts.

Once we believed that clocks measured time and that yardsticks measured space. In one sense, they still do. We further assumed that time and space were two different entities. Then came Einstein's theory of relativity, and time and space became locked into one concept: the time-space continuum. What is the difference between the old perspective and the new perspective? The way we think about, or interpret, the same information. The realities of time and space have not changed; the way we interpret them has.

Underlying and unifying any research project is its methodology. The research methodology directs the whole endeavor: It controls the study, dictates how the data are acquired, arranges them in logical relationships, sets up an approach for refining and synthesizing them, suggests a manner in which the meanings that lie below the surface of the data become manifest, and finally yields a conclusion or series of conclusions that leads to an expansion of knowledge. Thus, research methodology has two primary functions:

1. To control and dictate the acquisition of data
2. To corral the data after their acquisition and extract meaning from them

The second of these functions is what we mean by the phrase *interpretation of the data*.

Data demand interpretation. But no rule, formula, or algorithm can lead the researcher unerringly to a correct interpretation. Interpretation is inevitably subjective: It depends entirely on the hypotheses, assumptions, and logical reasoning processes of the researcher. In later chapters, we will present a number of potentially useful methods of organizing and interpreting data.

Now think about how we began this chapter. We suggested that certain activities cannot accurately be called research. At this point, you can understand why. None of those activities demands that the researcher draw any conclusions or make any interpretation of the data.

8. *Research is, by its nature, cyclical or, more exactly, helical.*   The research process follows a cycle and begins simply. It follows logical, developmental steps:
   a. A questioning mind observes a particular situation and asks, Why? What caused that? How come? (This is the subjective origin of research.)
   b. One question becomes formally stated as a problem. (This is the overt beginning of research.)
   c. The problem is divided into several simpler, more specific subproblems.
   d. Preliminary data are gathered that appear to bear on the problem.
   e. The data seem to point to a tentative solution of the problem. A guess is made; a hypothesis or guiding question is formed.
   f. Data are collected more systematically.
   g. The body of data is processed and interpreted.
   h. A discovery is made; a conclusion is reached.
   i. The tentative hypothesis is either supported by the data or is not supported; the question is either answered (partially or completely) or not answered.
   j. The cycle is complete.

The resolution of the problem or the tentative answer to the question completes the cycle, as is shown in Figure 1.1. Such is the format of all research. Different academic disciplines merely use different routes to arrive at the same destination.

But the neatly closed circle of Figure 1.1 is deceptive. Research is rarely conclusive. In a truer sense, the research cycle might be more accurately conceived of as a *helix*, or spiral, of research. In exploring an area, one comes across additional problems that need resolving, and so the process must begin anew. Research begets more research.

To view research in this way is to invest it with a dynamic quality that is its true nature— a far cry from the conventional view, which sees research as a one-time act that is static, self-contained, an end in itself. Here we see another difference between true research and the

The research cycle

THE RESEARCH PROCESS IS CYCLICAL

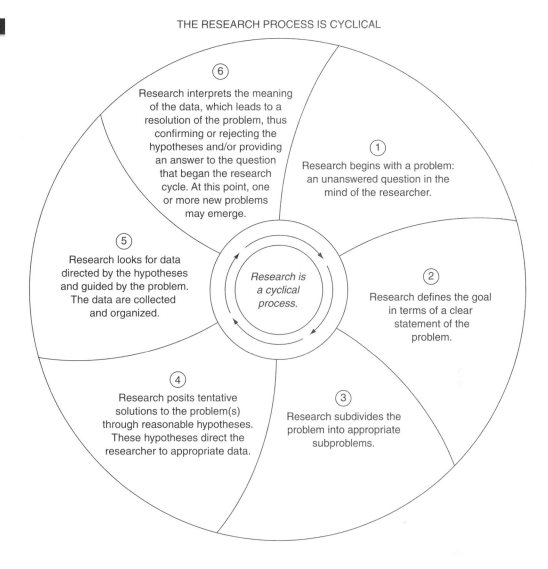

nonexamples of research with which this chapter opened. Every researcher soon learns that genuine research yields as many problems as it resolves. Such is the nature of the acquisition of knowledge.

DISCOVERING THE DISCIPLINE OF RESEARCH

Earlier in the chapter, we mentioned that academic research is popularly seen as an activity far removed from everyday living. Even graduate students working on theses or dissertations may consider their task to be mere academic busywork that has little or no relevance to the world beyond the university campus. Such is simply not true. Conducting the research required to write an acceptable thesis or dissertation is one of the most valuable educational experiences a person can have. Furthermore, it adds to our knowledge about the world in general and so can ultimately promote the welfare and comfort of everyone. Great discoveries that advance the frontiers of knowledge and enhance humankind's well-being are commonplace announcements in the contemporary media.

As a way of getting your feet wet in the world of research, take some time to read articles in research journals in your own academic discipline. You can do so by spending an hour or two in your local college or university library; you may also be able to find some relevant journals on the Internet.

BROWSING THE PERIODICALS SECTION OF THE LIBRARY

The library of any college or university houses numerous professional journals that describe a wide range of research studies in virtually any field of study. To find research studies related to a particular topic, you might begin with the paper indexes in the library's reference section or the online databases available through the library's computer system (more about such resources in Chapter 4). The research journals themselves are typically kept in a Periodicals section of the library. Following are examples of what you might find there:

American Educational Research Journal
American Journal of Distance Education
American Historical Review
Child Development
Communications Research
Early Childhood Research Quarterly
Educational Technology, Research and Development
Environmental Research
Hispanic Journal of Behavioral Science
Journal of Anthropological Research
Journal of Black Studies
Journal of Business Research
Journal of Educational Computing Research
Journal of Experimental Psychology
Journal of Management

Journal of Physical Education, Recreation, and Dance
Journal of Research in Crime and Delinquency
Journal of Speech, Language and Hearing Research
Nursing Research
Organizational Dynamics
Professional Geographer
Research in Consumer Behavior
Research in Nursing and Health
Research in Social Problems and Public Policy
Sex Roles
Sociological Methods and Research
Sociology and Social Research
Training and Development

Some libraries organize these journals alphabetically by title. Others organize them using the Dewey decimal system, which allows journals related to the same topic to be placed close together (more about the Dewey decimal system in Chapter 2).

Your professors should have suggestions about journals that are especially relevant to your academic discipline. Reference librarians can be helpful as well. In addition, especially if you are shy about asking other people for advice, you can get insights about important journals by scanning the reference lists in textbooks in your discipline.

Browse the journals related to your field just to get acquainted with them. Go first to those that pique your interest, and skim a few studies that relate to particularly intriguing topics. Then, get acquainted with as many of the journals in your discipline as you can. Competent researchers have general knowledge of the resources available in their field.

FINDING JOURNALS ON THE INTERNET

USING TECHNOLOGY

The **Internet** is a sprawling collection of computer networks linking millions of computers all over the world. Originally formed to link defense computers and scientists, the Internet has grown well beyond those boundaries. In recent years, it has become a powerful way to access a wide variety of information on an almost limitless number of topics. The Internet connects people for the purpose of sharing information. If you have not yet "traveled" on the Internet, this is the time to start!

Any exploration of the Internet requires some specialized equipment. First, the computer you use should have three features:

- A hook-up to a telephone or cable line
- A **modem,** a device that allows computer data to be transmitted over telephone or cable lines
- Computer software that allows you to access the Internet (e.g., Netscape Navigator, Microsoft Internet Explorer)

If Internet exploration is new to you, you may want to have a friend look over your shoulder and guide you as you take your first steps into cyberspace.

As you read later chapters of this book, you will learn about a wide variety of resources that the Internet can offer to both novice and expert researchers. For now, however, we'll limit our discussion to **online journals,** which are available in electronic form either instead of or in addition to paper form. As we write this edition of the book, only a small proportion of academic periodicals are completely available on the Internet, but more are going online all the time. Here are several examples of online journals and their Internet addresses:

> Sociological Research Online
> http://www.socresonline.org.uk/
>
> Online Journal of Issues in Nursing
> http://www.nursingworld.org/ojin/
>
> Online Journal of Peace and Conflict Resolution
> http://www.trinstitute.org/ojpcr/

You can find links to many other online journals on the following Web site at the University of California, San Diego:

> http://gort.ucsd.edu/newjour/

Keep in mind that the quality of research you find in your explorations of the library and the Internet may vary considerably. One rough indicator of the quality of a study is whether it has been juried or nonjuried. A **juried** (or *refereed*) research report has been judged by respected colleagues in one's field and deemed to be of sufficient quality and importance to warrant publication. For instance, the editors of many academic journals send submitted manuscripts to one or more reviewers who pass judgment on the manuscripts, and only manuscripts that meet certain criteria are published in the journal. A **nonjuried** (or *nonrefereed*) report is one that appears in a journal or on the Internet without first being screened by one or more experts. Some nonjuried reports are excellent, but others may not be.

PRACTICAL APPLICATION EVALUATING THE RESEARCH OF OTHERS

An important skill of a researcher is the ability to review the work of others and evaluate the quality of their methods, results, and conclusions. In some cases, this is quite easily accomplished; in others, it is more difficult. By developing your ability to evaluate other researchers' work, you get a better sense of how to improve your own research efforts. We suggest that you begin to sharpen your evaluation skills by locating several research articles relevant to your interests. As you read and study the articles, consider the questions in the following checklist.

✔ CHECKLIST
REFLECTIVE QUESTIONS TO CONSIDER WHEN EVALUATING RESEARCH

_____   1. In what source did you find the research article? Was it reviewed by experts in the field before it was published?

_____

_____

_____   2. Does the article have a stated research question or problem? That is, can you determine the focus of the author's work?

_____

_____

_____ 3. Does the article describe the collection of data, or does it describe and synthesize other studies in which data were collected?

_____

_____

_____ 4. Is the article logically organized and easy to follow? What could have been done to improve its organization?

_____

_____

_____ 5. Does the article contain a section that outlines and reviews previous studies on this topic? In what ways is this previous work relevant to the research problem?

_____

_____

_____ 6. If the author explained procedures that were followed in the study, are these procedures clear enough that you could repeat the work and get similar results? What additional information might be helpful or essential for you to replicate the study?

_____

_____

_____ 7. If data were collected, can you describe how they were collected and how they were analyzed? Do you agree with what was done? What additional things would you have done if you had been the researcher?

_____

_____

_____ 8. Do you agree with the interpretation of the results? Why or why not?

_____

_____

_____ 9. Finally, reflect over the entire article. What is, for you, most important? What do you find most interesting? What do you think are the strengths and weaknesses of this article? Will you remember this article in the future? Why or why not?

_____

_____

GUIDELINES   BENEFITING FROM OTHERS' RESEARCH

As you begin to evaluate selected articles by using the questions in the checklist, it may be wise to keep three guidelines in mind:

1. *Keep a research journal, writing log, notebook, or annotated bibliography of the articles you read.* Include bibliographic information such as

- The author's name
- The title of the article
- The name of the journal and the year, volume and issue numbers, and page numbers
- Keywords that capture the focus of the article

You may think that you will always be able to recall where you found an article and what you learned from it. However, our own experiences tell us that you probably *will* forget a good deal of what you read.

Now go to our
Companion Website at
http://www.prenhall.com/leedy to
assess your understanding of
chapter content and to complete
the projects that will help you
learn how to conduct research.

2. *Whenever you review someone else's work, take time to consider how you can improve your own work because of it.* Ask yourself, What have I learned that I would (or would not) want to incorporate into my own research? Perhaps it is a certain way of writing, a specific method of data collection, or a particular approach to data analysis. You should constantly question and reflect on what you read.

3. *Finally, don't read only one or two articles and think that you are done.* Get used to reading and evaluating; for a researcher, this is a lifelong endeavor. Always look for additional things you can learn.

FOR FURTHER READING

Anglin, G. J., Ross, S. M., & Morrison, G. R. (1995). Inquiry in instructional design and technology: Getting started. In G. Anglin (Ed.), *Instructional technology: Past, present, and future* (pp. 340–347). Englewood, CO: Libraries Unlimited.

Bouma, G. D. (1994). *The research process.* London: Oxford University Press.

Davitz, J. R., & Davitz, L. L. (1996). *Evaluating research proposals: A guide for the behavioral sciences.* Upper Saddle River, NJ: Prentice Hall.

Driscoll, M. (1995). Paradigms for research in instructional systems. In G. Anglin (Ed.), *Instructional technology: Past, present, and future* (pp. 322–327). Englewood, CO: Libraries Unlimited.

Goodwin, C. J. (2001). *Research in psychology: Methods and design* (3rd ed.). New York: Wiley.

Howe, R., & Lewis, R. (1994). *A student guide to research in social science.* New York: Cambridge University Press.

Leedy, P. (1981). *How to read research and understand it.* New York: Macmillan.

Luczun-Friedman, M. E. (1986). Introduction to research: A basic guide to scientific inquiry. *Journal of Post Anesthetic Nursing, 1,* 64–75.

McMillan, J. H., & Wergin, J. F. (2002). *Understanding and evaluating educational research* (2nd ed.). Upper Saddle River, NJ: Merrill/Prentice Hall.

Mutchnick, R. J., & Berg, B. L. (1996). *Research methods for the social sciences: Practice and applications.* Boston, MA: Allyn & Bacon.

Priest, S. H. (1996). *Doing media research: An introduction.* Thousand Oaks, CA: Sage.

Rosnow, R. L., & Rosenthal, R. (2002). *Beginning behavioral research: A conceptual primer* (4th ed.). Upper Saddle River, NJ: Prentice Hall.

Tools of Research

2

> *Every worker needs tools. The carpenter needs a hammer and a saw; the surgeon, a scalpel and forceps; the tailor, pins and scissors; and the researcher, an array of means by which data can be collected and made meaningful. The tools of research facilitate the ultimate goal of research itself: to derive conclusions from a body of data and discover what was hitherto unknown.*

Every artisan—and more generally, every professional—needs specialized tools to work effectively. Tools vary according to the job to be done. The tool is chosen to facilitate the task at hand and is often indispensable if the job is to be done at all. Without hammer and saw, the carpenter is out of business; without scalpel or forceps, the surgeon cannot practice. Every profession has its own particular equipment for carrying out the specific work it has to do. Researchers, likewise, have their own kit of tools to carry out their plans and achieve their goals.

The tools that researchers use to achieve their goals may vary considerably depending on the discipline. The microbiologist needs a microscope and culture media; the attorney, a library of legal decisions and statute law. Without these, researchers in these areas are immobilized. But these are special tools of research appropriate to a particular discipline or profession, and we do not discuss them in this chapter. Our concern here is with the general tools of research that the majority of researchers, regardless of discipline and situation, typically need to derive meaningful and insightful conclusions from the data they collect.

GENERAL TOOLS OF RESEARCH

We should be careful not to equate the *tools* of research with the *methodology* of research. A **research tool** is a specific mechanism or strategy the researcher uses to collect, manipulate, or interpret data. The **research methodology** is the general approach the researcher takes in carrying out the research project; to some extent, this approach dictates the particular tools the researcher selects.

Confusing the tool with the research method is immediately recognizable. Such phrases as "library research" and "statistical research" are telltale signs and largely meaningless. They suggest a failure to understand the nature of formal research, as well as a failure to differentiate between tool and method. The library is merely a place for locating or discovering certain data that will be analyzed and interpreted later in the research process. Likewise, statistics merely provide ways to summarize and analyze data, thereby allowing us to see their nature more clearly.

Following are six general tools of research:

1. The library and its resources
2. The computer and its software
3. Techniques of measurement
4. Statistics
5. The human mind
6. Language

Volumes have been written on each of these tools. In this text, we simply introduce them to help our readers begin to use them more effectively.

THE LIBRARY AND ITS RESOURCES AS A TOOL OF RESEARCH

For thousands of years, the library served primarily as a repository of books and manuscripts—a kind of literary mausoleum where documents were kept and added to as more literature and information became available. It was, for the most part, only a slowly expanding universe of knowledge, one that could be comfortably contained within masonry walls.

In the latter half of the 20th century, the role of the library changed. An explosion of information occurred. Research altered old ideas in almost every domain of human interest. Libraries had to come to grips with two important facts. First, they certainly could not hold all the world's information within their walls. Second, and perhaps more important, library patrons were becoming more sophisticated in their needs and desires and placed increasing priority on ease and speed of access to information. In response, libraries began acquiring new technologies for storing vast amounts of information (e.g., microforms, CD-ROMs, online databases) to augment the shelves of books and periodicals that lined their walls.

In the future, the library must continue to evolve. With advances in telecommunications, libraries may eventually exist, literally, without limits. Imagine using a computer and a cellular telephone connection to access a "virtual" library in which you can "walk" up and down the rows of books and pick selections from all available sources and languages known—all the while sitting in your home, office, classroom, car, or remote mountain cabin. These selections contain not only textual materials but also all forms of pictures, video, and audio media. If you want a "hard copy," you can print it out. If you want to browse the shelves for related works, you can do so. If you want to access a specific bit of information quickly, you can search the entire collection in a matter of milliseconds. All of these capabilities are already available to some extent.

When some doctoral student in the 21st century writes a dissertation on the information revolution of the 20th century, the most interesting chapter will probably be on the speed with which that revolution occurred. The shock waves associated with it have reached every segment of contemporary society. Directly above its epicenter, the college and university library has perhaps felt its most severe and uncompromising jolts.

THE LIBRARY OF THE QUIET PAST

Imagine, if you will, that you were a student in the 1950s or 1960s. When you went to the library to gather information, you headed straight to the card catalog—a series of drawers containing three index cards for each book in the library—and sorted through, card by card, the titles and content descriptions of the books in each category of interest. You jotted down call numbers to help you find the titles most likely to contain the information you needed. Next, you went to the stacks to inspect the volumes you selected.

Meanwhile, the periodical indexes were a primary means through which you found journal and newspaper articles about your topic. Ponderous volumes arranged in long rows on the reference shelves, they contained cross-indexed references to current literature and had titles such as

Readers' Guide to Periodical Literature, Education Index, New York Times Index, Business Periodicals Index, and *Psychological Abstracts.* You worked your way through each sizable volume until you found material on your area of interest, and then you made notes about the article: author, title, periodical, volume, pages, and date. Then you roamed long corridors in the periodicals section, tracking down the specific issues of specific journals. Finally, you found a few nuggets of information and carefully jotted them down on a notepad or on index cards.

Such was the acquisition of knowledge in the library of the quiet past. It was a laborious, time-consuming process that simply could not work efficiently under the sudden, torrential onrush of the information revolution.

THE LIBRARY OF THE STORMY PRESENT

In today's college library, a student's plan of attack is entirely different. In place of a card catalog (which might still be found in some out-of-the-way corner) are rows of computer terminals and keyboards where users can quickly generate lists of the library's holdings related to particular authors, titles, topics, or call numbers. On the same terminals, you can typically also find online databases that enable users to find journal articles on virtually any topic about which people have written.

Not only has the college library hardware changed, but the conventional view of knowledge has also changed (Lewis, 1988). Looking at a college course catalog, you would infer that human knowledge is an accumulation of separate disciplinary studies, each neatly boxed and bearing such labels as "anthropology," "biology," "chemistry," and "economics." In the typical college or university, these little boxes of knowledge are called "departments." Yet the quest for knowledge knows no boundaries or artificial departmentalization. Modern research does not operate under the concept of dichotomies, divisions, or cellular capsules of knowledge. Instead, the knowledge the human race has accumulated is, by nature, "a single, cohesive, interwoven whole" (Miksa, 1987, p. 8). Research has become less discipline-specific in both its problems and its methodologies. Hence, researchers need to have easy access to existing knowledge in a wide variety of disciplines.

HOW TO ACCESS INFORMATION QUICKLY AND EFFICIENTLY

Skilled researchers have several general library resources at their disposal to locate the information they need; key among these resources are library catalogs, indexes and abstracts, and reference librarians. Furthermore, many researchers find that just browsing among the library shelves is often time well spent.

Library Catalogs

Library book collections are still very much the core of information and ideas housed in a library today. The easiest way to find specific books is through the library catalog. Although you may occasionally find a local public library that still uses a card catalog, college libraries have, almost without exception, replaced such cumbersome systems with electronic catalogs that list their holdings. You sit at a computer terminal and type in one or two keywords, or perhaps you type in the title or author of a specific book. With the flick of a finger, information about one or more books—once contained on a catalog file card—is instantaneously displayed on the computer monitor.

DOES YOUR LIBRARY STILL HAVE THE CARD CATALOG?   For those who are still using the card catalog file to locate books, four simple rules govern the placing of individual cards in the file drawer:

1. Books *by* a person precede books *about* the person.
2. Collected works usually precede individual works.
3. When the same word is common for (a) a person, (b) a place, or (c) a thing, the cards in the catalog will be arranged in that order. For example, (a) cards pertaining to "Lincoln, Abraham" precede (b) cards pertaining to "Lincoln, Nebraska"; these precede (c) cards pertaining to "Lincoln Warehouse Corporation."
4. Saints, popes, kings, and others are arranged in their order of hierarchical precedence.

Indexes and Abstracts

During one of your next trips to the library, take some time to visit the reference section—the "heart" of the library for the researcher. Typically, this section of the library contains large volumes that can help you identify and locate needed information. Whether you are looking for general information or specific research articles in chemistry, psychology, history, nursing, education, engineering, or agriculture, indexes can help you locate relevant titles, authors, and abstracts for any conceivable topic.

Most libraries have both paper and electronic versions of indexes and abstracts. Depending on the subject and the number of years of work you wish to examine, a manual search through any one of the paper indexes may take considerable time and effort. This is where electronic databases become indispensable tools for the researcher. A college library typically provides access to a wide variety of *online databases*—not only indexes and abstracts, but also encyclopedias, dictionaries, and online journals—that enable you to locate sources of information that are available not only in the campus library itself but also in other libraries and institutions around the world. In the rare instance when a library does not provide access to online databases, it is likely to have a number of in-house electronic indexes, typically in the form of CD-ROMs (CD-ROM is short for compact disk—read-only memory), that each contain vast amounts of information—perhaps abstracts for tens of thousands of journal articles related to a particular discipline or perhaps the contents of an entire encyclopedia. With a computer and a CD-ROM drive, the researcher can access the information stored on the CD.

Indexes and abstracts are especially useful when you are conducting a literature review for your research project. According, we will look at such resources in more detail in Chapter 4.

The Reference Librarian

When you visit the reference section of your library, you will almost certainly see one or more librarians sitting at the reference desk. These individuals are there for one reason only: to help you and others find needed information. They can show you reference materials you never dreamed existed. They can show you how to use the computer catalog, online databases, paper and CD-ROM indexes, or any of the library's other resources.

Some new researchers are reluctant to approach a reference librarian for fear of looking foolish or stupid. Yet the reality is that library resources are changing so quickly that most of us cannot possibly keep up with them. Whatever you do, don't be afraid to ask librarians for assistance. Even as seasoned researchers, we seek the advice of these individuals frequently; by doing so, we can often save ourselves a great deal of time.

Browsing the Library Shelves

An important research skill is browsing the library, either physically by walking among the stacks or electronically by "browsing" the entries in the library's computer catalog. In many cases, when one goes to a library shelf to locate a book or journal, the information most useful is found not in the material that was originally targeted, but rather in a book nearby on the shelf. Skilled researchers not only look for the book they have originally designated but also scan nearby shelves and call numbers for related materials.

Books are coded and arranged on the library shelves in accordance with two principal systems for the classification of all knowledge: the Dewey decimal classification system and the Library of Congress system.

- *The Dewey decimal classification system.* Books are cataloged and shelved according to 10 basic areas of human knowledge and subsequent subareas, each divided decimally. The Dewey decimal system is the principal classification system in most public libraries and many other libraries and is probably the most generally accepted system throughout the world.
- *The Library of Congress (LC) classification system.* Books are assigned to particular areas of human knowledge that are given special alphabetical categories. This system is widely used in college and university libraries.

TABLE 2.1 A conversion chart: Dewey decimal classification system v. the Library of Congress classification system

DC	Subject	LC	DC	Subject	LC
630	Agriculture	S	400	Language	P
570	Anthropology	GN	340	Law	K
913	Archaeology	CC	020	Library Science	Z
700	Art	N	800	Literature	P
220	Bible	BS	810	Literature, American	PS
010–020	Bibliography	Z	820	Literature, English	PR
920.92	Biography	CT	840–860	Literature, Romance	PQ
560	Biology	QH	658	Management	HD
580	Botany	QK	510	Mathematics	QA
650	Business	HF	610	Medicine	R
540	Chemistry	QD	355–358	Military Science	U
155.4	Child Development	BF	780	Music	M
260–270	Church History	BR	560	Natural Science	QH
330	Economics	HB–HJ	359	Naval Science	V
370	Education	L	610	Nursing	RT
378	Education, Higher	LD	750	Painting	ND
030	Encyclopedias	AE	615	Pharmacy	RS
400	English	PE	100	Philosophy	B
600	Engineering	T	770	Photography	TR
700	Fine Arts	N	530	Physics	QC
440	French Language	PC	320	Political Science	J
000	General	A	150	Psychology	BF
910	Geography	G	200	Religions	B
550	Geology	QE	500	Science	Q
430	German Language	PF	730	Sculpture	NB
740	Graphic Arts	NC	300	Social Science	H
480	Greek Language	PA	301–309	Sociology	HM–HX
930–960	History (except American)	D	460	Spanish Language	PC
970–980	History, American (General)	E	790	Sports	GV
970–980	History, U.S. (Local)	F	310	Statistics	HA
250	Theology, Practical	BV	230	Theology, Doctrinal	BT
640	Home Economics	TX	590	Zoology	QL
070	Journalism	PN			

Note: This arrangement of the dual classification systems was conceived by Roger Miller, former director of the Murray Resources Learning Center, Messiah College, Grantham, PA.

Most libraries are organized according to one of these systems; a few classify their collections according to both.

For students who wish to browse or locate books in a particular category of knowledge, a guide to each system of classification may be helpful. Table 2.1 shows an equivalency chart of the two systems. Read down the "Subject" column to locate the area of knowledge in which the book may be located. The "DC" column of numbers to the left gives the Dewey decimal classification. The "LC" column of letters to the right indicates the corresponding Library of Congress classification symbols.

The best way to master the library as a research tool is to use it! Go in, explore, take stock of its resources, try electronic searching; browse in the reference room; go into the stacks and browse some more. You may be surprised at what a magnificent research tool the library really is.

THE COMPUTER AND ITS SOFTWARE AS A TOOL OF RESEARCH

As a tool of research, the personal computer is now commonplace. Over the past two or three decades, computer software packages have become increasingly user friendly, such that novice researchers can learn to use them quickly and easily.

To the uninitiated, computers may still have an aura of mystery. The variety of things they can do is incredible. The speed with which they work is incomprehensible. But, like any tool, no matter how powerful, they have their limitations.

Computers are not human brains. Yes, a computer can certainly calculate, compare, search, retrieve, sort, and organize data more efficiently and more accurately than you can. Compared to the intelligence and perceptiveness of the human brain, however, computers are relatively limited machines. In their present stage of development, they depend totally on a person to give them directions about what to do.

A computer is not a miracle worker. It cannot do your thinking for you. It can, however, be a fast and faithful assistant. When told exactly what to do, it is one of the researcher's best friends.

Throughout this book, you will find many "Using Technology" sections that describe specific ways in which, as a researcher, you can use computers to make your job easier. Table 2.2 provides suggestions for how you might use a computer to assist you in the research process. At this point, we describe one use of the computer that a researcher is likely to use *throughout* a research project: taking advantage of the Internet.

TAKING ADVANTAGE OF THE INTERNET

The Internet provides many resources that were simply not available to researchers 20 years ago. These resources include the World Wide Web, electronic mail, and news.

World Wide Web

Currently the most popular feature of the Internet is the **World Wide Web (WWW).** Web sites are the fastest growing part of the Internet, and for many people, these sites are the main reason for using the Internet. Each site includes one or more **Web pages** that you can read in much the same way you would read the pages of a book. Many pages have graphics, audio, and in some cases even digital video, in addition to text.

If you looked for any of the online journals mentioned in Chapter 1, then you were visiting the Web sites for those journals. The online databases we described in the preceding section on the library are also located on the Web. Every site on the Web has a particular address, or **URL** (short for Uniform Resource Locator). Following are examples:

University of New Hampshire
http://www.unh.edu/

National Aeronautics and Space Administration (NASA)
http://www.nasa.gov/

Ingenta (an online index of academic and professional journal articles)
http://www.ingenta.com/

If you want to access and use the WWW on your personal computer, you must have software known as a **Web browser,** such as Netscape Navigator or Microsoft Internet Explorer. This software allows users to go to various Web sites and move easily among connected sites. If you know the URL for the Web site you want to visit, you simply type it in the specified box in the browser. If you do not know the URL you need—or perhaps don't even know what sites might help you in finding the information you need—you can usually find the relevant URLs by using a *search engine,* such as Google, Yahoo, or AltaVista (we'll explain how to use these search engines in Chapter 4). Once you have electronically reached a site you want, you can often move

TABLE 2.2   The computer as a research assistant

Part of the Study	Team of Research Assistants
Planning the study	• Brainstorming assistance—software used to help generate and organize ideas for the research focus, to illustrate how different concepts could be related, and to consider how the process will be conducted. • Outlining assistance—software used to help structure the different aspects of the study and coordinate work efforts. • Project management assistance—software used to highlight and coordinate all the different efforts that need to occur in a timely fashion. • Budget assistance—spreadsheet software to help in outlining, estimating, and monitoring the potential costs involved in the research effort.
Literature review	• Background literature identification assistance—CD-ROM and online databases that identify and describe related published research that should be considered during the formative stages of the research endeavor. • Telecommunication assistance—computer technology used to communicate with other researchers and groups of researchers through e-mail, electronic bulletin boards, list servers, and the World Wide Web. • Electronic storage and retrieval assistance—use of electronic databases used to store valuable bibliographic citations and comments that can be readily sorted and accessed by title, author, keyword, and so on. • Writing assistance—software used to facilitate the writing, editing, formatting, and printing of the literature review.
Study implementation and data gathering	• Materials production assistance—software used for the development and use of instructional materials, graphic production, simulations, or actual interventions that are to be experienced by the participants. • Experimental control assistance—software used to control the effects of specific variables and restrict the occurrence of other potentially confounding variables. • Survey distribution assistance—database use coupled with word processing to identify and send specific communications to a targeted population. • Data collection assistance—software used to take fieldnotes or to monitor specific types of responses made by research participants.
Analysis and interpretation	• Organizational assistance—software used to assemble, categorize, code, integrate, and search potentially huge data sets (e.g., survey open-ended responses, qualitative interview data). • Conceptual assistance—software used to write and store ongoing reflections about data or to construct theories that integrate research findings. • Statistical assistance—statistical and spreadsheet software packages used to categorize and analyze various types of data sets. • Graphic production assistance—software used to depict data in graphic form to facilitate interpretation.
Reporting	• Communication assistance—telecommunication software used to distribute and discuss research findings and initial interpretations with colleagues and to receive their comments and feedback. • Writing and editing assistance—word processing software used to write and edit successive drafts of the final report. • Publishing assistance—desktop publishing software used to produce professional-looking documents that can be distributed at conferences and elsewhere to get additional comments and feedback. • Distribution assistance—the Internet, World Wide Web, and other networks used to electronically distribute a report of one's findings and to generate discussion for follow-up studies by others in the field.

to related sites by moving the cursor on the screen to a particular word or icon and then clicking the mouse; the software immediately transports you to another page via a **Web link.** Whenever you find pages that are particularly helpful, the software allows you to print them out.

Another useful feature of Web browsers is that they allow you to save particularly useful Web sites in an "address book" of sorts. Netscape software calls this feature "Bookmarks," whereas Microsoft calls it "Favorites." Whenever you reach a Web page you think might be helpful on future occasions, you can tell the software to "Add Bookmark" or "Add Page to Favorites." At some later date, you can then scroll down your list of saved addresses until you find the one you want, and the software immediately takes you there.

Electronic Mail

Electronic mail service, more commonly known as **e-mail,** allows people to communicate quickly with one another. As is true when using the national postal service (sometimes called *snail mail* by people too impatient to use it in this lightning-fast electronic age), the person who is sending the mail must know the address of the person who will be receiving it. A single message can be sent directly to one or many individuals at a single time (much like bulk mail). Unlike mail delivered by the postal service, a message sent through e-mail is generally delivered in a matter of seconds, no matter where in the world the receiver is. Additionally, the cost for sending or receiving the message is usually free or negligible. In most cases, people who use either university-based or commercial online services can send an unlimited amount of mail.

Although most e-mail messages contain short statements and questions, it is also possible to send or receive a lengthy, detailed message (e.g., a full manuscript of a research report), perhaps by adding it as an **attachment** to an e-mail message (depending on the software, an attachment may instead be called an *enclosure*). Furthermore, if you want more than one person (perhaps a research network of persons) to receive the message, you can send each a copy of the message simultaneously. E-mail technology can facilitate collaboration among people who have similar interests, in some cases without them ever meeting face to face.

News

The news feature of the Internet is like a huge bulletin board on which people post messages and comments to which others can react and add. Of particular value to the researcher are **list servers,** which provide a mechanism for electronic discussion groups. A list server is a mailing list, and any e-mail message sent to it is distributed to all the people who have subscribed to the list.

List servers have been formed on a wide variety of special interests. For example, if you like music, you can subscribe to a list server focusing on any number of special musical interests. As e-mail messages are received by this list server, you will automatically receive a copy.

Thousands of list servers on a wide variety of topics are available for subscription, often without charge. Through them, people can easily communicate with one another about topics of common interest.

ACCESSING THE INTERNET

The Internet can be accessed in several ways. For those at colleges and universities, access is generally quite easy through their institution's computer services. Likewise, many national, regional, and local commercial services (e.g., America Online, Prodigy, Comcast) provide access to the Internet for a monthly fee, which is often less than the cost of cable television.

LEARNING MORE ABOUT THE INTERNET

Using the Internet becomes a more user-friendly process all the time; even the most computer-anxious of researchers should have little or no trouble picking up the basics. You might ask a computer-literate friend to show you how it's done. You can find classes on using the Internet at almost any university or community college (check the "Continuing Education" or "Outreach" class schedule). You can also find a free tutorial on Internet basics at this address on the World Wide Web:

http://www.learnthenet.com/

This address is active as the eighth edition of this book goes to press. If it is no longer operational when you read the book, you will discover firsthand one of the many ways in which the World Wide Web continues to change and evolve over time.

PRACTICAL APPLICATION USING THE INTERNET TO FACILITATE COMMUNICATION

Read the following scenarios. In each case, think about how the researcher might use the Internet to solve his or her problem.

1. Arwin is a professor at a small college. Although his research is prominent in his field, few people on campus share his enthusiasm for his specialty—forensic pathology. Although Arwin avidly reads relevant academic journals, he looks forward to the annual meetings of his national organization, where he can exchange ideas with others who have similar interests. He wishes that such exchanges could occur more frequently.

2. Deirdre has a once-in-a-lifetime opportunity to spend 6 months in Australia collecting data about the various marine plants of the Great Barrier Reef. Although she is excited about the opportunity, she realizes that the work of her campus research group will suffer. Because of the distance, it will be difficult to provide feedback on the group's ongoing papers and projects. Although Deirdre and her colleagues can use the postal service to transport the work between them, this will definitely slow the progress of their work.

3. Recently, Alexis read about a new eye corrective procedure being investigated at a major medical research institution. The work appears potentially relevant to her own research, but she has questions about the procedures and long-term results. Hoping to get some quick answers, she writes a letter to the authors of the article, in care of their research institution, and waits for their reply.

How can the Internet help each of these researchers? For Arwin, being on one or more list servers might enable him to keep up with current developments in his field and communicate regularly with others in the field. During her time in Australia, Deirdre can stay in regular communication with her colleagues at home via e-mail, and she can easily send papers back and forth through attachments. To gain information about the corrective procedure in which she's interested, Alexis might visit the Web site of the hospital conducting the research, where she might find additional information about the procedure or the e-mail addresses of the individuals conducting the research.

PRACTICAL APPLICATION USING E-MAIL

If you have not yet discovered the joys of electronic mail, there's no time like the present to do so. Not only will e-mail help you communicate with fellow researchers around the world, but it will also help you stay in touch with family and friends. Within the past few years, we have seen our own e-mail messages (both sent and received) increase dramatically in number. We now use it even to reconnect with old friends from high school, schedule appointments, and pass along jokes received from other e-mailing acquaintances.

GUIDELINES GETTING STARTED ON E-MAIL

The best way to appreciate the advantages of e-mail is to try it. Here are some basic steps for getting started with e-mail.

1. *Get an e-mail account on a computer system.* If you are currently at a college or university, you can almost certainly get an account at your institution. When you get such an account, you will also get an e-mail address, perhaps one that looks something like this:

jeormro@bentley.unco.edu

The letters (and possibly numbers as well) appearing before the "at" sign (@) make up your user ID. Following the @ is information about the **server** (the specific computer and/or institution that handles the e-mail account) and the nature of that server's "host." In the address just presented, *jeormro* is the user ID, *bentley* is the name of the server, *unco* is the institution (University of Northern Colorado) where the server is located, and *edu* refers to the nature of the host (in this case, an educational institution).

An alternative is to get an account with a local or national Internet service provider, such as America Online or Prodigy. In such a situation, your e-mail address might look something like this:

jormrod@comcast.net

Pellis1974@aol.com

2. *Find out how to access the system and obtain the needed software to do so.* Ask the institution or company with whom you have obtained an account to provide instructions and software for sending and receiving e-mail. The agency should do so willingly, typically at little or no charge.

3. *Find the e-mail addresses of people you wish to contact.* In this day and age, many of your friends and acquaintances probably have e-mail addresses. You can also frequently find e-mail addresses in college directories and on business cards, product advertisements, and Web sites. When you have accumulated more than a few addresses, you may wish to use the *address book* feature of most e-mail software packages, which allows you to store the addresses directly on your computer and access them easily whenever you need them.

4. *Connect to the computer system that services your e-mail account and send a short message to a friend.* If a response does not return in a few days, try sending the message again. People don't always check their electronic mailboxes every day.

Most of our readers are probably already quite familiar with e-mail. Yet it is important for you to reflect on how you might use it specifically as a tool that can assist you in your research—for instance, as a means of facilitating communication and collaboration with people who have conducted studies similar to yours or who possess information and insights that may be critical to your own project.

MEASUREMENT AS A TOOL OF RESEARCH

Most researchers strive for objectivity: They believe that their observations should be influenced as little as possible—ideally not at all—by their own perceptions, impressions, and biases. (As we will note in Chapter 7, some qualitative researchers are an exception to this rule.) And one way of remaining objective is to identify a systematic way of measuring a phenomenon being studied.

But what is measurement? Most of us think of measurement in terms of such objects as rulers, scales, gauges, and thermometers. In research, **measurement** takes on a somewhat different meaning:

Measurement is limiting the data of any phenomenon—substantial or insubstantial—so that those data may be interpreted and, ultimately, compared to an acceptable qualitative or quantitative standard.

Let's look more closely at this definition. The first five words are *measurement is limiting the data.* When we measure something, we "set a limit" that "restrains" the data. We erect a barrier beyond which those data cannot go. What is a foot, a mile, a pound? Each is a unit of measure governed by a numerical restraint: 12 inches restrain a foot; 5,280 feet, a mile; and 16 ounces, a pound.

Now, let's look at the next six words: *of any phenomenon—substantial or insubstantial.* This phrase is all-inclusive. Nothing exists that the researcher cannot measure. In some cases, observable objects are measured. These are **substantial** measurements; that is, the things being measured have an obvious basis in the physical world. An engineer measures the span of a bridge; a chemist measures the mass of a compound both before and after transforming it in some way. A Greek scholar, Eratosthenes, attempted to measure the circumference of the earth by comparing two shadows of a gnomon (the rod of a sundial) in different cities. All of these are attempts to measure substantial phenomena.

We may also measure those things—if "things" they be—that are **insubstantial,** that exist only as concepts, ideas, opinions, feelings, or other intangible entities. For example, we might attempt to measure the economic "health" of business, the degree to which students have "learned," or the extent to which people "value" physical exercise. We seek to measure these intangibles, not with tape measures or scales, but with the Dow-Jones index, achievement tests, questionnaires, or interviews.

For certain researchers, such as those in the social sciences, humanities, and education, measuring intangibles is a primary stock-in-trade. The following example illustrates one way this might be accomplished.

MEASURING INSUBSTANTIAL PHENOMENA: AN EXAMPLE

A group of nine people, shown in Figure 2.1, work together in the personnel department of a large corporation. They are to attend a recognition dinner at an exclusive hotel.

They arrive in four cars. They enter the hotel in the following order: Terri, Sara, Greg, Tim, Gretchen, Matt, Peter, Jeff, and Joe. They greet each other and have time for a brief conversation before dinner. They position themselves in the conversation groups shown in Figure 2.2.

To the perceptive observer, the interpersonal dynamics within the group will soon become apparent. Who greets whom with enthusiasm or with indifference? Who joins in conversation with whom? Who seems to be a relative outsider? If there were "personal magnetic fields" among the guests, we might, with proper instrumentation, easily detect the presence of personal attraction, indifference, or rejection among various individuals within the group. But no such objective sensors of interpersonal relationships exist. *To merely observe the behavior of individuals in a particular situation is not to measure it.*

One possible approach to measuring the interpersonal dynamics of the group is to give each person in the group a slip of paper on which to record three choices: (a) one or more individuals

FIGURE 2.1

Recognition dinner participants

FIGURE 2.2

Interpersonal
relationships

Matt   Joe   Gretchen   Greg   Jeff   Terri   Peter   Sara   Tim

in the group whom the person likes most, (b) one or more individuals whom the person likes least, and (c) one or more individuals for whom the person has no strong feeling one way or another. When using this method, we must guarantee that every response will be kept confidential and, if possible, poll each person in the group individually.

We can then draw a chart, or **sociogram,** of these interpersonal reactions, perhaps in the manner depicted in Figure 2.3. We might also assign "weights" that place the data into three numerical categories: +1 for a positive choice, 0 for indifference, and −1 for a negative reaction.

FIGURE 2.3

Sociogram of
interpersonal dynamics

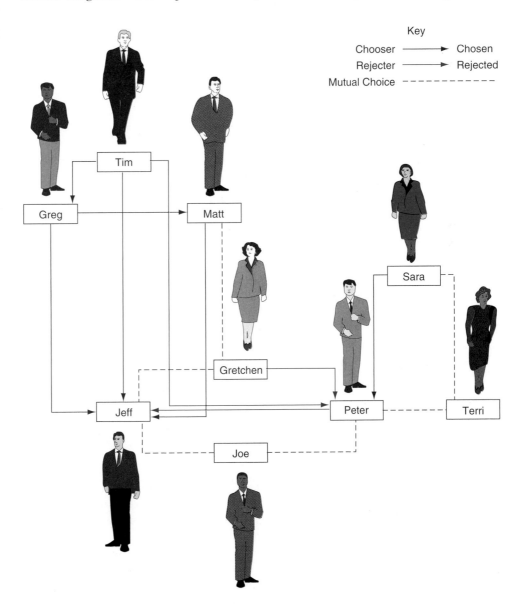

TABLE 2.3   Data from Figure 2.3 presented as a sociometric matrix

		Gretchen	Joe	Greg	Sara	Peter	Jeff	Tim	Matt	Terri
		How Each Person Was Rated by the Others								
How Each Person Rated the Others	Gretchen	—	0	0	0	−1	+1	0	+1	0
	Joe	0	—	0	0	+1	+1	0	0	0
	Greg	0	0	—	0	0	+1	0	+1	0
	Sara	0	0	0	—	+1	0	0	0	+1
	Peter	0	+1	0	0	—	−1	0	0	+1
	Jeff	+1	+1	0	0	0	—	0	0	0
	Tim	0	0	+1	0	−1	+1	—	0	0
	Matt	+1	0	0	0	0	+1	0	—	0
	Terri	0	0	0	+1	+1	0	0	0	—
	Totals	2	2	1	1	1	4	0	2	2

Categorizing the data in this way, we can then construct a sociometric matrix. To create a matrix, we arrange the names of each person twice: vertically down the left side of a grid and horizontally across the top of the grid. The result is shown in Table 2.3.

Certain relationships begin to emerge. As we represent group dynamics in multiple forms, certain clusters of facts suggest the following conclusions:

- Jeff is the informal or popular leader (sometimes called the "star") of the group. He received five choices and only one rejection. The sociogram confirms the matrix total.
- Probably some schism and tension are present in this group. Notice that Peter, Sara, and Terri form a subclique, or "island," that is separated from the larger clique that Jeff leads. The apparent liaison between these two groups is Joe, who has mutual choices with both Jeff and Peter.
- Friendship pairs may lend cohesion to the group. Notice the mutual choices: Matt and Gretchen, Peter and Joe, Jeff and Joe, Sara and Terri, Gretchen and Jeff. Only the sociogram reveals these alliances dramatically.
- Tim apparently is the isolate of the group. He received no choices; he is neither liked nor disliked. In such a position, he is probably the least influential member of the group.

We have presented this body of sociometric data in its various forms to show how intangible data can be measured. Many other approaches can be devised to measure similar phenomena. In fact, there are other methods of drawing sociograms aside from that just illustrated. For example, Chaatterjee and Srivastava (1982) have proposed a method useful for large populations, one that may be especially helpful in studying social forces within extended groups.

The analyses in Table 2.3 give us a mathematical insight into the social dynamics within a typical group. But *mathematics* is an easily misunderstood word, especially if we think of it in the narrow sense only—that is, as the science of mathematics. We must divorce ourselves from this connotation.

INTERPRETATION OF THE DATA

The ultimate criterion of any type of measurement is contained in the next seven words of our definition: *so that those data may be interpreted.* We have demonstrated what it means to interpret data by analyzing the interpersonal dynamics within a group of nine individuals, presumably amicably assembled for a dinner occasion. There, we looked below the surface to discover hidden social forces in their reactions to one another.

When researchers gain a sudden insight into the disparate data with which they have been working, they may experience a sense of excitement. The data have been *interpreted:* They have been transformed into small discoveries, revelations, enlightenments, and insights that the researcher has never seen before.

Now, we finish our definition: *and, ultimately, compared to an acceptable qualitative or quantitative standard.* A researcher must have a goal post, a true north, a point of orientation. In research, we call these standards *norms, averages, conformity to expected statistical distributions, goodness of fit, accuracy of description,* and the like.

Measurement is ultimately a comparison: a thing or concept measured against a point of limitation. We compare the length of an object with the scale of a ruler or a measuring tape. We "measure" an ideology against the meaning of it as articulated or suggested by the originator of the ideology. The essence of a religious belief resides in its sacred writings, in the precepts of its great teachers, and in its creed. The meaning of freedom is articulated in many political documents—for instance, in the Declaration of Independence and the Constitution of the United States. The essence of a philosophy arises from the writings and teachings of its founder: Platonism from Plato, Marxism from Karl Marx, and romanticism perhaps from Jean Jacques Rousseau. Against these original sources, it is possible to measure the thoughts and ideas of others and to approximate their similarity or deviance from them.

Data examined statistically are constantly being interpreted in comparison with statistical norms: the normal curve, a point of central tendency, the degree of dispersion, and other accepted statistical standards. Data analyzed qualitatively are compared across data sources, across methods, and across time.

We see, therefore, that our definition of measurement implies much more than a surface reading might suggest. Measurement is indeed a tool by which data may be inspected, analyzed, and interpreted so that the researcher may probe the meaning that lies below the surface.

FOUR SCALES OF MEASUREMENT

We might think of any form of measurement as falling into one of four categories, or **scales:** (1) nominal, (2) ordinal, (3) interval, and (4) ratio (Stevens, 1946). The scale of measurement will ultimately dictate the statistical procedures that can be used (if any) in processing the data. To appreciate this fact, we consider each scale of measurement and its characteristics.

Nominal Scale of Measurement

The word *nominal* comes from the Latin *nomen,* meaning "name." Hence, we can "measure" data to some degree by assigning names to them. Remember the earlier discussion of measurement, where we suggested that its basic meaning was to restrict, to limit. That's what a **nominal scale** does—and just about all that it does. Assign a specific name to anything, and you have restricted that thing to the meaning of its name. For example, we can measure a group of children by dividing it into two groups: girls and boys. Each subgroup is thereby measured—restricted—by virtue of gender to a particular category. By assigning a name, we create a measurement.

Things can be measured nominally in an infinite number of ways. We can further measure groups of girls and boys according to the home site of each child. Imagine that the town in which they live is divided into two sections by Main Street, which runs from east to west. Those children who live north of Main Street are "the Northerners"; those who live south of it are "the Southerners." In one period of U.S. history, we measured the population of the entire nation in just such a manner.

Nominal measurement is elemental and unrefined, but it does divide data into discrete categories that can then be compared with one another. Let's look at nominal measurement a bit more. We have six people: Zahra, Paul, Kathy, Binh, Ginger, and Nicky. They can be measured into six units of one each; they can also form two groups: Zahra, Kathy, and Ginger (the girls) in one and Paul, Binh, and Nicky (the boys) in the other. Let's think of them as a class that meets in Room 12 at Thompson's Corner School. By assigning a room number, we have provided the class with a name even though that "name" may be a number. That number, however, has no quantitative meaning: Room 12 is not necessarily bigger or better than Room 11, nor is it inferior to Room 13.

Only a few statistics are appropriate for analyzing nominal data. We can use the *mode* as an indicator of the most frequently occurring category within our data set; for instance, we might determine that there are more boys than girls in Room 12 at Thompson's Corner School. We can find the *percentage* of people in various subgroups within the total group; for instance, we could calculate the percentage of boys in each classroom. We can use a *chi-square test* to compare the relative frequencies of people in various categories; for instance, we might discover that more boys than girls live north of Main Street, but more girls than boys live south of Main Street. (We will discuss these statistics, as well as the statistics listed in the following discussions of the other three scales, in Chapter 11.)

Ordinal Scale of Measurement

With an **ordinal scale** of measurement, we can think in terms of the symbols > (greater than) or < (less than). We can compare various pieces of data in terms of one being greater or higher than another. In essence, this scale allows us to *rank-order* our data (hence its name *ordinal*).

We measure level of education grossly on the ordinal scale by classifying people as being unschooled or as having an elementary, high school, college, or graduate education. Likewise, we measure members of the workforce by grades of proficiency: unskilled, semiskilled, or skilled.

An ordinal scale expands the range of statistical techniques we can apply to our data. In addition to the statistics we can use with nominal data, we can also determine the *median,* or halfway point, in a set of data. We can use a *percentile rank* to identify the relative position of any item or individual in a group. We can determine the extent of the relationship between two characteristics by means of Spearman's *rank order correlation.*

Interval Scale of Measurement

An **interval scale** of measurement is characterized by two features: (1) it has equal units of measurement, and (2) its zero point has been established arbitrarily. The Fahrenheit (F) and Celsius (C) scales for measuring temperature are examples of interval scales: The intervals between any two successive numbers of degrees reflect equal changes in temperature, but the zero point is not equivalent to a total absence of heat. For instance, when Gabriel Fahrenheit was developing his Fahrenheit scale, he first took as his zero point the coldest temperature he observed in Iceland. Later, he made it the lowest temperature obtainable with a mixture of salt and ice. This was purely an arbitrary decision. It placed the freezing point of water at 32° and the boiling point at 212° above zero.

The rating scales employed by many businesses, survey groups, and professional organizations are often assumed to be on interval scales. For instance, many universities ask students to use rating scales to evaluate the teaching effectiveness of various professors. Following is an example of an item from one university's teaching evaluation form:

Place an X on the scale below at the point
where you would rate the availability of your
professor for conferences.

| 0 | 10 | 20 | 30 | 40 | 50 | 60 | 70 | 80 | 90 | 100 |

Never available   Seldom available   Available by appointment only   Generally available   Always available

Notice that the scale has 11 equidistant points ranging from 0 to 100. The equidistance creates what is presumed to be an interval scale for the measure. At five points along the scale are descriptive labels that can help students determine how they should rate their professor's availability. We might place descriptors at more places along the scale (perhaps at 10-point distances), thus potentially making the scale more sensitive or more accurate. For indicating the availability of a professor, such fineness of discrimination may not be either possible or desirable, but one may conceive of situations in which such a degree of discrimination may be necessary and appropriate.

Interval scales of measurement allow statistical analyses that are not possible with nominal or ordinal data. Because an interval scale reflects equal distances among adjacent points, any statistics that are calculated using addition or subtraction—for instance, *means, standard deviations,* and *Pearson product moment correlations*—can now be used.

Ratio Scale of Measurement

Two measurement instruments may help you understand the difference between the interval and ratio scales: a thermometer and a yardstick. If we have a thermometer that measures temperature on either the Fahrenheit or Celsius scale, we cannot say that 80°F is twice as warm as 40°F. Why? Because these scales do not originate from a point of absolute zero; a substance may have some degree of heat even though its measured temperature falls *below* zero. With a yardstick, however, the beginning of linear measurement is absolutely the beginning. If we measure a desk from the left edge to the right edge, that's it. There is no more desk in either direction beyond those limits. A measurement of "zero" means there's no desk there at all, and a "minus" distance isn't even possible.

More generally, a **ratio scale** has two characteristics: (1) equal measurement units (similar to an interval scale) and (2) *an absolute zero point,* such that 0 on the scale reflects a total absence of the quantity being measured.

Let's consider once again our "availability" scale for measuring professor effectiveness. This scale could never be considered a ratio scale. Why? Because there is only one condition in which the professor would be absolutely unavailable: if the professor were dead! Under that condition, all the rest of the degrees of availability would evaporate and the scale would vanish.

What distinguishes the ratio scale from the other three scales is that *the ratio scale can express values in terms of multiples and fractional parts* and the ratios are *true* ratios. A yardstick can do that: A yard is a *multiple* (by 12) of a 3-in. distance; 3 in. is one-fourth (a *fractional part*) of a foot. The ratios are 3:36 (or 1:12) and 3:12 (or 1:4).

Ratio scales outside the physical sciences are relatively rare. And whenever we cannot measure a phenomenon in terms of a ratio scale, we must refrain from making comparisons such as "this thing is three times as great as that" or "we have only half as much of one thing as another." Only ratio scales allow us to make comparisons that involve multiplication or division.

We can summarize our description of the four scales this way:

If you can say that

- One object is different from another, you have a *nominal scale;*
- One object is bigger or better or more of anything than another, you have an *ordinal scale;*
- One object is so many units (degrees, inches) more than another, you have an *interval scale;*
- One object is so many times as big or bright or tall or heavy as another, you have a *ratio scale.* (Senders, 1958, p. 51)

Table 2.4 provides a quick reference for the various types of scales, their distinguishing characteristics, and the statistical analysis possibilities for each scale. Later, when we consider the statistical interpretation of data, you may want to refer to this table to determine whether the type of data measurement you have employed will support the statistical operation you are contemplating.

VALIDITY AND RELIABILITY OF MEASUREMENT

Validity and *reliability* are two words that you will encounter repeatedly in research methodology, and these two terms are often used in connection with measurement. The validity and reliability of your measurement instruments influence the extent to which you can learn something about the phenomenon you are studying, the probability that you will obtain statistical significance in your data analysis, and the extent to which you can draw meaningful conclusions from your data.

TABLE 2.4 A summary of measurement scales, their characteristics, and their statistical implications

	Measurement Scale	Characteristics of the Scale	Statistical Possibilities of the Scale
Non-Interval Scales	Nominal scale	A scale that "measures" in terms of names or designations of discrete units or categories	Enables one to determine the mode, the percentage values, or the chi-square
	Ordinal scale	A scale that "measures" in terms of such values as "more" or "less," "larger" or "smaller," but without specifying the size of the intervals	Enables one also to determine the median, percentile rank, and rank correlation
Interval Scales	Interval scale	A scale that measures in terms of equal intervals or degrees of difference but whose zero point, or point of beginning, is arbitrarily established	Enables one also to determine the mean, standard deviation, and product moment correlation; allows one to conduct most inferential statistical analyses
	Ratio scale	A scale that measures in terms of equal intervals and an absolute zero point of origin	Enables one also to determine the geometric mean and the percentage variation; allows one to conduct virtually any inferential statistical analysis

Validity

The **validity** of a measurement instrument is the extent to which the instrument measures what it is supposed to measure. Certainly no one would question the notion that a yardstick is a valid means of measuring length. Nor would most people doubt that a thermometer measures temperature; for instance, in a mercury thermometer, the level to which the mercury rises is a function of how much it expands, which is a function of the degree to which it is hot or cold.

But to what extent does a standardized intelligence test actually measure a person's intelligence? How accurately do people's annual incomes reflect their social class? And how well does a sociogram capture the interpersonal dynamics in a group of nine people? Especially when we are measuring *insubstantial* phenomena—phenomena without a direct basis in the physical world—our measurement instruments may be somewhat suspect in terms of validity.

Let's return to the item we presented earlier to assess a professor's availability for students (see p. 26) and consider its validity as such a measure. Notice how fuzzy some of the category words are. The professor is "always available." What does *always* mean? Twenty-four hours a day? Could you call the professor at 3 A.M. any day of the week, or only whenever the professor is on campus? If the latter is the case, could you call your professor out of a faculty meeting or out of a conference with the president of the college? We might have similar problems in interpreting "generally available," "seldom available," and "never available." What seems at first glance to be a scale that anyone could understand is, on careful inspection, somewhat suspect in terms of its validity and, in fact, its practical usefulness as a measuring instrument for research purposes.

A test may be intended to measure a certain characteristic, and it may be *called* a measure of that characteristic, but these things don't necessarily mean that the test actually measures what its authors say it does. For example, consider a paper-and-pencil test of personality traits. With a series of check marks, the person indicates his or her most representative characteristics or behaviors in given situations; the person's responses on the test are presumed to reveal relatively stable personality traits. The question that validity asks is: Does such a test, in fact, measure the person's personality, or does it measure something else altogether? The answer depends, at least in part, on the extent to which the person is, or *can* be, truthful in responding. If the person responds in terms of characteristics and behaviors that he or she believes to be socially desirable, the test results may reveal not the person's actual personality, but rather an idealized portrait of how he or she would like to be seen by others.

Reliability

Imagine that you are concerned about your growing waistline and decide to go on a diet. Every day you put a tape measure around your waist and pull the two ends together snugly to get a measurement. But just how tight is "snug"? Quite possibly, the level of snugness might be different from one day to the next. In fact, you might even measure your waist with different degrees of snugness from one *minute* to the next. To the extent that you are not measuring your waist in a consistent fashion—even though you always use the same tape measure—you have a problem with reliability.

More generally, **reliability** is the consistency with which a measuring instrument yields a certain result when the entity being measured hasn't changed. As we have just seen in our waist-measuring situation, instruments that measure physical phenomena are not necessarily completely reliable. As another example, think of a beam balance that a storekeeper might use. When weighing out a pound of rice, the storekeeper won't always measure *exactly* the same amount of rice each time.

Instruments designed to measure psychological characteristics (insubstantial phenomena) tend to be even less reliable than those designed to measure physical (substantial) phenomena. For example, a student using the preceding scale for measuring professor availability might easily rate the professor as "70" one day and "90" the next, not because the professor's availability has changed overnight, but because the student's interpretations of the phrases "generally available" and "always available" *have* changed. Similarly, if we asked the nine people portrayed in Figure 2.1 (Gretchen, Joe, Greg, etc.) to indicate the people they liked best and least among their colleagues, they wouldn't necessarily always give us the same answers they gave us previously, even if the interpersonal dynamics within the group had remained constant.

We can measure something accurately only when we can also measure it consistently. Yet measuring something consistently doesn't necessarily mean measuring it accurately. In other words, *reliability is a necessary but insufficient condition for validity.*

Both validity and reliability, then, reflect the degree to which we may have *error* in our measurements. In many instances—and especially when we are measuring insubstantial phenomena—a measurement instrument may allow us to measure a characteristic only indirectly and so may be subject to a variety of biasing factors (e.g., people's responses on a rating scale are apt to be influenced by their interpretations, prejudices, memory lapses, etc.). In such cases, we have error due to the imperfect *validity* of the measurement instrument. Yet typically—even when we are measuring substantial phenomena—we may get slightly different measures from one time to the next simply because our measurement tool is imprecise (e.g., the waist size we measure may depend on how snugly we pull the tape measure). In such cases, we have error due to the imperfect *reliability* of the measure. Generally speaking, validity errors reflect biases in the instrument itself and are relatively constant sources of error. In contrast, reliability errors reflect *use* of the instrument and are apt to vary unpredictably from one occasion to the next.

Validity and reliability take different forms, depending on the nature of the research problem, the general methodology the researcher uses to address the problem, and the nature of the data that are collected. Accordingly, we will look at the various forms of validity and reliability when we discuss "Planning Your Research Design" in Chapter 5.

STATISTICS AS A TOOL OF RESEARCH

All tools are more suitable for some purposes than for others. Consider a screwdriver as an example. A screwdriver was designed for just a single purpose: to insert and remove screws. We've had friends, however, who have used screwdrivers for a wide variety of other tasks: to pry off lids, punch holes, scratch away unwanted paint, and so on. Certainly these friends often accomplished their objectives by using—or rather, misusing—a screwdriver in such ways, but the purpose for which the tool was designed was almost invariably ignored. So, too, with statistics. They can be a powerful tool when used correctly—in particular, when they are used for the specific kinds of data and research questions for which they were designed—but they can be misleading when they are applied in other contexts.

Statistics are typically more useful in some academic disciplines than in others. For instance, researchers use them quite often in such fields as psychology, sociology, and education; they use them less frequently in such fields as history, musicology, and literature. But whenever we use statistics, we must remember that the statistical values we obtain are never the end of a research endeavor nor the final answer to a research problem. The final question in research is, *What do the data indicate?*, not, What is their numerical configuration (where they cluster, how broadly they spread, or how closely they are related)? Statistics give us *information* about the data, but a conscientious researcher is not satisfied until the *meaning* of this information is revealed.

THE LURE OF STATISTICS

Statistics can be like the voice of a bevy of sirens to the novice researcher. For those who have forgotten their Homer, the *Odyssey* describes the perilous straits between Scylla and Charybdis. On these treacherous rocks sat an assembly of Sirens—svelte maidens who, with enticing songs, lured sailors in their direction and, by so doing, caused ships to drift and founder on the jagged shores.

For many beginning researchers, statistics hold a similar appeal. Subjecting data to elegant statistical routines may lure novice researchers into thinking they have made a substantial discovery, when in fact they have only calculated a few numbers that help them interpret the data. Behind every statistic lies a sizable body of data; the statistic may summarize these data in a particular way, but it cannot capture all the nuances of the data. The entire body of data collected, not any single statistic calculated, is what ultimately must be used to resolve the research problem. There is no substitute for the task the researcher ultimately faces: to discover the meaning of the data and its relevance to the research problem. Any statistical process you may employ is merely ancillary to this central quest.

Furthermore, even the most sophisticated statistical procedures can never make amends for a poorly conceived research study. An editorial in the journal *Research in Nursing and Health* makes this point quite poignantly:

> The use of elegant statistics can never compensate for inelegant conceptual bases. The new evaluative procedures are exciting because they enable examination of data in ways previously not possible. The bottom line remains the same, however. One cannot draw large savings out of an account into which little has been deposited. Neither can one draw useful meanings from studies into which less-than-important notions have been entered. ("Use of Elegant Statistics," 1987, p. iii)

PRIMARY FUNCTIONS OF STATISTICS

Statistics have two principal functions: to help the researcher (1) describe the data and (2) draw inferences from the data. **Descriptive statistics** summarize the general nature of the data obtained—for instance, how certain measured characteristics appear to be "on the average," how much variability exists among different pieces of data, how closely two or more characteristics are interrelated, and so on. In contrast, **inferential statistics** help the researcher make decisions about the data; for instance, they help one decide whether the differences observed between two groups in an experiment are large enough to be attributed to the experimental intervention rather than to a once-in-a-blue-moon fluke.

Both of these functions ultimately involve summarizing the data in some way. In the process of summarizing, statistical analyses often create entities that have no counterpart in reality. For instance, we usually accept the arithmetic mean, commonly called the *average,* without question or reservation. But take a simple example: Four students have part-time jobs on campus. One student works 24 hours a week in the library, the second works 22 hours a week in the campus bookstore, the third works 12 hours a week in the parking lot, and the fourth works 16 hours a week in the cafeteria. Data presented in this form are unorganized and random.

All data, as they come to us from the real world, are unorganized, separate bits of information. They have no focus; they need to be managed. How do we do this? Let's enlist the aid of statistics. How might we summarize the random work hours of the four students? One approach is to calculate the arithmetic mean. By doing so, we find that the students work, "on the average," 18.5 hours a week. Although we have "learned" something about these four students and their working hours, to some extent we have learned a myth: No student has worked exactly 18.5 hours a week. That figure represents absolutely no fact in the real world.

Apparently, we have solved one problem only to create another. We have created a dilemma. If statistics offer us only an unreality, then why use them? Why create myth out of hard, demonstrable data?

The answer lies in the nature of the human mind. Human beings can handle only so much information at a time. (If you have studied cognitive psychology, you may recognize that we are talking about the limited capacity of *working memory*.) Statistics help condense an overwhelming body of data into an amount of information that the mind can more readily comprehend. In the process, they can help the researcher "see" patterns and relationships in the data that might otherwise go unnoticed. More generally, statistics *help the human mind comprehend disparate data as an organized whole.* And as we shall see now, the human mind is another indispensable tool in the researcher's toolkit.

THE HUMAN MIND AS A TOOL OF RESEARCH

Statistics can tell us where the center of a body of data lies, how broadly the data are spread, how much two or more variables are interrelated—more generally, how the data stack up. But statistics cannot interpret those data and arrive at a logical conclusion as to their meaning. Only the mind of the researcher can do that.

The human mind is undoubtedly the most important tool on the researcher's workbench. Its functioning dwarfs all other gadgetry. Nothing equals its powers of comprehension, integrative reasoning, and insight.

Over the past several millennia, human beings have developed several strategies to help them make use of the human mind to better understand the unknown. Key among them are deductive logic, inductive reasoning, the scientific method, critical thinking, and collaboration with others.

DEDUCTIVE LOGIC

Deductive logic begins with one or more *premises.* These premises are statements or assumptions that are self-evident and widely accepted "truths." Reasoning then proceeds logically from these premises toward conclusions that must also be true. For example,

> If all tulips are plants, (premise 1)
>
> And if all plants produce energy through photosynthesis, (premise 2)
>
> Then all tulips must produce energy through photosynthesis. (conclusion)

To the extent that the premises are false, the conclusions will also be false. For example,

> If all tulips are platypuses, (premise 1)
>
> And if all platypuses produce energy through spontaneous combustion, (premise 2)
>
> Then all tulips must produce energy through spontaneous combustion. (conclusion)

The if-this-then-that logic is the same in both examples. We reach an erroneous conclusion in the second example (we conclude that tulips are likely to burst into flame on a regular basis) only because both of our premises are also erroneous.

Let's look back more than 500 years to Christopher Columbus's first voyage to the New World. At the time, people held many beliefs about the world that, to them, were irrefutable facts: Humans are mortal; God is good; the earth is flat. The terror that gripped Columbus's sailors as they crossed the Atlantic was a fear supported by deductive logic. If the earth is flat (premise), its flat surface should have boundaries. The boundaries of a flat surface should be the edges of that surface. If a ship continues to travel across a flat surface, it must eventually come to the edge of it and fall off.

The logic was sound; the reasoning, accurate; the conclusion, valid. Where the whole proposition went wrong was that the major premise was incorrect. The reasoning began with a preconceived idea that *seemed* to be true but in fact was not.

Deductive logic is extremely valuable for generating research hypotheses and testing theories. As an example, when developing her dissertation proposal, doctoral student Dinah Jackson was interested in the effects of *self-questioning*: asking oneself questions about the topic one is studying. She knew from well-established learning theory that forming associations among two or more pieces of information results in more effective learning than does trying to learn each piece of information separately from the others. She also found a body of research literature indicating that the kinds the questions people ask themselves (mentally) and try to answer as they learn (e.g., as they sit in class or read a textbook) affect what they learn and how effectively they remember it. (For instance, a student who is trying to answer the question, "What do I need to remember for the test?" might learn very differently from the student who is considering the question, "How might I apply this information to my own life?") Jackson's reasoning was as follows:

> If learning information in an integrative fashion is more effective than learning information piecemeal, (premise 1)
>
> If the kinds of questions learners ask themselves during a learning activity influence how they learn, (premise 2)
>
> If training in self-questioning techniques influences the kinds of questions that students ask themselves, (premise 3)
>
> And if learning is reflected in the kinds of notes that learners take during class, (premise 4)
>
> Then teaching students to ask themselves integrative questions as they study class material should lead to class notes that are more integrative in nature. (conclusion)

Such reasoning led Jackson to form and test the following hypothesis:

> Students who have formal training in integrative self-questioning will take more integrative notes than students who have not had any formal training. (Jackson, 1996, p. 12)

Happily, Jackson's dissertation research supported her hypothesis.

INDUCTIVE REASONING

Inductive reasoning begins, not with a preestablished truth or assumption, but with an observation. For instance, as a baby in a high chair many years ago, you may have observed that if you held a cracker in front of you and then let go of it, it fell to the floor. Hmmm, you may have thought, what happens if I do it again? So you took another cracker from the tray on your high chair, held it in front of you, and released it. It, too, fell to the floor. You followed the same procedure with several more crackers, and the result was always the same: The cracker traveled in a downward direction. Eventually you may have performed the same actions on other things—blocks, rattles, peas, milk, and so on—and inevitably observed the same result. You probably eventually drew the conclusion that all things fall when dropped—your first inkling about a force called *gravity*. (You may also have concluded that dropping things from your high chair greatly annoyed your parents, but that is another matter.)

In **inductive reasoning,** people use specific instances or occurrences to draw conclusions about entire classes of objects or events. In other words, they observe a sample and then draw conclusions about the population from which the sample comes. For instance, an anthropologist may draw conclusions about a certain culture after studying a particular community within that culture. A professor of special education may use a few case studies in which a particular instructional approach is effective with students who have autism to recommend that teachers use the instructional approach with other students who have autism. A sociologist may conduct two surveys, one in 1995 and a second in 2005, asking 500 people to describe their beliefs about AIDS and then drawing conclusions about how society's attitudes toward AIDS have changed over that time.

Figure 2.4 graphically depicts the nature of inductive reasoning. Let's look at an example of how this representation applies to an actual research project. Neurologists Silverman, Masland, Saunders, and Schwab (1970) sought the answer to a problem in medicine: How long can a person have a "flat EEG" (an isoelectric brain tracing indicating cerebral death) and still recover? Silverman and his colleagues observed 2,650 actual cases. They noted that, in all cases in which

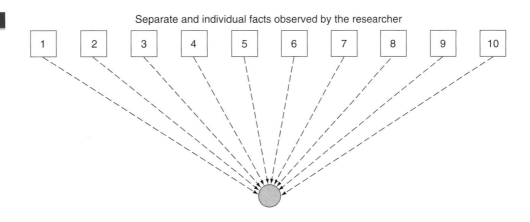

FIGURE 2.4
The inductive process

Separate and individual facts observed by the researcher

They all seem to lead to a single conclusion.

the flat EEG persisted for 24 hours or more, not a single recovery occurred. All the data pointed to the same conclusion: *It is unlikely that a recovery might take place with those who exhibit flat EEG tracings of 24 hours or more in duration.* We cannot, of course, rule out the unexplored cases, but *from the data observed,* the conclusion reached was that recovery seems impossible. The EEG line from *each* case led to that *one* conclusion.

THE SCIENTIFIC METHOD

During the Renaissance, people found that when data are assembled and studied dispassionately, the data may suggest previously undiscovered meaning. Thus was the scientific method born; the words literally mean "the method that searches after knowledge" (*scientia* is Latin for "knowledge" and derives from *scire,* "to know"). The scientific method gained momentum during the 16th century with such men as Paracelsus, Copernicus, Vesalius, and Galileo.

Traditionally, the **scientific method** is a means whereby insight into the unknown is sought by (1) identifying a problem that defines the goal of one's quest, (2) positing a hypothesis that, if confirmed, resolves the problem, (3) gathering data relevant to the hypothesis, and (4) analyzing and interpreting the data to see whether they support the hypothesis and resolve the question that initiated the research.

Figure 1.1 in Chapter 1, which depicts research as a cyclical process, illustrates quite clearly how the scientific method serves as a basis for research methodology. We should keep in mind, however, that not all research methodologies follow the steps we have outlined in exactly that sequence. For instance, as you will discover when you read Chapter 7, such approaches as ethnographic research and grounded theory research involve collecting data and *then* developing one or more hypotheses about them.

As you may already have realized, application of the scientific method often involves both deductive and inductive reasoning. Researchers may develop a hypothesis either from a theory (deductive logic) or from observations of specific events (inductive reasoning). Then, using deductive logic, they make predictions about the patterns they are likely to see in the data *if* the hypothesis is true. And often, using inductive reasoning, they generalize from data taken from a sample to describe the characteristics of a larger population.

CRITICAL THINKING

Before beginning a research project, effective researchers typically look at research studies and theoretical perspectives related to their topic of interest. But they don't just accept research findings and theories at face value; instead, they scrutinize them for faulty assumptions, questionable logic, weaknesses in methodology, inappropriate statistical analyses, and unwarranted conclusions. In other words, good researchers engage in critical thinking.

In general, **critical thinking** involves evaluating information or arguments in terms of their accuracy and worth (Beyer, 1985). Critical thinking may take a variety of forms, depending on the context. For instance, it may involve any one or more of the following (adapted from Halpern, 1998):

- *Verbal reasoning:*   Understanding and evaluating the persuasive techniques found in oral and written language.
- *Argument analysis:*   Discriminating between reasons that do and do not support a particular conclusion.
- *Decision making:*   Identifying and judging several alternatives and selecting the best alternative.
- *Critical analysis of prior research:*   Evaluating the value of data and research results in terms of the methods used to obtain them and their potential relevance to particular conclusions. Such critical analysis involves considering questions such as these:
  - Was an appropriate method used to measure a particular outcome?
  - Are the data and results derived from a relatively large number of people, objects, or events?
  - Have other possible explanations or conclusions been eliminated?
  - Can the results obtained in one situation be reasonably generalized to other situations?

Critical thinking sometimes takes different forms in different content areas. In history, it might involve scrutinizing various historical documents and looking for clues as to whether things *definitely* happened a particular way or only *maybe* happened that way. In psychology, it might involve critically evaluating the way in which a particular psychological characteristic (e.g., intelligence, personality) is being measured. In anthropology, it might involve observing people's behaviors over an extended period of time and speculating about what those behaviors indicate about the society being studied.

COLLABORATION WITH OTHERS

As the old saying goes, two heads are better than one. Typically, three or more are better still. Any single researcher is apt to have certain perspectives, assumptions, and theoretical biases—not to mention holes in his or her knowledge about the subject matter—that will limit how he or she approaches a research project. By bringing one or more professional colleagues onto the scene—ideally, colleagues who have perspectives, backgrounds, and areas of expertise somewhat different from the researcher's own—the researcher brings just that many more cognitive resources to bear on how to tackle the research problem and how to find meaning in the data obtained (e.g., see Nichols, 1998).

Sometimes these colleagues enter the picture as equal partners. On other occasions, they may simply offer suggestions and advice. For example, when a graduate student conducts research for a master's thesis or doctoral dissertation, the student is, of course, the key player in the endeavor. Yet the student typically has considerable guidance from an advisor and, especially in the case of a doctoral dissertation, from a faculty committee. The prudent student selects an advisor and committee members who have the expertise to help shape the research project into a form that will truly address the research question and, more generally, will make a genuine contribution to the student's field of study.

All of the processes just described—deductive logic, inductive reasoning, the scientific method, critical thinking, and collaboration with others—help the researcher take advantage of the human mind as a tool of research. We look at one final tool—language—in the next section.

LANGUAGE AS A TOOL OF RESEARCH

One of humankind's greatest achievements is language. Not only does it allow us to communicate with one another, but it also enables us to think more effectively. People can often think more clearly and efficiently about a topic when they can represent their thoughts in their heads with specific words and phrases.

Imagine, for a moment, that you are driving along a country road. In a field to your left, you see something with the following characteristics:

- Black and white in color, in a splotchy pattern
- Covered with a short, bristly substance
- Appended at one end by an object similar in appearance to a paintbrush
- Appended at the other end by a lumpy thing with four pointy objects sticking upward (two soft and floppy, two hard and curved around)
- Held up from the ground by four spindly sticks, two at each end

Unless you were born yesterday, you would almost certainly identify the object as a *cow*.

Words—even those as simple as *cow*—and the concepts that the words represent enhance our thinking in several ways (Ormrod, 2004):

1. *They reduce the world's complexity.* Classifying similar objects and events into categories and labeling those categories in terms of specific words make our experiences easier to understand. For instance, it is much easier to think to yourself, "I see a herd of cows," than to think, "There is a brown object, covered with bristly stuff, appended by a paintbrush and a lumpy thing, and held up by four sticks. Ah, yes, and I also see a black-and-white spotted object, covered with bristly stuff, appended by a paintbrush and a lumpy thing, and held up by four sticks. And over there is a brown-and-white object. . . ."

2. *They facilitate generalization and inference drawing in new situations.* When we learn a new concept, we associate certain characteristics with it. Then, when we encounter a new instance of the concept, we can draw on our knowledge of associated characteristics to make assumptions and inferences about the new instance. For instance, if you see a herd of cattle as you drive through the countryside, you can infer that you are passing through either dairy or beef country, depending on whether you see large udders hanging down between some of the spindly sticks.

3. *They allow abstraction of the environment.* An object that has bristly stuff, a paintbrush at one end, a lumpy thing at the other, and several spindly sticks at the bottom is a concrete entity. The concept *cow,* however, is more abstract: It connotes such characteristics as *female, supplier of milk,* and, to the farmer or rancher, *economic asset.* Concepts and the labels associated with them allow us to think about our experiences without necessarily having to consider all of their concrete characteristics.

4. *They enhance the power of thought.* When you are thinking about an object covered with bristly stuff, appended by a paintbrush and a lumpy thing, held up by four sticks, and so on, you can think of little else (as we mentioned earlier, human beings can think about only a very limited amount of information at any one time). In contrast, when you simply think *cow,* you can easily think about other ideas at the same time and perhaps form connections and interrelationships among them in ways you hadn't previously considered.

Just as *cow* helps us categorize certain experiences into a single idea, so, too, does the terminology of your discipline help you help you interpret and understand your observations. The words *tempo, timbre,* and *perfect pitch* are useful to the musicologist. Such expressions as *central business district, folded mountain,* and *distance to k* have special meaning for the geographer. The terms *lesson plan, portfolio,* and *charter school* communicate a great deal to the educator. Learning the specialized terminology of your field is indispensable to conducting a research study, grounding it in prior theory and research, and communicating your results to others.

THE VALUE OF KNOWING TWO OR MORE LANGUAGES

It should go without saying that not all significant research is reported in English. Accordingly, many doctoral programs require that students demonstrate a reading competency in one or two foreign languages in addition to proficiency in English. The choice of these languages is usually linked to the area of proposed research.

The language requirement is a reasonable one. Human enlightenment has spread across the world at an astounding rate because of research and discovery. The former Soviet Union, for example, made gigantic strides in science, especially in physics and space science. Japan has pushed back the frontiers of knowledge in electronics and robotics. Two of the most influential theorists in child development today—Jean Piaget and Lev Vygotsky—wrote in French and Russian, respectively. Many new discoveries are reported in the native language of the researcher. A researcher doing a doctoral dissertation that demands knowledge of research in other languages must be able to access that research through at least a reading competency in the languages in which the research is reported.

THE IMPORTANCE OF WRITING

All research, to be generally accessible to the larger scientific community and, ultimately, to society as a whole, must eventually be presented as a written document. To produce such a document, the researcher must possess the ability to use language with a degree of skill and accuracy that will clearly delineate all aspects of the research process. The written document is often referred to as the *research report*. The basic requirement for writing such a report is the ability to use language in a clear, coherent manner. We present some suggestions for writing effectively in the "Practical Application" section that immediately follows this section.

Although the conventional wisdom is that clear thinking precedes clear writing, we have learned through both our own work and that of others that writing can be a productive form of thinking in and of itself. When you write your ideas down on paper, you do several things:

- You must identify the specific ideas you do and do not know about your topic.
- You must clarify and organize your thoughts sufficiently to communicate them to your readers.
- You may detect gaps and logical flaws in your thinking.

Perhaps it is not surprising, then, that writing about a topic actually enhances the writer's understanding of that topic (Benton, 1997; Greene & Ackerman, 1995; Kellogg, 1994).

If you wait until all of your thoughts are clear before you start writing, you may never begin. Therefore, we recommend that you start writing your research proposal or report as soon as possible. Begin with a title and a purpose statement for your study. Commit your title to paper; keep it in plain sight as you focus your ideas. Although you are apt to change the title later as your research proceeds, creating a working title in the early stages of a project can provide both focus and direction. When you can draft a clear and concise statement that begins, "The purpose of this study is . . . ," you are well on your way to planning a focused research study.

PRACTICAL APPLICATION   COMMUNICATING EFFECTIVELY THROUGH WRITING

In our own experience, most students have a great deal to learn about how to write effectively. Yet we also know that, with effort, practice, expert guidance, and regular feedback, students *can* learn to write more effectively. Chapters 6 and 12 will present specific strategies for writing research proposals and research reports. Here we offer more general strategies for writing in a way that clearly communicates your ideas and reasoning to others. We also offer suggestions for using word processing software.

GUIDELINES   WRITING TO COMMUNICATE

The following guidelines are based on techniques often seen in effective writing. Furthermore, such techniques have consistently been shown to facilitate readers' comprehension of what others have written (e.g., Ormrod, 2004).

1. *Say what you mean to say.*   Precision is of utmost importance, not only in research proposals and reports, but in writing in general. Choose your words and phrases carefully so that you communicate your *exact* meaning, not some vague approximation. Many books and other resources offer suggestions for writing clear, concise, and effective sentences and combining those

sentences into unified and coherent paragraphs (e.g., see the sources in the "For Further Reading" list at the end of the chapter).

2. *Keep your primary objective in writing your paper in mind at all times, and focus your discussion accordingly.* All too often, novice researchers try to include everything they've learned, both from their literature review and from their data analysis, in their writing. But ultimately, everything you say should relate either directly or indirectly to your research problem. If you can't think of how something relates, leave it out! You'll undoubtedly have enough things to write about as it is.

3. *Provide an overview of what you will be talking about.* Your readers can more effectively read your work when they know what to expect as they read. Providing an overview of the topics to be discussed and their order, and possibly also showing how the various topics interrelate, is sometimes called an **advance organizer.** As a simple example, recall the doctoral student who studied the effects of self-questioning on the quality of classroom note taking. The student began the "Review of the Literature" in her dissertation as follows:

> The first part of this review will examine the theories, frameworks, and experimental research behind the research on adjunct questioning. Part two will investigate the transition of adjunct questioning to self-generated questioning. Specific models of self-generated questioning will be explored, starting with the historical research on question position [and progressing] to the more contemporary research on individual differences in self-questioning. Part three will explore some basic research on note taking, and tie note taking theory with the research on self-generated questioning. (Jackson, 1996, p. 17)

4. *Organize your ideas into general and more specific categories, and use headings and subheadings to guide your readers through your discussion of these categories.* Take a moment to flip through the pages of this book. Notice how often we use headings to let you know what we'll be talking about in the paragraphs to come. In our own experience, students often organize their thoughts (their literature reviews, for example) without communicating their organizational scheme to their readers. Using headings is one simple way to make that scheme crystal clear.

5. *Provide transitional phrases, sentences, or paragraphs that help your readers follow your train of thought.* If one idea, paragraph, or section leads logically to the next, say so! Furthermore, give readers some sort of signal when you change the course of your discussion. For instance, in her doctoral dissertation examining the various learning processes that students might use when listening to a lecture, Nancy Thrailkill finished a discussion of the effects of visual imagery (mental "pictures" of objects or events) and was making the transition to a more theoretical discussion of imagery. She made the transition easy to follow with this sentence:

> Although researchers have conducted numerous studies on the use and value of imagery in learning, they seem to have a difficult time agreeing on why and how it works. (Thrailkill, 1996, p. 10)

The first clause in this transitional sentence recaps the preceding discussion, whereas the second clause introduces the new (albeit related) topic.

6. *Use concrete examples to make abstract ideas more understandable.* There's a fine line between being abstract and being vague. Even as scholars who have worked in our respective academic disciplines for many years, we still find that we understand something better when the writer gives us a concrete example to illustrate an abstract idea. Let's look once again at the dissertation on self-questioning and class note taking. The author makes the point that how a researcher evaluates, or *codes,* the content of participants' class notes will affect what the researcher discovers about those notes; more specifically, she argues that a superficial coding scheme (e.g., counting the number of main ideas included in notes) fails to capture the true quality of the notes. She clarifies her point with a concrete example:

> For example, while listening to the same lecture, Student A may record only an outline of the lecture, whereas Student B may record an outline, examples, definitions, and

mnemonics. If a researcher only considered the number of main ideas that students included in their notes, then both sets of notes might be considered equivalent, despite the fact that the two sets differ considerably in the <u>type</u> of material recorded. (Jackson, 1996, p. 9)

7. *Use appropriate punctuation.*   Appropriate punctuation is not merely a bothersome formality. On the contrary, it can help you communicate your meanings. A colon will announce that what follows it explains the general statement that immediately precedes it. Similarly, the semicolon, the dash, quotation marks, parentheses, and italics are all tools for clarifying your thought. Also learn to use the comma correctly. Many style manuals have sections dealing with correct punctuation usage.

8. *Use figures and tables when such mechanisms can more effectively present or organize your ideas and findings.*   Although the bulk of your research proposal or report will almost certainly be prose, in some cases it might be helpful to present some information in figure or table form. Consider the sociogram and sociometric data presented earlier in Figure 2.3 and Table 2.3, respectively. We're sure you will agree that we couldn't possibly have presented the same information as effectively by describing it through words alone.

9. *At the conclusion of a chapter or major section, summarize what you've said.*   Chances are, you will be presenting a great deal of information in any research proposal or report that you write. Summarizing what you've said helps your readers identify the things that are, in your mind, the most important things for them to remember. For example, in a dissertation that examined children's beliefs about the mental processes involved in reading, Debby Zambo summarized a lengthy discussion about the children's understanding of what it means to pay attention:

> In sum, the students understand attention to be a mental process. They know their attention is inconsistent and affected by emotions and interest. They also realize that the right level of material, amount of information, and length of time helps their attention. The stillness of reading is difficult for some of the students but calming for others, and they appear to know this, and to know when reading will be difficult and when it will be calming. This idea is contrary to what has been written in the literature about struggling readers. (Zambo, 2003, 68)

10. *Anticipate that you will almost certainly have to write multiple drafts.*   All too often, we have had students submit research proposals, theses, or dissertations with the assumption that they have completed what they set out to do. Such students have invariably been disappointed (sometimes even outraged) when we've asked them to revise their work, usually several times over. The necessity to write multiple drafts applies not only to novice researchers but to experienced scholars as well. For instance, we would hate to count the number of times this book has undergone revision—certainly far more often than the label "eighth edition" indicates! Multiple revisions enable you to reflect on and critically evaluate your own writing, revise and clarify awkward passages, get feedback from peers and instructors who can point out where the manuscript lacks clarity, and spend more time ensuring that the final draft is as clear and precise as possible.

Fortunately, computer technology makes the revision process infinitely easier than it was in the days of manual typewriters. In the next section, we often some guidance for the novice word processor.

GUIDELINES   USING A WORD PROCESSOR

USING
TECHNOLOGY

One of the most common uses of the computer today is word processing. A **word processor** is a computer program for writing. By supporting the entering, editing, revising, formatting, storing, retrieving, and printing of text, a word processor can greatly enhance a researcher's personal productivity. Powerful word processing programs are now available that allow users to accomplish tasks that previously only professional typesetters could complete.

Most word processing programs include the following features:

▓ *Editing features.*   Common editing features allow you to enter information quickly, change wording, and delete unwanted letters, words, and paragraphs. As you examine what you have written, it is easy to move sections of text from one location to another. Editing features give the researcher more freedom to write, critically examine what has been written, and make modifications as necessary.

▓ *Formatting features.*   Common formatting features provide control over how the words appear on the page. If special emphasis is needed, a word can be highlighted by changing the type size or by <u>underlining</u>, *italicizing,* or using **boldface.** Text can be arranged in columns with various types of margins and alignments. Tables can be set up easily with borders and shading to highlight information. Many word processing programs also let the writer insert graphics quickly and easily into a body of text.

▓ *Special editing features.*   Several special features have proved invaluable to writers using word processors. These include an *outliner* to facilitate the initial planning and organization of the major sections of a writing project; a *spell checker* to call attention to and make suggestions for suspiciously spelled words; a *thesaurus* to help the writer identify alternative words and phrases; and a *grammar checker* to detect potential problems in how words have been put together.

▓ *Document storage and retrieval features.*   These features allow you to save your work and retrieve it later in exactly the same form. Moreover, it is possible to exchange the file you have saved with other people, who can access the copy from a disk or as an attachment to an e-mail message.

You will find that word processing software is an invaluable tool throughout the research process; in fact, we ourselves don't know how we lived without it for as long as we did. For example, as the *study is being planned,* word processing software can be used for brainstorming and organizing ideas. As *literature is being reviewed,* the software provides an efficient means of keeping track of bibliographic information, along with the ideas, theories, and research results found in various books, journal articles, and other resources. As the *study is being implemented,* the software can be used to generate various types of data collection instruments and to transcribe people's responses to such instruments as interviews and questionnaires. As the *data are being analyzed,* tables and graphics can be developed to help categorize and summarize patterns in the data. Finally, as the *final report is being completed,* it can be written in the proper form for review and potential publication.

We offer three general recommendations for using a word processor effectively:

1. *Save your document frequently.*   This seems like such an obvious point that we almost left it on the editing room floor, but then we remembered all the personal horror stories we have heard (and in some cases experienced ourselves) about losing data, research materials, and other valuable information. Every computer user eventually encounters some type of glitch that causes problems in the retrieval of information. Whether the disk goes bad, the electricity goes out before you can save a file, you get a system error, or your personal computer inexplicably crashes, data sometimes get lost. It is imperative that you get in the habit of saving your work. Save multiple copies so that if something goes awry in one place, you will always have a backup in a safe location. Here are a few things to think about:

- Save at least two copies of important files, and save them in different places—perhaps one file at home and another at the office, at a friend's house, or in a safe deposit box.
- Save your work-in-progress frequently, perhaps every 10 to 30 minutes.
- Save various versions of your work with titles that help identify each version—for instance, by including the date on which you completed each file.
- If something horrible does happen, some software programs (e.g., Norton Utilities) may be able to fix the damage and retrieve some or potentially all of the lost material.

2. *Use such features as the spell checker and grammar checker to look for errors, but don't rely on them exclusively.*   As we noted earlier in the chapter, although computers are marvelous machines, their "thinking" capabilities do not yet begin to approach those of the human mind. For instance, although a computer can detect spelling errors, it does so by comparing each word against a "dictionary" of correctly spelled words. Not every word in the English language will be included in

the dictionary; for instance, proper nouns (e.g., such surnames as Leedy and Ormrod) will *not* be. Furthermore, it may assume that *abut* is spelled correctly when the word you really had in mind was *about,* and it may very well not know that *there* should actually be *their.*

3. *Print out a paper copy for final editing.*   One of us once had a student who turned in a dissertation draft that was so full of spelling and grammatical errors as to be a very poor reflection on the student indeed—and this from a student who was, ironically, teaching a college-level English composition course at the time. A critical and chastising e-mail message to the student made her irate; she had checked her document quite thoroughly before submitting it, she replied, and was convinced that it was virtually error-free. When her paper draft was returned to her almost bloodshot with spelling and grammatical corrections, she was quite contrite. "I don't know how I missed them all!" she said. When asked if she had ever edited a printed copy of the draft, she replied that she had not, figuring that she could read her work just as easily on the computer monitor and thereby save a tree or two. But in our own experience, it's *always* a good idea to read a printed version of what you have written. For some reason, on a paper copy we can often catch errors that we have overlooked when they stared us in the face on the computer screen.

PRACTICAL APPLICATION IDENTIFYING IMPORTANT TOOLS IN YOUR DISCIPLINE

Throughout this chapter, we have discussed several key tools used by researchers as they go about their work. These tools can be effective and helpful only to the extent that they are used—and used correctly.

Some of the tools may be somewhat new to you. How will you learn when, how, and why you should use them? One effective means of learning about research tools is to work closely with an expert researcher in your field. Watch and observe this person in action as he or she uses one or more of these research tools.

Take the time to find a person who has completed a few research projects—perhaps someone who teaches a research methods class, someone who has published in several journals, someone who has repeatedly received research grants, or even someone who has recently finished a dissertation. Ask this individual the questions listed in the following checklist and, if possible, observe the person as he or she goes about research work. If you cannot locate anyone locally, it may be possible to contact one or more persons through e-mail (see the discussion of e-mail earlier in this chapter).

✔ CHECKLIST
INTERVIEWING AN EXPERT RESEARCHER

_____   1. How do you start a research project?

_____

_____

_____   2. What specific tools do you use (e.g., library resources, computer software, forms of measurement, statistics)?

_____

_____

_____   3. How did you gain your expertise with the various tools you use?

_____

_____

_____ 4. What are some important experiences you suggest for a novice researcher?

_____

_____

_____ 5. If I wanted to learn how to become a competent researcher, what specific tools would
you suggest I work with?

_____

_____

REFLECTIONS ON SIGNIFICANT RESEARCH

The time: February 13, 1929. The place: St. Mary's Hospital, London. The occasion: the reading of a paper before the Medical Research Club. The speaker: a member of the hospital staff in the Department of Microbiology. Such was the setting for the presentation of one of the most significant research reports of the early 20th century. The report was about a discovery that has transformed the practice of medicine. Dr. Alexander Fleming presented to his colleagues his research on penicillin. The group was apathetic. No one showed any enthusiasm for Fleming's paper. Great research has frequently been presented to those who are imaginatively both blind and deaf.

Fleming, however, knew the value of what he had done. The first public announcement of the discovery of penicillin appeared in the *British Journal of Experimental Pathology* in 1929. It is a readable report—one that André Maurois (1959) called "a triumph of clarity, sobriety, and precision." Get it; read it. You will be reliving one of the great moments in 20th-century medical research.

Soon after Fleming's paper, two other names became associated with the development of penicillin: Ernst B. Chain and Howard W. Florey (Chain et al., 1940; also see Abraham et al., 1941). Together, they developed a pure strain of penicillin. Florey was particularly instrumental in initiating its mass production and its use as an antibiotic for wounded soldiers in World War II (Coghill, 1944; also see Coghill & Koch, 1945). Reading these reports takes you back to the days when the medical urgency of dying people called for a massive research effort to make a newly discovered antibiotic available for immediate use.

October 25, 1945: The Nobel Prize in medicine was awarded to Fleming, Chain, and Florey.

If you wish to know more about the discovery of penicillin, read André Maurois's *The Life of Sir Alexander Fleming* (1959), the definitive biography done at the behest of Fleming's widow. The document will give you an insight into the way great research comes into being.

The procedures of great research are identical to those every student follows in doing a dissertation, a thesis, or a research report. All research begins with a problem, an observation, a question. Curiosity is the germinal seed. Hypotheses are formulated. Data are gathered. Conclusions are reached. What *you* are doing in research methodology is the same as what has been done by those who have pushed back the barriers of ignorance and made discoveries that have greatly benefited humankind.

Now go to our Companion Website at http://www.prenhall.com/leedy to assess your understanding of chapter content and to complete the projects that will help you learn how to conduct research.

FOR FURTHER READING

Tools of Research

Atkin, M. (Ed.) (1992). *Encyclopedia of educational research* (6th ed.). New York: Macmillan.

Barnes, A. S. (1994). *Research skills.* Dubuque, IA: Kendall/Hunt.

Berry, D. M. (1990). *A bibliographic guide to educational research* (3rd ed.). Metuchen, NJ: Scarecrow.

Dooley, D. (2001). *Social research methods* (4th ed.). Upper Saddle River, NJ: Prentice Hall.

Miller, D. C. (2002). *Handbook of research design and social measurement* (6th ed.). Thousand Oaks, CA: Sage.

The Library as a Research Tool

Chan, L. M. (1999). *A guide to the Library of Congress classification* (5th ed.). Englewood, CO: Libraries Unlimited.

Katz, W. A. (2002). *Introduction to reference work: Basic information sources* (Vol. 1, 8th ed.). New York: McGraw-Hill.

The Computer and Internet as Research Tools

Angell, D. (1994). *The elements of e-mail style: Communicate effectively via electronic mail.* Reading, MA: Addison-Wesley.

Bane, A. F., & Milheim, W. D. (1995). Internet insights: How academics are using the Internet. *Computers in Libraries, 15*(2), 32–36.

Edyburn, D. L. (1999). *The electronic scholar: Enhancing research productivity with technology.* Upper Saddle River, NJ: Merrill/Prentice Hall.

Fetterman, D. M. (1998). Webs of meaning: Computer and Internet resources for educational research and instruction. *Educational Researcher, 27*(3), 22–29.

Fisher, M. (1995). Desktop tools for the social scientist. In R. M. Lee (Ed.), *Information technology for the social scientist* (pp. 14–32). London: UCL Press.

Lee, R. M. (Ed.) (1995). *Information technology for the social scientist.* London: UCL Press.

Palme, J. (1995). *Electronic mail.* Boston: Artech House.

Robinson, P. R. (1992). *Delivering electronic mail: Everything you need to know about e-mail.* San Mateo, CA: M&T Books.

Roblyer, M. D. (2003). *Starting out on the Internet.* Upper Saddle River, NJ: Merrill/Prentice Hall.

Weitzman, E. A., & Miles, M. B. (1995). *Computer programs for qualitative data analysis.* Thousand Oaks, CA: Sage.

Young, M. L. (2002). *Internet: The complete reference* (2nd ed.). New York: McGraw-Hill.

Statistics as a Research Tool

Agresti, A., & Finlay, B. (1997). *Statistical methods for the social sciences.* Upper Saddle River, NJ: Prentice Hall.

Porkess, R. (1991). *The HarperCollins dictionary of statistics.* New York: Harper-Perennial.

Vogt, W. P. (1998). *Dictionary of statistics and methodology: A nontechnical guide for the social sciences* (2nd ed.). Thousand Oaks, CA: Sage.

Measurement as a Research Tool

Aft, L. (1992). *Productivity measurement and improvement* (2nd ed.). Upper Saddle River, NJ: Prentice Hall.

Earickson, R., & Harlin, J. (1994). *Geographic measurement and quantitative analysis.* Upper Saddle River, NJ: Prentice Hall.

Oppenheim, A. N. (1992). *Questionnaire design, interviewing, and attitude measurement.* New York: St. Martin's Press.

Thorndike, R. M. (1997). *Measurement and evaluation in psychology and education* (6th ed.). Upper Saddle River, NJ: Merrill/Prentice Hall.

Reasoning and the Scientific Method as Research Tools

Bicak, L. J., & Bicak, C. J. (1988). Scientific method: Historical and contemporary perspectives. *American Biology Teacher, 50,* 348–353.

Carey, S. S. (1994). *A beginner's guide to scientific method.* Belmont, CA: Wadsworth.

Giere, R. N. (1996). *Understanding scientific reasoning* (4th ed.). New York: Holt, Rinehart & Winston.

Poplin, M. S. (1987). Self-imposed blindness: The scientific method in education. *Remedial and Special Education, 8*(6), 31–37.

Shank, G. D. (2002). *Qualitative research: A personal skills approach.* Upper Saddle River, NJ: Merrill/Prentice Hall. [See Chapter 7]

Simonelli, R. (1994). Finding balance by looking beyond the scientific method. *Winds of Change, 9*(4), 106–112.

Storey, R. D. (1992). Why the scientific method? Do we need a new hypothesis? *Science Teacher, 59*(9), 18–21.

Effective Writing and Word Processing

American Psychological Association (APA). (2001). *Publication manual of the American Psychological Association* (5th ed.). Washington, DC: Author.

Flesch, R. (1974). *The art of readable writing.* New York: Harper & Row.

Lockard, J., & Abrams, P. (2001). *Microcomputers for twenty-first-century educators* (5th ed.). Boston: Allyn & Bacon.

Sternberg, R. J. (1977). *Writing the psychology paper.* Woodbury, NY: Barron's Educational Series.

Strunk, W., & White, E. B. (1995). *The elements of style.* Boston, MA: Allyn & Bacon.

Williams, J. M. (2002). *Style: Ten lessons in clarity and grace* (7th ed.). New York: Longman.

Part II
Focusing Your Research Efforts

3

The Problem: The Heart of the Research Process

The problem or question is the axis around which the whole research effort revolves. The statement of the problem must first be expressed with the utmost precision; it should then be divided into more manageable subproblems. Such an approach clarifies the goals and directions of the entire research effort.

The heart of every research project is the problem. It is paramount to the success of the research effort. To see the problem with unwavering clarity and to state it in precise and unmistakable terms is the first requirement in the research process.

FINDING RESEARCH PROJECTS

Problems for research are everywhere. Take a good look at the world around you. Where does your interest lie? Is it in agriculture, chemistry, economics, education, electronics, engineering, health sciences, language, literature, medicine, music, political science, physics, sociology, zoology, or perhaps in any one of dozens of other disciplines? Go to the library; inspect any volume of *Dissertation Abstracts International* under the general heading of your interest, and you will suddenly be aware how the world of research and the world of everyday life have become intertwined. You will see research intimately related to the ever-expanding and exploding universe of knowledge. There is every reason to believe that you can find a research problem to engage your enthusiasm and efforts.

Some research projects are intended to enhance basic knowledge about the physical, biological, psychological, or social world or to shed light on historical, cultural, or aesthetic phenomena. For example, a psychologist might study the nature of people's cognitive processes, and an ornithologist might study the mating habits of a particular species of birds. Such projects, which can advance human beings' theoretical conceptualizations about a particular topic, are known as **basic research.**

Other research projects are intended to address issues that have immediate relevance to current practices, procedures, and policies. For example, a nursing educator might compare the effectiveness of different strategies for training future nurses, and an agronomist might study the effects of various fertilizers on the growth of sunflowers. Such projects, which can inform human decision making about practical problems, are known as **applied research.**

Keep in mind, however, that the line between basic research and applied research is, at best, a blurry one. Answering questions about basic theoretical issues can often inform current practice in the everyday world; for example, by studying the mating habits of a particular species of birds, an ornithologist might lead the way in saving that species from extinction. Similarly, answering questions about practical problems may enhance theoretical understandings of particular phenomena; for example, the nursing educator who finds that one approach to training nurses is more effective than another may enhance psychologists' understanding of how, in general, people learn new skills.

Regardless of whether you conduct basic or applied research, a research project is likely to take a significant amount of your time and energy, so whatever problem you study should be *worth* that time and energy. As you begin the process of identifying a suitable research problem to tackle, keep two criteria in mind. First, your problem should address an important question, such that the answer can actually "make a difference" in some way. And second, it should advance the frontiers of knowledge, perhaps by leading to new ways of thinking, suggesting possible applications, or paving the way for further research in the field. To accomplish both of these ends, your research project must involve not only the collection of data but also the *interpretation* of those data.

Some problems are not suitable for research because they lack the "interpretation of data" requirement; they do not elicit a mental struggle on the part of the researcher to force the data to reveal their meaning. Following are four situations to avoid when considering a problem for research purposes:

1. *Research projects should not be a ruse for achieving self-enlightenment.*   All of us have large holes in our education, and filling them is perhaps the greatest joy of learning. But self-enlightenment is not the purpose of research. Gathering information to know more about a certain area of knowledge is entirely different from looking at a body of data to discern how it contributes to the solution of the problem.

A student once submitted the following as the statement of a research problem:

> The problem of this research is to learn more about the way in which the Panama Canal was built.

For this student, the information-finding effort would provide the satisfaction of having gained more knowledge about a particular topic, but it would *not* have led to *new* knowledge.

2. *A problem whose sole purpose is to compare two sets of data is not a suitable research problem.*   Take this proposed problem for research:

> This research project will compare the increase in the number of women employed over 100 years—from 1870 to 1970—with the employment of men over the same time span.

A simple table completes the project (*Historical Statistics*, 1975).

	1870	*1970*
Women employed	13,970,000	72,744,000
Men employed	12,506,000	85,903,000

The "research" project involves nothing more than a quick trip to the library to reveal what is already known.

3. *Calculating a coefficient of correlation between two sets of data to show a relationship between them is not acceptable as a problem for research.*   Why? Because the basic requirement for research is ignored: a human mind struggling with data. What we see here is a proposal to perform a statistical operation that a computer can do infinitely faster and more accurately than a person can. A correlation coefficient is nothing more than a statistic that expresses how closely two sets of data are related to each other. It tells us nothing about *why* that relationship exists.

Sometimes, we feel satisfied when we collect data and, by means of a statistical procedure, determine that two variables (e.g., the IQs of parents and their offspring) are closely related. We go off proclaiming to the world, "Research has shown that the correlation between the intelligence of the parents and that of their children is such-and-such." This is simply untrue. *Research* has not shown this; instead, *a tool of research* has given us this information. The fact, however, does suggest a problem for research: What is the cause of that relationship between children's and parents' intelligence? Is it genetic? Is it environmental? Is it a combination of both of these?

4. *Problems that result in a yes or no answer are not suitable problems for research.*   Why? For the same reason that merely finding a correlation coefficient is unsatisfactory. Both situations look at the froth on the top of the mug and mistake it for the substantive drink below!

"Is homework beneficial to children?" That is no problem for research, certainly not in the form in which it is stated. The researchable issue is not whether homework is beneficial, but wherein the benefit of homework, if there is one, lies. Which components of homework are beneficial? Which ones are counterproductive? If we knew the answers to these questions, then we could structure homework assignments with more purpose and greater intelligence—and thereby promote the learning of children—more effectively than we do now.

There is so much to learn and so many new, relevant, important questions being generated each day that we should look for significant problems and not dwell on those that will make little, if any, contribution. P. B. Medawar (1979), a Nobel laureate who investigated causes of the human body's rejection of organs and tissues transplanted from other human beings, gave wise advice to the young scientist when asked about conducting research:

> It can be said with complete confidence that any scientist of any age who wants to make important discoveries must study important problems. Dull or piffling problems yield dull or piffling answers. It is not enough that a problem should be "interesting"—almost any problem is interesting if it is studied in sufficient depth. (p. 13)

PRACTICAL APPLICATION: IDENTIFYING AND DESCRIBING THE RESEARCH PROBLEM

How can the beginning researcher formulate an important and useful research problem? Here we offer guidelines both for identifying a particular problem and for describing it in precise terms.

GUIDELINES   FINDING A LEGITIMATE PROBLEM

As a general rule, appropriate research projects don't fall out of trees and hit you on the head. You must be sufficiently knowledgeable about your topic of interest to know what projects might make important contributions to the field. Following are several strategies that are often helpful for novice and expert researchers alike.

1. *Look around you.* In many disciplines, questions that need answers—phenomena that need explanation—are everywhere. For example, let's look back to the early 17th century, when Galileo was trying to make sense of a variety of earthly and celestial phenomena. For example, why did large bodies of water (but not small ones) rise and fall in the form of tides twice a day? Why did sunspots consistently move across the sun's surface from right to left, gradually disappear, and then, about two weeks later, reappear on the right edge? Furthermore, why did sunspots usually move in an upward or downward path as they traversed the sun's surface, while only occasionally moving in a direct, horizontal fashion? Galileo correctly deduced that the various "paths" of sunspots could be explained by the facts that both the earth and sun were spinning on tilted axes and that (contrary to popular opinion at the time) the earth revolved around the sun rather than vice versa. Galileo was less successful in explaining tides, attributing them to the natural "sloshing" that would take place as the earth moved through space rather than to the moon's gravitational pull (Sobel, 2000).

We do not mean to suggest that novice researchers should take on such monumental questions as the nature of the solar system or oceanic tides. But smaller problems suitable for research exist everywhere. Perhaps you might see them in your professional practice or in everyday events. Continually ask yourself questions about what you see and hear: Why does such-and-such happen? What makes such-and-such tick? and so on.

2. *Read the literature.* One essential strategy is to find out what things are already known about your topic of interest; little can be gained by reinventing the wheel. In addition to

telling you what is already known, the existing literature is likely to tell you what is *not* known in the area—in other words, what still needs to be done. For instance, your research project might

- Address the suggestions for future research that another researcher has offered
- Replicate a research project in a different setting or with a different population
- Consider how various subpopulations might behave differently in the same situation
- Apply an existing perspective or explanation to a new situation
- Explore unexpected or contradictory findings in previous studies
- Challenge research findings that seem to contradict what you know or believe to be true (Neuman, 1994)

Reading the literature has other advantages as well. It gives you a theoretical base on which to build a rationale for your study. It provides potential research methodologies and methods of measurement. And it can help you interpret your results and relate them to what is already known in the field. (We address strategies for finding and reviewing related literature in Chapter 4.)

3. *Attend professional conferences.* Many researchers have great success finding new research projects at national or regional conferences in their discipline. By scanning the conference program and attending sessions of interest, they can learn "what's hot and what's not" in their field. Furthermore, conferences are a place where novice researchers can make contacts with experts in their field—where they can ask questions, share ideas, and exchange e-mail addresses with more experienced and knowledgeable individuals.

Some beginning researchers, including many students, are reluctant to approach well-known scholars at conferences, for fear that these scholars don't have the time or patience to talk with novices. Quite the opposite is true: Most experienced researchers are happy to talk with people who are just starting out. In fact, they may feel flattered that you are familiar with their work and that you would like to extend or apply it in some way.

4. *Seek the advice of experts.* Another simple yet highly effective strategy for identifying a research problem is simply to ask an expert: What needs to be done? What burning questions are still out there? What previous research findings seemingly don't make sense? Your professors will almost certainly be able to answer each of these questions, as will other scholars you may meet at conferences or elsewhere.

5. *Choose a topic that intrigues and motivates you.* As you read the professional literature, attend conferences, and talk with experts, you will uncover a number of potential research problems. At this point, you need to pick just one of them, and your selection should be based on what you personally want to learn more about. Remember, the project you're about to undertake will take you many months, quite possibly a couple of years or even longer. So it should be something that you truly believe is worth your time and effort. Peter Leavenworth, at the time a doctoral student in history, explained the importance of choosing an interesting dissertation topic this way: "You're going to be married to it, so you might as well enjoy it."

6. *Choose a topic that others will find interesting and worthy of attention.* Ideally, your work should not end with a thesis, dissertation, or other unpublished research report. If your research adds an important piece to what human beings know and understand about the world, then you will, we hope, want to share your findings with a larger audience. In other words, you will want to describe what you have done at a regional or national conference, publish an article in a professional journal, or both (we'll talk more about doing such things in Chapter 12). Conference coordinators and journal editors are often quite selective about the papers they accept for presentation or publication, and they are most likely to choose those papers that will have broad appeal.

Future employers, too, may make judgments about you, at least in part, based on the topic you have chosen for a thesis or dissertation. Your résumé or curriculum vitae will be more apt to attract their attention if, in your research, you are pursuing an issue of broad scientific or social concern or, more generally, a hot topic in your field.

GUIDELINES   STATING THE RESEARCH PROBLEM

As noted earlier, the heart of any research project is the problem. At every step in the process, successful researchers ask themselves: What am I doing? For what purpose am I doing it? Such questions can help focus your efforts toward achieving your ultimate purpose for gathering data: to resolve the problem.

Researchers get off to a strong start when they begin with an unmistakably clear statement of the problem. After identifying a research problem, therefore, you must articulate it in such a way that *it is carefully phrased and represents the single goal of the total research effort.* Following are some general guidelines to help you do just that:

1. *State the problem clearly and completely.* Your problem should be so clearly stated that anyone who reads English can read and understand it. If the problem is not stated with such clarity, then you are merely deceiving yourself that you know what the problem is. Such self-deception will cause you difficulty later on.

You can state your problem clearly only when you also state it completely. At a minimum, you should describe it in one or more *grammatically complete sentences.* As examples of what *not* to do, following are some meaningless half-statements—verbal fragments that only hint at the problem. Ask yourself whether you understand exactly what each student researcher plans to do.

> From a student in sociology:
>
> Welfare on children's attitudes.
>
> From a student in music:
>
> Palestrina and the motet.
>
> From a student in economics:
>
> Busing of schoolchildren.
>
> From a student in social work:
>
> Retirement plans of adults.

Unfortunately, all four statements lack clarity. It is imperative to think in terms of specific, researchable goals expressed in complete sentences. We take the preceding fragments and develop each of them into one or more complete sentences that describe a researchable problem.

Welfare on children's attitudes becomes:

> What effect does welfare assistance to parents have on the attitudes of their children toward work?

Palestrina and the motet becomes:

> This study will analyze the motets of Giovanni Pierluigi da Palestrina (1525?–1594) written between 1575 and 1580 to discover their distinctive contrapuntal characteristics and will contrast them with the motets of his contemporary William Byrd (1542?–1623) written between 1592 and 1597. During the periods studied, each composer was between 50 and 55 years of age.

Busing of schoolchildren becomes:

> What factors must be evaluated and what are the relative weights of those several factors in constructing a formula for estimating the cost of busing children in a Midwestern metropolitan school system?

Retirement plans for adults becomes:

> How do retirement plans for adults compare with the actual realization, in retirement, of those plans in terms of self-satisfaction and self-adjustment? What does an analysis of the difference between anticipation and realization reveal for a more intelligent approach to planning?

Notice that, in the full statement of each of these problems, the areas studied are carefully limited so that the study is of manageable size. The author of the Palestrina-Byrd study carefully limited the motets that would be studied to those written when each composer was between 50 and 55 years of age. A glance at the listing of Palestrina's works in *Grove's Dictionary of Music and Musicians* demonstrates how impractical it would be for a student to undertake a study of all the Palestrina motets. He wrote 392 of them!

2. *Think through the feasibility of the project that the problem implies.* Students sometimes rush into a problem without thinking through its implications. It's great to have ideas. It's much better to have practical ideas. Before your enthusiasm overtakes you, consider the following research proposal submitted by John:

> This study proposes to study the science programs in the secondary schools in the United States for the purpose of . . .

Let's think about that. The United States has more than 24,000 public and private secondary schools. These schools, north to south, extend from Alaska to the tip of Florida; east to west, from Maine to Hawaii. Certain practical questions immediately surface. How does John intend to contact each of these schools? By personal visit? Being very optimistic, he might be able to visit two schools per day—one in the morning and one in the afternoon. That would amount to more than 12,000 visitation days. The number of school days in the average school year is 180, so it would take more than 66 years for John to gather the data. Furthermore, the financial outlay for the project would be exorbitant; if we conservatively estimated $75 for daily meals, lodging, and travel, John would be spending more than $900,000 just to collect the data!

"But," John explains, "I plan to gather the data by mail with a questionnaire." Fine! Each letter to the 24,000 schools, with an enclosed questionnaire and a return postage-paid envelope, would cost about $.60 just for the postage. Thus, the total postage cost for letters to all the schools would be about $14,400. And we mustn't overlook the fact that John would need a second and perhaps a third mailing. A 50% return on the first mailing would be considered a good return. But, for the nonreturnees, a follow-up mailing would be needed, at a cost of approximately $8,000. That would bring the mailing bill to approximately $22,400. And we haven't even figured in the cost of envelopes, stationery, photocopying, and data analysis. All in all, we are talking about a project that would cost well over $30,000.

Obviously, John did not intend to send surveys to every school in the United States, yet that is what he wrote that he would do.

3. *Say precisely what you mean.* When you state your research problem, you should say exactly what you mean. You cannot assume that others will be able to read your mind. People will always take your words at their face value: You mean what you say. That's it.

Your failure to be careful with your words can have grave results for your status as a scholar and a researcher. In the academic community, a basic rule prevails: *Absolute honesty and integrity are assumed in every statement a scholar makes.*

Look again at John's problem statement. We could assume that John means to fulfill precisely what he has stated (although we would doubt it, given the time and expense involved). Had he intended to survey only some schools, then he should have said so plainly:

> This study proposes to survey the science programs *in selected secondary schools throughout the United States.*

Or, perhaps he could have limited his study to a specific geographical area or to a student population within certain designated limits. Such an approach would give the problem constraints that the original statement lacked and would communicate to others what John intended to do—what he realistically could commit to doing. Furthermore, it would have preserved his reputation as a researcher of integrity and precision.

One further haunting thought lingers regarding the statement of the problem. If a researcher cannot be thorough and precise in stating the nature of the problem, one might question whether such a researcher is likely to be any more thorough and precise in gathering and interpreting the data. And this doubt is very serious indeed, for it reflects on the basic integrity of the whole research effort.

We have discussed some common difficulties in the statement of the problem, including statements that are unclear or incomplete and statements that suggest impractical or impossible projects. Here's another difficulty: Occasionally, a researcher *talks about the problem* but never actually *states what the problem is*. Under the excuse that the problem needs an introduction or needs to be seen against a background, the researcher launches into a generalized discussion, continually obscuring the problem, never clearly articulating it. Take, for example, the following paragraph that appeared under the heading "Statement of the Problem":

> The upsurge of interest in reading and learning disabilities found among both children and adults has focused the attention of educators, psychologists, and linguists on the language syndrome. In order to understand how language is learned, it is necessary to understand what language is. Language acquisition is a normal developmental aspect of every individual, but it has not been studied in sufficient depth. To provide us with the necessary background information to understand the anomaly of language deficiency implies a knowledge of the developmental process of language as these relate to the individual from infancy to maturity. Grammar, also an aspect of language learning, is acquired through pragmatic language usage. Phonology, syntax, and semantics are all intimately involved in the study of any language disability.

Can you find a statement of problem here? Several problems are suggested, but none is articulated with sufficient clarity that we might put a finger on it and say, "There, that is the problem."

Earlier in this chapter, we invited you to go to *Dissertation Abstracts International* to see how the world of research and the real world of everyday living are intertwined. Now return to those abstracts and notice with what directness the problems are set forth. The problem is stated in the very first words of an abstract: "The purpose of this study is to . . ." No mistaking it, no background buildup necessary—just a straightforward plunge into the business at hand. All research problems should be stated with the same clarity.

4. *Edit your work.* You can avoid the difficulties we have been discussing by carefully editing your words. *Editing* is sharpening a thought to a gemlike point and eliminating useless verbiage. Choose your words precisely. Doing so will clarify your writing.

The sentences in the preceding paragraph began as a mishmash of foggy thought and jumbled verbiage. The original version of the paragraph contained 71 words. These were edited down to 37 words. This is a reduction of 52% and a great improvement in readability. Figure 3.1 shows the original version and the way it was edited. (The three lines under the *c* in *choose* means that the first letter should be capitalized. When we discuss editing in more detail in Chapter 6, we'll present some of the common editing marks and what they mean.)

Notice the directness of the edited copy. We eliminated unnecessarily wordy phrases—"relating to the statement of the problem," "a process whereby the writer attempts to bring what is said straight to the point"—replacing the verbosity with seven words: "sharpening a thought to a gemlike point."

Editing almost invariably improves your thinking and your prose. Many students think that any words that approximate a thought are adequate to convey it to others. This is not so. Approximation is never precision.

FIGURE 3.1

Editing to clarify your writing: An example

You can avoid the difficulties
∧ We have been discussing ~~several common difficulties~~
(~~relating to the statement of the problem. These can be~~
→ by carefully
~~improved or remedied through a careful~~ editing ~~of~~ your
sharpening a thought ~
words. Editing is ∧ ~~a process whereby the writer attempts~~
a gemlike
~~to bring what is said straight to∧the point~~) ~~Editing also~~
↳ and eliminating useless verbiage⊙
~~eliminates many meaningless expressions. We should~~
your   precisely⊙ Doing so
therefore, choose ~~our~~ words ~~carefully. By editing the words~~
≡
clarify your writing⊙
~~we have written our expression~~ will ~~take on new life.~~

The thought's the thing. It is clearest when it is clothed in simple words, concrete nouns, and active, expressive verbs. Every student would do well to study how the great writers and poets set their thoughts into words. These masters have much to say by way of illustration to those who have trouble putting their own thoughts on paper.

The following checklist can help you formulate a research problem that is clear, precise, and accurate.

✔ CHECKLIST
EVALUATING THE RESEARCH PROBLEM

_____   1. Write a clear statement of a problem for research.

_____

_____

_____

_____

_____   2. Review your written statement and ask yourself the following questions:

   • Is the problem stated in a complete, grammatical sentence?

   • Is it clear how the area of study will be limited or focused?

_____   3. On the basis of your answers to the questions in #2, edit your written statement.

_____

_____

_____

_____

_____   4. Look at your edited statement and reflect on the following questions:

   • Does the answer to this problem have the potential for providing important and useful answers and information?

   • Will the result be more than a simple exercise in gathering information, answering a yes/no question, or making a simple comparison?

   • Is the problem focused enough to be accomplished with a reasonable expenditure of time, money, and effort?

_____   5. Looking at the statement once more, consider this: Is the problem really what I want to investigate?

_____   6. Show other research students your work. Ask them to consider the questions listed in items 2 and 4 and then to give you their comments. With your compiled feedback, edit and rewrite your problem statement once again:

_____

_____

_____

_____

_____

DIVIDING THE RESEARCH PROBLEM INTO SUBPROBLEMS

Most research problems are too large or too complex to be solved without subdividing them. The strategy, therefore, is to divide and conquer. Almost every problem can be broken down into smaller units. From a research standpoint, these units are easier to address and resolve.

The subparts of the main problem are called **subproblems,** discussed briefly in the first chapter. By viewing the main problem through its subproblems, the researcher frequently gets a better idea of how to approach the entire research endeavor. So always think of a problem in terms of its component parts.

SUBPROBLEMS VERSUS PSEUDOSUBPROBLEMS

The researcher must distinguish subproblems that are an integral part of the main problem from things that look like problems but are nothing more than procedural issues. The latter, which we might call *pseudo-subproblems*, involve decisions the researcher must make before he or she can resolve the research problem and its subproblems. Consider the following as examples:

- What is the best way to choose a sample?
- How large should a representative sample of a population be?
- What instruments or methods should be used to gather the data?
- What statistical procedures should be used to analyze the data?
- How do I find the subproblems within the main problem?

Deal with pseudo-subproblems forthrightly by making a firm decision about them and then get on with the solution of the research problem. To deal with pseudo-subproblems, you must decide whether (a) a little common sense and some creative thinking might help in solving your "problem" or (b) you simply lack the knowledge to address the difficulty. In the latter case, you have three options:

1. Turn to the index of this text to see whether the pseudo-subproblem is discussed.
2. Carefully peruse the "For Further Reading" sections at the end of each chapter in this book to see whether they contain any references that may help you. Don't overlook general research methods books, such as *Educational Research* (Gay & Airasian, 2003) or *Qualitative Inquiry and Research Design* (Creswell, 1998). Consult these and similar works.
3. Go to a library, preferably a college or university library, and search for books under the subject heading "Research Methodology." Consult the indexes of these books, as you did with this text. Also check the leading periodical indexes under the heading "Research Methodology" to determine whether you can locate any articles related to your procedural issue. If your library does not have certain periodicals, you can typically obtain any article you need through interlibrary loan.

CHARACTERISTICS OF SUBPROBLEMS

Following are four key characteristics of subproblems:

1. *Each subproblem should be a completely researchable unit.*   A subproblem should constitute a logical subarea of the larger research undertaking. Each subproblem might be researched as a separate subproject within the larger research goal. The solutions to the subproblems, taken together, combine to resolve the main problem.

It is essential that each subproblem be stated clearly and succinctly. Often, a subproblem is stated in the form of a question. A question tends to focus the researcher's attention more directly on the research target of the subproblem than does a declarative statement. After all, an interrogative attitude is what marks a true researcher.

2. *Each subproblem must be clearly tied to the interpretation of the data.*   At some point in the statement of the subproblem—as within the main problem—the fact that data will be interpreted

must be clearly evident. This fact may be expressed as a part of each subproblem statement, or it may occupy an entirely separate subproblem.

3. *The subproblems must add up to the totality of the problem.*   After you have stated the subproblems, check them against the statement of the main problem to see that (a) nothing in excess of the coverage of the main problem is included and that (b) all significant areas of the main problem are covered by the subproblems.

4. *Subproblems should be small in number.*   If the main problem is carefully stated and properly limited to a feasible research effort, the researcher will find that it usually contains two to six subproblems. Sometimes, the inexperienced researcher will come up with as many as 10, 15, or 20 subproblems. When this happens, a careful review of the problem and its attendant subproblems is in order. If you find yourself in this situation, you should study the individual subproblems to see whether (a) some are actually procedural issues (pseudo-subproblems), (b) some might reasonably be combined into larger subproblems, or (c) the main problem is more complex than you originally believed. If the last of these is true, you may want to reconsider whether the solution to the overall research problem is actually achievable given the time and resources you have.

IDENTIFYING SUBPROBLEMS

Novice researchers frequently have difficulty identifying the subproblems within the main problem. You should begin with the problem itself. If the problem is correctly written, you will be able to detect the subproblem areas that may be isolated for further study. The old axiom that the sum of the parts equals the whole applies here. All the subproblems must add up to the total problem.

You can use either paper and pencil or "brainstorming" software to help you identify your subproblems. We describe each of these strategies briefly.

Taking a Paper-and-Pencil Approach

Using this approach, you write the problem on a piece of paper and then box off the subproblem areas. More specifically, you might follow these steps:

1. Copy the problem onto a clean sheet of paper, leaving considerable space between the lines.
2. Read the problem critically to discover the areas that should receive in-depth treatment before the problem can be resolved.
3. Make sure every subproblem contains a word that indicates the necessity to interpret the data within that particular subproblem (e.g., *analyze, discover, compare*). Underline this word.
4. Arrange the entire problem, which will now have the subproblems boxed off, into a skeletal plan that shows the research structure of the problem. You now have a structure of the whole research design.

This procedure for finding subproblems should work for any problem in any academic discipline. We use a problem in musicology to illustrate the technique. More specifically, we take the problem of the motets of Palestrina. As presented earlier in the chapter, this problem is as follows:

> This study will analyze the motets of Giovanni Pierluigi da Palestrina (1525?–1594) written between 1575 and 1580 to discover their distinctive contrapuntal characteristics and will contrast them with the motets of his contemporary William Byrd (1542?–1623) written between 1592 and 1597. During the periods studied, each composer was between 50 and 55 years of age.

Let's first delete the factual matter, such as life-span dates and the fact that the two men were contemporaries. These facts merely help in giving a rationale for certain elements within the problem. Modified to reflect its essential parts, the motet problem becomes the following:

The purpose of this study will be *to analyze* the motets of Palestrina written between 1575 and 1580 to discover their distinctive contrapuntal characteristics, *to analyze* the same characteristics in the motets of William Byrd written between 1592 and 1597, and to determine what *a comparative study of these two analyses* may reveal.

Notice that we have broken up the "will contrast them with" phrase in the original statement into two distinct tasks, *analyzing* Byrd's motets in the same manner that Palestrina's motets have been analyzed, and *comparing* the two analyses. The three underlined phrases in the revised problem statement reflect three subproblems, each of which involves interpretation of data that is necessary for resolving the main research problem.

Let's now arrange the problem so that we may see precisely what the design will be. Figure 3.2 is a graphic depiction of the problem. We have divided the problem into three subproblems. The first and second of these have the same general structural configuration: The analytical aspect of the subproblem is stated in the upper box and the purpose of the analysis is stated in the lower box. Addressing the third subproblem involves comparing the analyses conducted for the two preceding subproblems to determine what similarities and differences may exist. The last of the three subproblems—the comparison step—resolves the original main problem: characterizing Palestrina's motets.

Using Brainstorming Software

Some computer software facilitates the process of breaking problems into subproblems. Computer programs such as Inspiration, Semnet, Semantica, and IdeaFisher allow you to brainstorm research ideas and construct graphic networks of interrelated concepts, terms, and principles. For example, in Inspiration, you put the main problem, idea, or concept inside a box or oval in the middle of your computer screen. As you brainstorm other, related ideas, you put those on the screen as well, and you draw (and perhaps label) arrows to represent how various ideas are interconnected. You can break each concept or problem into subparts, and break down each subpart even further. The process is fast and flexible, and you can save and print your final diagram (Figure 4.1, presented in Chapter 4, is an example). Some brainstorming software, such as Inspiration, also allows you to convert your diagram into an outline that lists major topics and various levels of subtopics.

FIGURE 3.2

A structural representation of the Palestrina-Byrd problem

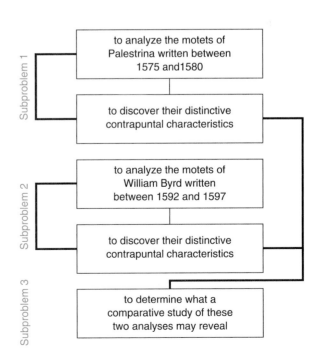

EVERY PROBLEM NEEDS FURTHER DELINEATION

Up to this point, we have been discussing only the problem and its subparts. The statement of the problem establishes the goal for the research effort. The subproblems suggest ways of approaching that goal in a manageable, systematic way. But a goal alone is not enough. To comprehend fully the meaning of the problem, we need other information as well. Both the researcher and those reading the research should ultimately have a clear understanding of every detail of the process.

In every research endeavor, the researcher should eliminate any possibility of misunderstanding by

- *Stating the hypotheses and/or research questions:*   Describing the specific hypotheses being tested or questions being asked.
- *Delimiting the research:*   Fully disclosing what the researcher intends to do and, conversely, does not intend to do.
- *Defining the terms:*   Giving the meanings of all terms in the statements of the problem and subproblems that have any possibility of being misunderstood.
- *Stating the assumptions:*   Presenting a clear statement of all assumptions on which the research will rest.

Taken as a whole, these elements comprise *the setting of the problem.* We look at each of them in more detail in the following sections. We also include a section on "Importance of the Study," as this topic is frequently discussed in dissertations and other research reports.

STATING THE HYPOTHESES AND/OR RESEARCH QUESTIONS

We discussed hypotheses in Chapter 1. There, we pointed out that hypotheses are tentative, intelligent guesses about how the research problem may be resolved. *Research questions* are somewhat different in that, in and of themselves, they don't offer any speculative answers related to the research problem. Hypotheses are essential to experimental research (see Chapter 10), whereas research questions are more common in many forms of qualitative research (see Chapter 7). Both hypotheses and questions provide guidance for the kinds of data the researcher should collect and suggest how the researcher should analyze and interpret those data. It is not unusual for a researcher to form hypotheses *and* ask questions related to a research problem.

Research hypotheses and questions may originate in the subproblems. Oftentimes, a one-to-one correspondence exists between the subproblems and their corresponding hypotheses or questions. In this situation, we have as many hypotheses or questions as we have subproblems.

In essence, a hypothesis or research question is to a researcher what a point of triangulation is to a surveyor: It provides a position from which the researcher may initiate an exploration of the problem or subproblem and also acts as a checkpoint against which to test the findings that the data reveal. After collecting and analyzing data, the researcher must ultimately ask: How do the data answer my research questions? What do they say about my research hypotheses?

Certainly, the data from a research study can (and should) answer each research question, and they may support or not support each research hypothesis. But notice how we just said that the data may *support* or *not support* each research hypothesis; we intentionally did *not* say that the data would prove or disprove a hypothesis. Hypotheses are nothing more than *tentative propositions set forth to assist in guiding the investigation of a problem or to provide possible explanations for the observations made.*

To set out deliberately to prove a hypothesis would defeat impartiality in research. The researcher might bias the procedure by looking only for those data that would support the hypothesis. Difficult as it may be at times, we must let the chips fall where they may. Hypotheses have nothing to do with proof. Rather, their acceptance or rejection is dependent on what the data—and the data alone—ultimately reveal. If you discover that your data do not support your research hypothesis, do not let such an outcome disturb you. It merely means that your educated guess about the outcome of the investigation was incorrect.

Distinguishing Null Hypotheses from Research Hypotheses

Because we can never really prove a hypothesis, we often set out to *dis*prove an opposite hypothesis. For instance, let's say that a team of social workers believe that one type of after-school program for teenagers (we'll call it Program A) is more effective than another program (we'll call it Program B) in terms of reducing high school dropout rates. The team's research hypothesis is:

> Teenagers enrolled in Program A will graduate from high school at a higher rate than teenagers enrolled in Program B.

Because the social workers cannot actually prove their hypothesis, they instead try to discredit an opposite hypothesis:

> There will be no difference in the high school graduation rates of teenagers enrolled in Program A and those enrolled in Program B.

If, in their research, the social workers find that there *is* a substantial difference in graduation rates between the two programs—and in particular, if the graduation rate is higher for youth in Program A—they can reject the "no differences" hypothesis and thus have, by default, supported their research hypothesis.

When we hypothesize that there will be *no* differences between groups, *no* relationships between variables, or, more generally, *no* patterns in the data, we are forming a **null hypothesis.** Null hypotheses are used primarily during statistical analyses; we support a research hypothesis by showing, statistically, that its opposite—the null hypothesis—probably is *not* true. Accordingly, we will look at null hypotheses again in our discussion of statistics in Chapter 11.

DELIMITING THE RESEARCH

We need to know precisely what the researcher intends to do. We also need to know precisely what the researcher does *not* intend to do.

What the researcher intends to do is stated in the problem. What the researcher is not going to do is stated in the *delimitations*. The limits of the problem should be as carefully bounded for a research effort as a parcel of land is for a real estate transfer.

Research problems typically emerge from larger contexts and larger problem areas. The researcher can easily be beguiled by discovering interesting information that lies beyond the precincts of the problem under investigation. For instance, in the Palestrina-Byrd problem, it is possible that, because the two men were contemporaries, Byrd may have met Palestrina or at least have come in contact with some of his motets. Such contact may have been a determinative influence on Byrd's compositions. But we are not concerned with *influences* on the motets of the two composers. We are interested only in the *characteristics* of the motets, including their musical style, musical individualism, and contrapuntal likenesses and differences. Study the contrapuntal characteristics—that is what a researcher of this problem will do. What the researcher will *not* do is become involved in any data extraneous to this goal—no matter how enticing or interesting such an exploratory safari may be.

Only a researcher who thinks carefully about the problem and its focal center can distinguish between what is relevant and what is not relevant to the problem. All irrelevancies to the problem must be firmly ruled out in the statement of delimitations. Figure 3.3 may make the matter of delimitations more understandable.

DEFINING THE TERMS

What precisely do the terms in the problem and the subproblems mean? For example, if we say that the purpose of the research is to analyze the harmonic characteristics of motets, what are we talking about? What are *harmonic characteristics*? Without knowing explicitly what a term means, we cannot evaluate the research or determine whether the researcher has carried out what was proposed in the problem statement.

FIGURE 3.3

Delimitation of a problem

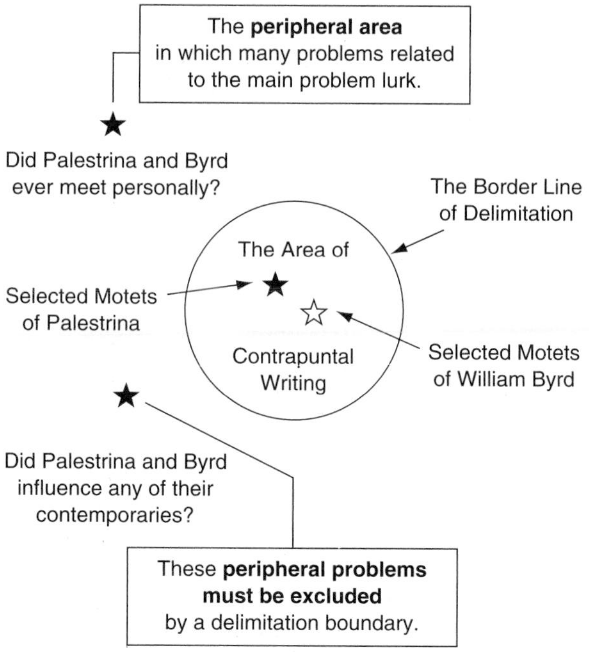

Each term must be defined operationally; that is, the definition must interpret the term *as it is used in relation to the researcher's project*. Sometimes, novice researchers rely on dictionary definitions, which are seldom either adequate or helpful. In defining a term, the researcher makes the term mean whatever he or she wishes it to mean within the context of the problem and its subproblems. We must know how the researcher defines the term. We need not necessarily agree with such a definition, but so long as we know what the researcher means when using the term, we are able to understand the research and appraise it appropriately.

A formal definition contains three parts: (a) the *term* to be defined; (b) the *genera*, or the general class to which the concept being defined belongs; and (c) the *differentia*, the specific characteristics or traits that distinguish the concept being defined from all other members of the general classification. For example, *harmonic characteristics* (the term to be defined) might be defined as *the manner* (the genera) in which tonal values are combined *to produce individualized polyphonic patterns associated with the works of a particular composer* (the differentia: telling what particular "manner" we mean).

The researcher must be careful to avoid *circular definitions*, in which the terms to be defined are used in the definitions themselves. A classic example is Gertrude Stein's "A rose, is a rose, is a rose." If we were to define *harmonic characteristics* in a circle, we might describe them as "those characteristics that derive from the harmonic patterns found in the works of a particular composer." Here the words *characteristics* and *harmonic* are used to define harmonic characteristics, giving others little if any guidance in understanding what the researcher means by the term.

STATING THE ASSUMPTIONS

We briefly discussed assumptions in Chapter 1. Assumptions are so basic that, without them, the research problem itself could not exist. For example, suppose we are attempting to determine, by means of a pretest and posttest, whether one method of instruction is superior to another. A basic assumption in such a situation is that the pretest and posttest measure knowledge of the subject matter in question.[1] We must assume, too, that the teacher(s) in the study can teach

---

[1] Alternatively, we might make no such assumption; instead, we might set out to determine the *validity* of the tests as measures in this situation. We introduced the concept of validity in Chapter 2 and will address it more fully in Chapter 5.

effectively and that the students are capable of learning the subject matter. Without these assumptions, we have no problem, no research.

In research, we try to leave nothing to chance in the hope of preventing any misunderstanding. All assumptions that have a material bearing on the problem should be openly and unreservedly set forth. If others know the assumptions a researcher makes, they are better prepared to evaluate the conclusions that result from such assumptions.

To discover your own assumptions, ask yourself, What am I taking for granted with respect to the problem? Ideally, your answer should bring your assumptions into clear view.

IMPORTANCE OF THE STUDY

In dissertations or research reports, researchers frequently set forth their reasons for undertaking the study. In a research proposal, such a discussion may be especially important. Some studies seem to go far beyond any relationship to the practical world. Of such research efforts one inwardly, if not audibly, asks, "Of what *use* is it? What *practical value* does the study have?"

In the 1970s, contemplating the exploration of the moon, the average citizen frequently asked, "What good is it? What's the use of it all? How will spending all this money on space flights benefit anyone?" Perhaps those engaged in space research did not set forth clearly and succinctly enough the reasons the missions were undertaken. Only now are we beginning to appreciate the practical value of those early missions.

ORDERING THE TOPICS IN A RESEARCH PROPOSAL

You may often find a one-to-one correspondence between the discussions in this text and the sequence of topics that typically appear in a research proposal or research report. In any document, the first order of business is to present the problem and its setting. Generally, the document opens with a statement of the problem for research. This is followed by subproblems, hypotheses, and questions presented in a logical order.

Once the problem and its component parts have been articulated, the remaining items comprising the setting of the problem are presented, typically including a statement of delimitations, definitions of terms, assumptions, and, in some instances, a statement about the importance of the study.

In a proposal or research report, such items often comprise the first chapter. The report then generally continues with a discussion of investigations that others have done, usually entitled "Review of the Related Literature." We discuss this topic in the next chapter.

A SAMPLE RESEARCH PROPOSAL

On the following pages, we present an excerpt from a research proposal submitted to the faculty of the School of Education of The American University in Washington, D.C. The proposal is not meant to be slavishly emulated. We present it here because its organization closely reflects some of the recommendations we've made in this chapter. Note, however, that, in the interest of space, we've shortened it considerably from the original.

The proposed research concerns a practical problem: developing a means of using an existing measurement instrument, the *Strong Vocational Interest Blank* (SVIB), to identify potential cartographers for the federal government. The SVIB assesses a person's interests in a wide variety of activities; the profile of interests that it generates is then compared with the interests of people in various occupations to identify occupations in which the person might find satisfaction and success. At the time the study was conducted, interest scales for 54 different occupational groups had been developed for the SVIB, but none had been developed for cartographers. The SVIB was published in two versions, the *SVIB for Men* and the *SVIB for Women*; to limit the scope of the project, the researcher focused only on the *SVIB for Men*.

The excerpt itself is presented on the left-hand side of the page, as are several editorial changes. On the right is a running commentary that points out the proposal's strengths and identifies suggestions that might make the proposal even more effective.

As you read the excerpt, notice the care with which the details of the proposed research are spelled out. The greater the anticipated investment of time, money, and effort, the fuller and more specific a research proposal should be.

DISSERTATION ANALYSIS *1*

THE PROBLEM AND ITS SETTING

The Statement of the Problem

This research^er proposes to identify and evaluate the existing discrete interests among Federally employed male cartographers and to develop a scale for the revised <u>Strong Vocational Interest Blank</u> to aid recruitment of cartographers into Federal employment.

<u>The Subproblems</u>

1. <u>The first subproblem.</u>   The first subproblem is to determine whether male cartographers employed by the Federal Government have a discrete pattern of interests different from those of men in general as measured by the <u>Strong Vocational Interest Blank for Men</u>.

2. <u>The second subproblem.</u>   The second subproblem is to construct a scoring key for the <u>Strong Vocational Interest Blank</u> to differentiate ^the interests of^ cartographers from those of ^   also from the interests of men in general and ^   other occupational groups.

3. <u>The third subproblem.</u>   The third subproblem is to analyze and interpret the treated data so as to evaluate the discovered interests in terms of their discreteness in recruiting cartographers.

The Hypotheses

The first hypothesis is that male cartographers employed by the Federal Government have a discrete pattern of interests different from those of men in general.

The second hypothesis is that the <u>Strong Vocational Interest Blank</u> can identify the existing discrete interests of cartographers differentially from ^those of^ men in general and ^those of^ other occupational groups.

The third hypothesis is that the development of an interest scale can aid the recruitment of cartographers into Federal employment.

The Delimitations

The study will not attempt to predict success of cartographers.

The study will not determine or evaluate the preparation and training of cartographers.

The study will be limited to male cartographers who have attained, within the U.S. Civil Service classification system, full performance ratings of GS-09 or higher in Occupation Series 1370.

The study will not evaluate ^any cartographers who may also be^ uniformed military personnel.

Comments

The headings clearly indicate the organization and outline of the proposal.

Research *doesn't "propose," hence our editorial change to* researcher. *The phrase "existing discrete" is unnecessary verbiage. If they are "discrete interests," they do "exist."*

The numbering here is superfluous. The indented subheading makes it apparent that this is the first subproblem. No need, therefore, to number it 1.

Here, the researcher is not saying what he means. He wants to differentiate the interests of cartographers. The edited additions bring the thought into correct perspective.

Notice that the three subproblems add up to the totality of the problem.

Notice the position of the hypothesis section. It immediately follows the subproblems. It facilitates seeing the one-to-one correspondence between the subproblem and the hypothesis pertaining to that subproblem.

The third hypothesis goes beyond the limits of the problem. The researcher does not intend to investigate the actual recruitment of cartographers so will not be able to either support or refute the hypothesis.

Again, the researcher is not saying what he means precisely. Our editing clarifies his meaning.

The Definitions of Terms

                           1   2   3

    <u>Cartographer.</u>   A cartographer is a professional employee who engages in the production of maps, including construction of projections, design, drafting (or scribing), and preparation through the negative stage for the reproduction of maps, charts, and related graphic materials.

    <u>Discrete interests.</u>   Discrete interests are those empirically derived qualities or traits common to an occupational population that serve to make them distinct from the general population or universe.

Abbreviations

    SVIB is the abbreviation used for the <u>Strong Vocational Interest Blank</u>.

    USATOPOCOM is an acronym for the U.S. Army Topographic Command.

    CIMR is an abbreviation used for the Center for Interest Measurement Research.

    SD is the abbreviation used for standard deviation.

Assumptions

    <u>The first assumption.</u>   The first assumption is that the need for cartographers in Federal service will continue.

    <u>The second assumption.</u>   The second assumption is that the revised <u>Strong Vocational Interest Blank</u> will continue in use as a vocational guidance tool.

    <u>The third assumption.</u>   The third assumption is that the recent revolutionary advances in the cartographic state of the art will not alter the interests of persons in the employment of the Federal Government as cartographers.

    <u>The fourth assumption.</u>   The fourth assumption is that the criterion group consisting of the population of cartographers employed by the USATOPOCOM at Washington, D.C.; Providence, Rhode Island; Louisville, Kentucky; Kansas City, Missouri; and San Antonio, Texas, is representative of the universe of Federally employed cartographers.

The Importance of the Study

    Cartographers and the nature of their work are little known in American society. The total annual production of graduates, at the bachelor's level, with competence in the broader field of survey engineering within which cartography is subsumed, is currently less than one percent of the annual requirement. The addition of a cartographer scale to the occupations routinely reported for the <u>Strong Vocational Interest Blank</u> would potentially bring to the attention of everyone involved with the existing vocational guidance system the opportunities within the field of map-making and serve to attract serious and capable students into the appropriate preparatory college programs.

NOTE: Excerpt is from a research proposal submitted by Arthur L. Benton to the American University, Washington, D.C., in partial fulfillment of the requirement for the degree of Doctor of Philosophy.

Notice that the word to be defined is given in the indented subheading. Then follows a complete definition comprising the three parts discussed in this chapter: (1) the term to be defined, (2) the genera, and (3) the differentia.

An abbreviations section is not discussed in the text, but it is perfectly appropriate. Whatever makes reading easier and aids in giving the problem an appropriate setting is worth including in this part of the proposal.

Notice that the assumptions are set up with appropriate paragraph subheadings. The earlier discussion of hypotheses might have been set up in a similar manner, perhaps using the subheadings "The first hypothesis," "The second hypothesis," and so on.

Clarity is most important in the writing and structuring of a proposal. Here the author's assumptions are spelled out clearly and succinctly.

This section gives the reader a practical rationale for undertaking the study.

PRACTICAL APPLICATION WRITING THE FIRST SECTIONS OF A PROPOSAL

In a Checklist earlier in this chapter, you stated your main problem for research. In doing so, you took the first step in creating a research proposal. Now you can add the subproblems and identify the setting of the problem by doing the following exercise. As you complete the exercise, you may occasionally find it helpful to refer back to the sample proposal just presented and to our comments beside it.

1. *State the subproblems.*   On a blank sheet of paper, write the research problem statement you developed earlier. Allow considerable space between the lines. Now inspect your problem carefully and do the following:
   a. Within the problem, box off those areas that must receive in-depth treatment if the problem is to be fully explored. Number the boxed-in areas consecutively.
   b. Underline the words that indicate your intention to interpret the data (e.g., analyze, compare).
   c. Below the problem, which has been thus treated, write the several subproblems of your study in complete sentences. Make sure each subproblem includes a word that reflects data interpretation.

2. *Write your hypotheses/questions.*   Read again what we have said about hypotheses and research questions in this chapter. Study the way the author of the sample proposal presented his hypotheses, and notice how they are precisely parallel to the subproblems. Then write your own hypothesis/question related to each of your subproblems.

3. *Write the delimitations.*   Review our earlier discussion of "Delimiting the Research." Look at the discussion of delimitations in the sample proposal. Now write down the specific things that your own research project will *not* address.

4. *Write the definitions of terms.*   Before writing your definitions, reread the section "Defining the Terms" earlier in the chapter. After writing your definitions, it may be helpful to box in the specific parts of each definition, labeling each box as "term," "genera," or "differentia." (Delete these labels in the final draft of your proposal.)

5. *Write the assumptions.*   Reread the section "Stating the Assumptions" in this chapter, and study the section of the sample proposal dealing with assumptions. Now write a list of the specific assumptions you will be making as you design and carry out your research project.

6. *Describe the importance of the study.*   Look once again at the section in the sample proposal that describes the importance of the study. Then, in a short paragraph, explain why your study is important. Generally, you will not need more than two or three paragraphs to accomplish this task. Edit out all but essentials.

7. *Type your proposal.*   Look at how the sample proposal appears, and type your own proposal using a similar style and format.

Now that you have written the first sections of a proposal, evaluate what you have done using the following checklist.

✔ CHECKLIST
EVALUATING YOUR PROPOSED RESEARCH PROJECT

_____   1. Have you read enough literature relevant to your topic to know that your research project is worth your time and effort?

   • Will the project advance the frontiers of knowledge in an important way?

_____

_____

- Have you asked a research expert in your field to advise you on the value of your research effort?

_____

_____

_____ 2. Have you looked at your research problem from all sides to minimize unwanted surprises?

- What is good about your potential project?

_____

_____

- What are the potential pitfalls of attempting this research effort?

_____

_____

_____ 3. What research procedure will you follow?

- Do you have a plan to review the literature?

_____

_____

- Do you have a plan for data collection?

_____

_____

- Do you have a plan for data analysis?

_____

_____

- Do you have a plan to interpret the data you collect?

_____

_____

_____ 4. What research tools are available for you to use? Make a list and check their availability. Determine how you will use them.

_____

_____

_____

_____

_____ 5. Have two or three peers review your proposal. Do they understand what you are proposing to do? What questions do they have? What concerns do they share?

- I have discussed this plan with _____ , _____ , and _____ .

- They have the following questions and concerns:

_____

_____

_____

PRACTICAL APPLICATION   REAPPRAISING A PROPOSED RESEARCH PROBLEM

In this chapter, we have given you numerous suggestions for identifying an appropriate problem or question for your research. Because the problem is the center and driving force of any research project, we have devoted considerable space to its discussion. We cannot overemphasize that if the problem is not correctly selected and stated, you may put time, energy, and resources into something that is less than what it could be.

GUIDELINES   FINE-TUNING YOUR RESEARCH PROBLEM

Earlier in the chapter, we presented guidelines for identifying and stating an appropriate research problem. Here we offer a few general suggestions for fine-tuning the problem you've identified:

1. *Conduct a thorough literature review.*   Make sure you know enough about your topic that you can ask important questions and then make solid decisions about how you might answer them through your research effort. You may find that you need to revise your research plan significantly once you've delved deep into the literature related to your topic. (We address strategies for conducting a literature review in Chapter 4.)

2. *Try to see the problem from all sides.*   What is good about this potential project? What is not? Try to get a full view of what you are proposing to do. Such a perspective will help minimize unwanted surprises.

3. *Think through the process.*   Once you have brought your research problem into clear focus, imagine walking through the whole research procedure, from literature review through data collection, data analysis, and interpretation. You can gain valuable insights as you mentally walk through the project. Pay close attention to specific bottlenecks and pitfalls that may cause problems later on.

4. *Use all available tools and resources at your disposal.*   Remember that research is always a learning experience. Allow time for learning about new tools or for learning how to use old tools in new ways.

5. *Discuss your research problem with others.*   Frequently, beginning researchers need to clarify their problem statement. One good way to do this is to present it to others in as clear a fashion as possible. If they do not understand, further explanation and clarity are needed. One can learn a great deal from trying to explain something to someone else.

6. *Hold up your project for others to examine and critique.*   Describe your proposed research to other people. Do not hide your project because you are afraid someone else may not like the idea or may want to steal it from you. Rarely will either of these events happen.

Continually ask for feedback from others. Ask other people questions about your research problem, and ask them to ask *you* questions about it. Don't be overly discouraged by a few individuals who may get some sense of satisfaction from impeding the progress of others. Many great discoveries have been made by people who were repeatedly told they couldn't do what they set out to do.

7. *Remember that your project will take time.*   All too often, we have had students tell us that they anticipate completing a major research project (such as a thesis or dissertation) in a semester or less. Such a belief is, in the vast majority of cases, unrealistic. Consider all the steps involved in research: formulating a research problem, doing the necessary literature search, collecting and interpreting the data, describing what you have done in writing, and improving on your research report through multiple drafts. If you think that you can accomplish all of these things within 2 or 3 months, you're almost certainly setting yourself up for failure and great disappointment. We would much rather you think of any research project—and especially your first project—as something that is a valuable learning experience in its own right. As such, it is worth however much of your time and effort it takes to do the job well.

 Now go to our Companion Website at http://www.prenhall.com/leedy to assess your understanding of chapter content and to complete the projects that will help you learn how to conduct research.

FOR FURTHER READING

Gall, M. D., Borg, W. R., & Gall, J. P. (2003). *Educational research: An introduction* (7th ed.). Boston: Allyn & Bacon. [See Chapter 4.]

Gay, L. R., & Airasian, P. (2003). *Educational research: Competencies for analysis and application* (7th ed.). Upper Saddle River, NJ: Merrill/Prentice Hall. [See Chapter 2.]

McBurney, D. H. (1995). The problem method of teaching research methods. *Teaching of Psychology, 22*(1), 36–38.

McMillan, J. H., & Schumacher, S. (1993). *Research in education: A conceptual introduction* (3rd ed.). New York: HarperCollins. [See Chapter 3.]

Medawar, P. B. (1979). *Advice to a young scientist.* New York: Harper & Row.

Neuman, W. L. (2003). *Social research methods: Qualitative and quantitative approaches* (5th ed.). Boston: Allyn & Bacon.

Schram, T. H. (2003). *Conceptualizing qualitative inquiry: Mindword for fieldwork in education and the social sciences.* Upper Saddle River, NJ: Merrill/Prentice Hall. [See Chapter 5.]

Wimmer, R. D., & Dominick, J. R. (2003). *Mass media research: An introduction* (7th ed.). Belmont, CA: Wadsworth. [See Chapter 2.]

Review of the Related Literature

Those who conduct research belong to a community of scholars, each of whom has journeyed into the unknown to bring back an insight, a truth, a point of light. What they have recorded of their journeys and findings will make it easier for you to explore the unknown: to help you also discover an insight, a truth, or a point of light.

As noted in Chapter 3, reading the literature related to your topic of interest can help you formulate a specific research problem. The related literature can help you in several other ways as well. In this chapter, we discuss the importance of the literature review and give you suggestions for reviewing the related literature thoroughly and efficiently.

UNDERSTANDING THE ROLE OF THE REVIEW

Research proposals and research reports typically have a section (in the case of a thesis or dissertation, an entire chapter) that reviews the related literature. The review describes theoretical perspectives and previous research findings regarding the problem at hand. Its function is to "look again" (*re + view*) at what others have done in areas that are similar, though not necessarily identical to, one's own area of investigation.

As a researcher, you should ultimately know the literature about your topic *very, very well*. In addition to helping you pin down your own research problem, a literature review has numerous other benefits:

1. It can offer new ideas, perspectives, and approaches that may not have occurred to you.
2. It can inform you about other researchers who conduct work in this area—individuals whom you may wish to contact for advice or feedback.
3. It can show you how others have handled methodological and design issues in studies similar to your own.
4. It can reveal sources of data that you may not have known existed.
5. It can introduce you to measurement tools that other researchers have developed and used effectively.

6. It can reveal methods of dealing with problem situations that may be similar to difficulties you are facing.
7. It can help you interpret and make sense of your findings and, ultimately, help you tie your results to the work of those who have preceded you.
8. It will bolster your confidence that your topic is one worth studying, because you will find that others have invested considerable time, effort, and resources in studying it.

Simply put, the more you know about investigations and perspectives related to your topic, the more effectively you can tackle your own research problem.

In most instances, researchers begin their review of the literature quite early in the game, and they draw on existing theories and prior research studies to help them pin down their research problem and accompanying hypotheses and questions. Only on rare occasions—when they intentionally choose *not* to let existing perspectives and research findings bias their data collection and interpretation—do researchers put off a thorough literature review until relatively late in the research process (e.g., see the discussion of grounded theory research in Chapter 7).

SOURCES AND STRATEGIES FOR LOCATING RELATED LITERATURE

You might find literature related to your topic in a number of different places—for instance, in books, journals, newspapers, government publications, conference presentations, and Web sites. Obviously, you cannot simply wander aimlessly through the library stacks or World Wide Web, hoping you will eventually stumble on items that may help you; you must focus your search from the very beginning.

A good way to start is to identify one or more **keywords**—words or short phrases summarizing your research topic—that can point you toward potentially useful resources. A prime source of such keywords is your statement of your research problem. For example, let's say that you are a psychologist who wants to study the effects of children's personal interests on their motivation to learn school subject matter. Obvious keywords for this topic are *interest*, *motivation*, and *learning*. These are very general, of course, but they should get you started. They will lead you to thousands, perhaps tens of thousands, of potential resources, however, and so you will soon want to identify more specific keywords. As you begin to look at books, journal articles, subject matter indexes, and other resources related to your topic and initial set of keywords, you should come across words and phrases that more closely capture what you want to study—perhaps including *intrinsic motivation*, *personal interest*, and Mihaly Csikszentmihalyi's concept of *flow*. Your set of keywords, then, is apt to change as your literature review progresses.

Armed with your initial keywords, you can proceed in several directions. In the following sections, we will look at three major starting points: (1) the library catalog, (2) indexes and abstracts in the library's reference section, and (3) online databases. We will then consider several additional strategies for zeroing in on relevant research literature.

USING THE LIBRARY CATALOG

A good college or university library will almost certainly have a number of books relevant to your research topic. Some books will be written solely by one or two individuals. Others may be collections of articles written by a variety of experts in the field. And don't overlook general textbooks in your discipline. A good textbook can give you a good general overview of a topic, including important concepts, theoretical perspectives, a sampling of relevant research, and critical references.

As a rule of thumb, use books with recent copyright dates. The more recently a book has been written, the more likely it is to give you a sense of current perspectives in your field and alert you to recent research findings that may be pertinent to your research problem. You should ignore this rule, of course, if you are specifically interested in how perspectives about your topic have changed over the years.

The most effective way to locate helpful books is through the library catalog. Although you may find a card catalog located in the reference section, you can usually search the library's holdings more effectively if you use the online catalog. You can access the catalog from computer terminals within the library or perhaps from your home computer via the library's Web site.

Accessing a Library Catalog from Home

USING
TECHNOLOGY

If you have access to the Internet from your home computer, then you already have access to countless online library catalogs around the world. These catalogs usually allow you to look for books by author, title, call number, or keyword. They will let you browse among related books quickly and easily. They will tell you on what floor of the library (and, if relevant, in what building or on what branch campus) a particular book is located. And they will typically tell you the status of a book—whether it's currently available and or when it's due to be returned.

You can explore how online catalogs work by visiting one or more of these university catalogs on the Internet:

> Brown University
> http://library.brown.edu/
>
> University of New Hampshire
> http://library.unh.edu/
>
> University of Northern Colorado
> http://www.unco.edu/library/

Typically, the Web home page for your own institution will have a link to the library and its catalog. If for some reason you have trouble finding your library's catalog on the Internet, ask a reference librarian for its Internet address.

USING INDEXES, ABSTRACTS, AND OTHER GENERAL REFERENCES

The journals in your library's periodicals section are, of course, another indispensable resource. The library catalog will tell you which journals the library owns and where each one is located. It will also tell you whether it owns the journal in paper form (in which case you can find it in the library stacks) or in *microform* (in which case you will probably find it in a cabinet in the library's periodicals section). The microforms area of the library is easy to spot, as it will have numerous cubicles with machines for viewing *microfilm*, *microfiche*, and the like. These machines may seem intimidating to the novice researcher, but they're quite easy to use once you've had a little practice. Don't be afraid to ask someone behind the periodicals desk to demonstrate how to use them.

However, although the library catalog will tell you which journals the library owns and in what form it owns them, it won't tell you the specific articles that each volume of a journal contains. Instead, you may need to consult the indexes and abstracts located in the reference section. An **index** lists articles and research reports in certain specified areas. An **abstract** is a summary of an article or research study; it also gives the source of the original study, should a reader wish to refer to it. Examples of commonly used indexes and abstract compilations are presented in Table 4.1. Your reference librarian can show you how to use such resources effectively and tell you which ones are available in electronic as well as paper form.

For contemporary events, do not overlook *Facts on File* and *The New York Times Index*. For a guide to the periodical literature of the 19th century, a work such as the *Nineteenth Century Readers' Guide* is indispensable.

TABLE 4.1   Examples of indexes and abstracts in various content areas

Indexes		Abstracts
Applied Science and Technology Index	*Index Medicus*	*Abstracts of Health Care Management Studies*
Art Index	*Index of Economic Articles in Journals and Collective Volumes*	*America, History and Life: Abstracts and Citations*
Bibliographic Index	*Index to Foreign Legal Periodicals*	*Bibliography of Bioethics*
Biography Index	*Index to Legal Periodicals*	*Biological Abstracts*
Biological and Agricultural Index	*International Index to Music Periodicals*	*Chemical Abstracts*
Book Review Index	*International Nursing Index*	*Child Development Abstracts and Bibliography*
British Education Index	*M.L.A. Index and Bibliography (Modern Language Association)*	*Dissertation Abstracts International*
British Humanities Index	*Music Index*	*Educational Administration Abstracts*
Business Periodicals Index	*New York Times Index*	*Historical Abstracts*
Canadian Periodical Index	*Poole's Index to Periodical Literature*	*International Political Science Abstracts*
Comprehensive Dissertation Index	*Readers' Guide to Periodical Literature*	*Nursing Abstracts*
Cumulative Index to Nursing and Allied Health Literature	*Resources in Education*	*Pollution Abstracts*
Current Index to Journals in Education (CIJE)	*Social Sciences Citation Index*	*Psychological Abstracts*
Education Index	*Social Sciences Index*	*Sage Public Administration Abstracts*
Essay and General Literature Index	*United Nations Documents Index*	*Sage Race Relations Abstracts*
Guide to Special Issues and Indexes of Periodicals	*Wall Street Journal Index*	*Sage Urban Studies Abstracts*
Humanities Index		*Social Work Research and Abstracts*
Illustration Index		*Sociological Abstracts*
		Urban Affairs Abstracts
		Women Studies Abstracts

Be sure to examine published bibliographies. One of the best current sources is the *Bibliographic Index*. Besterman's *Bibliography of Bibliographies* and similar standard reference sources are helpful. For locating books, *Books in Print, Cumulative Book Index, Book Review Digest*, and the various catalogs of the Library of Congress, the British Museum, the Bibliotheque Nationale, and other great libraries of the world are found in multivolume print form in many libraries.

You should also know about *Ulrich's International Periodicals Directory*. This five-volume set contains important information that can greatly reduce your search time. In it, you can find virtually all the titles of periodical indexes, bibliographies, and abstracts throughout the world. It includes online journals as well as more traditional paper journals.

Ask the reference librarian about any CD-ROM indexes that the library might have related to your subject area. A single CD-ROM contains a great deal more information than any single paper index can include, and it enables you to search its many entries quickly and efficiently. Furthermore, many CD-ROM reference indexes have built-in thesauruses that can help you identify keywords you may not have considered. Because you can conduct a search so quickly, you can try any number of keyword combinations and adjust your searches as needed. Yet the amount of information a CD-ROM will enable you to search pales in comparison to that of an online database, the resource we consider next.

USING ONLINE DATABASES

Most college and university libraries now provide access to **online databases,** enormous collections of citations or abstracts related to various subjects and disciplines. Table 4.2 lists some examples. Often, a library's home page on the World Wide Web will provide a direct link to these

TABLE 4.2

Examples of online databases

Database	Subject Area(s) Covered
Academic Search Premier	Education, humanities, multicultural issues, sciences, social sciences
America: History and Life	History of the United States and Canada
Applied Science and Technology Abstracts	Applied sciences and technology (e.g., aeronautics, computing, energy resources, engineering, food science, robotics)
Art Index and Art Index Retrospective	Art
Biological Abstracts	Biology, medicine
Books in Print	All disciplines (books)
Business Source Premier	Business, economics
Cumulative Index to Nursing and Allied Health Literature (CINAHL)	Health care, nursing
Dissertation Abstracts International	All disciplines (dissertations)
EconLit	Economics
Educational Resources Information Center (ERIC)	Education and education-related topics
Historical Abstracts	World history (excluding the United States and Canada; for these, use America: History and Life)
Ingenta	All disciplines (articles)
Linguistics and Language Behavior Abstracts (LLBA)	Language
MathSciNet	Mathematics (pure and applied), statistics
MEDLINE	Dentistry, health care, medicine, veterinary medicine
National Criminal Justice Reference Service Abstracts Database	Courts, crime, justice, law enforcement, victimization
PAIS (Public Affairs Information Service) International	Public and social policy, social sciences
PsycINFO	Psychology and psychological aspects of other disciplines (e.g., physiology, sociology, anthropology, education, medicine, business)
Social Work Abstracts	Social work and related topics (e.g., welfare, aging, substance abuse)
Sociological Abstracts	Sociology and related topics in the social and behavioral sciences
SPORT Discus	Physical education, physical fitness, recreation, sports medicine
Statistical Universe	Statistical information
Web of Science	Humanities, sciences, social sciences

databases, and users may be able to access them on their home computers as well as at the library. Because libraries typically pay ongoing fees for the databases, students who want to use them may need to enter their name and a university ID number before gaining access to them.[1]

Online databases allow searches of many thousands of journals and such other sources as books, chapters in edited books, dissertations, government documents, technical reports, and newspapers. A typical database allows you to limit your search in a variety of ways—perhaps by keywords, title, author, year, journal name, language, or any combination of these. As an example, let's consider PsycINFO, a database that includes information not only about sources in psychology but also about psychology-related sources in such disciplines as physiology, sociology, anthropology, education, medicine, and business. As this edition of *Practical Research* goes to press, PsycINFO works as follows:

1. When you enter the database, you type one to three words or phrases in boxes at the top of the screen. In pull-down menus to the right of the boxes, you can indicate whether each word or phrase you have typed is a title, author, key concept (i.e., keyword), date, word/phrase in the abstract, or some other entity.
2. In pull-down menus to the left of the boxes, you can tell the computer to
   a. Identify only those items that include *all* the words/phrases you have entered (for this, you select the "and" option)
   b. Identify items that include *any* of the words/phrases you have entered (for this, you select the "or" option)
   c. Exclude items that have one of the words/phrases you have entered (for this, you select the "not" option)
3. Options in the lower portion of the computer screen allow you to limit your search results still further, perhaps by specifying a particular journal, date, population, age group, or language.
4. Once you have limited your search to some degree (at a minimum by completing step 1), you click on the "Search" button in the upper right corner of your computer screen.
5. The next screen will either (a) give you one or more references or (b) tell you that it has come up empty-handed ("No results were found for your search query"). If references appear, you can click on their titles to view abstracts. If your search has been unsuccessful, you probably need to eliminate one or more of the limitations you imposed on your original search and click on the "Search" button again.
6. Once you've viewed the abstracts of potentially useful sources, PsycINFO lets you add them to a "folder" where you can save them and eventually print them out.

Some databases provide the sources themselves. For example, the *New York Times Digital Archive* allows you to search—and then also to read—news articles, editorials, letters to the editor, birth announcements, obituaries, advertisements, and virtually any other entry in any issue dating back to its first issue in 1851. *Congressional Universe* provides a compendium of recent U.S. laws, bills, regulations, publications, and a variety of other federal documents and activities.

ADDITIONAL STRATEGIES FOR ZEROING IN ON RELEVANT LITERATURE

In addition to using the library catalog, indexes and abstracts, and online databases, we suggest the following strategies: (1) looking at government publications, (2) surfing the World Wide Web, and (3) using the citations and reference lists of those who have gone before you.

---

[1] Occasionally, a researcher may have a Web browser that is incompatible with some part of the university's catalog system. For example, the second author of this book initially found that, although she could easily access her university's library catalog from her home computer, she was unable to access the university's online databases. After numerous failed attempts (which were followed by increasingly frustrated calls to the library's computer center), she learned that for some inexplicable reason, some Macintosh versions of Internet Explorer do not allow entry into the databases at her library. She switched to Netscape Communicator, which allowed her to access the databases easily.

Government Publications

One vast source of information you should not overlook is the Depository Libraries of the U.S. government. The U.S. Government Printing Office is the largest publisher of printed material in the world, and its publications are available through nearly 1,400 congressionally designated libraries (including many university libraries) throughout the United States. A few of the many publications available are *Statistical Abstract of the United States*, *Survey of Current Business*, *United States Government Manual*, *Public Papers of the Presidents*, and *Monthly Labor Review*. Other publications provide information about nutrition, environment and weather, careers, science and technology, business opportunities, health care, energy, and education. You can obtain more information about government publications and designated libraries by writing to the Superintendent of Documents, U.S. Government Printing Office, Washington, DC 20402, or by going to the office's Web site at

http://www.gpoaccess.gov/

Alternatively, you can find government documents (as well as those from industry and various public agencies) using the Global Information Locator Service (GILS) at

http://www.gils.net/

And, of course, don't forget the online database *Congressional Universe* mentioned earlier.

A comprehensive list of the government publications available in all regional depository libraries and in the subregional depository libraries is found in the nearly 200-page publication *List of Classes of United States Government Publications Available for Selection by Depository Libraries*. Not all depository libraries may carry the full contents of this list, but you should request it when you visit a depository library to appreciate the wide range of materials available through government sources.

World Wide Web

USING
TECHNOLOGY

In recent years, the World Wide Web has become an increasingly valuable source of information to researchers. If you have not already discovered the value of the Web in finding needed information, now is the time to begin. But be careful: Once you get the hang of Web surfing, you may find it so addictive that, like a good book, you can't stop reading it!

To conduct a search of the World Wide Web, you use your Web browser to travel to a **search engine,** a site on the Web that enables you to find information about particular topics. Here are a few search engine sites you might find helpful:

http://www.google.com/
http://www.altavista.com/
http://www.askjeeves.com/
http://www.excite.com/
http://www.hotbot.com/
http://www.infoseek.com/
http://www.yahoo.com/

These sites typically have a space in which you can type one or more keywords to start your search. Following are three general strategies to keep in mind when using search engines:

1. Use at least two keywords to limit your search. (For example, to locate research about children with autism, you might type the words *children* and *autism*.)
2. Type a plus sign (+) before any keyword that you definitely want used in your search. (For example, to limit your search only to children who have autism, you should type +*children* and +*autism*. Otherwise, you may get a listing of all resources involving children *or* autism, which would undoubtedly be a long list indeed.) An alternative to using + signs is to insert the word *and* between your keywords (e.g., typing *children and autism*).
3. If you want to look for a phrase rather than a single word, put quotation marks around the phrase. (For example, if you are looking for the home page of the Autism Society of America, you should type *"Autism Society of America,"* including the quotation

marks. This way, your search will be restricted to items specifically about that particular organization.)

Surfing the Web will lead you to a variety of locations. For instance, it may lead you to government office Web sites that can provide helpful information, including the U.S. Census Bureau, Department of Health and Human Services, Department of Education, Department of Labor, NASA, U.S. Geological Survey, and National Park Service. Many professional associations, such as the Autism Society of America, have Web sites as well, and these sites often provide a wealth of information about their areas of expertise.

Your Web search may also lead you to research articles and opinion papers that individual researchers have made available on the Internet, and you can typically print such documents or download them to your own computer. Keep in mind that such articles and papers vary widely in quality. Although most academic publications have a review process that enhances the quality of the research articles they include (recall our discussion of juried versus nonjuried reports in Chapter 1), many research reports posted on the Web have not yet been reviewed or judged by professional colleagues. Obviously, you will want to read *any* research report with a somewhat critical eye, but you should be especially careful when you read research reports on the Web that you cannot verify as the work of a credible scholar.

In many searches of the World Wide Web, you will almost certainly have to wade through many listings that are not terribly helpful. On the plus side, however, if you have access to the Internet from a home computer, you can browse anytime day or night—weekends, holidays, even 3 A.M. if you like. Libraries are sometimes closed, but the World Wide Web is always open.

Citations and Reference Lists of Those Who Have Gone Before You

No library or computer search, no matter how extensive, is foolproof. Ultimately any search depends on the particular keywords you use and the particular databases you include in your search. One additional—in our minds, *essential*—resource is the literature reviews of researchers whose own writings you've consulted. Such reviews, especially if they have been published recently, can give you valuable guidance about seminal research studies and cutting-edge ideas related to your research topic. As a rule of thumb, we urge you to track down *any references that you see cited by three or more other researchers*. Such references are clearly influencing current work in your field and should not be overlooked.

This brings us to another important point: Don't depend on what other authors say about a particular reference. Too often we have seen two or more authors misrepresent the work of a particular researcher in the same, particular way; apparently, they are reading one another's descriptions of that researcher's work rather than reading the researcher's own words! Whenever possible, *go to the original source and read it yourself*.

Considering all the resources described in this chapter, you might be thinking that you'll be spending the next 10 years conducting your literature review! Don't worry. In the section that follows, we describe how to conduct your literature search in an organized, efficient, and time-saving fashion.

PRACTICAL APPLICATION CONDUCTING A LITERATURE SEARCH

In Chapter 3, we discussed how to select a research problem or question. We also suggested that most problems, taken as a whole, are fairly complex and can be more easily solved when they are subdivided. Thus, we presented suggestions for identifying subproblems within the main problem.

The main problem and subproblems provide a way to focus your attention as you read the literature. One concrete and effective approach, using either paper and pencil or brainstorming software such as Inspiration, involves the following steps:

1. Write the problem in its entirety at the top of the page or computer screen.
2. Write down each subproblem in its entirety as well.
3. Identify the important words and phrases in each subproblem.

FIGURE 4.1

Using Inspiration
software to prepare for a
review of the literature

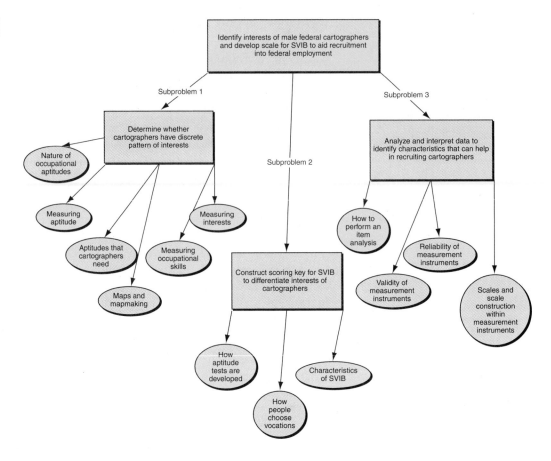

FIGURE 4.1

Using Inspiration
software to prepare for a
review of the literature

4. Translate these words and phrases into specific topics that you must learn more about.
   These topics become your "agenda" as you read the literature.
5. Go to the library to seek out resources related to your agenda.
6. Read!

Figure 4.1 shows the literature-review agenda we have identified for the research problem and subproblems identified in the sample proposal presented near the end of Chapter 3. We used Inspiration software to create the agenda. The four rectangles represent the research problem and its three subproblems. The ovals reflect the specific things we need to learn more about with respect to each subproblem.

The steps just described can help you keep your literature review within the realm of your research problem. It prevents you from wandering into other areas of the literature that, though potentially quite interesting, may be of little or no use to you when the time comes to write your literature review.

Now that you have an idea of what to search for in the library, let's discuss how to make your search efforts efficient and productive.

GUIDELINES   Using Your Library Time Efficiently

Make no mistake about it, conducting a thorough literature review takes a great deal of time. But it can take considerably *less* time if you plan ahead and approach your task in an organized and systematic fashion. Here are several suggestions for maximizing your efficiency at the library.

1. *Go to the library armed with data-gathering tools.* You will need a systematic way of recording the information you will be gathering—ideally, one that will also allow you to easily organize

FIGURE 4.2

Bibliography card

Call No. _____   Serial No. _____

Author(s) _____

Title of article _____

Journal title _____

Volume/Issue _____ Month/Year _____ Pages _____

Place of publication, publisher, date, edition (books only)

_____

Source in which item was found _____

How item relates to research problem _____

Comments (use space below and reverse side of card):

Note: The space for "Serial No." provides a place where you can record the order in which you read each source. You identify the first source as "1," the second source as "2," and so on. These numbers provide a quick and easy way of referring to each source later on.

what you've obtained. As is true for many aspects of the research process, you can use either paper and pencil or a computer (in this case, a laptop) to record what you find at the library.

A paper-and-pencil approach involves making bibliography cards that you use to record information about each source you locate and read. Figure 4.2 presents a suggested form for a bibliography card; it will ensure that you record all the information you will need if you use the source and so need to include it in your reference list. We suggest that you make a large number of these cards and take a supply whenever you go to the library. In addition to bibliography cards, you should also have a large number of blank cards on which you can write notes about the contents of each source. On each note card, you should identify the source in question by the same serial number you've assigned it on its bibliography card. To be consistent, you might want to write the serial number prominently in the upper right corner of each card.

An alternative approach is to bring a laptop computer to the library and enter the information you gather directly onto one or more computer files. It may seem cumbersome to carry a laptop computer with you as you work your way around the library. But computerizing the information you obtain at the very beginning of the literature review process will almost certainly save you time down the road. If you use a laptop at this stage of the game, you might want to bring a copy of Figure 4.2 with you as a way of helping you remember to record all the information you will need for each source. Alternatively, you can use computer database software, to be described shortly.

2. *Identify the materials (books, articles, etc.) you want to read, and determine whether your library has them.* You will probably identify many of the sources you need by consulting the library catalog and perusing indexes and abstracts in the reference section. As you make a list of the desired sources, keep the following suggestions in mind:

- *Keep track of the specific searches you conduct* (e.g., which indexes you consult, which keywords you use and in what order). Keeping such records ensures that you won't duplicate your efforts.
- *Let computers make your lists for you whenever possible.* For instance, if you are using an online database, you will probably be able to print out the sources you identify or, if you prefer, download your list to a computer disk.
- *Check the library holdings for the books and journals that you identify.* More specifically, find out if the library owns the sources you need and, if so, where they are located and whether they are currently on loan to another user. In the case of journals, you should also check to see whether they are in paper or microform (e.g., microfilm, microfiche). If the library does not

have something you need, keep the reference; we'll talk about alternative strategies for obtaining such materials shortly.

3. *Develop an organized plan of attack for finding the sources you've identified.* Arrange your sources according to where they are located in the library. For instance, you can organize books by call number. You can organize articles first by paper versus microform, and then by the specific journals in which they appear. If your university has multiple library sites, you will, of course, also want to organize your sources by the specific sites at which they are located.

4. *Track your sources down.* After you've organized your sources, you're ready to go find them and look them over. Keep track of whether each item is (a) found and used, (b) found but determined not to be helpful, or (c) not found. As you peruse the stacks, don't forget to browse (recall our discussion of browsing in Chapter 2).

5. *Record all basic information as you read each source.* "Make haste slowly" is a sound rule for any researcher. Be careful not to make careless, half-complete notes that, when consulted later, are either unintelligible or so lacking in essential information that they are practically useless. If you are using note cards to record your findings, write legibly or print clearly. If you can't distinguish between undotted *i*'s and closed-up *e*'s, or between carelessly made *a*'s and *o*'s, you may eventually find yourself scurrying back to sources for such details.

As you read each source, record any essential bibliographic information you have not previously obtained. In addition, specify exactly how the source relates to your research problem. (The bibliography card in Figure 4.2 includes a place for this information.) The competent researcher never forgets that everything is done for only one purpose: to contribute to the solution of the problem.

You will also want to write sufficient notes about the content of the source to enable you to recreate its ideas when, later, you are writing your literature review. As you do so, you may find it helpful to keep track of the pages on which you've found certain ideas; furthermore, page numbers are essential if you are quoting a source word for word. Suppose you are reading a work to which you've assigned the serial number 63. If you want to make notes on information contained on pages 24, 26, and 29, you might have three note cards, each with information from one of the three pages. You can label the cards simply as 63:24, 63:26, and 63:29, respectively. In some cases, of course, a source will have so much information that you will simply want to make a photocopy of relevant pages[2] or, in the case of a book, check it out and take it home.

6. *Identify strategies for obtaining sources that are not immediately available.* We can almost guarantee that you won't find everything you need the first time around. Some books may be currently checked out to other users. Other books and a few journals may not be among the library's holdings. Here are several strategies to consider in such situations.

   ▨ *Check at the circulation desk to see whether you can reserve, or possibly recall, a checked-out book.* If you discover that a book is out but due to be returned shortly, ask the librarian to put a *hold* on the book for you (some libraries allow you to do this yourself through the online catalog); the library will then contact you as soon as it's returned and save it for you at the circulation desk for a few days. If you discover that the book is checked out for a long period of time—perhaps for several months or longer—then ask if the book can be *recalled* for you. (Many university libraries allow professors to check out books for an entire semester or academic year, but they must return them earlier if someone else wants to use them.)
   ▨ *Submit a request for the source through interlibrary loan.* Most libraries have cooperative arrangements to exchange books with other libraries. In many cases, your library will gladly track down the books and journal articles you need and provide them to you at little or no charge except, perhaps, for photocopying.
   ▨ *Order books through a bookstore or online.* Most bookstores will gladly order any book that is currently in print and obtain it for you within a week or two. You can also order books online through Web sites such as these:

      http://amazon.com/
      http://barnesandnoble.com/

---

[2] In the United States, federal copyright law allows one copy for personal use.

http://www.borders.com/
http://www.dealpilot.com/
http://www.eastbaybooks.com/ (for out-of-print books)

■ *Use an online document delivery service.* Several sites on the World Wide Web provide a means of obtaining articles and research reports:

Ingenta (for journal articles)
http://www.ingenta.com/

ProQuest Digital Dissertations (UMI's Dissertation Abstracts database)
http://wwwlib.umi.com/dissertations/

ERIC Document Reproduction Service (for ERIC, a large database of educational documents)
http://edrs.com/

As you conduct your literature review, you will undoubtedly need to repeat this cycle of steps several times. You almost certainly won't identify every source you need the first time you visit the library. With each trip you make, however, you will become more and more of an expert about the topic you are pursuing. You will also become increasingly knowledgeable about the library and its resources.

ORGANIZING THE INFORMATION YOU HAVE COLLECTED

Imagine entering a new library to locate some books and articles, but this library doesn't have an organized system for storing its resources. Printed materials are placed on the most convenient shelves, not in any special place or order. The librarians leave it up to the users to look through all this material until they find what they need. How quickly you would become frustrated trying to locate the information you want! You will encounter similar frustration—albeit on a smaller scale—if you don't organize the information you gather from your literature search. As you begin to amass a substantial amount of information about your subject area, then, you will undoubtedly want to begin organizing it as well.

If you have been using bibliography cards to record information, you may want to make at least two copies of each card and set up two files. One would have the cards arranged alphabetically by the author's last name; the other would have the cards arranged in the order in which you read the sources (i.e., by the serial number you've assigned). It can be extremely helpful to have both types of files. For instance, perhaps you are reading an article that cites a source you think you may already have read. By having the author's last name, you can consult your alphabetical author file and readily find the information you've collected about the source in question. On other occasions, you will be reviewing your note cards, perhaps as you write your literature review. If you find a card labeled "63:29," you can turn to the cards you've arranged by serial number to find the author and title of the source in question. Ah, yes, you say to yourself, this information is on page 29 of source 63, which is . . . (you check your file) . . . M. J. Mahoney's *Human Change Processes* (1990, New York, Basic Books). No more mystery about where the note originated.

Putting your sources and notes on a computer, either while you're at the library or at a later time, can often help you keep track of and organize your sources more quickly and efficiently than using bibliography and note cards. Computer databases are one extremely useful tool in this regard.

CREATING COMPUTER DATABASES

Earlier we spoke of the databases that are available through online searches. In fact, you can create your *own* database for the literature you read. In general, a **database** is a collection of information that is organized in an easily accessible manner.

An analogy may be helpful. Most of us have an address book or file in which we keep track of the names, addresses, and telephone numbers of friends and relatives. At work or school, we may have a different address file that contains similar information for business associates, customers, or classmates. Suppose your home address file consists of a small recipe box that contains many index cards. If you were to pull out any specific card from the file, you would find important pieces of information. One piece might be the last name of one of your friends; other pieces would be his or her first name, telephone number, and so on. To be efficient at finding the appropriate name when needed, you may be organized enough to have put the cards in alphabetical order by last name.

In an electronic database, each kind of information that appears on every card in a file (e.g., name, telephone number) is called a **field**. Each card that holds a number of fields is referred to as a **record** (e.g., one record may contain all the information pertaining to your friend, Jerry Miller). And each set of records (e.g., the whole box of all your friends' addresses) is referred to as a **data file**.

Computer software (e.g., EndNote, ProCite) is available specifically for creating bibliographic databases. Such software allows you to create data files in which each source becomes a separate record. The data files have fields for title, author, date, journal reference, special keywords, an identification number, and any notes you take while reading the item.

By putting the information you collect in an electronic database, you can find anything you want in a second or two. For example, perhaps you want to find a book written by a specific author. You can search the author field in the entire database; each entry is compared with the author name you want. When a match is found, it is reported.

Furthermore, you can rapidly sort the data by whatever field you choose. For example, if you want all books listed in alphabetical order by author, the author field on each record within the database is identified and the records are rearranged into alphabetical order.

An additional advantage is that you can create your reference list directly from the database. Most bibliographic software packages allow you to create a reference list using whatever format (e.g., APA style, MLA style) your institution or academic discipline requires.

KNOWING WHEN TO QUIT

"When do I know that I have completed the review of the literature?" The novice researcher often asks this question. In theory, the answer might be "Never." As long as people continue to conduct research related to your topic, there will always be additional information that may be helpful to you. From a practical standpoint, however, you must finish your search, use what you have obtained, and get on with the study itself. But how will you know when that time has arrived?

The best advice we can give you is this: *Look for repetitive patterns in the materials you are finding and reading.* As you read more and more sources, eventually familiar arguments, methodologies, and findings will start to appear. Perhaps you will see the same key people and studies cited over and over. You will get a feeling of *déjà vu*—"I've seen this (or something similar to it) before." When you are no longer encountering new viewpoints, then you may be reasonably sure that you are familiar with the critical parts of the literature.

PRACTICAL APPLICATION BEGINNING YOUR REVIEW OF THE RELATED LITERATURE

In Chapter 3, you began to develop your own research proposal by stating the problem and the subproblems. In the following exercise, you will plan the review of related literature section of the proposal.

1. *Write your research problem.*   The literature that you review should be *only* that which is related to your research problem. To help you keep this fact foremost in your mind, write your problem in the following space:

   _____

   _____

   _____

2. *Identify the subproblems.*   Read your research problem and insert 1, 2, 3, 4, and so on before each separate subarea of the problem. By doing so, you can identify specific topics that you might use as you examine databases, indexes, abstracts, bibliographies, and similar reference works to find sources related to your problem. In the following spaces, list the keywords or phrases that will guide you in your search:

_____

_____

_____

3. *Go to the reference section of your library.*   Begin your search of the related literature by consulting a few of the general reference resources—databases, indexes, abstracts, bibliographies, and so on—listed earlier in the chapter. In the case of the paper resources you consult, make note of where in the library (or perhaps in which library) you found each one. Also list the edition, pages, or sections in which you found relevant material, plus any comments you wish to make. Table 4.3 gives you a sample format for your notes. This step will give you a general feel for the kind of work you will be doing early on in your search.

4. *Construct a set of bibliography cards or a bibliographic database.*   Decide whether you will use note cards or a computer database to record the information you find. You should then either (a) construct a bibliography card similar to that in Figure 4.2 (and make a minimum of 50 copies) or (b) set up a computer database and learn how to use it.

5. *Go back to the library with your information-gathering system.*   Use the cards or computer database to record the sources that you find in the general reference works. In each case, enter the author's name, the title of the book or article, the title of the journal (if you're dealing with an article), the publisher and publisher's location (if you're dealing with a book), the publication date, plus any other information that will help you find the reference. Also make note of the database, index, abstract, or other source in which you found the reference.

6. *Track down your references.*   Now comes the best part: You can actually start reading the literature and learning about your research area!

EVALUATING, ORGANIZING, AND SYNTHESIZING THE LITERATURE

Too many literature reviews do nothing more than report what other people have done and said. Such reviews, which are typically written by novice researchers, go something like this:

> In 1992, Jones found that such-and-such. . . . Furthermore, Smith (1994) discovered that such-and-such. . . . Black (1995) proposed that so-on-and-so-forth. . . .

We learn nothing new from such a review; we'd be better off reading the original articles for ourselves.

In a good literature review, the researcher doesn't merely report the related literature. He or she also *evaluates, organizes, and synthesizes what others have done.*

Turn back to the section "Practical Application: Evaluating the Research of Others" on page 9 of Chapter 1. There we urged you not only to read about others' work but also to critically evaluate their methods and conclusions. *Never take other people's conclusions at face value; determine for yourself whether their conclusions are justified based on the data presented.*

At this point you may be able to judge the work of other researchers only in a fairly superficial fashion, perhaps using the "Reflective Questions" checklist on pages 9–10 of Chapter 1. As you proceed through the rest of this book and learn more about research methodology, however, you will become increasingly knowledgeable about what kinds of conclusions are and are not warranted from various methodologies and types of data.

In addition to evaluating what you read, you must also organize the ideas you encounter during your review. The subproblems within your main problem should, in many cases, provide a general organizational scheme you can use. Looking at how other authors have organized literature reviews related to your topic may be helpful as well.

TABLE 4.3 Master key to reference materials

Title	Location	Edition	Page	Comments

Finally, and perhaps most importantly, you must *synthesize* what you've learned from your review. In other words, you must pull together the diverse perspectives and research results you've read into a cohesive whole. Here are some examples of what you might do:

- Compare and contrast varying theoretical perspectives on the topic.
- Show how approaches to the topic have changed over time.
- Describe general trends in research findings.
- Identify discrepant or contradictory findings, and suggest possible explanations for such discrepancies.
- Identify general themes that run throughout the literature.

When you write a literature review that does such things, you have contributed something new to the knowledge in the field even *before* you've conducted your own study. In fact, a literature review that makes such a contribution is often publishable in its own right. (We'll talk more about writing for publication in Chapter 12.)

PRACTICAL APPLICATION Writing the Section on the Related Literature

Once you have read, evaluated, organized, and synthesized the literature relevant to your research problem, you will, of course, eventually need to begin writing the section or chapter that describes your literature review. A few simple guidelines may help.

GUIDELINES Writing a Clear and Cohesive Review

As university professors, we've written many literature reviews ourselves. We've also read countless master's theses and dissertations written by novice researchers. From such experiences, we've developed the following general guidelines for writing a solid review of the related literature.

1. *Get the proper psychological orientation.* Be clear in your thinking. Know precisely what you are attempting to do. The review of the related literature section is a discussion of the studies, research reports, and scholarly writings that bear directly on your own effort.

You might think of the review of related literature section in your document to be a discussion with a peer about what others have written in relation to what you plan to do. Viewing the literature section in this way can help you see your own effort within the context of the efforts of other researchers. A conscientious and thorough review of the literature related to your problem can open up new possibilities and new ways of looking at the problem that might have been totally overlooked otherwise.

2. *Have a plan.* Writing a review of the related literature takes planning and organization. This effort requires thought, structure, and coherence.

Before beginning to write the review of the related literature, outline what you plan to say. Perhaps one of the best guides for such an outline is the problem itself. A careful consideration of the problem should suggest relevant areas for discussion and the order in which they should be addressed (refer back to Figure 4.1 for an example).

Begin your discussion of the related literature from a comprehensive perspective, like an inverted pyramid—broad end first. Then, as you proceed, you can deal with more specific ideas and studies and focus in more and more on your own particular problem.

Early in the game, you will probably want to consider the classic works—those groundbreaking studies that have paved the way for much of the research about the topic. Such studies give an overall historical perspective and provide a context for your own efforts. As an example, the scientists who developed the laser built on the efforts and writings of those who explored relativistic quantum mechanics and the nature of matter and light in electromagnetic fields.

Throughout your discussion of the related literature, your organizational scheme should be clear. As noted in Chapter 2, you can enhance the clarity of your organization by such devices as overviews (advance organizers), headings and subheadings, and transitional sentences.

3. *Emphasize relatedness.* Keep your reader constantly aware of how the literature you are discussing is related to your problem. Point out precisely what the relationship is. Remember that you are writing a review of the *related* literature.

Literature reviews should never be a chain of isolated summaries of the writings of others (Jones says . . . ; Smith says . . . ; Black says . . .). Such is not a discussion of related literature; no attempt is made to demonstrate the relatedness of the literature to the problem being researched.

Whenever you cite a study, explain clearly how it relates to your own research problem. If you cannot identify a relationship, you would do well to consider whether you should include the study at all.

As a way of helping you make frequent connections between your discussion of the literature and the research that you are doing, we suggest the following procedure:

a. Write your research problem prominently at the top of a sheet of paper or word processing document. In this location, it will be a constant reminder of the central axis around which everything else revolves.
b. Divide the problem by numbering its various subparts.
c. Divide the remainder of the page or word processing document into two columns. If you are using paper, you can simply draw a line down the middle. If you are using a word processing document, you might want to insert a table that has 2 columns and at least 10 rows.
d. Gather together all the citations that refer to a particular aspect of the problem so that you have as many groups as you have subdivisions of your main problem.
e. In the left-hand column, list each study in your review.
f. In the right-hand column, opposite each study, note the particular subdivision of the problem to which the study relates and your rationale for including it in the literature review.
g. Add additional pages (for a paper list) or table rows (for a word processing document) as you need them until you've listed every study.

4. *Give credit where credit is due.* In writing the literature review, always, *always* credit those authors whose ideas you are using or whose research results you are reporting. The specific way in which you do this (e.g., with footnotes or with citations in parentheses in the text itself) will depend on the particular style manual you are using, which, in turn, will depend on your particular discipline. We will provide more details about various style manuals in Chapter 12 (see the section "Getting Started" and Table 12.1).

In a few cases, you may even want to present other authors' actual words, either within quotation marks (for a phrase or sentence) or in an indented passage such as that on page 30 of this book (for a longer quotation). You should use lengthy quotations only when you have a very good reason—for instance, when the specific words that an author uses are as important as the ideas that the author presents. The law allows "fair use" of a quotation, but some publishers have their own rules of thumb about how much you can quote. When in doubt, check with the publisher.[3]

5. *Review the literature. Don't reproduce it!* As important as what others say about their research, and perhaps even more important, is what *you* say about their research. Your emphasis should always be on how a particular idea or research finding relates to your own problem—something that only you can discuss.

6. *Summarize what you have said.* Perhaps the most important question that any researcher can ask—and *should* ask continually throughout the progress of the research study—is, What does it all mean? Every discussion of related literature should end with a brief summary section in which you gather up all that has been said and describe its importance in terms of the research problem. Under the simple heading "Summary," you can condense your review into a synopsis of how the existing literature on your topic contributes to an understanding of the specific problem you are trying to solve.

---

[3] Many publishers now include on their Web sites their guidelines about what and how much you can use without seeking their permission. If you do need their permission for what you want to use, you can often submit a permission request online.

7. *Remember that your first draft will almost certainly NOT be your last draft.* As pointed out in Chapter 2, you should expect to write multiple drafts of your research report, including your literature review. In fact, writing the first draft will help you identify parts of the literature that are still unclear to you and places where you may need additional information or references. One strategy that we authors use as we write a literature review is to leave blanks for information we realize we still need, tag the blanks with paper clips or Post-It notes, and then make a final visit to the library to fill them in.

Even when you've obtained all the information you need for a complete review, you will typically not be able to express your thoughts with complete clarity the first time around. Write the review, print it out, and let it sit for a few days. Then reread it with a critical eye, looking for places where you've been ambiguous, incomplete, or perhaps even self-contradictory.

8. *Ask others for advice and feedback.* We have frequently suggested that you seek feedback from others on various parts of your study, and the literature review is no different. Ask others to read your rough draft, talk with others about what you have found, and get ideas about additional avenues you may need to explore. Use e-mail to contact people who have an interest in this area of study (e.g., contact the authors of studies that have influenced your own work). Explain where you are working, send them a copy of what you have written, and ask for their feedback and suggestions. You will be amazed at how helpful and supportive people can be when you tell them that you have read their work and would appreciate their opinion.

A Sample Research Proposal

At this point, it may be helpful to look at excerpts from what, in our opinion, is a well-written review of the related literature for a doctoral dissertation proposal. The author, Kay Corbett, was a doctoral student in educational psychology at the University of Northern Colorado. For her research project, she wanted to identify possible relationships between cognitive development and motor development (i.e., between the development of children's thinking abilities and that of their movement patterns), particularly during ages 4 through 8. Thus, the literature review focused on both the cognitive and motor development of young children.

Two qualities of the proposal are particularly worth noting. First, the author does not present the studies she has read in a piecemeal, one-at-a-time fashion; instead, she continually synthesizes the literature into a cohesive whole. Second, the author's organizational scheme is obvious throughout; she uses an advance organizer, numerous headings and subheadings, and transitional paragraphs to help the reader follow her as she moves from one topic to the next.

As was true for the sample proposal in Chapter 3, excerpts from the proposal itself appear on the left-hand side and our commentary appears on the right. The ellipses (. . .) indicate places where we have omitted some of the text. In some cases, we've summarized the content of what we've omitted within brackets.

Now go to our Companion Website at http://www.prenhall.com/leedy to assess your understanding of chapter content and to complete the projects that will help you learn how to conduct research.

DISSERTATION ANALYSIS 2

REVIEW OF LITERATURE

The literature review will include three areas: (a) empirical studies relating motor and cognitive development, (b) motor development, and (c) the neo-Piagetian theories of development as they relate to both motor and cognitive development. The present review is limited to investigations of children within the 4- to 8-year-old age range. Studies targeting children with special needs are excluded.

[The remainder of the chapter is divided into three main sections: "Motor and Cognitive Development," "The Development of Gross Motor Skills," and "The Neo-Piagetian Theories of

Comments

The author begins with an advance organizer that outlines the upcoming chapter and describes the scope of the literature review.

Notice how the three sections correspond roughly to the "a," "b," and "c" that the author described in the first paragraph.

Development." We pick up the chapter midway through the section on "The Development of Gross Motor Skills."]

The Development of Gross Motor Skills

. . . [T]he early childhood period is when many fundamental motor patterns are most efficiently learned. During this age period, children must have daily practice and participation in movement education programs to develop the fundamental movement skills to a mature pattern (Gallahue, 1993, 1995b, 1996; Halverson & Roberton, 1984; Haubenstricker & Seefeldt, 1986; Haywood, 1993; Miller, 1978, cited in Gallahue, 1989; Williams, 1983). If opportunity for this practice is not provided, children may move into adolescence with immature motor patterns that will hinder their ability to enter games or sports activities (Gallahue, 1995a; Haubenstricker & Seefeldt, 1986). Mature patterns can be acquired later in the developmental life span, but it requires much more time and practice to relearn the patterns.

. . . The fundamental patterns for the 4- to 8-year-old age range include four categories of movements: (a) locomotor movement, (b) stability movements, (c) manipulative movements, and (d) axial movements (Gallahue, 1995b).

The locomotor movements acquired and/or refined during this period of childhood are running, jumping, hopping, galloping and sliding, leaping, skipping, and climbing (Gallahue, 1995b). These movements "involve a change in location of the body relative to a fixed point on the surface" (Gallahue, 1989, p. 46).

Stability movements refer to the "ability to maintain one's balance in relationship to the force of gravity even though the nature of the force's application may be altered or parts of the body may be placed in unusual positions" (Gallahue, 1989, p. 494). Stability movements include weight transfer skills (Haywood, 1993). Weight transfer skills include inverted supports, in which the body assumes an upside-down position for a number of seconds before the movement is discontinued. "Stabilization of the center of gravity and maintenance of the line of gravity within the base of support apply to the inverted posture as well as to the erect standing posture" (Gallahue, 1989, p. 275). Other stability movements are dodging, one-foot balancing, beam walking, and rolling.

The manipulative movements involve giving force to objects and receiving force from them (Gallahue, 1989). Movements practiced during childhood are overhand throwing, catching, kicking, striking, dribbling, ball rolling, trapping (feet or body is used to absorb the force of the ball instead of the hands and arms), and volleying.

The axial movements are "movements of the trunk or limbs that orient the body while it remains in a stationary position" (Gallahue, 1989, p. 271). Bending, stretching, twisting, turning, swinging, swaying, reaching, and lifting are all axial movements. They are used in combination with other movements to execute more complex movement skills.

Researchers investigating the development of fundamental movement skills focus on qualitative changes as children's developing movement patterns become more smooth and efficient. The following section will review studies investigating the development of fundamental movement patterns in children four to eight years of age.

Notice how the author integrates and summarizes the results of several studies—an approach that is quite appropriate when researchers have all come to a similar conclusion. Several of the studies are (at the time the proposal is written) quite recent, communicating the (probably accurate) impression that the author is presenting an up-to-date perspective on the topic. A citation such as "Miller, 1978, cited in Gallahue, 1989" should be used only when the original source (in this case, Miller, 1978) is difficult to obtain.

Notice how this sentence alerts the reader to the organizational structure that follows.

To indicate that she is using Gallahue's definition of locomotor movements, the author uses quotation marks and, within the citation, lists the page on which she found the definition.

The author quotes Gallahue several times. As a general rule, you should limit your quotations to situations in which an author's presentation of ideas or information is exceptionally vivid, precise, or in some other way highly effective. Otherwise, just paraphrase what your sources have said, giving them appropriate credit, of course, for their ideas.

This paragraph helps the reader follow the author's train of thought as she makes the transition from one topic to another, related one.

Development of Locomotor Skills

The locomotor skills, from earliest acquisition until mature patterns are established, develop through qualitatively different stages (e.g., Gallahue, 1995b; Haywood, 1993; Haubenstricker & Seefeldt, 1986). The studies reviewed investigated qualitative changes that occur as fundamental locomotor patterns are developed.

Walking.   The mature walking pattern is achieved between the fourth and seventh year (Eckert, 1987; Guttridge, 1939; Wickstrom, 1983; Williams, 1983). At this level, there is a reflexive arm swing, narrow base of support (feet are placed no further apart than the width of the shoulders), the gate is relaxed, the legs lift minimally, and there is definite heel-toe contact (Gallahue, 1989). Although the mature pattern is achieved during the early childhood period, walking is not targeted in movement education programs as a skill needing concentrated focus (Gallahue, 1989, 1996; Werder & Bruininks, 1988).

Running.   Many investigators have studied the running pattern. Roberton & Halverson (1984) document the development of running by rating arm action separately from leg action but base the documentation on earlier work (Wickstrom, 1983; Seefeldt et al., 1972, cited in Gallahue, 1989). Gallahue (1995b) proposes a whole-body sequence of development based on the same earlier work. Running patterns develop from flat-footed, uneven patterns with arms swinging outward to smoother patterns with step length increased, and a narrower base of support. The mature pattern includes a reflexive arm swing, narrow base of support, relaxed gait, minimal vertical lift, and a definite heel to toe contact. Several University of Wisconsin studies of children between 1.5 and 10 years of age have documented the qualitative changes in the running pattern (Haywood, 1993).

Jumping.   Early developmentalists defined age norms for children's jumping achievements (Wickstrom, 1983). The children step down from a higher surface from one foot to the other, before jumping off the floor with both feet. Then they learn to jump from progressively greater heights onto both feet. Later, they can jump forward, and over objects (Haywood, 1993).

Developmental sequences in both the horizontal and vertical jump are based on research on the standing long jump (Clark & Phillips, 1985; Hellebrandt et al., 1961; Seefeldt et al., 1972, cited in Gallahue, 1989; Wickstrom, 1983; Roberton, 1984; Roberton & Halverson, 1984). The one-footed takeoff is one salient characteristic of the earliest jump pattern and persists in some children well into their elementary school years (Roberton, 1984). The jumping motor patterns develop during the ages from two to seven years (Haubenstricker & Seefeldt, 1986). Some elements of the jumping pattern remain stable across ages and type of jump, specifically, 3-, 5-, 7-, and 9-year olds and adults all use the same pattern of leg coordination. All people do not obtain a mature pattern in childhood. In fact many immature patterns are found in adults (Haywood, 1993). . . .

[The author devotes additional sections to "Hopping," "Galloping and sliding," "Skipping," and "Leaping and Climbing," She then proceeds to the development of other categories of motor skills and, eventually, to a discussion of the third major topic of the chapter—neo-Piagetian theories.]

NOTE: Excerpt is from a research proposal submitted by Katherine E. Corbett to the University of Northern Colorado, Greeley, in partial fulfillment of the requirement for the degree of Doctor of Philosophy. Reprinted with permission.

Here the headings "Walking," "Running," "Jumping," and so on, under the more general "Development of Locomotor Skills" heading, communicate quite clearly how the section is organized.

Notice how, in this paragraph, the author synthesizes what previous researchers have found. She intentionally does not describe studies one by one when they all point to the same conclusion. The result is a smooth-flowing, easy-to-read, summary of work that has been done related to the topic.

In the second and third sentences of the "Running" paragraph, the verbs document, base, and proposes should be documented, based, and proposed (past tense). In general, use past tense (e.g., proposed or has proposed) to describe what has been done in the past. Use present tense to represent general ideas that are not restricted to a single time period. For instance, present tense is appropriately used in the paragraph's fourth sentence ("Running patterns develop from . . .").

In this paragraph the author clarifies the types of studies (i.e., research on the standing long jump) on which certain conclusions have been drawn. By doing so, she helps the reader put the conclusions in perspective and, perhaps, judge the quality of those conclusions.

Throughout the chapter, various levels of headings continue to be important guideposts that reflect this overall organizational scheme.

FOR FURTHER READING

Review of the Related Literature

Brink, P. J., & Wood, M. J. (1994). *Basic steps in planning nursing research* (4th ed.). Boston: Jones & Bartlett. [See Chapter 5, "Critical Review of the Literature."]

Cooper, H., & Hedges, L. V. (Eds.). (1994). *Handbook of research synthesis*. New York: Russell Sage.

Cooper, H. M. (1989). *Integrating research: A guide for literature reviews* (2nd ed.). Thousand Oaks, CA: Sage.

Fink, A. (1998). *Conducting research literature reviews: From paper to the Internet*. Thousand Oaks, CA: Sage.

Gall, M. D., Borg, W. R., & Gall, J. P. (2003). *Educational research: An introduction* (7th ed.). Boston: Allyn & Bacon. [See Chapter 4, "Reviewing the Literature."]

Gay, L. R., & Airasian, P. (2003). *Educational research: Competencies for analysis and application* (7th ed.). Upper Saddle River, NJ: Merrill/Prentice Hall. [See Chapter 2.]

Krathwohl, D. R. (1998). *Methods of educational and social science research: An integrated approach* (2nd ed.). Boston: Allyn & Bacon. [See the discussion of "Finding Links to Past Research."]

Notter, L. E., & Hott, J. R. (1988). *Essentials of nursing research* (4th ed.). New York: Springer. [See Chapter 4, "The Literature Search."]

Polit, D., & Hungler, B. (2002). *Nursing research: Principles and methods* (6th ed.). Philadelphia: J. B. Lippincott. [See the discussion of "Locating and Summarizing Existing Information on a Problem."]

Online Databases

Gale Research, Inc. (yearly). *Gale guide to Internet databases*. Detroit: Author.

O'Leary, M. (1996). *The online 100: Online Magazine's field guide to the 100 most important online databases*. Brandenton, FL: Online.

Stoker, D. (1996). *Electronic information sources: An evaluative guide*. New Providence, NJ: Bowker-Saur.

5

Planning Your Research Project

Before the construction of a building, architects develop a meticulous set of plans. These plans ensure success in construction of the building. Researchers should be no less detailed and precise in the planning of a research design. Plans, specifications, criteria, and design: All of these serve well the architect, the builder, and the researcher alike.

Architectural planning and research planning have much in common. Each requires a conceptualization of the overall organization of a project and a detailed specification of the steps to be carried out; only after such planning has occurred can work on the project actually begin. For successful completion, a building requires plans that are clearly conceived and accurately drawn. A research project should be no less completely visualized and precisely detailed.

PLANNING A GENERAL APPROACH

When we talk about a general strategy for solving a research problem, we are talking about a **research design**. The research design provides the overall structure for the procedures the researcher follows, the data the researcher collects, and the data analyses the researcher conducts. Simply put, research design is *planning*.

Nothing helps a research effort be successful so much as planning the overall design carefully. More research effort is wasted by going off half-prepared, with only a vague set of ideas and procedures, than in any other way. You will be much more efficient and effective as a researcher if you identify your resources, your procedures, and your data—always with the central goal of solving your research problem in mind—at the very beginning of your project.

THE BASIC FORMAT OF ALL RESEARCH

The research process follows a basic format. No matter which academic discipline gives rise to the research endeavor, the general research procedure is fundamentally the same. Although you will sometimes hear people refer to "social science research," "nursing research," or "educational research," in fact the search for information to solve a problem or to answer a question seldom fits squarely within the bounds of a single academic discipline.

85

In planning a research design, the researcher in quest of new knowledge and understanding cannot be shackled by discipline-specific methodological restraints. The course of a research project will frequently lead the investigator into new and unfamiliar territories that have historically been associated with other content areas. The sociologist trying to resolve a problem in sociology may come face to face with problems that are psychological or economic. The educational researcher exploring the causes of a learning disability may need to consider the domains of neurophysiology, psychopathology, endocrinology, and family counseling. The student in criminal justice may venture into the realms of abnormal psychology and behavioral genetics on the way to finding a solution for a problem in criminology. Any good researcher must be *eclectic,* willing to draw on whatever sources seem to offer productive methods or evidence for resolving the research problem.

Figure 5.1 presents the basic format for the research process. It is important to note, however, that a research project does not always follow these steps in the exact sequence depicted here. Particularly in the case of qualitative research—an approach we will describe later in the chapter—a researcher may order the steps somewhat differently. For instance, in some forms of qualitative research (to be described briefly later in this chapter and in more detail in Chapter 7), the researcher formulates a hypothesis and reads much of the literature only *after* collecting a substantial amount of data.

Instead of limiting their thinking to departmentalized knowledge, researchers might do much better to think of problems as arising out of broad generic areas within whose boundaries all research falls: people, things, records, thoughts and ideas, and dynamics and energy. Let's briefly consider some research problems that may fall within each of these areas.

- *People.*   In this category are found research problems relating to individuals; groups; populations; folklore; nationalities; families; sex; community groups and subgroups; employees; management; the disadvantaged; the wealthy; students; ancestors; tribes; mental and physical processes; medical, psychological, educational, and social problems; learning; motivation; crime; criminals; rehabilitation; nutrition; language and linguistics; and religion.
- *Things.*   In this category are found research problems relating to biological and vegetable life, viruses, bacteria, inanimate objects (rocks, soil, buildings, furniture), matter

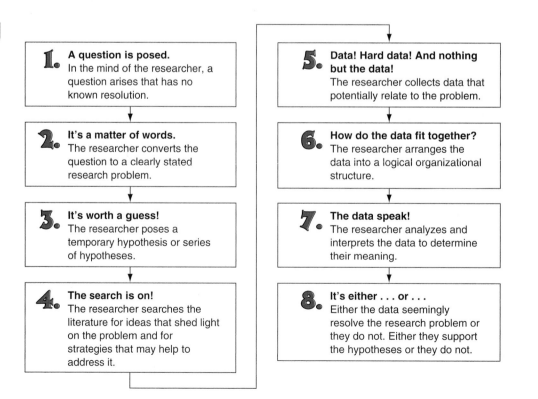

FIGURE 5.1

The basic format of the research process

1. **A question is posed.**
In the mind of the researcher, a question arises that has no known resolution.

2. **It's a matter of words.**
The researcher converts the question to a clearly stated research problem.

3. **It's worth a guess!**
The researcher poses a temporary hypothesis or series of hypotheses.

4. **The search is on!**
The researcher searches the literature for ideas that shed light on the problem and for strategies that may help to address it.

5. **Data! Hard data! And nothing but the data!**
The researcher collects data that potentially relate to the problem.

6. **How do the data fit together?**
The researcher arranges the data into a logical organizational structure.

7. **The data speak!**
The researcher analyzes and interprets the data to determine their meaning.

8. **It's either . . . or . . .**
Either the data seemingly resolve the research problem or they do not. Either they support the hypotheses or they do not.

(molecules, atoms, subatomic matter), chemical and pharmacological problems, space, stars, galaxies, the universe, machines, food, and clothing.

 ▨ *Records.*   In this category are found research problems relating to letters, legal documents, lists, journals, memoranda, books, registers, diaries, memoirs, incunabula, interviews, minutes, speeches, monuments, tablets, recordings, census reports, financial and corporate statements, mementos, artifacts, archeological remains, files, newspapers, sketches, drawings, paintings, music, and manuscripts.

 ▨ *Thoughts and ideas.*   In this category are found research problems relating to opinions, reactions, concepts, theories, viewpoints, philosophical ideas, political theory, religious beliefs, perceptions, observations, issues, language and semantics, judgments, literature, mathematical concepts and theories, confessions, journalistic columns, cartoons, and caricatures.

 ▨ *Dynamics and energy.*   In this category are found research problems relating to human energy and activity, metabolism, bionics, excitation states, radiation, radio and microwave transmission, quantum mechanics, hydrodynamics, hydrologic cycles, atomic and nuclear energy, wave mechanics, thinking, gravity, gravitation, thermodynamics, atmospheric and oceanic energy systems, solar energy, quasars, black holes, and extragalactic radiation.

We do not intend the preceding lists to be all-inclusive. We merely present them to give you an idea of the many research possibilities that each category suggests.

In its planning and design, research approaches all problems through certain methodological channels that are particularly appropriate to the nature and type of data the investigation of the problem requires. This being so, the researcher must differentiate critically between the terms *research design* (or *planning*) and *research methodology*.

RESEARCH PLANNING VERSUS RESEARCH METHODOLOGY

Do not confuse overall research planning with research methodology. Whereas the general approach to planning a research study may be similar across disciplines, the specific methods one uses to collect and analyze data may be specific to a particular academic discipline. This is because data vary so widely in nature. You cannot deal with a blood cell in the same way that you deal with a historical document, and the problem of finding the sources of Coleridge's "Kubla Khan" is entirely different from the problem of finding the sources of radio signals from extragalactic space. You cannot study chromosomes with a questionnaire, and you cannot study attitudes with a chemical analysis.

In planning the research design, therefore, it is extremely important for the researcher not only to choose a viable research problem but also to consider the kinds of data that an investigation of the problem will require and feasible means of collecting and interpreting those data. Many beginning researchers become so entranced with the glamour of the problem that they fail to consider practical issues related to data availability, collection, and interpretation.

Comparing the brain wave patterns of gifted and nongifted children may be an engaging project for research, but consider the following issues:

 ▨ Will you be able to find a sufficient number of people who are willing to participate in the study?
 ▨ Do you have an electroencephalograph at your disposal?
 ▨ If so, do you have the technical skills to use it?
 ▨ Are you sufficiently knowledgeable to interpret the electroencephalographic tracings you obtain?
 ▨ If so, do you know how you would interpret the data and organize your findings so that you could draw conclusions from them?

Unless the answer to all these questions is yes, it probably is better that you give up this project in favor of one that you have the knowledge, resources, and skills to carry through to completion. Your research should be *practical* research, built on precise and realistic *planning* and executed within the framework of a clearly conceived and feasible *design*.

GENERAL CRITERIA FOR A RESEARCH PROJECT

As you plan your research project, certain features common to all research should serve as guidelines. All research is ultimately tested by certain criteria that must be built into the research design in the planning stage. Here, briefly, are those criteria.

UNIVERSALITY.   The research project should be such that it could be carried out by *any* competent person. The researcher is merely a catalyst, an agent whose function is to collect, organize, and report what the collected data seem to indicate. Another individual, one who is equally capable of carrying out the research, might take your place and complete the project with essentially the same results. (We will find an exception to this criterion later in the chapter, when we discuss the nature of data collection in qualitative research.)

REPLICATION.   The research should be repeatable. Any other competent researcher should be able to take the problem and, collecting data under the same circumstances and within the identical parameters that you have used, achieve results comparable to those you have obtained.

CONTROL.   The researcher must isolate, or *control,* those factors that are central to the research problem. Control is important for replication: An experiment should be repeated under the identical conditions and in the identical way in which it was first carried out. Control is also important for consistency within the research design. For instance, if we want to compare the effects of two different treatments on some other factor, then we should keep everything else (aside from the specific treatments we are studying) as similar as possible.

Control is more easily achieved in some areas than in others. In the physical sciences, for example, control of such factors as temperature, pressure, electrical potential, humidity, and the like is possible to a high degree. Control is more challenging—but certainly possible—in research areas concerned with human behavior.

Control is especially important in experimental research designs. Accordingly, we will talk more about this issue in Chapter 10.

MEASUREMENT.   The data should be able to be measured in some way. This, again, is easily accomplished in the physical sciences. Measurement is typically less precise and less accurate in the humanities and social sciences. Later in the chapter, we will discuss strategies for enhancing measurement procedures in these areas.

THE NATURE AND ROLE OF THE DATA IN RESEARCH

Research is a viable approach to a problem only when there are data to support it. The term *data* is plural (singular is *datum*) and comes from the past participle of the Latin verb *dare,* which means "to give." Data are those pieces of information that any particular situation *gives* to an observer.

WHAT ARE DATA?

Researchers must always remember that data are not absolute reality—the pure, undisguised, naked Truth that underlies all the phenomena we observe. Rather, data are *manifestations* of that reality. No one has ever looked upon Truth itself. We are like those who live in a dungeon, across the floor of which a beam of sunlight passes. That light gives us an idea of what the sun must be like, but if we can never behold the sun, we shall never know the difference between it and the shaft of light on the dungeon floor.

The researcher is in a factual dungeon. He or she will never be able to see the original source of the data. For instance, we often see what other people do—the behaviors they exhibit, the things they create, and the effects of their actions on others. But the actual people "inside"—those individuals we shall never know!

Research seeks, through data, to discover underlying truths. Yet such is probably an endless pursuit. Experienced researchers are constantly aware that the Truth they most ardently seek is forever just beyond what is represented by the data and, hence, just beyond human grasp. For instance, the scientist probing the nature of subatomic matter may detect tiny entities that make up larger bits of matter. Yet the scientist knows, too, that such entities are probably made up of sub-sub-subentities that, like the will-o'-the-wisp, beckon yet evade measurement and investigation.

The mind yearns to understand the Truth. To pursue that goal, we have chosen the path of research. But the path always ends at the farthest reaches of the data, which are at the brink of the canyon in whose depths lies the inaccessible, ultimate Truth.

DATA ARE TRANSIENT AND EVER CHANGING

Whenever we look at data analytically, we gain new insights. But at the same time, we also discern new problems that demand further research.

Data are not only elusive but also transient. Data that the researcher is permitted to glimpse may exist for only a split second. Consider, as an example, this research situation. A sociologist is interested in conducting a survey to learn about people's attitudes and opinions in a certain city. The sociologist's research assistants start by administering the survey in a particular city block. By the time they move on to the next block, the data they've collected are already out of date. Some people in the previous block who indicated that they held a particular opinion have now changed their minds and have a somewhat different opinion. They have seen a television program or heard a discussion that has changed it. Some people have moved away, and others have moved in; some have died, and others have been born. Tomorrow, next week, next year—what we thought we had "discovered" may have changed completely.

Data are, therefore, transient. We catch merely a fleeting glance of what seems to be true at one point in time but is not necessarily true the next.

Researchers must recognize that even the most carefully collected data may have an elusive quality about them and that, at a later point in time, they may have no counterpart in reality whatsoever. Data are volatile: They evaporate quickly.

PRIMARY DATA VERSUS SECONDARY DATA

The researcher's only perceptions of Truth are various layers of truth-revealing fact. In the layer closest to the Truth are **primary data;** these are often the most valid, the most illuminating, the most truth-manifesting. Farther away is a layer consisting of **secondary data,** which are derived not from the Truth itself, but from the primary data instead.

Earlier, we used the analogy of the researcher as one who sits in a dungeon and tries to understand the sun only by looking at a shaft of sunlight that falls upon the floor. This direct beam of sunlight represents the *primary data*. Although the shaft is not the sun itself, it has come directly from the sun. But now imagine that the imprisoned researcher sees the sunlight, not as a direct beam, but as a shimmering light on the floor. The sunlight (primary data) has fallen onto a mirror and then been reflected—distorted by the imperfections within the mirror—to an image like, yet also unlike, the original shaft of light. This reflection of light is secondary data.

As another example, consider the following incident: You see a car veer off the highway and careen into a ditch. You have witnessed the entire event. Afterward, the driver says he had no awareness of the possibility of an accident until the car went out of control. Neither of you will ever be able to determine the absolute truth underlying the accident. Did the driver have a momentary seizure of which he was unaware? Did the car have an imperfection that the damage caused by the accident obscured? Were other factors involved that neither of you noticed? The answers lie beyond an impenetrable barrier. The true cause of the accident may never be known, but the things that you witnessed, incomplete as they may be, are primary data that emanated directly from the accident itself.

Now along comes a newspaper reporter who interviews both you and the driver of the car. The reporter writes an account of the accident for the local paper. When your sister reads the account in the paper the next morning, she gets, as it were, the sunlight-reflection-upon-the-floor

FIGURE 5.2

The relation between
data and Truth

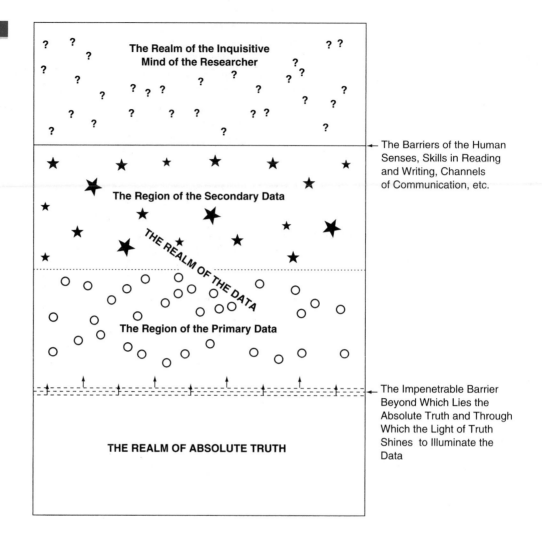

version of the event. The article in the newspaper provides secondary data. The data are, of necessity, distorted—albeit ever so little—by the channels of communication through which they must pass to you. The reporter's writing skills, your sister's reading skills, and the inability of language to reproduce every nuance of detail that a firsthand observation can provide all distort, however slightly, what you actually observed.

What we have been saying about data and their relation to Truth is represented by Figure 5.2. Lying farthest away from the researcher—and, hence, most inaccessible—is The Realm of Absolute Truth. It can be approached by the researcher only by passing through two intermediate areas that we have labeled The Realm of the Data. Notice that an impenetrable barrier exists between The Realm of Absolute Truth and The Region of the Primary Data. Small bits of information leak through the barrier and manifest themselves as data. Notice, too, the barrier between The Realm of the Data and The Realm of the Inquisitive Mind of the Researcher. This barrier is comprised of many things: the distortions and insensitivities of the human senses, the weaknesses of instrumentation, the inability of language to communicate thoughts exactly, the inability of two human beings to witness the same event and to report it in precisely the same way, and so on.

Researchers should never forget the overall idea behind Figure 5.2. Keeping it in mind may prevent them from making exaggerated claims or drawing unwarranted conclusions. No researcher can ever glimpse Absolute Truth, nor can anyone even perceive the data that reflect that Truth except through imperfect senses and imprecise channels of communication. Such a humiliating awareness helps researchers be cautious in the interpretation and reporting of research findings—for instance, by using such words as *perhaps*, *it seems*, *one might conclude*, and *it would appear to be*.

CRITERIA FOR THE ADMISSIBILITY OF DATA

Not all data that come to the researcher's attention are acceptable for use in a research project. Data can be defective. If they are, they may affect the validity of the researcher's conclusions. The imperfections in the data stem from the imperfections and irregularities of nature. If researchers include in the mass of data those that are imperfect or irregular—those that are distorted, inaccurate, hopelessly entangled with other data, and so on—they corrupt the entire body of data.

One axiom of research is that any research effort should be *replicable;* that is, it should be able to be repeated by any other researcher at any other time under *precisely the same conditions.* To ensure such precision, certain criteria must be adopted, certain limits established, certain standards set up that all data must meet in order to be admitted for study.

For example, imagine that an agronomist wants to determine the effect of ultraviolet light on growing plants. *Ultraviolet* is a vague term: It may include any light radiation between 500 and 4,000 angstroms. The agronomist must narrow the parameters of the data so that they will fall within certain specified limits. What precisely does she or he mean by *ultraviolet light?* Within what angstrom range will ultraviolet emission be acceptable? At what intensity? With what time duration? With plants at what distance from the source of emission? What precisely does the researcher mean by the phrase "effect of ultraviolet light on growing plants"? All plants? A specific genus? A particular species? The agronomist must be quite specific about all of these things so that another researcher can achieve very similar conditions in replicating the study.

By prescribing such criteria and insisting on standards, we can control the type of data admitted and regulate the conditions under which the research effort proceeds. Any data not meeting the criteria are excluded from the study. It is, of course, much easier to control data in the physical sciences, where we can measure the data quantitatively, but such control is also possible in the humanities, the social sciences, and the arts. In these latter disciplines, the criteria are usually established by definition, and admissible data must meet the definitive parameters.

We hem in the data on all sides, placing on them the restriction of criterion after criterion, so that we are able to isolate only those data that are acceptable for our use. The rest of the data are inadmissible. The restrictions we identify are what we call the **criteria for the admissibility of data.**

When we standardize the data, admitting only those that comply with the criteria, we can more nearly control the research effort and conclude with greater certainty what appears to be true. Therefore, to ensure the integrity of the research, we must set forth *beforehand* precisely what standards the data must meet. These criteria must be set forth clearly in both the research proposal and the research report. Only in this way can we make the consumer of the research a party to the criteria so that both the researcher and the consumer come to an intelligent understanding of what is being studied.

IDENTIFYING APPROPRIATE MEASUREMENT INSTRUMENTS

We will almost invariably want to pin down what we observe by *measuring* it in some way. Sometimes we will be able to use one or more existing measurement instruments—perhaps an oscilloscope to measure patterns of sound, a published personality test to measure a person's tendency to be either shy or outgoing, or a rating scale that a previous researcher has developed to assess parents' child-rearing practices. In other situations, we may have to develop our *own* measurement instruments—perhaps a survey to assess people's opinions about welfare reform, a paper-and-pencil test to measure what students have learned from a particular instructional unit, or a checklist to evaluate the quality of a new product.

Measurement instruments provide a basis on which the entire research effort rests. Just as a building with a questionable foundation is unlikely to be safe for habitation, so, too, will a research effort employing faulty measurement tools provide little of value in solving the problem under investigation.

As you plan your research project, then, you should determine clearly and definitively the nature of the measurement instruments you will use. Furthermore, you should describe any instrument in explicit, concrete terms. For instance, if you are assessing some aspect of human thought or behavior, you should describe the questions asked or tasks administered, the overall length of the instrument (e.g., number of items, time required for administration), and the method of scoring responses.

You should also provide evidence that the instruments you use have a reasonable degree of validity and reliability for your purposes. In the following sections, we briefly discuss the kinds of validity and reliability you may need to consider.

Determining the Validity of Measurement Instruments

As you should recall from Chapter 2, the *validity* of a measurement instrument is the extent to which the instrument measures what it is actually intended to measure. Validity takes different forms, each of which is important in different situations:

- **Face validity** is the extent to which, on the surface, an instrument *looks like* it's measuring a particular characteristic. Face validity is often useful for ensuring the cooperation of people who are participating in a research study. But because it relies entirely on subjective judgment, it is not, in and of itself, terribly convincing evidence that an instrument is truly measuring what the researcher wants to measure.

- **Content validity** is the extent to which a measurement instrument is a representative sample of the content area (domain) being measured. Content validity is often a consideration when a researcher wants to assess people's *achievement* in some area—for instance, the knowledge they've learned during classroom instruction or the job skills they've acquired in a rehabilitation program. A measurement instrument has high content validity if its items or questions reflect the various parts of the content domain in appropriate proportions and if it requires the particular behaviors and skills that are central to that domain.

- **Criterion validity** is the extent to which the results of an assessment instrument correlate with another, presumably related measure (the latter measure is, in this case, called the *criterion*). For example, a personality test designed to assess a person's shyness or outgoingness (the extent to which one is *introverted* or *extroverted*) has criterion validity if its scores correlate with other tests of introversion versus extroversion. An instrument designed to measure a salesperson's effectiveness on the job should correlate with the number of sales the individual actually makes during the course of a business day.

- **Construct validity** is the extent to which an instrument measures a characteristic that cannot be directly observed but must instead be inferred from patterns in people's behavior (such a characteristic is a *construct*). Motivation, creativity, racial bias, bedside manner—all of these are constructs, in that none of them can be *directly* observed and measured. When researchers ask questions, present tasks, or observe behaviors as a way of assessing an underlying construct, they should obtain some kind of evidence that their approach does, in fact, measure the construct in question.

Sometimes there is universal agreement that a particular instrument provides a valid instrument for measuring a particular characteristic. We could all agree that a ruler measures length, a thermometer measures temperature, and a barometer measures air pressure. But whenever we do *not* have such universal agreement, we must provide evidence that an instrument we are using has validity for our purpose.

A detailed discussion of how to determine validity is beyond the scope of this book; measurement textbooks, such as those listed in the "For Further Reading" section at the end of the chapter, provide more detailed information. Nevertheless, here we offer a few examples of what researchers sometimes do to demonstrate that their measurement instruments have validity for their purposes:

- **A multitrait-multimethod approach** (Campbell & Fiske, 1959).   Two or more different characteristics are each measured using two or more different approaches. The different measures of the *same* characteristic should be highly correlated. The same ways of measuring *different* characteristics should *not* be highly correlated. For example, in a classroom situation, the constructs *achievement motivation* and *social motivation* might each be measured both by self-report inventories and by teacher observation checklists. Statistical analyses should reveal that the two measures of achievement motivation are highly correlated and that the two measures of social motivation are also highly correlated. Results from the two self-report inventories—because they are intended to assess different characteristics—should *not* be highly correlated, nor should results from the two teacher checklists.

- **A table of specifications.** To construct a measurement instrument that provides a representative sample of a particular content domain—in other words, to establish content validity—the researcher often constructs a two-dimensional grid (*table of specifications*) listing the specific topics and behaviors that reflect achievement in the domain. In each cell of the grid, the researcher indicates the relative importance of each topic-behavior combination. He or she then develops a series of tasks or test items that reflects the various topics and behaviors in appropriate proportions.
- **Judgment by a panel of experts.** Several experts in a particular area are asked to scrutinize an instrument to ascertain its validity for measuring the characteristic in question.

Although none of the approaches just described guarantees the validity of a measurement instrument, each one increases the likelihood of such validity.

Determining the Reliability of Measurement Instruments

As explained in Chapter 2, the *reliability* of a measurement instrument is the extent to which it yields consistent results when the characteristic being measured hasn't changed. Like validity, reliability takes different forms in different situations. Following are several forms of reliability that are frequently of interest in research studies:

- **Interrater reliability** is the extent to which two or more individuals evaluating the same product or performance give identical judgments.
- **Internal consistency reliability** is the extent to which all the items within a single instrument yield similar results.
- **Equivalent forms reliability** is the extent to which two different versions of the same instrument (e.g., "Form A" and "Form B" of a scholastic aptitude test) yield similar results.
- **Test-retest reliability** is the extent to which the same instrument yields the same result on two different occasions.

You can find additional information about each of these in almost any general measurement textbook.

A researcher can enhance the reliability of a measurement instrument in several ways. First, the instrument should always be administered in a consistent fashion; in other words, there should be **standardization** in use of the instrument from one situation or person to the next. Second, to the extent that subjective judgments are required, specific *criteria* should be established that dictate the kinds of judgments the researcher makes. And third, any research assistants who are using the instrument should be *well trained* so that they obtain similar results.

As pointed out in Chapter 2, we can measure something accurately only when we can also measure it consistently. In other words, in order to have validity, we must also have reliability. The more valid and reliable our measurement instruments are, the more likely we are to draw appropriate conclusions from the data we collect and, thus, to solve our research problem in a credible fashion.

LINKING DATA AND RESEARCH METHODOLOGY

Earlier in the chapter, we described data as a link between Absolute Truth and the researcher's inquiring mind. Data are like ore: They contain pieces of the truth but are in a rather unrefined state. To extract meaning from the data, we employ what is commonly called *research methodology*.

Data and methodology are inextricably interdependent. For this reason, the methodology to be used for a particular research problem must always take into account the nature of the data that will be collected in the resolution of the problem.

An example may help to clarify this point. Imagine that a man from a remote village decides to travel to the big city. While he is there, he takes his first ride on a commercial jetliner. No one in his village has ever flown before, so naturally when he returns home, they are curious about his trip. One afternoon, two friends ask him about his experience, yet each one asks very different questions. The first friend asks, "How fast did you move?" "How far did you go?" and "How high did you fly?" The second friend asks, "How did you feel when you were moving so fast?" "What was it like being above the clouds?" and "What did the city look like from so high?" Both friends are asking questions that can help them learn more about the experience of flying in an airplane. Yet they differ considerably in what they want to know. Because they ask different kinds of questions, they obtain different kinds of information. If they were to recount what they had learned about "flying in a jetliner," they would most likely describe very different things. Although neither of them has the "wrong" story, neither does each have the whole story.

In research, too, different questions yield different types of information. Different research problems lead to different research designs and methods, which in turn result in the collection of different types of data and different interpretations of those data.

Furthermore, many kinds of data may be suitable only for a particular methodology. To some extent, *the data dictate the research method*. As an example, consider historical data, those pieces of information gleaned from written records of past events. You cannot extract much meaning from historical documents by using a laboratory experiment. An experiment is simply not suited to the nature of the data.

Over the years, numerous research methodologies have emerged to accommodate the numerous different forms that data are likely to take. Accordingly, we must take a broad view of the approaches the term *research methodology* encompasses. Above all, we must not limit ourselves to the belief that only a true experiment constitutes "research." Such an attitude prohibits us from agreeing that we can better understand Coleridge's poetry by reading the scholarly research of John Livingston Lowes (1927, 1955) or from appreciating Western civilization more because of the historiography of Arnold Toynbee (1939–1961).

No single highway leads us exclusively toward a better understanding of the unknown. Many highways can take us in that direction. They may traverse different terrain, but they all converge on the same destination: the enhancement of human knowledge.

In Chapters 7 through 11 of this book, we will discuss a wide variety of research methodologies. But many researchers tend to categorize research studies into two broad categories: quantitative research and qualitative research. We now look at this distinction.

COMPARING QUANTITATIVE AND QUALITATIVE APPROACHES

In general, **quantitative research** is used to answer questions about relationships among measured variables with the purpose of explaining, predicting, and controlling phenomena. This approach is sometimes called the *traditional*, *experimental*, or *positivist* approach.

In contrast, **qualitative research** is typically used to answer questions about the complex nature of phenomena, often with the purpose of describing and understanding the phenomena from the participants' point of view. The qualitative approach is also referred to as the *interpretative*, *constructivist*, or *postpositivist* approach.

Both approaches involve similar processes (e.g., formation of one or more hypotheses, review of the related literature, collection and analysis of data). Yet these processes are often combined and carried out in different ways, leading to distinctly different research methods. For instance, quantitative researchers usually start with a specific hypothesis to be tested. They isolate the variables they want to study, control for extraneous variables, use a standardized procedure to collect some form of numerical data, and use statistical procedures to analyze and draw conclusions from the data. In contrast, qualitative researchers often start with general research questions rather than specific hypotheses, collect an extensive amount of verbal data from a small number of participants, organize those data into some form that gives them coherence, and use verbal descriptions to portray the situation they have studied.

A quantitative study usually ends with confirmation or disconfirmation of the hypotheses that were tested. A qualitative study is more likely to end with tentative answers or hypotheses about what was observed. These tentative hypotheses may form the basis of future studies (perhaps quantitative in nature) designed to test the proposed hypotheses. In this way, qualitative and quantitative approaches represent complementary components of the research process.

To some extent, quantitative and qualitative research designs are appropriate for answering different kinds of questions. As a result, we learn more about the world when we have both quantitative and qualitative methodologies at our disposal than when we are limited to only one approach or the other (e.g., Creswell, 1998; Glesne & Peshkin, 1992; Moss, 1996).

Let's consider how the two approaches might look in practice. Suppose two researchers are interested in investigating the "effectiveness of the case-based method of teaching business management practices." The first researcher asks the question, "How effective is case-based instruction in comparison with lecture-based instruction?" She finds five instructors who are teaching case-based business management classes; she also finds five instructors who are teaching the same content using lectures. At the end of the semester, the researcher administers an achievement test to students in all 10 classes. Using statistical analyses, she compares the scores of students in case-based and lecture-based courses to determine whether the achievement of one group is significantly higher than that of the other group. When reporting her findings, she summarizes the results of her statistical analyses. This researcher has conducted a *quantitative* study.

The second researcher is also interested in the effectiveness of the case method but asks the question, "What makes case-based instruction effective or ineffective?" To answer this question, he assumes the role of a participant observer in a case-based business management course for an entire year. He spends an extensive amount of time talking with the teacher and some of the students to try to understand the participants' perspectives on case-based instruction. He carefully scrutinizes his data for patterns and themes in the responses. He then writes an in-depth description and interpretation of what he has observed in the classroom setting. This researcher has conducted a *qualitative* study.

Distinguishing Characteristics of Quantitative and Qualitative Approaches

Table 5.1 presents a summary of differences between quantitative and qualitative approaches. We briefly discuss these differences in the next few paragraphs, not to persuade you that one approach is better than the other, but to help you make a more informed decision about which approach might be better for your own research question.

PURPOSE.   Quantitative researchers seek explanations and predictions that will generalize to other persons and places. The intent is to establish, confirm, or validate relationships and to develop generalizations that contribute to theory.

Qualitative researchers seek a better understanding of complex situations. Their work is often exploratory in nature, and they may use their observations to build theory from the ground up.

PROCESS.   Because quantitative studies represent the mainstream approach to research, carefully structured guidelines exist for conducting them. Concepts, variables, hypotheses, and methods of measurement tend to be defined before the study begins and remain the same throughout. Quantitative researchers choose methods that allow them to objectively measure the variable(s) of interest. They also try to remain detached from the research participants so that they can draw unbiased conclusions.

The qualitative research process is more holistic and "emergent," with the specific focus, design, measurement instruments (e.g., interviews), and interpretations developing and possibly changing along the way. Researchers enter the setting with open minds, prepared to immerse themselves in the complexity of the situation and interact with their participants. Categories (variables) emerge from the data, leading to "context-bound" information, patterns, and/or theories that help to explain the phenomenon under study.

DATA COLLECTION.   Quantitative researchers identify one or a few variables that they intend to study and then collect data specifically related to those variables. Specific methods of measuring each variable are identified, developed, and standardized, with attention to the validity and reliability of the

TABLE 5.1

Distinguishing characteristics of quantitative and qualitative approaches

Question	Quantitative	Qualitative
What is the purpose of the research?	• To explain and predict • To confirm and validate • To test theory	• To describe and explain • To explore and interpret • To build theory
What is the nature of the research process?	• Focused • Known variables • Established guidelines • Predetermined methods • Somewhat context-free • Detached view	• Holistic • Unknown variables • Flexible guidelines • Emergent methods • Context-bound • Personal view
What are the data like, and how are they collected?	• Numeric data • Representative, large sample • Standardized instruments	• Textual and/or image-based data • Informative, small sample • Loosely structured or nonstandardized observations and interviews
How are data analyzed to determine their meaning?	• Statistical analysis • Stress on objectivity • Deductive reasoning	• Search for themes and categories • Acknowledgment that analysis is subjective and potentially biased • Inductive reasoning
How are the findings communicated?	• Numbers • Statistics, aggregated data • Formal voice, scientific style	• Words • Narratives, individual quotes • Personal voice, literary style

measurement instruments. Data are collected from a population, or from one or more large samples that represent the population, in a form that is easily converted to numerical indices.

Qualitative researchers operate under the assumption that reality is not easily divided into discrete, measurable variables. Qualitative researchers are often described as *being* the research instrument because the bulk of their data collection is dependent on their personal involvement (interviews, observations) in the setting. Rather than sample a large number of people with the intent of making generalizations, qualitative researchers tend to select a few participants who can best shed light on the phenomenon under investigation. Both verbal data (interview comments, documents, field notes) and nonverbal data (drawings, photographs, videotapes) may be collected.

DATA ANALYSIS.   All research requires logical reasoning. Quantitative researchers tend to rely more heavily on deductive reasoning, beginning with certain premises (e.g., hypotheses, theories) and then drawing logical conclusions from them. They also try to maintain objectivity in their data analysis, conducting predetermined statistical procedures and using objective criteria to evaluate the outcomes of those procedures.

In contrast, qualitative researchers make considerable use of inductive reasoning: They make many specific observations and then draw inferences about larger and more general phenomena. Furthermore, their data analysis is more subjective in nature: They scrutinize the body of data in search of patterns—subjectively identified—that the data reflect.

It is important to note here that quantitative research is not exclusively deductive, nor is qualitative research exclusively inductive. Researchers of all persuasions typically use both types of reasoning in a continual cyclic fashion. Quantitative researchers often formulate a theory by inductive reasoning—for instance, by observing a few situations—and then try to support their theory by drawing, and then testing, the conclusions that follow logically from it. Similarly, after qualitative researchers have identified a theme in their data using an inductive process, they move into a more deductive mode to verify or modify it with additional data.

REPORTING FINDINGS.   Quantitative researchers typically reduce their data to means, medians, correlations, and other summarizing statistics. It is not necessary or helpful to look at individual scores; rather, the power of interpretation rests in the large number of scores that depict the norm, or average, of the group's performance. The results are usually presented in a report that employs a formal, scientific style using passive voice and impersonal language.

Qualitative researchers construct interpretive narratives from their data and try to capture the complexity of the phenomenon under study. They use a more personal, literary style, and they often include the participants' own language and perspectives. Although all researchers must be able to write clearly, effective qualitative researchers must be especially skilled in this area.

We draw such distinctions, in part, as a way of pointing out the relative strengths and weaknesses of the two approaches. For example, a common weakness of quantitative research is that it is sometimes conducted in a laboratory—and therefore somewhat artificial—setting. Although contrived circumstances can give the researcher considerable control over the events that occur, the results obtained may in some cases not generalize to more naturalistic settings. In contrast, qualitative research occurs within natural contexts and so, in this respect, is more "true to life." Yet the findings of qualitative studies may be so specific to a particular context that they do not apply (generalize) to other contexts.

By making the distinction between quantitative and qualitative research, we do not mean to imply that these approaches are mutually exclusive—that a researcher must choose to use one or the other of them for any particular study. In fact, researchers often combine elements of both approaches in what is sometimes called a **mixed-method design.** For example, it is not unusual for researchers to *count* (and therefore quantify) certain kinds of data in what is, for all intents and purposes, a qualitative investigation (Eisner, 1998; Silverman, 1993). Nor is it unusual for quantitative researchers to report participants' perceptions of, or emotional reactions to, various experimental treatments.

CONSIDERING THE VALIDITY OF YOUR METHOD

No matter what research methodology you choose, you must think about the *validity* of your approach. We have already described the importance of validity in measurement instruments. Here we are talking about the validity—the accuracy, meaningfulness, and credibility—of *the research project as a whole*. Your research effort will be worth your time and effort only to the extent that it allows you to draw meaningful and defensible conclusions from your data.

When we consider the validity of a research study, we need to ask two basic questions. First, does the study have sufficient controls to ensure that the conclusions we draw are truly warranted by the data? And second, can we use what we have observed in the research situation to make generalizations about the world beyond that specific situation? The answers to these two questions address the issues of *internal validity* and *external validity,* respectively.

INTERNAL VALIDITY

The **internal validity** of a research study is the extent to which its design and the data it yields allow the researcher to draw accurate conclusions about cause-and-effect and other relationships within the data. To illustrate, we present three situations in which the internal validity of a study is suspect:

1. A marketing researcher wants to study how humor in television commercials affects sales. To do so, the researcher studies the effectiveness of two commercials that have been developed for a new soft drink called Zowie. One commercial, in which a well-known but serious television actor describes how Zowie has a zingy and refreshing taste, airs

during the months of March, April, and May. The other commercial, a humorous scenario in which several teenagers spray one another with Zowie on a hot summer day, airs during the months of June, July, and August. The researcher finds that in June through August, Zowie sales are almost double what they were in the preceding three months. "Humor boosts sales," the researcher concludes.

2. An industrial psychologist wants to study the effects of soft classical music on the productivity of a group of typists in a typing pool. At the beginning of the month, the psychologist meets with the typists to explain the study, gets their consent to play the music during the working day, and then begins to have music piped into the office where the typists work. At the end of the month, the typists' supervisor reports a 30% increase in the number of documents completed by the typing pool that month. "Soft music increases productivity," the psychologist concludes.

3. An educational researcher wants to study the effectiveness of a new method of teaching reading to first graders. The researcher asks all 30 of the first-grade teachers in a particular school district if they would like to receive training in the new method and then use it during the coming school year. Fourteen teachers volunteer to learn and use the new method; 16 teachers say that they would prefer to use their current approach. At the end of the school year, students who have been instructed with the new method have significantly higher average scores on a reading achievement test than students who have received more traditional reading instruction. "The new method is definitely better than the old one," the researcher concludes.

Did you detect something wrong with the conclusions that these researchers drew? If not, go back and read the three descriptions again. *None of the conclusions is warranted from the study conducted.*

In the first research study, the two commercials apparently differed from each other in many ways (e.g., the presence of teenagers, the amount of action) in addition to humor. And, of course, we shouldn't overlook the fact that the humorous commercial aired during the summer months. People are more likely to drink soft drinks (including Zowie) when they are hot!

In the second study, the typists *knew* that they were participating in a research study; they also knew the nature of the researcher's hypothesis. Sometimes the participants in a research study change their behavior simply because they know they are in a research study—an effect known as **reactivity** or the **Hawthorne effect**. Perhaps the typists typed more because they liked the researcher and wanted to help him support his hypothesis. Perhaps they simply liked getting a little attention for a change. Furthermore, the researcher didn't consider the number of people who were working before and after the music started. Perhaps productivity increased simply because two people in the typing pool had just returned from vacation!

In the third study, notice that the researcher looked for volunteers to use the new method for teaching reading. Were the volunteer teachers different in some way from the nonvolunteers? Were they better educated or more motivated? Did they teach with more enthusiasm and energy because they *expected* the new method to be more effective—a phenomenon known as **experimenter expectancy?** Or did the volunteer teachers happen to teach in areas of the school district where children had a better "head start" in learning to read? Perhaps the children in the volunteers' classrooms performed better on the achievement test not because the instructional method was more effective, but because, as a group, they had been read to more frequently by their parents, gone to better preschools, and so on.

To ensure the internal validity of a research study, we need to take whatever precautions we can to *eliminate other possible explanations for the results we observe*. Following are several strategies researchers sometimes use to increase the probability that *their explanations are the most likely ones* for the observations they have made:

- **A controlled laboratory study.** An experiment is conducted in a laboratory setting so that environmental conditions can be carefully regulated.
- **A double-blind experiment.** In a situation where two or more different methods are being compared, neither the participants in the study nor the people administering the methods (e.g., teachers, research assistants) know what the researcher's hypothesis is or which method is expected to be more effective. In other words, both the participants and

the method-deliverers are "blind" with regard to whether they are in a group hypothe-sized to be more or less effective than another group.

- **Unobtrusive measures.**   People are observed in such a way that they do not know their actions are being recorded. We offer two real-life examples to illustrate. In one case, a uni-versity library measured student and faculty use of different parts of the library by look-ing at wear-and-tear patterns on the carpet. In another situation, researchers for the National Park Service looked at hikers' frequency of using different hiking trails by in-stalling electronic counters in hard-to-notice locations beside the trails (Ormrod & Tra-han, 1982). (Note that ethical issues sometimes arise when we observe people without their permission; we discuss ethics a little later in the chapter.)
- **Triangulation.**   Multiple sources of data are collected with the hope that they will all converge to support a particular hypothesis or theory. This approach is especially com-mon in qualitative research; for instance, a researcher might engage in many informal ob-servations in the field *and* conduct in-depth interviews, then look for common themes that appear in the data gleaned from both methods. Triangulation is also common in mixed-method designs, in which both quantitative and qualitative data are collected to answer a single research question.

Internal validity is especially of concern in experimental designs (described in Chapter 10), where the specific intent is to identify cause-and-effect relationships. But to some degree, inter-nal validity is important in any research study. The researcher must have confidence that the con-clusions drawn are warranted from the data collected.

EXTERNAL VALIDITY

The **external validity** of a research study is the extent to which its results apply to situations be-yond the study itself—in other words, the extent to which the conclusions drawn can be *generalized* to other contexts. As a general rule, we contribute more to humanity's knowledge about the world when we conduct research that has implications that extend far beyond the spe-cific situation studied.

Following are three commonly used strategies that enhance the external validity of a research project:

- **A real-life setting.**   Earlier we mentioned that researchers sometimes use laboratory ex-periments to help them control the environmental conditions in which a study takes place. There is a downside to laboratory studies, however: They provide an artificial set-ting that may be quite different from real-life circumstances. Research that is conducted in the outside world, although it may not have the tight controls of a laboratory project, may be more valid in the sense that it yields results with broader applicability to other real-world contexts.[1]
- **A representative sample.**   Whenever we conduct research to learn more about a par-ticular category of objects or creatures—whether we are studying rocks, salamanders, or human beings—we will often study a *sample* from that category and then draw conclu-sions about the category as a whole. (Here is a classic example of inductive reasoning.) To study the properties of granite, we might take pieces of granite from anywhere in the world and assume that our findings based on those pieces would be generalizable to gran-ite found in other locations. The same might hold true for salamanders if we limited our conclusions to the particular species we have studied.

---

[1] The artificial nature of laboratory research has been a concern in psychology for many years. Anderson, Lindsay, and Bushman (1999) compared the results of laboratory and field studies related to a wide variety of psychological phenomena. They discov-ered that the two kinds of studies typically yield similar results—that studies conducted in the lab and those conducted in nat-ural settings lead to the same conclusions about human nature. In their own words, "the psychological laboratory has generally produced psychological truths, rather than trivialities" (p. 3).

Human beings are another matter. The human race is incredibly diverse in terms of culture, child-rearing practices, educational opportunities, personality characteristics, and so on. To the extent that we restrict our research to people with a particular set of characteristics, we may not be able to generalize our findings to those with a very different set of characteristics. Ideally, we want the participants in a research study to be a *representative sample* of the population about which we wish to draw conclusions. In Chapter 9, we will consider a number of strategies for obtaining representative samples.

■ **Replication in a different context.**   Imagine that one researcher draws a conclusion from a particular study in a specific context, and another researcher who conducts a similar study in a very different context reaches the same conclusion, and perhaps additional researchers also conduct similar studies in dissimilar contexts and, again, draw the same conclusion. Under such circumstances, these studies, taken together, provide evidence that the conclusion has validity and applicability across diverse contexts and situations.

Ideally, the researcher should consider both internal validity and external validity when designing a research project. One's conclusions are valid and meaningful only to the extent that they are warranted based on the data collected *and* have applicability beyond the specific research situation itself.

VALIDITY IN QUALITATIVE RESEARCH

The concepts of internal and external validity originated in discussions of experimental research (Campbell & Stanley, 1963). In recent years, some qualitative researchers have begun to question their relevance to qualitative designs (Creswell, 1998; Guba & Lincoln, 1988; Lather, 1991; Wolcott, 1994). In fact, Lincoln and Guba (1985) and Creswell (1998) have suggested that such words as *credibility, dependability, confirmability, verification,* and *transferability* be used instead of the term *validity*.

As noted earlier, qualitative researchers frequently use triangulation—comparing multiple data sources in search of common themes—to support the validity of their findings. Following are several additional strategies they employ:

■ **Extensive time in the field.**   The researcher may spend several months, perhaps even a year or more, studying a particular phenomenon, forming tentative hypotheses, and continually looking for evidence that either supports or disconfirms those hypotheses.

■ **Negative case analysis.**   The researcher actively looks for cases that contradict existing hypotheses, then continually revises his or her explanation or theory until all cases have been accounted for.

■ **Thick description.**   The situation is described in sufficiently rich, "thick" detail that readers can draw their own conclusions from the data presented.

■ **Feedback from others.**   The researcher seeks the opinion of colleagues in the field to determine whether they agree or disagree that the researcher has made appropriate interpretations and drawn valid conclusions from the data.

■ **Respondent validation.**   The researcher takes his or her conclusions back to the participants in the study and asks quite simply, Do you agree with my conclusions? Do they make sense based on your own experiences?

As you can see, then, researchers use a wide variety of approaches to support the validity of their findings. Different approaches are appropriate in different situations, depending on the nature of the data and the specific methodologies used.

Regardless of the kind of study you decide to conduct, you must address the validity of your study at the very beginning of your project—that is, *at the planning stage*. If you put off validity issues until later in the game, you may end up conducting a study that has little apparent validity, either in terms of minimizing alternative explanations for the results obtained (internal validity) or in terms of being generalizable to the world "out there" (external validity). As a result, you are almost certainly wasting your time and effort on what is, for all intents and purposes, a useless enterprise.

ETHICAL ISSUES IN RESEARCH

Within certain disciplines—the social sciences, education, criminology, medicine, and similar areas of study—the use of human subjects in research is, of course, quite common. And whenever human beings are the focus of investigation, we must look closely at the ethical implications of what we are proposing to do.

Most ethical issues in research fall into one of four categories: protection from harm, informed consent, right to privacy, and honesty with professional colleagues. In this section we raise concerns related to each of these categories. We also describe the internal review boards and professional codes of ethics that provide guidance for researchers.

PROTECTION FROM HARM

Researchers should not expose research participants to undue physical or psychological harm. As a general rule, the risk involved in participating in a study should not be appreciably greater than the normal risks of day-to-day living. Participants should not risk losing life or limb, nor should they be subjected to unusual stress, embarrassment, or loss of self-esteem. In cases where the nature of a study involves creating a small amount of psychological discomfort, participants should know this ahead of time, and any necessary debriefing or counseling should follow immediately after their participation.

INFORMED CONSENT

Research participants should be told the nature of the study to be conducted and given the choice of either participating or not participating. Furthermore, they should be told that, if they agree to participate, they have the right to withdraw from the study at any time. *Any participation in a study should be strictly voluntary.*

A dilemma sometimes arises as to *how* informed participants should be. If people are given too much information—for instance, if they are told the specific research hypothesis being tested—they may behave differently than they would under more normal circumstances (recall our discussion of reactivity earlier in the chapter). A reasonable compromise is to give potential participants a general idea of what the study is about (e.g., "This study is investigating the effects of an exercise program on people's overall mental health") and to describe what specific activities their participation will involve—in other words, to give them sufficient information to make a reasonable, informed judgment about whether they wish to participate.

On rare occasions (e.g., in some studies of social behavior), telling participants the true nature of a study may lead them to behave in ways that would defeat the purpose of the study. In general, deception of any kind is frowned upon and should be used *only* when the study cannot meaningfully be conducted without it. Even then, the degree of deception should be as minimal as possible, and participants should be told the true nature of the research as soon as their involvement is over. (An internal review board, to be described shortly, can give you guidance in this respect.)

Earlier we mentioned the use of unobtrusive measures as a strategy for measuring behavior. Strictly speaking, unobtrusive measures violate the principle of informed consent. But if people's behaviors are merely being recorded in some way during their normal daily activities—if people are not being asked to do something they ordinarily would not do—and if they are not being scrutinized in any way that might be potentially invasive or embarrassing, then unobtrusive measures are quite appropriate. Recall our two earlier examples, examining the frequency with which people use different parts of the library and the frequency with which they hike along certain trails in a national park. Both of these were behaviors within the scope of participants' normal activities.

One common practice (and one required for certain kinds of research at most research institutions) is to present an **informed consent form** that describes the nature of the research project, as well as the nature of one's participation in it. Such a form should contain the following information:

- A brief description of the nature of the study
- A description of what participation will involve, in terms of activities and duration

- A statement indicating that participation is voluntary and can be terminated at any time without penalty
- A list of any potential risk and/or discomfort that participants may encounter
- The guarantee that all responses will remain confidential and anonymous
- The researcher's name, plus information about how the researcher can be contacted
- An individual or office that participants can contact, should they have questions or concerns about the study
- An offer to provide detailed information about the study (e.g., a summary of findings) upon its completion
- A place for the participant to sign and date the letter, indicating agreement to participate (when children are asked to participate, their parents must read and sign the letter)

An example of such a form is presented in Figure 5.3.

RIGHT TO PRIVACY

Any research study should respect participants' right to privacy. Under no circumstances should a research report, either oral or written, be presented in such a way that others become aware of how a particular participant has responded or behaved (unless, of course, the participant has specifically granted permission, in writing, for this to happen).

In general, a researcher must keep the nature and quality of participants' performance strictly confidential. For instance, the researcher might give each participant a code number and then label any written documents with that number rather than with the person's name. And if a particular person's behavior is described in depth in the research report, he or she should be given a pseudonym to assure anonymity.

HONESTY WITH PROFESSIONAL COLLEAGUES

Researchers must report their findings in a complete and honest fashion, without misrepresenting what they have done or intentionally misleading others about the nature of their findings. And under no circumstances should a researcher fabricate data to support a particular conclusion, no matter how seemingly "noble" that conclusion may be.

Within this context, we should also recall Chapter 4's discussion about giving appropriate credit where credit is due. Any use of another person's ideas or words demands full acknowledgment; otherwise, it constitutes plagiarism and documentary theft. Full acknowledgment of all material belonging to another person is mandatory. To appropriate the thoughts, ideas, or words of another—even if you paraphrase the borrowed ideas in your own language—without acknowledgment is unethical and highly circumspect. Honest researchers do not hesitate to acknowledge their indebtedness to others.

INTERNAL REVIEW BOARDS

In the United States, any college, university, or research institution will have an **internal review board (IRB)**[2] that scrutinizes all proposals for conducting human research under the auspices of the institution. This board, which is made up of scholars and researchers across a broad range of disciplines, checks proposed research studies to be sure that the procedures are not unduly harmful to participants, that appropriate procedures will be followed to obtain participants' informed consent, and that participants' privacy and anonymity are assured.

It is important to note that the research is reviewed at the proposal stage. *A proposal must be submitted to the IRB board and approved by the board before a single datum is collected.* Depending on the extent to which the study intrudes in some way on people's lives and imposes risk to participants, the board's chairperson may quickly declare it *exempt from review*, give it an *expedited review*,

---

[2] You might also see this committee called something along the lines of "Committee for Protection of Human Subjects."

Understanding How Students Organize Knowledge

You are being asked to participate in a study investigating ways in which students organize their knowledge.

We are interested in determining how students organize their knowledge in memory and use that knowledge. It is hoped that the results of this study can be useful in helping teachers understand why students perform differently from one another in the classroom.

As a future teacher, you will most likely have to use your knowledge in a variety of situations. However, relatively little is known about relationships among factors involved in knowledge application. Your participation may help to clarify some of these relationships so that we can better identify why students perform differently. And, although you may not directly benefit from this research, results from the study may be useful for future students, both those you teach and those who, like yourself, plan to be teachers.

If you agree to participate, you will complete two activities. In addition, we need to use your anonymous grade point average (GPA) as a control variable in order to account for initial differences among students. To ensure anonymity, we will submit only your social security number to the UNC Registrar, who will use this number to locate your GPA. The Registrar will black out the first three digits of your social security number before giving us this information, and the remaining six-digit number will be used only to keep track of your performance on the other activities. You will not be putting your name on anything except for this form. And, there will be no attempt to link your name with the last six digits of your social security number because individual performance is not of interest in this study. Only group results will be reported.

In the first activity, you will be asked to complete a 15-minute Self-Rating Checklist. This checklist consists of statements about knowledge application which you will judge to be true or false according to how each statement applies to you. In the second activity (which will be administered two days later), you will be given a list of concepts and asked to organize them on a sheet of paper, connect concepts you believe to be related, and describe the type of relationship between each connected pair of concepts. This activity should take about 30 minutes.

Although all studies have some degree of risk, the potential in this investigation is quite minimal. All activities are similar to normal classroom procedures, and all performance is anonymous. You will not incur any costs as a result of your participation in this study.

Your participation is voluntary. If at any time during this study you wish to withdraw your participation, you are free to do so without prejudice.

If you have any questions prior to your participation or at any time during the study, please do not hesitate to contact us.

AUTHORIZATION: I have read the above and understand the nature of this study. I understand that by agreeing to participate in this study I have not waived any legal or human right and that I may contact the researchers at the University of Northern Colorado (Dr. Jeanne Ormrod or Rose McCallin, 303-555-2807) at any time. I agree to participate in this study. I understand that I may refuse to participate or I may withdraw from the study at any time without prejudice. I also grant permission to the researchers to obtain my anonymous grade point average from the UNC Registrar for use as a control variable in the study. In addition, I understand that if I have any concerns about my treatment during the study, I can contact the Chair of the Internal Review Board at the University of Northern Colorado (303-555-2392) at any time.

Participant's signature: _____   Date: _____

Social Security Number: _____

Researcher's signature: _____   Date: _____

FIGURE 5.3

Example of an informed consent form

Adapted from *Knowledge Application Orientation, Cognitive Structure, and Achievement* (pp. 109–110), by R. C. McCallin, 1988, unpublished doctoral dissertation, University of Northern Colorado, Greeley. Adapted with permission.

NOTE. The form was used to recruit college students who were enrolled in a class in a teacher preparation program. It is missing one important ingredient: an offer to provide information about the study upon its completion. Instead, Ms. McCallin appeared in class a few weeks after she had collected data to give a summary of the study and its implications for teachers.

or bring it before the board for a *full review*. In any case, the researcher cannot begin the study until (a) the board has given its seal of approval to the study as originally designed or (b) the researcher has made any modifications that the board requests.

The IRB criteria and procedures vary slightly from one institution to another. For examples of institutional policies and procedures, you may want to visit the following Web sites

McGill University, Faculty of Medicine
http://www.medicine.mcgill.ca/research/irb/

The Rockefeller University
   http://rucares.org/irb/

or

   http://clinfo.rockefeller.edu/irb/

University of Mississippi
   http://www.olemiss.edu/depts/research/irb/

You can find other helpful sites on the World Wide Web by using a search engine (e.g., http://www.google.com) and such keywords as "IRB," "human participants," and "human subjects."

We should note here that universities and other research institutions have review boards for animal research as well. Any research that causes suffering, distress, or death to animals must be described and adequately justified to an **institutional animal care and use committee (IACUC)**. Furthermore, the researcher must minimize or prevent such suffering and death to research animals to the extent that it is possible to do so. As examples of research institutions' IACUC policies and procedures, we refer you to:

University of Maryland
   http://www.umresearch.umd.edu/IACUC/

University of Arizona
   http://www.ahsc.arizona.edu/uac/iacuc/

PROFESSIONAL CODES OF ETHICS

Many disciplines have their own codes of ethical standards governing research that involves human subjects and, when applicable, research involving animal subjects as well. A listing of some of these codes can be found in "For Further Reading" at the end of the chapter.

Another source of discipline-specific ethical codes is, of course, the World Wide Web. For instance, you can find the codes of the American Anthropological Association, American Association for Public Opinion Research, and the American Psychological Association at the following Web sites, respectively:

   http://www.aaanet.org/
   http://www.aspor.org/
   http://www.apa.org/

PLANNING FOR DATA COLLECTION

After identifying the research design and methodology, considering issues related to validity and reliability, and addressing the ethical implications of a project, the researcher must also make decisions about how to acquire and interpret the data necessary for resolving the overall research problem. Such decisions must be made before the researcher begins to write the research proposal.

Basic to the research design are four fundamental questions about the data. If the researcher is to avoid serious trouble later on, these questions must be answered specifically, concretely, and without mental evasion or reservation. The forthright answers to these questions will bring any research planning and design into clear focus.

1. *What data are needed?*   This question may seem like an overly simple one, but in fact a visualization of the data, an appreciation of their nature, and a clear understanding of their treatment are fundamental to any research effort. Certain questions demand resolution. On a sheet of paper, write down the answers to the following questions: To resolve the problem, what data are mandatory? What is their nature? Are they documentary? statistical? interview data? questionnaire replies? observations? measurements made before and after an experimental intervention? Specifically, what data do you need, and what are their characteristics?

2. *Where are the data located?*   Those of us who have taught research methodology are constantly amazed at students who come up with perfectly fascinating problems for research projects. But then we ask a basic and obvious question: "Where will you get the data to resolve the problem?" The student either looks bewildered and remains speechless or else mutters something such as, "Well, they must be available *somewhere*." Not *somewhere*, but *precisely where*? If you are doing a documentary study, where are the documents you need? At precisely what library and in what collection will you find them? What society or what organization has the files you must see? Where are these organizations located? Specify geographically—by town, street address, and zip code! Suppose a nurse or a nutritionist is doing a research study about Walter Olin Atwater, who has been instrumental in establishing the science of human nutrition in the United States. Where are the data on Atwater located? The researcher can go no further until that basic question is answered.

3. *How will the data be secured?*   To know where the data are is not enough; you need to know how they may be obtained. With privacy laws, confidentiality agreements, and so on, securing the information you need may not be as easy as you might think. You may indeed know what data you need and where they are located, but an equally important question is, How will you get them? In designing a research project, this question cannot be ignored. Careful attention to the matter marks the difference between a viable research project and a pipe dream.

4. *How will the data be interpreted?*   This is perhaps the most important question of all. The three former hurdles have been overcome. You have the data in hand. Now, spell out precisely what you intend to do with the data to solve the research problem or one of its subproblems.

At this point, go back and carefully read how you've worded your research problem. How must you treat the data to resolve the problem? If you process the data as you propose, what will the result be? How do you propose to measure the data? How can you be assured that your measurement instruments have adequate validity and reliability? If you are planning to conduct certain statistical analyses, are the statistical procedures appropriate for the characteristics of the data? Are you proposing a statistical technique that requires interval data when the data you have will be nominal or ordinal? As you can see, a great many questions must be addressed before you begin to carry out your research project.

PRACTICAL APPLICATION Choosing a Research Approach

Although we believe that many research studies would be enhanced by combining both quantitative and qualitative methods, we also realize that novice researchers may not have the time, resources, or expertise to effectively combine approaches for their initial research attempts. Therefore, we advise you to choose one or the other of these approaches for the overall design of your first few studies. Furthermore, we urge you to make the choice based on the research problem you want to address and the skills you have as a researcher, *not* on what tasks you want to avoid. For example, disliking mathematics and wanting to avoid conducting statistical analyses are *not* good reasons for choosing a qualitative study.

GUIDELINES Deciding Whether to Use a Quantitative or Qualitative Approach

Table 5.2 is designed to guide you in your choice between quantitative and qualitative approaches. Keep in mind that the items in the table are not necessarily ordered from most to least important. Each item should factor into your decision. Consider each component carefully before making your final selection.

TABLE 5.2	Use This Approach If:	Quantitative	Qualitative
Which approach should I use?	1. You believe that:	There is an objective reality that can be measured	There are multiple possible realities constructed by different individuals
	2. Your audience is:	Familiar with/supportive of quantitative studies	Familiar with/supportive of qualitative studies
	3. Your research question is:	Confirmatory, predictive	Exploratory, interpretive
	4. The available literature is:	Relatively large	Limited
	5. Your research focus:	Covers a lot of breadth	Involves in-depth study
	6. Your time available is:	Relatively short	Relatively long
	7. Your ability/desire to work with people is:	Medium to low	High
	8. Your desire for structure is:	High	Low
	9. You have skills in the area(s) of:	Deductive reasoning and statistics	Inductive reasoning and attention to detail
	10. Your writing skills are strong in the area of:	Technical, scientific writing	Literary, narrative writing

Qualitative studies have become increasingly popular in recent years, even in some disciplines that have historically placed heavy emphasis on quantitative approaches. Yet we have met many students who've naively assumed that qualitative studies are easier or in some other way more "comfortable" than quantitative designs. Be forewarned: Qualitative studies require as much effort and rigor as quantitative studies, and data collection alone often stretches over the course of many months. In the following paragraphs, we briefly discuss each of the components in Table 5.2 from the perspective of someone who might be inclined to "go qualitative."

1. *Consider your own comfort with the assumptions of the qualitative tradition.*   If you believe that no single reality underlies your research problem, but that, instead, different individuals may have constructed different, and possibly equally valid, realities relevant to your problem, then qualitative research is more appropriate.

2. *Consider the audience for your study.*   If your intended audience (e.g., a dissertation committee, a specific journal editor, journal readers) is not accustomed to or supportive of qualitative research, it makes little sense to spend the time and effort needed to do a good qualitative study (e.g., see Miller, Nelson, & Moore, 1998).

3. *Consider the nature of the research question.*   Qualitative designs can be quite helpful for addressing exploratory or interpretive research questions. But they may be of little use in testing a priority hypotheses about cause-and-effect relationships.

4. *Consider the extensiveness of the related literature.*   If the literature base is weak, underdeveloped, or altogether missing, a qualitative design can provide the researcher with the freedom and flexibility needed to explore a specific phenomenon so that important variables might be identified.

5. *Consider the depth of what you wish to discover.*   If you want to examine a phenomenon in depth with a relatively small number of participants, a qualitative approach is ideal. But if you are skimming the surface of a phenomenon and wish to do so using a large number of individuals, a quantitative study will be more efficient.

6. *Consider the amount of time you have available for conducting the study.*   Qualitative studies typically involve an extensive amount of time both on site and off site. If your time is limited, you may not be able to complete a qualitative study satisfactorily.

7. *Consider the extent to which you are willing to interact with the people in your study.*   Qualitative researchers must be able to establish rapport and trust with their participants and interact with them on a fairly personal level. Furthermore, gaining initial entry into a research site involves much advance planning and numerous preliminary contacts.

8. *Consider the extent to which you feel comfortable working without much structure.* Qualitative researchers typically work without specific rules and procedures; their work is exploratory in many respects. Therefore, they need a high tolerance for ambiguity.

9. *Consider your ability to organize and draw inferences from a large body of information.* Qualitative research typically involves the collection of a great many field notes, interview responses, and so on, that are not clearly organized at the beginning of the process. Working with extensive amounts of data and reasoning inductively about them require considerable self-discipline and organizational ability. In comparison, conducting a few statistical analyses—even for those who have little affection for mathematics—is a much easier task.

10. *Consider your writing skills.* Qualitative researchers must have excellent literary writing skills. Communicating findings is the final step in all research projects; the success of your research ultimately will be judged by how well you accomplish this final component of the research process.

Once you have decided whether to take a quantitative or qualitative approach, you need to pin down your research method more precisely. Table 5.3 lists some common research methodologies and the types of problems for which each is appropriate.

PRACTICAL APPLICATION JUDGING THE FEASIBILITY OF A RESEARCH PROJECT

Many beginning researchers avoid looking closely at the practical problems of research. Envisioning an exotic investigation, an appealing problem, or a solve-the-problems-of-the-world project sometimes keeps a researcher from making an impartial judgment about the practicability of the project. The following checklist can help you wisely plan and accurately evaluate the research project you have in mind.

To determine the feasibility of your research project, study the checklist and fill it out completely. After you have finished, review your responses. Then, answer this question: Can you reasonably accomplish this study? If your answer is no, determine where the unfeasibility of the project lies. Identify approaches you might use to make it more realistically accomplishable.

✔ CHECKLIST
DETERMINING WHETHER A PROPOSED RESEARCH PROJECT IS REALISTIC AND PRACTICAL

THE PROBLEM

_____ 1. With what area(s) will the problem deal?
  _____ People
  _____ Things
  _____ Records
  _____ Thoughts and Ideas
  _____ Dynamics and Energy

_____ 2. Are data that relate directly to the problem available for each of the categories you've just checked? _____ Yes _____ No

_____ 3. What academic discipline is primarily concerned with the problem?

_____

_____ 4. What other academic disciplines are possibly also related to the problem?

_____

TABLE 5.3 Methodology and concomitant research goals

Method	Characteristics of the Method and the Research Goals the Method Attempts to Achieve
Action research	A type of applied research that focuses on finding a solution to a local problem in a local setting. For example, a teacher investigates whether a new spelling program she has adopted leads to improvement in her students' achievement scores. (See G. E. Mills' *Action Research*, 2003, for guidance on conducting action research.)
Case study	A type of qualitative research in which in-depth data are gathered relative to a single individual, program, or event, for the purpose of learning more about an unknown or poorly understood situation. (See Chapter 7.)
Content analysis	A detailed and systematic examination of the contents of a particular body of material (e.g., television shows, advertisements, textbooks) for the purpose of identifying patterns, themes, or biases within that material. (See Chapter 7.)
Correlational research	A statistical investigation of the relationship between two or more variables. Correlational research looks at surface relationships but does not necessarily probe for causal reasons underlying them. For example, a researcher might investigate the relationships among high school seniors' achievement test scores and their grade point averages a year later when they are first-year college students. (See Chapter 9.)
Developmental research	An observational-descriptive type of research that either compares people in different age groups (a *cross-sectional study*) or follows a particular group over a lengthy period of time (a *longitudinal study*). Such studies are particularly appropriate for looking at developmental trends. (See Chapter 9.)
Ethnography	A type of qualitative inquiry that involves an in-depth study of an intact cultural group in a natural setting. (See Chapter 7.)
Experimental research	A study in which participants are randomly assigned to groups that undergo various researcher-imposed treatments or interventions, followed by observations or measurements to assess the effects of the treatments. (See Chapter 10.)
Ex post facto research	An approach in which one looks at conditions that have already occurred and then collects data to investigate a possible relationship between these conditions and subsequent characteristics or behaviors. (See Chapter 10.)
Grounded theory research	A type of qualitative research aimed at deriving theory through the use of multiple stages of data collection and interpretation. (See Chapter 7.)
Historical research	An attempt to solve certain problems arising out of a historical context through gathering and examining relevant data. (See Chapter 8.)
Observation study	A type of quantitative research in which a particular aspect of behavior is observed systematically and with as much objectivity as possible. (See Chapter 9.)
Phenomenological research	A qualitative method that attempts to understand participants' perspectives and views of social realities. (See Chapter 7.)
Quasi-experimental research	A method similar to experimental research but without random assignment to groups. (See Chapter 10.)
Survey research	A common method used in business, sociology, and government. Surveys are used to describe the incidence, frequency, and distribution of certain characteristics in a population. (See Chapter 9.)

_____ 5. What special aptitude do you have as a researcher for this problem?

_____ Interest in the problem

_____ Experience in the problem area

_____ Education and/or training

_____ Other (specify):

_____

_____

THE DATA

_____ 6. How available are the data to you?

       _____ Readily available

       _____ Available, with permission

       _____ Available with great difficulty or rarely available

       _____ Unavailable

_____ 7. How often are you personally in contact with the source of the data?

       _____ Once a day   _____ Once a week   _____ Once a month

       _____ Once a year   _____ Never

_____ 8. Will the data arise directly out of the problem situation?

       _____ Yes   _____ No

       If your answer is "no," where or how will you secure the data?

       _____

       _____

       _____

_____ 9. How do you plan to gather the data?

       _____ Observation _____ Questionnaire _____ Tests or inventories

       _____ Photocopying of records _____ Interview and tape recording

       _____ Other (explain): _____

       _____

       _____

       _____

_____ 10. Is special equipment or are special conditions necessary for gathering or processing the data?

       _____ Yes   _____ No

       If your answer is "yes," specify: _____

       _____

       _____

_____ 11. If you will need special equipment, do you have access to such equipment and the skill to use it?

       _____ Yes   _____ No

       If the answer is "no," how do you intend to overcome this difficulty?

       _____

       _____

_____ 12. What is the estimated cost in time and money to gather the data?

       _____

_____ 13. What evidence do you have that the data you gather will be valid and reliable indicators of the phenomena you wish to study?

       _____

       _____

CRITERIA-BASED EVALUATION

_____ 14. Does your research project meet the four criteria applicable to all research? (For a refresher on these criteria, see the section "General Criteria for a Research Project.")

       Universality   _____ Yes   _____ No

       Replication   _____ Yes   _____ No

Control	_____ Yes	_____ No
Measurement	_____ Yes	_____ No

_____ 15. As you review your responses to this checklist, might any of the factors you've just considered, or perhaps any other factors, hinder a successful completion of your research project?

_____ Yes   _____ No

If your answer is "yes," list those factors. _____

_____

_____

WHEN YOU CAN'T ANTICIPATE EVERYTHING IN ADVANCE: THE VALUE OF A PILOT STUDY

Did you have trouble answering some of the questions in the checklist? For instance, did you have difficulty estimating how much time it would take you to gather or process your data? Did you realize that you might need to develop your own questionnaire, test, or other measurement instrument but then wonder how valid and reliable the instrument might be for your purpose?

Up to this point, we have been talking about planning a research project as something that occurs all in one fell swoop. In reality, a researcher may sometimes need to do a brief exploratory investigation, or **pilot study**, to try out particular procedures, measurement instruments, or methods of analysis. *A brief pilot study is an excellent way to determine the feasibility of your study.* Furthermore, although it may take some time initially, it may ultimately save you time by letting you know, after only a small investment on your part, which approaches will and will not be effective in helping you solve your overall research problem.

PRACTICAL APPLICATION ESTABLISHING RESEARCH CRITERIA AND JUSTIFYING YOUR RESEARCH METHODOLOGY

In this exercise you will continue developing your research proposal, for which you have already conducted a review of the related literature (see Chapter 4). In writing proposals, we leave nothing unspecified. Here, we explore how to treat each subproblem in terms of its data, the criteria for the admission of those data into your study, and a justification of the methodology you propose to employ. In the form presented in Figure 5.4 (extend it as needed), we suggest the following approach to justify your research methods:

1. Write your principal problem at the top of the page, and divide the rest of the page into the two columns.
2. In the left-hand column, write the first subproblem.
3. Immediately below the subproblem, write a description of the data that you will need to resolve that subproblem.
4. In the right-hand column, write the criteria that you will establish for the admissibility of those data into your research design. Be specific. Avoid vague, overgeneralized statements.
5. Repeat steps 2–4 for the remaining subproblems.

Now refer to the earlier sections on "Comparing Quantitative and Qualitative Approaches" and "Guidelines: Deciding Whether to Use a Quantitative or Qualitative Approach." Then do the following:

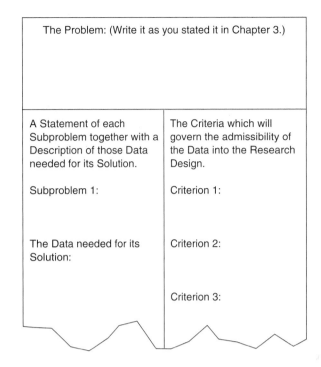

FIGURE 5.4

Justifying your research approaches

The Problem: (Write it as you stated it in Chapter 3.)

A Statement of each Subproblem together with a Description of those Data needed for its Solution.	The Criteria which will govern the admissibility of the Data into the Research Design.
Subproblem 1:	Criterion 1:
The Data needed for its Solution:	Criterion 2:
	Criterion 3:

1. Describe the characteristics that the data in your research project will exhibit.
2. For the data you have just described, identify the approach, quantitative or qualitative or perhaps some combination of the two, that would be most appropriate for collecting, analyzing, and interpreting those data. Justify your choice.

PRACTICAL APPLICATION DEVELOPING A PLAN OF ATTACK

Once you have determined that your research project is feasible, you can move ahead. Yet particularly for a novice researcher, all the things that need to be done—writing and submitting the proposal, getting IRB approval, arranging for access to one or more research sites, setting up any experimental interventions you have planned, collecting the data, analyzing and interpreting it, and writing the final research report—may, in combination, seem like a gigantic undertaking. We recall, with considerable disappointment and sadness, the many promising doctoral students we've known who took all of the required courses, passed their comprehensive exams with flying colors, and then never earned their doctoral degrees because they couldn't persevere through the process of completing a dissertation.

The most effective strategy we can suggest here is to *develop a research and writing schedule*. Figure 5.5 provides a workable format for your schedule. In the left-hand column, list all of the specific tasks you need to accomplish for your research project (writing the proposal, getting approval from the IRB and any other relevant faculty committees, conducting any needed pilot studies, etc.) in the order in which you need to accomplish them. In the second column, estimate the number of weeks or months it will take you to complete each task, always giving yourself a little more time than you think you will need. In the third column, establish appropriate target dates for accomplishing each task, taking into account any business trips, vacations, and other breaks in your schedule that you anticipate. Use the right-hand column to check off each step as you complete it.

Task to Complete	Estimated Amount of Time Needed	Target Date for Completion	Task Completed (indicate with a ✔)

FIGURE 5.5

Establishing a schedule for your project

USING PROJECT MANAGEMENT SOFTWARE AND ELECTRONIC PLANNERS

In the business world, project management software (e.g., FastTrack Schedule, TopDown Flowcharter, SmartDraw) has become popular. This type of software can be used to organize and coordinate the various aspects of a research project. For example, it lets you outline the different phases of the project, the times at which those phases need to be completed, the ways in which they are interrelated, and the person who is responsible for completing each task. This information can be displayed in graphic form with due dates and milestones highlighted.

Project management software is especially helpful when a research project has many separate parts that all need to be carefully organized and coordinated. For example, suppose a large research effort is being conducted in a local school district. The effort requires a team of observers and interviewers to go into various schools and observe teachers in class, interview students during study hall, and discuss administrative issues with the principals. Coordinating the efforts of the many observers, teachers, students, and administrators is a complex task that can be easily laid out and scheduled by project management software.

You might consider computerizing your schedule even if you don't expect your research project to be as multifaceted as the one we've just described. For instance, computerized versions of day planners (e.g., Now Up-to-Date) are widely available. These customized databases can store and organize the various tasks you need to accomplish. You can insert electronic reminders that you need to do certain things on such-and-such a date. And you can easily revise your long-term schedule if unforeseen circumstances occur.

KEEPING AN OPTIMISTIC AND TASK-ORIENTED OUTLOOK

In our own experiences, we have found that a schedule goes a long way in helping us complete a large task. In fact, this is exactly the approach we took when we wrote various editions of this book. Make no mistake about it, writing a book can be even more overwhelming than conducting a research project!

A schedule in which you break your project into small, easily doable steps accomplishes several things for you simultaneously. First, it gives you the confidence that you *can* complete your project if you simply focus on one piece at a time. Second, it helps your persevere by giving you a series of target dates that you strive to meet. And last (but certainly not least!), checking off the tasks in the right-hand column provides a regular reminder that you are making progress toward your final goal of solving the research problem.

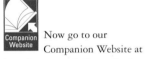

Now go to our Companion Website at http://www.prenhall.com/leedy to assess your understanding of chapter content and to complete the projects that will help you learn how to conduct research.

FOR FURTHER READING

Planning Your Research Design

Berg, K., & Latin, R. (1994). *Essentials of modern research methods in health, physical education, and recreation.* Upper Saddle River, NJ: Prentice Hall.

Bordens, K. S., & Abbott, B. A. (1995). *Research design and methods: A process approach* (3rd ed.). Mountain View, CA: Mayfield.

Brink, P. J., & Wood, M. J. (1994). *Basic steps in planning nursing research: From question to proposal* (4th ed.). Boston: Jones & Bartlett.

Brink, P. J., & Wood, M. J. (1997). *Advanced design in nursing research.* Thousand Oaks, CA: Sage.

Brockopp, D. Y., & Hastings-Tolsma, M. T. (2003). *Fundamentals of nursing research* (3rd ed.). Boston: Jones & Bartlett.

Creswell, J. W. (2002). *Educational research: Planning, conducting, and evaluating quantitative and qualitative research.* Upper Saddle River, NJ: Merrill/Prentice Hall.

Ethridge, D. (1995). *Research methodology in applied economics: Organizing, planning, and conducting economic research.* Ames: Iowa State University Press.

Firestone, W. A. (1987). Meaning in method: The rhetoric of quantitative and qualitative research. *Educational Researcher, 16*(7), 16–21.

Gebremedhin, T. G., & Tweeten, L. G. (1994). *Research methods and communication in the social sciences.* Westport, CT: Praeger.

Goodwin, C. J. (2001). *Research in psychology: Methods and design* (3rd ed.). New York: Wiley.

Hedrick, T. E., Bickman, L., & Rog, D. J. (1993). *Applied research design: A practical guide.* Thousand Oaks, CA: Sage.

Jacob, H. (1984). *Using published data: Errors and remedies.* Thousand Oaks, CA: Sage.

Jung, S. (1995). *The logic of discovery: An interrogative approach to scientific inquiry.* New York: Peter Lang.

Lehmann, D. R., Gupta, S., & Steckel, J. H. (1998). *Marketing research*. Upper Saddle River, NJ: Prentice Hall.

Mertens, D. M., & McLaughlin, J. (1994). *Research methods in special education*. Thousand Oaks, CA: Sage.

Neuman, W. L. (2003). *Social research methods: Qualitative and quantitative approaches* (5th ed.). Boston: Allyn & Bacon.

Neuman, W. L., & Wiegand, B. (2000). *Criminal justice research methods: Qualitative and quantitative approaches*. Boston: Allyn & Bacon.

Singleton, R., Jr., Straits, B. C., & Straits, M. M. (1993). *Approaches to social research* (2nd ed.). London: Oxford University Press.

Westmeyer, P. M. (1994). *A guide for use in planning, conducting, and reporting research projects* (2nd ed.). Springfield, IL: Charles C Thomas.

Measurement

Aft, L. (1992). *Productivity measurement and improvement* (2nd ed.). Upper Saddle River, NJ: Prentice Hall.

Earickson, R., & Harlin, J. (1994). *Geographic measurement and quantitative analysis*. Upper Saddle River, NJ: Prentice Hall.

Oppenheim, A. N. (1992). *Questionnaire design, interviewing, and attitude measurement*. New York: St. Martin's Press.

Thorndike, R. M. (1997). *Measurement and evaluation in psychology and education* (6th ed.). Upper Saddle River, NJ: Merrill/Prentice Hall.

Ethics

American Educational Research Association. (1992). Ethical standards of the American Educational Research Association. *Educational Researcher*, 21(7), 23–36.

American Psychological Association. (2002). Ethical principles of psychologists and code of conduct. *American Psychologist*, 57, 1060–1073.

Bankowski, Z., & Levine, R. J. (1993). *Ethics and research on human subjects: International guidelines*. Albany, NY: World Health Organization.

Cheney, D. (Ed.). (1993). *Ethical issues in research*. Frederick, MD: University Publishing Group.

Christians, C. G. (2000). Ethics and politics in qualitative research. In N. K. Denzin & Y. S. Lincoln (Eds), *Handbook of qualitative research* (2nd ed., pp. 133–155). Thousand Oaks, CA: Sage.

Eiserman, W. C., & Behl, D. (1992). Research participation: Benefits and considerations for the special educator. *Teaching Exceptional Children, 24*, 12–15.

Elliott, D., & Stern, J. E. (Eds.) (1997). *Research ethics: A reader*. Hanover, NH: University Press of New England.

Erwin, E., Gendin, S., & Kleiman, L. (Eds.). (1994). *Ethical issues in scientific research: An anthology*. New York: Garland.

Loue, S., & Case, S. L. (2000). *Textbook of research ethics: Theory and practice*. New York: Plenum Press.

Neuman, W. L. (2003). *Social research methods: Qualitative and quantitative approaches* (5th ed.). Boston: Allyn & Bacon. [Provides an excellent discussion of ethical issues.]

Penslar, R. L. (Ed.). (1995). *Research ethics: Cases and materials*. Bloomington: Indiana University Press.

Sieber, J. E. (1992). *Planning ethically responsible research*. Thousand Oaks, CA: Sage.

Sim, M. (Ed.). (1994). *Ethics of scientific research*. Lanham, MD: Rowman & Littlefield.

Stanley, B., Sieber, J. E., & Melton, G. B. (Eds.). (1996). *Research ethics: A psychological approach*. Lincoln: University of Nebraska Press.

Tashakkori, A., & Teddlie, C. (1998). *Mixed methodology: Combining qualitative and quantitative approaches*. Thousand Oaks, CA: Sage

Vanderpool, H. (1995). *Research ethics: Facing the 21st century*. Frederick, MD: University Publishing Group.

6

Writing the Research Proposal

Research is never a solo flight, an individual excursion. It begins by researchers communicating their thoughts, plans, methods, and objectives for others to read, discuss, and act upon. The mechanism that begins such a research dialogue is the research proposal. As a point of departure, it must be a precision instrument from the first word to the last.

Research is never a solitary activity. It involves many people and requires access to and use of resources far beyond one's own. For that reason, it must be carefully planned, laid out, inspected, and, in nearly every instance, approved by others. The graduate student conducting research for a thesis or dissertation must get the approval of an academic committee. A researcher seeking grant funding must get approval from the university or the organization for which he or she works, and the project must be deemed worthy of funding by the grant-awarding agency. Any researcher who plans to work with human subjects must get the approval of an internal review board, and one who plans to work with animals must get that of an institutional animal care and use committee (see Chapter 5). Such approvals are usually secured through the submission of a document known as a *research proposal*. The proposal lays out the problem for research, describes exactly how the research will be conducted, and outlines in precise detail the resources—both factual and instrumental—the researcher will use to achieve the desired results.

RESEARCHER AND ARCHITECT: PLANNERS IN COMMON

A proposal is as essential to successful research as an architect's plans are to the construction of a building. No one would start building a structure by rushing out to dig a hole for the foundation without knowing in detail how the building will look when it is finished. Before one turns a shovelful of earth, many questions must be addressed, many decisions made. What kind of building is desired? Is it a personal residence? If so, will it be a two-story colonial, a split-level, or a one-story ranch? How will the building be placed on the lot? Where will the doors be located? What kind of pitch will the roof have, and how will it be shingled? What kind of heating system will be used? Each of these questions is important, and each should be addressed *before* a pound of dirt is excavated or a nail driven.

Even after all these decisions have been made, does the digging begin? Not at all! Further planning is necessary. The architect draws a floor plan of the entire structure, floor by floor, showing to the inch precisely where every room, closet, and door will be located. The architect also draws a series of elevations of the proposed building, showing each wall to scale as it will appear when completed. Finally, the architect draws up a set of specifications for the building, indicating exactly what lumber is to be used, how far apart certain beams will be placed, what kinds of doors and windows will be put in what locations, and all other details. Nothing is left to chance.

So is it now time to stake off the position of the building and start digging for the foundation? Not so fast! Before the construction crew can do anything, they need *permission*. The contractor must get a building permit. Most communities have building codes that govern the kinds of buildings that can be constructed—codes regarding plumbing, electrical wiring, distance from the street, and so on. A permit provides a means of ensuring that new buildings meet these codes. The point is this: *Permission is essential to the plan*. This principle holds true both in planning a building and in proposing research.

Like the architect who presents detailed plans for a building, the researcher develops a written proposal for a research project. In this proposal, the problem and its attendant subproblems are clearly stated, hypotheses or questions are articulated, all necessary terms are defined, delimitations are carefully spelled out, and the reason for conducting the study—why it's important—is explained. The researcher then specifies every anticipated detail of acquiring, organizing, analyzing, and interpreting the data. Parallel to the architect's specifications, the researcher sets forth the resources at hand for carrying out the research: his or her qualifications (and those of any assistants), the availability of the data, the means by which the data will be secured, any needed equipment and facilities, and any other aspects of the total research process that merit explanation. Nothing is overlooked. All questions that may arise in the minds of those who review the proposal are anticipated and answered. Any unresolved matter is a weakness in the proposal and may seriously affect its approval.

We cannot overemphasize the importance of the proposal. It is the key that unlocks the door to the research endeavor. If it is not clearly and explicitly delineated, it may cause the whole project to be turned down.

Sometimes young researchers think the proposal is merely a necessary formality and thus do not give it the serious consideration it deserves. They try to set forth the project in a few, hastily written pages. Such an approach often fails. Those sponsoring a project, whether a graduate committee or a funding agency, realize that a researcher invests considerable time, effort, and (sometimes) money when doing research. Accordingly, no one should rush into a project without a clearly conceived goal and a thorough, objective evaluation of all aspects of the research endeavor.

No matter whether you are seeking funding for a project from a grant foundation or seeking approval for a thesis or dissertation from a university faculty committee, a clear, well-written proposal is essential. Nothing is a substitute for an explicit setting forth of both problem and procedure. Other names for a proposal are *prospectus, plan, outline, statement,* and *draft*. If you are asked to present any of these, you are being asked to present a research proposal.

CHARACTERISTICS OF A PROPOSAL

Research demands that those who undertake it be able to think clearly, without confusion. The proposal will demonstrate, fortunately or unfortunately, whether the author possesses that ability. When one reads a proposal that is hazily focused, poorly organized, and lacking in essential details, one gets the impression that the mind that produced such a document is incapable of thinking logically, systematically, and thoroughly about the job that needs to be done. Unwelcome as the fact may be, the perceived qualifications of a researcher, more often than not, rest squarely upon the quality of the proposal submitted.

Therefore, as you embark on the task of writing a research proposal, you should understand exactly what characteristics a proposal should have.

A Proposal Is a Straightforward Document

A proposal should not be cluttered with extraneous and irrelevant material. Right off the bat, it opens with a straightforward statement of the problem to be researched. It needs no explanatory props—no introduction, prologue, or statement telling why the researcher became interested in the problem or feels a burning desire to research it. Such information may be interesting, but none of it is necessary or appropriate. Those who will review your proposal are not interested in such autobiographical excursions. These, indeed, suggest that you cannot separate essentials from irrelevancies and so will neither enhance your stature as a researcher nor recommend you as one who can think in a clear and focused manner.

Whatever does not contribute directly to the delineation of the problem and its solution must be eliminated. Anything else is a distraction. Remember the architect's drawing: clean, clear, and economical. It contains all that is necessary, not one detail more.

Journalists are taught—or if not taught, soon learn—that the first words they write are the most important ones. You capture or lose your reader with the first sentence. It is impossible to overemphasize the importance of the beginning, whether it be of a speech, a news story, an article, or a proposal.

Imagine a proposal that begins with these words: "Five decades ago, the social and economic status of minority groups in the United States was . . ." A reader's reaction might easily be: "Who cares, at this moment, what the social and economic status of minorities was 50 years ago? That's history. What does the researcher *propose* to do *in the near future*? C'mon, what's the problem? *State it!*"

You see, if your first sentence irritates your reader, you are put immediately at a disadvantage, and you have possibly sacrificed your reader's interest. More seriously, the reader may infer that you cannot distinguish between history and future planning and so wonder about your ability as a researcher to think clearly and critically.

Keep in mind the meaning of *proposal*. The word suggests looking forward, to what the researcher *plans to do in the future*. If a writer intends to make an analytical comparison of the past and present social and economic conditions of minority groups, he or she might begin, "This study *will* analyze the social and economic status of certain minority groups today in comparison with their similar status five decades ago for the purpose of . . ." This is a no-nonsense beginning, and it indicates that the writer knows what a proposal should be.

A Proposal Is Not a Literary Production

An architect's drawing is not a work of art. Similarly, a proposal is not a creative, "literary" production. The purpose of both is simply to communicate clearly. Just as an architect's drawings present a plan for construction with economy of line and precision of measurement, a proposal describes a future research project with an economy of words and precision of expression.

The language must be clear, sharp, and precise. The proposal provides a chance to show with what ultimate clarity and detail the researcher can state a problem, delineate the treatment of the data, and establish the logical validity of a conclusion.

To those who have been taught that writing should be stylistically interesting and artistically creative, the preceding statements may come as a bit of a shock. Yet writing a superb proposal calls for skills of expression just as demanding as those needed for forging an unforgettable sentence.

A Proposal Is Clearly Organized

Proposals are written in conventional prose style, and thoughts are expressed in simple paragraph form. The organization of the thoughts is outlined by the proper use of headings and subheadings. Organization and outline are essential. They hint at an orderly and disciplined mind—one of the highest tributes to a researcher's qualifications.

Turn back to Chapter 2, "Tools of Research." Look only at the headings in that chapter. They indicate the overall organization of ideas presented in the chapter.

Following, in outline form, is the organization of Chapter 2 as reflected in its heading and subheadings. We begin by listing the name of the chapter itself; after all, the chapters of this book represent the major categories we are using to organize what we want to say about practical research.

II. Tools of Research
   A. General tools of research
   B. The library and its resources as a tool of research
      1. The library of the quiet past
      2. The library of the stormy present
      3. How to access knowledge quickly and efficiently
         a. Library catalogs
         b. Indexes and abstracts
         c. The reference librarian
         d. Browsing the library shelves
   C. The computer and its software as a tool of research
      1. Taking advantage of the Internet
         a. World Wide Web
         b. Electronic mail
         c. News
      2. Accessing the Internet
      3. Learning more about the Internet
   D. Practical application: Using the Internet to facilitate communication
   E. Practical application: Using e-mail
      1. Guidelines: Getting started on e-mail
   F. Measurement as a tool of research
      1. Measuring insubstantial phenomena: An example
      2. Interpretation of the data
      3. Four scales of measurement
         a. Nominal scale of measurement
         b. Ordinal scale of measurement
         c. Interval scale of measurement
         d. Ratio scale of measurement
      4. Validity and reliability of measurement
         a. Validity
         b. Reliability
   G. Statistics as a tool of research
      1. The lure of statistics
      2. Primary functions of statistics
   H. The human mind as a tool of research
      1. Deductive logic
      2. Inductive reasoning
      3. The scientific method
      4. Critical thinking
      5. Collaboration with others
   I. Language as a tool of research
      1. The value of knowing two or more languages
      2. The importance of writing
   J. Practical application: Communicating effectively through writing
      1. Guidelines: Writing to communicate
      2. Guidelines: Using a word processor
   K. Practical application: Identifying important tools in your discipline
      1. Checklist: Interviewing an expert researcher
   L. Reflections on significant research
   M. For further reading

In professional writing, headings and subheadings are the single most commonly used strategy to express the writer's overall organizational scheme. Examine your textbooks—even current magazine articles—and you will discover how frequently headings are used to indicate the organizational structure of what has been written. You should communicate the outline of your thoughts to your own readers in the same fashion.

ORGANIZING A RESEARCH PROPOSAL

Proposals follow a simple, logical train of thought. Although there are conceivably many ways to arrange the various topics within a proposal, most proposals use similar formats, especially in quantitative studies. The following is an example of a format you might use in a quantitative proposal:

I. The problem and its setting
   A. The statement of the problem and subproblems
   B. The hypotheses
   C. The delimitations
   D. The definitions of terms
   E. The assumptions
   F. The importance of the study
II. The review of the related literature
III. The data and the treatment of the data
   A. The data needed and the means for obtaining the data
   B. The research methodology
   C. The specific treatment of the data for each subproblem
      1. Subproblem 1 (*The subproblem is restated here.*)
         a. The data needed to address the subproblem
         b. The treatment of the data
      2. Subproblem 2 (*The same format for Subproblem 1 is followed here.*)
      3. Additional subproblems are discussed in the same manner.
IV. The qualifications of the researcher and any assistants
V. An outline of the proposed study (steps to be taken, timeline, etc.)
VI. References
VII. Appendixes

Qualitative proposals sometimes use a slightly different format. The following format is an example of an outline for a qualitative proposal:

I. Introduction
   A. General background for the study
   B. Purpose of the study
   C. Guiding questions
   D. Delimitations and limitations
   E. Significance of the study
II. Methodology
   A. Theoretical framework
   B. Type of design and the assumptions that underlie it
   C. Role of the researcher (including qualifications and assumptions)
   D. Selection and description of the site and participants
   E. Data collection strategies
   F. Data analysis strategies
   G. Methods of achieving validity
III. Findings
   A. Relationship to literature
   B. Relationship to theory

      C. Relationship to practice
   IV. Management plan, timeline, feasibility
    V. References
   VI. Appendixes

One rule governs the writing of proposals and final documents: *The arrangement of the material should be presented in such a manner that it forms for the reader a clear, progressive presentation.* It keeps items together that belong together—for example, the problem and its resultant subproblems, the subproblems and their corresponding hypotheses.

FORMATTING HEADINGS AND SUBHEADINGS

You must use different formats to indicate the different levels of headings you use. For instance, if you have five different levels of headings, following is one possible scheme you might use:[1]

- *Level 1 heads,* the most important ones, are in **ALL CAPITAL LETTERS** and centered on the page. These are headings of the largest units of writing; for instance, they may be the titles of the various chapters in a proposal or research report. They correspond with Roman numerals I, II, III, and so on, in an outline.
- *Level 2 heads* are in **Capital and Lowercase Letters** and centered on the page. They correspond with the capital letters A, B, C, and so on, in an outline.
- *Level 3 heads* are in ***Italicized Capital and Lowercase Letters*** and centered on the page. They correspond with the numbers 1, 2, 3, and so on, in an outline.
- *Level 4 heads* are in ***Italicized Capital and Lowercase Letters*** and flush with the left margin. They correspond with the letters a, b, c, and so on, in an outline.
- *Level 5 heads* have a ***Single capital letter followed by lowercase letters.*** They are italicized and indented, and they are followed on the same line by the beginning of the first paragraph in the section. Such heads are sometimes known as *run-in heads.* They correspond with the numbers (1), (2), (3), and so on, that you sometimes see in an outline.

If you used this format, your various headings would look like this on the page:

FIRST LEVEL HEAD

Second Level Head

Third Level Head

Fourth Level Head

   Fifth level head. The first paragraph of this section begins here. . . .

To help the headings stand out on the page, you will, in most cases, want to have an extra space (that is, an empty line) just preceding each one.

The format we suggest here is not the only one you might use. When choosing appropriate formats for your headings, you should check with any style manuals in your discipline and, if you are a student, with any graduate school requirements. For example, many style manuals ask that writers leave a blank line before headings; however, the fifth edition of the American Psychological Association's *Publication Manual* (2001) asks that writers *not* do so.

Above all, you should be *consistent* in how you format your headings. We have seen too many proposals, theses, and dissertations in which headings of equal importance appear in ALL CAPITALS and in Capitals and Lowercase, or perhaps they appear both

Centered

and

Flush Left.

Such inconsistency points to a careless, sloppy writer and, a proposal reviewer might think, perhaps an equally careless and sloppy researcher.

---

[1] This scheme is similar to that suggested in the American Psychological Association's *Publication Manual* (2001).

PRACTICAL APPLICATION WRITING YOUR PROPOSAL

Challenging as writing a proposal can be, especially for the beginning researcher, it isn't rocket science. Here we offer two sets of guidelines, one each for writing a first draft and for revising your proposal.

GUIDELINES WRITING THE FIRST DRAFT

The following suggestions are based both on our own experiences as proposal writers and as faculty members who have advised numerous master's and doctoral students.

1. *Use a computer or other word processor.* Whether you begin writing your proposal on a word processor or on paper should depend on which medium allows you to think and write most easily. For example, if you have had considerable experience using a keyboard and can type as fast as you write, then you will undoubtedly want to use a word processor from the get-go. In contrast, if you use the more tedious hunt-and-peck approach and have considerable trouble finding such letters as *Q, X,* and *Z,* then you might want to start off with paper and pencil. At some point, however, you should put your first draft on a word processor to make those inevitable revisions (there will be many!) easier.

Early in the game, take the time to learn any special features of your word processing software that you will need for typing your proposal or your final research report. For instance, learn how to insert tables, graphs, footnotes, and other specially formatted features. If you will be including words with accent marks or using punctuation marks different from those in English (e.g., *déjà, señor, Günter, ¿*), find out how to type them. If you will need to use certain symbols (e.g., α, Σ, π) or mathematical formulas, learn how to include them in your document.

2. *Adhere to any guidelines required by the institution, organization, or funding agency to which you are submitting the proposal.* If the group to which you are submitting the proposal requires that you (a) use certain headings, (b) follow a particular style manual (e.g., APA style), or (c) include certain information, do it! Blatant disregard for such guidelines is, for many proposal reviewers, a red flag that the researcher may not have his or her act together sufficiently to conduct the proposed research.

3. *When writing the first draft, focus more on organization and logical thought sequences than on exact wording, grammatical correctness, and spelling.* In Chapter 2, we mentioned that human beings can think about only a limited number of things at one time. All the processes that skillful writing involves—organizing thoughts, following a logical sequence, expressing ideas clearly and succinctly, using acceptable grammar and punctuation, spelling words correctly, and so forth—may far exceed that capacity. In other words, you may very well *not* be able to do it all at once!

In the first draft, you should focus your attention on the big picture—that is, on presenting your ideas in a logical, organized, and coherent fashion. At this point, don't worry about picky details. If you can't think of the right word, leave a blank where it should go and move on. If you can't remember how a word is spelled, spell it in whatever way you can for the time being and then perhaps indicate your uncertainty by adding a question mark in parentheses. If you're not sure about where the commas go, either insert them or don't, and then check a style manual later on.

As you write, you may even discover that you're missing an important piece of information, perhaps something that you need to track down at the library. Never mind, let it go for now. Leave a blank and make a note of what you need. Chances are that you will need several such bits of information. You can track them all down later, *after* you've finished your first draft.

4. *Present the research problem at the beginning of the first chapter.* As we stated earlier in the chapter, *always* lead off with your research problem. After all, the problem is at the very center of, and so drives, the entire project.

5. *Convince the reader of the importance of your project.* You must convince your readers that your planned research is not a trivial, meaningless undertaking—that, on the contrary, it can potentially make a substantial contribution to the body of human knowledge and may even, in some small way, help to make the world a better place. Although you won't want to get emotional in your presentation, you nevertheless want to generate interest in what you are doing: You want your readers to *want to know* what the outcome of your project will be.

6. *Assume that your readers know nothing whatsoever about your proposed project.* Novice researchers often leave out critical pieces of information, assuming, somehow, that their readers are already aware of these things. (We have found this to be especially true for students who are writing a proposal for a faculty committee that already has some knowledge about the planned research.) Such omissions can lead to many misunderstandings along the way, and these misunderstandings may get you in trouble later on.

Your proposal is the mechanism through which you describe, in a permanent written form, what you intend to do from beginning to end. In this respect, it is very much like a contract to which you and your reviewers will ultimately agree. Accordingly, leave nothing unsaid, no question unanswered.

7. *Describe your methods with as much detail and precision as possible.* The extent to which you can describe your method will depend to some degree on whether you are using a quantitative or qualitative approach. If you are using a quantitative approach, you will need to specify your sample, measurement instruments, and procedures with the utmost detail. If you are using a qualitative approach, you will probably be making some sampling and procedural decisions as the study proceeds. Even so, you should, at the proposal stage, outline your sources of data and procedures as specifically as possible. Remember, the more information your reviewers have about your proposed project, the better position they will be in to determine its worth and potential contribution.

8. *If you intend to use data that already exist, describe where the data are located and how you plan to secure them.* In some studies, and especially in historical research, a researcher may need certain kinds of records. In such a situation, the researcher should know their exact location. Many novice researchers begin research projects by assuming that records are available but learn too late that either no records exist or the needed records are in an inaccessible location or under such heavy restriction that they are not available. Answer the question, Where are the data located? in no uncertain terms, and determine that you have access to them.

Suppose that the necessary data are letters written by an important historical figure and that they are in the possession of the person's family. You may know where the letters are located, but do you know how will get them for your research purposes? Perhaps, in a case like this—or in any situation in which records are under the control of others—you might provide the names and addresses of the people who possess the data. You might also state that these custodians of the data have consented to your using the data for research purposes. Such details should be clearly stated in the proposal so that your sponsor, your academic committee, the funding agency, or whoever else is reading your proposal can clearly see that you will have ready access to the data.

9. *Describe how you will use the data to answer your research problem.* Even though you have not yet collected your data, you will nevertheless need to describe how you intend to organize, analyze, and interpret them so that you can solve your research problem. Do not assume that others will know what you intend to do. Spelling out the treatment and interpretation of the data is a tedious, time-consuming process. But the alternative—attempting to relegate it to the broad sweep, the quick and easy statement, the careless approach—almost invariably courts disaster. Interpretation of the data is the step that gives meaning to the entire enterprise and makes it a genuine research endeavor, and so it must be planned and specified well in advance.

To see how some novice researchers fail to answer this most important question—How will the data be interpreted?—let's examine an excerpt from an economics doctoral student's proposal for a dissertation about labor relations. The excerpt appears in Figure 6.1. The student's main research problem is to "analyze the attitudes of professional employees toward certain aspects of management policy and to evaluate the relationship between these attitudes and the responsibility of management to articulate such policy for its employees." The student has organized his discussion of the data in terms of specific subproblems, describing both data collection and data interpretation with respect to each subproblem. In the excerpt, we see how the student says he will resolve the following subproblem:

What does an analysis of the attitudes of employees toward management policy for salary increases and merit pay reveal?

FIGURE 6.1

Where is the interpretation of the data? An excerpt from a student's proposal

Restatement of *Subproblem 1*. The first subproblem is to determine through an analysis of employee responses the attitudes of employees toward certain aspects of management policy for salary increases and merit pay.

THE DATA NEEDED

The data needed to resolve this subproblem are those employee responses to questions concerning salary increases and merit pay.

WHERE THE DATA ARE LOCATED

The data are located in the employee responses to questions 3, 7, and 13 of the questionnaire, "Survey of Employee Attitudes Toward Management."

HOW THE DATA WILL BE SECURED

The data will be secured by accurately tabulating all of the responses of employees to the above questions on the questionnaire.

HOW THE DATA WILL BE INTERPRETED

From the responses of the questions, a table will be constructed similar to the following structural model. It will indicate the employee attitudes, their frequency, and the percentages of these attitudes of the total attitude response to each question.

Attitude	Frequency	Percentage
Totals		

A graph will then be constructed to show which attitudes received the greatest number of reactions and which had the least number of reactions. The median and the mean will also be found for the total group as a basis for comparison.

First read the student's restatement of the subproblem, his description of the data needed to resolve the problem, and his discussion of how he intends to secure those data. With these things in mind, read the section "How the Data Will Be Interpreted." What does the researcher really intend to do? Is he really going to *interpret* the data, to derive meaning from them? Is he going to "determine" anything *through an analysis of employee responses?*

Unfortunately, the student is not talking about interpreting the data. He is merely planning to *tabulate* and *graph* the data. He will rearrange them and present them in another form. The data remain almost as raw as they were originally in the questionnaire. The researcher also tells us that he will find two points of central tendency ("averages") for the data: the median and the mean. The median and mean of *what?* The frequencies? The percentages? Both? And *why* will he calculate the median and mean? What do these statistics tell us about "attitudes of employees toward certain aspects of management policy"? These are critical questions that should be answered *in the proposal*. In the student's proposal as it presently exists, there is no discussion of how the data relate to *attitudes of employees,* even though an understanding of these attitudes is central to resolving the subproblem.

What might the student do to interpret his data? After tabulating the data in the manner he describes, he might collapse the responses into two categories, or perhaps into a continuum of categories, that reflect either support of or opposition to management policies. Then he could carefully review each category to identify the characteristics of each. Were people who supported management lukewarm in their support? What keywords did they use in their responses? What did the overall category response indicate about the attitudes of the employees?

Despite its obvious weakness, the excerpt in Figure 6.1 does illustrate one effective strategy for discussing the analysis and interpretation of the data. In particular, it can be quite helpful to *address each subproblem separately.* In particular, for each subproblem, you might:

a. Restate the subproblem.
b. Clearly identify the data that relate to the subproblem.
c. Explain fully and unequivocally how you intend to analyze and interpret the data to resolve the subproblem.

More generally, *the plan for the treatment of the data should be so unequivocal and so specific that any other qualified person could carry out your research project, without your assistance, by means of your proposal alone.* Every contingency should be anticipated; every methodological problem should be resolved. The degree to which you delineate how the data will be interpreted will play a significant role in the success or failure of your research endeavor. The method of data interpretation is the key to research success, and it should be described with utmost care and precision.

10. *Use appendices to present informed consent letters, specific measurement instruments, and other detailed materials.* Although you need to describe your procedures precisely and completely, too much detail can interfere with the overall flow of your writing. Appendices provide an easy way to present any necessary details that are not central to the points you are trying to make. Simply refer to each appendix as it is relevant to your discussion, perhaps like this: "To recruit participants, the nature of the study will be described, and volunteers will be asked to read and sign an informed consent letter (Appendix D)."

GUIDELINES   REVISING YOUR PROPOSAL

You must remember that your first draft will almost certainly *not* be your last one. This is true not only for research proposals and reports but for other major writing projects as well. Here we offer some suggestions for polishing your proposal into its final form:

1. *Set the proposal aside for a few days.* After writing your first draft, put it aside for a while so that, later, you can approach it with a fresh eye. If you reread it too soon, you will read it with what you *thought you had said* still fresh in your mind and so won't necessarily read what you *actually wrote.*

2. *Read a paper (rather than electronic) copy of your first draft.* As we mentioned in Chapter 2, paper copies often reveal problems with a text that somehow escape our attention on the computer screen. We're not sure why this is, but we've repeatedly found it to be so.

Your proposal should, at this point at least, be double-spaced rather than single-spaced and have wide margins, thereby leaving you lots of room for writing corrections and comments. You should expect that *you will write all over your first draft.* Figure 6.2 presents many commonly used editing marks for small-scale changes. For more significant changes (e.g., adding and moving text), you may want to use arrows, indicate pages where sentences or paragraphs should be moved to or from, and have blank sheets of paper (or perhaps your computer) nearby for major rewrites.

3. *Carefully scrutinize what you have written, looking for disorganized thoughts and illogical thinking.* Look for places where you move unpredictably from one topic to another, go off on unnecessary tangents, or draw unwarranted conclusions. Also, look at each paragraph under each one of your headings: All paragraphs under a particular heading should deal specifically with the topic that the heading identifies.

4. *Look for places where you are not as clear as you might be.* Ambiguous phrases and sentences—those with several possible meanings and those with no obvious meaning at all—can wreak havoc in a research proposal. As an example, consider this excerpt from a review of the literature written by a former master's student:

It appears to be the case that not only is note taking superior for recall immediately after lecture, but that the entire memory storage and recall process is further strengthened as time goes on when one takes notes on a lecture. And, of course, this is generally how American college students are tested.

FIGURE 6.2

Commonly used editing marks

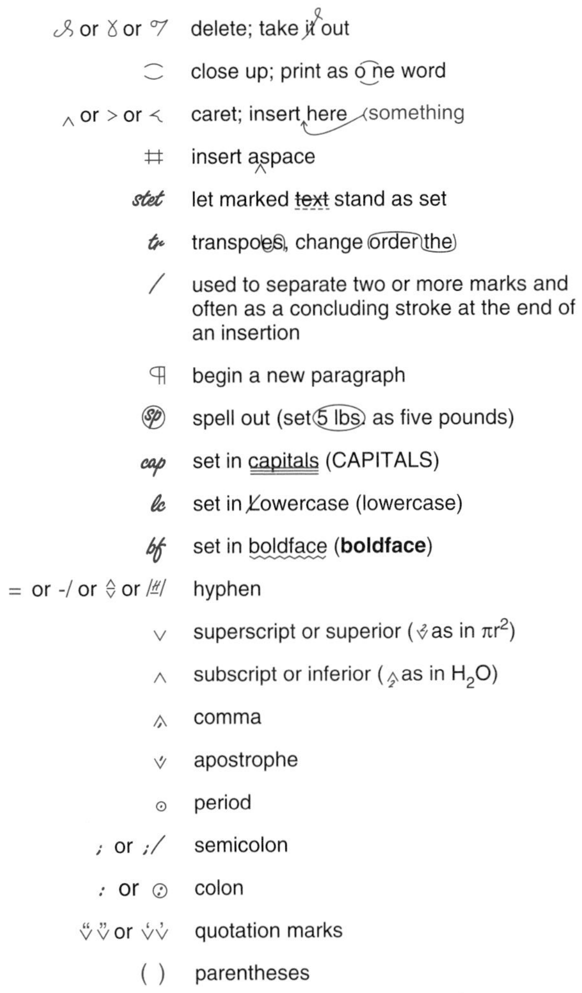

ℛ or 𝒳 or ℐ	delete; take it out
⌒	close up; print as one word
∧ or > or ＜	caret; insert here something
#	insert a space
stet	let marked text stand as set
tr	transpose, change order the
/	used to separate two or more marks and often as a concluding stroke at the end of an insertion
¶	begin a new paragraph
ⓢⓟ	spell out (set 5 lbs as five pounds)
cap	set in capitals (CAPITALS)
lc	set in lowercase (lowercase)
bf	set in boldface (**boldface**)
= or -/ or ⌃ or /#/	hyphen
∨	superscript or superior (∨ as in πr^2)
∧	subscript or inferior (∧ as in H_2O)
∧	comma
∨	apostrophe
⊙	period
; or ;/	semicolon
: or ⊙	colon
∨∨ or ∨∨	quotation marks
( )	parentheses

What does the student mean by the phrase "the entire memory storage and recall process is further strengthened"? And to what does the word *this* refer in the second sentence? Even though one of us authors is an educational psychologist who knows a great deal about both human memory processes and American testing procedures, neither of us has any idea what this student was trying to communicate.

5. *Keep your sentences simple and straightforward.* As a general rule, try to keep your sentences short. Vary the length, of course, but break up those long, contorted sentences into shorter, more succinct ones. Be alert to how and where you use adjectives, adverbs, and other modifiers. Misplaced phrases and clauses can create havoc with the thought you want to communicate.[2]

6. *Choose your words carefully.* A thesaurus—perhaps a book, the "thesaurus" feature in your word processing software, or an online thesaurus[3]—can help you find the exact word you need. Never use a long word where a short one will do. In a straightforward discussion, use one- or two-syllable words rather than longer ones. Use professional jargon only when you need it to relate your ideas to existing theory and literature in the discipline.

7. *Check carefully for errors in grammar, punctuation, and spelling.* Now is the time to attend to grammar, punctuation, spelling, and other minor details. Ultimately you want your proposal to

---

[2] Consider this example of misplaced modification in a classified ad: "Piano for sale by a woman with beautifully carved mahogany legs that has arthritis and cannot play anymore." Move the prepositional phrase and add a comma, and the ad makes much more sense: "FOR SALE: A piano with beautifully carved mahogany legs, by a woman who has arthritis and cannot play anymore."

[3] You can find Merriam-Webster's online dictionary and thesaurus at www.m-w.com/.

be, if not perfect, then as close to perfect as any human being can make it. Careless errors and other signs of sloppiness may suggest to your reviewers that the way you conduct your research project may be equally careless and sloppy.

Your word processing software will, of course, be helpful in this respect. For instance, *use the grammar checker*. Grammar checkers can search for word expressions, clichés, multiple negation, too many prepositional phrases, and other common problems. Some word processors even have a built-in function to measure the reading level of your writing; such information might be helpful in ensuring that you are writing at the appropriate level for your audience.

In addition, *use the spell checker, but don't rely on it exclusively*. As we pointed out in Chapter 2, a spell checker typically does nothing more than check each word to see if it is a "match" with a word in the English language or in some other list that you specify. It will not tell you whether you have used the right words in every case. So even if you take advantage of the spell checker, always, *always* follow up by reading your document, word for word, to be sure that every word is spelled correctly. If you're a poor speller, then ask someone else (a good speller, obviously) to proofread the entire document for errors.

8. *Consider the feasibility of your project once again.* Now that you've laid everything out in the proposal, check one more time to be sure that you have the time, resources, and energy to do everything you say you are going to do.

9. *Print out your second draft, and read your proposal carefully once again.* Look critically at each thought as it stands on paper. Do the words say exactly what you want them to say? Read carefully phrase by phrase. See whether one word will carry the burden of two or more. Throw out superfluous words.

10. *Seek the feedback of others.* We cannot stress this point enough. No matter how hard you try, you cannot be as objective as you'd like to be when you read your own writing. Ask people to read and critique what you've written. Don't ask friends or relatives who are likely to give you a rubber stamp of approval; instead, ask people who will read your work thoroughly, give you critical feedback, and make constructive suggestions.

One final comment: *Get used to writing.* Researchers write continuously—sometimes to communicate with others, at other times to facilitate their own thinking. Paper or a word processor can be effective for personal brainstorming sessions. Take time to sit back and use pencil or keyboard as to help you clarify your thoughts and ideas.

COMMON WEAKNESSES IN RESEARCH PROPOSALS

Proposals submitted to funding agencies undergo a rigorous screening process. The agencies typically receive many more proposals than they can possibly support, and so they can be quite picky about the research projects they select. In fact, the agencies *should* be picky. There is little value in funding a project with a poorly conceived design, inappropriate data, or questionable statistical analysis, because any conclusions that emerge from the project will be shaky at best.

Allen (1960) and Cuca and McLoughlin (1987) have described the kinds of weaknesses they saw in proposals submitted to the National Institutes of Health (NIH)—weaknesses that prevented the proposed research projects from being funded. In Figure 6.3, we list many of the shortcomings these authors have described. In our experience, the list is equally applicable to a wide range of disciplines.

Proposals submitted by students for academic research projects (e.g., for theses and dissertations) tend to have many of the weaknesses listed in Figure 6.3. We urge you to study the figure carefully so that you can avoid such problems.

At this point, a comment by George N. Eaves in *Grants Magazine* is particularly apropos:

> I have concluded that the single most important qualification for a beginning investigator's successful competition for a grant is a demonstration of outstanding qualifications. These qualifications are not the kind usually presented in a biographical sketch, such as advanced degrees and publications, but the demonstrated ability to think clearly and logically, to express logical thought concisely and cogently, to discriminate between the significant and the inconsequential, to display technical prowess, to handle abstract thought, to analyze data objectively and accurately,

Weaknesses related to the *Research Problem:*
- The description of the project is so nebulous and unfocused that the purpose of the research is unclear.
- The problem is unimportant or unlikely to yield new information.
- The hypothesis is ill-defined, doubtful, or unsound, or it rests on insufficient evidence.
- The problem is more complex than the investigator realizes.
- The problem is of interest only to a particular, localized group, or in some other way has limited relevance to the field as a whole.

Weaknesses related to the *Research Design and Methodology:*
- The description of the design and/or method is so vague and unfocused as to prevent adequate evaluation of its worth.
- The data the investigator wishes to use are either difficult to obtain or inappropriate for the research problem.
- The proposed methods, measurement instruments, or procedures are inappropriate for the research problem.
- Appropriate controls are either lacking or inadequate.
- The equipment to be used is outdated or inappropriate.
- The statistical analysis has not received adequate consideration, is too simplistic, or is unlikely to yield accurate and clear-cut results.

Weaknesses related to the *Investigator:*
- The investigator does not have sufficient training or experience for the proposed research.
- The investigator appears to be unfamiliar with the literature relevant to the research problem.
- The investigator has insufficient time to devote to the project.

Weaknesses related to *Resources:*
- The institutional setting is unfavorable for the proposed research.
- The proposed use of equipment, support staff, or other resources is unrealistic.

Based on data presented by Allen (1960) and Cuca and McLoughlin (1987).

and to interpret results confidently and conservatively. These capabilities characterize scholarship, and it is through scholarship that an applicant for a research grant can demonstrate his [or her] qualifications. (Eaves, 1984, p. 151)

We might also add that this same constellation of qualities is what graduate professors look for in candidates for the doctoral degree.

PRACTICAL APPLICATION STRENGTHENING YOUR PROPOSAL

Once you have written what you believe to be your final proposal, you should scrutinize it one more time, preferably after you've set it aside for a few days. *Take a critical approach, looking for what's wrong rather than what's right.* The following checklist can provide guidance about what to look for.

 **CHECKLIST**

FEATURES DETRACTING FROM PROPOSAL EFFECTIVENESS

Check each item to be sure that your proposal exhibits *none* of the following characteristics:

FOR ANY RESEARCH PROPOSAL:

_____ 1. The statement of the problem is vague, or it is so obscured by discussions of other topics that it is impossible to find.

_____ 2. The methodology is incompletely described; an explanation of exactly how the research will be conducted is not specifically delineated.

_____   3. The proposed treatment of each subproblem is general and cursory; it does not convey clearly how the data will be used and interpreted to resolve the subproblem or the overall research problem.

_____   4. Criteria for the admissibility of the data are weak or nonexistent.

_____   5. The proposal lacks sharpness. It is not logically organized. Without clear divisions that set forth the areas of the research project, it rambles. The reader has difficulty isolating the discussion of the problem, the subproblems, the related studies, the methodology, the interpretation of the data, and other related parts of the proposal.

_____   6. The proposal is phrased in terms that are too general, ambiguous, or imprecise to be useful for evaluation. Such phrases as "tests will be given" and "tests will be made" are largely meaningless.

_____   7. The format of the proposal deviates from the guidelines set forth in the informational literature of the approval group or funding agency.

FOR A PROPOSAL TO A FUNDING AGENCY:

_____   8. The problem does not address the research area outlined by the funding agency.

_____   9. The proposal is too ambitious for the grant money available.

_____   10. Items included in the budget are disallowed by the terms of the grant.

_____   11. A clear and explicit budget statement outlining program expenditures is lacking, or the summary of estimated costs is ambiguous and indefinite.

_____   12. The section of the proposal explaining the study's importance is not set forth clearly enough for the funding agency to see a relationship of the study to the purpose for which the grant is awarded.

FINAL THOUGHTS ABOUT PROPOSAL WRITING

Perhaps the most challenging part of a proposal, at least for beginning researchers, is the discussion of how the data will be handled. This is also the most tedious part of the proposal to write; most of us are reluctant to spell out every minute detail of procedure and to support our choices with a rationale based solidly on accepted research methodology and analytical thinking. The weakness of many proposals is the hope that what we find too tedious to state specifically, others will nevertheless *assume* that we will do. In a proposal, you cannot ask your reader to make such a journey of faith.

When drawing up a contract, an attorney meticulously includes all the rights and obligations of the parties included in the contract. The proposal writer should prepare a proposal with the same precision. For, in a sense, a proposal is, under certain circumstances, a form of contract, or what we might call a *quasi* contract.

Are you submitting a proposal for a grant to underwrite a research project? If so, you (as the party of the first part) are proposing to undertake a research project in exchange for a monetary consideration from the agency providing the grant (the party of the second part). Regarded from a legal standpoint, your proposal, on acceptance by the granting agency, is a formal contractual relationship.

Now let's look at the situation from an academic standpoint. Certainly there are differences between a proposal presented to a funding agency and a proposal presented by a student to an academic advisor. Yet in another way, the two kinds of proposals are very similar: In both cases, the basic elements of the research problem, the methodology, the data, and any other factors critical to conducting the inquiry must be clearly set forth and mutually agreed on before the actual research activity can begin.

Usually, faculty advisors will want to review the proposal periodically as it is being developed; they will also want to monitor your progress as you proceed with your study. Such a process of ongoing guidance from an experienced professional and researcher is to be welcomed, not avoided. It is perhaps the single best way you can learn the tricks of the research trade.

Proposals are mandatory for many academic research projects. For instance, any thesis or dissertation must begin with a proposal, and any project involving human subjects must get IRB approval before it ever gets off the ground. But even when a proposal is not mandatory, it is always *advisable,* regardless of the magnitude of the project or its academic sophistication. From a student's perspective, a proposal has two distinct advantages:

1. It helps the student organize the research activity.
2. It communicates to the student's advisor what the student intends to do, thereby enabling the advisor to provide counsel and guidance in areas that may pose exceptional difficulty.

A proposal for any research endeavor merits words that are carefully chosen, a style that is clear and concise, an attention to the most minute procedural detail, and for each procedure, a rationale that is logically and clearly stated. This is a tall order, but the result reveals the scholarship of the proposal author as perhaps no other academic assignment can ever do.

It is an awesome fact to contemplate, but to no small degree *your proposal is you*! It defines your ability to think critically and to express your thoughts clearly. *It is the practical application of your educational competence laid bare upon a sheet of paper.*

A SAMPLE RESEARCH PROPOSAL

We conclude this chapter by presenting an example of what a research proposal—in this case, a proposal for a doctoral dissertation at the University of Northern Colorado—might look like. The author, Rosenna Bakari, uses the very first paragraph of the proposal to present the research problem clearly and concisely:

> Attitudes that teachers bring into the classroom are a critical factor in the academic failure of African American students (Irvine, 1990). Preliminary research suggests that many in-service and prospective teachers do not hold positive attitudes toward teaching African American students (Irvine, 1990). As a result, many researchers see attitudes and values clarification of preservice teachers concerning race as a critical aspect of multicultural teacher education (Gay, 1994; Wiggins & Follo, 1999; Zeichner, 1996). However, there are no adequate instruments available to measure preservice teachers' attitudes about teaching African American students. Hence, the intent of this research is to develop and validate an instrument to measure preservice teachers' attitudes toward teaching African American students. (p. 1)

Now go to our Companion Website at http://www.prenhall.com/leedy to assess your understanding of chapter content and to complete the projects that will help you learn how to conduct research.

We now fast-forward to Bakari's methodology section. As we have in previous chapters, we present the proposal itself on the left and add our observations on the right.

DISSERTATION ANALYSIS 3

METHODOLOGY	Comments
This study is intended to develop and validate a survey instrument that assesses preservice teachers' attitudes toward teaching African American students. The survey instrument was developed based on educational recommendations and research literature indicating that culture is an important consideration in educating African American students effectively. Two pilot studies were conducted as preliminary investigations. This chapter will summarize the pilot studies and discuss the methodology of the current study. [*The student describes the two pilot studies she conducted previously relative to her present study. We pick the proposal up later, as she describes her proposed sample, measurement instruments, data collection, and data analysis.*]	*The author begins by reminding the reader of the purpose of the proposed research. The repetition of the research problem at this point, though not essential, is helpful to the reader, who can then put the procedures that follow into proper perspective.* *The first paragraph is an* advance organizer *for the reader, who then can follow the author's subsequent train of thought more easily.*

Sample

Three sub-groups will be solicited for participation. The first group will represent institutions where preservice teachers have little exposure to African American issues in education. The majority of participants are expected to be White and have little exposure to African American populations.

In the second group, preservice teachers will be solicited from teacher education programs that have more program goals or objectives related to teaching African American students. For example, diversity courses may be a requirement for graduation. In addition, preservice teachers are likely to have greater exposure to African American student populations during student teaching, in their university courses, or in their living communities than group one. However, the majority of participants are still expected to be White.

The third group of preservice teachers will be solicited from historically Black colleges or universities (HBCUs). Although HBCUs may differ in many respects, their focus is a "commitment, dedication, and determination to enhance the quality of life for African Americans" (Duhon-Sells, Peoples, Moore, & Page, 1996, p. 795). The majority of participants from this group are expected to be African American.

A minimum of 100 students will be solicited from each group. Sample size is critical because it provides a basis for the estimation of sampling error (Hair, Anderson, Tatham & Black, 1995). A sample size of at least 100 is recommended to conduct a confirmatory factor analysis because a sample less than 100 may not provide enough statistical power to reject the null hypothesis. A small sample could lead to acceptance of a model which is not necessarily a good fit, simply because there was not enough statistical power to reject the model. On the other hand, if the sample is too large, the model may be rejected due to sensitivity in detecting small differences, because the larger the sample, the more sensitive the test is to detecting differences (Hair, Anderson, Tatham & Black, 1995). Hair, Anderson, Tatham, and Black (1995) recommend a sample size between 100 and 200.

In order to achieve the minimum participant requirement for each group, involvement from more than one university may be necessary. For instance, four universities may represent group one while two universities may represent group two. This flexibility is important due to the variability in size of teacher education programs. Moreover, the reliance on instructors' willingness to contribute class time to this research may minimize the number of participants. All participants will be undergraduate or graduate preservice teachers and enrolled in a required course for a teacher preparation program. Graduate students must also be in pursuit of initial teacher certification. Students may be in any phase of their teacher preparation program. Preservice teachers who are not currently enrolled in any of the classes where the instrument will be distributed will not be selected for participation. Further, only students who are in attendance on the day the instrument is distributed will be selected for participation. For those students solicited to participate, participation will be voluntary, and anonymous.

Instrumentation

Four instruments will be employed for data collection in this research. They include the demographic data sheet, Attitudes toward Teaching African American Students Survey, Responding Desirably on Attitudes and Opinions measurement (RD-16), and General Attitudes toward Teaching Survey. The demographic data sheet and the Teachers' Attitudes toward Teaching African American Students Survey (TAASS) were both designed by the

---

Earlier in the proposal the author presented her rationale for giving the instrument to three different groups. She predicted that the three groups would, on average, respond differently to the instrument, thereby providing evidence for the validity of the instrument (see Chapter 5).

Although the author is expecting the three groups to have different proportions of students from different racial groups, she will nevertheless seek information in support of her prediction through a demographic information sheet that she describes later in her proposal.

Always "spell out" what an abbreviation stands for before using it. For instance, here the author refers to "historically Black colleges or universities" and identifies the abbreviation HBCU in parentheses. She can then use "HBCU" in future discussions and her readers will know to what she is referring.

Here the author provides a justification for her sample size. We discuss the issue of statistical power in Chapter 11; at that point, we also revisit the concept of a null hypothesis.

The author explains why she is drawing her sample from several universities. It appears that she is predicting, and then answering, the kinds of questions the reader might have about her method.

The author gives enough information about her sample to enable any qualified reader to conduct the study she proposes. In addition, by describing the nature of her sample, she provides information about the population to which her study's results could reasonably be generalized.

Once again we see an advance organizer for the discussion that follows.

The author uses abbreviations (TAASS and RD-16) for two of her instruments. To be consistent, she should probably introduce them both in the second sentence of the paragraph, rather than leave TAASS for the third sentence as she does here.

researcher for this particular study. The General Attitudes toward Teaching Survey is an adaptation from a published Teacher Efficacy Scale and the TAASS. The RD-16 is a published instrument designed to measure social desirability. A description of the four instruments follows.

[*Under four separate subheadings, the author describes each instrument in detail, including the specific items that each one includes and any known information about validity and reliability.*]

Data Collection

Participants will be contacted in their classes, where the instructor has agreed to allow class time to conduct this research. Participants will be told that the objective of the research is to gather information about future teachers, particularly, who they are (demographics) and what they believe about teaching. To avoid a social desirability response set, participants will not be informed about the specific focus of the study (developing and validating an instrument to measure preservice teachers' attitudes toward teaching African American students). A statement will be read aloud to the class that informs students of their right to refuse to participate without any negative consequences, as well as the possibility of being requested to participate in follow-up research (test-retest reliability for the TAASS).

Requests for names and student identification numbers will be prohibited as any part of the data collection. However, participants will be asked to create identifications for themselves that cannot be traced to them by others. Pseudo-identification is necessary for students to remain anonymous, yet allows the researcher to conduct a retest for reliability measures. Examples of anonymous identifications will be given, such as a favorite noun, verb, or adjective (chair, jump, lazy). Students will be duly cautioned about selecting identifications that can be traced to them, such as mothers' maiden names, any part of their social security numbers, or nicknames.

Individual surveys will not be seen by anyone other than the participant once they are completed. Students will be requested to place their completed surveys in a designated "return" envelope. The last student to return the surveys will be requested to seal the return envelope. Only when the last survey is placed in the return envelope, and the envelope is sealed, will the administrator be permitted to handle the materials.

In classes where the researcher does not administer the instruments, research packets will be prepared for the person who does. Research packets will contain a disclosure statement to be read aloud to the participants. In addition to the disclosure sheet, the packets will include a demographic information sheet, the TAASS, and only one of the validity criteria instruments. Half of the participants will receive the RD-16 in their packet, and the other half will receive the General Attitudes Scale. The order of the instruments will also vary in the packets, with the exception of the demographic data sheet. The demographic data sheet will always appear last. Administrators will be instructed to avoid interpreting items on any of the three survey instruments. If students ask for interpretation of any items on the surveys, administrators will be instructed to respond, "Please use your best interpretation to answer all the items." However, clarifications may be made about the demographic information, if requested.

Three weeks after the initial research data has been collected, classes will be selected (based on availability) for retest of the TAASS. Participants will be solicited in a minimum of three classes that participated in the initial research. Only the TAASS will be administered for the retest. Students will be required to use the pseudo-identification selected in the initial research.

The heading "Procedure" is more commonly used than "Data Collection" in human subjects research, but the latter is acceptable as well.

Here the author describes her procedures regarding informed consent.

Here she describes the steps she will take to ensure participants' right to privacy.

Notice how the author uses future tense *to describe her proposed methodology. Later, when she rewrites the methodology section for her final research report, she will, of course, change her description of procedures to* past tense.

The author will vary the order in which participants respond to the instrument, presumably as a way of determining whether taking one instrument affects how a participant responds to the instruments that follow.

The author is taking steps to increase the reliability *of the instrument by* standardizing *its administration (see Chapter 5).*

The author will administer the TAASS to some participants twice so that she can determine its test-retest reliability *(see Chapter 5).*

Data Analysis

   LISREL and SPSS statistical software will be used for all analyses. As Hair, Anderson, Tatham, and Black (1995) point out, there is no method of dealing with missing data that is free of disadvantages. Anytime missing data is imputed there is a risk of biasing the results (e.g., distributions, or correlation). Even the option of using the complete case approach has disadvantages. When only completed data is used, there is a risk of reducing the sample size to an inappropriate number. Moreover, the results may no longer be generalizable to the intended population if the missing data is systematized rather than randomized (Hair, Anderson, Tatham & Black, 1995). Before any approach will be decided as to how to handle missing data, the missing data will be reviewed for systematic avoidance of response.

   [The author then describes the specific analyses she plans to conduct and how they relate to her research problem.]

Notice that the author describes her proposed methods of data analysis as well as her methods of data collection. By doing so, she helps the reader determine whether her analyses will be appropriate for her research questions.

Notice, too, that the author will consider the nature of the data before and during her data analyses.

A book by Hair, Anderson, Tatham, and Black (1995) is cited several times in the methodology section. To be consistent with APA style (which she adheres to in her proposal), the author should list all four authors only for the first citation; after that, she can shorten the citation to "Hair et al. (1995)."

NOTE. Excerpt is from a research proposal submitted by Rosenna Bakari to the University of Northern Colorado, Greeley, in partial fulfillment of the requirement for the degree of Doctor of Philosophy. Reprinted with permission.

FOR FURTHER READING

Beebe, L. (Ed.). (1992). *Professional writing for the human services.* Washington, DC: National Association of Social Workers Press.

Bjelland, H. (1992). *Business writing the modular way.* Ann Arbor, MI: Books on Demand.

Bowman, J. P. (1992). *How to write proposals that produce.* Phoenix, AZ: Oryx.

Brewer, E. W. (1993). *Finding funding: Grantwriting for the financially challenged educator.* Thousand Oaks, CA: Corwin Press.

Carlson, M. (1995). *Winning grants step by step.* San Francisco: Jossey-Bass.

DeBakey, L. (1976). The persuasive proposal. *Journal of Technical Writing and Communication, 6*(1), 5–25.

Ges and Williams, Inc. (1991). *Grantsmanship and proposal writing manual.* Dubuque, IA: Kendall/Hunt.

Krathwohl, D. R. (1988). *How to prepare a research proposal: Guidelines for funding and dissertations in the social and behavioral sciences.* Syracuse, NY: Syracuse University Press.

Miner, L. E., & Miner, J. T. (2003). *Proposal planning and writing* (3rd ed.). Phoenix, AZ: Oryx Press.

Moore, P. (1991). Grant workshop: To win over reviewers, make their job easy. *Federal Grants and Contracts Weekly, 15*(21), 7–8.

Ogden, T. E., & Goldberg, I. A. (Eds.). (2002). *Research proposals: A guide to success* (3rd ed.). San Diego, CA: Academic Press.

Reif-Lehrer, L. (1995). *Grant application writer's handbook* (3rd ed.). Boston: Jones & Bartlett.

Ries, J. B. (1995). *Applying for research funding: Getting started and getting funded.* Thousand Oaks, CA: Sage.

Rudestam, K. E., & Newton, R. R. (1992). *Surviving your dissertation.* Thousand Oaks, CA: Sage.

Smith, M. C., & Carney, R. N. (1999). Strategies for writing successful AERA proposals. *Educational Researcher, 28*(1), 42–45, 58.

Wagner, P. D. (1991). On writing a grant application: A personal view. *Physiologist, 34,* 29–31.

Part III
Qualitative Research Methodologies

7

Qualitative Research

To answer some research questions, we cannot skim across the surface. We must dig deep to get a complete understanding of the phenomenon we are studying. In qualitative research, we do indeed dig deep: We collect numerous forms of data and examine them from various angles to construct a rich and meaningful picture of a complex, multifaceted situation.

The term **qualitative research** encompasses several approaches to research that are, in some respects, quite different from one another. Yet all qualitative approaches have two things in common. First, they focus on phenomena that occur in natural settings—that is, in the "real world." And second, they involve studying those phenomena in all their complexity. Qualitative researchers rarely try to simplify what they observe. Instead, they recognize that the issue they are studying has many dimensions and layers, and so they try to portray the issue in its multifaceted form.

As noted in Chapter 2, most researchers strive for objectivity in their research. They believe that their observations should be influenced as little as possible by any perceptions, impressions, and biases they may have. By maintaining objectivity, they hope to maximize their chances of determining the ultimate Truth we spoke of in Chapter 5. But some qualitative researchers are an exception in this regard. They argue that, although objective methods may be appropriate for studying physical events such as electricity, chemical reactions, and black holes, an objective approach to studying human events—interpersonal relationships, social structures, creative products, and so on—is neither desirable nor, perhaps, even possible (Eisner, 1998; Moss, 1996; Wolcott, 1994). Qualitative researchers believe that the researcher's ability to interpret and make sense of what he or she sees is critical for understanding any social phenomenon. In this sense, *the researcher is an instrument* in much the same way that a sociogram, rating scale, or intelligence test is an instrument.

Furthermore, some qualitative researchers believe that there isn't necessarily a single, ultimate Truth to be discovered. Instead, there may be multiple perspectives held by different individuals, with each of these perspectives having equal validity, or truth (Creswell, 1998; Guba & Lincoln, 1988). One goal of a quality study, then, might be to reveal the nature of these multiple perspectives.

We see qualitative studies in many academic disciplines, including anthropology, sociology, history, political science, medicine, psychology, and education. In some disciplines, such as psychology and education, qualitative approaches were once frowned upon (due largely to their subjective nature) and have only recently gained wide acceptance as legitimate research.

Yet we should hardly think of qualitative research as being "new" or "modern." In fact, many researchers believe that all inquiry starts out in a qualitative form (e.g., Lauer & Asher, 1988). When little information exists on a topic, when variables are unknown, when a relevant theory base is inadequate or missing, a qualitative study can help define what is important—that is, *what needs to be studied*. The field of medicine, as one example, makes extensive use of qualitative methods when unique or puzzling cases are first observed. Early efforts in biology to classify species and to create taxonomies were certainly qualitative efforts. The analysis of historical data is almost completely qualitative. And social scientists often look subjectively for patterns in the complex phenomena they observe.

In this chapter, we give you a general idea of what qualitative research is and what it strives to accomplish. Included in the chapter are descriptions of five kinds of qualitative studies: case studies, ethnographies, phenomenological studies, grounded theory studies, and content analyses. We will describe a sixth kind, historical research, in Chapter 8.

THE NATURE OF THE RESEARCH PROBLEM AND PLANNING IN QUALITATIVE RESEARCH

In Chapter 3, we emphasized the importance of pinning down the problem with utmost precision. Here, too, we sometimes find an exception in qualitative research. Qualitative researchers often formulate only general research problems and ask only general questions about the phenomenon they are studying. For example, they might ask, What is the nature of the culture of people living in Samoa?, or What is it like to live with someone who has Alzheimer's disease?, or How can a teacher use principles from behaviorist psychology to help a student with autism succeed in an elementary school classroom? Such research problems and questions do not remain so loosely defined, however. As a study proceeds, the qualitative researcher gains increasing understanding of the phenomenon under investigation and so becomes increasingly able to ask specific questions and formulate specific hypotheses.

Because qualitative researchers tend to ask open-ended questions at the beginning of an investigation, they sometimes have difficulty identifying ahead of time the exact methods they will use. Initially, they may select only a general approach suitable for their purpose, perhaps selecting a case study, ethnography, or content analysis. As they learn more about what they are studying and so can ask more specific questions, so, too, can they better specify what methods they should use to answer those questions.

The methodology in a qualitative study, then, continues to evolve over the course of the investigation. Despite this fact, we must emphasize that *qualitative research requires considerable preparation and planning*. The researcher must be well trained in observation techniques, interview strategies, and whatever other data collection methods are likely to be necessary to answer the research problem. The researcher must have a firm grasp of previous research related to the problem so that he or she knows what to look for and can separate important information from unimportant details in what he or she observes (a grounded theory study is an exception here, for reasons you will discover shortly). And the researcher must be adept at wading through huge amounts of data and finding a meaningful order in what, to someone else, may seem like chaos. For these reasons, a qualitative study can be a challenging task indeed. It is definitely *not* the approach to take if you're looking for quick results and easy answers.

WHEN TO CHOOSE A QUALITATIVE APPROACH

Qualitative research studies typically serve one or more of the following purposes (Peshkin, 1993):

- *Description.* They can reveal the nature of certain situations, settings, processes, relationships, systems, or people.
- *Interpretation.* They enable a researcher to (a) gain new insights about a particular phenomenon, (b) develop new concepts or theoretical perspectives about the phenomenon, and/or (c) discover the problems that exist within the phenomenon.

▓ *Verification.*   They allow a researcher to test the validity of certain assumptions, claims, theories, or generalizations within real-world contexts.

▓ *Evaluation.*   They provide a means through which a researcher can judge the effectiveness of particular policies, practices, or innovations.

As a general rule, qualitative studies do *not* allow the researcher to identify cause-effect relationships—to answer questions such as What caused what? or Why did such-and-such happen? You will need quantitative research, especially experimental studies, to answer questions of this kind.

QUALITATIVE RESEARCH DESIGNS

In this section, we describe five common qualitative research designs. We give you enough information to help you determine whether one of these approaches might be suitable for your research question, and we briefly describe the specific nature of the method, data analysis, and research report. Later in the chapter, we discuss data collection strategies and data analysis strategies that are more broadly applicable to qualitative designs.

A single chapter cannot cover everything you would need to know to carry out a solid qualitative research project. Should you choose to conduct a qualitative study, we urge you to take advantage of the resources listed in the "For Further Reading" section at the end of the chapter.

Remember, too, that of all the designs we describe in this book, qualitative research methods are the least prescriptive (Eisner, 1998). There are no magic formulas, no cookbook recipes for conducting a qualitative study. This book, as well as any others that you may read, can give you only general guidelines based on the experiences of those qualitative researchers who have gone before you. In a qualitative study, the specific methods that you use will ultimately be constrained only by the limits of your imagination.

CASE STUDY

In a **case study**, a particular individual, program, or event is studied in depth for a defined period of time. For example, a medical researcher might study the nature, course, and treatment of a rare illness for a particular patient. An educator might study and analyze the instructional strategies that a master teacher uses to teach high school history. A political scientist might study the origins and development of a politician's campaign as he or she runs for public office. Case studies are common not only in medicine, education, and political science, but also in law, psychology, sociology, and anthropology.

Sometimes researchers focus on a single case, perhaps because its unique or exceptional qualities can promote understanding or inform practice for similar situations. In other instances, researchers study two or more cases—often cases that are different in certain key ways—to make comparisons, build theory, or propose generalizations; such an approach is called a *multiple* or *collective* case study.

A case study may be especially suitable for learning more about a little known or poorly understood situation. It may also be useful for investigating how an individual or program changes over time, perhaps as the result of certain circumstances or interventions. In either circumstance, it is useful for generating or providing preliminary support for hypotheses. Its major weakness is that, especially when only a single case is involved, we can't be sure that the findings are generalizable to other situations.

METHOD.   In a case study, the researcher collects extensive data on the individual(s), program(s), or event(s) on which the investigation is focused. These data often include observations, interviews, documents (e.g., newspaper articles), past records (e.g., previous test scores), and audiovisual materials (e.g., photographs, videotapes, audiotapes). In many instances, the researcher may spend an extended period of time on site and interact regularly with the people who are being studied.

The researcher also records details about the context surrounding the case, including information about the physical environment and any historical, economic, and social factors that have bearing on the situation. By identifying the context of the case, the researcher helps others who read the case study draw conclusions about the extent to which its findings might be generalizable to other situations.

DATA ANALYSIS.   Data analysis in a case study typically involves the following steps (Creswell, 1998; Stake, 1995):

1. *Organization of details about the case.*   The specific "facts" about the case are arranged in a logical (e.g., chronological) order.
2. *Categorization of data.*   Categories are identified that can help cluster the data into meaningful groups. (For instance, a researcher studying the course of a political campaign might think in terms of "campaign strategies," "fund-raising activities," "news media accounts," "setbacks," etc.)
3. *Interpretation of single instances.*   Specific documents, occurrences, and other bits of data are examined for the specific meanings they might have in relation to the case.
4. *Identification of patterns.*   The data and their interpretations are scrutinized for underlying themes and other patterns that characterize the case more broadly than a single piece of information can reveal.
5. *Synthesis and generalizations.*   An overall portrait of the case is constructed. Conclusions are drawn that may have implications beyond the specific case that has been studied.

Particularly when only a single case is studied, any generalizations made are, of course, tentative and must await further support from other studies—perhaps support from additional case studies, other kinds of qualitative studies, or experimental research.

A case study researcher often begins to analyze the data during the data collection process; preliminary conclusions are likely to influence the kind of data he or she seeks out and collects in later parts of the study. Ultimately the researcher must look for convergence (*triangulation*) of the data: Many separate pieces of information must all point to the same conclusion.

THE RESEARCH REPORT.   If you conduct a case study, you will probably want to include the following in your report:

1. *A rationale for studying the case.*   Explain why the case was worthy of in-depth study—in other words, how it will contribute to human beings' knowledge about the world.
2. *A detailed description of the facts related to the case.*   Describe the specific individual(s), program(s), or event(s) you studied, as well as the setting and any other uncontested facts about the case. At this point, you should be as thorough and as objective as possible.
3. *A description of the data you collected.*   Tell your readers what observations you made, whom you interviewed, what documents you examined, and so on.
4. *A discussion of the patterns you found.*   Describe any trends, themes, personality characteristics, and so on, that the data suggest. At this point, you are going beyond the facts themselves to your *interpretation* of the facts. Support each pattern you identify with sufficient evidence to convince the reader that the pattern does, in fact, accurately portray the data. If some data contradict the patterns you propose, however, you should describe those as well. *Even though you are interpreting as well as reporting data, you want to present as complete and unbiased an account of the case as you possibly can.*
5. *A connection to the larger scheme of things.*   In some way, you need to answer the question, So what? In what way does the case study contribute to our knowledge about some aspect of the human experience? The connection(s) you make here might take one or more of several forms. You might compare the case with other, previously reported cases and note similarities and dissimilarities. You might argue that the case either supports or disconfirms an existing hypothesis or theory. Or you might use the case to support your contention that a particular intervention—perhaps a medical treatment, teaching method, or campaign strategy—can be a highly effective one.

ETHNOGRAPHY

In a case study, the researcher looks at a particular person, program, or event in considerable depth. In an **ethnography,** the researcher looks at an *entire group*—more specifically, a group that shares a common culture—in depth. The researcher studies the group in its natural setting for a lengthy period of time, often several months or even several years. The focus of investigation is on the everyday behaviors (e.g., interactions, language, rituals) of the people in the group, with an intent to identify cultural norms, beliefs, social structures, and other cultural patterns.

Ethnographies were first used in cultural anthropology, but they are now seen in sociology, psychology, and education as well. The conception of the type of "culture" that can be studied has also changed over time: Whereas ethnographies once focused on large cultural units (e.g., the island of Samoa), in recent years they have been used to study such "cultures" as massage parlors, kindergartens, and homeless shelters (Bateman, 1990).

An ethnography is especially useful for gaining an understanding of the complexities of a particular, intact culture. It allows considerable flexibility in the choice of methods used to obtain information about the culture. Such flexibility can be either an advantage (to the astute researcher who knows what to look for) or a disadvantage (to the novice who may be overwhelmed and distracted by unimportant details). Hence, if you decide that an ethnography is the approach most suitable for your research problem, we urge you to get a solid grounding in cultural anthropology before you venture into the field (Creswell, 1998).

METHOD.   Site-based fieldwork is the *sine qua non*—the essence—of any ethnography. Prolonged engagement in the cultural group's natural setting gives the researcher time to observe and record processes that would be almost impossible to learn about by using any other approach.

The first step in an ethnographic study is to gain access to a site appropriate for answering the researcher's general research problem or question. Ideally, the site should be one in which the researcher is a "stranger" and has no vested interest in the outcome of the study. A site that the researcher knows well (perhaps one where he or she is acquainted with some of the group members) may be more accessible and convenient, but by being so close to the situation, the researcher may have difficulty looking at it with sufficient detachment to gain a realistic perspective of the processes he or she is observing (Creswell, 1998).

To gain access to a site, the researcher must often go through a **gatekeeper,** a person who can provide a smooth entrance into the site. This individual might be a tribal chief in a community in a developing country, a principal or teacher in a school or classroom, or a program director in a shelter for the homeless.

After gaining entry into the site, the researcher must establish rapport with the people being studied and gain their trust. At the same time, the researcher must be open about why he or she is there. The principle of *informed consent* described in Chapter 5 is just as essential in an ethnography as it is in any other type of research.

Initially, the researcher uses a "big net approach" (Fetterman, 1989), intermingling with everyone and getting an overall sense of the cultural context. Gradually, the researcher identifies **key informants** who can provide information and insights relevant to the research question and can facilitate contacts with other helpful individuals.

In some ethnographic studies, the researcher engages in **participant observation,** becoming immersed in the daily life of the people. In fact, over the course of the study, the researcher's role may gradually change from "outsider" to "insider." The advantage here is that he or she may gain insights about the culture that could not be obtained in any other way. The disadvantage is that he or she may become so emotionally involved as to lose the ability to assess the situation accurately. In some situations, the researcher may even "go native," joining the cultural group and therefore becoming unable to complete the study (Creswell, 1998).

Throughout the fieldwork, the researcher is a careful observer, interviewer, and listener. Furthermore, he or she takes extensive fieldnotes (written either on site at the time or in private later in the day) in the form of dialogues, diagrams, maps, and so forth. Lengthy conversations and significant events can be recorded using audiotapes and videotapes. The researcher may also collect artifacts (e.g., tools, ritualistic implements, artistic creations) and records (e.g., accounting ledgers, personal journals, lesson plans) from the group.

We must caution you that conducting a good ethnography requires both considerable patience and considerable tolerance. One experienced ethnographer has described the process this way:

> It requires a great patience under any circumstances for me to "sit and visit." A rather inevitable consequence of being inquisitive without being a talker is that my conversational queries usually prompt others to do the talking. During fieldwork, I make a conscious effort to be sociable, thus providing opportunities for people to talk to me. My work ethic takes over to help me become not only more social but more attentive and responsive, and out pour the informants' stories and explanations so essential to good fieldwork.
>
> (Parenthetically, I note my suspicion that many fieldworkers talk too much and hear too little. They become their own worst enemy by becoming their own best informant. . . .)
>
> . . . I never confront informants with contradictions, blatant disbelief, or shock, but I do not mind presenting myself as a bit dense, someone who does not catch on too quickly and has to have things explained. . . . (Wolcott, 1994, p. 348)

DATA ANALYSIS.   As is true in case study research, data collection and data analysis in an ethnographic study often occur somewhat simultaneously. The analysis typically proceeds in the following fashion (Wolcott, 1994):

1. *Description.*   The information obtained is organized into a logical structure. Ethnographers have used a variety of strategies to organize and describe the cultures they have observed, including the following:
    * Describing events in chronological order
    * Describing a typical day in the life of the group or of an individual within the group
    * Focusing on a critical event for the group
    * Developing a story, complete with plot and characters
2. *Analysis.*   The data are categorized according to their meanings. Patterns, regularities, and critical events are identified.
3. *Interpretation.*   The general nature of the culture is inferred from the categories, meanings, and patterns identified in step 2. Existing theoretical frameworks in the field may lend structure and support during the interpretation process.

Experienced ethnographers readily admit that it is virtually impossible (and perhaps not even desirable) to analyze their data with total objectivity. Wolcott (1994) has proposed that the researcher should instead strive for *rigorous subjectivity*; to achieve this end, he has suggested, the researcher should aim for balance, fairness, completeness, and sensitivity in the final analysis and interpretation of the data.

THE RESEARCH REPORT.   The final report for an ethnography is rarely written in the impersonal style that is typical for many other forms of research. On the contrary, it is often a personal, literary narrative designed to engage the reader's attention and interest. When writing the report, the ethnographer may act as much like a storyteller as like a scholar and researcher.

When you write about an ethnographic study, you will want to include the following information (Creswell, 1998, 2002):

1. *An introduction that provides a rationale and context for the study.*   Present your research question at the beginning of the report (at this point in the book, such a suggestion should hardly be a surprise!), and describe the nature of your study as it relates both to your question and to one or more theoretical perspectives. More generally, explain why the study was an important one for you to conduct and for others to read about.
2. *A description of the setting and methods.*   Describe the group you studied and the methods you used to study it. Go into considerable detail about what people do and say, how they interact with one another, what systems and rituals they have in place, and so on. In other words, engage in the *thick description* described in Chapter 5. Ideally, an ethnographic report should "place the reader figuratively in the setting . . . transport the reader to the actual scene . . . make it real" (Creswell, 2002, pp. 491–492).

3. *An analysis of the culture studied.*   Describe the patterns and themes you observed (e.g., the stated or unstated norms and conventions for behavior, the social hierarchy, the belief system). Present evidence (e.g., descriptions of artifacts, conversations with group members) to support your claims. Use the participants' actual words—perhaps including their language or dialect as well—to give your account realism and "life."

4. *A conclusion.*   Relate your findings to your research question and to concepts and theories in your discipline.

To the extent that different group members have different perspectives, you should present those perspectives. Ethnographers give their research participants *voice*: They often use participants' own words to convey a sense of what it is like to live and work within the culture.

Although it may be impossible for you to be completely objective when you describe the culture you have studied, you should nevertheless try to avoid making judgments. Even small changes in wording can make a significant difference in this regard. For instance, rather than saying, "Only one villager had ever graduated from high school," you might say, "One villager had graduated from high school" (Wolcott, 1994, pp. 352–353). And rather than saying, "Few pupils were at task," you might instead say, "Five pupils appeared to be engaged in the assignment" (Wolcott, 1994, p. 353).

Ultimately you want to construct an in-depth portrait of the culture in all its complexities. Your portrait should give your readers a better understanding of the culture and help them develop a sense of empathy for the group's members. And it should be sufficiently detailed that a stranger could join the group and have some idea of how to participate in a meaningful fashion (Creswell, 1998).

PHENOMENOLOGICAL STUDY

In its broadest sense, the term *phenomenology* refers to a person's perception of the meaning of an event, as opposed to the event as it exists external to the person. A **phenomenological study** is a study that attempts to understand people's perceptions, perspectives, and understandings of a particular situation. In other words, a phenomenological study tries to answer the question, What is it like to experience such-and-such? For instance, a researcher might study the experiences of people caring for a dying relative, living in an abusive relationship, or home-schooling a child.

In some cases, the researcher has had personal experience related to the phenomenon in question and wants to gain a better understanding of the experiences of others. By looking at multiple perspectives on the same situation, the researcher can then make some generalizations of *what something is like* from an insider's perspective.

METHOD.   Phenomenological researchers depend almost exclusively on lengthy interviews (perhaps one to two hours in length) with a carefully selected sample of participants. A typical sample size is from 5 to 25 individuals, all of whom have had direct experience with the phenomenon being studied (Creswell, 1998).

The actual implementation of a phenomenological study is as much in the hands of the participants as in the hands of the researcher. The phenomenological interview is often a very unstructured one in which the researcher and participants work together to "arrive at the heart of the matter" (Tesch, 1994, p. 147). The researcher listens closely as participants describe their everyday experiences related to the phenomenon and must be alert for subtle yet meaningful cues in participants' expressions, questions, and occasional sidetracks. A typical interview looks more like an informal conversation, with the participant doing most of the talking and the researcher doing most of the listening.

Throughout the data collection process, the researcher suspends any preconceived notions or personal experiences that may unduly influence what the researcher "hears" the participants saying. Such suspension (sometimes called *bracketing* or *epoché*) can be extremely difficult for a researcher who has personally experienced the phenomenon under study. Yet it is essential if the researcher is to gain an understanding of the typical experiences that people have had.

DATA ANALYSIS.   The central task during data analysis is to identify common themes in people's descriptions of their experiences (Barritt, 1986). After transcribing the interviews, the researcher typically takes the following steps (Creswell, 1998):

1. *Identify statements that relate to the topic.*   The researcher separates relevant from irrelevant information in the interview and then breaks the relevant information into small segments (e.g., phrases or sentences) that each reflect a single, specific thought.
2. *Group statements into "meaning units."*   The researcher groups the segments into categories that reflect the various aspects ("meanings") of the phenomenon as it is experienced.
3. *Seek divergent perspectives.*   The researcher looks and considers the various ways in which different people experience the phenomenon.
4. *Construct a composite.*   The researcher uses the various meanings identified to develop an overall description of the phenomenon as people typically experience it.

The final result is a general description of the phenomenon as seen through the eyes of people who have experienced it firsthand. The focus is on common themes in the experience despite diversity in the individuals and settings studied.

THE RESEARCH REPORT.   There is no specific structure for reporting a phenomenological study. As is true for virtually any form of research, you will want to present the research problem or question, describe your methods of data collection and analysis, draw a conclusion about the phenomenon you have studied (in the form of a composite of your participants' experiences), relate your findings to an existing body of theory and research, and discuss any practical implications of your findings. Your report should be sufficiently vivid that your readers come away feeling that "I understand better what it is like for someone to experience that" (Polkinghorne, 1989, p. 46).

GROUNDED THEORY STUDY

Of all the research designs we describe in this book, a grounded theory study is the one *least* likely to begin from a particular theoretical framework. On the contrary, the major purpose of a grounded theory approach is to *begin with the data and use them to develop a theory*. More specifically, a **grounded theory study** uses a prescribed set of procedures for analyzing data and constructing a theoretical model from them. The term *grounded* refers to the idea that the theory that emerges from the study is derived from and "grounded" in data that have been collected in the field rather than taken from the research literature. Grounded theory studies are especially helpful when current theories about a phenomenon are either inadequate or nonexistent (Creswell, 2002).

Typically, a grounded theory study focuses on a *process* (including people's actions and interactions) related to a particular topic, with the ultimate goal of developing a theory about that process (Creswell, 2002). The approach has its roots in sociology (Glaser & Strauss, 1967) but is now used in anthropology, education, nursing, psychology, and social work as well (Strauss & Corbin, 1994). It has been used effectively for such diverse topics as the interactions between building contractors and future homeowners, the ways in which scientists work, the management of a difficult pregnancy, experiences with chronic illness, remarriage following divorce, and spousal abuse (Strauss & Corbin, 1994).

METHOD.   As is true for the qualitative designs previously described, data collection is field-based, flexible, and likely to change over the course of the study. Interviews typically play a major role in data collection, but observations, documents, historical records, videotapes, and anything else of potential relevance to the research question may also be used. The only restriction is that the data collected *must* include the perspectives and voices of the people being studied (Charmaz, 2002; Strauss & Corbin, 1994).

Data analysis begins almost immediately, at which point the researcher develops *categories* to classify the data. Subsequent data collection is aimed at *saturating* the categories—in essence, learning as much about them as possible—and at finding any disconfirming evidence that may suggest revisions in the categories identified or in interrelationships among them. This process of moving back and forth between data collection and data analysis, with data analysis driving later data collection, is sometimes called the **constant comparative method**. The theory that ultimately evolves is one that includes numerous concepts and interrelationships among those concepts; in other words, it has *conceptual density* (Schram, 2003).

DATA ANALYSIS.   Experts disagree about the best approach to analyzing data in a grounded theory study. One widely used approach is that proposed by Strauss and Corbin (1990, 1998), who suggest the following steps:

1. *Open coding.*   The data are divided into segments and then scrutinized for commonalities that reflect categories or themes. After the data are categorized, they are further examined for *properties*—specific attributes or subcategories—that characterize each category. In general, open coding is a process of reducing the data to a small set of themes that appear to describe the phenomenon under investigation.
2. *Axial coding.*   Interconnections are made among categories and subcategories. Here the focus is on determining more about each category in terms of
    - The conditions that give rise to it
    - The context in which it's embedded
    - The strategies that people use to manage it or carry it out
    - The consequences of those strategies

    The researcher moves back and forth among data collection, open coding, and axial coding, continually refining the categories and their interconnections as additional data are collected.
3. *Selective coding.*   The categories and their interrelationships are combined to form a *story line* that describes "what happens" in the phenomenon being studied.
4. *Development of a theory.*   A theory, in the form of a verbal statement, visual model, or series of hypotheses, is offered to explain the phenomenon in question. The theory depicts the evolving nature of the phenomenon and describes how certain conditions lead to certain actions or interactions, how those actions or interactions lead to *other* actions, and so on, with the typical sequence of events being laid out. No matter what form the theory takes, *it is based entirely on the data collected.*

We've described these steps only in the most general terms. Strauss and Corbin's *Basics of Qualitative Research* (1998) offers more specific guidance and some helpful examples.

The steps just listed provide a structured and relatively systematic way of boiling down a huge body of data into a concise conceptual framework that describes and explains a particular phenomenon; as such, it has a semblance of rigor and objectivity that many researchers find appealing. Yet in some experts' eyes, these steps are *too* structured, to the point that they limit a researcher's flexibility and may predispose the researcher to identify categories prematurely (Charmaz, 2000; Glaser, 1992). Should you decide that a grounded theory study is the best way to tackle your research problem, we urge you to read diverse descriptions of the form that such a study might take (especially see Charmaz, 2000, 2002; Glaser, 1992; Strauss & Corbin, 1990, 1998).

THE RESEARCH REPORT.   The style of writing used to describe a grounded theory study is typically objective and impersonal. Building on Creswell's (1998) recommendations, we suggest that you include the following in your report:

1. *A description of the research question.*   Describe your general research problem and explain how you delineated it more precisely over the course of the study.
2. *A review of the related literature.*   Do *not* use the literature to provide concepts or theories for your study, but *do* use it to provide a rationale and context for your study.
3. *A description of your methodology and data analysis.*   Describe the approach you took at the beginning of the study and how your approach evolved over time. Outline the nature of the sample and setting, as well as the specific methods (interviews, observations, etc.)

you used. Explain the categories and properties you identified. Describe how your data collection was driven by your data analysis.

4. *A presentation of your theory.*   Present the theory you've developed in a verbal or visual form, or, even better, both verbally and visually. Use some of your actual data (e.g., excerpts from interviews) to illustrate and support the theory.

5. *A discussion of implications.*   Show how your theory is similar to or dissimilar from other theoretical perspectives. Explain how it relates to existing knowledge about the topic. Discuss potential implications of the theory for practice or future research.

CONTENT ANALYSIS

A **content analysis** is a detailed and systematic examination of the contents of a particular body of material for the purpose of identifying patterns, themes, or biases. Content analyses are typically performed on *forms of human communication*, including books, newspapers, films, television, art, music, videotapes of human interactions, and transcripts of conversations. For instance, a researcher might use a content analysis to determine whether television commercials reflect traditional sex-role stereotypes, what religious symbols appear in works of art, how teachers spend their time in the classroom, or what attitudes are reflected in the speeches or newspaper articles of a particular era in history. As you might gather from these examples, content analyses are found in a wide variety of disciplines, including psychology, history, art, education, journalism, and political science.

Of the five designs described in this chapter, a content analysis involves the greatest amount of planning at the front end of the project. The researcher typically defines a specific research problem or question at the very beginning (e.g., "Do contemporary television commercials reflect traditional gender stereotypes?", "What religious symbols appeared in early Byzantine architecture, and with what frequency, during the years 527–867?"). The researcher also identifies the sample to be studied and the method of analysis early in the process.

Content analyses are not necessarily stand-alone designs. For instance, a content analysis might be incorporated into a *cross-sectional study* (see Chapter 9) to discover developmental trends in children's conceptions of history or geography (e.g., Forbes, Ormrod, Bernardi, Taylor, & Jackson, 1999; Ormrod, Jackson, Kirby, Davis, & Benson, 1999). It might be used in an *ex post facto study* (see Chapter 10) to determine how people in different academic disciplines interpret and understand new information differently (Ormrod, Ormrod, Wagner, & McCallin, 1988). Or it might be used in a *quasi-experimental study* (see Chapter 10) to find out how different instructional techniques affect the kinds of class notes that college students take (Jackson, 1996).

METHOD.   As a general rule, a content analysis is quite systematic, and measures are taken to make the process as objective as possible. The following steps are typical:

1. The researcher identifies the specific body of material to be studied. If this body is relatively small, it is studied in its entirety. If it is quite large (e.g., if it consists of all newspaper articles written during a particular time period), a sample (perhaps a random sample) is selected.

2. The researcher defines the characteristics or qualities to be examined in precise, concrete terms. The researcher may identify specific examples of each characteristic as a way of defining it more clearly.

3. If the material to be analyzed involves complex or lengthy items (e.g., works of literature, transcriptions of conversations), the researcher breaks down each item into small, manageable segments that are analyzed separately.

4. The researcher scrutinizes the material for instances of each characteristic or quality defined in step 2. When judgments are entirely objective (e.g., when the study involves looking for the appearance of certain words in a text), only one judge, or *rater*, is necessary. When judgments are more subjective (e.g., when the study involves evaluating a teacher's behaviors for the specific activities that each behavior reflects), two or three raters are typically involved, and a composite of their judgments is used.

DATA ANALYSIS.   Almost invariably, one crucial step in a content analysis is to tabulate the frequency of each characteristic found in the material being studied. Thus, a content analysis is quantitative as well as qualitative. In some situations, appropriate statistical analyses are performed on the frequencies or percentages obtained to determine whether significant differences exist relevant to the research question. The researcher then uses such tabulations and statistical analyses to interpret the data as they reflect on the problem under investigation.

THE RESEARCH REPORT.   If you conduct a content analysis, either as your sole methodology or in combination with other designs, you should include the following in your research report:

1. *A description of the body of material you studied.*   Describe the overall body of material you wanted to investigate and any sampling procedures that you used to select specific items or artifacts from it.
2. *Precise definitions and descriptions of the characteristics you looked for.*   Define each characteristic precisely enough that another researcher could replicate your study. Consider using specific examples from your data to illustrate each characteristic.
3. *The coding or rating procedure.*   Describe the procedure that the rater(s) used to evaluate the material and, if applicable, how multiple ratings were combined.
4. *Tabulations for each characteristic.*   Report frequencies or percentages (or both) for each characteristic. Consider using tables or graphs as a way of reporting this information in a concise, organized fashion.
5. *A description of patterns that the data reflect.*   Identify themes or trends in the material (e.g., as reflected in your tabulations).

Table 7.1 summarizes the nature of the five designs we've just discussed. Keep in mind, however, that these designs are not necessarily as distinctly different as Table 7.1 might indicate. In fact, any particular study may include elements of two or more designs. Remember, much qualitative research is, by its very nature, flexible and open-ended, and so it continues to evolve over the course of the project. To the extent that your research question leads you to believe that two or more designs are equally relevant to your purpose, think creatively about how you might combine them into a single study.

Such flexibility should *not*, however, lead you to believe that you can conduct a qualitative research project in a sloppy, poorly-thought-through manner. On the contrary, the flexible nature of a qualitative study makes it just that much more challenging, especially for the novice researcher. *For anything you do in a qualitative study, you must have a definite rationale and a distinct purpose, and you must keep your overall goal—to answer your research question—clearly in sight at all times.*

COLLECTING DATA IN QUALITATIVE RESEARCH

As you have seen, qualitative researchers often use multiple forms of data in any single study. They might use observations, interviews, objects, written documents, audiovisual materials, electronic documents (e.g., e-mail messages, Web sites), and anything else that can help them answer their research question. Furthermore, many qualitative studies are characterized by an *emerging design*: Data collected early in the investigation often influence the kinds of data that the researcher subsequently gathers.

In qualitative research, the potential sources of data are limited only by the researcher's open-mindedness and creativity. For example, in an educational setting, a researcher might consider where various students are seated in the lunch room, what announcements are posted on the walls, or what messages are communicated in graffiti (Eisner, 1998). In an ethnography or phenomenological study, a researcher might ask one or more participants to keep a daily journal or to discuss the content and meaning of photographs and art objects (Creswell, 1998).

Regardless of the kinds of data involved, data collection in a qualitative study takes a great deal of time. The researcher should record any potentially useful data thoroughly, accurately, and systematically, using fieldnotes, audiotapes, sketches, photographs, or any other suitable means. As they collect data, many qualitative researchers also begin jotting notes (sometimes called **memos**) about their initial interpretations of what they are seeing and hearing.

TABLE 7.1	Distinguishing characteristics of different qualitative designs			
Design	Purpose	Focus	Methods of Data Collection	Methods of Data Analysis
Case study	To understand one person or situation (or perhaps a very small number) in great depth	One case or a few cases within its/their natural setting	• Observations • Interviews • Appropriate written documents and/or audiovisual material	• Categorization and interpretation of data in terms of common themes • Synthesis into an overall portrait of the case(s)
Ethnography	To understand how behaviors reflect the culture of a group	A specific field site in which a group of people share a common culture	• Participant observation • Structured or unstructured interviews with "informants" • Artifact/document collection	• Identification of significant phenomena and underlying structures and beliefs • Organization of data into a logical whole (e.g., chronology, typical day)
Phenomenological study	To understand an experience from the participants' point of view	A particular phenomenon as it is typically lived and perceived by human beings	• In-depth, unstructured interviews • Purposeful sampling of 5–25 individuals	• Search for "meaning units" that reflect various aspects of the experience • Integration of the meaning units into a "typical" experience
Grounded theory study	To derive a theory from data collected in a natural setting	A process, including human actions and interactions and how they result from and influence one another	• Interviews • Any other relevant data sources	• Prescribed and systematic method of coding the data into categories and identifying interrelationships • Continual interweaving of data collection and data analysis • Construction of a theory from the categories and interrelationships
Content analysis	To identify the specific characteristics of a body of material	Any verbal, visual, or behavioral form of communication	• Identification and possible sampling of the specific material to be analyzed • Coding of the material in terms of predetermined and precisely defined characteristics	• Tabulation of the frequency of each characteristic • Descriptive or inferential statistical analyses as needed to answer the research question

It is essential that data collection methods are consistent with the ethical principles presented in Chapter 5. The people being studied must know the nature of the study and be willing participants in it (this is *informed consent*), and any data collected should not be traceable back to particular individuals (thus maintaining their *right to privacy*). One common way of keeping personal data confidential is to assign various pseudonyms to different participants and to use those pseudonyms both during data collection and in the final research report.

Common to all qualitative studies is a need to identify an appropriate *sample* from which to acquire data. Another feature that most qualitative studies share (content analyses excepted) is heavy reliance on *observations*, *interviews*, or both, as a source of data. Let's look at each of these topics more closely.

SAMPLING

As we have seen, qualitative researchers draw their data from many sources—not only from a variety of people, but perhaps also from objects, textual materials, and audiovisual and electronic records. The particular entities they select comprise their **sample**, and the process of selecting them is called **sampling**.

Only rarely—for instance, when a researcher conducts a content analysis of a small group of items—can a researcher look at *everything* that has potential relevance for the research problem. More typically, the researcher must be choosy about the data that he or she gathers and analyzes and, as a result, will get an incomplete picture of the phenomenon in question. One experienced qualitative researcher has described the situation this way:

> Whether observing, interviewing, experiencing, or pursuing some combination of strategies, you cannot be everywhere at once or take in every possible viewpoint at the same time. Instead . . . you develop certain perspectives by engaging in some activities or talking to certain people rather than others. . . . You build assertions toward the never-quite-attainable goal of "getting it right," approximating realities but not establishing absolutes.
>
> Your task, both derived from and constrained by your presence, is thus inherently interpretive and incomplete. The bottom line is that there is no bottom line: It is not necessary (or feasible) to reach some ultimate truth in order for your study to be credible and useful. (Schram, 2003, p. 97)

How you identify your sample must depend on what research question(s) you want to answer. If you want to draw inferences about an entire population or body of objects, then you must choose a sample that can be presumed to *represent* that population or body. Ideally, this sample is chosen through a completely random selection process or one that reflects appropriate proportions of each subgroup within the overall group of people or objects. We consider several such sampling strategies in our discussion of descriptive quantitative research in Chapter 9. (Truly effective researchers often draw on methodologies from diverse research traditions.)

More often, qualitative researchers are intentionally nonrandom in their selection of data sources. Instead, their sampling is *purposeful*: They select those individuals or objects that will yield the most information about the topic under investigation. For example, grounded theory researchers tend to engage in **theoretical sampling**, choosing data sources that are most apt to help them develop a theory of the process in question. Later, they may employ **discriminant sampling**, returning to those data sources that are most apt to help them validate that theory (Creswell, 2002).

OBSERVATIONS

The qualitative researcher may make observations either as a relative outsider or, especially in the case of an ethnography, as a participant observer. Unlike observations conducted in quantitative studies (see Chapter 9), observations in a qualitative study are intentionally unstructured and free-flowing: The researcher shifts focus from one thing to another as new and potentially significant objects and events present themselves. The primary advantage of conducting observations in this manner is flexibility: The researcher can take advantage of unforeseen data sources as they surface.

Such an approach has its drawbacks, of course. The researcher (especially a novice researcher) won't always know what things are most important to look for, especially at the beginning, and so may waste considerable time observing and recording trivialities while overlooking entities that are more central to the research question. A second disadvantage is that *by his or her very presence*, the researcher may alter what people say and do and how significant events unfold.

Recording events can be problematic as well. Written notes are often insufficient to capture the richness of what one is observing. Yet audiotapes and videotapes aren't always completely dependable either. Background noises may make tape-recorded conversations only partially audible. A video camera can capture only the events happening in a particular direction. And the very presence of tape recorders and video cameras may make participants uncomfortable.

If you decide to conduct observations as part of a qualitative study, we offer these suggestions:

1. Before you begin your study, experiment with various data recording strategies (fieldnotes, audiotapes, videotapes), identify the particular methods that work best for you, and practice using them in other contexts.
2. When you begin your observations, have someone introduce you to the people you are watching. At this point, you should briefly describe your study and get participants' consent.

3. As you observe, remain relatively quiet and inconspicuous, yet be friendly to anyone who approaches you. You certainly don't want to discourage people from developing relationships with you and, perhaps later, taking you into their confidence.

4. If you take fieldnotes, consider dividing each page of your notebook into two columns. Use the left column to record your observations (making notes, drawing maps, etc.), and use the right column to write your preliminary interpretations.

The last suggestion is a particularly important one. *It is essential that you not confuse your actual observations with your interpretations of them*, for two reasons. First, you need to be as objective as you can in the records you keep. And second, your interpretations of what you've seen and heard are apt to change over the course of the study.

INTERVIEWS

Interviews can yield a great deal of useful information. The researcher can ask questions related to any of the following (Silverman, 1993):

- Facts (e.g., biographical information)
- People's beliefs and perspectives about the facts
- Feelings
- Motives
- Present and past behaviors
- Standards for behavior (i.e., what people think *should* be done in certain situations)
- Conscious reasons for actions or feelings (e.g., why people think that engaging in a particular behavior is desirable or undesirable)

Keep in mind, however, that, especially when a researcher asks about *past* events, behaviors, and perspectives, interviewees must rely on their memories, and human memory is rarely as accurate as a tape recorder or video recorder might be. In fact, people's memories are subject to considerable distortion: People are apt to recall what *might* or *should* have happened (based on their attitudes or beliefs) rather than what actually *did* happen (Schacter, 1999; Schwarz, 1999).

Interviews in a qualitative study are rarely as structured as the interviews conducted in a quantitative study (more about quantitative study interviews in Chapter 9). Instead, they are either open-ended or semistructured, in the latter case revolving around a few central questions. Unstructured interviews are, of course, more flexible and more likely to yield information that the researcher hadn't planned to ask for; their primary disadvantage is that the researcher gets different information from different people and may not be able to make comparisons among the interviewees.

In some cases, a researcher may want to interview several participants simultaneously in a **focus group**. To conduct a focus group, the researcher gathers several people (usually no more than 10 or 12) to discuss a particular issue for 1 to 2 hours. A moderator (who may or may not be the researcher) introduces the issues to be discussed, makes sure no one dominates the discussion, and keeps people focused on the topic. Focus groups are especially useful when

- Time is limited
- People feel more comfortable talking in a group than alone
- Interaction among participants may be more informative than individually conducted interviews
- The researcher is having difficulty interpreting what he or she has observed (Creswell, 1998; Neuman, 1994)

PRACTICAL APPLICATION Conducting Interviews in a Qualitative Study

Conducting an informative interview is not as easy as it might seem. In this section we offer guidelines for the novice researcher and suggest computer technology that can make the task easier.

GUIDELINES   CONDUCTING A PRODUCTIVE INTERVIEW

The following suggestions are based partly on our own experiences and partly on guidance offered by Creswell (1998), Eisner (1998), Shank (2002), and Silverman (1993):

1. *Identify some questions in advance.* Conducting an unstructured interview effectively requires considerable experience and skill: The researcher must sense when the conversation is drifting in an unproductive direction and gently guide it back on course. Novice researchers often have better success when they prepare a few questions in advance and make sure that all are addressed during the course of the interview. These questions should, of course, be related to the research questions and overall research problem. As an example, in a qualitative study she conducted for her doctoral dissertation, Debby Zambo examined how children with reading disabilities believe that their minds work when they read. She worked with and extensively studied 11 children in grades five through nine, interviewing them 10 to 15 times over the course of her investigation. Figure 7.1 presents an excerpt from her dissertation, in which she shows how her interview questions aligned with her research questions.

For any single interview, limit your list of questions to a small number, perhaps five to seven. (Although Debby Zambo had many more questions than this, she spread them throughout a dozen or so interviews with each child.) You will find that you won't necessarily need to ask every question explicitly, as the answers to some may emerge while a participant is responding to others.

Ideally, interview questions should encourage people to talk about a topic without hinting that they give a particular answer. In other words, avoid leading questions. Questions such as "What is going on now?" "What is it like to work here?" and "What's a typical day like?" can stimulate an informative conversation without suggesting that one kind of response is somehow more desirable than another (Shank, 2002).

2. *Make sure your interviewees are representative of the group.* You should choose people whom you expect to give you typical perceptions and perspectives. In some cases, you may intentionally pick "extremists" or other exceptional individuals, but when you do so, you should identify them as such in your notes.

3. *Find a suitable location.* In theory, you can conduct an interview anywhere that people are willing to talk to you. But you will probably have a more successful interview if you find a quiet place where you and your interviewee are unlikely to be distracted or interrupted.

4. *Get written permission.* Explain the nature of the study and your plans for using the results. Ask the participant (or, in the case of a child, the participant's parent or guardian) to sign an informed consent form. Offer to provide an abstract or copy of the research report once you have completed the study.

5. *Establish and maintain rapport.* Begin the conversation with small talk that can break the ice. Be courteous and respectful at all times. Show genuine interest in what the person has to say.

Interviews in qualitative studies are typically quite informal, to the point where they may appear similar to casual conversation. There is one critical difference between a qualitative interview and normal dialogue, however: The researcher wants to gain information from the interviewee without also revealing his or her own perspectives. In other words, a critical element of most intimate conversations—disclosure of one's thoughts, beliefs, and feelings—is lopsided, with only one member of the pair doing the disclosing. To maintain rapport and general feelings of closeness and trust, therefore, you must show compassion and interest in other ways, perhaps through body language (smiling, maintaining eye contact, leaning forward) and such neutral encouragements as "Go on" and "What do you mean?" (Shank, 2002).

6. *Focus on the actual rather than on the abstract or hypothetical.* You are more likely to get revealing information if you ask what a person *does or would do in a specific situation*. For example, if you are interviewing a teacher, ask questions about teaching strategies rather than about educational philosophy; otherwise, you might get nothing more than what Eisner (1998) describes as "pious, canned proclamations that seem as though they had been snatched from a third-rate philosophy of education text" (p. 183).

FIGURE 7.1

Example of how a researcher might align interview questions with research questions

From *Uncovering the Conceptual Representations of Students with Reading Disabilities* (pp. 140–142), by D. Zambo, 2003, unpublished doctoral dissertation, Arizona State University, Tempe. Reprinted with permission.

Research Question	Interview Question
1. What do students with reading disabilities think about reading and themselves? a. What are their thoughts about reading?	What do they think reading is all about? What do they find easy/difficult to read? Who do they think good/poor readers are and what do good/poor readers do? How do you become good/poor at reading?
b. What are their ideas about themselves and reading?	What are they reading? What do they think is easy/difficult to read? What goes on in their head when they read easy/difficult things? What is their activity level (calm/fidgety) when they read? What body parts do they use when they read? How do they think reading has/will impact their lives in the past, present, and future?
2. What emotions are evoked when they read?	Do they get frustrated when they read? What other emotions may be involved when they read? Does believing they can get better at reading help them be a better reader? Does hoping they can get better at reading help them be a better reader? Does wishing they can get better at reading help them be a better reader?
3. What do children with reading difficulties know about the cognitive processes of reading? a. What do they know about attention?	What is attention? Do they recognize that they must focus their attention when they read? What do they focus on? Why do they focus on that? Do they have difficulty with attention? If so, what do they do? Is their attention easy or difficult to capture when they read? Can they sustain their attention enough when they read? What do they do to sustain their attention? How consistent is their attention? What do they do to make their attention consistent? Is their attention better on some days and when is it better? What do they do if their attention is better on some days? What distracts them when they read? Do ideas and memories pop into their heads and distract them when they read?
b. What do they know about their memory and reading?	What do they know about memory in general? What do they do to put things into their memory? What do they do to keep things in their memory? How do they remember what they read? How do they remember/understand what they have read?

FIGURE 7.1

Continued

Research Question	Interview Question
4. What do students with dyslexia know about the brain and reading?	Do they understand the brain is interconnected with external body parts? Analogy—Can they create an analogy for the brain? Metacognition—Thinking About Thinking—What do they wonder about their mind/brain? [What do they] think about their thinking? Can they differentiate mental entities (thoughts, dreams, and memories) from close imposters?
5. What do children with dyslexia know about their dyslexic mind?	How do their brains work when they read? Are their brains like or different than other's brains when they read? Do they listen/see/feel things in their brains when they read? How do they do this? Do they think their minds are active when they read? What happens in their minds when they read? What do they do to make this happen? Are they aware of what is in their minds as they read? Are their minds excited when they read? How do things get from a book to their brains?

7. *Don't put words in people's mouths.* Let people choose their own way of expressing their thoughts. A good interviewer is, above all, a good listener who lets people say what they want to say in the way they want to say it. Furthermore, a good interviewer recognizes that people may reveal inconsistences in their recollections, attitudes, and logic: Their perceptions won't necessarily all fit together in a neat little package (Kvale, 1996).

8. *Record responses verbatim.* Whether you use handwritten notes, shorthand, a tape recorder, or laptop computer, capture everything the person says, especially if the interview is an unstructured one. If you suspect that an interviewee may have said something other than what he or she intended to communicate, read or play back the response and ask if it accurately reflects his or her thoughts.

9. *Keep your reactions to yourself.* Although you won't necessarily want to maintain a continual "poker face," you are more likely to get accurate information if you don't show surprise or disapproval of what someone tells you.

10. *Remember that you are not necessarily getting the facts.* As confident and convincing as some of your participants may be, you should always treat their responses as *perceptions* rather than as facts.

11. *When conducting a focus group, take group dynamics into account.* Whenever you gather two or more individuals into a single interview, these individuals will rarely act as true "equals." Some participants are likely to dominate the conversation. Others may be reluctant to express their views, perhaps because they are shy or feel uncertain that their perspectives are valid. In most cases, you will get more representative (and hence more useful) data if you make sure that everyone in the group has a chance to answer each question. Accordingly, you should keep your list of questions for a focus group quite short. And if you are recording the focus group session, ask participants to identify themselves by name at the beginning of the session; having them do so will help you identify different speakers when you transcribe the session later on.

USING TECHNOLOGY TO FACILITATE DATA COLLECTION AND TRANSCRIPTION

Some computer software lets you to turn a laptop computer into a tape recorder; it also lets you mark key points in the interview, retrieve desired pieces of information quickly, and slow down what you've recorded so that you can transcribe it more easily. Other software programs will even do your transcribing for you! The capabilities of this software are expanding all the time. We urge you to look at such software as IBM VoiceType Simply Speaking, Naturally Speaking, Power Secretary, and

ViaVoice to see how their latest versions might make your recording and interviewing tasks easier and less time-consuming.

In some cases, you can conduct qualitative interviews long-distance through e-mail, two-way textual communication software known as *instant messaging*, or computer-based *video conferencing* (e.g., Creswell, 2002). Keep in mind, however, that ethical standards don't fly out the window simply because you're conversing with people in cyberspace rather than in the same room. You must still seek participants' (or parents') informed consent, and you must protect participants' privacy. Furthermore, you must ensure that participants have appropriate characteristics and qualifications for your investigation—something that may be difficult to determine if you never meet these individuals in the flesh (Creswell, 2002).

ORGANIZING AND ANALYZING THE DATA FROM QUALITATIVE STUDIES

As you have undoubtedly realized by this time, there is usually no single "right" way to analyze the data in a qualitative study. The researcher begins with a large body of information and must, through inductive reasoning, sort and categorize it and gradually boil it down to a small set of abstract, underlying themes. Even in content analysis—an approach that, on the surface, may seem quite straightforward and matter-of-fact—the researcher often determines the specific characteristics to be studied only after carefully scrutinizing the body of material in search of potentially meaningful characteristics to identify and count.

In the quantitative designs that we'll consider in Chapters 9 and 10, data analysis and data interpretation are, in large part, two separate steps, with numerical data being mathematically manipulated and statistically analyzed, and then the results of those manipulations and analyses being interpreted with respect to the original research questions and hypotheses. In most qualitative research, however, data analysis and interpretation are closely interwoven, and both are often enmeshed with data collection as well. Schram (2003) expresses this idea quite eloquently:

> **Qualitative inquiry is fundamentally interpretive**. . . . Experiences do not speak for themselves; nor do features within a research setting directly or spontaneously announce themselves as worthy of your attention. As a qualitative fieldworker, you cannot view your task simply as a matter of gathering or generating "facts" about "what happened." Rather, you engage in an active process of *interpretation*: noting some things as significant, noting but ignoring others as not significant, and missing other potentially significant things altogether. . . .
>
> Consider the deceptively straightforward task of transcribing a taped interview. Given the common lack of clear-cut endings in ordinary speech, how do you determine when and how to punctuate to indicate a completed phrase or sentence? Is it a function of *how* the interviewee said what she said? How do you determine *how* something was said? How does your decision affect the intent or meaning of what was actually spoken? And ultimately, how do you determine the degree of trust you should attach to what was said? In other words, even a transcript is the product of ongoing interpretive (and ethical) decisions about the significance that you give to what other people convey as meaningful. (pp. 9–10)

Creswell (1998) has described a **data analysis spiral** that is, in our view, equally applicable to a wide variety of qualitative studies. Using this approach, you go through the data several times, taking the following steps:

1. Organize the data, perhaps using index cards, manila folders, or a computer database. You may also break down large bodies of text into smaller units, perhaps in the form of stories, sentences, or individual words.

2. Peruse the entire data set several times to get a sense of what it contains as a whole. In the process, you should jot down a few memos (e.g., writing in the margins or using Post-It notes) that suggest possible categories or interpretations.

3. Identify general categories or themes, and perhaps subcategories or subthemes as well, and then classify each piece of data accordingly. At this point, you should be getting a general sense of patterns—a sense of *what the data mean*.

4. Integrate and summarize the data for your readers. This step might include offering propositions or hypotheses that describe relationships among the categories. It might

FIGURE 7.2

The data analysis spiral

(based on Creswell, 1998)

THE FINAL REPORT

Synthesis
• Offering hypothesis or propositions
• Constructing tables, diagrams, hierarchies

Classification
• Grouping the data into categories or themes
• Finding meanings in the data

Perusal
• Getting an overall "sense" of the data
• Jotting down preliminary interpretations

Organization
• Filing
• Creating a computer database
• Breaking large units into smaller ones

THE RAW DATA

also involve packaging the data into an organizational scheme such as a table, figure, matrix, or hierarchical diagram.

We depict this spiral graphically in Figure 7.2.

No matter how you proceed, the data analysis for a qualitative study is a complex and time-consuming process. You must wade through a great deal of information, some of which will be useful and some of which will not. Furthermore, the data you obtain are multifaceted and may reflect several different meanings simultaneously.

In a qualitative study, the interpretation of the data will inevitably be influenced by the researcher's biases and values to some extent, reflecting the notion of *researcher as instrument* that we spoke of earlier. Nevertheless, we urge you to do as much as you can to minimize the extent to which your prior expectations and opinions enter into your final analysis, perhaps by using some or all of the following strategies:

- Collect two or more different kinds of data (e.g., observations, interviews) related to any particular phenomenon.
- Get multiple and varying perspectives on any single issue or event.
- Make a concerted effort to look for evidence that contradicts your hypotheses.
- In your final research report, acknowledge any biases you have, so that your readers can take them into account when reading the report.

USING COMPUTER DATABASES TO FACILITATE DATA ORGANIZATION AND INTERPRETATION

USING TECHNOLOGY

We're guessing that you will use word processing software to record interviews and perhaps some of your other data as well. By storing your data on a computer, you can easily retrieve any piece of information using a relevant keyword, you can sort your data quickly and in multiple ways, and, as a precaution against some unforeseen catastrophe (e.g., a flood or fire), you can back up your files onto a separate computer disk and store them in a safe deposit box or other safe location.

We suggest that you also consider using a computer database to help you organize and interpret your data. Some computer database programs (e.g., DataEase, Ethnograph, FileMaker Pro, HyperQual, HyperRESEARCH, Kwalitan, NUD*IST, NVivo, WinMAX) are especially suited for qualitative research studies. They provide a ready means of storing, segmenting, and organizing lengthy fieldnotes, and they are designed to help you find patterns in your notes. Typically, you can transfer (in computer language, you can *import*) word processing files into such programs. Some computer database programs are easier to learn and use than others, but the easy ones tend to be less powerful (Fetterman, 1998). Remember that spending additional preparation time learning how to use a program is likely to save you time in the long run.

PRACTICAL APPLICATION PLANNING A QUALITATIVE STUDY

As you have seen, a qualitative research project is not something to be entered into casually. The flexibility of qualitative methodologies is an advantage for experienced researchers but often a disadvantage for novices, who may not have sufficient background or training to make wise decisions about how to proceed. Furthermore, data collection and data analysis may be far more complex and time consuming than the researcher anticipated.

If you think that a qualitative approach may be suitable for your purposes, you may want to do a pilot study first to find out whether you feel comfortable with the ambiguity and lack of structure in the process (Creswell, 1998). We urge you, too, to learn as much as you can about qualitative research strategies, perhaps by reading some of the references listed at the end of the chapter. Once you have determined that you have both the time and skills to conduct a qualitative study, you may find the following checklist helpful in your planning.

✔ CHECKLIST
PLANNING A QUALITATIVE STUDY

WHAT IS THE PURPOSE OF THE PROJECT?

_____ 1. What is the current status of knowledge pertaining to the question?

_____

_____

_____

_____ 2. Why is the study important?

_____

_____

_____

WHAT IS THE SPECIFIC FOCUS AND DESIGN OF THE PROJECT?

_____ 3. Will the focus be on individuals, groups, cultures, experiences, processes, or content?

_____

_____

_____

_____ 4. Will the design be a case study, ethnography, phenomenological study, grounded theory study, content analysis, a combination of two or more of these, or none of these?

_____

_____

_____

WHAT DATA ARE NEEDED?

_____   5. How will you gain access to the site?

_____

_____

_____

_____   6. How much time will you need?

_____

_____

_____

_____   7. What resources are needed and available?

_____

_____

_____

_____   8. Are there any existing constraints on data collection?

_____

_____

_____

HOW WILL THE DATA BE COLLECTED?

_____   9. How will the participants or materials be sampled?

_____

_____

_____

_____   10. What role will you, as the researcher, assume?

_____

_____

_____

_____   11. How will you ensure anonymity and confidentiality for the participants?

_____

_____

_____

_____   12. What procedures will you follow, and in what order?

_____

_____

_____

HOW WILL THE ANALYSIS BE CONDUCTED?

_____   13. What is the unit of analysis (person, event, story, etc.)?

_____

_____

_____

_____ 14. What methods of analysis will you use?

_____

_____

_____

_____ 15. How will you make sure that you and others can have confidence in your findings?

_____

_____

_____

HOW WILL THE FINDINGS BE COMMUNICATED?

_____ 16. How will you describe the context?

_____

_____

_____

_____ 17. How will you convey the participants' perspectives?

_____

_____

_____

_____ 18. What format(s) will you use to synthesize the data?

_____

_____

_____

CRITERIA FOR EVALUATING QUALITATIVE RESEARCH

How do readers, reviewers, and practitioners assess the worth of a qualitative proposal or research study? What characteristics are essential to a "good" study? What makes one study "excellent" and another only "marginal"?

Experienced qualitative researchers have offered a variety of standards that might be used to evaluate a qualitative study (Altheide & Johnson, 1994; Creswell, 1998; Eisner, 1998; Gall, Borg, & Gall, 1996; Glaser, 1992; Howe & Eisenhardt, 1990). We've boiled their suggestions down to nine general criteria:

1. *Purposefulness.*   The research question drives the methods used to collect and analyze data, rather than the other way around.
2. *Explicitness of assumptions and biases.*   The researcher identifies and communicates any assumptions, beliefs, values, and biases that may influence data collection and interpretation.
3. *Rigor.*   The researcher uses rigorous, precise, and thorough methods to collect, record, and analyze data. The researcher also takes steps to remain as objective as possible throughout the project.
4. *Open-mindedness.*   The researcher shows willingness to modify hypotheses and interpretations when newly acquired data conflict with previously collected data.
5. *Completeness.*   The researcher depicts the object of study in all its complexity. The researcher spends sufficient time in the field to understand all the nuances of the phenomenon; describes the physical setting, behaviors, and perceptions of the participants; and gives readers a total, multifaceted picture of the phenomenon (i.e., *thick description*).

6. *Coherence.*   The data yield consistent findings, such that the researcher can present a portrait that "hangs together." Multiple data sources converge onto consistent conclusions (*triangulation*), and any contradictions within the data are reconciled.
7. *Persuasiveness.*   The researcher presents logical arguments, and the weight of the evidence suggests one interpretation to the exclusion of others.
8. *Consensus.*   Other individuals, including the participants in the study and other scholars in the discipline, agree with the researcher's interpretations and explanations.
9. *Usefulness.*   The project yields conclusions that promote better understanding of the phenomenon, enable more accurate predictions about future events, or lead to interventions that enhance the quality of life.

PRACTICAL APPLICATION EVALUATING A QUALITATIVE STUDY

Drawing from the preceding criteria, as well as from guidelines presented by Good (1993), we offer the following checklist to help you evaluate either a proposal or a final report for a qualitative research project.

✔ CHECKLIST
EVALUATING QUALITATIVE RESEARCH STUDIES
METHODS

		YES	NO
_____	1. Is the context/setting of the study adequately described?	___	___
_____	2. Are techniques for data collection appropriate for the research problem? Are they thoroughly and precisely described?	___	___
_____	3. Are multiple data sources used?	___	___
_____	4. Are sufficient data collected from a variety of participants over an appropriate length of time?	___	___
_____	5. Are criteria for the selection of participants, informants, or materials presented? Is the sample described in sufficient detail?	___	___
_____	6. Are the roles of the researcher(s) and participants made clear?	___	___
_____	7. Does the researcher identify any assumptions, beliefs, values, or biases that might influence data collection or analysis?	___	___

FINDINGS AND INTERPRETATIONS

		YES	NO
_____	8. Is the data analysis appropriate for the research question, methodology, and theoretical framework?	___	___
_____	9. Are data analysis techniques explicitly described?	___	___
_____	10. Do data analysis techniques allow for revision and reinterpretation as new data come to light?	___	___
_____	11. Is triangulation of the various data sources addressed?	___	___
_____	12. If used, are tables, figures, and other graphics easy to read and interpret? Do they enhance the reader's ability to understand the study?	___	___
_____	13. Are sufficient data reported to support the conclusions drawn?	___	___
_____	14. Are any irrelevant and unnecessary data reported? If so, what should be deleted?	___	___
_____	15. Are discrepant data discussed and reconciled?	___	___
_____	16. Have the setting and observations been sufficiently described to present a convincing case?	___	___

_____   17. Are participant "voices" used to support the assertions and
             present multiple perspectives?   ____ ____

_____   18. Is the report detailed enough that the findings can be compared
             to other studies in other contexts?   ____ ____

_____   19. Is the discussion congruent with the research question and
             rationale for the study?   ____ ____

_____   20. Are implications for theory and/or practice discussed?   ____ ____

_____   21. Have other scholars in the field reviewed the proposal or report?
             If so, do they agree that the approach, methodology, and
             conclusions are appropriate?   ____ ____

_____   22. Have participants in the project read the report? Do they agree
             with its findings?   ____ ____

WRITING STYLE

_____   23. Is the writing style (e.g., expository, narrative) appropriate for
             the study?   ____ ____

_____   24. If a narrative is used, are the stories understandable? Are
             they authentic?   ____ ____

_____   25. Is the writing style concise? Is the argument clear?   ____ ____

_____   26. Are the writer's arguments logical and persuasive?   ____ ____

A SAMPLE DISSERTATION

Now go to our
Companion Website at
http://www.prenhall.com/leedy to
assess your understanding of
chapter content and to complete
the projects that will help you
learn how to conduct research.

As an illustration of how the methodology of a qualitative research study might look, we present excerpts from Robin Smith's doctoral dissertation conducted at Syracuse University (Smith, 1999). The study was a multiple case study that also incorporated elements of grounded theory research and content analysis.

The study focused on five high school students who had significant intellectual disabilities. In particular, it examined the nature of the students' involvement and participation in high school classrooms. It looked, too, at teachers' perceptions and interpretations of the students' disabilities and academic performance.

The dissertation's "Method" chapter begins with an overview of the research strategies used and a rationale for selecting the individuals to be studied. It then presents more specific information about each of the five students: Gerald, Trish, Nick, Tyrone, and Abe. We pick up the chapter at the point where it begins a discussion of data collection. As we have done in preceding chapters of this book, we present excerpts on the left and a running commentary on the right.

DISSERTATION ANALYSIS

Data Collection Processes

Data gained in the varied academic settings of the five students assisted in understanding the patterns of academic participation and the meanings and relationships of the five students regarding their academic participation in high school. I gathered data from the following sources:

Observations

Over three school semesters, I conducted observations of five high school students who were attending high school and enrolled in at least one academic subject in the general high school curriculum. These observations totaled 52 visits ranging in length . . . the shortest was 15 minutes . . . the longest, 6 hours. . . . *[The author continues with a detailed discussion of the kinds of observations made and the circumstances in which she made them.]*

Conversations and Interviews

I had conversations and interviews with adults involved and concerned with the students, such as general and special education teachers, assistants, and parents. I recorded and described these conversations in field notes and transcriptions. . . .

The semi-structured interviews with the parents of each student included the following kinds of questions:

1. Tell me about the history of your child's schooling.
2. What are the child's strengths? That is, what is he or she good at?
3. Where does it get hard for the student?
4. How does he or she like high school? How can you tell?
5. What do you see your child learning?
6. What are your goals and dreams for your child?
7. What else should I know about your child to better understand what is happening for him or her in school?

I conducted similar interviews with the special education teachers, which included discussion of their educational goals for the student. I conducted one formal interview with each special education teacher, with further interviews as necessary to enhance my understanding of my data. These other interviews were often in the form of brief conversations during or in between class, interviews by appointment, and phone conversations.

I also conducted interviews with the general education teachers in the form of formal, informal, or brief conversations that fit into the teachers' schedules. . . . I also had some conversations with the general education teachers by staying a few minutes after class and asking them questions about what I had observed that day or how they thought the student was doing. . . .

I taped and had transcribed in-depth interviews, and I embedded observer comments in the transcribed text as I reviewed it. I wrote down informal conversations as soon as possible, and when possible, wrote during the conversations according to the comfort level of the participants with note taking. I used a Hewlett Packard 200LX-palmtop computer, which enabled me to take legible and detailed notes and add more detail soon after an observation.

Official Records and Documents

Official records and documents were another source of information. At the very end of my study I went to the district office of special education, which kept the official records of all five of the students. I looked in each file to learn what I could about the students' grades and progress reports, along with the professional assessments and recommendations regarding the students' schooling. I took notes on my hand-held computer and read long quotes into

Comments

Here the author provides information about the amount of time she spent in the field. Her observations varied considerably in duration depending on the situation; we are more apt to see such flexibility in a qualitative study than in a quantitative one.

The interviews were presumably structured in this manner so that similar kinds of information would be obtained about each child.

The author used follow-up unstructured interviews to gather additional information as needed. This strategy is consistent with a grounded theory approach, in which the researcher moves back and forth between data collection and data analysis.

The author used audiotapes and transcriptions to capture the details of in-depth interviews; she also wrote notes about shorter, more informal conversations as soon after they took place as possible. The phrase "according to the comfort level of the participants with note taking" might have been better worded as "to the extent that participants felt comfortable with my note taking." However, the phrase reflects an appropriate sensitivity about taking notes only when it did not make a participant feel uneasy. And notice the author's use of a small computer to facilitate data collection!

Why did the author wait until the end to look at school records and documents? Later in this excerpt you will see her reason: She was worried that early knowledge of these records would bias her interpretations of what she observed in the classroom.

my tape recorder for later reference and transcription. I took notes on students' work in class and from some student work I found in the files, and collected samples of their work where possible.

Finally, I relied heavily on very detailed field notes. At first I wrote everything I saw. As I narrowed my focus I consistently included the students' interactions with adults and peers, their reactions to what was going on, and what other students were doing at the same time. Describing interactions of the nonspeaking students was challenging; due to the crowded conditions of several of the general education classes and my being in a wheelchair, I was not always able to be close enough to the student to observe facial expressions. Fortunately, each student was accessible to me most of the time, especially when I was well into the study and a couple of sympathetic teachers invited the student to sit where I could be close by. Thus many of my observations were able to include whispered dialogue between the student and support person helping with an assignment.

This narrowing of focus as the study proceeds is frequently found in qualitative research.

Notice how the author is looking for nonverbal as well as verbal information. Notice, too, how cooperative participants (in this case, some "sympathetic teachers") can facilitate data collection.

Coding and Analysis

. . . As I collected and analyzed data from preliminary observations, I found issues to explore . . . questions arose that created a need for further observing or interviewing. Using the constant comparative method of analysis (Glaser & Strauss, 1967), I collected data, looked for emerging themes and recurrent events, categorized them, and reevaluated my themes and categories. As I collected more data, I wrote analytic memos about my data, and reevaluated my previous theories as I compared old data with new (Bogdan & Biklen, 1992, pp. 72–75). The themes of academic engagement, generated by my pilot study, continued to expand in depth and breadth, and they generated more themes that guided the development of my study.

For example, Nick, one of the students I observed, sat with his assistant in the last row by the door, separated by another row of desks from the class; he seemed an observer in class lectures and discussions. When his assistant supported him to participate in hands-on activities, the assistant did the task for the student. The educators in the room said to me, "He doesn't understand much of what's going on," and they did not expect him to benefit from the actual curriculum content ("He's not getting much out of it."). In contrast, Trish, a student with even less physical coordination and verbal expression, followed a full academic schedule, and many of her teachers considered her to be involved, interested, and learning. This led me to look for signs of expectations of the student and how people evaluated the students. Thus, early data codes such as "expectation," "perception," and "assessment" led to a chapter regarding expectations and another regarding types of assessments.

I used Q.S.R. Nudist (QSR-NUD*IST, 1995) to code my data. This program enabled me to identify text segments in various ways, including participants' names and roles, as well as assigned categories such as "engaged," "disengaged," and "academics," that resulted in 98 data codes. A few of these original codes survived my ongoing revisions and collapsing of categories to my final analysis. I printed categories out in groups and coded them again by hand, testing new coding categories by merging several categories and reexamining the data. For example, many of the text segments that I had labeled "expectation" evolved into "assessment." Once I had determined that assessment was an important category, I subdivided it into "formal," "informal," and "professional," each with its own set of categories which are explained in my data chapter, "Patterns of Assessment.". . . Further hand coding yielded the categories I finally used in the chapter on "participation.". . .

The constant comparative method *is central to grounded theory research.*

Here we see that the author conducted an earlier pilot study—*something we urge any beginning researcher to do, particularly when planning a qualitative study.*

Notice the author's attention to Nick's physical distance from other students—a clear, nonverbal indicator that Nick is essentially a nonparticipant, an outsider, in this classroom.

The ability to contrast one situation with another is a key advantage of a multiple case study.

Here we see open coding, *the first step in data analysis in a grounded theory study.*

*NUD*IST is a computer database program especially suited for data collection in qualitative research.*

Here data analysis has moved on to axial coding, *where the author is refining her categories and their interconnections.*

[The author continues the discussion of data coding and other issues and then turns to the subject of values.]

<u>Exposing Researcher Values</u>

During this research I have continuously inspected my expectations and values as a continuing reminder of the role that values have in inquiry. . . . Ongoing self-reflection in memos and discussions with mentors throughout the course of the study helped me identify and account for the interference of my assumptions in my study. . . . For example, sometimes I was tempted to express findings about expectations in cause and effect terms. . . .

In this section, the author reveals her biases and the strategies she used to counteract those biases. Regular conversations with her university advisor and others helped her identify assumptions she didn't initially realize she was making.

I expose my values in my narrative as playing a significant role in my inquiry. In sharing my values in the introduction, and further here, I have attempted to take them into account as I share my data and analysis. For example, as a disability rights advocate, I have hoped that my research regarding students with disabilities would be a contribution toward achieving equality and full integration of people with disabilities. I remained aware of my bias against the self-contained setting, where four of the students in the study were based, in order to see what might actually benefit the students in that setting. I am aware that my bias is related to my advocacy stance against segregation and to the negative accounts of friends who have experienced segregated special education. I also had a prejudice against professional assessments along with the likelihood . . . that I might be influenced by the contents if I read them early in the study. To counter inappropriate influence of this prejudice, I read the assessments at the end of my study and took a class in how to administer psychoeducational assessments. . . .

Here the author describes her bias in favor of inclusion, where students with disabilities learn in general education classrooms alongside their nondisabled peers, rather than self-contained classrooms, in which students with disabilities are segregated from nondisabled students.

Here we discover why the author waited until the end of her study to look at school records.

As I listened to my informants, I was aware of my own assumption that students benefit from academic inclusion and that all students have the right to attain knowledge . . . for my observations and interviews, I kept an open mind to the notion that special education settings do not preclude learning, may even enhance it, and that observing the special education academic experiences could also inform me about student engagement and how they [students] participated in the academic activities.

Here the author is looking for disconfirming evidence, one effective strategy for minimizing the influence of a researcher's biases on data interpretation.

<u>Leaving the Field</u>

The process of leaving the field was gradual. I was learning less and less from observations by the end of spring. Completing ceasing the first school year observation was precipitated by the beginning of the university summer session and my assignment to spend all day in a suburban school as a student teacher. I was assigned to Trish's summer school class the second summer session and took notes on that experience. I visited her twice in the fall but was excluded from her general education classes due to overcrowding. Also in the fall, I spent two days with Tyrone. . . . By then I had been analyzing data and felt the main thing lacking was the assessment of material from official records. Waiting until the following summer to look into the records proved wise, as I was able to find them a rich source of data. I actually eased my way out of the field (Bogdan & Biklen, 1992, pp. 104–105) rather than leaving, keeping contacts with many of my informants and calling to find out what is going on with a student or to clarify a question.

In grounded theory terminology, the author has probably saturated her categories at this point: Any additional information is shedding little or no new light on the subject matter.

Notice that the author didn't just "disappear" from the scene. Instead, she continued to maintain contact with her participants after her research was completed.

NOTE. From *Academic Engagement of High School Students with Significant Disabilities: A Competence-Oriented Interpretation* (pp. 18–30) by R. M. Smith, 1999, unpublished doctoral dissertation, Syracuse University, Syracuse, New York. Reprinted with permission.

FOR FURTHER READING

Agar, M. H. (1980). *The professional stranger: An informal introduction to ethnography*. San Diego: Academic Press.

Bernard, H. R. (1999). *Social research methods: Qualitative and quantitative approaches*. Thousand Oaks, CA: Sage.

Chandler, S. (Ed.). (1992). Qualitative issues in educational research. *Theory into Practice*, *31*, 87–186.

Coffey, A., & Atkinson, P. (1996). *Making sense of qualitative data: Complementary research strategies*. Thousand Oaks, CA: Sage.

Creswell, J. W. (1998). *Qualitative inquiry and research design: Choosing among five traditions*. Thousand Oaks, CA: Sage.

Creswell, J. W. (2002). *Educational research: Planning, conducting, and evaluating quantitative and qualitative research*. Upper Saddle River, NJ: Merrill/Prentice Hall.

Denzin, N. K., & Lincoln, Y. S. (Eds.). (2000). *Handbook of qualitative research* (2nd ed.). Thousand Oaks, CA: Sage.

Edyburn, D. L. (1999). *The electronic scholar: Enhancing research productivity with technology*. Upper Saddle River, NJ: Merrill/Prentice Hall.

Eisner, E. W. (1998). *The enlightened eye: Qualitative inquiry and the enhancement of educational practice*. Upper Saddle River, NJ: Prentice Hall.

Fetterman, D. M. (1989). *Ethnography: Step by step*. Thousand Oaks, CA: Sage.

Fielding, N. G., & Lee, R. M. (Eds.). (1998). *Computer analysis and qualitative research*. Thousand Oaks, CA: Sage.

Glaser, B. (1992). *Basics of grounded theory analysis*. Mill Valley, CA: Sociology Press.

Hammersley, M., & Atkinson, P. (1995). *Ethnography: Principles in practice* (2nd ed.). New York: Routledge.

Hatch, A. J. (1995). *Qualitative research in early childhood settings*. New York: Praeger.

Hutchinson, S. (1988). Education and grounded theory. In R. R. Sherman & R. B. Webb (Eds.), *Qualitative research in education: Focus and methods* (pp. 123–140). London: Falmer.

Jorgensen, D. L. (1989). *Participant observation: A methodology for human studies*. Thousand Oaks, CA: Sage.

Kvale, S. (1996). *InterViews: An introduction to qualitative research interviewing*. Thousand Oaks, CA: Sage.

Lather, P. (1991). *Getting smart: Feminist research and pedagogy within the postmodern*. New York: Routledge.

Lincoln, Y. S., & Guba, E. G. (1985). *Naturalistic inquiry*. Thousand Oaks, CA: Sage.

Locke, L. F. (1989). Qualitative research as a form of scientific inquiry in sport and physical education. *Research Quarterly for Exercise and Sport*, *60*, 1–20.

Meloy, J. M. (1994). *Writing the qualitative dissertation: Understanding by doing*. Hillsdale, NJ: Erlbaum.

Merriam, S. B. (1988). *Case study research in education: A qualitative approach*. San Francisco: Jossey-Bass.

Merriam, S. B. (1995). What can you tell from an N of 1? Issues of validity and reliability in qualitative research. *PAACE Journal of Lifelong Learning*, *4*, 51–60.

Miles, M. B., & Huberman, A. M. (1994). *Qualitative data analysis* (2nd ed.). Thousand Oaks, CA: Sage.

Morgan, D. L. (1998). *The focus group guidebook*. Thousand Oaks, CA: Sage.

Morris, D. (1994). *Guidelines for writing a qualitative research report*. Chicago: American Marketing Association.

Morse, J. M., & Field, P. A. (1995). *Qualitative research methods*. Thousand Oaks, CA: Sage.

Moustakas, C. (1994). *Phenomenological research methods*. Thousand Oaks, CA: Sage.

Munhall, P. L., & Boyd, C. O. (1993). *Nursing research: A qualitative perspective*. New York: National League for Nursing.

Peshkin, A. (1988). Understanding complexity: A gift of qualitative research. *Anthropology and Education Quarterly*, *19*, 416–424.

Polkinghorne, D. E. (1989). Phenomenological research methods. In R. S. Valle & S. Halling (Eds.), *Existential-phenomenological perspectives in psychology* (pp. 41–60). New York: Plenum.

Richardson, J. T. E. (1999). The concepts and methods of phenomenological research. *Review of Educational Research*, *69*, 53–82.

Schram, T. H. (2003). *Conceptualizing qualitative inquiry: Mindword for fieldwork in education and the social sciences*. Upper Saddle River, NJ: Merrill/Prentice Hall.

Shank, G. D. (2002). *Qualitative research: A personal skills approach*. Upper Saddle River, NJ: Merrill/Prentice Hall.

Smith, M. L. (1987). Publishing qualitative research. *American Educational Research Journal*, *24*, 173–183.

Stake, R. (1995). *The art of case study research*. Thousand Oaks, CA: Sage.

Strauss, A., & Corbin, J. (1990). *Basics of qualitative research: Grounded theory procedures and techniques*. Thousand Oaks, CA: Sage.

Strauss, A., & Corbin, J. (1994). Grounded theory methodology: An overview. In N. Denzin & Y. Lincoln (Eds.), *Handbook of qualitative research* (pp. 273–285). Thousand Oaks, CA: Sage.

Strauss, A., & Corbin, J. (1998). *Basics of qualitative research: Techniques and procedures for developing grounded theory* (2nd ed.). Thousand Oaks, CA: Sage.

Tashakkori, A., & Teddlie, C. (1998). *Mixed methodology: Combining qualitative and quantitative approaches*. Thousand Oaks, CA: Sage

Weaver, A., & Atkinson, P. (1994). *Microcomputing and qualitative data analysis*. Aldershot, UK: Avebury.

Weaver, A., & Atkinson, P. (1996). From coding to hypertext. In R. G. Burgess (Ed.), *Using computers in qualitative research* (pp. 141–168). Greenwich, CT: JAI.

Weitzman, E. A., & Miles, M. B. (1995). *Computer programs for qualitative data analysis*. Thousand Oaks: Sage.

Wolcott, H. F. (1994). *Transforming qualitative data: Description, analysis, and interpretation*. Thousand Oaks, CA: Sage.

Yin, R. K. (1989). *Case study research: Design and method*. Thousand Oaks, CA: Sage.

8

Historical Research

Looking at a string of seemingly random events, the historical researcher develops a rational explanation for their sequence, speculates about cause-and-effect relationships among them, and draws inferences about the effects of events on individuals and the society in which they lived.

In and of itself, history consists of nothing more than an ever-flowing stream of events and the continuing changes in human life and its institutions—its languages, customs, philosophies, religions, art, architecture, and so on. Historical research tries to make sense of this maelstrom. It considers the currents and countercurrents of present and past events, with the hope of discerning patterns that tie them all together. At its core, **historical research** deals with the *meaning of events*.

Most of us have never been formally introduced to historical research. In higher education, it is often assumed that anyone who has had a course or two in history should be able to conduct historical research. This assumption is, of course, unwarranted. Although many people confuse the *study of history* with the *historical method*, these are two entirely different entities and should not be equated.

Many of us may have the impression that historical research involves gathering significant facts about a major event—perhaps a war, an economic depression, or the growth of a nation—and organizing these facts into a sequence, usually chronological. Such an enterprise may yield a historical narrative. It is not, however, true historical research. The heart of the historical method is, as with any other type of research, not the accumulation of the facts, but rather the *interpretation* of the facts. Nothing can take the place of that. The interpretation of the data is central in all research. Without it, there is no research.

Like so many pieces of a jigsaw puzzle, events may, on the surface, seem to happen randomly. But if you study any sequence of events, you will inevitably begin to see patterns that tie them together and make them meaningful. Like the continents, historical events sometimes drift slowly, but the discerning mind can detect, below the mass of data, considerable motion. The task of the historical researcher is not merely to describe *what* events happened but to present a *factually supported rationale* to explain *why* they happened.

Events do crystallize into meaningful clusters. Just as cause and effect exist in the physical world, so are they equally present in the historical world—in interactions among human beings, as well as in interactions between humanity and the environment.

Historical research is certainly not the domain of historians alone. On the contrary, we see it in such disciplines as geography, anthropology, psychology, literature, and linguistics. As you will see, it is largely a qualitative endeavor, although historical researchers often make use of quantitative data as well.

DATA SOURCES IN HISTORICAL RESEARCH

The historical researcher digs deep. The researcher makes every effort to find firsthand accounts and artifacts of an event—newspaper clippings, original memos, diary entries, eyewitnesses, relevant objects—and from such basic sources tries to establish a coherence that gives meaning to the event. When this happens, it is truly the historical researcher's finest hour.

In Chapter 5, we distinguished between *primary data* and *secondary data*, with the former being closer to the reality, or Truth, that the researcher wants ultimately to uncover. In historical research, this distinction is often referred to in terms of primary sources versus secondary sources. **Primary sources** are those that appeared first in time. They take such diverse forms as letters, diaries, sermons, laws, census reports, immigration records, probate documents, deeds, photographs, paintings, films, buildings, and tools. As an example, Matthew McKenzie, a doctoral student in history at the University of New Hampshire, studied the impact of the Boston Marine Society on political decision making and scientific advancements in colonial America and the early decades of the United States. Matt made extensive use of the society's minutes and other documents, as he explained in the following excerpt from his dissertation:

> [A]s an organization of [sea] captains predicated upon fellowship and mutual aid and with a distinct role within the port [Boston Harbor], the Society went to great lengths to follow proper parliamentary procedures and to act only on decisions taken unanimously. As part of this process, the Society maintained meeting minutes recording the Society's (though not individuals') opinions, resolutions, and approved actions. Consequently, throughout its 250-year history, the society left committee reports, resolutions, and clear statements that reveal its collective will and motivations. These records allow historians to uncover not only what the organization did, but why. (McKenzie, 2003, pp. 2–3)

Another source of primary data, at least for fairly recent events, is interviews of people who participated in them. This approach is sometimes known as **narrative research** or **oral history**. An excellent example is Kevin C. Kearns's *Dublin Tenement Life* (1994), which pulls data from interviews from many residents of inner-city tenement buildings into a vivid description of inner-city Irish life in the early 1900s. We present a brief excerpt from Kearns's description of teenage courting practices to give you a taste of this approach:

> Flirtation between tenement children began around the age of twelve, usually during street games. If a young girl "fancied a fella" she would boldly snatch his cap and dash off hoping to be pursued. During teenage years contact between boys and girls took place mostly within the group settings. But by age eighteen or thereabouts "marriage was their highest ambition," claims Peggy Pigott [a former tenement resident whom Kearns interviewed]. It was around this time that young women liked to go "clicking" in pairs. Clicking was an acceptable practice whereby respectable young women would stroll together along fashionable Dublin streets ostensibly window-viewing but in reality hoping to meet decent lads. When May Hanaphy [another interviewee] and one of her pals went clicking back in the 1920s, it was a perfectly proper way to meet a prospective husband:
>
> > *Oh, clicking then was very popular. See, that's how flirting went on. That's how many a girl got her husband, going out at night time. Oh, you'd go out for that purpose at that time. We'd go clicking along mostly O'Connell Street or maybe down Henry Street, you know, slow walking . . . strolling, and two fellas's come along and say 'there's two mots.' (Kearns, 1994, p. 46)*

Interview data often give life to historical events. But just as is true in conducting any interview, the researcher must remember that participants' recollections are not always accurate. Only when several people recall events similarly can a researcher have reasonable confidence in what the interviews reveal. More generally, the guidelines for "Conducting a Productive Interview" presented in Chapter 7 are as applicable to historical researchers as to other qualitative researchers.

Historical researchers don't necessarily limit themselves to words, images, and objects; they often use *numbers* as well. For instance, they might draw inferences about people's interests during a particular time period by looking at the numbers of books on various topics that were sold during that period (Marius, 1989). Or they might examine the frequencies with which the Puritans of colonial America named their children after figures in the Bible, chart trends in these frequencies over time, and then speculate about what the trends might mean for religious practices and beliefs (Marius, 1989). In his study of the Boston Marine Society, McKenzie (2003) used early tax rolls to determine the wealth of society members, and he used society records of new members to show the decline in the society's popularity and influence in the early 1800s (see Figures 8.1 and 8.2). In research for his masters' thesis, Peter Leavenworth (1998) used early deeds to find patterns in land sales in New England during the 1600s, with a focus on land sold by native Americans to British colonists. At one point in his analysis, Leavenworth plotted the frequency of land sales for each month of the year (see Figure 8.3). In the following excerpt from his thesis, he found considerable meaning in the month-to-month frequency data:

> One last use of the deed index is to chart times of the year when transactions were more prevalent. . . . [T]he dips in overall Indian deed activity shown in February and May are consistent throughout the century. The February dip was either hunting- or weather-related, while the May dearth may have been either a time of Indian removal to summer habitations, or the period of spring fishing runs, or both. Many early accounts, including missionary John Eliot's, mention

FIGURE 8.1

Using tax rolls to determine the wealth of Boston Marine Society members

From *Vocational Science and the Politics of Independence: The Boston Marine Society, 1754–1812* (p. 25) by M. G. McKenzie, 2003, unpublished doctoral dissertation, University of New Hampshire, Durham. Reprinted with permission.

Wealth Bracket	No. in bracket	Assessed Tax in 1771 (£ s)	Proportion of Population
Top 20%	8	£37 12s–£46 13s	11%
2nd	6	£28 6s–£37 12s	8%
3rd	19	£18 18s–£28 4s	26%
4th	19	£9 10s–£18 16s	26%
5th	20	0–£9 8s	28%
Total Population	72		100%

Source: Pruitt, *Massachusetts Tax Evaluation;* and Baker, *Boston Marine Society,* 318–361

FIGURE 8.2

Using new membership data to reveal the decline in the Boston Marine Society's popularity and influence during the early 1800s

From *Vocational Science and the Politics of Independence: The Boston Marine Society, 1754–1812* (p. 198) by M. G. McKenzie, 2003, unpublished doctoral dissertation, University of New Hampshire, Durham. Reprinted with permission.

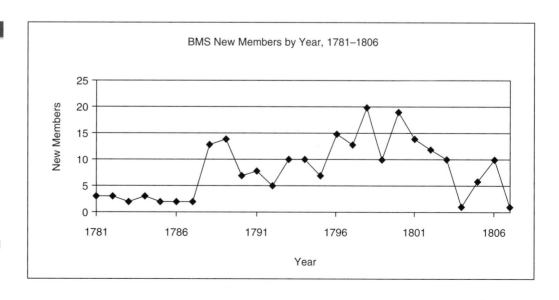

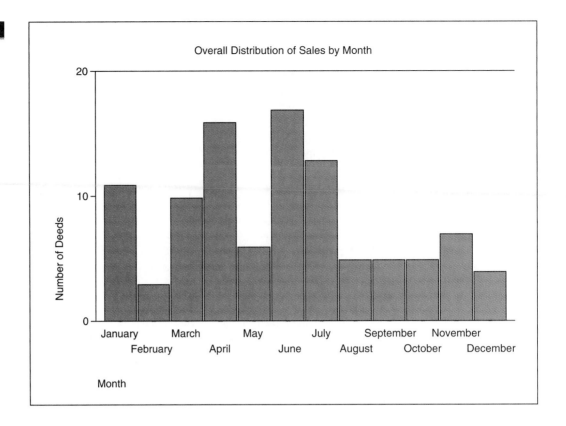

large annual spring gatherings of many bands at traditional fishing locations on the Merrimack and Piscataqua Rivers. When distribution is separated by decade, large spikes in land sales increasingly cluster in the spring later in the century. This may point to a growing native need for sustenance from the English marketplace after the hardships of the winter months, especially as their increasing proximity to white society did not raise their standard of living. Both Indian and English land sale patterns, not surprisingly, display a marked decrease at harvest time. (Leavenworth, 1998, pp. 88–89)

In the examples we've just seen, the raw numerical values sufficed for the researchers' purposes. In other instances, however, historical researchers may perform statistical analyses on the numerical data they collect; in such instances, historical research is truly a blend of qualitative and quantitative methodologies. An excellent resource for beginning historical researchers is Haskins and Jeffrey's *Understanding Quantitative History* (1990), which suggests many potentially useful sources of quantitative information and describes a variety of ways to analyze quantitative historical data.

In contrast with primary sources, **secondary sources** are the works of historians who have interpreted and written about primary sources. Secondary sources inevitably reflect the assumptions and biases of the people who wrote them. Such may be the case even when the sources were written soon after the primary sources were created.

Yet they, too, can reflect the biases of their creators, as explained in the following excerpt from a geography dissertation that analyzed changes in Jamaican agricultural practices during the early 1800s:

The sources of data are primarily printed documents published during the period of crisis, plus some surviving correspondence. Most important are island newspapers, the annual almanac, books, pamphlets, and government records. As with any historical data, [they] are incomplete in their coverage of contemporary events and may present a biased picture of the times. Some are also suspect as personal interpretations of interested parties participating in the events described. These problems are not insurmountable so long as we are aware of them and interpret source information in terms of its contemporary context. In fact, the opinions and biases reflected in much of the data [are themselves] an important component in our portrait of adaptive change. (R. K. Ormrod, 1974, pp. 217–218)

Notice how the author acknowledges the probable presence of bias in some of the secondary sources he used, even those published during the time period he was studying. In fact, he uses that bias to his advantage: as a way of getting a better handle on the prevailing perspectives of the time.

As noted in Chapter 5, researchers can probably never determine the ultimate, objective "Truth" that lies beneath a body of data. This frustrating state of affairs characterizes historical research as well as other research traditions (e.g., see Novick, 1988). Primary sources are generally regarded as being closer to whatever is or was "true" than secondary sources. Primary sources are those data that historians view as being closest to the ultimate "Truth" about historical events.

COLLECTING HISTORICAL RECORDS

Historical researchers often find it helpful to make copies of the primary sources (letters, minutes, deeds, etc.) that they find in archival collections at libraries, museums, historical societies, and the like. Many institutions provide photocopies for a small fee. An alternative approach is to photocopy the sources using a *digital camera*, which requires less light than photocopying and so is less likely to inflict environmental "wear and tear" on fragile documents. Photographs from digital cameras can be loaded directly onto a personal computer, allowing for easy cutting-and-pasting into a research report.

As researchers collect their documents, however, they should keep track of where each one came from, perhaps in a form similar to the footnotes they might eventually use to describe the documents in a final research report. For paper photocopies, small Post-It notes attached at a corner and written comments on the flip side are obvious strategies. When a digital camera is used, an ongoing log of what each shot is and where and when it is taken is essential.

ONLINE DATABASES ABOUT HISTORICAL EVENTS

Some historical documents and records can be found only in the archives of various libraries, museums, and historical societies around the world, and you may have to travel a great distance to see them. But many others have been painstakingly captured in electronic form and made available online. For example, many university libraries subscribe to such online databases as the following:

- *Making of America:* Copies of thousands of books and tens of thousands of journal articles published in the 1800s.
- *Accessible Archives:* Copies of several American newspapers and magazines from the 1800s.
- *New York Times Digital Archive:* Every page of every issue of the *New York Times* since its first issue in 1851.
- *Ancestry Plus:* A genealogical database that includes such documents as census records; birth, marriage, and death certificates; and immigration and naturalization records.

In addition, government Web sites offer many historical documents online. One especially helpful site is that of the Library of Congress (http://www.loc.gov/), which provides documents related to both American and world history and also gives links to other helpful Web sites around the world.

Access to such sources of information opens up many possibilities for people who previously were restricted by location, time, disabilities, or other challenges. In addition, simple word-processing functions such as "copy" and "paste" are invaluable time savers. As you locate relevant quotations, references, and so forth that you want to keep for future reference, it is possible to highlight the desired sections, copy them, and then paste them into your own database in a matter of seconds. (If you do such copying and pasting, you must take appropriate precautions to avoid copyright infringement, and you must not use the words and ideas of others without proper citation.)

PRACTICAL APPLICATION HANDLING HISTORICAL DATA SYSTEMATICALLY

In historical research, most of the data collected will be recorded in terms of hundreds, perhaps even thousands, of notes. It is imperative that the researcher have some means of gathering and controlling the data so that he or she reaps the greatest return from the innumerable hours spent in archives, document rooms, and libraries.

It is easy to read and take notes, but for many novice researchers, it is difficult to organize those notes into a format that facilitates interpretation. Historical data collection demands a systematic plan, not only for collecting data but also for retrieving and analyzing them. Before beginning historical research, therefore, you should have a specific plan for the acquisition, organization, storage, and retrieval of your data. Here we suggest two approaches you might take: a paper-and-pencil approach and a computerized approach.

A PAPER-AND-PENCIL APPROACH

Look back at Chapter 4 and review our suggestions for using note cards and bibliography cards. You may want to alter the formats described in that chapter to fit the nature of historical data. Earlier, we discussed the multidimensional nature of historical data. A fact may lie simultaneously in the province of time, of space, of personality, and perhaps of subject matter. Take, for example, a note that you might make when studying Edgar Allan Poe's poem "Annabel Lee." Poe wrote the poem in 1849 while living in a small cottage in the Fordham section of the Bronx in what is now New York City. As a researcher, you may wish to look at the note within the contexts of (a) Poe's life in Fordham; (b) Poe's poetry written in 1849; (c) poems that Poe wrote about his wife, Virginia Clemm; and (d) all information collected about the poem "Annabel Lee." Thus, you might want to study this single note from four different angles.

To facilitate analyzing a single note card from multiple perspectives, you should ideally make multiple copies, perhaps three or four, depending on your ultimate analysis of the data. For instance, you might want to organize your note cards by (a) chronological order, (b) geographical location, (c) historical figures, and (d) specific subtopics within your overall research topic.

As you've undoubtedly gathered, the approach we've just described can be both time- and space-consuming. The very process of making multiple copies takes a great deal of time; photocopying provides a faster, but more expensive, alternative. And unless you make duplicate copies of everything, you run the risk of losing all the data you've collected in the event of a fire, flood, or other catastrophe. Furthermore, the many notes you take may occupy a great deal of space in what is, for many researchers, tight living or working quarters. A more efficient alternative is to use a computer to record and organize your data.

A COMPUTERIZED APPROACH TO COLLECTING AND ORGANIZING YOUR DATA

USING
TECHNOLOGY

Technology facilitates data collection in several ways. We begin with the note-taking process. Instead of using the note card and manual copying of the data, take a cassette recorder to the library or archives or wherever the data may be available. Dictate the data (notes) instead of transcribing them. Better yet, take a laptop computer and either type or dictate your notes directly into the computer. (As noted in Chapter 7, some computer software lets you turn a laptop into a tape recorder.) When you return home, enter your notes into a database or word processing file.

From here on, the management of your data is limited only by the capabilities of your software. Most word processing programs let you search through your documents for recurring words or phrases; you can then copy these into a separate file. Many database software programs also sort, alphabetize, create tables and summaries, and arrange data in an ascending or descending order by date and event. Computerizing the data offers a broad range of techniques for data management. Your best guide for availability of data management features is the manual for your software package. Scan the index; it outlines the features available.

EVALUATING AND INTERPRETING HISTORICAL DATA

Once researchers have located historical data relevant to a research problem, they must decide what is fact and what is fiction. In other words, they must determine the *validity* of their data.

The data of historical research are subject to two types of evaluation. First, a researcher must judge whether a document or artifact is authentic. Second, he or she must decide, if the item is indeed authentic, what it means. In these two situations, the researcher is reviewing the data to determine their **external evidence** and **internal evidence,** respectively. (You may also see these referred to as *external criticism* and *internal criticism*.) We briefly discuss each of these concepts to give you a fuller appreciation of their use in historical research.

EXTERNAL EVIDENCE

External evidence is primarily concerned with the question, Is the article genuine? Counterfeits and frauds are not uncommon, nor is their acceptance by the naive scholar and researcher unusual.

External evidence for the validity of a document is of paramount importance for the credibility of the research. Establishing authenticity of documents may in some cases involve carbon dating, handwriting analysis, identification of ink and paper, vocabulary usage and writing style, and other approaches. This aspect of historical methodology is a study in itself, and we cannot discuss it at length in a text as brief as this one.

INTERNAL EVIDENCE

Quite apart from the question of genuineness is the equally important question, What does it mean? When considering a manuscript or a statement, the researcher asks such questions as, What was the author trying to say? To what individuals or events do certain phrases refer? What interpretations can be extracted from the words?

Take a well-known utterance. The time is November 19, 1863. Abraham Lincoln is speaking at the dedication of a national cemetery in Gettysburg, Pennsylvania. In that brief but famous dedicatory address, the President said, "But, in a larger sense, we cannot dedicate—we cannot consecrate—we cannot hallow this ground. The brave men, living and dead, who struggled here, have consecrated it, far above our power to add or detract."

What did Lincoln mean by "the brave men, living and dead"? Did he mean only the brave men of the Union forces? (We must remember that he was dedicating a Union cemetery.) Did he mean the brave Confederate men as well? Or did he mean brave men, indiscriminately, with no thought of North or South but merely of courage and valor? To a researcher studying the life of Abraham Lincoln, it is essential to know precisely what the President did mean by those words.

The matter of internal evidence applies not only to articles from the distant past but to more contemporary documents as well. What does the decision of a court mean? What do the words of the decision convey about the intent and will of the court? The question comes up all the time in legal interpretation. In such instances, the primary question is, *What do the words mean?* This is the sole concern of internal evidence.

Considerable historical meaning can be found in graphic documents as well as verbal ones. For example, in his dissertation about the Boston Marine Society, McKenzie analyzed nautical charts of New England coastline created during the society's era. He noticed that one early mapmaker, DesBarres—whose nautical charts were typically rendered in painstaking detail—had a glaring omission in a map of the Bar Harbor area of Maine. McKenzie interpreted the omission in light of political concerns of the time:

> In at least one case, DesBarres consciously changed the shape of the coastline to suit imperial [British] needs, thus pitting local needs against imperial desires. In his chart of the coast of Maine from Frenchman Bay to Mosquito Harbor, DesBarres failed to indicate Northeast Harbor, the best harbor in the region, or anything that might resemble a harbor along the southern coast of Mount Desert island. . . . DesBarres' omission was almost certainly intentional, as the rest of the island's features, including its topography, coves, and hazardous rocks, were laid out in

DesBarres' characteristic detail, and in more detail than the rest of land areas on the chart. DesBarres most likely left this strategically important harbor out of consideration for military reasons. In this case, imperial concerns outweighed the need for accurate local charts for free commerce. (McKenzie, 2003, p. 79)

When interpreting historical data, the researcher will inevitably impose certain assumptions on them. For instance, when looking at the laws that a democratic government created during a particular era, the researcher may assume that the laws reflected the *needs and beliefs of the majority of voting citizens* (Marius, 1989). Or, more generally, when tracking the course of events in a particular society, a researcher may assume that the events reflected *economic or social progress* (Breisach, 1994). A good historical researcher will identify, explicitly and concretely, the assumptions that guide his or her interpretation of historical data. As an example, we look once again at the previously excerpted geography dissertation, this time focusing on the researcher's interpretation of events during a crisis in Jamaican sugar planting practices during the early 19th century:

> Our interpretation [of the data] will depend upon two primary assumptions: (1) an adaptation imperative existed which demanded that the island society respond to the events threatening its pattern of livelihood, and (2) most of the behaviors involved in the response, bounded by the constraints inherent in the functioning cultural ecosystem, were goal directed. These assumptions lead us to expect an orderly response to crisis rather than a random one and lead us to seek a behavior system which sought to relieve the stresses on the society. Although such a behavior system would function in a probabilistic manner rather than as a closely determined one, we should nevertheless be able to construct an orderly framework of interpretation around our data. . . . (R. K. Ormrod, 1974, p. 227)

CONSIDERING HISTORICAL TIME AND HISTORICAL SPACE

The student of historical research must distinguish carefully between two concepts that are frequently confused under the general umbrella of "the study of history." One of these concepts is genuine historical research—*historiography*, as it is sometimes called. The other concept is *chronology*, the setting down of occurrences and events in the order in which they happened. Toynbee's *A Study of History* is historiography (historical research); the *Anglo-Saxon Chronicle* is an example of chronology.

Chronology is often nothing more than a listing of dates and events. It is not defined as research because it does not interpret the meaning of the events; it does not address the significance of any single event within the larger constellation of events.

The following is chronology:

1492	*Columbus discovers America.*
1607	*The first permanent English settlement in America is established at Jamestown, Virginia.*
1620	*The Pilgrims land at Plymouth, Massachusetts.*
1624	*The Dutch settle New Amsterdam.*
1630	*The Puritans establish Massachusetts Bay Colony.*
1634	*Lord Calvert settles Maryland.*
1682	*William Penn founds the colony of Pennsylvania.*
1733	*James Oglethorpe founds the colony of Georgia.*
1754–1763	*The French and Indian War is fought.*
1775–1783	*The War of American Independence is fought.*
1789	*George Washington is inaugurated as the first President of the United States of America.*
1792	*The first political parties appear in the United States; the Industrial Revolution begins in the United States with the introduction of Eli Whitney's cotton gin.*

The list is merely a succession of 12 dates marking a series of events in the first three centuries of the history of the original 13 colonies.

Yet changing the format does not change the genre. The mere recasting of a chronological list into paragraph form with detailed prose and appropriate documentary footnotes does not transform an unimaginative chronicle into historical research. The paragraph still recounts only a sequence of events—nothing more.

The historical researcher should be concerned primarily with historiography—with the interpretation of historical events. As we have said so many times before, interpretation is the indispensable element in all research.

This is not to imply that chronology does not fill an important place in historical study. It does. It is the grist of the research mill and is often the first step in the research process. You can recognize how essential chronology is in historical research if you attempt to visualize the disadvantage that would result from attempting to reconstruct the history of early England without the *Anglo-Saxon Chronicle*.

In view of what we have just noted, let's now look analytically at the chronology just presented. What, in fact, do these events say? What do they mean? Are they merely isolated happenings, or do they have relationships to one another and to the whole 300-year time span? These are questions the historical researcher is always asking of data. Such questions represent a basic attitude in historical research. If we are to do historical research, we must seek not only to identify the chain of events that comprise history but also to understand the meaning of these events, in terms of their relationships both to one another and to the problem under study.

History is dimensional. It has the dimensions of *historical time* and *historical space*. Both of these dimensions are important in interpreting historical data. We first discuss the concept of historical time; we then explore the idea of historical space.

HISTORICAL TIME

Some beginning researchers fail to familiarize themselves with the time dimension; hence, they do not appreciate the significance that the temporal context gives to the data. The more angles from which data are regarded, the more meaningful those data become. Historical data are no exception.

In the chronology we presented, the time span was 300 years: 1492 to 1792. To get a better sense of this time span, we draw a line 150 mm long and, for our 300-year span, make each millimeter equal to 2 years. We put the year 1492 at one end of the line and the year 1792 at the other end; we then insert the various events in the chronology in the appropriate places. The chronology now appears as shown in Figure 8.4.

How different the chronology now appears. It is no longer merely a list of items. It has become a series of events placed along a time continuum. The dynamics of history are now becoming apparent. Notice also the *rhythms* along the timeline. An event happens—the discovery of America. Then, an apparently sterile 115 years (1492–1607) elapse between that event and the first permanent English settlement at Jamestown, Virginia. But such was not the case. The total stage of history was, of course, crowded with events during that 115-year period. In what is now the United States of America, Spanish conquistadors and missionaries were busy in the Southwest and Florida. The French were in the Mississippi Valley. But if we look at the activity in the original 13 colonies, the historical record just depicted offers only silence during that span of years.

Then, beginning in 1607, events occur in rapid succession for slightly more than a quarter of a century: The English settle in Virginia and Massachusetts, the Dutch settle in New Amsterdam, and the Calvertists settle in Maryland. Other events, unmentioned of course, were also taking place: Roger Williams and the Antinomians settled in Rhode Island; the Swedes, in Delaware; John Mason and David Thomson, in New Hampshire. This quarter century of American colonial history teemed with activity! But for the purposes of this particular chronology, we have not mentioned these other events.

The timeline proceeds. Another century is unbroken except for one event, the founding of Pennsylvania. Then, the final half of the third century is again a time of renewed activity, of turbulent events: the birth of a nation and the beginning of an industrial revolution.

We need only a little imagination to realize that the device we have been discussing briefly—and merely for the purpose of presenting a historiographical method—has great potential. It also

FIGURE 8.4

FIGURE 8.4

Using a chronological timeline

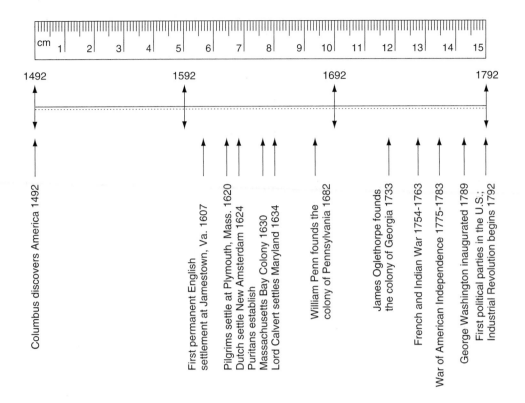

has considerable flexibility. The historical researcher who is studying more than one set of chronological data within the same time frame may gain increased insight by arranging multiple timeline scales side by side. We might superimpose onto the timeline in Figure 8.4 another series of events—for example, the principal events in the history of England that determined the discoveries and settlements in the New World. Similarly, we could plot on a third scale important events in mainland Europe over the same 300-year period. We would then read the chart as mathematicians read a slide rule: one scale against the other.

Because historical data often relate to events many years or centuries before the researcher's era, they have a tendency to telescope and appear closer together in time than they really were. Historical time can be deceptive unless we are alert to its realities. A pencil and some simple subtraction will reveal a great deal that may otherwise escape our awareness. If we compare a particular historical period against a period closer to us in time, we see more clearly the pace with which events moved in days gone by. For instance, into the block of time that elapsed between the discovery of America and the establishment of the first permanent English settlement at Jamestown, we could pack all of American history from the invention of the telephone in 1876 to the creation of the Internet in the 1980s.

HISTORICAL SPACE

We have been discussing history as a time phenomenon, and we have demonstrated the role of time in seeking the meaning of historical data. But events also happen in a particular place. They have a *space dimension*.

In trying to understand the significance of historical data, the *where*, or spatial dimension, is often just as important as the *when*. Let's now consider the geographical locations of some of the events on our earlier timeline. Study the map shown in Figure 8.5. Notice how English colonization began at the extremes (Virginia and Massachusetts), with the Dutch settling at New Amsterdam approximately 275 miles north of Jamestown and 225 miles south of the Massachusetts Bay Colony. Calvert founded Maryland. Half a century later, Penn settled Pennsylvania. In the interim, the Swedes had come to Delaware, and New Jersey was being negotiated between the Dutch and the English, with the whole situation complicated by conflicting deeds and per-

FIGURE 8.5

The spatial dimension of history

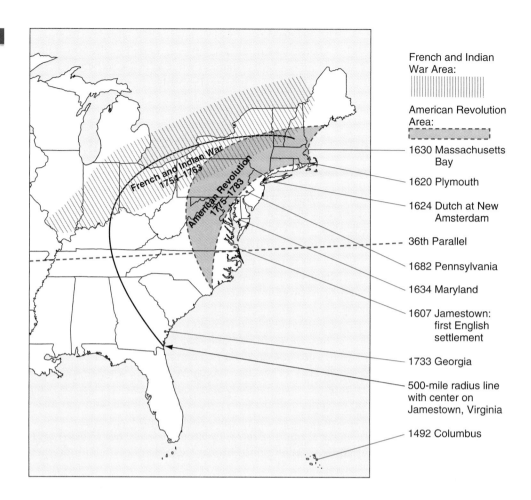

missions granted by authorities ignorant of one another's actions. The colonization that began at the fringes was now closing in toward the center. Only a map can reveal this phenomenon.

See what we have done with a single set of facts? We have arranged the same historical data in three ways: first, in a simple chronological listing; second, along a timeline continuum; and, third, in geographical relationship. Each arrangement provides a different insight into the meaning of the data. In each instance, we have more fully answered the basic question every researcher asks of any data, What do these data mean? The geographical placement of the information reveals a number of new insights aside from those apparent through the chronological and timeline presentations:

1. Colonization was not equally spread along the Atlantic coast. It clustered north of the 36th parallel.
2. The first English colony, at Jamestown, was pivotally located. It was just about equidistant from the northernmost and southernmost points of colonization activity.
3. We draw an arc on the map using Jamestown as the pivotal point and including the area in which almost all the events of the first 300 years of colonial American history took place. If we compare the radius of the arc to the scale of miles, we see that most activity in colonial America occurred within 500 miles of Jamestown.
4. The French and Indian War took place in the hatched area that lies partly in the northwest portion of the arc and partly outside the limits of the arc. Using a little imagination, we might suspect that the war seemed as remote to the colonists of Jamestown, Philadelphia, and New York as events in the Middle East seem to many North American residents today. (If we were to view a map of key events during the War for American Independence, we would find that, unlike the French and Indian War, it was a very close-to-home struggle. It swept through the colonies in a north-to-south direction. The only variation to this pattern was the Vincennes exploit of George Rogers Clark in 1779.)

5. The landing of Columbus on San Salvador is perhaps the only event lying outside the area of principal activity as bounded by the 500-mile radial line. Not only is it some 950 miles south of Jamestown, but it is also removed from the settlement at Jamestown by 115 years of history. Probably, this one event does indeed lie outside the corpus of historical data we are studying and is convenient only as a point of chronological reference.

PSYCHOLOGICAL OR CONCEPTUAL HISTORICAL RESEARCH

Thus far, we have discussed conventional historical research, the study of significant events and the individuals who played a role in them. But this chapter would not be complete without a brief discussion of another type of historical research—namely, that concerned with the origin, development, and influence of ideas and concepts. Ideas and concepts can influence the course of history just as surely as events and people do.

As an example, the idea of *democracy* was born in Greece; its development has run parallel to the events of the Greco-Roman world, the Middle Ages, and modern times. Over the years the idea has evolved into such concepts as *representative government* and *political campaign*. The initial concept of democracy that began in ancient Athens is, perhaps, found in its purest form today in the New England town meeting.

Consider other key ideas that have guided the course of civilization: capitalism, socialism, rationalism, individualism, communism, utopianism. Each of them, as well as other ideas akin to them, has its own developmental history, which is just as "real" as the history of Western civilization, the United States, or your hometown. Open any comprehensive encyclopedia to some of the principal ideas of civilization just listed, and you may well find some discussion of how these ideas have evolved over time.

Look, too, at Arnold Toynbee's monumental *A Study of History*. Here, you will find not the traditional approach to history—the description and interpretation of events—so much as the dynamic ideas that have powered the histories of nations and civilizations and that have been instrumental in bringing about cataclysmic changes in those histories.

THE FASCINATION OF SEARCHING FOR ROOTS

We mentioned in Chapter 5 the fascinating research of John Livingston Lowes, which is presented in *The Road to Xanadu*. Lowes's book is remarkable because it is, in a sense, research in reverse. In it, Lowes searches for "the genesis of two of the most remarkable poems in English, 'The Rime of the Ancient Mariner' and 'Kubla Khan'" (Lowes, 1927, p. 3).

This type of research, which is the counterpart of a genealogical search of one's family origins, begins with such questions as, Where did it come from? and How did it all begin? This is precisely the type of research that astronomers and astrophysicists conduct to try to account for the creation of the universe. One does not have to design a research project on such a cosmic scale to engage in the same kind of detective work that reels backward in search of answers instead of forward, as is usually done.

The process of beginning with a phenomenon and going backward in time to identify possible causal factors is sometimes called *ex post facto research*. We will consider ex post facto within a different context—how people's backgrounds may potentially affect their current characteristics and behaviors—in Chapter 10.

PRACTICAL APPLICATION Historical Research Writing

Written accounts of historical research vary widely, depending on the researcher and his or her style of writing. Research reports dealing with historical research need not be dull, and in fact those historians whose works often appear on best-seller lists infuse their descriptions of history with many colorful events and interesting personalities.

To appreciate how various scholars have handled the same subject matter, take one significant event in history—the Peloponnesian War, the Battle of Tours, or the march of Hannibal across the Alps—and compare the treatment of the event by various historical writers. In view of the matters discussed in this chapter, compare the historical accounts on the basis of the following checklist. We suggest using a word processor to answer the questions.

✔ CHECKLIST
COMPARING TWO RECORDS OF A SIGNIFICANT EVENT IN HISTORY

1. Identify two sources that describe the same event in history and list them below:

Author: _____   Author: _____

Title of work: _____   Title of work: _____

Reference: _____   Reference: _____

2. Evaluate each record in terms of the following questions:

_____ Is there an attempt to evaluate the sources of evidence? If yes, in what ways?

_____

_____

_____ Does the account show an awareness of "historical time"? If yes, in what ways?

_____

_____

_____ Does the account show an awareness of "historical space"? If yes, in what ways?

_____

_____

_____ Is the account a prose form of chronology? If yes, in what ways?

_____

_____

_____ Is the account interspersed with interpretations of the historical data? If yes, in what ways?

_____

_____

_____ Is there an attempt to evaluate the sources of evidence? If yes, in what ways?

_____

_____

_____ Does the account show an awareness of "historical time"? If yes, in what ways?

_____

_____

_____ Does the account show an awareness of "historical space"? If yes, in what ways?

_____

_____

_____ Is the account a prose form of chronology? If yes, in what ways?

_____

_____

_____ Is the account interspersed with interpretations of the historical data? If yes, in what ways?

_____

_____

3. Compare the two columns of information. Are the accounts essentially the same? If not, describe the difference between them.

_____

_____

Reflect on what you learned from each account. How did the study and comparison of the two works help you gain a greater understanding of the topic? What additional information would also have been helpful?

For a variation on the preceding project, look up some event in the *Cambridge Ancient* (or *Modern*) *History* and choose the identical event in, for example, Will Durant's *The Story of Civilization*. The purpose of this project is to give you an opportunity to develop skill at critically evaluating historiography and historical research.

GUIDELINES   WRITING THE HISTORICAL RESEARCH REPORT

Many of the suggestions we offer about writing in Chapters 2, 4, 6, and 12 apply to historical research as well as to any other type of research. In addition, Marius (1989) has offered several useful *rules for argument* that you should keep in mind when, in particular, you are writing about a historical research study.

1. *State your own argument early in the game.*   Remember, you are not only presenting the data, but you are also *interpreting* it. You should be up-front about your interpretation and not keep your readers guessing.

2. *Provide examples to support any assertion you make.*   You make a more convincing case when you give examples of data that lend credence to your position.

3. *Give the fairest possible treatment of any perspectives different from your own.*   You may very well be presenting an interpretation that differs from those of other scholars. Describe competing interpretations and provide evidence that supports them as well as evidence that casts doubt upon them.

4. *Point out the weaknesses of your own argument.*   Better to shoot holes in your own case than to have others do it for you. You portray yourself as a credible researcher when you appear to be objective, rather than blindly one-sided, in your analysis and interpretation of your data.

With regard to the fourth guideline, we should remind you that your research project, while answering your initial research question, may also yield new, unanswered questions. You can turn any inconsistent findings that you uncover into "unresolved issues" or "suggestions for future research."

A SAMPLE DISSERTATION

 Now go to our Companion Website at http://www.prenhall.com/leedy to assess your understanding of chapter content and to complete the projects that will help you learn how to conduct research.

We now return to Matthew McKenzie's dissertation on the Boston Marine Society, which Matt completed for his doctoral degree in history at the University of New Hampshire (McKenzie, 2003). We have already shown brief snippets of the dissertation to illustrate certain aspects of historical research, but we now present a larger chunk with a running commentary. You will see that, overall, the dissertation has a different feel to it than the proposal and dissertation excerpts that appear in previous chapters. Unlike those earlier excerpts, this dissertation is written as a *narrative*, with historical events and interpretations seamlessly interwoven throughout the discussion. Matt spent an extra year overhauling major sections of his dissertation, and his efforts show clearly in the quality of his writing. Notice, too, how Matt used footnotes to identify his sources, reflecting the style that historians typically use in their research reports (more about various styles in Chapter 12).

DISSERTATION ANALYSIS 5

INTRODUCTION

In the spring of 1755, Captain Hector McNeill was in command of a merchant vessel in a small flotilla convoying an army up the Bay of Fundy. The fleet had left Boston a few days before with the task of safely delivering 2,000 New England soldiers to fight against their French imperial rivals at Fort Beaussejour. As the fleet sailed along the current-swept, rocky

Comments

In Chapter 6, we suggested that you always state your research problem at the very beginning of your research proposal. In a research report, however, researchers often begin with a few paragraphs of background

shores, [Colonel] Robert Monckton worried about the fate of his army. Back in Boston, there had been almost no charts for him to consult, and even fewer descriptions of the currents and tides that made this region so dangerous. Moreover, his and his army's fate rested in the hands of a few Boston merchant skippers, like Captain McNeill, none of whom likely knew the latest and best techniques in navigation.

Despite his fears, however, and the dangerous shoals and hazardous headlands, the fleet proceeded safely. When Monckton approached McNeill about their progress, curious as to how a colonial trading skipper could successfully undertake such a hazardous job, McNeill showed him information which no British commander in North America or London knew existed. Trading along the coast, McNeill had collected five years of nautical observations, including (presumably) tides, currents, coastal descriptions, and manuscript drawings. From these observations, McNeill had drawn a chart covering the coast from Cape Cod to Cape St. Mary's including the Bay of Fundy. McNeill's chart impressed the British commander. And shortly after the Boston skipper safely delivered his regiments, Monckton dislodged the French from Beaussejour.[1]

McNeill was not alone in his interest in marine cartography in New England. In 1760, he joined a group of master mariners in Boston, called the Boston Marine Society (BMS), which had also been systematically collecting navigational observations since 1754. Both McNeill and the Marine Society understood that local navigational knowledge carried commercial, political, and imperial opportunities. Consequently, when the organization united senior captains for mutual aid, they also recognized that they stood in an important position between London imperial agents in North America and the coastline that interested them. Furthermore, they were actively collecting data as every member returned to Boston—a feature that they would try to barter for greater influence in Boston and within the [British] Empire.

Historians are fortunate in the Marine Society's meticulous record keeping and parliamentary procedure. Two key issues help modern researchers see the society's collective will and motivation. First, as membership was limited to captains alone, the Society was self-conscious that they spoke as an elite body in Boston's maritime community. Second, as an organization of captains predicated upon fellowship and mutual aid and with a distinct role within the port, the Society went to great lengths to follow proper parliamentary procedures and to act only on decisions taken unanimously. As part of this process, the Society maintained meeting minutes recording the Society's (though not individuals') opinions, resolutions, and approved actions. Consequently, throughout its 250-year history, the society left committee reports, resolutions, and clear statements that reveal its collective will and motivations. These records allow historians to uncover not only what the organization did, but why.

This is not the first study of the Boston Marine Society. Earlier studies of the Marine Society have cataloged in some detail the work the Marine Society undertook during its long history. Nathaniel Spooner stitched together a rough narrative in his 1879 *Gleanings of the Boston Marine Society* (Boston, 1879, 1999). In 1982, William A. Baker's *A History of the Boston Marine Society* (Boston, 1982) integrated the Marine Society's history more closely with changes in Boston politics and economics and assembled systematic information on the

information that provides a context for the research problem. A common strategy in historical writing is to begin with a story—a real-life drama of sorts—that draws readers in and motivates them to continue reading.

Here we get a glimpse of what will be one major thrust of the dissertation: describing and tracking the nature of early nautical charts, whose use and promotion were partly attributable to efforts of the Boston Marine Society.

Notice the use of footnotes to identify the sources for certain statements. The author is using the style required by the Journal of American History *(available online on the journal's Website at http://www.indiana. edu/~jah/). Footnotes are also consistent with the Chicago Manual of Style (2003).*

Notice the smooth flow of the narrative from one event to another. In our experience, narrative writing is more challenging than traditional "scientific" report writing. However, when well executed (as is the case here), narrative reports are also more engaging than scientific reports tend to be.

Here we see the context in which the discussion of the society's minutes (excerpted earlier in the chapter) appeared.

---

[1] Hector McNeill to Lord Colville, January 17, 1763, Boston Marine Society Papers (Massachusetts Historical Society, Boston, Mass.).

society's more than 3,000 members. Both of these works greatly aided the project that follows. Yet neither delved into the society's influence upon the history of American science, [and] with the exception of Baker's study of the Society during the American Revolution, neither Baker nor Spooner were interested in examining how the society operated as an active agent in Boston's historical development.

This study seeks to examine the society within the context of the history of American Science. Academic centers and learned societies have been the focus for most considerations of American science because of their prominence in the nineteenth and twentieth centuries. The Marine Society's scientific interests indicate, however, that colonial groups could and did develop their own scientific agenda that they pursued through methods adapted from common vocational practices. In doing so, the Marine Society's navigational work draws important parallels to the history of colonial science in other areas during the late eighteenth century. In the simplest form, I argue that colonial Boston shipmasters were not dependent upon learned societies for their navigational research needs. Rather, they adapted their mutual aid society and developed methodologies to collect navigational observations, analyze them for reliability and accuracy, and in a few cases, publish their findings for the benefit of the community. Furthermore, given the close ties between seafaring, economic growth and political influence in a mercantile economy, the Marine Society's work in navigational research granted them social and political influence in Boston. With this added influence—power would be too strong a term for it—the Marine Society tried to stabilize post-Revolutionary Boston politics, and to legitimate their efforts to become one of the town's new elites. Ultimately, the Marine Society lost its political influence as changes in navigational research, shifts in Boston and national politics, and new market centers for scientific information combined to weaken the society's position in both the political and navigational research world.

The Marine Society gives us a glimpse of the rise and fall of what I call "vocational science." In many previous studies discussed below, science and research were considered as a purely intellectual—"academic"—exercise, centered in learned academies, universities, and laboratories. I argue, to the contrary, that those who used navigation to carry their vessels safely into port, and expanded navigational knowledge, pursued science just as much as those who approached navigation from theoretical understandings of geodesy, mathematical astronomy, and spherical trigonometry. Whether using complex mathematical models to develop an absolute understanding of coastal features, or using piloting techniques, rule of thumb guidelines, simple instruments, and best-as-possible guess-work, both vocational and academic researchers formed part of a larger process by which the knowledge of New England's coast expanded.

The idea of vocational science also highlights an important mechanism by which specific groups used science to shore up their economic, social and political positions within their local area. While most prior work on American science has shown how the pursuit of scientific knowledge translated into improved cultural and social reputation, most have seen these efforts as a neutral desire to expand humanity's understanding of the world. Yet in this case, engagement in scientific research carried immediate economic, political and social benefits that were anything but neutral. As Joyce Chaplin has shown, colonial Carolina low-country planters sent botanical specimens to the Royal Society and the Royal Society of Arts in exchange for agricultural innovations. These innovations—seeds, water control mechanisms,

---

Here the author explains how his own research extends the boundaries of what is known and believed about the Boston Marine Society's role in American history.

Here the author also explains how his research represents a divergence from the traditional approach to the history of science: Rather than studying the effects of traditional academic groups (universities and academic organizations), he is studying the impact of a less academic, yet definitely influential, group.

The author makes his central hypothesis clear at this point: He believes that early shipmasters relied on one another rather than on traditional scientific investigations to get the information they needed to travel safely along the northern Atlantic coastline.

He posits a second hypothesis as well: The society's significant involvement in the local economy gave it considerable influence in early Boston.

The author introduces a new concept— vocational science—to describe the phenomenon he uncovers in his research.

The author contrasts his own viewpoint with more traditional views.

The author argues convincingly that, contrary to the popular perception of scientists as individuals who are more concerned about the general quest for knowledge than about their personal needs,

and processing machinery—helped them secure political control over Carolina politics during the Early Republic and helped create the land-owning elite of the Ante-bellum south.[2] James McClellan argues that while French planters in Saint Domingue did not embrace science as openly as their Carolina counterparts, science did serve the mercantilist interests of the state, and helped perpetuate slavery in the French Caribbean.[3] Finally, John Lauritz Larson has shown that experimental engineering designs for locks, dams, and internal waterways promised America's post-Revolutionary elite a means to promote private improvement schemes with public funds and in the face of public opposition.[4] In all these situations, science—whether tied to European centers or not—worked to bolster a specific group's local political and economic positions. Not pursued solely for knowledge in its own right, science expanded knowledge of the natural world, yet at the same time advanced specific interests.

these "vocational scientists" often had fairly self-serving motives at the root of their endeavors. He draws analogies to advancements in other locations and other times, where people may have been equally self-promoting. In doing so, he situates his research within a larger body of research literature that has preceded his own work.

Readers will find the terms "science," "navigational knowledge," and "research" used quite liberally and perhaps over-interchangeably in the pages that follow. This is intentional. The structured and distinct practices that we associate with science today had yet to develop in the second half of the eighteenth century. The lines between "amateur," "practitioner," and "interested gentleman" were blurry to say the least. As others have shown, to impose such categories on inquiries into the natural world and the inquirers themselves clouds more than clarifies. Only after science underwent dramatic changes in the early nineteenth century would science have such clear structures.[5]

Here the author anticipates and addresses a potential source of confusion for his readers. In particular, he provides a reasonable rationale for why he will use several terms interchangeably.

[*The report continues with a discussion of earlier researchers' explanations of the interplay among science, politics, and social dynamics in colonial American and the early decades following the American Revolution.*]

---

[2] Joyce Chaplin, *An Anxious Pursuit: Agricultural Innovation and Modernity in the Lower South, 1730–1815* (Chapel Hill, 1993), 131–142.

[3] James E. McClellan III, *Colonialism and Science: Saint Domingue in the Old Regime* (Baltimore, 1993), 9, 289–292.

[4] John Lauritz Larson, *Internal Improvement: National Public Works and the Promise of Popular Government in the Early United States* (Chapel Hill, 2001), 1–37.

[5] See McClellan, *Colonialism and Science*, 7; and Roy MacLeod, "On visiting the Moving Metropolis: Reflections on the Architecture of Imperial Science," in Scientific Aspects of European Expansion, ed. William K. Storey (Hampshire, 1996), 24–27.

NOTE. From *Vocational Science and the Politics of Independence: The Boston Marine Society, 1754–1812* (pp. 1–6), by M. G. McKenzie, 2003, unpublished doctoral dissertation, University of New Hampshire, Durham. Reprinted with permission.

We have said enough about the historical method for the purposes of the beginning researcher. We now turn to an entirely different approach to the discovery of knowledge. Chapters 7 and 8 have dealt with qualitative methodologies; Chapters 9, 10, and 11 will explore quantitative research.

FOR FURTHER READING

Barzun, J., & Graff, H. (1992). *The modern researcher* (5th ed.). San Diego, CA: Harcourt Brace. [Provides a comprehensive survey of historians' work]

Breisach, E. (1994). *Historiography: Ancient, medieval, and modern* (2nd ed.) Chicago: University of Chicago Press.

Brundage, A. (1997). *Going to the sources: A guide to historical research and writing* (2nd ed.). Wheeling, IL: Harlan Davidson.

Burstyn, J. N. (1987). History as image: Changing the lens. *History of Education Quarterly, 27,* 167–180.

Button, H. W., & Provenzo, E. F., Jr. (1989). *History of education and culture in America* (2nd ed.). Upper Saddle River, NJ: Prentice Hall.

Case, D. O. (1991). The collection and use of information by some American historians: A study of motives and methods. *Library Quarterly, 61*(1), 61–82.

Clive, J. (1989). *Not by fact alone: Essays on the writing and reading of history*. New York: Knopf.

de Certeau, M. (1988). *The writing of history*. New York: Columbia.

Edson, C. H. (1986). Our past and present: Historical inquiry in education. *Journal of Thought, 21,* 13–27.

Errante, A. (2000). But sometimes you're not part of the story: Oral histories and ways of remembering and telling. *Educational Researcher, 29*(2), 16–27.

Floud, R. (1980). *Introduction to quantitative methods for historians* (2nd ed.). New York: Routledge, Chapman & Hall.

Gilmore, M. B. (1992). Historians, books, computers, and the library. *Library Trends, 40,* 667–686.

Gray, W. (1991). *Historian's handbook: A key to the study and writing of history* (2nd ed.). Prospect Heights, IL: Waveland.

Harvey, C., & Press, J. (1996). *Database systems and historical research: Software, methods, and applications*. New York: St. Martin's Press.

Haskins, L., & Jeffrey, K. (1990). *Understanding quantitative history*. New York: McGraw-Hill.

Hill, M. R. (1993). *Archival strategies and techniques*. Thousand Oaks, CA: Sage.

Jarausch, K. H. (1991). *Quantitative methods for historians: A guide to research, data, and statistics*. Chapel Hill: University of North Carolina Press.

Lewis, M. J., & Lloyd-Jones, R. (1996). *Using computers in history: A practical guide*. New York: Routledge.

Marius, R. (1989). *A short guide to writing about history*. New York: HarperCollins.

Novick, P. (1988). *That noble dream: The "objectivity question" and the American historical profession*. Cambridge, England: Cambridge University Press.

Poulton, H. J., & Howland, M. S. (1972). *The historian's handbook: A descriptive guide to reference works*. Norman: University of Oklahoma Press.

Slavens, T. P. (1994). *Sources of information for historical research*. New York: Neal-Schuman.

Veyne, P. (1984). *Writing history: Essay on epistemology*. Hanover, NH: University Press of New England.

Zweig, R. W. (1993). Electronically generated records and twentieth-century history. *Computers and the Humanities, 27*(2), 73–83.

Part IV

Quantitative Research Methodologies

9

Descriptive Research

To behold is to look beyond the fact; to observe, to go beyond the observation. Look at the world of people, and you will be overwhelmed by what you see. But select from that mass of humanity a well-chosen few, and observe them with insight, and they will tell you more than all the multitudes together.

In this chapter, we discuss types of quantitative study that fall under the broad heading *descriptive quantitative research*. This type of research involves either identifying the characteristics of an observed phenomenon or exploring possible correlations among two or more phenomena. In every case, descriptive research examines a situation *as it is*. It does not involve changing or modifying the situation under investigation, nor is it intended to determine cause-and-effect relationships.

As you proceed through the chapter, you will find several strategies—sampling, making observations, interviewing—that you encountered previously in Chapter 7's discussion of qualitative research. This is old news, you might think. On the contrary, such strategies take on a very different form when we want them to yield quantitative data, and so we will essentially be starting from scratch when we talk about them here.

DESCRIPTIVE RESEARCH DESIGNS

In the next few pages, we describe observation studies, correlational research, developmental designs, and survey research. All of these approaches yield quantitative information that can be summarized through statistical analyses. We devote a significant portion of the chapter to survey research, because this approach is used so frequently in such diverse disciplines as business, government, public health, sociology, and education.

OBSERVATION STUDIES

In qualitative studies, observations are usually recorded in great detail, perhaps with fieldnotes or videotapes that capture the wide variety of ways in which people act and interact. From these data, the researcher constructs a complex yet integrated picture of how people spend their time. (We refer you back to Chapter 7 for a second look at the nature of observations in qualitative research.)

In quantitative research, an **observation study** is quite different. Typically, the focus is on a *particular* aspect of behavior. Furthermore, the behavior is quantified in some way. In some situations, each occurrence of the behavior is counted to determine its overall frequency. In other situations, the behavior is rated for accuracy, intensity, maturity, or some other dimension. But regardless of approach, the researcher strives to be *as objective as possible* in assessing the behavior being studied. To maintain such objectivity, he or she is likely to use strategies such as the following:

▧ Define the behavior being studied in a precise, concrete manner so that the behavior is easily recognized when it occurs.

▧ Divide the observation period into small segments and then record whether the behavior does or does not occur during each segment. (Each segment might be 30 seconds, 5 minutes, 15 minutes, or whatever other time span is suitable for the behavior being observed.)

▧ Use a rating scale to evaluate the behavior in terms of specific dimensions (more about rating scales later in the chapter).

▧ Have two or three people rate the same behavior independently, without knowledge of one another's ratings.

▧ Train the rater(s) to follow specific criteria when counting or evaluating the behavior, and continue training until consistent ratings are obtained for any single occurrence of the behavior.

A study by Kontos (1999) can give you a flavor for what a researcher might do in an observational study. Kontos's research question was this: What roles do preschool teachers adopt during children's free-play periods? (She asked the question within the context of theoretical issues that are irrelevant to our purposes here.) The study took place during free-play sessions in Head Start classrooms, where 40 preschool teachers wore cordless microphones that transmitted what they said (and what people near them said as well) to a remote audiotape recorder. Each teacher was audiotaped for 15 minutes on each of two different days as they assumed their normal classroom activities. Following data collection, the tapes were transcribed and broken into 1-minute segments. Each segment was coded in terms of the primary role that the teacher assumed during that time, with five possible roles being identified: *interviewer* (talking with children about issues unrelated to a playtime activity), *stage manager* (helping children get ready to engage in a play activity), *play enhancer/playmate* (joining a play activity in some way), *safety/behavior monitor* (managing children's behavior), or *uninvolved* (not attending to the children's activities in any fashion). Two research assistants independently coded the transcripts after first being trained until they were consistent in their judgments at least 90% of the time. (The researcher found, among other things, that teachers' behaviors were to some degree a function of the activities in which the children were engaging. Her conclusions, like her consideration of theoretical issues, go beyond the scope of this book.)

As should be clear from the preceding example, an observational study involves considerable advance planning, meticulous attention to detail, a great deal of time, and, often, the help of one or more research assistants. Furthermore, a pilot study to iron out any wrinkles in identifying and classifying the behavior(s) under investigation is essential; embarking on a full-fledged study without pilot-testing the methodology first may result in many hours of wasted time.

Ultimately, an observational study can yield data that portray much of the richness and complexity of human behavior. In some situations, then, it provides a quantitative alternative to such approaches as ethnographies and grounded theory studies.

CORRELATIONAL RESEARCH

A **correlational study** examines the extent to which differences in one characteristic or variable are related to differences in one or more other characteristics or variables. A **correlation** exists if, when one variable increases, another variable either increases or decreases in a somewhat predictable fashion.

In correlational studies, researchers gather data about two or more characteristics for a particular group of people or other appropriate units of study. These data are numbers that reflect specific measurements of the characteristics in question; for instance, they might be test scores, grade point averages (GPAs), ratings assigned by an expert observer, or frequencies of certain behaviors.

An example may be helpful. As you well know, as children grow older, they become better readers. In other words, there is a *correlation* between age and reading ability. Imagine that a researcher has a sample of 50 children and knows two things about these children: their age and their scores on a reading achievement test (the test scores indicate the approximate "grade level" at which the children are reading). The researcher might plot the data on a **scatterplot** (also known as a *scattergram*) to allow a visual inspection of the relationship between the two variables. Figure 9.1 presents this hypothetical scatterplot. Chronological age is on the vertical axis (the *ordinate*) of the graph, and reading level is on the horizontal axis (the *abscissa*). Each dot represents a particular child; its placement on the scatterplot indicates both the child's age and his or her reading level.

If age and reading ability were two completely unrelated characteristics, the dots would be scattered all over the graph. When the dots instead form a rough elliptical shape (as the dots in Figure 9.1 do), or perhaps a skinnier sausage shape, then we know that the two characteristics are correlated to some degree. The diagonal line running through the middle of the dots (sometimes called the *line of regression*) reflects a hypothetical perfect correlation between age and reading level; if all the dots fell on this line, then a child's age would tell us *exactly* what the child's reading level is. In actuality, only four of the dots fall on the dotted line. Some dots lie below the line, showing children whose reading level is, relatively speaking, advanced for their age. Other dots lie above the line, indicating children who are lagging a bit in reading.

As we examine the scatterplot, we can say several things about it. First, we can *describe* the homogeneity or heterogeneity of the two variables—the extent to which the children are similar to or different from one another with respect to age and reading level. For instance, if the data were to include only children ages 6 and 7, then we would have greater homogeneity with respect to age than would be the case for a sample of children ages 6 through 13. Second, we can *describe* the degree to which the two variables are intercorrelated, perhaps by computing a statistic known as a *correlation coefficient* (we'll describe the nature of this coefficient in Chapter 11). But third, and most importantly, we can *interpret* these data and give them meaning. For instance, the upward trend of the dots from left to right tells us that as children grow older, their reading level improves. We can also conclude that a child's age should help us estimate or predict the child's reading level to some degree.

A Caution About Interpreting Correlational Results

In all correlational studies, be alert for faulty logic. When two variables are correlated, researchers sometimes conclude that one of the variables must in some way influence the other. In

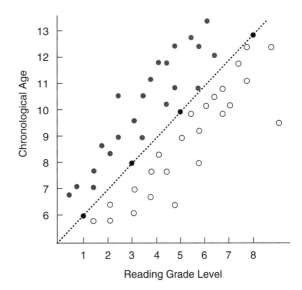

FIGURE 9.1

Example of a scatterplot: Correlation between age and reading level some instances, such influence may indeed be present; for example, chronological age (or at least the amount of experience that one's age reflects) almost certainly has a direct bearing on children's mental development, including their reading ability. But ultimately we can never infer a cause-and-effect relationship on the basis of correlation alone. Simply put, *correlation does not, in and of itself, indicate causation*.

Take a logically absurd yet statistically demonstrable example. We could conceivably find a statistical correlation between the number of elephants in Thailand in any given year and the size of the Florida orange crop that same year. The facts may be very clear: As the size of the elephant population increases over time, the Florida orange crop also increases. Yet it is ludicrous to think that because we can show a positive correlation there must therefore be a causal bond at the root of the relationship. There is no connection whatsoever between the elephant population in Thailand and the production of oranges in Florida (at least none *we* can think of!). The correlation is simply a fluke and has no meaning. One variable correlates meaningfully with another only when a common causal bond links the phenomena of both variables in a logical relationship. However, identifying the exact nature of this causal bond is beyond the scope of a simple correlational study.

In the extreme situation of the elephants–oranges correlation, the faulty logic is readily apparent. Yet we often see similarly faulty reasoning proposed in correlational research reports. For instance, imagine that a researcher finds a correlation between socioeconomic level and academic performance: Children from lower socioeconomic groups have lower GPAs than children from higher socioeconomic groups. It would be all too easy to draw the conclusion that socioeconomic status directly *affects* (i.e., has a causal influence on) academic achievement. We might think that because the family paycheck, the family living conditions, and so forth are inadequate, the achievement of the boys and girls of such families is also below par. If a family's economic status could be improved, we conclude, the learning ability of the family's children would also improve.

No, no, no! We *cannot* make an inference about causation on the basis of correlated data alone. It's possible that paycheck size does have an impact on children's grades, but it's equally possible that it does not. Perhaps, instead, an undetermined third variable (e.g., parents' education levels or the degree to which family members are subjected to racial or ethnic discrimination) influences both the size of the family paycheck and the children's school performance.

If we were to infer that socioeconomic status directly affects academic achievement, not only would we be going far beyond the data we have, but we would also have trouble accounting for all of the world's geniuses and intellectual giants, some of whom have been born of indigent parents and grown up in poverty. For example, Robert Burns, the greatest of Scottish poets, did not have even a common school education because of the poverty of his family. Enrico Caruso, the great Italian tenor, was born in Naples of a poor family. George Washington Carver, a famous American botanist, was born of slaves. The father of Franz Schubert, the Austrian composer, was a peasant, and his mother was a cook; Schubert himself lived in poverty most of his life. The case of Abraham Lincoln, born in a log cabin, walking miles to borrow a book, also discredits the impoverished environment-deprived child theory.

The data may not lie, but the causal conclusions we draw from the data may, at times, be extremely suspect. Nevertheless, a good researcher must not be content to stop at the point of finding a correlational relationship, because *beneath the correlation* lie some potentially quite interesting dynamics. One way to explore these dynamics is through *structural equation modeling*, a statistical procedure we'll describe briefly in Chapter 11. Another approach—one that will yield more solid conclusions about cause-and-effect relationships—is to follow up a correlational study with one or more experimental studies (described in Chapter 10) to test various hypotheses about what causes what.

DEVELOPMENTAL DESIGNS

Earlier, we presented a hypothetical example of how children's ages might correlate with their reading achievement levels. Oftentimes when researchers want to study how a particular characteristic changes as people grow older, they use one of two developmental designs, either a cross-sectional study or a longitudinal study.

In a **cross-sectional study**, people from several different age groups are sampled and compared. For instance, a developmental psychologist might study the nature of friendships for children at ages 4, 8, 12, and 16. A gerontologist might consider how retired people in their 70s, 80s, and 90s are most likely to spend their leisure time.

In a **longitudinal study**, a single group of people is followed over the course of several months or years, and data related to the characteristic(s) under investigation are collected at various times. For example, a psycholinguist might examine how children's spoken language changes between 6 months and 10 years of age. Or an educational psychologist might get measures of academic achievement and social adjustment for a group of fourth graders and then, 10 years later, find out which students had completed high school (and what their GPAs were) and which ones had not. (In the latter example, the researcher might also compute correlations between the measures taken in the fourth-grade and the students' high school GPAs; thus, the project would be a correlational study as well as a longitudinal one.)

Obviously, cross-sectional studies are easier to conduct than longitudinal studies, because the researcher can collect all the needed data at a single time. In contrast, a researcher who conducts a longitudinal study must collect data over a lengthy period and invariably loses some participants along the way, perhaps because they move to unknown locations or perhaps because they no longer want to participate. An additional disadvantage of a longitudinal design is that when people respond repeatedly to the same measurement instrument, they are likely to improve simply because of their *practice* with the instrument, even if the characteristic being measured hasn't changed at all.

But cross-sectional designs have their disadvantages as well. For one thing, the different age groups sampled may have been raised under different environmental conditions. For instance, imagine that we wanted to find out whether logical thinking improves or declines between the ages of 20 and 70. If we took a cross-sectional approach, we might get samples of 20-year-olds and 70-year-olds and then measure their logical thinking ability, perhaps by using a standardized multiple-choice test. Now imagine that the 20-year-olds obtained higher scores on our logical thinking test than the 70-year-olds. Does this mean that logical thinking ability declines with age? Not necessarily. At least two other possible explanations readily come to mind. The quality of education has changed in many ways over the past century, and the younger people have probably had a superior education to that of the older people. And the younger folks have almost certainly had more experience taking multiple-choice tests than the older folks have.

A second disadvantage of a cross-sectional design is that we cannot compute correlations between characteristics at different age levels. Consider, again, the educational psychologist who wants to use students' academic achievement and social adjustment in fourth grade to predict their tendency to drop out in high school. In a cross-sectional study, there would be different students in the two age groups, and so any predictions from one age to the next would, of course, be impossible.

Both cross-sectional and longitudinal designs are used in a variety of disciplines, but, as you might guess, they are most commonly seen in developmental research (e.g., studies in child development or gerontology). Should you wish to conduct a developmental study, we urge you to browse in such journals as *Child Development* and *Developmental Psychology* for ideas about specific research strategies.

SURVEY RESEARCH

Some scholars use the term *survey research* to refer to almost *any* form of descriptive, quantitative research (Gay & Airasian, 2003; Johnson, 2001). We use a more restricted meaning here: **Survey research** involves acquiring information about one or more groups of people—perhaps about their characteristics, opinions, attitudes, or previous experiences—by asking them questions and tabulating their answers. The ultimate goal is to learn about a large population by surveying a sample of that population; thus, we might call this approach a *descriptive survey* or *normative survey*.

Reduced to its basic elements, a **survey** is quite simple in design: The researcher poses a series of questions to willing participants; summarizes their responses with percentages, frequency counts, or more sophisticated statistical indexes; and then draws inferences about a particular population from the responses of the sample. It is a common approach, used with more or less sophistication in many areas of human activity. From the individual citizen who asks neighbors to sign a petition in support of a proposed town ordinance, to the Gallup Poll that seeks to discover people's attitudes about various candidates for political office, surveys are commonplace features of contemporary life. This is not to suggest, however, that because of its frequent use, a survey is any less demanding in its design requirements or any easier for the researcher to conduct than any other type of research. Quite the contrary, the survey design makes critical demands on the researcher that, if not carefully respected, may place the entire research effort in jeopardy.

Survey research captures a fleeting moment in time, much as a camera takes a single-frame photograph of an ongoing activity. By drawing conclusions from one transitory collection of data, we may extrapolate about the state of affairs over a longer time period. At best, the extrapolation is a conjecture, and sometimes a hazardous one at that, but it is our only way to generalize from what we see. So often, survey reports that we read seem to suggest that what the researcher found in one sample population at one particular time can be accepted for all time as a constant. Far more misleading is the strongly implied assumption that these results can be entered into the Book of Eternal Certainties as ever-abiding Truth. Remember the wisdom of Heraclitus: There is nothing permanent but change.

An additional consideration in survey research is that we are relying on *self-report* data: People are telling us what they believe to be true or, perhaps, what they think we want to hear. As we noted in our discussion of interviews in Chapter 7, people's memories for events are often distortions of reality: What they think happened isn't always what *did* happen. Furthermore, people's descriptions of their attitudes and opinions are often constructed on the spot—oftentimes, they haven't really thought about certain issues until a researcher poses a question about them—and so may be colored by recent events or the current context (Schwarz, 1999). An additional problem is that some people may intentionally misrepresent the facts (at least, the "facts" as they know them) in order to present a favorable impression to the researcher. For example, if we were to ask parents the question "Have you ever abused your children?" the percentage of parents who told us "yes" would be close to zero, and so we would almost certainly underestimate the prevalence of child abuse in our society.

Survey research typically employs a face-to-face interview, a telephone interview, or a written questionnaire. We discuss these techniques briefly here and then offer practical suggestions for conducting them in "Practical Application" sections later on. We'll describe a fourth approach—using the Internet—in a later "Practical Application" that addresses technology-based methods of data collection.

Face-to-Face and Telephone Interviews

In qualitative research studies, interviews are often quite open-ended, perhaps addressing one or a few central issues but otherwise going in different directions for different participants. In survey research, however, interviews are fairly structured. In a **structured interview**, the researcher asks a standard set of questions and nothing more. In a **semi-structured interview**, the research may follow the standard questions with one or more individually tailored questions to get clarification or probe a person's reasoning.

Another difference between qualitative and quantitative studies is the general "feel" of the interview: It tends to be informal and friendly in a qualitative study but more formal and emotionally neutral in a quantitative one. Participants in a qualitative interview may feel as if they're simply engaging in a friendly chat with the researcher, who is typically someone they've come to know and trust. In contrast, participants in survey research are continually aware that, yes, this is an interview, and that the temporary relationship they've formed with the researcher will end once the interview is complete. This is not to say, however, that a survey researcher shouldn't strive to establish rapport with participants. Quite the contrary, the researcher is more likely to gain participants' cooperation and encourage them to respond honestly if he or she is likable and friendly and shows a genuine interest in what they have to say.

Face-to-face interviews have the distinct advantage of enabling the researcher to establish rapport with potential participants and therefore gain their cooperation; thus, such interviews yield the highest **response rates**—the percentages of people agreeing to participate—in survey research. However, the time and expense involved may be prohibitive if the needed interviewees reside in a variety of states or countries.

Telephone interviews are less time-consuming and less expensive (they involve only the cost of long-distance calls), and the researcher has ready access to virtually anyone on the planet who has a telephone. Although the response rate is not as high as for a face-to-face interview (many people are apt to be busy, annoyed at being bothered, or otherwise not interested in participating), it is considerably higher than for a mailed questionnaire. The researcher cannot establish the same kind of rapport that is possible in a face-to-face situation, and the sample will be biased to the extent that people without phones are part of the population about whom the researcher wants to draw inferences.

Personal interviews, whether they be face-to-face or over the telephone, allow the researcher to clarify ambiguous answers and, when appropriate, seek follow-up information. Because such interviews take time, however, they may not be practical when large sample sizes are important.

Questionnaires

Paper-pencil questionnaires can be sent to a large number of people, including those who live thousands of miles away. Thus, they may save the researcher travel expenses, and postage is typically cheaper than a lengthy long-distance telephone call. The social scientist who collects data with a questionnaire and the physicist who determines the presence of radioactivity with a Geiger counter are at just about the same degree of remoteness from their respective sources of data: Neither sees the source from which the data originate. From the perspective of survey participants, this distance becomes an additional advantage: Participants can respond to questions with assurance that their responses will be anonymous, and so they may be more truthful than they would be in a personal interview, particularly when they are talking about sensitive or controversial issues.

Yet questionnaires have their drawbacks as well. Typically, the majority of people who receive questionnaires don't return them—in other words, there may be a low **return rate**—and the people who do return them are not necessarily representative of the originally selected sample. Even when people are willing participants in a questionnaire study, their responses will reflect their reading and writing skills and, perhaps, their misinterpretation of one or more questions. Furthermore, by specifying in advance all of the questions that will be asked—and thereby eliminating other questions that *could* be asked about the issue or phenomenon in question—the researcher is apt to gain only limited, and possibly distorted, information (Dowson & McInerney, 2001).

Questionnaires often make use of checklists and rating scales. We describe these devices in the next section.

USING CHECKLISTS AND RATING SCALES

Observation studies look at people's behaviors, and developmental studies, correlational studies, and survey research frequently use questionnaires to learn about people's behaviors, characteristics, attitudes, and opinions. Behaviors and attitudes are often quite complex and so not, at least on the surface, easily evaluated or quantified. Two techniques that facilitate both evaluation and quantification in such circumstances are the checklist and the rating scale.

A **checklist** is a list of behaviors, characteristics, or other entities that a researcher is investigating. Either the researcher or participants (depending on the study) simply check(s) whether each item on the list is observed, present, or true; or else *not* observed, present, or true.

A **rating scale** is more useful when a behavior, attitude, or other phenomenon of interest needs to be evaluated on a continuum of, say, "inadequate" to "excellent," "never" to "always," or "strongly disapprove" to "strongly approve." Rating scales were developed by Rensis Likert in the 1930s to assess people's attitudes; accordingly, they are sometimes called **Likert scales**.[1]

---

[1] Although we have occasionally heard *Likert* pronounced as "lie-kert," the correct pronunciation is "lick-kert."

We illustrate the use of both techniques with a simple example. In the late 1970s, park rangers at Rocky Mountain National Park in Colorado were concerned about the heavy summertime traffic traveling up a narrow mountain road to Bear Lake, a popular destination for park visitors. So in the summer of 1978, they provided buses that would shuttle visitors up to Bear Lake and back again. This being a radical innovation at the time, the rangers wondered about people's reactions to the buses; if there were strong objections, other solutions to the traffic problem would have to be identified for the following summer.

Park officials asked a sociologist friend of ours to address their research question: How do park visitors feel about the new bus system? The sociologist decided that the best way to approach the problem was to conduct a survey. He and his research assistants waited at the parking lot to which buses returned after their trip up to Bear Lake; they randomly selected people who exited the bus and administered the survey. With such a "captive" audience, the response rate was very high: 1246 of the 1268 people who were approached agreed to participate in the study, giving the researcher a response rate of 98%.

We present three of the interview questions in Figure 9.2. Based on people's responses, the sociologist concluded that people were solidly in favor of the bus system (Trahan, 1978). As a result, it continues to be in operation today, many years after the survey was conducted.

One of us authors once sat on a doctoral committee for a student who, as part of her dissertation, developed a creative way of presenting a Likert scale to children (Shaklee, 1998). The student was studying the effects of a particular approach to teaching elementary school science, and she wanted to find out whether students' beliefs about the nature of science, as well as about school learning in general, would change as a result of the approach. Both before and after the instructional intervention, she read a series of statements and asked students either to agree or to disagree with them by pointing to one of four faces. The statements and the rating scale that the students used to respond to them are presented in Figure 9.3.

Notice that in the rating scale items in the Rocky Mountain National Park survey, park visitors were given the option of remaining "neutral" about a question. In the elementary school study, however, the children always had to answer yes or no. Experts have mixed views about letting respondents remain neutral in interviews and questionnaires. If you use rating scales in your own research, you should consider the implications of letting your respondents

---

FIGURE 9.2

Excerpts from a survey at Rocky Mountain National Park. Item 4 is a *checklist*. Items 5 and 6 are *rating scales*

From Trahan, 1978, Appendix A

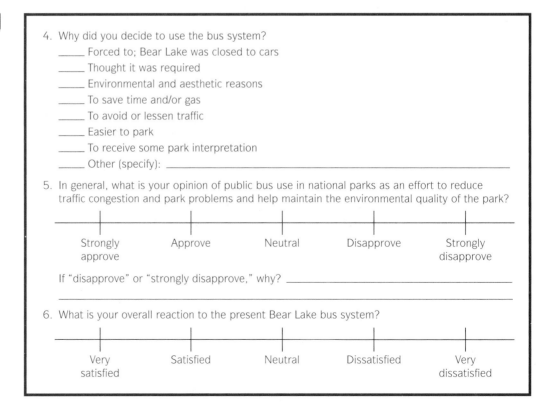

4. Why did you decide to use the bus system?
_____ Forced to; Bear Lake was closed to cars
_____ Thought it was required
_____ Environmental and aesthetic reasons
_____ To save time and/or gas
_____ To avoid or lessen traffic
_____ Easier to park
_____ To receive some park interpretation
_____ Other (specify): _____

5. In general, what is your opinion of public bus use in national parks as an effort to reduce traffic congestion and park problems and help maintain the environmental quality of the park?

| Strongly approve | Approve | Neutral | Disapprove | Strongly disapprove |

If "disapprove" or "strongly disapprove," why? _____
_____

6. What is your overall reaction to the present Bear Lake bus system?

| Very satisfied | Satisfied | Neutral | Dissatisfied | Very dissatisfied |

FIGURE 9.3

Asking elementary school children about science and learning

From *Elementary Children's Epistemological Beliefs and Understandings of Science in the Context of Computer-Mediated Video Conferencing with Scientists* (pp. 132, 134), by J. M. Shaklee, 1998, unpublished doctoral dissertation, University of Northern Colorado, Greeley. Reprinted with permission.

Students responded to each statement by pointing to one of the faces below.

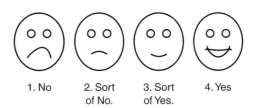

1. No   2. Sort of No.   3. Sort of Yes.   4. Yes

Students who were unfamiliar with Likert scales practiced the procedure using items A and B; other began with item 1.

A. Are cats green?
B. Is it a nice day?
1. The best thing about science is that most problems have one right answer.
2. If I can't understand something quickly, I keep trying.
3. When I don't understand a new idea, it is best to figure it out on my own.
4. I get confused when books have different information from what I already know.
5. An expert is someone who is born really smart.
6. If scientists try hard enough, they can find the truth to almost everything.
7. Students who do well learn quickly.
8. Getting ahead takes a lot of work.
9. The most important part about being a good student is memorizing the facts.
10. I can believe what I read.
11. Truth never changes.
12. Learning takes a long time.
13. Really smart students don't have to work hard to do well in school.
14. Kids who disagree with teachers are show-offs.
15. Scientists can get to the truth.
16. I try to use information from books and many other places.
17. It is annoying to listen to people who can't make up their minds.
18. Everyone needs to learn how to learn.
19. If I try too hard to understand a problem, I just get confused.
20. Sometimes I just have to accept answers from a teacher even if they don't make sense to me.

"straddle the fence" by including a "no opinion" or other neutral response, and design your scales accordingly.

Whenever you use checklists or rating scales, you simplify and more easily quantify people's behaviors or attitudes. In the process, however, you may lose valuable information (Delandshere & Petrosky, 1998). Ultimately you will have to determine whether the trade-off is worth it for the particular research problem you are investigating.

PRACTICAL APPLICATION PLANNING AND CONDUCTING INTERVIEWS

Interviewing involves much more than just asking questions. The questions for the interview should be carefully planned and precisely worded to yield the kinds of data the researcher needs to answer his or her research question. In the following two sections, we offer guidelines for conducting interviews in a quantitative study and present an example of how one student successfully planned and conducted the interviews he needed for a research project.

GUIDELINES CONDUCTING INTERVIEWS IN A QUANTITATIVE STUDY

In Chapter 7, we presented guidelines for conducting interviews in qualitative research. Most of those guidelines are equally applicable in quantitative research, and so we list them again here:

1. Make sure your interviewees are representative of the group.

2. Find a suitable location.

3. Get written permission.

4. Establish and maintain rapport.

5. Focus on the actual rather than on the abstract or hypothetical.

6. Don't put words in people's mouths.

7. Record responses verbatim.

8. Keep your reactions to yourself.

9. Remember that you are not necessarily getting the facts.

But interviews are typically more structured in quantitative studies than they are in qualitative studies. Therefore, we add several additional guidelines for conducting interviews in quantitative research.

10. *As you write the questions, consider how you can quantify the responses, and modify the questions accordingly.* Remember, you are conducting a *quantitative* study. Thus, you will, to some extent, be coding people's responses as numbers and, quite possibly, conducting statistical analyses on those numbers. You will be able to assign numerical codes to responses more easily if you identify an appropriate coding scheme ahead of time.

11. *Consider asking questions that will elicit qualitative information as well.* You do not necessarily have to quantify *everything.* People's responses to a few open-ended questions may support or provide additional insights into the numerical data you obtain from more structured questions.

12. *Pilot-test the questions.* When you plan your interview, you will, of course, be trying hard to develop clear and concise questions. Despite your best intentions, however, you may write questions that are ambiguous or misleading or that yield uninterpretable or otherwise useless responses. You can save yourself a great deal of time over the long run if you fine-tune your questions before you begin data collection. You can easily find the weak spots in your questions by asking a few volunteers to answer them in a pilot study.

13. *Restrict each question to a single idea.* Don't try to get too much information in any single question; in doing so, you may get multiple kinds of data—"mixed messages," so to speak—that are difficult to interpret (Gall, Borg, & Gall, 1996).

14. *Save controversial questions for the latter part of the interview.* If you will be touching on sensitive topics (e.g., attitudes about AIDS, opinions about gun control), put them near the end of the interview, after you have established rapport and gained the person's trust (Gall et al., 1996).

15. *Seek clarifying information when necessary.* Be alert for responses that are vague or otherwise difficult to interpret. Simple probes such as "Can you tell me more about that?" may produce the additional information you need (Gall et al., 1996).

AN EXAMPLE IN INTERNATIONAL RELATIONS

A student wanted to interview certain United Nations personnel to get their opinions concerning issues related to his study. He hoped to gather his data quickly but systematically, and he planned his approach to achieve that goal. He wanted to go to New York City for a series of interviews and, to conserve both time and expense, wished to schedule them as tightly as possible. His procedure was organized and logical.

Approximately 6 weeks before going for the interviews, the student wrote the United Nations representatives with whom he wished to confer; he told them when he would be in New York and requested an interview that would last not more than half an hour. He asked each prospective interviewee for an indication of several time slots when the interview might be scheduled. In his letter, he explained clearly what information he was seeking and why he was seeking it. His reasons were mature and meaningful and were phrased so that they held some interest for those he was to interview. (*Not* among his reasons was the fact that he was writing a thesis! If you must reveal that you are collecting data for a thesis, use the word *study* in lieu of *thesis*. Look at the world realistically. Aside from the student and the graduate advisor, theses hold very little glamour in the everyday world. Studies are much more acceptable.)

With the letter, the student enclosed a separate sheet containing the questions he intended to ask during the interview, arranged in the order he would ask them. He also suggested that, if the interviewee had no objections, taping the conference would facilitate matters considerably, conserving time and lessening the distraction of handwritten notes. He provided a check box on a return postcard for the interviewee to indicate whether he or she had any objection to recording the interview.

After he received his replies, he set up a master chart of appointments and places and confirmed immediately, by letter, the appointment time, thanking the interviewee for his or her cooperation. Where a time conflict arose, he sought to resolve it by suggesting alternative times that were still open.

Ten days before the interview, the student mailed a reminder, together with another copy of the interview questions, just in case the interviewee had misplaced the copy previously sent. He also enclosed his full interview schedule so that his interviewee might appreciate the time exigencies under which he was working.

On the day of the interview, the student arrived promptly. He introduced himself, stated briefly that he had come in accordance with previously made arrangements, asked whether his interviewee wished a copy of the questions he had previously sent, and began with the first question. He tried to guide the interview, always keeping to his agenda of questions and seeking to preserve an easy, friendly, yet professional atmosphere.

As each interview drew to a close, he thanked his interviewee for the courtesy of giving his or her time and went off to his next appointment.

In 3½ days, he had interviewed 35 United Nations representatives and had more than four-fifths of his data on tape. He transcribed the substance of the interviews and, within 10 days of his visit, sent a typed transcript to each interviewee, together with a letter thanking that person for granting the interview. He asked each individual to read the transcript carefully and, if it was correct, to sign a statement that it was a correct record of the interview. If the person found it inexact or incorrect in any place, he or she could correct the script or edit it as desired. The transcript had wide margins and was double spaced, thereby providing ample room for corrections.

In the same mailing, the researcher included a request for permission to use whatever part of the interview might provide data for his study, with the full understanding that, before the study was released, the interview material would again be submitted to the interviewee for complete approval. This was done, of course, before submitting the report as a final document for the degree. In the final thesis, the researcher acknowledged his interviewees and noted that they had inspected and approved all their quoted statements. This is the only way a researcher or an author can be protected against the accusations of falsification of the facts, libel suits, and other legal entanglements.

In summary, the researcher's use of the following steps led to a highly productive research effort:

1. Set up the interview well in advance.
2. Send the agenda of questions you will ask the interviewee.
3. Ask for permission to tape the conference.
4. Confirm the date immediately in writing.
5. Send a reminder, together with another agenda of questions, 10 days before you expect to arrive.
6. Be prompt; follow the agenda; have a copy of your questions for your interviewee in case he or she has mislaid the original copy.
7. Following the interview, submit a transcript of the interview and get either a written acknowledgment of its accuracy or a corrected copy from the interviewee.
8. After you have incorporated the material into your research report, send that section of the report to the interviewee for final approval and written permission to use the data in your report.

PRACTICAL APPLICATION CONSTRUCTING AND ADMINISTERING A QUESTIONNAIRE

Questionnaires seem so simple, yet in our experience they can be tricky to construct and administer. One false step can lead to uninterpretable data or an abysmally low return rate. We have numerous suggestions that can help you make your use of a questionnaire fruitful and efficient. We've divided them into two categories: constructing your questionnaire and maximizing your return rate. We also present some ideas for how you might use computer technology to develop your materials and tabulate your data more easily.

GUIDELINES   CONSTRUCTING A QUESTIONNAIRE

Following are twelve guidelines for developing a questionnaire that encourages people to be cooperative and yields responses you can use and interpret. We apologize for the length of the list, but, as we just said, questionnaire construction is a tricky business.

1. *Keep it short.* Your questionnaire should be as brief as possible and solicit only that information essential to the research project. You should test every item by two criteria: (a) What do I intend to do with the information I am requesting? and (b) Is it absolutely essential to have this information to solve part of the research problem?

2. *Use simple, clear, unambiguous language.* Write questions that communicate exactly what you want to know. Avoid terms that your respondents may not understand, such as obscure words or technical jargon. Also avoid words that do not have precise meanings, such as *several* and *usually*.

3. *Check for unwarranted assumptions implicit in your questions.* Consider a very simple question: "How many cigarettes do you smoke each day?" It seems to be a clear and unambiguous question, especially if we accompany it with certain choices so that all the respondent has to do is to check one of them:

How many cigarettes do you smoke each day?

(Check one of the following.)

_____ more than 25   _____ 25–16   _____ 15–11   _____ 10–1   _____ 5–1   _____ none

One obvious assumption here is that the person is a smoker, which probably is not the case for all participants. A second assumption is that a person smokes the same number of cigarettes each day, but for many smokers, this assumption doesn't hold water. At the office, when the pressure is on and they are working at full speed, people may be chain smokers. But at home on weekends and holidays, they may relax and smoke only one or two cigarettes a day or go without smoking at all. How are the people in this group supposed to answer the above question? What box does this type of smoker check?

Had the author of the question considered the assumptions on which the question was predicated, he or she might first have asked questions such as these:

Do you smoke cigarettes?

____ Yes

____ No (If you mark "no," skip the next two questions.)

Are your daily smoking habits reasonably consistent; that is, do you smoke about the same number of cigarettes each day?

____ Yes

____ No (If you mark "no," skip the next question.)

4. *Word your questions in ways that do not give clues about preferred or more desirable responses.* Take another question: "What strategies have you used to try to quit smoking?" By implying that the

respondent has, in fact, tried to quit, it may lead him or her to describe strategies that have never been seriously tried at all.

5. *Check for consistency.* When an issue about which you are asking is such that some respondents may give answers that are socially acceptable rather than true, you may wish to incorporate a "countercheck" question into your list at some distance from the first question. This strategy helps verify the consistency with which a respondent has answered questions. For instance, take the following two items appearing in a questionnaire as items 2 and 30. (Their distance from each other increases the likelihood that a person will answer the second without recalling how he or she answered the first.) Notice how one individual has answered them:

2. Check one of the following choices:

_X_ In my thinking, I am a liberal.

____ In my thinking, I am a conservative.

30. Check one of the following choices:

____ I find new ideas stimulating and attractive, and I would find it challenging to be among the first to try them.

_X_ I subscribe to the position of Alexander Pope:
"Be not the first by whom the new is tried
Nor yet the last to lay the old aside."

The two responses are inconsistent. In the first, the respondent claims to be a liberal thinker but later, when given the liberal and the conservative positions in another form, indicates a position generally thought to be more conservative than liberal. Such an inconsistency might lead you to question whether the respondent is truly the liberal thinker that he or she claims to be.

6. *Determine in advance how you will code the responses.* As you write your questions, perhaps even *before* you write them, develop a plan for recoding participants' responses into numerical data that you can statistically analyze. Data processing procedures may also dictate the form a questionnaire should take. If, for example, people's response sheets will be fed into a computer scanner, the questionnaire must be structured differently than if the responses will be tabulated using paper and pencil.

7. *Keep the respondent's task simple.* Make the instrument as simple to read and respond to as possible. Remember, you are asking for people's *time*, a precious commodity for many people these days.

Discussion items—those that present open-ended questions and ask people to respond with lengthy answers—are time-consuming and mentally exhausting for both the participants and the researcher. Don't forget that you will have to wrestle with the participants' words to try to determine exactly what their answers mean. Those who write in the "Yes/no, and I'll tell you why" style are few and far between. The usefulness of responses to discussion items rests entirely on participants' skill to express in words the thoughts they wish to convey. Respondents may ramble, engaging in discussion that doesn't answer the question or is beside the point.

Save your respondents and yourself from this ordeal. After answering 15 to 20 discussion questions, your respondents will think you are demanding a book! Such a major compositional exercise is unfair to those from whom you are requesting a favor.

8. *Provide clear instructions.* Communicate exactly how you want people to respond. For instance, don't assume that they are familiar with Likert scales. Some of them may never have seen such scales before.

9. *Give a rationale for any items whose purpose may be unclear.* We can't say this enough: You are asking people to do you a favor by responding to your questionnaire. Give them a reason to *want* to do the favor. At a minimum, each question should have a purpose, and in one way or another, you should make that purpose clear.

10. *Make the questionnaire attractive and professional looking.* Your instrument should have clean lines, crystal-clear typing (and certainly no typos!), and, perhaps, two or more colors.

TABLE 9.1 Guide for the construction of a questionnaire

Write the question in the space below.	Why are you asking the question? How does it relate to the research problem?	Multiple Choice	Yes/No Answer	Open-Ended Discussion	Countercheck*

*A "countercheck" question is one included to verify that the reply given on another question in the questionnaire was accurate and/or honest.

11. *Conduct a pilot test.* Give the questionnaire to at least half a dozen friends or colleagues to see whether they have difficulty understanding any items. Have them actually fill out the questionnaire; this way, you can see the kinds of responses you are likely to get and make sure that, down the road, the "real" responses you obtain will be of sufficient quality to help you answer your research question.

12. *Scrutinize the almost-final product carefully to make sure it addresses your needs.* Item by item, a questionnaire should be quality tested again and again for precision of expression, objectivity, relevance, and probability of favorable reception and return. Have you concentrated on the recipient of the questionnaire, putting yourself in the place of someone who is asked to invest time on your behalf? If you received such a questionnaire from a stranger, what would your honest reaction be? These questions are important and should be answered impartially.

Above all, you should make sure that *every question is essential for you to address the research problem.* Table 9.1 can help you examine your items with this criterion in mind. Make as many copies as you might need to accommodate the length of your questionnaire. Write each item in the left-hand column and then, in the next column, explain why you need to include it. If you can't explain how an item relates to your research problem, throw it out!

GUIDELINES   MAXIMIZING YOUR RETURN RATE FOR A MAILED QUESTIONNAIRE

As university professors, we've sometimes been asked to distribute questionnaires in our classes that relate, perhaps, to some aspect of the university's student services or to students' preferences for the university calendar. The end-of-semester student evaluation forms that you often fill out are questionnaires as well. Even though participation in such surveys is voluntary, the response rate when one has such a captive audience is typically quite high, and often 100%.

Mailing questionnaires to people one doesn't know is quite another matter. Potential respondents have little or nothing to gain by answering and returning the questionnaire, and so many of them do not. As a result, the typical return rate for a mailed questionnaire is 50% or less, and in recent years it has steadily declined (Rogelberg & Luong, 1998).

We think of one student who recently conducted dissertation research in the area of reading. As part of her study, she sent a questionnaire to reading teachers to inquire about their beliefs and attitudes about a certain kind of children's literature. Initially, the student sent out 103 questionnaires; 14 teachers completed and returned them (a return rate of 13%). In a second attempt, she sent out 72 questionnaires to a different group of teachers; 12 responded (a return rate of 15%). In one final effort, she sought volunteers on the Internet by using two lists of teachers' e-mail addresses; 57 teachers indicated that they were willing to fill out her questionnaire, and 20 of them actually did so (a return rate of 35%).

Was the student frustrated? Absolutely! Yet she had made a couple of mistakes that undoubtedly thwarted her efforts from the beginning. First, the questionnaire had 36 questions, 18 of which were open-ended ones that required lengthy written responses. A quick glance would tell any discerning teacher that the questionnaire would take an entire evening to complete. Second, the questionnaires were sent out in the middle of the school year, when teachers were probably already quite busy planning lessons, grading papers, and so on. Even teachers who truly wanted to help this struggling doctoral student (who was a former teacher herself) may simply not have found the time to do it. Fortunately for the student, the questionnaire was only one small part of her study, and so she was able to complete her dissertation successfully with the limited (and almost certainly nonrepresentative) sample of responses she received.

Should you decide that a mailed questionnaire is the most suitable approach for answering your research question, the following guidelines can help you increase your return rate:

1. *Consider the timing.* The student just described mailed her questionnaires in the winter and early spring because she wanted to graduate at the end of the summer. The timing of her mailing was convenient for her; however, it was *not* convenient for the people to whom she sent the questionnaire, and her response rate (and her study!) suffered as a result. Consider the characteristics of the sample you are surveying, and try to anticipate when respondents will be most likely to have time to answer a questionnaire. And as a general rule, stay away from peak holiday and vacation times, such as mid-December through early January.

2. *Make a good first impression.* Put yourself in the place of a potential respondent. Imagine a stranger sending you the questionnaire you propose to send. What is your initial impression as you draw the questionnaire from the envelope? Is it inordinately long and time-consuming? Is it cleanly and neatly typed? Does it have adequate margins, giving the impression of relaxation and uncluttered ease? Are the areas for response adequate and clearly indicated? Is the tone courteous, and are the requests reasonable?

3. *Motivate potential respondents.* Give people a reason to *want* to respond. Occasionally, researchers may actually have the resources to pay people for their time or offer other concrete inducements. But more often than not, you will have to rely on the power of persuasion to gain cooperation. Probably the best mechanism for doing so is the cover letter you include with your questionnaire.

One researcher who conducted a particularly successful questionnaire study handled it this way: After selecting her population, she sent to each person a letter describing the potential value of the study. The letter emphasized the importance of the study to the addressee, and it invited the addressee to cooperate by answering the questionnaire. A copy of the researcher's letter of inquiry with marginal comments on some of its features appears in Figure 9.4.

Compare the letter in Figure 9.4 with the brief note in Figure 9.5 that was sent to one of us and that, unfortunately, is all too typical of students' first attempts at drafting such a letter. A lack of common courtesy in letters of this sort may be another reason for the poor return of questionnaires when beginning researchers attempt to use the survey method.

The cover letter is extremely important. It should be carefully and thoughtfully composed and should stress the concerns of the recipient rather than any selfish interests of the sender. Some students forget this and, in doing so, unintentionally reveal their own self-centeredness.

4. *Include a self-addressed envelope with return postage.* Accompany your questionnaire with a self-addressed stamped envelope for your respondent's convenience in returning the questionnaire. To

FIGURE 9.4

An annotated letter of inquiry

THE AMERICAN UNIVERSITY
Massachusetts and Nebraska Avenues, N.W.
Washington, DC 20016

The School of Nursing

August 15, 1999

Dear Alumna,

Your School of Nursing is appealing to you for help. We are not asking for funds—all we ask is a few minutes of your time.

It is to your advantage to be recognized as a graduate of a school that has an excellent reputation for the education and training of nurses to meet the realities of nursing practice. You can assist us to maintain—and to improve—this reputation by cooperating in the evaluation of the program of Nursing Education at The American University. What we would like to ask you is to give us your candid, honest opinion of the nursing program in effect when you were a student nurse in training at The American University. We have a questionnaire that we would like to send you, with your permission, and that will take no more than fifteen minutes of your time to answer.

The Lucy Webb Hayes School of Nursing at The American University is growing. With your help it can grow in professional stature and educational excellence. We are sure you will be willing to cooperate with us toward those desired goals.

As an enclosure with this letter, you will find a return postcard on which you may indicate your willingness to cooperate with us by answering the questionnaire. Thank you for the courtesy of your assistance.

Very sincerely yours,

Ruth G. Thomas

Ruth G. Thomas, R.N.

The questionnaire was designed to gather information on one of the subproblems of the study: "How adequately do the graduates consider the program to have been in preparing them for a professional nursing career?"

The author quickly indicates this is not an appeal for money—only a few minutes of time.

The researcher points out that it is to the advantage of the addressee to answer the questionnaire.

Notice the phrase "with your permission"! Also, the estimate of time required helps to convince the reader to cooperate.

The positive is emphasized: We are growing; we want to grow in excellence—but we need you!

This is a splendid device for getting a commitment. (The card is reproduced as Figure 9.6.)

Notice the tone. The courteous tone is carried out to the very end of the letter.

impose on a person's time and spirit of cooperation and then to expect that person also to supply the envelope and pay the postage is unreasonable.

5. *Offer the results of your study.* In return for the investment of time and the courtesy of replying to your questions, offer to send your respondent a summary of the results of your study if he or she wishes it. You might provide a check space, either at the beginning or at the end of your instrument, where a respondent can indicate the desire to have such a summary, together with a place for name, address, and zip code. In questionnaires for which anonymity is desirable, a separate postcard may be included to indicate the desire for a summary. It, too, should request name, address, and zip code, along with the suggestion that it be mailed separately from the questionnaire to maintain anonymity.

6. *Be gently persistent.* Experts often suggest that when people do not initially respond to a questionnaire, you can increase your response rate by sending two follow-up reminders, perhaps send-

FIGURE 9.5

A poorly worded request for cooperation

X Y Z UNIVERSITY
Campus Station

April 1, 1999

Dear Sir:

I am a graduate student at X Y Z University, and the enclosed questionnaire is sent to you in the hope that you will assist me in obtaining information for my Master's thesis.

I should appreciate your early reply since I am attempting to get my degree this June.

Yours truly,

John Doe

John Doe

FIGURE 9.6

Questionnaire response card

Dear Mrs. Thomas:
☐ Please send the questionnaire; I will be happy to cooperate.
☐ I am sorry, but I do not wish to answer the questionnaire.
Comments:

Date: _____   _____
                          Name

ing each one out a week or two after the previous mailing (e.g., Neuman, 1994; Rogelberg & Luong, 1998). But if the questionnaire is meant to be anonymous, how do you know who has returned it and who has not?

To address this problem, many researchers put a different code number on each copy they send out and keep a list of which number they have sent to each person in their sample. When a questionnaire is returned, they remove the number and person's name from the list. When it is time to send a follow-up letter, they send it only to the people who are still on the list. (Researchers should use the list of names and code numbers *only* for this purpose. At no point should they use it to determine who responded in what way to each question.)

Let's return to the letter in Figure 9.4. It mentioned an enclosed card (see Figure 9.6) that gave the recipient an opportunity to express a willingness to answer the questionnaire. The card was simple and straightforward. It was addressed and stamped and required only a check mark and a signature from the recipient.

After receiving a card that indicated willingness to cooperate, the researcher mailed the questionnaire immediately. She kept a log of questionnaires mailed, the people to whom they were mailed and their addresses, and the date of mailing. If a reply was not received within three weeks' time, she sent a reminder letter. The reminder was written in the same tone as the initial letter. This second letter, with comments, appears in Figure 9.7.

The letter brought results. The researcher was being firm and persuasive, but with considerable skill and tact. Courtesy, understanding, and respect for others pay large dividends in a situation in which a researcher needs others' cooperation. This is especially true in questionnaire studies.

FIGURE 9.7

A follow-up letter

THE AMERICAN UNIVERSITY
Massachusetts and Nebraska Avenues, N.W.
Washington, DC 20016

The School of Nursing

September 5, 1999

Dear Alumna,

All of us are busier these days than we should be, and most of us have a hard time keeping abreast of those obligations that are essential and required. We know how the little extras sometimes receive our best intentions, but we also know that in reality none of us has the time we desire to fulfill those intentions.

From the questionnaire that reached you—we hope—about three weeks ago, we have had no reply. Perhaps you mislaid the questionnaire, or it may have miscarried in the mail—any one of dozens of contingencies could have happened.

In any event, we are enclosing another copy of the questionnaire. We are sure you will try to find fifteen minutes somewhere in your busy schedule to check its several items and drop it in the nearest postal box. Most of them have been returned. We'd like to get them all back. Will you help us?

Thanks. We shall appreciate your kindness.

Very sincerely yours,

Ruth G. Thomas

Ruth G. Thomas, R.N.

This letter applies tactfulness, diplomacy, psychology, and human relations techniques at their very best.

Note the "understanding" tone of the letter: "All of us are busier these days . . ." It removes any reason to feel gulit about the failure to reply.

No need for the recipient of this letter to make excuses; the writer has disarmed the situation by offering two and suggesting that there may be dozens more.

By enclosing a second questionnaire, the writer gives the recipient no excuse for not returning the questionnaire that she had previously agreed to complete. Note how gently the suggestion is made that she is one of the few delinquent ones.

The faith in this letter is boundless. It would be difficult indeed not to respond in the face of such confidence that you will do so.

USING DATABASES, WORD PROCESSING, AND MAIL MERGE IN DEVELOPING QUESTIONNAIRE MATERIALS

 USING TECHNOLOGY

Computer databases can be readily adapted for use with research involving questionnaires. Information regarding participants' names and addresses, as well as information regarding which materials have been sent and received, can be incorporated into such a database. A search through the database can quickly identify people who have and have not received a letter of inquiry, those who have or have not yet responded, and those who need a first or second reminder letter.

Combining the database with a word processing program can also be helpful. For example, mailing labels can be quickly produced, thus decreasing the amount of time needed to address various mailings to potential participants. Many word processors (and some databases) come with prepared templates for many kinds of mailing labels. By identifying the type of label you have for your printer, you can print any or all of the names from your database directly onto the labels.

Inquiry letters, thank-you letters, and other correspondence can be personalized by using the *merge* function of most word processors. This function allows you to combine the information in your database with the documents you wish to send out. For example, when printing the final version of your cover letter, you can include the person's name immediately after the greeting (e.g., "Dear Carlos Asay")—a simple touch that is likely to yield a higher return rate than letters addressed to "Potential Respondent" or "To whom it may concern." The computer inserts the names for you; you need only tell it where to find the names in your database. The same process is used on every item of junk mail you receive that addresses you personally or that shows your name on a $10,000,000 check (that you may already have won!) and asks you to order magazines so you can collect your prize. Advertisers have realized the importance of personalization for quite some time. When individuals are addressed by name, they feel special and are more inclined to invest a little of their time.

USING SCANNERS TO FACILITATE DATA TABULATION

When you need a large sample to address your research problem adequately, you should consider in advance how you will tabulate the responses after the questionnaires are returned to you. One widely used strategy is to have a computer scan preformatted answer sheets and automatically sort and organize the results. To use this strategy, your questions must each involve a small set of possible answers; for instance, they might be multiple choice, have yes/no answers, or incorporate a 5-point rating scale. You will want the participants to respond using a number 2 pencil. Enclosing one with the questionnaire you send is common courtesy. Furthermore, anything you can do to make participants' task easier—even something as simple as providing the writing implement—will increase your response rate.

PRACTICAL APPLICATION COMPUTERIZING DATA COLLECTION IN DESCRIPTIVE RESEARCH

If you are conducting a descriptive research study, you are likely to find that computerizing some aspects of data collection makes your task easier and more efficient. Depending on your research design and methodology, you may find one or more of the following strategies helpful:

1. *Directly enter data as an observation is being made.* For example, if you are conducting an observation study, you might use the number keypad on the keyboard to record different types of observations; you might also key in numbers to record your ratings when you use a rating scale to evaluate specific behaviors. If you are a fast typist, you can even enter narrative information during your observations.

2. *Use your computer as a tape recorder.* As we mentioned in Chapter 7, some computer software programs allow you to record interviews directly onto a laptop computer and then transform these conversations into written text. Examples of such software include IBM VoiceType Simply Speaking, Naturally Speaking, Power Secretary, and ViaVoice.

3. *Look for peripheral devices that may aid data collection.* By *peripheral devices,* we mean pieces of equipment that you can attach to your computer to enhance its capabilities. For example, Gall and colleagues (Acheson & Gall, 1992; Gall et al., 1996) have described an approach in which observers use a bar code reader and a special list of bar codes to record different types of behaviors. Each code is associated with a specific type of behavior. When a particular behavior is observed, the bar code reader is swept over the appropriate bar code, and immediately the type and time of the behavior are recorded. In this way, all observations are entered into the computer and categorized for analysis in a single motion.

4. *Administer a questionnaire on a computer.* Electronic questionnaires can be highly effective when participants feel comfortable with computers. When participants enter their responses directly onto a computer, you obviously save a great deal of time. Furthermore, a computer has the capability to record how quickly people respond—information that may in some situations be relevant to your research question.

5. *Use the computer to monitor the quality of the data being collected.* The computer can be used to "clean up" the data by locating coding errors and detecting apparently misrecorded, nonsensical responses.

6. *Explore the possibility of using the Internet for data collection.* Some researchers are now experimenting with data collection on the Internet. They may put a questionnaire on a Web site and ask people who visit the site to respond. One such site is "Psychological Research on the Net,"

where one can find a wide variety of online research projects.[2] As we write this eighth edition of the book, the site is hosting projects on such diverse issues as memory, logical reasoning, emotions, attitudes, language, visual perception, interpersonal relationships, perinatal stress, chronic illness, and traffic safety. It also provides links to other online research labs. John Krantz, who maintains the site, checks to be sure that each project has been approved by the appropriate Internal Review Board and incorporates informed consent procedures. There is no fee for using the site (J. Krantz, personal communication, May 2003).

An Internet-based approach to data collection is, of course, a relatively new one, and we still have much to learn about its viability for yielding useful information for important research questions. Some evidence indicates that, at least for investigation of certain psychological processes (e.g., cognition, visual perception), online research studies yield data comparable to those obtained in a laboratory (McGraw, Tew, & Williams, 2000).

Should you choose to collect data on the Internet, keep in mind that your sample will hardly be representative of the overall population of human beings. After all, participants will be limited to people who (a) are comfortable with computers, (b) spend a fair amount of time on the Internet, (c) enjoy participating in research studies, and (d) have been sufficiently enticed by your research topic to participate. In many cases, they will be college students who are earning course credit for their participation (McGraw et al., 2000). In short, *your sample will be biased to a considerable degree.*

Sampling is a concern for any researcher, but it is especially so for the researcher who wants to draw inferences about a large population. In the following section, we look at strategies for selecting an appropriate sample and consider how bias in sampling procedures may distort the data obtained.

CHOOSING A SAMPLE IN A DESCRIPTIVE STUDY

The researcher who conducts a descriptive study wants to determine *the nature of how things are.* Especially when conducting survey research, the researcher will want to describe one or more characteristics of a fairly large population—perhaps the logical thinking capabilities of 10-year-olds, the teaching behaviors of preschool teachers, or the attitudes that visitors to Rocky Mountain National Park have about a bus shuttle system. Whether the population is 10-year-olds, preschool teachers, or park visitors, we are talking about *very large* groups of people; for instance, more than 3 million people visit Rocky Mountain National Park every year.

In such situations, the researcher will, of course, usually not study the entire population of interest. Instead, he or she will select a subset, or **sample,** of that population. But the researcher can use the results obtained from the sample to make generalizations about the entire population only if *the sample is truly representative of the population.* Here we are talking about the *external validity* of a research study, a concept introduced in Chapter 5.

When phrasing their research problems, many novice researchers forget that they will be studying a sample rather than a population. They announce, for example, that their goal is "to survey the legal philosophies of the attorneys of the United States and to analyze the relationship of these several philosophical positions with respect to the recent decisions of the Supreme Court of the United States." Someone who words a problem in this way has simply not thought through the meaning of the words themselves: "The attorneys of the United States"! The American Bar Association consists of more than 400,000 attorneys distributed over more than 3.5 million square miles in the 50 states. As we look at the problem more closely, we begin to discern other, more serious difficulties. What are "philosophical attitudes"? How does one isolate these attitudes to study them? How can one show a "relationship of philosophical positions" to "recent decisions of the Supreme Court"? How will this relationship be expressed? Will it be expressed statistically? If so, how would one quantify "philosophical positions" and "decisions"? If not, then how will the relationship be shown?

In the previously stated research problem, the difficulty basically arises out of the way the problem is worded. If, on the one hand, the researcher has said what he or she means, then he or

---

[2] You can reach the site by going to APS's home page, http://www.psychologicalscience.org/; click on "Psychology links" and then on "Online Psychology Experiments." Alternatively, you can go directly to the site, which, as this book goes to press, is located at http://psych.hanover.edu/research/exponnet.html.

she proposes to survey "the attorneys"—all of them! If, on the other hand, the researcher intends to survey only a certain cross section of the attorneys, then the statement of the problem should have said that with such qualifying and accurately descriptive words as *selected, representative, typical, certain, a random sample of,* and so on. Careful researchers say precisely what they mean. Notice the difference in the meaning between "The purpose of this research is to survey the representative legal philosophies of a random sample of attorneys . . ." and the original wording, "The purpose of this research is to survey the legal philosophies of the attorneys of the United States. . . ."

How, then, is sampling done? In a number of ways. The sampling procedure depends on the purpose of the sampling and a careful consideration of the parameters of the population.

Look through the wrong end of a telescope. You will see the world in miniature. This is precisely what the sampling procedure chosen for any particular project should seek to achieve. *The sample should be so carefully chosen that, through it, the researcher is able to see all the characteristics of the total population in the same relationship that they would be seen were the researcher, in fact, to examine the total population.*

Ideally, samples are population microcosms. In optics, unless lenses are precision-made and accurately ground, one is likely to get distortion through the spyglass. Similarly, unless the sampling procedure is carefully planned, the conclusions that the researcher draws from the data are likely to be distorted. Such distortion is called *bias.* We discuss this topic a bit later in this section. For the moment, however, we concern ourselves with various sampling designs.

SAMPLING DESIGNS

Different sampling designs may be more or less appropriate in different situations. Here we consider eight different approaches to sampling, which fall into two major categories: probability sampling and nonprobability sampling.

Probability Sampling

In **probability sampling,** the researcher can specify in advance that each segment of the population will be represented in the sample. This is the distinguishing characteristic that sets it apart from nonprobability sampling.

Generally, the components of the sample are chosen from the larger population by a process known as random selection. **Random selection** means choosing a sample in such a way that each member of the population has an equal chance of being selected. When such a random sample is selected, the researcher can assume that the characteristics of the sample approximate the characteristics of the total population.

Let's explain that. Suppose we have a beaker that contains 100 ml of water. Another container holds 10 ml of a concentrated acid. We combine the water and acid in proportions of 10:1. After thoroughly mixing the water and acid, we should be able to extract 1 ml from any part of the solution and find that the sample contains precisely 10 parts water and 1 part acid. In the same way, if we have a population with considerable variability in race, wealth, education, social standing, and other factors, and if we have a perfectly selected random sample (a situation usually more theoretical than practical), we will find in the sample those same characteristics that exist in the larger population, and we will find them in the same proportions.

A sample is no more representative of the total population than the degree to which it has been randomly selected. There are, of course, many methods of random selection. For instance, we could assign each person in the population a different number and then use an arbitrary method of picking certain numbers, perhaps by using a roulette wheel (if the entire population consists of 75 or fewer members), drawing numbers out of a hat, or using a computer's random number generator. In today's world of advanced computer applications, an electronic spreadsheet often provides a reliable way of generating random numbers. Microsoft Works, for example, has a built-in function that automatically generates a new random number each time the application is recalculated.

A tried-and-true, and therefore widely used, method of selecting a random sample is to use a **table of random numbers,** such as that presented in Table 9.2. The researcher typically does not start at the beginning of the table; instead, he or she identifies a starting point randomly.

TABLE 9.2 Random numbers table

	1	2	3	4	5	6	7	8	9	0
1	38 01 08 18 62	82 52 01 82 29	02 56 28 19 24	88 42 92 63 07	23 99 90 93 57	78 10 48 55 21	29 84 46 25 60	50 24 21 62 40	56 88 09 95 57	01 78 78 86 35
	51 10 40 21 24	04 69 90 71 43	04 78 84 81 84	41 31 82 31 79	40 79 15 65 18	28 86 32 62 70	55 33 27 42 50	35 64 53 48 31	15 24 21 63 23	17 59 94 69 95
	72 73 42 19 31	72 73 42 19 31	84 53 15 16 78	98 77 86 76 75	66 51 70 90 93	87 83 76 49 08	32 14 91 93 50	47 49 89 17 52	05 46 40 33 05	77 27 15 16 31
	94 72 67 55 42	52 52 26 41 89	32 38 14 58 97	71 94 93 90 49	66 42 05 69 12	28 08 82 64 25	27 79 96 81 66	29 86 00 94 07	84 54 57 62 22	70 80 69 62 87
	77 75 72 87 20	86 70 64 02 44	89 24 08 35 53	32 96 00 84 78	48 68 39 83 83	56 47 81 77 42	39 59 64 69 02	10 19 94 50 51	40 34 19 81 31	38 54 97 22 17
2	92 44 11 50 85	05 70 08 70 64	91 81 58 48 16	61 87 43 52 08	60 42 80 59 20	34 28 49 91 25	19 73 63 65 72	86 97 13 99 06	08 03 07 62 52	33 68 42 59 38
	60 04 91 78 89	71 40 77 32 66	11 30 10 01 21	49 12 88 73 47	68 54 94 32 12	20 77 44 49 64	06 44 46 32 33	29 70 98 08 59	64 16 94 48 45	32 22 40 94 41
	28 39 28 16 75	92 57 77 21 95	56 93 73 19 17	94 62 18 76 31	00 85 74 86 15	67 31 42 98 65	39 93 31 64 30	75 28 25 82 38	25 99 97 68 63	98 45 70 95 46
	88 49 94 80 45	16 20 72 31 64	74 04 31 00 86	97 79 33 98 04	55 26 34 15 70	76 70 92 40 97	79 70 00 64 33	24 29 27 30 25	86 96 27 96 51	67 14 98 05 49
	71 23 62 84 00	35 01 41 52 70	05 91 02 35 24	53 74 60 11 41	36 34 18 08 46	80 67 41 60 61	29 06 20 72 42	53 96 06 98 42	81 13 97 04 71	27 27 63 85 31
3	96 96 31 54 02	00 91 92 76 35	15 68 62 95 24	32 12 73 38 93	77 48 20 37 37	38 54 96 41 02	71 55 92 52 72	83 88 14 67 44	60 20 86 72 56	55 39 83 52 20
	42 24 86 51 17	60 92 31 00 55	68 99 02 84 40	43 90 67 66 07	93 58 14 66 19	24 57 83 41 75	81 17 09 22 06	62 51 63 29 07	48 78 30 39 28	07 12 36 20 41
	48 04 03 20 10	64 51 11 11 69	31 07 84 90 36	84 56 50 31 14	58 67 15 93 17	36 07 58 97 44	23 49 17 02 59	56 11 41 67 04	46 66 29 36 60	25 24 38 04 18
	24 82 46 95 57	73 54 42 99 51	33 72 12 89 86	63 44 34 78 78	62 23 04 30 78	31 36 77 96 03	07 00 17 98 53	40 50 52 29 34	71 77 22 68 97	18 04 81 99 29
	81 67 50 87 94	68 85 73 36 83	04 80 31 52 66	70 04 32 61 56	87 67 45 06 85	39 67 65 57 22	79 93 95 80 66	97 60 51 95 17	94 12 85 08 16	20 28 59 36 47
4	13 45 91 94 98	03 88 43 86 42	98 65 79 38 10	91 12 81 98 30	31 11 40 95 83	14 00 22 00 49	95 99 76 05 42	73 99 91 91 12	62 89 71 43 96	57 23 16 02 17
	72 24 96 81 87	52 68 73 61 17	51 94 47 58 01	13 88 40 38 70	51 11 02 00 63	66 16 46 92 60	98 74 78 50 78	17 07 25 83 52	18 65 27 13 89	55 91 08 06 12
	55 05 71 44 11	66 04 57 07 14	92 20 82 92 33	30 08 96 22 15	50 11 40 49 53	07 91 17 27 71	46 03 95 14 94	47 94 10 17 21	23 03 23 69 95	40 24 39 29 92
	92 36 97 30 14	88 41 90 80 35	07 75 80 26 05	94 14 31 80 07	55 41 14 57 90	52 12 46 94 70	44 39 99 50 47	19 52 92 92 66	26 20 82 10 07	95 75 73 66 54
	89 92 58 84 08	73 41 65 61 95	43 97 81 33 05	74 67 22 23 00	86 26 66 99 63	08 89 21 14 83	40 34 50 36 28	86 84 82 22 34	25 82 86 47 85	06 38 07 97 44
5	26 83 98 13	77 10 83 11 03	00 44 16 60 42	30 88 02 35 74	26 31 51 32 71	73 00 22 00 49	22 32 76 37 24	67 99 80 12 23	12 06 07 80 23	39 20 96 85 52
	10 71 47 27 12	75 45 51 26 23	59 59 86 21 70	98 76 96 40 12	97 70 77 57 74	44 22 44 97 62	42 28 17 09 55	55 45 12 45 69	88 80 59 76 58	28 90 74 84 74
	41 04 81 62 78	06 77 53 27 14	52 71 25 82 93	52 02 54 04 07	51 23 05 30 59	52 40 03 90 79	48 44 83 66 71	68 67 24 41 65	83 90 16 72 41	62 28 75 86 34
	33 85 26 45 29	22 81 84 43 83	11 60 71 38 45	93 07 22 30 42	99 30 52 21 40	89 18 59 29 95	23 43 14 58 06	49 06 40 32 58	59 56 50 23 90	39 01 75 86 33
	45 50 56 50 40	26 05 25 93 64	78 17 59 58 83	80 47 43 71 41	03 06 18 79 54	16 23 18 55 60	08 65 50 82 07	33 78 77 53 41	88 04 45 86 61	16 87 80 32 14
6	92 53 64 22 75	68 24 20 99 94	21 95 33 19 10	23 01 49 45 26	34 34 81 38 89	60 81 53 27 72	13 93 48 56 37	24 88 10 64 90	78 18 95 35 38	72 70 45 72 58
	99 41 50 17 32	32 35 95 10 22	34 50 81 80 34	12 13 53 83 62	86 07 50 83 86	82 21 93 36 48	56 58 87 36 67	03 90 19 50 76	07 50 95 86 69	90 00 55 69 31
	82 40 93 92 43	88 84 79 42 86	15 16 07 30 59	92 54 78 72 92	34 17 73 57 56	31 46 75 31 06	65 20 76 65 17	52 50 16 84 22	73 57 74 10 88	98 63 77 24 70
	86 48 92 62 86	04 86 51 39 73	61 17 22 69 09	03 39 10 59 24	06 79 60 36 93	93 97 68 61 23	15 40 89 22 72	20 67 30 37 14	39 84 53 12 90	78 65 10 23 09
	89 52 47 59 01	52 00 88 05 98	80 62 64 78 59	33 74 08 06 67	41 77 42 65 24	77 95 26 51 27	38 18 74 92 72	46 70 52 78 60	06 90 74 56 50	76 31 58 65 83
7	22 21 03 21 90	20 37 19 57 62	99 37 27 35 26	12 68 43 81 53	71 92 33 99 26	78 69 45 98 85	87 39 43 19 80	58 31 70 14 75	49 07 71 35 11	95 06 72 41 00
	90 53 60 07 99	17 18 66 37 53	74 41 09 90 62	44 56 94 44 36	31 74 10 57 63	79 62 84 26 54	88 56 10 22 55	14 82 30 95 52	01 07 97 96 23	64 99 36 57 51
	26 37 79 96 33	88 52 34 17 95	31 23 24 58 77	75 88 64 08 53	05 81 86 00 75	87 59 13 45 98	63 38 70 31 41	80 85 48 37 86	47 97 87 19 83	66 94 71 49 11
	43 02 16 18 53	51 79 03 90 34	30 34 88 89 36	85 70 92 05 82	01 57 58 98 83	81 19 21 57 98	63 34 00 57 50	65 48 83 28 97	72 80 43 01 65	55 64 58 40 56
	20 95 76 51 15	97 32 97 58 43	39 55 93 17 32	03 16 16 65 24	34 21 10 91 88	58 22 98 68 41	54 15 20 20 14	61 33 44 76 24	54 70 39 17 47	08 99 19 55 89
8	37 42 58 13 23	44 82 67 97 98	54 38 79 75 11	75 72 16 32 68	74 59 37 13 10	34 52 36 07 27	72 43 90 64 99	10 49 51 53 27	52 04 26 28 62	10 70 98 42 50
	31 51 93 66 48	35 56 04 55 20	29 19 24 55 97	32 79 45 92 58	76 37 11 35 79	05 68 00 86 87	32 46 69 85 86	24 47 32 60 28	29 45 36 58 21	30 84 54 36 35
	26 19 62 67 67	70 61 22 01 70	18 84 36 99 94	00 57 54 28 92	45 72 40 05 06	60 23 19 24 02	89 71 17 57 63	79 51 34 10 11	12 97 06 05 00	96 77 28 11 35
	42 55 29 27 78	76 81 16 63 13	04 93 73 21 04	84 91 77 67 10	50 00 21 92 50	96 91 83 66 19	81 15 86 62 40	81 15 69 78 10	18 40 92 93 88	13 01 90 70 82
	90 27 74 26 17	61 75 82 44 09	42 16 28 32 77	98 36 41 39 73	97 45 85 85 08	15 25 93 29 16	76 34 85 81 21	04 93 90 43 54	92 77 48 04 07	70 52 35 99 32
9	91 78 11 76 19	19 09 29 73 14	94 09 50 52 42	00 57 41 82 55	34 52 10 83 68	17 58 82 71 68	72 43 90 64 99	10 49 51 53 27	52 04 26 28 62	10 70 98 42 50
	53 42 75 49 95	48 74 48 88 94	52 58 34 96 85	31 34 96 82 31	47 55 84 13 48	86 83 54 45 38	32 46 69 85 86	24 47 32 60 28	29 45 36 58 21	30 84 54 36 35
	09 48 74 77 55	89 30 05 25 52	93 01 06 07 66	98 09 08 65 43	51 91 90 05 91	79 45 73 93 80	89 71 17 57 63	79 51 34 10 11	12 97 06 05 00	96 77 28 11 35
	23 43 73 69 25	89 55 18 26 26	87 69 88 38 12	40 83 94 06 23	96 55 93 14 80	49 89 86 62 40	81 15 86 62 40	81 15 69 78 10	18 40 92 93 88	13 01 90 70 82
	59 47 86 32 53	50 76 46 09 82	07 81 75 38 35	53 87 71 45 94	64 24 70 27 23	45 39 48 71 66	76 34 85 81 21	04 93 90 43 54	92 77 48 04 07	70 52 35 99 32
0	80 73 71 10 81	52 63 88 33 59	35 11 58 95 64	10 50 63 30 30	07 31 89 22 05	68 24 20 99 94	21 95 33 19 10	58 31 70 14 75	23 01 49 45 26	34 34 81 38 89
	67 44 30 85 08	18 69 78 50 15	88 24 02 62 46	36 89 70 02 89	78 50 98 86 01	32 35 95 10 22	34 50 81 80 34	14 82 30 95 52	12 13 53 83 62	86 07 50 83 86
	35 15 98 11 06	18 64 51 44 49	37 38 41 40 68	14 65 00 37 23	87 63 85 50 66	88 84 79 42 86	15 16 07 30 59	80 85 48 37 86	92 54 78 72 92	34 17 73 57 56
	66 17 63 96 90	44 57 17 04 05	85 84 64 44 05	34 06 31 13 81	92 30 29 21 61	61 17 22 69 09	65 48 83 28 97	61 17 22 69 09	03 39 10 59 24	06 79 60 36 84
	53 52 48 13 33	85 33 38 32 53	77 67 16 86 82	50 81 83 25 84	53 65 33 12 88	80 62 64 78 59	54 15 20 20 14	80 62 64 78 59	33 74 08 06 67	41 77 42 65 24

One fundamental principle must be kept in mind: *The purpose of randomness is to let blind chance determine the outcomes of the selection process to as great a degree as possible.* Hence, in determining a starting point for the selection of random numbers, *pure chance* must always initiate the process.

Consider the table of random numbers presented in Table 9.2 (similar tables can be found in most introductory statistics textbooks). It includes 100 blocks of numbers, arranged in 10 rows and 10 columns. The rows and columns are numbered merely to assist us in choosing a starting point for using the table. Any block within the table will be at the intersection of two guide numbers. To enter the table, we need an entry number of two digits; one digit will be used to designate the row, and the other the column, for the block at which we will begin.

But how do we find an entry number? Pull a dollar bill from your wallet. The one we have just pulled as we write this book has the serial number C 45 391827A. We choose the first two digits of the serial number, which makes the entry number 45. But which is the row and which is the column? We flip a coin. If it comes down heads, the first digit will designate the row; otherwise, the digit will designate the column. The coin comes down tails. This means that we will begin in the fourth column and the fifth row. The block where the two intersect is the block where we begin within the table.

We don't have to use a dollar bill to determine the entry point. We could use any source of numbers, such as a telephone directory, a license plate, an almanac, a friend's social security number, or the stock quotations page in a newspaper. Only one rule governs the final determination of an entry point: *Pure chance dictates the choice.*[3]

Having determined the "starting block," we must now determine the size of the proposed sample. If it is to be fewer than 100 individuals, we will need only two-digit numbers; if it is to be fewer than 1,000, we will need three digits to accommodate the sample size.

Let's go back to the total population for a moment to consider the group from which the sample is to be drawn. It will be necessary to designate individuals in some manner. It is advantageous, therefore, to arrange the members of the population in a logical order (e.g., alphabetically by surname) and to assign each person a serial number for identification.

Now we are ready for the random selection. We start with the upper left-hand digits in the designated block and work downward through the two-digit column in the rest of the table. If we need additional numbers, we proceed to the top of the next column, work our way down, and so on, until we have selected the sample we need.

Figure 9.8 illustrates the process we've just described. You will recall that our random number from the dollar bill was 45. This we selected as the entering number to find the starting point within the table. For purposes of illustration, we will assume that the total population consists of 90 individuals from which we will select a sample of 40. We will need random numbers of two digits each. Beginning in the upper left-hand corner of the designated block and remembering that only 90 individuals are in the total population, we see that the first number in the leftmost column is 30, so we choose from the total population individual number 30. The next number (98) does not apply because only 90 persons are in the population. Our next choice is 52, we ignore 93, and then we choose 80. Proceeding to the next block down, we choose 23 and 12, ignore 92, choose 3 and 33. We continue down the column and proceed to any additional columns we need, ignoring the numbers 91–99 and 00 and any numbers we have already selected, until we get a sample of 40.

We have probably said enough about the use of a table of random numbers. We turn now to specific probability sampling techniques.

SIMPLE RANDOM SAMPLING.   Simple random sampling is the least sophisticated of all sampling designs. The sample is chosen by simple random selection, whereby every member of the population has an equal chance of being selected.

Simple random sampling is easy when the population is small and all of its members are known. For example, one of us once used it in a study to evaluate the quality of certain teacher

---

[3] One of our readers has correctly pointed out that not all of the sources just suggested reflect strictly random numbers; rather, they may show a predictable pattern, with some numbers appearing more frequently than others. Nevertheless, using such a source ensures that the entry point into the table is chosen *arbitrarily,* eliminating any chance that the researcher might, either intentionally or unintentionally, tilt the sample selection in one direction or another.

FIGURE 9.8

Choosing the starting point in a random numbers table

	1	2	3	(4)	5
	38 01 08 18 62	82 52 01 82 29	02 56 28 19 24	88 42 92 63 07	23 99 90 93 57
	51 10 40 21 24	04 69 90 71 43	04 78 84 81 84	41 31 82 31 79	40 79 15 65 18
1	92 12 24 41 22	72 73 42 19 31	84 53 15 16 78	98 77 86 76 75	66 51 70 90 93
	94 72 67 55 42	52 52 26 41 89	32 38 14 58 97	71 94 93 90 49	66 42 05 69 12
	77 75 72 87 20	86 70 64 02 44	89 24 08 35 53	32 96 00 84 78	48 68 39 83 83
	92 44 11 50 85	05 70 08 70 64	91 81 58 48 16	61 87 48 52 08	60 42 80 59 20
	60 04 91 78 89	71 40 77 32 66	11 30 10 01 21	49 12 88 73 47	68 54 94 32 12
2	28 39 28 16 75	92 57 77 21 95	56 93 73 19 17	94 62 18 76 31	00 85 74 86 15
	88 49 94 80 45	16 20 72 31 64	74 04 31 00 86	97 79 33 98 04	55 26 34 15 70
	71 23 62 84 00	35 01 41 52 70	05 91 02 35 24	53 74 60 11 41	36 34 18 08 46
	96 96 31 54 02	00 91 92 76 35	15 68 62 95 24	32 12 73 38 93	77 48 20 37 37
	42 24 86 51 17	60 92 31 00 55	68 99 02 84 40	43 90 67 66 07	93 58 14 66 19
3	48 04 03 20 10	64 51 11 11 69	31 07 84 90 36	84 56 50 31 14	58 67 15 93 17
	24 82 46 95 57	73 54 42 99 51	33 72 12 89 86	63 44 34 78 78	62 23 04 30 78
	81 67 50 87 94	68 85 73 36 83	04 80 31 52 66	70 04 32 61 56	87 67 45 06 85
	13 45 91 94 98	03 88 43 86 42	98 65 79 38 10	91 12 81 98 30	31 10 49 95 83
	72 24 96 81 87	52 68 73 61 17	51 94 47 58 01	13 88 40 38 70	51 11 02 00 63
4	55 05 71 44 11	66 04 57 07 14	92 20 82 92 33	30 08 96 22 15	50 11 40 49 63
	92 36 97 30 14	88 41 90 80 35	07 75 80 26 05	94 14 31 80 07	55 41 14 57 90
	89 92 58 84 08	73 41 65 61 95	43 97 81 33 05	74 67 22 23 00	86 26 66 99 63
	26 80 83 98 13	77 10 83 11 03	00 44 16 60 42	30 88 02 35 74	26 31 51 32 71
	10 71 47 27 12	75 45 51 26 23	19 59 86 21 70	98 76 96 40 12	97 70 77 57 74
(5)	~~44 94 81 62 78~~	~~00 77 55 27 14~~	~~52 71 25 82 30~~	52 02 54 04 07	51 23 05 30 59
	33 85 26 45 29	22 81 84 43 83	11 60 71 38 45	93 07 22 30 42	99 30 52 21 40
	45 50 56 50 40	26 05 25 93 64	78 17 59 58 83	80 47 43 71 41	03 06 18 79 54
	92 53 64 22 75	68 24 20 99 94	21 95 33 19 10	23 01 49 45 26	34 34 81 38 89
	99 41 50 17 32	32 35 95 10 22	34 50 81 80 34	12 13 53 83 62	86 07 50 83 86
6	82 40 93 92 43	88 84 79 42 86	15 16 07 30 59	92 54 78 72 92	34 17 73 57 56
	86 48 92 62 86	04 86 51 39 73	61 17 22 69 09	03 39 10 59 24	06 79 60 36 84
	89 52 47 59 01	52 00 88 05 98	80 62 64 78 59	33 74 08 06 67	41 77 42 65 24
	22 21 03 21 90	20 37 19 57 62	99 37 27 35 26	12 68 43 81 53	71 92 33 99 26
	90 53 60 07 99	17 18 66 37 53	74 41 09 90 62	44 56 94 44 36	31 74 10 57 63
7	26 37 79 96 33	88 52 34 17 95	31 23 24 58 77	75 88 64 08 53	05 81 86 00 75
	43 02 16 18 53	51 79 03 90 34	30 34 88 89 36	85 70 92 05 82	01 57 58 98 83
	20 95 76 51 15	97 32 97 58 43	39 53 93 17 32	03 16 16 65 24	34 21 10 91 88

training institutes during the summer of 1992 (Cole & Ormrod, 1995). Fewer than 300 people had attended the institutes, and we knew who and where they all were. But for very large populations (e.g., all 10-year-olds or all lawyers), simple random sampling is neither practical nor, in many cases, possible.

STRATIFIED RANDOM SAMPLING. Think of Grades 4, 5, and 6 in a public school. This is a *stratified population.* It has three different layers (*strata*) of distinctly different types of individuals. In stratified random sampling, the researcher samples equally from each one of the layers in the overall population.

If we were to sample a population of fourth-, fifth-, and sixth-grade children in a particular school, we would assume that the three strata are roughly equal in size (i.e., there are similar numbers of children at each grade level), and so we would take equal samples from each of the three grades. Our sampling method would look like Figure 9.9.

Stratified random sampling has the advantage of guaranteeing equal representation of each of the identified strata. It is, of course, most appropriate when those strata are equal in size in the overall population as well.

FIGURE 9.9

Stratified random
sampling design

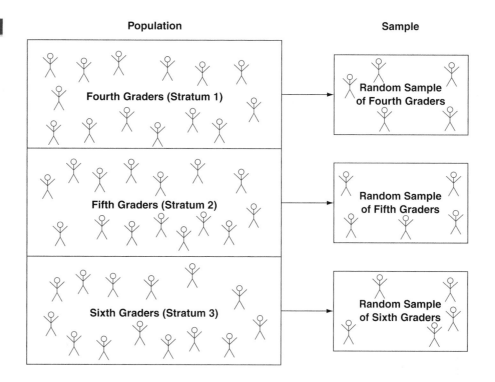

PROPORTIONAL STRATIFIED SAMPLING.   In the simple stratified random sampling design, all the strata of the population are essentially equal in size. But now we come to a different situation. Consider a community that has, for example, 1,000 Jewish people, 2,000 Catholics, and 3,000 Protestants. Let's imagine a survey situation. A local newspaper publishes a section dealing with interfaith church news, religious events, and syndicated articles of interest to the religious community in general. The editor wants to obtain certain information and opinions from the paper's readers and so decides to conduct a survey.

In this situation, the editor chooses his sample in accordance with the proportions of each religious group in the paper's readership. For every Jewish person, there should be two Catholics and three Protestants. In this situation, the people are not obviously segregated into the different strata, so the first step is to identify the members of each stratum and then select a random sample from each one. Figure 9.10 schematically represents this type of sampling.

CLUSTER SAMPLING.   Sometimes the population of interest is spread out over a large area. It may not be feasible to make up a list of every person living within the area and, from the list, select a sample for study through normal randomization procedures. Instead, we might obtain a map of the area showing political boundaries or other subdivisions. We can then subdivide an expansive area into smaller *units*. For example, a city can be subdivided into precincts, clusters of city blocks, or school boundary areas; a state can be divided into counties or townships. In cluster sampling, it is important that the clusters be as similar to one another as possible, with each cluster containing an equally heterogeneous mix of individuals.

A subset of the identified clusters is randomly selected. The sample consists of the people within each of the chosen clusters. Using our example of community religious groups, let's assume the community is a large city that we have divided into 12 areas, or clusters. We randomly select clusters 1, 4, 9, and 10, and their members become our sample. This sampling design is depicted in Figure 9.11.

SYSTEMATIC SAMPLING.   Systematic sampling involves selecting individuals (or perhaps clusters) according to a predetermined sequence. The sequence must originate by chance. For instance, we might scramble a list of units that lie within the population of interest and then select every 10th unit on the list.

Let's take the cluster diagram presented in Figure 9.11. The population has 12 cells, or clusters. Half of the cell numbers are odd, and the other half are even. Using the systematic sampling

FIGURE 9.10

Proportional stratified
sampling design

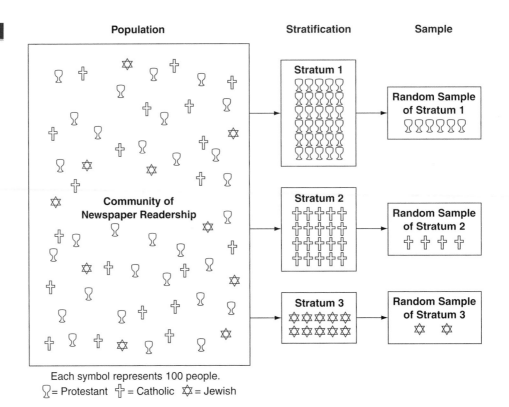

Each symbol represents 100 people.
♀ = Protestant   ✝ = Catholic   ✡ = Jewish

FIGURE 9.11

Cluster sampling design

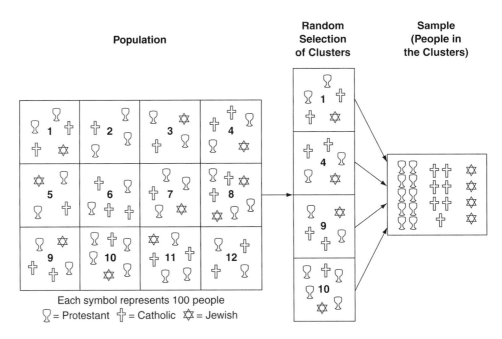

Each symbol represents 100 people
♀ = Protestant   ✝ = Catholic   ✡ = Jewish

technique, we choose, by *predetermined sequence,* the clusters for sampling. Let's toss a coin. Heads dictates that we begin with the first odd-numbered cluster; tails dictates that we begin with the first even-numbered cluster. The coin comes down tails, which means that we start with the first even-numbered digit, which is 2, and select the systematically sequential clusters 4, 6, 8, 10, 12. Figure 9.12 shows the systematic sampling design as used for sampling clusters.

At this point, let's consider the various kinds of populations for which different probability sampling techniques may be appropriate in a research study.

1. The population may be generally homogeneous. The individual units within the population may be similar with respect to the characteristics of interest.

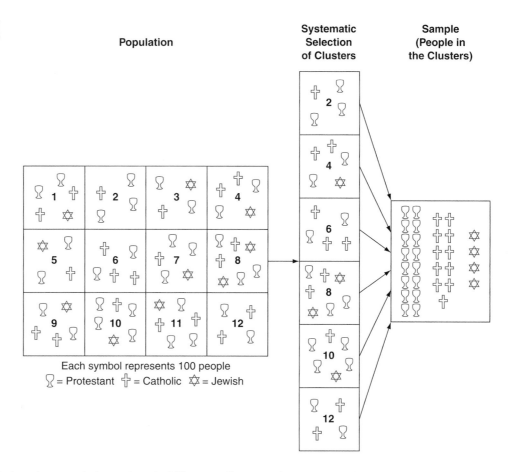

FIGURE 9.12
Systematic sampling design

Population

Systematic Selection of Clusters

Sample (People in the Clusters)

Each symbol represents 100 people
♟ = Protestant ✝ = Catholic ✡ = Jewish

TABLE 9.3 Population characteristics and probability sampling techniques appropriate for each population type

Population Characteristic	Example of Population Type	Appropriate Sampling Technique(s)
1: Population is generally a homogeneous group of individual units.	A particular variety of flower seeds, which a researcher wants to test for germination potential.	Simple random sampling Systematic sampling of individual units (for large populations)
2: Population contains definite strata that are approximately equal in size.	A school with six grade levels: kindergarten, first, second, third, fourth, and fifth.	Stratified random sampling
3: Population contains definite strata that appear in different proportions within the population.	A community in which residents are Catholic (25%), Protestant (45%), Jewish (15%), Muslim (5%), or nonaffiliated (10%).	Proportional stratified sampling
4: Population consists of discrete clusters with similar characteristics. The units within each cluster are as heterogeneous as units in the overall population.	Travelers in the nation's 20 leading air terminals. (All air terminals are similar in atmosphere, purpose, design, etc. The passengers who use them differ widely in such characteristics as age, gender, national origin, socioeconomic status, and belief system, with such variability being similar from one airport to the next.)	Cluster sampling Systematic sampling (of clusters)

2. The population may contain definite strata that are roughly equal in size.

3. The population may contain definite strata that occupy varying proportions of the overall population.

4. The population may consist of clusters whose characteristics are similar, but the individual units (e.g., people) within each cluster show variability in characteristics that is similar to the variability in the overall population.

Table 9.3 lists these four possibilities and suggests probability sampling designs appropriate for each one.

A sampling design should not be chosen blindly or willy-nilly. Each of the designs we've just discussed is uniquely suited to a particular kind of population, and so you should consider the nature of your population when selecting your sampling technique. The design diagrams presented in Figures 9.9 through 9.12 can assist you in your choice.

Nonprobability Sampling

In nonprobability sampling, the researcher has no way of forecasting or guaranteeing that each element of the population will be represented in the sample. Furthermore, some members of the population have little or no chance of being sampled. Here we discuss three types of nonprobability samplings.

CONVENIENCE SAMPLING. Convenience sampling (also known as *accidental sampling*) makes no pretense of identifying a representative subset of a population. It takes people or other units that are readily available—for instance, those that arrive on the scene by mere happenstance.

Convenience sampling may be appropriate for some less demanding research problems. For example, suppose you own a diner and want to sample the opinions of your patrons on the quality of food and service at the diner. You open for breakfast at 6 A.M. Each morning for a week, you question the first 40 patrons who arrive. Customers who have on one occasion expressed an opinion are eliminated on subsequent arrivals. The opinions you eventually get are from 38 men and 2 women. It is a heavily lopsided poll in favor of men, perhaps because the people who arrive at 6 A.M. are likely to be in certain occupations—laborers, construction workers, truck drivers—that are predominantly male.

The data from this convenience sample give you the thoughts of robust, hardy men about your breakfast menu at the diner. That's all. Yet such information may be all you need for the purpose you have.

Not all research data need to be collected through careful, thoughtful sampling procedures. But without such safeguards, the conclusions drawn from the research may not be trustworthy.

QUOTA SAMPLING. Quota sampling is a variation of convenience sampling. It selects respondents in the same proportions that they are found in the general population, but not in a random fashion. Let's consider a population in which the number of African Americans equals the number of European Americans. Quota sampling would choose, say, 20 African Americans and 20 European Americans, but without any attempt to select these individuals randomly from the overall population.

For example, suppose you are a reporter for a television station. At noon, you position yourself with microphone and television camera at a cross street in the center of a particular city. As people pass, you interview them. The fact that European Americans or African Americans may come in clusters of two, three, or four is no problem. All you need are the opinions of 20 people from each category of the population. This type of sampling regulates only the size of each category within the sample; in every other respect, the selection of the sample is nonrandom and, in most cases, convenient.

PURPOSIVE SAMPLING. In purposive sampling, people or other units are chosen, as the name implies, for a particular *purpose*. For instance, we might choose people who we have decided are "typical" of a group or those who represent diverse perspectives on an issue.

Agencies that forecast elections frequently use purposive sampling: They may choose a combination of voting districts that, in past elections, have been quite useful in predicting the final outcomes.

Purposive sampling may be very appropriate for certain research problems. However, the researcher should always provide a rationale explaining why he or she selected the particular sample of participants.

SAMPLING IN SURVEYS OF VERY LARGE POPULATIONS

Nowhere is sampling more critical than in survey research. Frequently the researcher reports that x percent of people believe such-and-such, that y percent do so-and-so, or that z percent are in favor of a particular political candidate. *Such percentages are meaningless unless the sample is representative of the population about which inferences are to be drawn.*

A basic rule governs survey research: Nothing comes out at the end of a long and involved study that is any better than the care, precision, and thought that went into the basic planning of the research design and the selection of the population. The results of a survey are no more trustworthy than the representativeness of the sample. Population parameters and sampling procedures are of paramount importance and become critical factors in the success of the study.

But now imagine that a researcher wants to conduct a survey of the country's *entire adult population*. How can the researcher possibly hope to get a random, representative sample of such a large group of people? The Survey Research Center of the University of Michigan's Institute for Social Research (1976) has used what it calls a *multistage sampling of areas*:

1. *Primary area selection.*   The Center divides the country into small "primary areas," each consisting of a specific county, a small group of counties, or a large metropolitan area. It randomly selects a predetermined number of these areas.
2. *Sample location selection.*   Each of the selected primary areas is divided into smaller sections ("sample locations"), such as specific towns. The Center randomly selects a small number of these locations.
3. *Chunk selection.*   The sample locations are divided into still smaller "chunks" that have identifiable boundaries such as roads, streams, or the edges of a city block. Most chunks have 16 to 50 dwellings, although the number may be larger in large cities. Once again, a random sample is selected.
4. *Segment selection.*   Chunks are subdivided into areas containing a relatively small number of dwellings, and some of these "segments" are, again, chosen randomly.
5. *Housing unit selection.*   Approximately four dwellings are selected (randomly, of course) from each segment, and the residents of those dwellings are asked to participate in the survey. If a doorbell is unanswered, the researcher returns at a later date and tries again.

This sampling method is depicted graphically in Figure 9.13.

As you may have deduced, the center's approach is a multistage version of cluster sampling. At each stage of the game, units are selected randomly. "Randomly" does not mean haphazardly or capriciously. Instead, a mathematical procedure is employed to ensure that selection is entirely random and the result of blind chance. This process should yield a sample that is, in all important respects, representative of the country's population.

Two other sampling issues should arise in the mind of the practical researcher: How large a sample does one need, and to what extent will *bias* in one's sample selection procedures limit the generalizability and interpretability of the results? We turn to these matters next.

IDENTIFYING A SUFFICIENT SAMPLE SIZE

The basic rule is, *the larger the sample, the better*. But such a generalized rule is not too helpful to a researcher who has a practical decision to make about a specific research situation. Obviously, we need to provide more guidance here. Gay and Airasian (2003, p. 113) have offered the following guidelines for selecting a sample size:

- For small populations (with fewer than 100 people or other units), there is little point in sampling. Survey the entire population.
- If the population size is around 500, 50% of the population should be sampled.
- If the population size is around 1,500, 20% should be sampled.
- Beyond a certain point (at about 5,000 units or more), the population size is almost irrelevant, and a sample size of 400 should be adequate.

Generally speaking, then, the larger the population, the smaller the percentage (but not the smaller the number!) one needs to get a representative sample.

To some extent, the size of an adequate sample depends on how homogeneous or heterogeneous the population is—how alike or different its members are with respect to the characteristics of research interest. If the population is markedly heterogeneous, a larger sample will be necessary than if the population is fairly homogeneous. Important, too, is the degree of precision with which the researcher wishes to draw conclusions or make predictions about the population under study.

FIGURE 9.13

Multistage sampling

From the *Interviewer's Manual* (rev. ed., p. 36), by the Survey Research Center, Institute for Social Research, 1976, Ann Arbor: University of Michigan. Reprinted with permission.

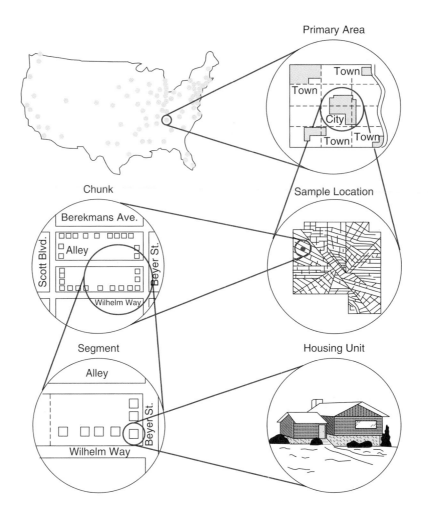

Statisticians have developed formulas for determining the desired sample size for a given population. Such formulas are beyond the scope of this book, but you can find them in many introductory statistics books (e.g., Mason & Lind, 1990; Ott, Larson, Rexroat, & Mendenhall, 1991).

BIAS IN RESEARCH SAMPLING

Look back at the five steps that the University of Michigan's Survey Research Center uses to obtain a sample for a national survey. Notice the last sentence in the fifth step: "If a doorbell is unanswered, the researcher returns at a later date and tries again." The researcher does *not* substitute one housing unit for another; doing so would introduce *bias* into the sampling design. The Center's *Interviewer's Manual* describes such bias well:

> The house on the muddy back road, the apartment at the top of a long flight of stairs, the house with the growling dog outside must each have an opportunity to be included in the sample. People who live on back roads can be very different from people who live on well paved streets, and people who stay at home are not the same as those who tend to be away from home. If you make substitutions, such important groups as young men, people with small families, employed women, farmers who regularly trade in town, and so on, may not have proportionate representation in the sample. (Survey Research Center, 1976, p. 37)

In research, **bias** is any influence, condition, or set of conditions that singly or together distort the data. Data are, in many respects, delicate and sensitive to unintended influences. We talk about the hard facts, the solid truth, and yet every researcher soon learns that data are neither so hard nor so solid as the phrases might suggest. Data are highly susceptible to distortion.

Bias can creep into a research project in a variety of subtle and undetected ways. It can be easily overlooked by even the most careful and conscientious researcher. For instance, when conducting an interview, the researcher's personality may affect the responses of the interviewee. In asking questions, the researcher's tone of voice or the inflection or emphasis within the sentence may influence how a respondent replies.

Bias attacks the integrity of the facts. It is particularly vicious when it enters surreptitiously into the research system and goes undetected. It can render suspect even the most carefully planned research effort.

Among the conditions that lead to bias is any influence that may have disturbed the randomness by which the choice of a sample population has been selected. Here we are talking about **sampling bias**.

The best way to appreciate sampling bias is to see it at work. Suppose a researcher decides to use a city telephone directory as a source for selecting a random sample for a telephone interview. She opens to a page at random, closes her eyes, puts the point of her pencil down on the page, and selects the name that comes closest to the pencil point. You can't get much more random than that, she reasons. But the demon of bias is there. The selection made does not represent the entire spectrum of the general population. Individuals in the lower economic strata of the population will not be adequately represented because many of them cannot afford telephone service. Nor will wealthy individuals be proportionally represented because many of them have unlisted telephone numbers. Hence, the sample will consist of a greater percentage of people at middle-income levels than exists in the general population.

Mailed questionnaire studies frequently fall victim to bias as well, often without the researcher's awareness. Let's take a simple situation. Suppose a questionnaire is sent to 100 citizens, asking, "Have you ever been audited by the Internal Revenue Service to justify your income tax return?" Of the 70 questionnaires returned, 35 are from people who indicate they have been audited, whereas 35 are from people who indicate they have never been audited. The researcher might therefore conclude that 50% of American citizens are likely to be audited by the IRS at one time or another.

The researcher's generalization may not be accurate, however. We need to consider how the nonrespondents (who, after all, were 30% of the original sample) might be different from those who responded to the questionnaire. Many people consider an IRS audit to be a reflection of their integrity. Perhaps for this reason, the nonrespondents may not have wanted to indicate they had been audited and so may have thrown the questionnaire in the wastebasket. The bias growing out of their efforts to preserve their integrity may have distorted the truth of the situation. Perhaps, instead of a 50–50 split, an estimate of 65% (people audited) versus 35% (people not audited) may have been more accurate; the researcher does not have the data to make such an estimate, however.

The examples just presented illustrate two different ways in which bias may creep into the research sample. In the case of the telephone survey, *sample selection* itself was biased because not everyone in the population had an equal chance of being selected. In fact, people not listed in the telephone directory had *zero* chance of being selected. Here we see the primary disadvantage of nonprobability sampling, and especially of convenience sampling: People who happen to be readily available for a research project—those who are in the right place at the right time—are almost certainly *not* a random sample of the overall population.

In the example concerning IRS audits, *response rate*, and potential differences between respondents and nonrespondents, was the source of bias. In that particular situation, the researcher's return rate of 70% was quite high. More often, however, the return rate in a questionnaire study is 50% or less, and the more nonrespondents there are, the greater the likelihood of bias.

Nonrespondents to questionnaires are often different from respondents in one or more ways (Rogelberg & Luong, 1998). They may have less interest in the topic being studied. They may have illnesses, disabilities, or language barriers that prevent them from responding. And on average, they have lower educational levels. To the extent that such variables affect how people respond to a questionnaire, then bias will exist in the data that the questionnaire yields.

Acknowledging the Probable Presence of Bias

It is almost impossible for people to live in this world without coming into contact with disease-bearing germs and other microorganisms. Likewise, in the research environment, the researcher cannot avoid having data contaminated by bias of one sort or another. What is unprofessional, however, is for the researcher to fail to acknowledge the likelihood of biased data or to fail to recognize the possibility of bias in the study. When formulating conclusions about the data, a researcher must be sure to consider the effect that bias may have had in distorting them.

In survey research, you should *always* report the percentages of people who have and have not consented to participate, such as those who have agreed and refused to be interviewed or those who have and have not returned questionnaires. Furthermore, you should be candid about possible sources of bias that result from differences between participants and nonparticipants. Rogelberg and Luong (1998) have suggested several strategies for identifying possible bias in questionnaire research; we list three especially useful ones here:

1. Carefully scrutinize the questionnaire for items that might be influenced by one's education level, interest in the topic, or other factors that frequently distinguish respondents from nonrespondents.
2. Compare the responses on questionnaires that were returned quickly with responses on those that were returned later, perhaps after a second reminder letter or after the deadline you imposed. The late ones may, to some extent, reflect the kinds of responses that nonrespondents would have given. Significant differences between the early and late questionnaires probably indicate bias in your results.
3. Randomly select a small number of nonrespondents and try to contact them by mail or telephone. Present an abridged version of your survey, and, if some people reply, match their answers against those in your original set of respondents.

One of us authors once used a variation on the third strategy in the study of summer training institutes that we mentioned earlier in the chapter (Cole & Ormrod, 1995). A research assistant had sent questionnaires to all attendees at one summer's institutes so that the institutes' leaders could improve the training sessions the following year, and she had gotten a return rate of 50%. She placed telephone calls to small random samples of both respondents and nonrespondents and asked a few of the questions that had been on the questionnaire. She obtained similar responses from both groups, leading the research team to conclude that the responses to the questionnaire were probably fairly representative of the entire population of institute participants.

Good researchers demonstrate their integrity by admitting, without reserve, that bias is omnipresent and may well have influenced their findings. Ideally, they point out precisely how bias may have infiltrated the research design. With this knowledge, others may then appraise the research realistically and judge its merits honestly.

As researchers, we must learn to live with bias, but at the same time we must guard against its infective destruction. In research, we cannot force the data to support anything. The data should be, as much as possible, immune to influence of any kind and should speak for themselves. If they are tainted with bias, we must accept that as an inevitable condition in most research and should not be unduly upset.

PRACTICAL APPLICATION POPULATION ANALYSIS FOR A DESCRIPTIVE SURVEY

Select a particular population and conduct an analysis of its structure and characteristics. Analyze the population you have chosen by completing the following checklist.

✔ CHECKLIST
ANALYZING A POPULATION

_____   1. On the following line, identify the population you have chosen:

_____

_____   2. Now answer the following questions with respect to the *structure of the population*:

	YES	NO
a. Is the population a relatively homogeneous group of individuals or other units?	____	____
b. Could the population be considered to consist generally of equal "layers," each of which is fairly homogeneous in structure?	____	____
c. Could the population be considered to be composed of separate homogeneous layers differing in size and number of units comprising them?	____	____
d. Could the population be envisioned as isolated islands or clusters of individual units, with the clusters being similar to one another in composition?	____	____

_____   3. Through what means would you extract a representative sample from the total population? Describe your procedure on the following lines:

_____

_____

_____   4. Refer to Table 9.3. Is your sampling procedure appropriate for the characteristics of the population? _____ Yes _____ No

_____   5. Have you guaranteed that your sample will be chosen by chance and yet will be representative of your population? _____ Yes _____ No

_____   6. If the preceding answer is yes, explain how this has been done.

_____

_____

_____

_____   7. Indicate what means will be employed to obtain the information you need from the sample:

_____

_____

_____   8. What are the weaknesses inherent in this method of obtaining the data?

_____

_____

_____   9. What safeguards have you established to counteract any potential bias in your approach to data collection? Be specific.

_____

_____

_____

INTERPRETING DATA IN DESCRIPTIVE RESEARCH

Data are of little or no value merely as data. In our discussion of descriptive research methods, we have principally discussed the acquisition of data: how to obtain the data from the general population with appropriate techniques (observations, interviews, questionnaires, sampling) and how to protect those data against distortion of bias. We have been thinking of the process of data collection only.

At this juncture, we remind you of two basic principles of research:

1. The purpose of research is to seek the answer to a problem in the light of the data that relate to the problem.
2. Although collecting data for study and organizing it for inspection take care and precision, extracting meaning from the data—what we have called the interpretation of the data—is all-important.

A descriptive study is often a very "busy" research method: The researcher must decide on a population; choose a technique for sampling it; minimize the entrance of bias into the study; develop a valid means of collecting the desired information; and then actually collect, record, organize, and analyze it all. The activities connected with descriptive research are complex, time-consuming, and distracting. Therein lies an element of danger. With all this action going on, it would not be surprising if the researcher lost sight of the problem and subproblems. But the problem and its subproblems are precisely the reason for all the rest of the activity.

All research activity is subordinate to the research problem itself. Sooner or later, the entire effort must result in an interpretation of the data and a setting forth of conclusions, drawn from the data, to resolve the problem being investigated. Inexperienced researchers may forget this. Activity for activity's sake is seductive. Amassing great quantities of data can provide a sense of well-being. Like Midas looking at his hoard of gold, researchers might lose sight of the ultimate demands that the problem itself makes on those data. Presenting the data in displays and summaries—graphs, charts, tables—does nothing more than demonstrate the researcher's acquisitive skills and consummate ability to present the same data in different ways. Descriptive research ultimately aims to solve problems through the interpretation of the data that have been gathered.

SOME FINAL SUGGESTIONS

As we approach the end of the chapter, it is important to reflect on several issues related to descriptive research. Consider each of the following questions within the context of the research project you have in mind:

- Why is a description of this population and/or phenomenon valuable?
- What specific data will I need to solve my research problem and its subproblems?
- What procedures do I need to get the necessary information? How should I implement those procedures?
- How do I get a sample that will truly be reflective of the entire population about which I am concerned?
- How can I collect my data in a way that ensures no misrepresentation or misunderstanding?
- How do I control for possible bias in the collection and description of the data?
- What do I do with the data once I have collected them? How do I organize and prepare them for analysis?

A SAMPLE DISSERTATION

We conclude the chapter by illustrating how questionnaires might be used in a correlational study to address the topic of violence in intimate relationships (e.g., husband and wife, boyfriend and girlfriend) in American society. The excerpts we present are from Luis Ramirez's doctoral dissertation in sociology completed at the University of New Hampshire (Ramirez, 2001).

Now go to our Companion Website at http://www.prenhall.com/leedy to assess your understanding of chapter content and to complete the projects that will help you learn how to conduct research.

The doctoral student hypothesizes that violence (in particular, assault) between intimate partners is, in part, a function of ethnicity, acculturation (e.g., adoption of mainstream American behaviors and values), criminal history, and social integration (e.g., feelings of connectedness with family and friends). He further hypothesizes that, as a result of such factors, differences in intimate partner violence might be observed in Mexican Americans and non-Mexican Americans.

He begins Chapter 1 by discussing the prevalence of violence (especially assault) in intimate relationships. We pick up Chapter 1 at the point where he identifies his research questions and hypotheses. We then move into Chapter 2, where he describes his methodology. As has been true for earlier proposal and dissertation samples, the research report appears on the left-hand side, and our commentary appears on the right.

DISSERTATION ANALYSIS 6

RESEARCH QUESTIONS	Comments

[T]he following questions will be addressed: What role does acculturation into American society have on intimate partner violence for Mexican Americans? What are the effects of a person's criminal history on intimate partner violence? What is the extent and the relation of criminal history to intimate partner violence, and is criminal history restricted to one type of crime or is it a more general tendency (violent versus property crimes)? Are crimes that are committed early in life more indicative of a pattern of crime as compared to crimes that begin later in life? Do people who assault their partners possess weak social bonds with the society they live in? Finally, this study will ask the question, "Are there differences between criminal history and bond to society for Mexican Americans and Non-Mexican Whites, and how do these factors affect intimate partner violence?"

To understand factors underlying violence in intimate partner relationships—his main research problem—the author identifies a number of subproblems, which he expresses here as research questions.

If relations are found between these characteristics, it suggests that social agencies that deal with intimate partner violence need to adjust their policies and intervention procedures to better meet the characteristics of their clients. The focus of primary prevention could be put on the social bonding process, the criminal history of the individual, or the acculturation process in order to help solve future problems. Furthermore, a comparative study of intimate partner assault among ethnic groups could provide further clarification to a body of literature and research that has produced mixed results.

Here the author addresses the importance of the study, *both pragmatic (results have potential implications for social policy and practice) and theoretical (results may shed light on inconsistencies in previous research studies).*

[T]he author briefly reviews theoretical frameworks related to ethnicity and acculturation, criminal history, and control theory, which he then uses as a basis for his hypotheses.

HYPOTHESES

The theoretical frameworks reviewed led to the following hypotheses:

Ethnicity and Acculturation

1. The rate of intimate partner violence is lower for Mexican Americans than Non-Mexicans.
2. The higher the acculturation into American Society, the higher the probability of assaulting a partner for Mexican Americans.

The hypotheses are organized by the theoretical frameworks from which they have been derived, helping the reader connect them to rationales the author has previously provided.

Criminal History

3. Criminal history is more prevalent for Mexican Americans than for Non-Mexicans.

4. The more crimes committed in the past, the higher the probability of physically assaulting a partner.

5. Criminal history is more associated with an increased risk of intimate partner violence for Mexican Americans than Non-Mexicans. Criminal history is more associated with an increased risk of intimate partner violence for Mexican Americans than Non-Mexicans.

6. Early onset crime is more associated with an increased risk of intimate partner violence than criminal behavior beginning later in life.

7. Previous violent crime is more associated with an increased risk of intimate partner violence than property crime.

Social Integration

8. Mexican Americans are more socially integrated than Non-Mexican Whites.

9. The more socially integrated an individual is, the lower the probability of physically assaulting a partner.

10. Social Integration is more associated with a decreased risk of intimate partner violence for Mexican Americans than Non-Mexicans.

A more detailed review of the literature will be presented in . . . following chapters. Literature for all hypotheses will be reviewed in their respective chapters.

Figure 1.1 is a diagramed representation of what I believe is the causal process that could affect intimate partner violence. It includes demographic and control variables, the main independent variables (acculturation, criminal history, social integration), and intimate partner violence. These variables will be described in detail in the next chapter.

Notice how the hypotheses are single spaced. Single-spaced hypotheses often appear in theses and dissertations, but check the guidelines at your own institution to see whether such formatting is desired.

An in-depth review of the literature is postponed until Chapters 3 through 5, where the author also relates his own results to previous research findings. Although this is an unusual organizational structure, it works well in this situation, allowing the reader to connect results relative to each hypothesis to the appropriate body of literature. Note the transition to the next chapter, which immediately follows.

Figure 1.1 Model of Intimate Partner Violence

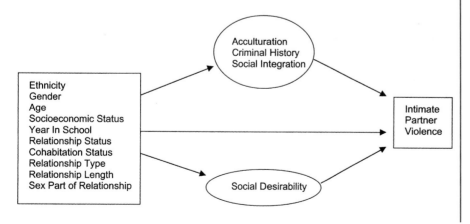

Figure 1.1 effectively condenses and summarizes the researcher's hypotheses.

CHAPTER 2

METHODS

Sample

The issues discussed in the previous chapter will be investigated using data from a sample of college students who have been or are currently in a dating or married relationship. A sample of college students is appropriate for this study for the following reasons: 1) The National Crime Victimization Survey found that the rates of non-lethal intimate partner violence was greatest for the 20 to 24 year age group, followed by the 16 to 19 age group, and then the 25 to 34 age group (Renison & Welchans, 2000). The majority of college students fall into the high-risk age categories. Sugarman and Hotaling (1989) identified eleven studies that provided rates for physical assault of dating partners and concluded the rates of assaulting a partner range from 20% to 59%. 2) College students make up about a third of the 18 to 22 year old population. College students are a sizable population in reference to the general population (about 15 million). 3) College students are in a formative period of their lives in relation to the habits that they develop with an intimate partner. These habits could surface in other intimate relations (O'Leary, Malone, & Tyree, 1994; Pan, Neidig, & O'Leary, 1994).

It is important to mention that a sample of college students is not a representative sample of the general population in the United States. This group generally has lower levels of criminal behavior, substance abuse, and marriage rates. Additionally, college students may be more socially integrated into society and are engaged in education as a tool for upward mobility. In short, this is a segment of society that plays by the rules.

Data Collection

Six hundred and fifty questionnaires were passed out to students at The University of Texas at El Paso and Texas Tech University during the fall 1999, spring 2000, and summer 2000 semesters. Students who were enrolled in Sociology, Anthropology, and History classes [were] the respondents.

Respondents filled out the questionnaire (Appendix A) in a classroom setting. Each respondent received a booklet consisting of: (1) a cover sheet explaining the purpose of the study, the participant's rights, and the name of a contact person and telephone number for those who might have questions after the test session was over; (2) the demographic questions; (3) the instruments described in this section. The purpose, task demands, and rights were explained orally as well as in printed form at the beginning of each session. Respondents were told that the questionnaire would include questions concerning attitudes, beliefs, and experiences they may have had. They were guaranteed anonymity and confidentiality of their responses and they were told that the session would take an hour or slightly more. In actuality, the range of time that it took students to finish was between 30 minutes to 1 hour. All students were asked to sign a written consent form before completing their questionnaires. Students were also given instructions on how to properly fill out three scantron sheets before they were left to fill out the questionnaire at their own pace.

A debriefing form was given to each participant as they turned in their questionnaire. It explained the study in more detail and provided names and telephone numbers of local mental health services and community resources, such as services for battered women. Students that voluntarily participated in the study were offered extra credit points by their professors.

Some style manuals suggest that an author include at least a small amount of text between two headings of different levels. For example, before beginning the "Sample" section, the author might provide an advance organizer, describing the topics he will discuss in the chapter and in what order.

The author clearly realizes that his sample (college students) is not representative of the entire U.S. population. He presents a good case that the sample is quite appropriate for his research questions. At the same time, he acknowledges that his sample has some shortcomings.

The author, whose home town is El Paso, has numerous acquaintances at both institutions and so can easily gain access to these students. He must, of course, seek approval from the Internal Review Boards at the two institutions, as well as at the institution where he is completing his doctorate.

The author has combined his informed consent forms and questionnaires into a single booklet that he can easily distribute. Doing so is quite common in descriptive research, especially with adult samples, and increases the efficiency of data collection.

The author is using technology (scantron sheets) in his data collection. Give the nature of his sample (college students) and his sample size (576), this approach is reasonable.

Given the sensitive nature of some questionnaire items, the debriefing that follows data collection appropriately includes information about community resources for individuals who have been victims of partner violence.

The initial sample consisted of 650 respondents of which 576 chose to complete the questionnaire. Of these, 33 questionnaires were omitted because they were non-legible or partially completed. Finally, of the 543 remaining questionnaires, 348 were selected for this study because they met the criteria of having no missing data for any specific question, were either Mexican American/Mexican National or Non-Mexican White, and had been in a heterosexual romantic relationship for a month, or longer during the previous 12 months.

Here the author describes his criteria for including completed questionnaires in his data set. In essence, he is addressing the issue of admissibility of the data (see Chapter 5).

NOTE: From *The Relation of Acculturation, Criminal History, and Social Integration of Mexican American and Non-Mexican Students to Assaults on Intimate Partners* (pp. 3–4, 14–20) by I. L. Ramirez, 2001, unpublished doctoral dissertation, University of New Hampshire, Durham. Reprinted with permission.

FOR FURTHER READING

Alreck, P. L., & Settle, R. B. (1995). *The survey research handbook* (2nd ed.). Burr Ridge, IL: Irwin.

Babbie, E. (1990). *Survey research methods* (2nd ed.). Belmont, CA: Wadsworth.

Berdie, D. R., Anderson, J. F., & Niebuhr, M. A. (1986). *Questionnaires: Design and use* (2nd ed.). Metuchen, NJ: Scarecrow Press.

Bourque, L. B., & Clark, V. A. (1992). *Processing data: The survey example.* Thousand Oaks, CA: Sage.

Bourque, L. B., & Fielder, E. P. (Eds.) (2002). *How to conduct self-administered and mail surveys* (2nd ed.) Thousand Oaks, CA: Sage.

Bourque, L. B., & Fielder, E. P. (2002). *How to conduct telephone surveys.* Thousand Oaks, CA: Sage.

Delandshere, G., & Petrosky, A. R. (1998). Assessment of complex performances: Limitations of key measurement assumptions. *Educational Researcher, 27,* 14–24.

Fink, A. (2002). *How to design survey studies* (2nd ed.) Thousand Oaks, CA: Sage.

Fink, A. (2002). *How to sample in surveys* (2nd ed.) Thousand Oaks, CA: Sage.

Fink, A. (2002). *The survey handbook* (2nd ed.). Thousand Oaks, CA: Sage.

Fowler, F. J., Jr. (2001). *Survey research methods* (3rd ed.). Thousand Oaks, CA: Sage.

Frey, J. H., & Oishi, S. M. (1995). *How to conduct interviews by telephone and in person.* Thousand Oaks, CA: Sage.

Gay, L. R., & Airasian, P. (2003). *Educational research: Competencies for analysis and application* (7th ed.). Upper Saddle River, NJ: Merrill/Prentice Hall. [See Chapters 10 and 11.]

Gibbons, J. D. (1993). *Nonparametric measures of association.* Thousand Oaks, CA: Sage.

Gubrium, J. F., & Holstein, J. A. (Eds.) (2002). *Handbook of interview research: Context and method.* Thousand Oaks, CA: Sage.

Henry, G. T. (1990). *Practical sampling.* Thousand Oaks, CA: Sage.

Litwin, M. S. (2002). *How to measure survey reliability and validity.* Thousand Oaks, CA: Sage.

Magnusson, D., Bergman, L. R., Rudinger, G., & Torestad, B. (Eds.). (1991). *Problems and methods in longitudinal research: Stability and change.* New York: Cambridge University Press.

Oppenheim, A. N. (1992). *Questionnaire design, interviewing, and attitude measurement* (2nd ed.). New York: St. Martin's Press.

Rea, L. M., & Parker, R. A. (1997). *Designing and conducting survey research* (2nd ed.). San Francisco: Jossey-Bass.

Rogelberg, S. G., & Luong, A. (1998). Nonresponse to mailed surveys: A review and guide. *Current Directions in Psychological Science, 7,* 60–65.

Rosenfeld, P. (1993). Computer-administered surveys in organizational settings: Alternatives, advantages, and applications. *American Behavioral Scientist, 36,* 485–511.

Salant, P., & Dillman, D. A. (1994). *How to conduct your own survey.* New York: Wiley.

Schuman, H., & Presser, S. (1982). *Questions and answers: Experiments in the form, wording, and context of survey questions.* San Diego: Academic Press.

Schwarz, P. N., & Sudman, S. (1996). *Answering questions: Methodology for determining cognitive and communicative processes in survey research.* San Francisco: Jossey-Bass.

Thach, L. (1995). Using electronic mail to conduct survey research. *Educational Technology, 35*(2), 27–31.

10

Experimental and Ex Post Facto Designs

Progress is relative. We measure progress by noting the amount of change between what was and what is. And we attempt to account for the change by identifying the dynamics that have caused it. Ideally, we must manipulate one possible causal factor while keeping all other possible causal factors constant; only in this way can we determine whether the manipulated factor has an effect on the phenomenon we're studying. To the extent that multiple factors all vary simultaneously, we learn little about true underlying causes.

In the designs we've discussed up until now, we've made no systematic attempt to determine the causes of the phenomena being studied. But ultimately we often do want to know what causes what; in other words, we want to identify *cause-and-effect relationships*.

A researcher can most convincingly identify cause-and-effect relationships by using an **experimental design.** In such a design, the researcher considers many possible factors that might cause or influence a particular condition or phenomenon. The research then attempts to control for all influential factors *except* those whose possible effects are the focus of investigation.

An example can help to clarify the point. Imagine that we have two groups of people. We take steps to make sure that these two groups are, on average, so similar that we can, for all intents and purposes, call them equivalent. We give them a pretest to measure a particular characteristic in which we're interested (perhaps blood pressure, academic achievement, or spending habits). Then we expose only one of the groups to a **treatment** or intervention of some sort (perhaps a new drug, an instructional method, or an advertising campaign) that we think may have an effect on the characteristic we are studying. Afterward, we give both groups a posttest to measure the characteristic once again. If the characteristic changes for the group that received the intervention but does not change for the other group, and if everything about the two groups has been the same *except for the intervention*, then we can reasonably conclude that the treatment or intervention brought about the change we observed. Because we have not only observed the situation but also *manipulated* it, we have used an experimental design.

We must clarify the difference between an *experiment* and an *experimental design*. An experiment does not necessarily involve an experimental design. As an illustration, consider a problem that arose in Thomas Edison's laboratory in the early days of the incandescent electric lightbulb. Edison had given his engineers a lightbulb that was both round and tapering in shape and asked them to calculate its volume. Each engineer drew on a wealth of mathematical knowledge to solve the problem, yet each arrived at a different answer. Edison then went into his laboratory, filled a container with water, measured the water's volume, immersed the incandescent bulb into it, and snipped off the pointed glass tip. Water rushed into the bulb (because it was a vacuum) and filled it completely. Edison removed the water-filled bulb from the container and then measured the amount of water that remained. The difference between the amount of water in the container before and after the lightbulb had been filled was the volume of the bulb.

That was an experiment. It was not research, nor was it an experimental design. The experiment merely determined a fact (the volume of the lightbulb), and for that particular fact there was no further meaning to be derived. Had Edison been able to *interpret* his findings in some additional way, then his experiment would have been a research experiment.

Some of the research designs we describe in this chapter are true experimental designs; as such, they allow us to identify cause-and-effect relationships. Other designs in this chapter eliminate some—but not all—alternative explanations of an observed change. All of the designs in this chapter have one thing in common: clearly identifiable independent and dependent variables. In the following sections, we distinguish between independent and dependent variables and explore the importance of control for studying cause-and-effect relationships. After that, we introduce you to a variety of research designs that involve an environmental intervention of some sort—either an intervention that a researcher directly manipulates (resulting in an experimental design or one of its relatives) or one that the environment has provided before a research study begins (resulting in an ex post facto design).

INDEPENDENT AND DEPENDENT VARIABLES

In previous chapters, we have occasionally used the term *variable*, but we haven't stopped to define it. We do so now: A **variable** is any quality or characteristic in a research investigation that has two or more possible values. For instance, variables in studies of how effectively children learn in classrooms might include instructional methods used; teachers' educational backgrounds, emotional warmth, and beliefs about classroom discipline; children's intelligence, personality characteristics, prior learning experiences, reading skills, and study strategies; and of course, how much children actually learn in class. Variables in studies of how well seeds germinate might include amounts of sun and water, kinds of soil and fertilizer, presence or absence of various parasites and microorganisms, genetic makeup of the seeds, speed of germination, and hardiness of the resulting plants.

When we investigate cause-and-effect relationships, we are, of course, looking at the extent to which one variable (the *cause*) influences another variable (the *effect*). A variable that the researcher studies as a possible cause of something else—in many cases, this is one that the researcher directly manipulates—is called an **independent variable.** A variable that is potentially influenced by the independent variable—that "something else" we just mentioned—is called a **dependent variable,** because it is influenced by, and so to some extent *depends* on, the independent variable. In research in the social sciences and education, the dependent variable is often some form of human behavior. In medical research, it might be people's physical health or well-being. In agricultural research, it might be quality or quantity of a particular crop.

To illustrate the two kinds of variables, we take a simple situation in the physical world. Suppose an investigator connects a potentiometer to a source of electricity and then connects a voltmeter to the potentiometer. The potentiometer, a resistor, allows the investigator to control the voltage that reaches the voltmeter: By turning a knob in one direction or the other, the investigator can allow more or less voltage to travel forward, and the voltmeter measures the voltage that reaches it. In this situation, the voltage that the potentiometer delivers is the independent variable. The reading on the voltmeter—where the needle points on the face of the instrument—depends on the voltage and so is the dependent variable.

Let's now consider an example in medical research. Imagine that we want to compare the relative effectiveness of two different drugs that are used to treat high blood pressure. We take a sample of 60 men who have high blood pressure and randomly assign each man to one of two groups: The men in one group take one drug, and the men in the other group take the other drug.

Later, we compare the blood pressure measurements for the men in the two groups. In this situation, we are manipulating the particular drug that each person takes; the drug, then, is the independent variable. Blood pressure is the variable that is presumably influenced by the drug taken and so is the dependent variable.

As a final example, let's look at a dissertation in educational psychology (Thrailkill, 1996). The researcher wanted to study the effects of three different kinds of lecture material on people's ability to remember information contained in the lecture. Working with undergraduate students, she presented different parts of a lecture on an obscure American Civil War battle in one of three ways: (1) she described certain historical figures and events in such a manner that they were easy to imagine and visualize (*imagery* condition), (2) she included attention-grabbing phrases (*attention* condition), or (c) she did neither of these things (*control* condition). In the following examples, the underscored phrases illustrate the modifications made for each of the three conditions; other variations in wording made the three lectures equivalent in length:

> Imagery: Lincoln also created the Army of Virginia, incorporating several forces which had been under different commanders. Lincoln set the dimpled, baby-faced young blond Major General John Pope in charge of this new combined force. Being put under his command was objectionable to some of the former commanders. . . .

> Attention: Lincoln also created the Army of Virginia, incorporating several forces which had been under different commanders. Listen to me now. Lincoln set the less experienced Major General John Pope in charge of this new combined force. Being put under the command of Pope was objectionable to some of the former commanders. . . .

> Control: Lincoln also created the Army of Virginia, incorporating several forces which had been under different commanders. Lincoln set the less experienced junior officer Major General John Pope in charge of this new combined force. Being put under the command of Pope was objectionable to some of the former commanders. . . . (Thrailkill, 1996, p. 62, some underscoring added)

After presenting different parts of the lecture under the three conditions, the researcher measured the students' recall for the lecture in two ways. She first gave them blank sheets of paper and asked them to write down as much of the lecture as they could remember (a "free recall" task). When they had completed the task, she gave them a multiple-choice test that assessed their memory for specific facts within the lecture. In this study, the independent variable was the nature of the lecture material: easily visualized, attention-getting, or neutral. There were two dependent variables, both of which reflected students' ability to recall facts within the lecture: performance on the free recall task and scores on the multiple-choice test. Thrailkill's hypothesis was confirmed: The students' ability to recall lecture content *depended*, to some extent, on the way in which the content was presented.

THE IMPORTANCE OF CONTROL

In Chapter 5, we introduced you to the concept of *internal validity*. The internal validity of a research study is the extent to which its design and the data it yields allow the researcher to draw accurate conclusions about cause-and-effect and other relationships. In experimental designs, internal validity is essential; without it, any results the researcher obtains are uninterpretable.

As an example, suppose we have just learned about a new method of teaching science in elementary school. We want to conduct an experiment to investigate the method's effect on students' science achievement test scores. We find two fifth-grade teachers who are willing to participate in the study. One teacher agrees to use the new method in the coming school year; in fact, she is quite eager to try it. The other teacher wants to continue using the same approach he has always used. Both teachers agree, too, that at the end of the school year we can give their students a science achievement test.

Are the two classes the same in every respect *except for the experimental intervention?* If the students taught with the new method obtain higher science achievement test scores at the end of the year, will we know that the method was the *cause* of the higher scores? The answer to both questions is a resounding *no!* The teachers are different: One is female and the other male, and they almost certainly have different personalities, educational backgrounds, teaching styles, and so on. In addition, the two groups of students may be different; perhaps the students instructed by the new method are, on average, more intelligent or motivated than the other, or perhaps they live in a more affluent school district. Other, more subtle differences may be at work as well, including the interpersonal dynamics in the two classes, and the light, temperature, and noise levels within each classroom. Any one of these factors, and perhaps others that we haven't thought of, may have contributed to the differences in achievement test scores we obtained.

Whenever we compare two or more groups that are or might be different in ways *in addition to* the particular treatment or intervention we are studying, we have **confounding variables** in our study. The presence of such variables makes it extremely difficult to draw conclusions about cause-and-effect relationships, because we cannot pin down *what* is the cause of any phenomenon we observe after the intervention.

To maximize internal validity when a researcher wants to identify cause-and-effect relationships, then, the researcher needs to control confounding variables so that these variables are ruled out as explanations for any effects observed. Researchers use a variety of strategies to control for confounding variables. Following are several common ones:

1. *Keep some things constant.*   When a factor is the *same* for everyone, it cannot possibly account for any differences that we see. Oftentimes researchers ensure that different treatments are imposed in the same or similar environments. They may also seek research participants who share a certain characteristic, such as sex, age, grade level, or socioeconomic status. (Keep in mind, however, that restricting the nature of one's sample may lower the *external validity*, or generalizability, of any findings obtained; see Chapter 5's discussion of this concept.)

2. *Include a control group.*   In Chapter 5, we described a study in which an industrial psychologist begins playing classical music as employees in a typing pool go about their daily task of typing documents. At the end of the month, the psychologist finds that the typists' productivity is 30% higher than it was the preceding month. The increase in productivity may or may not be due to the classical music. There are too many possible confounding variables—personnel changes, nature of the documents being typed, numbers of people out sick or on vacation during the 2 months, even just the knowledge that an experiment is being conducted—that may also account for the typists' increased productivity.

To better control for such extraneous variables, researchers frequently include a **control group,** a group that receives either no intervention or a "neutral" intervention that should have little, if any, effect. They then compare the performance of this group to an **experimental group** (also known as a **treatment group**) that participates in an intervention.

As you should recall from Chapter 5, people sometimes show improved performance simply because they know they are participating in a research study, an effect known as *reactivity* or the *Hawthorne effect*. To take this fact into consideration, a researcher sometimes gives the people in a control group a **placebo** that has the appearance of having an effect but in reality does not have an effect. For instance, a researcher studying the effects of a new arthritis medication might give some participants a particular dosage of the medicine and give others a similar-looking sugar pill. Or a researcher investigating a new approach to treating test anxiety might use the new treatment with some individuals but give other individuals general relaxation training that, although possibly beneficial in other ways, won't necessarily address their test anxiety.

We must stress quite strongly that any researcher who incorporates placebos in a study must consider *three ethical issues* related to the use of placebos. First is the principle of informed consent: Participants in the study must be told that the study includes a placebo treatment as well as an experimental one and that they will not know which treatment they have received until the study has ended. Second, if participants in the study have actively sought help for a medical, psychological, or other serious problem, those who initially receive the placebo treatment should, at the conclusion of the study, be given the opportunity to receive more effective treatment. (This is assuming, of course, that the treatment *is* more effective than the placebo.) Third, and most important, when studying a treatment related to life-threatening situations (e.g., a new drug for terminal cancer, a new psychotherapeutic technique for suicidal teenagers), the researcher must seriously weigh (a) the benefits of the new knowledge that can be gained by including a control group that receives no treatment versus (b) lives that may be saved by including all participants in the treatment group.

Our last point raises an issue we cannot possibly resolve for you here. Should you find yourself having to make a decision about the best research design to use in a life-and-death situation, you should consult with your professional colleagues, the Internal Review Board at your institution, and, of course, your own conscience.

3. *Randomly assign people to groups.*   In Chapter 9, we spoke at length of the value of selecting people at random to participate in a research study; such random selection enhances the probability that any results obtained for the sample also apply to the population from which the sample has been drawn. In experimental studies, researchers use random selection for a different purpose: to assign participants within their sample to various groups.

In any research study involving human beings or other living things, members of the sample are likely to be different from one another in ways that are relevant to the variables under investigation. For example, earlier in the chapter we described a situation in which a researcher wants to compare two methods of teaching elementary school science. The students in the study will almost certainly differ from one another in intelligence, motivation, educational opportunities at home, and other factors that will affect their performance on the science achievement test given at the end of the school year. It would be virtually impossible to control for such variables by having all students in the study have the *same* intelligence, the *same* motivation, the *same* kinds of outside opportunities, and so on.

As an alternative to keeping some characteristics the same for everyone, a researcher can, instead, randomly assign participants to groups. When people have been selected for one group or another on a random basis, then the researcher can reasonably assume that *on average, the groups are quite similar* and that *any differences between them are due entirely to chance.* In fact, many inferential statistical tests—especially those that allow the researcher to make comparisons among two or more groups—are based on the assumption that group membership is randomly determined and that any pretreatment differences between the groups result from chance alone.

4. *Assess equivalence before the treatment with one or more pretests.*   Sometimes random assignment to two different groups simply isn't possible; for instance, researchers may have to study groups that already exist (e.g., students in classrooms, participants in different medical treatment programs). An alternative in this situation is to assess other variables that might influence the dependent variable and determine whether the groups are similar with respect to these variables. If the groups *are* similar, then the researcher reduces or eliminates the possibility that such variables could account for any group differences that are later observed.

Another strategy is to identify **matched pairs:** pairs of people—one in each of two groups being compared—who are identical or very similar with respect to characteristics that are relevant to the study. For instance, a researcher comparing the achievement test scores of students in two different instructional programs might identify pairs of students of the same sex and age who have similar IQ scores. A researcher comparing two different treatments for a particular illness might match patients according to sex, age, and duration and intensity of the illness. In either case, the researcher does not study the data collected for *all* people in the two groups, only the people who are part of "matched sets" that he or she has identified. A researcher who uses this approach will, in the final research report, explain in what way(s) the participants in the study have been matched. For example, he or she might say, "pairs were matched on the basis of age, gender, and socioeconomic status."

One problem with assessing before-treatment equivalence with pretests is that the researcher rules out *only the variables that he or she has actually assessed and determined to be equivalent across groups.* The design does not rule other influential factors that the researcher has not assessed and perhaps not even considered.

5. *Expose participants to both or all experimental conditions.*   Still another strategy for controlling for individual differences is to *use participants as their own controls*—that is, to have every participant in the study undergo all experimental and control treatments and then assess the effects of each treatment independently. Such an approach is known as a *within-subjects design* or a *repeated measures design.*

As an example, let's return to the dissertation involving three different lecture methods and their possible effects on recall for lecture content (Thrailkill, 1996). The researcher's sample consisted of volunteer students who were enrolled in three sections of an undergraduate class in educational psychology, and she planned to give the lecture just three times, once to each class. The lecture was about an American Civil War battle sufficiently obscure that participants were unlikely to have had any prior knowledge about it; thus, participants' prior knowledge about the battle was a constant (they all had zero prior knowledge) rather than a confounding variable. The researcher divided the lecture into three parts of approximately equal length and wrote three versions of each part, one version each for the imagery, attention, and control conditions. She combined the three versions of the three lecture parts such that each class received the different treatments in a different sequence, as follows:

	PART OF LECTURE		
	First Part	**Middle Part**	**Last Part**
Group 1	Attention	Imagery	Control
Group 2	Control	Attention	Imagery
Group 3	Imagery	Control	Attention

In this manner, all participants in her study were exposed to the two treatments and the control condition, and each condition occurred in all possible places (first, second, and third) in the sequence.

In the study just described, the researcher had three groups whose members were not randomly assigned, and so she gave all three interventions (imagery, attention, and control) to all three groups. Sometimes researchers use a similar strategy with just a single group, and in some cases with just a single individual. You will learn some strategies for showing causation in single-group and single-individual studies later in the chapter, when we explore *quasi-experimental designs*.

6. *Statistically control for confounding variables.*   Sometimes researchers can control for known confounding variables, at least in part, through statistical techniques. Such techniques as *partial correlation*, *analysis of covariance* (ANCOVA), and *structural equation modeling* are suitable for this purpose. We'll briefly describe each of these in Chapter 11. Should you choose to use one of them in your own research, we urge you to consult one or more statistics books for guidance about their use and appropriateness for various research situations.

Keep in mind, however, that controlling confounding variables statistically is no substitute for controlling for them in one's research design if at all possible. *A carefully controlled experimental design is the only approach that allows you to draw definitive conclusions about cause-and-effect relationships.*

OVERVIEW OF EXPERIMENTAL AND EX POST FACTO DESIGNS

In true experimental research, the researcher manipulates the independent variable and examines its effects on another, dependent variable. A variety of research designs have emerged that differ in the extent to which the researcher manipulates the independent variable and controls for confounding variables. In the upcoming sections, we will present a number of possibilities, which we've divided into three general categories: (a) *pre-experimental designs*, (b) *true experimental designs*, and (c) *quasi-experimental designs*. We will also describe designs in which a researcher studies the possible effects of an environmental factor that has occurred prior to the study itself; such designs are often called *ex post facto designs*. Finally, we will consider studies in which the effects of two independent variables are examined simultaneously; such studies involve *factorial designs*. Altogether, we will introduce 16 different designs that illustrate various ways—some more effective than others—of identifying possible cause-and-effect relationships. Much of our discussion will be based on a classic book chapter by Campbell and Stanley (1963).[1]

---

[1] In particular, Designs 1–6 and Designs 8–11 are based on those that Campbell and Stanley described. However, when describing Design 11, we use the contemporary term *reversal design* rather than Campbell and Stanley's original term *equivalent time-samples design*.

We will be illustrating the designs using tables that have this general format:

Group	Time—>		
Group 1			
Group 2			

Each group in a design will be shown in a separate row, and the things that happen to the group over time will be shown in separate cells within the row. The cells will have one of four notations:

Tx: Indicates that a *treatment* (reflecting the independent variable) is presented.

Obs: Indicates that an *observation* (reflecting the dependent variable) is made.

—: Indicates that nothing occurs during a particular time period.

Exp: Indicates a previous *experience* (an independent variable) that some participants have had and others have not; the experience has not been one that the researcher could control.

The nature of these tables will become more apparent as we proceed.

As you read about the 16 designs, keep in mind that they are hardly an exhaustive list; researchers may modify or combine them in various ways. For example, although we will be limiting ourselves to studies with only one or two groups (perhaps one treatment group and one control group), it is entirely possible to have two or more treatment groups (each of which is exposed to a different variation of the independent variable) and, in some cases, two control groups (perhaps one getting a placebo and another getting no intervention at all). More generally, the designs we describe here should simply provide a starting point that gets you thinking about how you might best tackle your own research problem.

PRE-EXPERIMENTAL DESIGNS

In **pre-experimental designs,** it is not possible to show cause-and-effect relationships, because either (a) the independent "variable" doesn't vary or (b) experimental and control groups are not comprised of equivalent or randomly selected individuals. Such designs are helpful only for forming tentative hypotheses that should be followed up with more controlled studies.

DESIGN 1: ONE-SHOT EXPERIMENTAL CASE STUDY

The one-shot experimental case study is probably the most primitive type of experiment that might conceivably be termed "research." An experimental treatment (Tx) is introduced, and then a measurement (Obs)—a posttest of some sort—is administered to determine the effects of the treatment. This design is shown in the following table:

Group	Time—>	
Group 1	Tx	Obs

The design has low internal validity because it is impossible to determine whether participants' performance on the posttest is the result of the experimental treatment per se. Many other variables may have influenced participants' performance, such as physiological maturation, experiences in the participants' home lives, or a significant event in the society in which the participants live. Perhaps the condition observed after the treatment existed *before* the treatment as well. The reality is that, with a single measurement or observation, we have no way of knowing whether the situation has changed or not, let alone whether it has changed as a result of the intervention.

One-shot experimental case studies may be at the root of many common misconceptions. For example, imagine that we see a boy sitting on the damp ground in mid-April. The next day, he has a sore throat and a cold. We conclude that sitting on the damp earth caused him to catch cold. Thus, the design of our "research" thinking is something like this:

Exposure to cold, damp ground (Tx) —> Child has a cold (Obs)

Such "research" may also "support" such superstitious folk beliefs as these: If you walk under a ladder, you will have bad luck; Friday the 13th is a day of catastrophes; a horseshoe above the door brings good fortune to the house. Someone observed an event, then observed a subsequent event, and linked the two together as cause and effect.

Be careful not to confuse the one-shot experimental case study method with the case study design of many qualitative studies. As described in Chapter 6, case study research involves extensive engagement in a research setting—a far cry from basing conclusions on a single observation.

Although the one-shot experimental case study is simple to carry out, its results are, for all intents and purposes, meaningless. At the very least, researchers should use the design described next.

DESIGN 2: ONE-GROUP PRETEST-POSTTEST DESIGN

In a one-group pretest-posttest design, a single group (a) has a pre-experimental evaluation, then (b) is administered the experimental treatment, and finally (c) is evaluated after the treatment. This design is represented as follows:

Group	Time—>		
Group 1	Obs	Tx	Obs

Suppose an elementary school teacher wants to know if listening to a story on a tape recorder improves the reading skills of students in her class. She gives her students a standardized reading pretest, has them listen to a tape-recorded story every day for 8 weeks, and then tests them with an alternate form of the same standardized test. If the students' test scores improve over the 8-week period, she might conclude—perhaps accurately, but perhaps not—that listening to the stories was the cause of the improvement.

Suppose an agronomist hybridizes two strains of corn. He finds that the hybrid strain is more disease-resistant and has a better yield than either of the two parent types. He concludes that the hybridization process has made the difference. Once again we have an Obs-Tx-0bs design: The agronomist measures the disease level of the parent strains (Obs), develops a hybrid of the two strains (Tx), and then measures the disease level of the next generation (Obs).

In a one-group pretest-posttest design, we at least know that a change has taken place. However, we have not ruled out other possible explanations for the change. In the case of the elementary school teacher's experiment, improvement in reading scores may have been due to other activities within the classroom curriculum, to more practice taking the reading test, or simply to the fact that the students were 8 weeks older. In the case of the agronomist's experiment, changes in rainfall, temperature, or soil conditions may have been the primary reason for the healthier corn crop.

DESIGN 3: STATIC GROUP COMPARISON

The static group comparison involves both an experimental group and a control group. Its design takes the following form:

Group	Time—>	
Group 1	Tx	Obs
Group 2	—	Obs

An experimental group is exposed to a particular experimental treatment; the control group is not. After the treatment, both groups are observed and their performance compared. In this design, however, no attempt is made to obtain equivalent groups or at least to examine the groups to determine whether they are similar before the treatment. Thus, we have no way of knowing if the treatment actually causes any differences we observe between the groups.

The three designs just described, though commonly employed in many research projects, leave much to be desired in terms of drawing conclusions about what causes what. The experimental designs we describe next are far superior in this respect.

TRUE EXPERIMENTAL DESIGNS

In contrast with the somewhat simple designs we have just described, **experimental designs** offer a greater degree of control and, as a result, greater internal validity. The first three designs we discuss here share one thing in common: People or other units of study are *randomly assigned to groups*. Such random assignment guarantees that any differences between the group are probably quite small and, in any case, are due entirely to chance. The last design in this section involves a different strategy: administering different treatments to a single group.

DESIGN 4: PRETEST-POSTTEST CONTROL GROUP DESIGN

In a pretest-posttest control group design, an experimental group and a control group are carefully selected through appropriate randomization procedures. The experimental group is observed, subjected to the experimental treatment, and observed once again. The control group is isolated from any influences of the experimental treatment; it is simply observed both at the beginning and at the end of the experiment. The paradigm for the pretest-posttest control group design is as follows:

	Group	Time—>		
Random Assignment	Group 1	Obs	Tx	Obs
	Group 2	Obs	—	Obs

Such a design, simple as it is, solves two major problems associated with pre-experimental designs. We can determine whether a change takes place after the treatment, and, if so, we can eliminate other possible explanations (in the form of confounding variables) as to why the change has taken place. Thus, we have a reasonable basis on which to draw a conclusion about a cause-and-effect relationship.

DESIGN 5: SOLOMON FOUR-GROUP DESIGN

One potential problem in the preceding design is that the process of observing or assessing people before administering the experimental treatment may, in and of itself, influence how people respond to the treatment. For instance, perhaps the pretest increases people's motivation: It makes them want to benefit from the treatment they receive. Such an effect is similar to the reactivity effect that we described in Chapter 5 and referred to earlier in this chapter.

To address the question, What effect does pretesting have?, Solomon (1949) proposed an extension of the pretest-posttest control group design that involves four groups, as depicted in the following table:

	Group	Time—>		
Random Assignment	Group 1	Obs	Tx	Obs
	Group 2	Obs	—	Obs
	Group 3	—	Tx	Obs
	Group 4	—	—	Obs

The addition of two groups who are not pretested provides a distinct advantage. If the researcher finds that, in the final observation, Groups 3 and 4 differ in much the same way that

Groups 1 and 2 do, then the researcher can more easily generalize his or her findings to situations in which no pretest has been given. In other words, the Solomon four-group design enhances the *external validity* of the study.

Obviously, this design involves a considerably larger sample and demands more time and energy on the part of the researcher. Its principal value is in eliminating pretest influence; where such elimination is desirable, the design is unsurpassed.

DESIGN 6: POSTTEST-ONLY CONTROL GROUP DESIGN

Some life situations defy pretesting. You cannot pretest the forces in a thunderstorm or a hurricane, nor can you pretest growing crops. Additionally, at times you may be unable to locate a suitable pretest, or, as just noted, the very act of pretesting can influence the results of the experimental manipulation. In such circumstances, the posttest-only control group design offers a possible solution. The design may be thought of as the last two groups of the Solomon four-group design. The paradigm for the posttest-only approach is as follows:

	Group	Time—>	
Random Assignment	Group 1	Tx	Obs
	Group 2	—	Obs

Random assignment to groups is, of course, critical in the posttest-only design. Without it, the researcher has nothing more than a static group comparison (Design 3), from which, for reasons previously noted, the researcher has a difficult time drawing inferences about cause and effect.

DESIGN 7: WITHIN-SUBJECTS DESIGN

Throughout the book we have been using the term *participants* when referring to people who participate in a research study. Some disciplines (e.g., psychology) often use the term *subjects* instead. This term has a broader meaning than *participants* in that it can be used to refer to a wide variety of populations—perhaps human beings, dogs, pigeons, or laboratory rats.

By *within-subjects design*, we mean that all participants receive two (or possibly more) different treatments simultaneously, and the potential effects of each treatment are observed. If we use the subscripts a and b to designate the different treatments and treatment-specific measures, then, in its simplest form, the design is as follows:

Group	Time—>	
Group 1	Tx_a	Obs_a
	Tx_b	Obs_b

You may also see the term *repeated-measures design* used for such a study, because the dependent variable is measured more than once, with the effect of each treatment being assessed separately.

As an example, imagine that a researcher wants to study the effects of illustrations in teaching science concepts to sixth graders. The researcher creates a short textbook that presents, say, 20 different concepts. In the textbook, all 20 concepts are defined and described with similar precision and depth. In addition, the text illustrates 10 of those concepts (chosen randomly) with pictures or diagrams. After students read the book, they take a test that assesses their understanding of the 20 concepts, and the researcher computes separate test scores for the illustrated and nonillustrated concepts. If the students perform better on test items for illustrated concepts than on items for nonillustrated ones, the researcher can reasonably conclude that, yes, illustrations help students learn science more effectively. In other words, the researcher has identified a cause-and-effect relationship.

For a within-subjects design to work, the various forms of treatment must be such that their effects are fairly localized and unlikely to "spread" beyond specifically targeted behaviors. This is the case in the study just described: The illustrations help students learn the particular concepts that have been illustrated but do not help students learn science more generally. In contrast, it would not make sense to use a within-subjects design to study the effects of two different psychotherapeutic techniques to reduce adolescents' criminal behaviors: If the same group of adolescents receives both treatments and then shows a significant reduction in juvenile offenses, we might suspect that either treatment could have had a fairly broad impact.

Ideally, too, the two different treatments should be administered repeatedly, one after another, in a balanced, but somewhat random order. For example, in the textbook that presents both illustrated and nonillustrated science concepts, we might begin with an illustrated concept, then have two nonillustrated ones, then another illustrated one, another nonillustrated one, two illustrated ones, and so on, with the presentation of the two conditions being evenly balanced throughout the book.

With the last point in mind, let's return to the dissertation involving the history lecture described earlier. Each group received each of the three treatments: the imagery, attention, and control conditions. The logistics of the study were such that it was difficult to intermingle the three treatments throughout the lecture; instead, the researcher administered first one treatment (e.g., attention), then another (e.g., imagery), and finally the third (e.g., control). Had she limited her study to a single group, she could not have ruled out an alternative explanation—when in the lecture the information appeared (whether it appeared near the beginning, in the middle, or at the end)—for the results she obtained. By using three different groups, each of which had each condition in a different order, she was able to eliminate that alternative explanation. Strictly speaking, however, because the researcher could neither randomize assignment to groups nor randomly distribute different treatment conditions throughout the lecture, her study is probably better characterized as a quasi-experimental study than a true experimental study. We look more closely at quasi-experimental designs now.

QUASI-EXPERIMENTAL DESIGNS

In the preceding discussion of true experimental designs, we emphasized the importance of *randomness*, either in the selection of group members in a multiple-groups study or in the presentation of different treatments in a single-group study. Sometimes, however, randomness is not possible or practical. In such situations, researchers often use **quasi-experimental designs.** When they conduct quasi-experimental studies, they do not control for all confounding variables and so cannot completely rule out some alternative explanations for the results they obtain. They must take whatever variables and explanations they have not controlled for into consideration when they interpret their data.

DESIGN 8: NONRANDOMIZED CONTROL GROUP PRETEST-POSTTEST DESIGN

The nonrandomized control group pretest-posttest design can perhaps best be described as lying somewhere between the static group comparison (Design 3) and the pretest-posttest control group design (Design 4). Like Design 3, it involves two groups to which participants have not been randomly assigned. But it incorporates the pretreatment observations of Design 4. In sum, the nonrandomized control group pretest-posttest design can be depicted as follows:

Group	Time—>		
Group 1	Obs	Tx	Obs
Group 2	Obs	—	Obs

Without random assignment, there is, of course, no guarantee that, prior to the experimental treatment or intervention, the two groups are similar in every respect—that any differences between them are due entirely to chance. However, an initial observation (e.g., a pretest) can confirm that the two groups are at least similar in terms of the dependent variable under investigation.

If, after one group has received the experimental treatment, we then find group differences with respect to the dependent variable, we might reasonably conclude that the posttreatment differences are probably the result of that treatment.

Identifying matched pairs in the two groups is one way of strengthening the pretest-posttest control group design. For instance, if we are studying the effect of a particular preschool program on children's IQ scores, we might find pairs of children—each pair including one child who is enrolled in the preschool program and one who is not—who are the same sex and age and have similar IQ scores before the program begins. Although we cannot rule out all other possible explanations in this situation (e.g., it may be that the parents who enroll their children in the preschool program are more concerned about their children's cognitive development in general), we can at least rule out *some* alternative explanations.

DESIGN 9: SIMPLE TIME-SERIES DESIGN

In its simplest form, a time-series design consists of making a series of observations (i.e., measuring the dependent variable on several occasions), introducing an intervention or other new dynamic into the system, and then making additional observations. If a substantial change results in the second series of observations, we may reasonably assume that the cause of the change was the factor introduced into the system. This design thus looks something like the following:

Group	Time—>								
Group 1	Obs	Obs	Obs	Obs	Tx	Obs	Obs	Obs	Obs

In such studies, the sequence of observations made prior to the treatment is often referred to as **baseline** data.

Such a design has been widely used in the physical and biological sciences. Sir Alexander Fleming's discovery that *Penicillium notatum* (a mold) could inhibit staphylococci (a type of bacteria) is an example of this type of design. Fleming had observed the growth of staphylococci on a culture plate *n* number of times. Then, unexpectedly, a culture plate containing well-developed colonies of staphylococci was contaminated with the spores of *Penicillium notatum*. Fleming observed that the colonies near the mold seemed to disappear. He repeated the experiment with the bacteria and the mold in company with each other. Each time, his observation was the same: no staph germs near the mold.

The major weakness of this design is the possibility that some other, unrecognized event may occur at the same time that the experimental treatment does (a confounding variable sometimes known as *history*). If this other event is actually the cause of the change, then any conclusion that the treatment has brought about the change will, of course, be an erroneous one.

DESIGN 10: CONTROL GROUP, TIME-SERIES DESIGN

In a variation of the time-series design, two groups are observed over a period of time, but one group (a control) does not receive the experimental treatment. The design is configured as follows:

Group	Time—>								
Group 1	Obs	Obs	Obs	Obs	Tx	Obs	Obs	Obs	Obs
Group 2	Obs	Obs	Obs	Obs	—	Obs	Obs	Obs	Obs

This design has greater internal validity than the simple time-series design (Design 8). If an outside event is the cause of any changes we observe, then presumably the performance of *both* groups will be altered after the experimental treatment takes place. If, instead, the experimental treatment is the factor that affects performance, then we should see a change only for Group 1.

DESIGN 11: REVERSAL TIME-SERIES DESIGN

The reversal design uses a within-subjects approach as a way of minimizing (though not entirely eliminating) the probability that outside effects might bring about any changes observed. The intervening experimental variable is sometimes present, sometimes absent, and we measure the dependent variable at regular intervals. Thus, we have the following design:

Group	Time—>							
Group 1	Tx	Obs	—	Obs	Tx	Obs	—	Obs

To illustrate, suppose we are interested in whether audiovisual materials help students learn astronomy. On some days we might include audiovisual materials in a lesson, and on other days we might omit them. We can then measure how effectively students learn under both conditions. If the audiovisual materials do, in fact, promote student learning, then we should see consistently better student performance on those days.

DESIGN 12: ALTERNATING TREATMENT DESIGN

A variation on the reversal design involves including two or more different forms of the experimental treatment in the design. Referring to the two different forms of treatment with the notations Tx_a and Tx_b, we can depict such a design in the following manner:

Group	Time—>												
Group 1	Tx_a	Obs	—	Obs	Tx_b	Obs	—	Obs	Tx_a	Obs	—	Obs	Tx_b	Obs

If such a sequence were pursued over a long enough time span, then we would presumably see different effects for the two different treatments.

DESIGN 13: MULTIPLE BASELINE DESIGN

Designs 11 and 12 are based on the assumption that the effects of any single treatment are temporary and limited to the immediate circumstances. But what do we do if a treatment is likely to have long-lasting and perhaps more general effects? If the treatment is truly apt to be beneficial, then ethical considerations may discourage us from including an untreated control group. In such instances, a multiple baseline design provides a good alternative. This design requires at least two groups. Prior to the treatment, baseline data is collected for all groups, and then the treatment itself is introduced at a different time for each group. In its simplest form, a multiple baseline design might be configured as follows:

Group	Time—>					
	Baseline—>		*Treatment—>*			
Group 1	—	Obs	Tx	Obs	Tx	Obs
	Baseline—>				*Treatment—>*	
Group 2	—	Obs	—	Obs	Tx	Obs

A study by Heck, Collins, and Peterson (2001) provides an example of this approach. The researchers wanted to determine if instruction in playground safety would decrease elementary school children's risky behaviors on the playground. The treatment in this case involved a 5-day intervention in which a woman visited the classroom to talk about potentially risky behaviors on slides and climbing equipment, as well as about the unpleasant consequences that might result from such behaviors. The woman visited four classrooms on different weeks;

FIGURE 10.1

Instances of risky behavior on slides and climbers by grade level; third graders and kindergartners shared a combined recess

Reprinted from "Decreasing Children's Risk Taking on the Playground" by A. Heck, J. Collins, and L. Peterson, 2001, *Journal of Applied Behavior Analysis, 34*, p. 351. Reprinted with permission of the Society for the Experimental Analysis of Behavior, Inc.

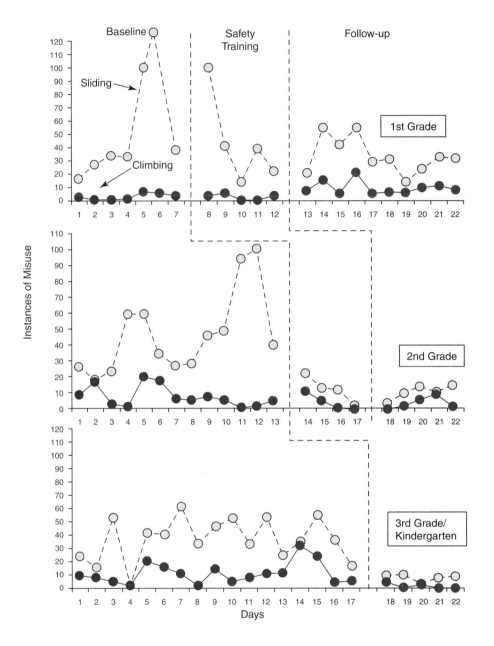

a random selection process resulted in her visiting the first grade class one week, the second grade class the following week, and the kindergarten and third grade classes (which went to recess at the same time) the week after that. Meanwhile, two independent observers simultaneously counted the number of risky behaviors on the playground before, during, and after the intervention. The data they collected are depicted in Figure 10.1; number of risky behaviors on the slide are shown with the lighter dots, whereas those on the climbing equipment are shown with the darker dots. Notice how each group has data for three time periods: a pre-intervention baseline period, the 5-day safety-training period, and a post-training follow-up period. As you can see, the children showed fairly rapid declines in risky behavior on the slide once safety training began. Those groups who used the climbing equipment most frequently (the second and third graders) showed a concurrent decline in risk taking on that equipment. Because the behavior changes occurred at different times for the three groups, and in particular when each group began the safety training, the researchers reasonably concluded that the training itself, rather than something else in the school environment or elsewhere, was probably the reason for the change.

USING DESIGNS 11, 12, AND 13 IN SINGLE-SUBJECT STUDIES

Reversal, alternating treatment, and multiple baseline designs can be used not only with groups but also with single individuals, in what are collectively known as **single-subject designs.** A study by Deaver, Miltenberger, and Stricker (2001) illustrates how a researcher might use two of these, reversal and multiple baseline, simultaneously. A 2-year-old girl named Tina had been referred for treatment because she often twirled her hair with her fingers so vigorously that she pulled out some of her hair. On one occasion she wrapped the hair around a finger so tightly that it began to turn blue and the hair had to be removed with scissors. Tina engaged in such behavior primarily when she was alone (e.g., at naptime); hence, there was no parent or other adult present to discourage it. The researchers identified a simple treatment—putting thin cotton mittens on her hands—and wanted to document its effect. They videotaped Tina's behaviors when she was lying down for a nap in either of two settings, her bedroom at home or her daycare center, and two observers independently counted the number of hair twirling incidents as they watched the videotapes. Initially, the observers collected baseline data. Then, during separate time periods for the bedroom and daycare settings, they gave Tina the mittens to wear during naptime. After reversing back to baseline in both settings, they had Tina wear the mittens once again. The percentages of time that Tina twirled her hair in the two settings over the course of the study are presented in Figure 10.2.

In both the bedroom and daycare settings, the researchers alternated between baseline and treatment; this is the *reversal* aspect of the study. Furthermore, they initiated, and then later reinitiated the treatment, at different times in the two settings; this is the *multiple baseline* aspect of the study. Figure 10.2 consistently shows dramatic differences in hair twirling during baseline versus mittens conditions, leading us to conclude that the mittens, rather than some other factor, were almost certainly the reason for the disappearance of hair twirling.

FIGURE 10.2

Percentage of session time in which hair twirling was observed both in the bedroom and at daycare

Reprinted from "Functional Analysis and Treatment of Hair Twirling in a Young Child" by C. M. Deaver, R. G. Miltenberger, & J. M. Stricker, 2001, *Journal of Applied Behavior Analysis*, *34*, p. 537. Reprinted with permission of the Society for the Experimental Analysis of Behavior, Inc.

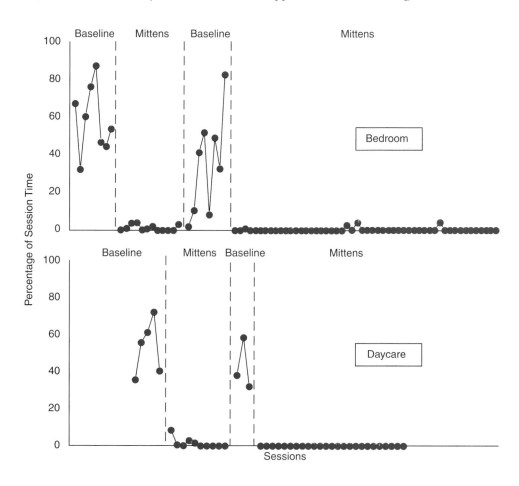

Ex Post Facto Designs

In many situations, it is unethical or impossible to manipulate certain variables in order to investigate their potential influence on other variables. For example, one cannot introduce a new virus, withhold instruction, ask parents to abuse their children, or modify a person's personality to compare the effects of these factors on the dependent variables in one's research problem.

Ex post facto designs[2] (the term *ex post facto* literally means "after the fact") provide an alternative means by which a researcher can investigate the extent to which specific independent variables (a virus, a modified curriculum, a history of family violence, or a personality trait) may possibly affect the dependent variable(s) of interest. Although experimentation is not feasible, the researcher identifies events that have already occurred or conditions that are already present and then collects data to investigate a possible relationship between these factors and subsequent characteristics or behaviors. After observing that different circumstances have prevailed among two or more groups (e.g., some children are vaccinated against chicken pox, whereas others are not; one preschool provides extensive training in drawing and art, whereas another does not), an astute researcher attempts to determine whether these different circumstances preceded an observed difference on some dependent variable (e.g., reported number of cases of chicken pox, development of artistic skills).

Ex post facto designs are often confused with correlational or experimental designs because they have similarities with both types of designs. Like correlational research, ex post facto research involves looking at existing conditions. But like experimental research, it has clearly identifiable independent and dependent variables.

Unlike experimental studies, however, ex post facto designs involve no direct manipulation of the independent variable: The presumed "cause" has already occurred. To the extent that such manipulation is not possible, the researcher cannot draw firm conclusions about cause and effect. The problem here is that the experimenter cannot control for confounding variables that may provide alternative explanations for any group differences that are observed.

Although an ex post facto study lacks the control element—and so does not allow us to draw definite conclusions about cause and effect—it is nevertheless a legitimate research method that pursues truth and seeks the solution of a problem through the analysis of data. Science has no difficulty with such a methodology. Medicine uses it widely in its research activities. Physicians discover an illness and then inaugurate their search "after the fact." They sleuth into antecedent events and conditions to discover a possible cause for the illness. Such was the approach of medical researchers when the AIDS virus emerged in the 1980s.

Like experimental designs, ex post facto designs may take a variety of forms. Here we present one possible design for illustrative purposes. We will also present a second ex post facto design in the subsequent section on factorial designs.

Design 14: Simple Ex Post Facto Design

Design 14 is similar to the static group comparison (Design 3), which we included in our discussion of pre-experimental designs. The sole difference here is one of timing: In this case, the "treatment" in question occurred long before the study began; hence, we will call it an *experience* rather than a treatment because the researcher has not been responsible for imposing it. A simple ex post facto design can be depicted as follows, where Exp refers to a prior experience that one group has had and another has not:

Group	Time—>	
	Prior event(s)	*Investigation period*
Group 1	Exp	Obs
Group 2	—	Obs

---

[2] Ex post factor designs are also known as *causal-comparative* designs. However, as Johnson (2001) has so eloquently pointed out, the latter term may mislead novice researchers to believe that such designs show cause and effect as clearly and definitely as true experimental designs. In reality, of course, such designs never eliminate all other possible explanations for an observed effect; thus, they cannot truly show cause and effect.

An obvious variation on this design is one in which Group 2 has an experience as well, albeit a different experience from that of Group 1.

Such designs are common in studying the possible effects of environmental variables such as television viewing habits, child abuse, and malnutrition. They are also used in studying the potential influences of preexisting (and often hereditary or congenital) characteristics such as gender, mental illness, and physical disability. (In the latter instances, we might want to replace the term *experience* with a term such as *characteristic*.) The most we can conclude from these studies is that certain behaviors or characteristics tend to be *associated* with certain preexisting conditions; we can never determine that those behaviors or characteristics were actually caused by those conditions.

FACTORIAL DESIGNS

Thus far, we have been describing designs in which only one independent variable is studied. Yet in many situations, a researcher examines the effects of two or more independent variables in a single study; this approach is known as a **factorial design.**

DESIGN 15: RANDOMIZED TWO-FACTOR DESIGN

In its simplest form—one involving two independent variables, which we'll call *Variable 1* and *Variable 2*—such a design might look something like the following:

Group	Time—>		
	Treatments related to the two variables may occur simultaneously or sequentially		
	Treatment related to Variable 1	*Treatment related to Variable 2*	
Group 1	Tx_1	Tx_2	Obs
Group 2	Tx_1	—	Obs
Group 3	—	Tx_2	Obs
Group 4	—	—	Obs

(Random Assignment)

We can determine the effects of the first independent variable by comparing the performance of Groups 1 and 2 with that of Groups 3 and 4. We can determine the effects of the second independent variable by comparing Groups 1 and 3 with Groups 2 and 4. If you think you've seen this design before, in a way you have. This is simply a more generalized form of the Solomon four-group design (Design 5), but we are no longer limiting ourselves to having the presence or absence of a pretest be one of our independent variables.

Such a design allows us to determine not only the possible effects of two independent variables but also whether those variables *interact* in some way as they influence the dependent variable. For instance, imagine that, after presenting both treatments, we find that Groups 2, 3, and 4 show similar performance but that Group 1 outperforms the other three. Such a result may indicate that neither independent variable produces a particular effect on its own—that *both* variables are necessary to bring about the effect.

DESIGN 16: COMBINED EXPERIMENTAL AND EX POST FACTO DESIGN

In the factorial design just presented, participants are randomly assigned to groups in a true experimental study. But it is also possible to combine elements of experimental research and ex post facto research into a single factorial design. In its simplest form, such a design might look like the following:

Group   Time—>

	Prior event(s)	Investigation period—>			
Group 1	Exp$_a$	Random Assignment	Group 1a	Tx$_a$	Obs
			Group 1b	Tx$_b$	Obs
Group 2	Exp$_b$	Random Assignment	Group 2a	Tx$_a$	Obs
			Group 2b	Tx$_b$	Obs

In this case, the researcher initially divides the sample into two groups based on the participants' previous experiences or preexisting conditions; this is the *ex post facto* part of the study. Then the researcher randomly assigns members of each group into one of two treatment groups (or perhaps a treatment group and a control group); this is the *experimental* part of the study. The result is four groups that represent all four possible combinations of the previous experience/preexisting characteristic and the treatment variable. Such a design enables the researcher to study how an experimental manipulation may influence some dependent variable *and* how a previous experience or preexisting characteristic may possibly interact with that manipulation.

As a variation on such a design, the experimental manipulation might be a within-subjects variable rather than a between-groups variable. As an example, one of us authors once joined forces with two colleagues and a graduate student to test the hypothesis that people with different educational backgrounds interpret and remember maps differently and, more specifically, that only people with a background in geography apply general principles of geography when they interpret maps (Ormrod, Ormrod, Wagner, & McCallin, 1988). We constructed two maps to test our hypothesis. One map (see Figure 10.3) was arranged in accordance with the patterns of a typical city; for instance, a downtown business district was located at a point where it could be easily reached from different directions (this is typical), and factories, a lumberyard, and low-income

FIGURE 10.3

The logical map in Ormrod et al.'s (1988) factorial study

Reprinted from "Reconceptualizing Map Learning" by J. E. Ormrod, R. K. Ormrod, E. D. Wagner, & R. C. McCallin, 1988, *American Journal of Psychology, 101,* p. 428. Reprinted with permission of University of Illinois Press.

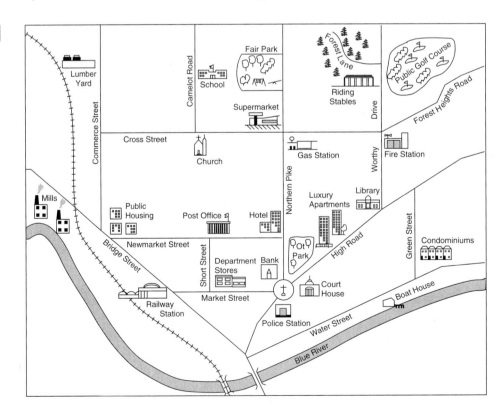

FIGURE 10.4

The illogical map in
Ormrod et al.'s (1988)
factorial study

Reprinted from
"Reconceptualizing Map
Learning" by J. E. Ormrod,
R. K. Ormrod, E. D. Wagner, &
R. C. McCallin, 1988,
*American Journal of
Psychology, 101,* p. 429.
Reprinted with permission of
University of Illinois Press.

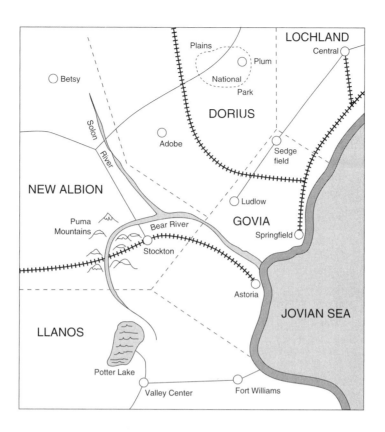

housing were situated near railroad tracks (also typical). The second map (see Figure 10.4) was less "logical" in the sense that it violated basic geographic principles; for instance, a river originated in the plains and ran up into a mountain range, and various transportation networks did not interconnect in the way that they normally do. The two different maps reflected one of our independent variables: logic (or lack thereof) of the spatial arrangement of features within a map.

Three groups of college professors—geographers, sociologists, and educational psychologists—provided the basis for our second independent variable: educational background. We asked each professor to study each of the two maps aloud for three 2-minute intervals (we recorded what they said during the study sessions) and then, after each interval, to draw as much of the map as he or she could remember.

Thus, if we call the two maps Tx_a (logical map) and Tx_b (illogical map), our design looked like the following:

Group	Time—>							
Geographers	Tx_a	Obs	Obs	Obs	Tx_b	Obs	Obs	Obs
Sociologists	Tx_a	Obs	Obs	Obs	Tx_b	Obs	Obs	Obs
Educational psychologists	Tx_a	Obs	Obs	Obs	Tx_b	Obs	Obs	Obs

In this situation, one independent variable—the logic or illogic of the map presented—was a variable we directly manipulated, and we presented it to all participants in a *within-subjects* (repeated-measures) manner. The second independent variable, educational background, was a preexisting condition and therefore something we could *not* control; this was the *ex post facto* part of the design.

The upshot of the study was that there was an *interaction* between the two independent variables, map logic and educational background. In particular, the geographers remembered more of the logical map than they did of the illogical map; in contrast, the sociologists and educational psychologists remembered each map with equal accuracy. We interpreted this result to indicate that only the geographers were applying geographic principles to study the maps and that they could use such principles effectively only with the geographically logical one. We supported our conclusion by conducting content analyses of the professors' study sessions: Indeed, the geographers applied many geographic principles to the logical map (but not the illogical one); meanwhile, the sociologists and educational psychologists studied both maps in a haphazard fashion, and with few attempts to interpret them.

A summary of the pre-experimental, experimental, quasi-experimental, ex post facto, and factorial designs described in the preceding sections appears in Table 10.1. Keep in mind that, as stated earlier, this is not an exhaustive list of experimental and ex post facto designs. You can combine and expand on these designs in a number of ways—and perhaps incorporate elements of qualitative or descriptive-quantitative designs (e.g., content analysis or longitudinal data collection) as well—to more effectively address your own research question.

TABLE 10.1   Summary of experimental designs

Name of the Design	Aim of the Research	Notation Paradigm*	Comments on the Design
Pre-Experimental Designs			
1. One-shot experimental case study	To show that one event (a treatment) precedes another event (the observation)	Group Time—> / Group 1 | Tx | Obs	Shows a before-and-after sequence but cannot substantiate that this is a cause-and-effect relationship.
2. One group pretest-posttest design	To show that change occurs after a treatment	Group Time—> / Group 1 | Obs | Tx | Obs	Provides a measure of change but yields no conclusive results about its cause.
3. Static group comparison	To show that a group receiving a treatment behaves differently than one receiving no treatment	Group Time—> / Group 1 | Tx | Obs / Group 2 | — | Obs	Fails to determine pre-treatment equivalence of groups.
True Experimental Designs			
4. Pretest-posttest control group design	To show that change occurs following, but only following, a particular treatment	Group Time—> / Random Assignment: Group 1 | Obs | Tx | Obs / Group 2 | Obs | — | Obs	Controls for many potential threats to internal validity.
5. Solomon four-group design	To investigate the possible effect of pretesting	Group Time—> / Random Assignment: Group 1 | Obs | Tx | Obs / Group 2 | Obs | — | Obs / Group 3 | — | Tx | Obs / Group 4 | — | — | Obs	Enables the researcher to determine how pretesting may affect the final outcome observed.
6. Posttest-only control group design	To determine the effects of a treatment when pretesting cannot or should not occur	Group Time—> / Random Assignment: Group 1 | Tx | Obs / Group 2 | — | Obs	Uses the last two groups in the Solomon four-group design; random assignment to groups is critical for ensuring group equivalence.

TABLE 10.1 Summary of experimental designs *(continued)*

Name of the Design	Aim of the Research	Notation Paradigm*	Comments on the Design

True Experimental Designs, *continued*

7. Within-subjects design
Aim: To compare the relative effects of different treatments for the same participants

Group Time—>

Group 1	Tx$_a$	Obs$_a$
	Tx$_b$	Obs$_b$

Comments: Useful only when effects of each treatment are temporary and localized.

Quasi-Experimental Designs

8. Nonrandomized control group pretest-posttest design
Aim: To show that two groups are equivalent with respect to the dependent variable prior to the treatment, thus eliminating initial group differences as an explanation for post-treatment differences

Group Time—>

Group 1	Obs	Tx	Obs
Group 2	Obs	—	Obs

Comments: Differs from experimental designs because test and control groups are not totally equivalent; equivalence on the pretest assures equivalence only for variables that have specifically been measured.

9. Simple time-series experiment
Aim: To show that, for a single group, change occurs during a lengthy period only after the treatment has been administered

Group Time—>

Group 1	Obs	Obs	Tx	Obs	Obs

Comments: Provides a stronger alternative to Design 2; external validity is increased by repeating the experiment in different places under different conditions.

10. Control group, time-series design
Aim: To bolster the internal validity of the preceding design with the addition of a control group

Group Time—>

Group 1	Obs	Obs	Tx	Obs	Obs
Group 2	Obs	Obs	—	Obs	Obs

Comments: Involves conducting parallel series of observations on experimental and control groups.

11. Reversal time-samples design
Aim: To show, in a single group or individual, that a treatment consistently leads to a particular effect

Group Time—>

Group 1	Tx	Obs	—	Obs	Tx	Obs

Comments: Is an on-again, off-again design in which the experimental variable is sometimes present, sometimes absent.

12. Alternating treatment design
Aim: To show, in a single group or individual, that different treatments have different effects

Group Time—>

Group 1	Tx$_a$	Obs	—	Obs	Tx$_b$	Obs

Comments: Involves sequentially administering different treatments at different times and comparing their effects against the possible consequences of nontreatment.

13. Multiple baseline design
Aim: To show the effect of a treatment by initiating it at different times for different groups or individuals, or perhaps in different settings for a single individual

Group Time—>

Group 1	—	Obs	Tx	Obs	Tx	Obs
Group 2	—	Obs	—	Obs	Tx	Obs

Comments: Involves tracking two or more groups or individuals over time, or tracking a single individual in two or more settings, for a lengthy period of time, as well as initiating the treatment at different times for different groups, individuals, or settings.

(continued)

TABLE 10.1   Summary of experimental designs *(continued)*

Name of the Design	Aim of the Research	Notation Paradigm*	Comments on the Design

Ex Post Facto Designs

Name of the Design	Aim of the Research	Notation Paradigm*	Comments on the Design
14. Simple ex post facto design	To show the possible effects of an experience that occurred, or a condition that was present, prior to the investigation	Group Time—> Group 1 Exp Obs Group 2 — Obs	May show a difference between groups but does not conclusively demonstrate that the difference is due to the prior experience/condition in question.

Factorial Designs

Name of the Design	Aim of the Research	Notation Paradigm*	Comments on the Design
15. Randomized two-factor design	To study the effects of two experimenter-manipulated variables and their possible interaction	Group Time—> *Random Assignment:* Group 1 Tx_1 Tx_2 Obs Group 2 Tx_1 — Obs Group 3 — Tx_2 Obs Group 4 — — Obs	Requires a larger sample size than two-group studies; random assignment to treatments is essential.
16. Combined experimental and ex post facto design	To study the effects of an experimenter-manipulated variable, a previously existing condition, and the interaction between the two	Group Time—> Group 1 Exp_a *Random Assignment:* Group 1a Tx_a Obs Group 1b Tx_b Obs Group 2 Exp_b *Random Assignment:* Group 2a Tx_a Obs Group 2b Tx_b Obs	Requires a larger sample size than two-group studies; random assignment to the experimenter-manipulated variable is essential.

*The symbols in each paradigm are explained fully in the discussion of each design type in the text.

META-ANALYSES

As we have seen, we can conclude that a cause-and-effect relationship exists between an independent variable and a dependent variable only when we have directly manipulated the independent variable and have controlled for confounding variables that might offer alternative explanations for any observed changes in the dependent variable. Even when we've taken such precautions, however, there is the possibility that our alleged "cause" doesn't really produce the effect we think it does—that the situation we've just observed is a once-in-a-lifetime fluke.

In Chapter 5, we introduced the idea of *replication:* A research study should be repeatable. In fact, we gain greater confidence in our research findings when a study is repeated over and over again—perhaps with a different population, in a different setting, or with slight variations on the treatment implementation.

Once researchers have conducted many such replications, another researcher may come along and conduct a **meta-analysis**—that is, an analysis of the analyses. In particular, the researcher combines the results of many experimental and/or ex post facto studies to determine whether they yield consistent, predictable results. A meta-analysis is primarily a statistical technique, and so we will look at this procedure more closely in Chapter 11.

CONDUCTING EXPERIMENTS ON THE INTERNET

 USING TECHNOLOGY

In the section "Computerizing Data Collection in Descriptive Research" in Chapter 9, we mentioned that some researchers now conduct research studies on the Internet. Although most of these studies can best be categorized as descriptive studies, we occasionally see experimental studies as well. For instance, one of us authors once visited the Web site "Psychological Research on the Net," which provides links to numerous sites that host online research projects.[3] To learn more about this growing approach to data collection, she became a participant in several of the online studies that were active at the time. Although most of the studies involved completing questionnaires and so appeared to be correlational or survey studies, one of them was clearly an experimental study. In particular, she was asked to (a) read and study a story that was illustrated by several photographs; (b) read three additional stories, one of which was quite similar to the initial story; and (c) answer a series of questions about details in the stories. In a subsequent debriefing on the Web site, she learned that she had been randomly assigned to the experimental group in the second part of the study; other participants were assigned to a control group, in which all three stories were quite different from the initial story. The researcher was investigating the possible effects that a similar story in Part b might have on recall for the story in Part a.

In some instances, an Internet-based research study may be quite suitable for your research question. Keep in mind, however, that the sample you get will hardly be representative of the overall population; for instance, it is likely to consist primarily of college-education, computer-literate people who enjoy participating in research studies. An additional problem is that you cannot observe your participants to determine whether they are accurately reporting demographic information (their age, gender, etc.) and whether they are truly following the instructions you present. Accordingly, we suggest that you use an Internet-based study only to formulate tentative hypotheses or to pilot-test experimental materials you plan to use in a more controlled and observable situation.

TESTING YOUR HYPOTHESES, AND BEYOND

Experimental and ex post facto studies typically begin with specific research hypotheses, and subsequent statistical analyses will, of course, be conducted to test these hypotheses. Such analyses often take the form of a *t* test, analysis of variance, or analysis of covariance (more about such procedures in Chapter 11).

Yet one's analyses need not be restricted *only* to the testing of initially stated hypotheses. Oftentimes a study may yield additional results—results that are unexpected yet intriguing—that merit analysis. There is no reason why the researcher can't examine these findings—perhaps statistically, perhaps not—as well.

PRACTICAL APPLICATION IDENTIFYING RESEARCH DESIGNS

As a way of reviewing the designs we've described in this chapter, we offer a little "pop quiz." Following are brief summaries of five research studies. The studies don't necessarily fit exactly into one of the design categories presented, but each one is definitely *experimental*, *quasi-experimental*, or *ex post facto* in nature. Identify the type of research that each study reflects. The answers appear after the suggested readings at the end of the chapter.

1. A team of researchers has a sample of elementary school boys, some of whom have been identified as having attention-deficit hyperactivity disorder (ADHD) and some of

---

[3] As noted in Chapter 9, you can reach the site by going to APS's home page, http://www.psychologicalscience.org/; click on "Psychology links" and then on "Online Psychology Experiments." Alternatively, you can go directly to the site, which, as this book goes to press, is located at http://psych.hanover.edu/research/exponnet.html.

whom have not. One of the researchers asks each boy to interpret several social situations that are depicted in a series of black-and-white drawings (e.g., one sequence of drawings shows a sequence of events at a Halloween party). Some of the situations involve antisocial behavior (e.g., aggression), and other situations involve prosocial behavior (e.g., sharing). The researchers compare the interpretations that boys with ADHD make with the interpretations that boys without ADHD make (Milch-Reich, Campbell, Pelham, Connelly, & Geva, 1999).

2. Two researchers want to see if a particular training program is effective in teaching horses to enter a horse trailer without misbehaving in the process (without rearing, trying to turn around, etc.). Five horses (Red, Penny, Shadow, Sammy, and Fancy) go through the training, with the training beginning on a different day for each horse. For each horse, an observer counts the number of misbehaviors every day prior to and during training, with data being collected for a time span of at least 45 days (Ferguson & Rosales-Ruiz, 2001).

3. Two researchers wonder whether an eyewitness's memory of an event is affected by questions that he or she is asked subsequent to the event. To find out, the researchers shows adults a film that depicts a car accident. Each adult is then asked one of five questions (randomly selected) about the accident:
   • About how fast were the cars going when they *contacted* each other?
   • About how fast were the cars going when they *hit* each other?
   • About how fast were the cars going when they *bumped into* each other?
   • About how fast were the cars going when they *collided into* each other?
   • About how fast were the cars going when they *smashed into* each other?

   The researchers compute the average speed given in response to each of the five questions to determine whether the questions have influenced participants' "memory" for the accident (Loftus & Palmer, 1974).

4. A researcher studies the effects of two different kinds of note-taking training (one of which is a placebo) on the kinds of notes that college students take. Her sample consists of students enrolled in two sections of an undergraduate course in educational psychology; with the flip of a coin, she randomly determines which section will be the treatment group and which will be the control group. She analyzes the content of students' class notes both before and after the training, making the prediction that the two groups' notes will be similar before the training but qualitatively different after the training (Jackson, 1996).

5. At the request of the National Park Service, two researchers at Rocky Mountain National Park are investigating the degree to which signs along hiking trails might influence hikers' behaviors. Park Service officials are concerned that the heavy traffic on one particular hiking trail, the trail to Emerald Lake, may be having a negative impact on the local environment; they would like to divert some traffic to a lesser-used trail to Lake Haiyaha, which begins at the same place as the Emerald Lake trail. One day in early summer, the researchers hide battery-operated, optic counters at key locations along the two trails to record the number of hikers. The study has four phases: (1) at the spot where the two trails originate, only signs indicating the destinations of the two trails are present; (2) a "positively worded" sign is added that describes the attractive features of the Lake Haiyaha trail and encourages hikers to use it; (3) the positively worded sign is replaced by a "negatively worded" sign that describes the crowdedness of the Emerald Lake trail and discourages its use; and (4) both the positively worded and negatively worded signs are posted. The researchers compare the frequency of hikers during each of the four phases (Ormrod & Trahan, 1982).

A SAMPLE DISSERTATION

To illustrate how an experimental study might appear in its written form, we present excerpts from Virginia Kinnick's doctoral dissertation conducted at the University of Colorado (Kinnick, 1989). The researcher, a faculty member in the School of Nursing at another university, had considerable experience teaching nursing students the knowledge and skills they would need when working with women who were in the process of delivering a baby, and her interest lay in learning more about teaching such knowledge and skills effectively.

During a woman's labor prior to the delivery of her baby, a fetal monitor is often used to assess the baby's heart rate, and the maternity nurse must frequently check the monitor for signs that the baby may be experiencing exceptional and potentially harmful stress. The researcher wanted to determine whether a particular method of teaching concepts (Tennyson & Cocchiarella, 1986) might be more effective for teaching fetal monitoring skills than the method traditionally used in nursing education programs. In her own words, the researcher's problem statement was as follows:

> This study is designed to determine if use of an instructional design model for concept attainment in teaching the critical concepts related to fetal monitoring will make a significant difference in preparation of nursing students in this skill, compared to the traditional teaching method which exists in most schools. (Kinnick, 1989, p. 8)

The research design is not one of the designs we've specifically described in this chapter. Instead, it involves administering three different instructional treatments to three (randomly selected) treatment groups and then observing the effects of the treatments at two different times: once immediately after instruction and then later after students had completed the clinical rotation portion of their nursing program. Thus, the design of the study was the following:

	Group	Time—>		
Random Assignment	Group 1	Tx_1	Obs	Obs
	Group 2	Tx_2	Obs	Obs
	Group 3	Tx_3	Obs	Obs

In the following pages, we present excerpts from the methodology chapter of the researcher's dissertation. Our comments and observations appear on the right-hand side.

Now go to our Companion Website at http://www.prenhall.com/leedy to assess your understanding of chapter content and to complete the projects that will help you learn how to conduct research.

DISSERTATION ANALYSIS 7

METHODOLOGY

[After an introductory paragraph outlining the chapter's contents, the author describes the sample—students enrolled in maternity nursing courses at two universities—used in the study. Then, as she begins a discussion of her procedure, she explains that the experimental treatments were based on the Tennyson-Cocchiarella concept-teaching model (1986) and presents the key elements of the model. We pick up the methodology chapter at the point where the author describes the specific treatments used for each of the three treatment groups.]

Description of the Treatment Groups

[The author first explains that, for each of the three groups, treatment consisted of instruction in the basic concepts of fetal monitoring, plus additional instructional strategies, or "teaching variables," that differed for the groups.] . . . Starting with a basic class and adding new teaching variables to each treatment group, however, did require additional time. The length of time required for teaching the three treatment groups varied between 1 and 2 hours. These timeframes were established based on the results of the survey of baccalaureate nursing schools, in which 36% of the schools responding had less than 1 hour to teach fetal monitoring theory, and 52% had 1 to 2 hours (Kinnick, 1989).

The teaching variables for the first treatment group included labels and definitions, and presentation of best examples. According to Merrill and Tennyson, these variables usually

Comments

The author points out a possible confounding variable *in her study: the three forms of instruction took varying amounts of time.*

The survey to which the author refers was administered during a pilot study that she conducted prior to conducting the dissertation itself. She published the pilot study as a research article, which she cites here.

include additional information needed to aid in the clarification and understanding of the concepts (Merrill & Tennyson, 1977, p. 100). Therefore, the design of this didactic presentation began with a very basic overview of physiology at the uterofetoplacental unit. Electronic fetal monitoring patterns are a reflection of uterofetoplacental physiology. Understanding the normal physiology and changes in the physiology that cause inadequate fetal oxygenation help the learner to identify the various patterns, and whether patterns are normal or abnormal. Understanding the physiology is also the basis to identifying appropriate nursing intervention which promotes normal physiology (reduction or even elimination of fetal distress) when abnormal patterns occur.

When the classes were taught, the majority of students did not have any theory about the process of labor and delivery. In addition, they had not seen a fetal monitor. Methods of monitoring the fetus and a brief description and discussion of external versus internal monitoring, therefore, needed to be discussed. In addition, it was necessary to show the students a print-out of a fetal monitor as well as explain what the graphs meant. Before the basic concepts related to interpretation of the fetal heart could be taught, the student also needed to recognize critical characteristics of a contraction pattern as seen on a monitor strip. Contraction patterns can be a cause of physiological changes at the uterofetoplacental site. After these areas had been covered, the concept label, definitions, and best examples were presented. . . .

This 1 hour presentation included labels, definitions, best examples, and clarifying information. In the experience of this researcher, this presentation reflects closely the method for teaching fetal monitoring used in most schools of nursing, especially when the allocated time for teaching this content is limited. This treatment group is referred to as Group 1 throughout the study.

The second treatment group began with the same presentation used with the first treatment group, plus the addition of expository presentations for each major concept. An expository presentation was added after the labels, definition, and best examples of each set of coordinate concepts had been completed. For example, following the definition and display of the best examples of baseline fetal heart rate and its coordinate concepts, an expository presentation was done of the coordinate concepts. When that was completed, the concept of baseline variability was introduced and the same order of teaching variables was used. The addition of the expository presentations added approximately half an hour, so that this treatment group was scheduled for one and one-half hours. This group (labels, definitions, best examples and expository presentation) is referred to as Group 2.

The design in Group 2 was chosen based on the results of Dunn's research (1984) on concept learning with college age students. . . . *[The author briefly describes Dunn's findings and their relevance for the instruction presented to Group 2.]*

The treatment design for the third group used the same teaching variables as in Group 2, plus the addition of an interrogatory presentation to follow each expository presentation. This involved the addition of . . . transparencies specifically developed for the interrogatory presentation. When a fetal monitor pattern was shown on the screen, students were requested to compare it with their handout [of] definitions (list of critical characteristics) and best examples, and to identify the concept shown on the fetal monitoring pattern. This treatment design incorporated all of the teaching variables of the Tennyson-Cocchiarella concept-teaching model.

Here the author describes the treatment used for each treatment group; in a later "Procedure" section, she describes the general procedure she used to conduct the study. More often, a researcher will include a description of how each group was treated within the procedure section itself. Either approach is acceptable, however, as long as the writer makes the organization of the methodology section clear (e.g., through headings and subheadings).

This description of what most students knew (and did not know) before instruction gives the reader greater confidence that the results observed after instruction (i.e., students' test performance) were probably due to the instructional treatments, rather than to any earlier learning experiences that the students may have had.

Notice that the author's notion of what is "traditional" instruction is based on her own experiences, and she says so here.

After describing Group 1, the author proceeds to descriptions of Group 2 and then Group 3 in a logical and systematic fashion. The use of three subheadings (something along the lines of Treatment for Group 1 or Group 1 Instruction) might have been helpful, however.

By "expository presentation," the author means giving a short explanation or lecture about important ideas and concepts.

A rationale for a particular experimental treatment strengthens any research report. A brief rationale can easily be incorporated into the description of procedures; a longer one should probably be presented earlier in the research report.

By "interrogatory presentation," the author means asking questions to assess students' understanding of, and ability to apply, what they have learned.

Development of the Instruments

[In this section, the author describes the tests she used to assess what participants knew about fetal monitoring following instruction, as well as a short questionnaire she used to determine the extent to which each participant had learned something about fetal monitoring before instruction.]

Procedure

Prior to implementing this research, approval for the project was obtained from the Human Research Committee at the University of Colorado, and the Internal Review Board for Research at the University of Northern Colorado (Appendix E). The researcher then met with all students in each maternity nursing course during their first class, to explain the research and ask their consent to participate. Consent forms were provided for each student (Appendix E). Once this process was completed, the research design was implemented.

Because the author conducted the study at two universities, she followed the necessary human research review procedures at both institutions.

Each maternity nursing course had three groups participating in the research. Students in each of the courses were randomly assigned to one of these three groups. One group received the instructional method described in the Tennyson-Cocchiarella model of concept attainment. A second group received the same instructional method with the exception of the interrogatory presentation. The third group had a didactic presentation using only tables, definitions, best examples and clarifying information. In other words, both the expository and interrogatory presentations were eliminated from the presentation for the third group. In both schools, the researcher taught all three methods. A script (or lecture) was developed for the researcher to use in all the treatment groups so that the content was the same in each group (Appendix F). The students were tested in a class session within 2 to 3 days following the class (treatment).

As noted earlier in Chapter 10, random assignment is one effective way of ruling out the possible effects of confounding variables.

The first group mentioned here ("one group") is actually Group 3, and the last ("the third group") is actually Group 1; this reversal might cause confusion for the reader.

The use of a "script" here should help the researcher teach the content similarly for all three treatment groups (except, of course, for the things she intentionally wanted to do differently for the three groups). Thus, it should help to minimize any effects due to researcher expectancy (see Chapter 5).

After the completion of the clinical experience of all groups in each university, a parallel form of the classification test was again administered. The sequence can be summarized as follows:

Class instruction——> Posttest—> Clinical

Rotation—> Delayed Test upon Completion of

Clinical Rotation

This graphic display of the procedure used is a helpful summary for the reader.

In addition, each student was requested to keep a record of the number of contacts each of them had with fetal monitoring tracings, the context, and type of pattern (Appendix G). For example, the student may have been assigned to a labor patient who had a normal pattern. The contact, however, could have been in clinical conference where actual monitor strips of patients were discussed, or also in a prenatal clinic where a nonstress test was done on a patient. The purpose of keeping these records [was] to identify the number of interrogatory examples the students encountered clinically and the range of examples. This information [could] be compared with the post test results.

The author presumably asked students to keep such records as a way of helping her interpret any unexpected results related to the delayed (post-clinical rotation) test. Keep in mind, however, that such self-reporting techniques, dependent as they are on participants' diligence and memories, will not always yield totally accurate information.

Ideally, none of the students were to have had any contact in the clinical setting before the instruction and first test were done. However, it was impossible to schedule all three treatments before students in each maternity nursing course were assigned to the clinical setting since they began their clinical experiences the second week of classes. A few students in this situation were assigned to patients with fetal monitors attached. Since they did not have any theory on fetal monitoring, they were not responsible for interpretation of fetal monitor patterns. However, staff nurses and/or clinical instructors may have demonstrated

Here the author points out a potential (probably minor) weakness in her study:

how to attach and detach the equipment and talked about tracings seen by each student on their individual patients.

Statistical Analysis

[The author continues with a discussion of the statistical analyses she used to compare the performance of the three groups.]

NOTE. From *Learning Fetal Monitoring Under Three Conditions of Concept Teaching* (pp. 58–69) by V. Kinnick, 1989, unpublished doctoral dissertation, University of Colorado, Boulder. Reprinted with permission.

Some students had additional exposure to fetal monitoring after the instruction she had given them in their respective treatment groups. The exposure was apparently minimal, however, and so probably did not jeopardize the quality of her study. Such honesty is essential in any research report.

FOR FURTHER READING

Ary, D., Jacobs, L. C., & Razavieh, A. (2001). *Introduction to research in education* (6th ed.). New York: Wadsworth.

Bausell, R. B. (1994). *Conducting meaningful experiments: 40 steps to becoming a scientist.* Thousand Oaks, CA: Sage.

Campbell, D. T., & Stanley, J. C. (1966). *Experimental and quasi-experimental designs for research.* Chicago: Rand McNally.

Cook, T. D., & Campbell, D. T. (1979). *Quasi experimentation: Design and analysis issues for field settings.* Chicago: Rand McNally.

Deming, S. N., & Morgan, S. L. (1993). *Experimental design* (2nd ed.). New York: Elsevier Science.

DePoy, E., & Gitlin, L. N. (1993). *Introduction to research: Strategies for health and human services.* St. Louis: Mosby-Year Book.

Friedman, D., & Sunder, S. (1994). *Experimental methods: A primer for economists.* New York: Cambridge University Press.

Froelicher, E. S. W. (1988). Understanding and reducing measurement error. *Cardiovascular Nursing, 24,* 48.

Gall, M. D., Borg, W. R., & Gall, J. P. (2003). *Educational research: An introduction* (7th ed.). Boston: Allyn & Bacon.

Glass, G. V. (1988). Quasi experiments: The case of interrupted time series. In R. M. Jaeger (Ed.), *Complementary methods for research in*
education (pp. 445–464). Washington, DC: American Educational Research Association.

Heath, D. (1994). *An introduction to experimental design and statistics for biology.* Bristol, PA: Taylor & Francis.

Hinkelmann, K., & Kempthorne, O. (1994). *Design and analysis of experiments: Vol. 1. Introduction to experimental design.* New York: Wiley.

Kirk, R. E. (1994). *Experimental design: Procedures for the behavioral sciences* (3rd ed.). Pacific Grove, CA: Brooks/Cole.

Lorenzen, T. J., & Anderson, V. L. (1993). *Design of experiments: A no-name approach.* New York: Marcel Dekker.

Morgan, D. L., & Morgan, R. K. (2001). Single participant research design: Bringing science to managed care. *American Psychologist, 56,* pp. 119–127.

Phillips, D. C. (1981). Toward an evaluation of the experiment in educational contexts. *Educational Researcher, 10*(6), 13–20.

Pukelsheim, F. (1993). *Optimal design of experiments.* New York: Wiley.

Solso, R. S., & MacLin, K. (2002). *Experimental psychology: A case approach* (7th ed.). Boston: Allyn & Bacon.

Answers to the Practical Application ("Identifying Research Designs") on page 239

1. This is an *ex post facto* study, because the researchers do not (and *cannot*) manipulate the independent variable: the presence or absence of attention-deficit hyperactivity disorder.

2. This is a *quasi-experimental* study. In particular, it involves a multiple baseline design: Each of the horses begins training on a different day. In the section of the chapter "Using Designs 11, 12, and 13 in Single-Subject Studies," a multiple baseline study involving a single 2-year-old girl is described. Here we see the approach being used with five horses, each of which is treated identically except for the date on which training begins.

3. This is an *experimental* study in which the researchers randomly assign participants to one of five groups, each of which is asked a different question.

4. Don't let the random selection of treatment and control groups fool you. This is a *quasi-experimental* study because the participants are not randomly assigned as *individuals* to the treatment and control groups. More specifically, the study is a nonrandomized control group pretest-posttest design (Design 8).

5. This, too, is a *quasi-experimental* study. It is a time-series design in which the effects of no intervention (phase 1) are compared to the effects of two different interventions (the two new signs) imposed either singly or in combination. Of the designs described in this chapter, it is probably most similar to Design 12. Note, however, that no phase of the study is repeated; this omission is a decided weakness in the design.

11

Statistical Techniques for Analyzing Quantitative Data

With statistics, we can summarize large bodies of data, make predictions about future trends, and determine when different experimental treatments have led to significantly different outcomes. Thus, statistics are among the most powerful tools in the researcher's toolbox.

In quantitative research, we try to make better sense of the world by using numbers. Sometimes these numbers represent aspects of the observable, physical world, such as the temperature of an object, the pull of gravity on physical mass, or the number of people engaging in a particular activity. We may also use numbers to represent nonphysical phenomena, such as intelligence, academic achievement, the strength of personal preferences and beliefs, or the worth of an employee to an organization. We can then summarize and interpret the numbers by using statistics. More generally, we can think of *statistics* as a group of computational procedures that allow us to find patterns and meaning in numerical data.

To beginning researchers, the field of statistics sometimes appears to be a never-never land where obtuse concepts are elusively conjured up by the mathematical imagination. But in reality, statistics are invaluable and often indispensable tools in research. They provide a means through which numerical data can be made more meaningful, so that the researcher may see their nature and better understand their interrelationships. The first and last question of statistics is precisely the same question that every researcher needs to ask: What do the data mean? In other words, what message do they communicate?

EXPLORING AND ORGANIZING A DATA SET

Before employing any statistical procedure, look closely at your data and explore various ways of organizing them. Using an open mind and imagination, see what patterns you can detect without the benefit of computational complexity. Nothing takes the place of looking carefully, inquiringly, critically—perhaps even naively—at the data.

We take a simple example to illustrate the point. Following are the scores on a test of reading achievement for 11 children: Ruth, 96; Robert, 60; Chuck, 68; Margaret, 88; Tom, 56; Mary, 92; Ralph, 64; Bill, 72; Alice, 80; Adam, 76; Kathy, 84. What do you see? Stop at this point. Jot down as many observations as possible before reading any further.

Now let's try various arrangements of the scores to see just how much information we can extract from them before subjecting them to statistical treatment. Some of the information may

FIGURE 11.1

The 11 children in our reading achievement test sample

be irrelevant to our research problem. No matter. We are after what we can see by the process of looking. Careful researchers discover everything possible about their data, whether the information is immediately useful or not.

We begin by forming an alphabetical list of the children's names and their test scores:

Adam	76	*Mary*	92
Alice	80	*Ralph*	64
Bill	72	*Robert*	60
Chuck	68	*Ruth*	96
Kathy	84	*Tom*	56
Margaret	88		

When we display the children's test scores in this manner, the scores are no more meaningful, but we have at least isolated individuals and scores so that we can inspect them more easily. Does this arrangement show us anything? Yes. It shows that the highest score was earned by a girl and that the lowest score was earned by a boy. Silly, you say, and meaningless. Perhaps. But it's an observable fact, and it may come in handy at a future time.

Let's keep the arrangement but view it in another way. In Figure 11.1, we see these 11 boys and girls lined up in a row, still arranged in alphabetical order according to first names. Look! Now, we can discern a symmetrical pattern in these children that was not apparent before. No matter whether we start from the left or from the right, we have *one* boy, then *one* girl, then *two* boys, *three* girls, *two* boys, *one* girl, and *one* boy. Putting adjacent children of the same sex together, the arrangement is this:

$$\male \quad \female \quad \male\male \quad \female\female\female \quad \male\male \quad \female \quad \male$$

or:

$$1 \quad 1 \quad 2 \quad 3 \quad 2 \quad 1 \quad 1$$

Now let's arrange the data differently, separating girls from boys:

Girls		Boys	
Alice	80	Adam	76
Kathy	84	Bill	72
Margaret	88	Chuck	68
Mary	92	Ralph	64
Ruth	96	Robert	60
		Tom	56

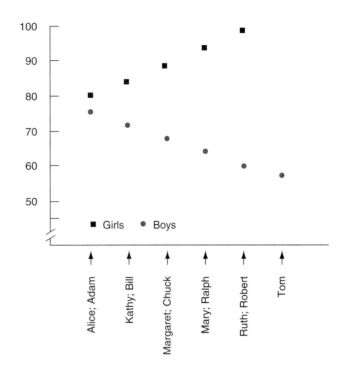

FIGURE 11.2

A visual representation
of the reading
achievement test scores

Represented graphically in Figure 11.2, the trends are quite dramatic: The girls' scores increase as we proceed through the alphabet, and the boys' scores decrease.

Not only is there a divergence of trends, but now we are aware of a very obvious fact that may, up to this point, have escaped our attention: The scores are equidistant from one another. Each score is 4 points either above or below the preceding one.

What have we seen? Whatever we have seen may have no relevance whatsoever for our project, but because it represents *dynamics within the data*, it is important that we see it. That is the point: The researcher should be aware of the dynamics, the phenomena, that are active within the data, whether those phenomena are important to the purpose of the research or not. The astute researcher overlooks nothing.

The preceding exercise was, of course, an artificial one. We would be hard pressed to find much meaning in diverging trends for girls versus boys that appear simply through an alphabetical arrangement of first names. Yet for the researcher working in an area of science, observations of a similar kind may reveal important new knowledge. Take the case of a paleontologist and an astronomer who noticed data recorded in the form of growth marks on the shells of the chambered nautilus (Kahn & Pompea, 1978). They noticed that each chamber had an average of 30 growth lines and deduced that (a) the growth lines had appeared at the rate of 1 per day and (b) one chamber had been laid down every lunar month, specifically every 29.53 days. They also concluded that, if their interpretation of the data was correct, it might be possible to determine from fossil shells the length of the ancient lunar months. Because the distance of the moon from the earth can be calculated from the length of the lunar month, the scientists examined nautilus fossils—some of them 420 million years old—and noticed a gradual decrease in the number of growth lines in each chamber as the fossils came from farther and farther back in prehistoric time. This finding indicated that the moon was once closer to the earth and revolved around it more rapidly than it does now—an observation consistent with generally accepted scientific theory.

From these two examples, certain basic principles about the exploration of data emerge. Where two variables are concerned (e.g., test scores and names, or growth rings and lunar cycles), one of the variables becomes dominant and governs the meaning that emerges from the other. In the data we inspected for the 11 children, meaning emerged from the last arrangement of data primarily because we used an alphabetized list of the students' names. Another arrangement of the data would have probably made a different meaning more apparent. This suggests a fundamental guideline for looking at the data: *Whatever the researcher does with the data to prepare it for inspection or interpretation will affect the meaning that those data reveal. Therefore, every researcher should be able to provide a clear, logical rationale for the procedure used to arrange and organize the data.*

We had no rationale whatever for arranging the data according to the children's first names. Had we used their last names, which would have been equally illogical, we would still have seen that the girls had higher scores than the boys, but we would not necessarily have seen the diverging trends depicted in Figure 11.2.

In research questions dealing with the physical world, the method for organizing data is apt to be fairly straightforward. Data often come to the scientist prepackaged and prearranged. The sequence of growth rings on a nautilus shell is already there. It cannot be altered. What such data need for interpretation are a pair of keen eyes and a curious and inquiring mind. Therefore, the researcher working in the physical or biological sciences may not have the same problem of arranging data for interpretation that a colleague in the social sciences, education, or the humanities may face.

ORGANIZING DATA TO MAKE THEM EASIER TO THINK ABOUT AND INTERPRET

As we first mentioned in Chapter 2, the human mind can think about only so much information at one time. A data set of, say, 5000 different pieces of information is well beyond a human being's mental capacity. In fact, unless the researcher has obtained *very* few pieces of data (perhaps only seven or eight numbers), then he or she will want to organize them in one or more ways to make them easier to inspect and think about.

In the preceding example of 11 children and their reading achievement test scores, we experimented with several simple organizational schemes in an effort to find patterns in the data. Let's take another everyday example. Joe is in high school. During February, he gets the following grades: 92, 69, 91, 70, 90, 89, 72, 87, 73, 86, 85, 75, 84, 76, 83, 83, 77, 81, 78, 79. Here Joe's grades are listed in a *simple linear sequence*—the order in which they were earned. These are the raw numerical facts—the data—directly from a life situation. As they appear in the preceding list, they do not say very much, other than that Joe's performance seems to be inconsistent.

Let's organize Joe's grades in a *two-dimensional table*, under the respective day of the week, Monday through Friday:

Grade Record for February

	Monday	*Tuesday*	*Wednesday*	*Thursday*	*Friday*
First week	92	69	91	70	90
Second week	89	72	87	73	86
Third week	85	75	84	76	83
Fourth week	83	77	81	78	79

The table reveals some patterns in Joe's grades. If we compare the five columns to one another, the grades on Monday, Wednesday, and Friday are considerably higher than those on Tuesday and Thursday. And if we look at successive scores in each column, we see that they get progressively worse on Mondays, Wednesdays, and Fridays, but progressively better on Tuesdays and Thursdays.

Now let's represent Joe's grades in the form of a simple *line graph* (Figure 11.3). In this graph, we see phenomena that were not readily apparent in the two-dimensional table. It is hard to miss the considerable variability in grades during the first and second weeks of the period. Just as apparent is the gradual leveling-out process seen in the third and fourth weeks. A profile of this sort should prompt the alert researcher to explore the data further in an attempt to explain the erratic behavior that the graph reflects.

Graphing data is often quite useful for revealing patterns in a data set. For example, let's return to a study first described in a Practical Application exercise near the end of Chapter 10:

Two researchers want to see if a particular training program is effective in teaching horses to enter a horse trailer without misbehaving in the process (without rearing, trying to turn around, etc.). Five horses (Red, Penny, Shadow, Sammy, and Fancy) go through the training, with the training

FIGURE 11.3

Line graph of Joe's daily
grades

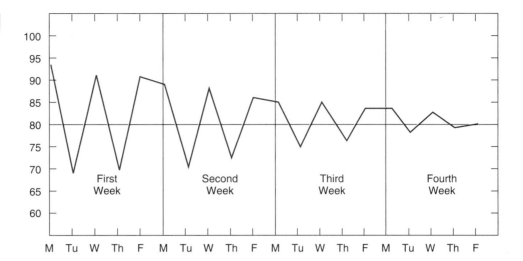

beginning on a different day for each horse. For each horse, an observer counts the number of
misbehaviors every day prior to and during training, with data being collected for a time span of
at least 45 days (Ferguson & Rosales-Ruiz, 2001).

In the preceding chapter, we were concerned only with the design of this study, concluding that it
was a quasi-experimental (and more specifically, a multiple baseline) study. But now let's look at the
results of the study. When the researchers plotted the number of misbehaviors (categorized as head
tossing, standing, turning, freezing, or rearing) for each horse before and during training, they constructed the graph presented in Figure 11.4. Was the training effective? Absolutely yes! Once training began, Penny had one really bad day plus another day in which she turned a couple of times, and
Shadow and Fancy each tossed their heads during one of their loading sessions. Aside from these four
occasions, the horses behaved perfectly throughout the lengthy training period, despite the fact that
all five had been quite ornery prior to training. These data have what we might call a *hit-you-between-
the-eyes* quality: We don't need a fancy statistical analysis to tell us that the training was effective.

Time-series studies often yield data that show clear hit-you-between-the-eyes patterns; for
other examples, return to Figures 10.1 and 10.2 on pages 230 and 231, respectively. But generally speaking, simply organizing the data in various ways will not, in and of itself, reveal everything that the data have to offer. Instead, a researcher—especially one who has conducted a
quantitative study—will need to perform statistical analyses to fully discover the patterns and
meanings the data hold. Before we turn to the nature of statistics, however, let's briefly look at
how a researcher can use computer software to assist with the data organization process.

USING COMPUTER SPREADSHEETS TO ORGANIZE AND ANALYZE DATA

The process of organizing large amounts of data was once a cumbersome, time-consuming, and
tedious task. Fortunately, the advent of computers has made the process much simpler and more
efficient. One important tool is an **electronic spreadsheet**, a software program that allows a researcher to manipulate data displayed in a table (Microsoft Excel and Lotus 1–2–3 are two widely
used examples). The table, known as a *spreadsheet*, is divided into rows and columns to form a grid;
you simply insert the data you've collected into appropriate cells within the grid.

The beauty of electronic spreadsheets is that once you enter data into them, the software can
quickly and easily make desired calculations. For example, you can add test scores in several
columns together to create a new column that you might call "Total of Test Scores," or you might
divide the numbers in one column by the numbers in another to get proportions that are potentially meaningful in the context of your study. If you change a data point—for example, perhaps
you discover you miskeyed a test score and so must correct it—all of the relevant calculations are
automatically updated. The software typically also lets you copy (or *import*) data from databases,
word processing documents, or other spreadsheets into your spreadsheet.

FIGURE 11.4

Inappropriate trailer-loading behaviors for five horses before and after training.

Source: Reprinted from "Loading the Problem Loader: The Effects of Target Training and Shaping on Trailer-Loading Behavior of Horses" by D. L. Ferguson & J. Rosalez-Ruiz, 2001, *Journal of Applied Behavior Analysis*, *34*, p. 419. Reprinted with permission of the Society for the Experimental Analysis of Behavior, Inc.

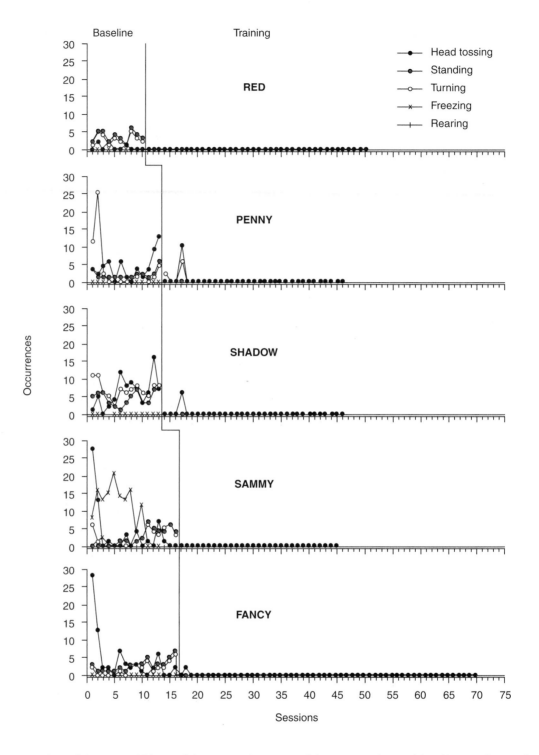

Spreadsheets would be useful to researchers even if they were only capable of listing data and adding up different columns and rows. But in fact, they allow the researcher to do many other things as well:

▨ *Sorting.*   Once the data have been organized into rows and columns, it is possible to reorganize them in any way you wish. For example, suppose you have reading test scores for a large number of children of various ages. You originally entered the scores in the order in which you obtained them. But now you decide that you want to consider them on the basis of the children's ages. In a matter of seconds, an electronic spreadsheet can sort the scores by age and list them from youngest to oldest child, or vice versa.

▓ *Searching.* With large sets of data, it is often difficult and time-consuming to find specific bits of information. Most spreadsheets have the ability to search for desired information. For example, if you need to locate information about a specific individual or a specific measurement, the program can quickly find it for you.

▓ *Recoding.* A spreadsheet typically allows you to make a new column that reflects a transformation of data in another column. For instance, imagine that you have reading scores for children from ages 7 to 15. Perhaps you want to compare the scores for children in three different age groups: Group 1 will consist of children who are 7 to 9 years old, Group 2 will include 10- to 12-year-olds, and Group 3 will include 13- to 15-year-olds. You can tell the computer to form a new column called "Group" and give each child a group number (1, 2, or 3) depending on the child's age.

▓ *Graphing.* Most spreadsheet programs have graphing capabilities. After you highlight the appropriate parts of the data, the program will automatically produce a graph from those data. Generally, the type of graph produced is selected from several options (e.g., scattergrams, line charts, pie charts, bar charts). Users can select how the axes are labeled, how the legend is created, and how the data points are depicted.

▓ *Formulas.* As we have mentioned, the electronic spreadsheet can carry out simple calculations, but this is only the tip of the iceberg! Current spreadsheet programs have the capability to calculate many complex mathematical and statistical formulas. Once the data are organized into rows and columns, you can specify formulas that describe and analyze one or more groups of data. For example, you can enter the formula for computing the average, or mean, of a set of numbers, and the spreadsheet will then perform the necessary calculations. Many commonly used formulas are often preprogrammed, so you merely select the statistic or function you need (e.g., you might select "AVERAGE") and highlight the data you wish to include in the calculation. The software does the rest.

▓ *"What Ifs."* Because of the speed and ease with which an electronic spreadsheet can calculate and recalculate formulas, the researcher has an important tool for gaining further insights. For example, if you are looking at a set of data and decide that an additional comparison between groups might prove interesting, the spreadsheet can complete the comparison in a matter of seconds. This capability allows you to continually ask "what if . . .": What if the data were analyzed on the basis of gender, rather than on the basis of grade level? What if results from administering one level of a specific medication were analyzed instead of grouping all levels together? This "what if . . ." capability allows the researcher to explore the data in many possible ways quickly and easily.

As with other computer applications, the spreadsheet allows the researcher to save, store, recall, and easily update information as needed and to print it when desired.

We have said enough about organizing a data set. We now turn to some of the most important tools in a researcher's toolbox—statistics. We must caution you that we cannot possibly describe the wide variety of available statistical procedures in a single chapter. Here we must limit ourselves to a description of basic statistical concepts and principles and a brief overview of some of the most commonly used procedures. We are assuming that you have taken or will take at least one course in statistics (better still, take two or three!) to get a firm foundation in this essential research tool.

CHOOSING APPROPRIATE STATISTICS

In a preceding section, we looked at Joe's academic performance in three ways: a simple linear sequence, a two-dimensional table, and a line graph. All of these depicted his day-to-day performance. Now, instead, let's begin to summarize what we are seeing in Joe's test scores. We can, for example, use a statistic known as a *mean*—more commonly called an *average*—to take out the jagged irregularities of daily performance. In Figure 11.5, we represent Joe's average scores for the four different weeks with four broken lines. When we do this, we get an entirely new view of Joe's achievement. Whereas the graph originally showed only an erratic zigzagging between daily

FIGURE 11.5

Line graph of Joe's
weekly average grades

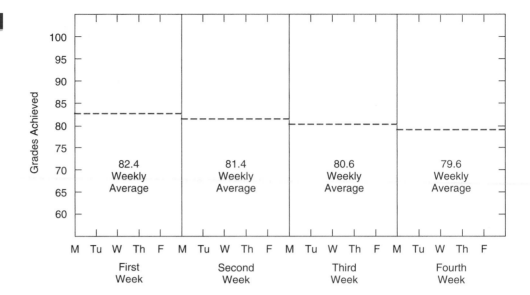

extremes, with the zigzags becoming less extreme as the weeks went by, the dotted lines show that, week by week, very little change actually occurred in Joe's average level of achievement.

Yet it may be that we also want to summarize how much Joe's grades *vary* each week. The means presented in Figure 11.5 tell us nothing about how consistent or inconsistent Joe's grades are in any given week. We would need a different statistic—perhaps a *range* or a *standard deviation*—to summarize the variability we see each week. (We'll describe the nature of such measures of variability shortly.)

Thus far, we have discovered an important point: *Looking at data in only one way yields an incomplete view of those data and, hence, provides only a small segment of the full meaning that those data contain.* For that reason, we have many statistical techniques, each of which is suitable for a different purpose. Each technique extracts a somewhat different meaning from a particular set of data. Every time you apply a new statistical treatment to your data, you derive new insights and see more clearly the meaning of those data.

In the next few pages, we consider two basic functions that statistics can serve. We also discuss the various ways in which the nature of the data may dictate the particular statistical procedures that can be used. In subsequent sections, we examine two major groups of statistics: descriptive and inferential.

FUNCTIONS OF STATISTICS

Statistics have two major functions. Some statistics describe what the data look like—where their center or midpoint is, how broadly they are spread, how closely the variables within the data are correlated with one another, and so on. Such statistics, appropriately enough, are called **descriptive statistics**.

But other statistics, known as **inferential statistics**, serve a different purpose: They allow us to make *inferences* about large populations by collecting data on relatively small samples. For example, imagine that you are an immigration officer. Although you have never been to Australia, you have met numerous Australians as they debark from incoming planes and ships. Perhaps you have even become well acquainted with a small number of Australians. From this small sample of the Australian population, you might infer what Australian people in general are like. (Your inferences may or may not be accurate because your sample, which consists entirely of immigrants to this country, is not necessarily representative of the entire population of Australia. However, that is a sampling problem, not a statistical one.)

More generally, inferential statistics involve using a small sample of a population and then *estimating* the characteristics of the larger population from which the sample has been drawn. For instance, we might estimate a population mean from the mean we obtain for a sample. Or we

	The Symbol Used to Designate the Factor	
The Factor in Question	Population Parameter	Sample Statistic
The mean	μ	$\bar{X}$ or M
The standard deviation	σ	s or SD
Proportion or probability	P	p
Number or total	N	n

might determine whether two or more groups of people are different based on differences we observe between samples taken from each of those groups. Inferential statistics provide a way of helping us make reasonable guesses about a large, unknown population by examining a small sample that *is* known. In the process, they also allow us to test our hypotheses regarding what is true for that large population.

Statistics as Estimates of Population Parameters

Especially when we use statistics to draw inferences about a population from which a research sample has been drawn, we are essentially using them as *estimates of population parameters*. A **parameter** is a characteristic or quality of a population that, in *concept*, is a constant; however, its *value* is variable.

Consider a circle. One of the parameters, or characteristics, of a circle is its radius, which has a functional relationship to the circle. In concept, the radius is a constant: It is always the same for every circle—the distance from the center of the circle to the perimeter. In value, it varies, depending on the size of the circle. Large circles have long radii; small circles, short radii. The value—that is, the length of the radius in linear units (centimeters, inches, feet)—is variable. Thinking of a parameter in this way, we see that each circle has several parameters: The diameter is always twice the radius (r), the circumference is always $2\pi r$, and the area is always πr^2. These concepts are constants, even though their particular values vary from one circle to the next.

Within the context of this discussion, a parameter is a particular characteristic (e.g., a mean or standard deviation) of the entire population—which is sometimes called a *universe*—about which we want to draw conclusions. In most cases, we can study only a small sample of that population. Any calculation we perform for the sample rather than the population (the sample mean, the sample standard deviation, etc.) is called a **statistic**. Statisticians distinguish between population parameters and sample statistics by using different symbols for each. Table 11.1 presents a few commonly used symbols used in statistical notation.

CONSIDERING THE NATURE OF THE DATA

As you begin to think about the statistical procedures that might be most appropriate for your research problem, keep in mind that different statistics are appropriate for different kinds of data. In particular, you should consider whether your data

  ■ Have been collected for a single group or, instead, for two or more groups
  ■ Involve continuous or discrete variables
  ■ Represent nominal, ordinal, interval, or ratio scales
  ■ Reflect a normal or non-normal distribution

After we look at each of these distinctions, we will relate them to another distinction—that between parametric and nonparametric statistics.

Single-Group Versus Multi-Group Data

In some cases, a research project yields data about a single group of people or objects. In other cases, it may yield parallel sets of data about two or more groups. Analyzing characteristics of a single group will often require different statistical techniques than making comparisons among two or more groups.

Continuous Versus Discrete Variables

In Chapter 10, we defined a *variable* as a quality or characteristic in a research investigation that has two or more possible values. Simply put, a variable *varies*. However, it may vary in different ways. A **continuous variable** reflects an infinite number of possible values falling along a particular continuum. A simple example is chronological age. The participants in a research study can be an infinite number of possible ages. Some might be 2 years old, others might be 92, and we might have virtually any age (including fractions of years) in between. Even if the study is limited to a small age range—say, 2- to 4-year-old children—we might have children who are exactly 2 years old, children who are 2 years and 1 month old, children who are 2 years and 2 months old, and so on. We could, in theory, be even more precise, perhaps specifying participants' ages in days, hours, minutes, seconds, or even fractions of a second.

In contrast, a **discrete variable** has a finite and small number of possible values. A simple example is a student's high school grade level. At a 4-year high school, a student can be in only one of four grades: 9th, 10th, 11th, or 12th. At most high schools, it isn't possible to be anything else. One cannot be somewhere between two grade levels, such as in the "9.25th grade."

Nominal, Ordinal, Interval, and Ratio Data

In Chapter 2, we described four different scales of measurement; these scales, in turn, dictate how we can statistically analyze the numbers we obtain relative to one another. To refresh your memory, we briefly review each of the scales again here.

- *Nominal data* are those for which numbers are used only to identify different categories of people, objects, or other entities; they do not reflect a particular quantity or degree of something. For instance, a researcher might code all males in a data set as 1 and all females as 2. The researcher might also code political affiliation with numbers, perhaps using 1 for Republicans, 2 for Democrats, 3 for Independents, and so on. In neither case do the numbers indicate that participants have more or less "sex" or "political affiliation" relative to one another.

- *Ordinal data* are those for which the assigned numbers reflect a particular order or sequence. They tell us that people, objects, or other entities fall along a continuum in terms of a particular variable; they do not, however, tell us anything about how great the differences are between them. For example, in a group of graduating high school seniors, each student might have a class rank that reflects his or her relative academic standing in the group: A class rank of 1 indicates the highest grade point average (GPA), a rank of 2 indicates the second highest GPA, and so on. These numbers tell us which students surpassed others in terms of GPA, but it does not tell us precisely how similar or different the GPAs of any two students are.

- *Interval data* reflect standard and equal units of measurement. As is true for ordinal data, the numbers reflect differences in degree or quantity. But, in addition, differences between the numbers tell us *how much difference* exists in the characteristic being measured. As an example, scores on intelligence tests (IQ scores) are, because of the way in which they are derived, assumed to reflect an interval scale. Thus, if we take four scores at equal intervals—say 85, 95, 105, and 115—we can assume that the 10-point difference between each pair reflects equivalent differences in intelligence between the people who have obtained those scores. The one limitation of interval data is that a value of zero (0) does *not* necessarily reflect a complete lack of the characteristic being measured. For example, it is sometimes possible to get an IQ score of 0, but such a score does not mean that a person has no intelligence whatsoever.

- *Ratio data* are similar to interval data but have an additional feature: a true zero point. Not only do the numbers reflect equal intervals between values for the characteristic being measured, but in addition a value of 0 tells us that there is a complete absence of that characteristic. An example would be income level: People with an annual income of $30,000 make $10,000 more than people with an annual income of $20,000, and people with an annual income $40,000 make $10,000 more than people with an annual income of $30,000. Furthermore, people who make $0 a year have *no* income.

Normal and Non-Normal Distributions

Theorists propose that many characteristics of human populations reflect a particular pattern, one that looks like this:

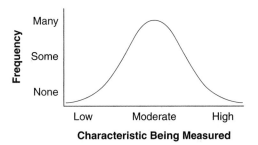

This pattern, commonly called the **normal distribution** or **normal curve** (you may also see the term *bell curve*), has several distinguishing characteristics:

- *It is horizontally symmetrical.*   One side is the mirror image of the other.
- *Its highest point is at its midpoint.*   More people (or whatever other entities are the focus of investigation) are located at the midpoint than at any other point along the curve. In statistical terms, three widely used measures of central tendency—the mode, the median, and the mean (all to be described shortly)—are the same.
- *Predictable percentages of the population lie within any given portion of the curve.*   If we divide the curve according to its standard deviation (also to be described shortly), we know that certain percentages of the population lie within each portion. In particular, approximately 34.1% of the population lies between the mean and one standard deviation below the mean, and another 34.1% lies between the mean and one standard deviation above the mean. Approximately 13.6% of the population lies between one and two standard deviations below the mean, with another 13.6% lying between one and two standard deviations above the mean. The remaining 4.6% lies two or more standard deviations away from the mean, with 2.3% at each end of the distribution. This pattern is reflected in Figure 11.6. (The proportions of the population lying within any particular section of the normal distribution can be found in most introductory statistics books.)

To better understand the normal distribution, take any fortuitous happening and analyze its distribution pattern—the corn production of Iowa in any given year, for example. If we could survey the per-acre yield of every farmer in Iowa (literally, the total population, the universe of the

Percentages within each portion of the normal distribution

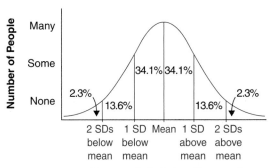

cornfields and corn farmers in Iowa), we would probably find that a few farmers had a remarkably poor yield of corn per acre for no discernible reason except that "that's the way it happened." A few other farmers, for an equally unaccountable reason, had remarkably heavy yields from their fields. Generally, however, most farmers will have had a middle-of-the-road yield, sloping gradually in either direction toward the greater-yield or the lesser-yield direction. The normal curve will describe the Iowa corn production. No one planned it that way; it is simply the way nature behaves.

Walk into any clothing store. Take an inventory of men's suit sizes or women's dress sizes, and you are likely to see a normal distribution. Take the heights and weights of all the children in a given school system, and again the normal curve will be evident.

Watch an approaching thunderstorm. An occasional flash of lightning will herald the coming of the storm. Soon, the flashes will occur more frequently. At the height of the storm, the number of flashes per minute will reach a peak. Gradually, with the passing of the storm, the number of flashes will subside. The normal curve is at work once again.

We could think of thousands of situations, only to find that nature often behaves according to the normal distribution. The curve is a constant. It is always bell-shaped. In any one situation, the *values* within it vary. The mean is not always the same number; the overall shape may be more broadly spread or more compressed, depending on the situation being represented.

Sometimes, however, a variable does not fall in a normal distribution. For instance, its distribution might be lopsided, or **skewed**. If the peak lies to the left of midpoint, we call such a distribution **positively skewed**; if the peak lies to the right of midpoint, the distribution is **negative skewed**. Or perhaps a distribution is unusually pointy or flat, such that the percentages within each portion of the distribution are different from those depicted in Figure 11.6. Here we are talking about **kurtosis**, with an unusually peaked, or pointy, distribution reflecting a **leptokurtic curve** and an unusually flat one being a **platykurtic curve** (see Figure 11.7).

Of course, some data sets don't resemble a normal distribution, not even a lopsided, pointy, or overly flattened variation of one. In general, ordinal data, by virtue of how they are created, will *never* fall into a normal distribution. For instance, a data set might look more like a stairway that progresses upward in regular intervals. Take a graduating class. If each student is given a class rank according to academic grade point average, Luis might rank first, Janene might rank second, Marietta third, and so on. We don't see a normal distribution in this situation, because we have only one student at each academic rank. If we construct a graph that depicts the frequencies of the class ranks, we see a low, flat distribution rather than one that rises upward and peaks in the middle.

Percentile ranks, too, form a flat distribution rather than a bell-shaped curve. Percentile ranks are frequently used to report performance on aptitude and achievement tests. To calculate them, a researcher must first look at the *raw score*—the number of test items answered correctly or number of points accumulated—that each person in the sample earns on a test or other research instrument. A particular individual's percentile rank is then calculated as follows:

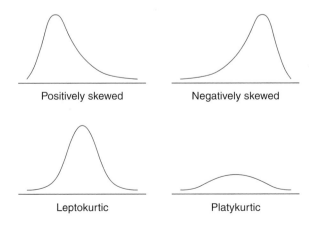

FIGURE 11.7

Common departures from the normal distribution

Positively skewed   Negatively skewed

Leptokurtic   Platykurtic

$$\%\text{ile rank} = \frac{\text{Number of other people scoring } \textit{lower} \text{ than the individual}}{\text{Total number of people in the sample}}$$

Percentile ranks, by the very nature of how they are calculated, spread people evenly over the number of possible ranks one might get; for instance, there will be roughly the same number of people earning percentile ranks of 95, 65, 35, and 5. Furthermore, while percentile ranks tell us how people have performed relative to one another, they do not tell us *how much* they differ from one another in the characteristic being assessed. In essence, then percentile ranks are *ordinal data* and must be treated as such.

Choosing Between Parametric and Nonparametric Statistics

Your choice of statistical procedures will depend, to some degree, on the nature of your data and the extent to which they reflect a normal distribution. Some statistics, known as **parametric statistics**, are based on certain assumptions about the nature of the population in question. Two of the most common assumptions are these:

- The data reflect an interval or ratio scale.
- The data fall in a normal distribution (e.g., the distribution has a central high point, and it is not seriously skewed, leptokurtic, or platykurtic).

When either of these assumptions is violated, the statistical results one obtains may be suspect.

Other statistics, called **nonparametric statistics**, are not based on such assumptions. For instance, some nonparametric statistics are appropriate for data that are ordinal rather than interval in nature. Others may be useful when a population is highly skewed in one direction or the other.

You may be thinking, Why not use nonparametric statistics all the time to avoid having to make (and possibly violate) any assumptions about the data? The reason is simple: Our most complex and powerful inferential statistics are based on parametric statistics. Nonparametric statistics are, by and large, appropriate only for relatively simple analyses.

On an optimistic note, we should point out that some statistical procedures are **robust** with respect to certain assumptions; that is, they yield generally valid results even when an assumption isn't met. For instance, a particular procedure might be as valid with a leptokurtic or platykurtic distribution as it is with a normal distribution; it might even be valid with ordinal rather than interval data. When using any statistical technique, you should consult with a statistics textbook to determine what assumptions are essential for that technique and what assumptions can easily be overlooked.

DESCRIPTIVE STATISTICS

As their name implies, descriptive statistics *describe* a body of data. Here we discuss how to determine three things we might want to know about a data set: points of central tendency, amount of variability, and the extent to which different variables are related to one another.

POINTS OF CENTRAL TENDENCY

By *point of central tendency*, we mean a central point around which the data revolve, a middle point around which the data regarding a particular variable are equally distributed. In statistical language, we use the term *measures of central tendency* to refer to techniques for finding such a point. Of these, the most commonly employed are the mode, the median, and the mean. Each of these measures has its own characteristics and applications.

The **mode** is the single number or score that occurs most frequently. For instance, in this data set

3   4   6   7   7   9   9   9   9   10   11   11   13   13   13   15   15   21   26

the mode is 9, because 9 occurs more frequently (four times) than any other number. Similarly, if we look at the list of Joe's grades (see p. 248), we see that only one score (83) appears more than once; thus, 83 is the mode. As a measure of central tendency, the mode is of limited value, in part because it will not always appear near the middle of the distribution and in part because it is not very stable from sample to sample. However, the mode is the *only* appropriate measure of central tendency for nominal data.

The **median** is the numerical center of a set of data, with exactly as many scores above it as below it. The word *median* comes from the Latin word for "middle," and so the median score is the one precisely in the middle of the series. Recall that Joe's record has 20 grades. Thus, 10 grades are above the median, and 10 are below it. The median is midway in the series between the 10th and 11th scores, or in this case, midway between the scores of 81 and 83—that is, 82 (see Figure 11.8).

You might think of the **mean** as the fulcrum point for a set of data: It represents the single point at which the two sides of a distribution "balance." Mathematically, the mean is the *arithmetic average* of the scores within the data set. To find it, we calculate the sum of all the scores (adding each score every time it occurs) and then divide by the total number of scores. If we use the symbol X to refer to each score in the data set and the symbol N to refer to the total number of scores, we calculate the mean as follows:

$$M = \frac{X_1 + X_2 + X_3 + \ldots + X_N}{N}$$

Statisticians frequently use the symbol Σ (uppercase sigma) to designate adding all the numbers related to a particular variable; thus, we can rewrite the formula for a mean as follows:

$$M = \frac{\Sigma X}{N}$$

Using the formula, we find that the mean for Joe's grades is 81, as illustrated in Figure 11.8. (The variation in Joe's grades, depicted in the figure as *measures of variability*, is discussed later in this chapter.)

The mean is the measure of central tendency that researchers and statisticians most commonly use. However, it is appropriate only for interval or ratio data, because it makes mathematical sense to compute an average only when the numbers reflect equal intervals along a particular scale.

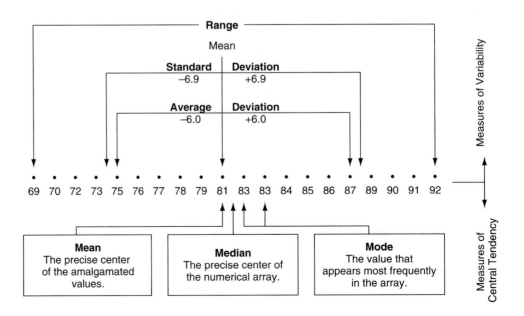

FIGURE 11.8

Measures of central tendency and variability for Joe's grades

The median is more appropriate for dealing with ordinal data. The median is also used frequently when a researcher is dealing with a data set that is highly skewed in one direction or the other. As an example, consider this set of scores:

3   4   5   5   6   9   15   17   125

The mean for these scores is 21, a number that doesn't give us a very good idea of the point near which most of the scores are located. The median, which in this case is 6, is a better reflection of central tendency because it isn't affected by the single extreme score of 125. Similarly, medians are often used to reflect central tendency in family income levels, home values, and other such "financial" variables; most family incomes and home values are clustered at the lower end of the scale, with only a very few extending into the million-dollar range.

Curves Determine Means

The mean as we've just described it—sometimes known as the *arithmetic mean*—is most appropriate when we have a normal distribution, or at least a distribution that is somewhat symmetrical. But not all phenomena fit a bell-shaped pattern. Growth is one. It follows an ogive curve that eventually flattens into a plateau (see Figure 11.9).

Growth is a function of geometric progression. As an example, consider Thomas Robert Malthus, an English clergyman and economist, who was the first to warn the human race about the population explosion and the possibility of worldwide famine. Malthus's *An Essay on the Principle of Population as It Affects the Future Improvement of Society* was the first serious discussion of the effects of growth mathematics. He contended that population, when unchecked, increases in a *geometric* ratio: 2, 4, 8, 16, 32, 64, 128 . . . , whereas subsistence increases only in *arithmetic* ratio: 2, 4, 6, 8, 10, 12, 14 . . . . Malthus also predicted that the eventual flattening of the growth curve would be determined by the arithmetic progression factor, *subsistence*. A growth curve tends to resemble an *S*, as illustrated in Figure 11.9.

If we are recording the growth of bean stalks in an agronomy laboratory, we do not find the average growth by assuming a normal distribution and calculating the arithmetic mean. The statistical technique does not fit the natural fact. Instead, we use the **geometric mean**, which is computed by multiplying all the scores together and then finding the Nth root of the product. In other words, the geometric mean, which we can symbolize as *Mg*, is calculated as follows:

$$M_g = \sqrt[N]{(X_1)\ (X_2)\ (X_3)\ldots(X_N)}$$

For growth phenomena, we use the geometric mean because that is the way things grow. That is the way cells divide—geometrically.

FIGURE 11.9

Typical growth curve

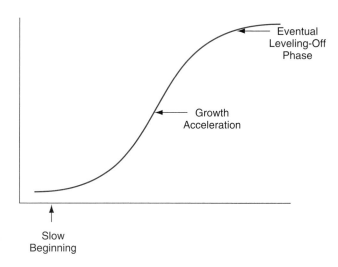

Biologists, physicists, ecologists, and economists all encounter growth phenomena (and decay phenomena as well) in one form or another. They all witness the same typical aspects of change: a slow beginning (a few settlers in an uninhabited region, a few bacteria on a culture); then, after a period of time, rapid expansion (the boom period of city growth, the rapid multiplication of microorganisms); and the leveling-off period (the land becomes scarce and the city sprawl is contained by geographical and economic factors, the bacteria have populated the entire culture). Following are examples of situations in which the application of the geometric mean is appropriate:

- Biological growth situations
- Population growth situations
- Increments of money at compound interest
- Averaging ratios or percentages
- Decay or simple decelerative situations

In every situation, one basic principle applies: The configuration of the data dictates the measure of central tendency most appropriate for that particular situation. If the data fall in a distribution that approximates a normal curve (as most data do), they call for one measure of central tendency. If they assume an ogive curve configuration (characteristic of a growth or developmental situation), they demand another measure. A *polymodal distribution*—one with several peaks—might call for still a third approach; for instance, the researcher might describe it in terms of its two or more modes. Only after careful and informed consideration of the characteristics of the data can the researcher select the most appropriate statistical measure. Such sensitive discrimination in the choice of a statistical tool is a distinguishing mark of the skilled researcher.

Thus, we come to the first rule for researchers who use statistics in their research: *The nature of the data—the facts of life—governs the statistical technique, not the other way around.* Just as the physician must know what drugs are available for specific diseases and disorders, so the researcher must know what statistical techniques are suited to specific research demands. Table 11.2 presents a summary of the measures of central tendency and their uses, together with the various types of data for which each measure is appropriate.

Measures of Central Tendency as Predictors

Some researchers regard the matter of central tendency from a somewhat different standpoint. They consider it from the perspective of optimal chance: What is the best prediction?

TABLE 11.2

Using measures of central tendency for different types of data

Measure of Central Tendency	How It's Determined (N = number of scores)	Data for Which It's Appropriate
Mode	The most frequently occurring score is identified.	• Data on nominal, ordinal, interval, and ratio scales • Multimodal distributions (two or more modes may be identified when a distribution has multiple peaks)
Median	The scores are arranged in order from smallest to largest, and the middle score (when N is an odd number) or the midpoint between the two middle scores (when N is an even number) is identified.	• Data on ordinal, interval, and ratio scales • Data that are highly skewed
Arithmetic mean	All the scores are added together, and their sum is divided by the total number (N) of scores.	• Data on interval and ratio scales • Data that fall in a normal distribution
Geometric mean	All the scores are multiplied together, and the nth root of their product is computed.	• Data on ratio scales • Data that fall in an ogive curve (e.g., growth data)

As an example, consider this situation. Suppose you are walking down the street. Suddenly you come upon a crowd of people forming in a normal-curve-like manner. Where, based on your best prediction, will you find the cause for the crowd forming? The answer is simple. Where the crowd is deepest, where the greatest number of people are, you will probably find the cause for the gathering. It may be a street fight, an accident, a woman giving away wooden nickels. But whatever the occasion, your best guess about the cause of the gathering lies at the point where the human mass is at its peak.

Similarly, we can often make reasonable predictions about a population based on our knowledge of central tendency. When we speak of "the average citizen," "the average student," and "the average wage earner," we are referring to those citizens, students, and wage earners who are huddled around the point of central tendency. In the broad spectrum of possibilities, we are betting on the average being the best guess as to what is most characteristic of the total population.

MEASURES OF VARIABILITY: DISPERSION AND DEVIATION

Up to this point, we have been discussing the question, What is the best guess? Now we turn to the opposite question: What are the worst odds? This, too, is important to know. The more that the data cluster around the point of central tendency, the greater the probability of making a correct guess about where any particular data point lies. The farther the data are dispersed from the central axis, the greater the margin of predictive error becomes. Consider, for example, the two curves shown in Figure 11.10. The data are more uniform when they cluster about the mean. Scatter them, and they lose some of their uniformity. They become more diverse, more heterogeneous. As specific data points recede farther from the mean, they lose more and more of the quality that makes them "average."

Statistics and surveying are somewhat similar. Each needs a point of origin from which to make further measurements. With surveying, the origin of measurement is a triangulation point; with statistics, one parameter of the data, usually the mean, establishes a measurement point for the mass of data. If we can establish a mean, then from it we can make further measurements. In this way, we can learn more about the data and discern their characteristics.

To make a sound judgment, it is important to see two parameters of the data. We must discern not only their centrality but also their spread. And it helps to see these characteristics in terms of quantitative values. Researchers are like cartographers charting an unknown land; they must "chart" the data, appreciate the meaning of the "peaks and valleys," and evaluate the effect of the expansiveness or narrowness of the spread. Such information aids greatly in interpreting the data later on.

How Great Is the Spread?

Perhaps the simplest measure of variability is the **range**. The range indicates the spread of the data from lowest to highest value:

Range = Highest score − Lowest score

For instance, the range for Joe's test scores is $92 - 69$, or 23 (see Figure 11.8).

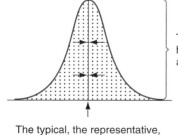

The data tend to be closely clustered around the mean.

The typical, the representative, the "most common" data.

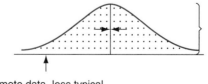

As data are dispersed farther and farther from the mean, they tend less and less to resemble the data qualities of the mean.

Remote data, less typical, less representative.

FIGURE 11.10

Distributions that differ in variability

Although the range is easy to compute, it has limited usefulness as a measure of variability and may even be misleading if the extreme upper or lower limits are atypical of the other values in the series. Let's take an example. Following are the numbers of children in each of ten families: 1, 3, 3, 3, 4, 4, 5, 5, 6, 15. We might say that the families range from one with an only child to a family of 15 children (a range of 15 − 1, or 14). But this figure is misleading: It suggests that the sample shows a great deal of variability in family size. We give a more realistic estimate of variability in this sample when we say that 80% of the families have from 3 to 6 children.

Other measures of variability use the median or mean as a starting point. One such measure is the **interquartile range**. If we divide the distribution into four equal parts, Quartile 1 lies at a point where 25% of the members of the group are below it. Quartile 2 divides the group into two equal parts and is identical to the median. Quartile 3 lies at a point where 75% of the values are below it.[1] The interquartile range is equal to Quartile 3 (the 75th percentile point) minus Quartile 1 (the 25th percentile point), as follows:

$$\text{Interquartile range} = \text{Quartile } 3 - \text{Quartile } 1$$

Thus, the interquartile range gives us the range for the middle 50% of the cases in the distribution. Because quartiles are associated with the median, any statistical approach employing the median as a measure of central tendency should also consider the quartile deviation as an appropriate statistical measure for variability.

But now let's use the mean as a starting point instead. Imagine that we determine how far away from the mean each piece of data in the distribution is; that is, we calculate the *difference* between each score and the mean score (we call this difference the *deviation*). If we were to add up all these differences (ignoring the plus and minus signs) and then divide the sum by the *number* of scores (which reflects the number of differences as well), we get the *average* of the differences between any score and the mean. This number is sometimes called the *average deviation* (AD). The equation for the average deviation is:

$$AD = \frac{\sum |X - M|}{N}$$

Here $|X - M| = X - M$ without regard for plus and minus signs; in other words, it is the *absolute value* of the difference between each score and the mean.

The average deviation is easily understood and, for that reason, has some merit. It is acceptable when no further statistical procedure is contemplated. It is a little-used value, however, and the measures of standard deviation and variance have largely replaced it in most research projects.

The **standard deviation** (σ or s) is the standard measure of variability in most statistical procedures. To understand the reason for using the standard deviation, we must think about what happens mathematically when we find the average deviation, which we have just discussed. Imagine that we were to compute the average deviation without using the absolute values of the differences. For any number lying to the left of the mean (and thus having a lesser value than the mean), the difference between the number and the mean ($X - M$) would be a negative number. In contrast, any number lying to the right of the mean would yield a positive $X - M$ value. When we added all the positive and negative deviations together, they would cancel one another out, yielding an overall sum of zero. To circumvent this problem, of course, the average deviation uses absolute values, thereby allowing us to ignore the plus and minus signs. Yet this is a rather dubious procedure. It is neither sound mathematics nor sound statistics to ignore what we do not like. We can, however, change negatives to positives in a perfectly acceptable mathematical manner. In algebra, if we multiply a negative value by itself, it becomes positive. Thus, when we square all negative differences, they become positive.

To calculate a standard deviation, we follow a procedure similar to calculating an average deviation. However, rather than taking the absolute value of the score-mean differences, we *square* the differences. After we have added the squared differences together and then divided by the

---

[1] If, instead of dividing the data into 4 equal parts, we divide them into 10 equal parts, then each part is called a *decile*; if into 100 equal parts, each part is called a *percentile*.

number of scores, we find the square root of the quotient. Thus, the formula for a standard deviation is as follows:

$$s = \sqrt{\frac{\Sigma(X - M)^2}{N}}$$

It is important to note that we square the differences first and *then* we add them together. If we were to add them together first and then square their sum, we would get an entirely different (and incorrect) result!

The average deviation and standard deviation are usually similar but not identical values. As an example, if we calculate them for Joe's grades, we get an average deviation of 6.0 and a standard deviation of 6.9 (see Figure 11.8).

Many statistical procedures use still another measure of variability. This statistic is known as the **variance**, which is simply the standard deviation squared:

$$s^2 = \frac{\Sigma(X - M)^2}{N}$$

The various measures of variability that we've discussed (omitting the average deviation, which, as we've said, is rarely used) are summarized in Table 11.3.

Using the Mean and Standard Deviation to Calculate Standard Scores

Earlier we mentioned the term *raw score*, the number of correct answers or points that a person gets on a test or other research instrument. Such scores typically need some context to make them meaningful. For instance, if we say that Mary has gotten a score of 35 on a test of extroversion (i.e., on a test assessing her tendency to be socially outgoing), you might ask: What does that score *mean*? Is it high? low? somewhere in the middle? Without a context, a score of 35 has no meaning. We have no idea how extroverted or introverted Mary is.

Sometimes researchers provide context by converting raw scores to **norm-referenced scores**, scores that reflect where each person in the group is relative to the characteristic being measured. We have already seen one example of a norm-referenced score: A *percentile rank* is the percentage of people in the group that a particular individual has scored *better than*. For example, if Mary scores at the 95th percentile on a test of extroversion, then we know that she is quite outgoing—more so than 95% of the people who have taken the test. But as we have seen, percentile ranks have a

TABLE 11.3 Using measures of variability for different types of data	Measure of Variability	How It's Determined (N = number of scores)	Data for Which It's Appropriate
	Range	The difference between the highest and lowest scores in the distribution	• Data on ordinal, interval, and ratio scales*
	Interquartile range	The difference between the 25th and 75th percentiles	• Data on ordinal, interval, and ratio scales • Especially useful for highly skewed data
	Standard deviation	$s = \sqrt{\dfrac{\Sigma(X - M)^2}{N}}$	• Data on interval and ratio scales • Most appropriate for normally distributed data
	Variance	$s^2 = \dfrac{\Sigma(X - M)^2}{N}$	• Data on interval and ratio scales • Most appropriate for normally distributed data • Especially useful in inferential statistical procedures (e.g., analysis of variance)

* Measures of variability are usually inappropriate for nominal data. Instead, frequencies or percentages of each number are reported.

definite limitation. They are ordinal data rather than interval data, and so such basic arithmetic operations as addition and subtraction are impossible. Thus, we will be very limited in the statistical procedures we can perform on them.

More useful in statistical analyses are standard scores. Simply put, a **standard score** tells us how far an individual's performance is from the mean with respect to standard deviation units. The simplest standard score is a z-score, which is calculated by using an individual's raw score (which we'll symbolize as X), along with the mean and standard deviation for the entire group, as follows:

$$z = \frac{X - M}{s}$$

As an illustration, let's return to Mary's score of 35 on the extroversion test. If the mean of the scores on this test is 25, and if the standard deviation is 5, then we could calculate Mary's z-score as follows:

$$z = \frac{35 - 25}{5} = \frac{10}{5} = 2$$

When we calculate z-scores for the entire group, we get a distribution that has a mean of 0 and a standard deviation of 1.

Because about half of the z-scores for any group of people will be a negative number (remember, the *mean* for the group is 0), researchers sometimes change z-scores into other standard-score scales with different means and standard deviations. To convert a z-score to another scale, we would simply multiply the z by the new scale's standard deviation (s_{new}) and then add the new scale's mean (M_{new}) to the product obtained, as follows:

New standard score = $(z \times s_{new}) + M_{new}$

Let's take an example. One common standard-score scale is the **IQ** scale, which uses a mean of 100 and a standard deviation of 15. (As you might guess, this scale is the one on which intelligence test scores are typically based.) If we were to convert Mary's extroversion score to the IQ scale, we would plug her z-score of 2, plus a standard deviation of 15 and a mean of 100, into the preceding formula:

IQ score = $(2 \times 15) + 100 = 130$

Thus, using the IQ-scale, Mary's score on the extroversion test would be 130.

Another commonly used standard-score scale is the **stanine**. Stanines have a mean of 5 and a standard deviation of 2. Mary's stanine would be 9, as we can see from the following calculation:

stanine = $(2 \times 2) + 5 = 9$

Stanines are *always* a whole number from 1 to 9. If our calculations gave us a number with a fraction or decimal, we would round it off to the nearest whole number. If some of our calculations resulted in numbers of 0 or less, or 10 or more, we would change those scores to 1 and 9, respectively.

Standard scores provide context for the scores: If we know the mean and standard deviation on which the scores are based, then we also know where in the distribution any particular score lies. For instance, an IQ score of 70 is two standard deviations (30 points) below the mean of 100, and a stanine score of 6 is one-half of a standard deviation (1 is half of 2) above the mean of 5.

Converting data to standard scores does not change the shape of the distribution; it merely changes the mean and standard deviation of that distribution. But imagine that, instead, we *do* want to change the nature of the distribution. Perhaps we want to change a skewed distribution into a more balanced, normally distributed one. Perhaps, in the process, we also want to change ordinal data into interval data. Several procedures exist for doing such things, but describing them would divert us from the basic nature and functions of statistics that we need to focus on here. You can find discussions of *normalizing* a data set in many basic statistics textbooks; another good resource is Harwell and Gatti (2001).

Keeping Central Tendency and Variability in Perspective

Statistics related to central tendency and variability provide us with a beginning point from which to view our data. Of course, we must first examine the data to observe their configuration and fundamental characteristics, and then second, through statistical means, we must analyze the data, seeing (through the eyes of statistical procedures) what the mass of data appears to be like.

So as not to lose perspective, we should remind ourselves that statistical manipulation of the data is not research. Research goes one step further and demands *interpretation* of the data. In finding medians, means, interquartile ranges, or standard deviations, we have not interpreted the data, not extracted any *meaning* from them. We have merely described the center and spread of the data. We have attempted only to see what the data look like. After learning their basic nature, we can then attempt to say what those data mean. That is, we can look for the conditions that are forcing the data to behave as they do. For example, if we toss a die 100 times and a 5 comes up 65 times out of the 100, we will have a distribution much different than what we would expect. This may suggest to us that a reason lurks behind the particular results we have obtained. For example, perhaps we are playing with a loaded die!

MEASURES OF RELATIONSHIP: CORRELATION

The statistics we have discussed so far—measures of central tendency and variability—relate to only a single variable. Oftentimes, however, we also want to know how two or more variables are interrelated. For example, relationships exist between age and reading ability (refer to Figure 9.1), between emotional state and physical health, between the amount of rainfall and the price of food in the marketplace. Consider, too, the relationships between temperature and pressure, between the intensity of light and the growth of plants, between the administration of a certain medication and the resultant platelet agglutination in the blood. We could go on and on. Relationships between two variables are everywhere. One function of statistics is to describe or indicate the strength of such relationships.

The statistical process by which we discover the nature of relationships among different variables is called *correlation*. The resulting statistic, called a **correlation coefficient**, is a number between −1 and +1; most correlation coefficients are decimals (either positive or negative) somewhere between these two extremes. A correlation coefficient for two variables simultaneously tells us two different things about the relationship between those variables:

▓ *Direction.*   The direction of the relationship is indicated by the *sign* of the correlation coefficient—in other words, by whether the number is a positive or negative one. A positive number indicates a **positive correlation**: As one variable increases, the other variable also increases. For example, there is a positive correlation between self-esteem and school achievement: Students with higher self-esteem achieve at higher levels (e.g., Marsh, 1990). In contrast, a negative number indicates an inverse relationship, or **negative correlation**: As one variable increases, the other variable decreases. For example, there is a negative correlation between speed and accuracy in answering questions: People who take longer to answer questions tend to make fewer errors in answering them (e.g., Shipman & Shipman, 1985).

▓ *Strength.*   The strength of the relationship is indicated by the *size* of the correlation coefficient. A correlation of +1 or −1 indicates a *perfect* correlation: If we know the degree to which one characteristic is present, we know exactly how much of the other characteristic exists. For example, if we know the length of a horseshoe crab in inches, we also know exactly what its length is in centimeters. A number close to either +1 or −1 (e.g., +.89 or −.76) indicates a *strong* correlation: The two variables are closely related, so knowing the level of one variable allows us to predict the level of the other variable with considerable accuracy. For example, we often find a strong relationship between two intelligence tests taken at the same time: People tend to get similar scores on both tests, especially if both tests cover similar kinds of content (e.g., McGrew, Flanagan, Zeith, & Vanderwood, 1997). In contrast, a number close to 0 (e.g., +.15 or −.22) indicates a *weak* correlation: Knowing the level of one variable allows us to predict the level of the other variable, but

TABLE 11.4

Examples of correlational
statistics

Statistic	Symbol	Data for Which It's Appropriate
		Parametric Statistics
Pearson product moment correlation	r	Both variables involve continuous data.
Coefficient of determination	R^2	This is the square of the Pearson product moment correlation; thus, both variables involve continuous data.
Point biserial correlation	r_{pb}	One variable is continuous; the other involves discrete, dichotomous, and perhaps nominal data (e.g., Democrats vs. Republicans, males vs. females).
Biserial correlation	r_b	Both variables are continuous, but one has been artificially divided into an either-or dichotomy (e.g., "above freezing" vs. "below freezing," "pass" vs. "fail").
Phi coefficient	ϕ	Both variables are true dichotomies.
Triserial correlation	r_{tri}	One variable is continuous; the other is a trichotomy (e.g., "low," "medium," "high").
Partial correlation	$r_{12 \cdot 3}$	The relationship between two variables exists, in part, because of their relationships with a third variable, and the researcher wants to "factor out" the effects of this third variable (e.g., what is the relationship between motivation and student achievement when IQ is held constant statistically?).
Multiple correlation	$R_{1 \cdot 23}$	One variable is related to two or more variables; here the researcher wants to compute the first variable's *combined* relationship with the others.
		Nonparametric Statistics
Spearman rank order correlation (Spearman's rho)	ρ	Both variables involve rank-ordered data and so are ordinal in nature.
Kendall coefficient of concordance	W	Both variables involve rankings (e.g., rankings made by independent judges regarding a particular characteristic) and hence are ordinal data, and the researcher wants to determine the degree to which the rankings are similar.
Contingency coefficient	C	Both variables involve nominal data.
Kendall's tau correlation	τ	Both variables involve ordinal data; the statistic is especially useful for small sample sizes (e.g., $N < 10$).

we cannot predict with much accuracy. For example, there is a weak relationship between intellectual giftedness and emotional adjustment: Generally speaking, people with higher IQ scores show greater emotional maturity than people with lower scores (e.g., Janos & Robinson, 1985), but many people are exceptions to this rule. Correlations in the middle range (for example, those in the .40s and .50s, positive or negative) indicate a *moderate* correlation.

Mention correlation coefficient, and most students think of the Pearson product moment correlation, sometimes called the Pearson *r*. Although this is probably the most common of all correlational statistics, there are perhaps a dozen more. As in the case of the mean, the nature of the data determines the technique that is most appropriate for calculating correlation. In Table 11.4, we present several parametric and nonparametric correlational techniques and the kinds of data for which they are appropriate.

One statistic that is particularly worth noting in Table 11.4 is the *coefficient of determination*, or R^2. This statistic, which is the square of the Pearson *r*, tells us *how much of the variance is accounted for* by the correlation. Although you will see this expression used frequently, researchers usually don't stop to explain what it means. By *variance*, we are specifically referring to a particular measure of variability mentioned earlier: the square of the standard deviation, or s^2. For example, if we find that, in our data set, the R^2 between Variable 1 and Variable 2 is .30, we know that 30% of the variability in Variable 1 is reflected in its relationship with Variable 2. This knowledge will allow us to control for some of the variability in our data set through such statistical procedures as partial correlation and analysis of covariance.

Always keep in mind that the nature of the data governs the correlational procedure that is appropriate to those data. Don't forget the cardinal rule: *Look at the data!* Determine their nature, scrutinize their characteristics, and then select the correlational technique suitable for the type of data with which you are working.

How Validity and Reliability Affect Correlation Coefficients

Beginning researchers should be aware that the extent to which a researcher finds a statistical correlation between two characteristics depends, in part, on how well those characteristics have been measured. Even if, logically, there *should* be a correlation between two variables, the researcher won't necessarily find one if the measurement instruments he or she uses have poor validity and reliability. For instance, we are less likely to find a correlation between age and reading level if the reading test we use is neither a valid (accurate) nor reliable (consistent) measure of reading achievement.

Over the years, we've had many students find disappointingly low correlation coefficients between two variables that they hypothesized would be highly correlated. By looking at the correlation coefficient alone, a researcher cannot determine the reason for a low correlation any more than he or she can determine the reason for a high one. Yet one thing is for certain: *You will find substantial correlations between two characteristics only if you can measure both characteristics with a reasonable degree of validity and reliability.* We refer you back to Chapter 5's section on "Identifying Appropriate Measurement Instruments," where you can find strategies for maximizing both of these essential qualities of sound measurement.

A Reminder About Correlation

Whenever you find evidence of a correlation within your data, you must remember one important point: *Correlation does not necessarily indicate causation.* For example, if you find a correlation between motivation and classroom achievement, you cannot necessarily conclude that students' motivation *influences* their achievement. Only experimental studies, such as those described in Chapter 10, allow you to draw definitive conclusions about the extent to which one thing causes or influences another.

Finding a correlation in a data set is equivalent to discovering a signpost. That signpost points to the fact that two things are related, and it reveals the nature of the relationship (positive or negative, strong or weak). It should then lead you to wonder, What is the underlying cause of the relationship? But the statistic alone will not be able to answer that question.

INFERENTIAL STATISTICS

As mentioned earlier, inferential statistics allow us to make inferences about large populations from relatively small samples. More specifically, inferential statistics have two main functions:

1. To estimate a population parameter from a random sample
2. To test statistically based hypotheses

In this text, we do not have the space to venture too far into these areas; statistics textbooks will give you more detailed information. We comment briefly, however, about several general concepts and principles.

ESTIMATING POPULATION PARAMETERS

When we conduct research, more often than not we use a sample to learn about the larger population from which the sample has been drawn. Typically we compute various statistics for the sample we have studied. Inferential statistics can tell us how closely these sample statistics approximate parameters of the overall population. For instance, we often want to estimate population parameters related to central tendency (the mean, or μ), variability (the standard deviation, or σ), and proportion or probability (P). These values in the population compare with the $\overline{X}$ (or M), the s, and the p of the sample (refer back to Table 11.1, p. 253).

To show you what we mean by estimation, we use a simple illustration. Jan is a production manager of a manufacturing corporation. She has a sample lot of connecting-rod pins. These pins fit snugly into assembly units, permitting the units to swivel within a given arc. The diameter of the pins is critical: If the diameter is too small, the assembly will wobble while turning; if too large, the assembly will stick and refuse to move. Jan has received complaints from customers that some of the pins are faulty. She wishes to estimate, on the basis of a sample, how many units may have to be recalled for replacement. The sample is presumably random and representative. From this sample, Jan wants to know three facts about the hundreds of thousands of pins that have been manufactured and sold:

1. What is the average diameter of the pins?
2. How widely do the pins vary in diameter?
3. What proportion of the pins produced will be acceptable in the assemblies already marketed?

The problem is to determine population parameters on the basis of the sample statistics. From the sample, Jan can estimate the mean, the variability, and the probability of acceptable pins within the population universe. These are the values represented by μ, the σ, and the P.

Statistical estimates of any kind are based on the assumption that *the sample is randomly chosen and representative of the total population*. Only when we have a random, representative sample can we make guesses about how closely our statistics estimate population parameters. To the extent that a sample is nonrandom and therefore nonrepresentative—to the extent that its selection has been *biased* in some way—our statistics may be poor reflections of the population from which it has been drawn.

An Example: Estimating a Population Mean

Imagine that we want to estimate the average (mean) height of 10-year-old boys in the state of New Hampshire. Measuring the heights of the entire population would be incredibly time-consuming, so we decide instead to measure the heights of a random and presumably representative sample of, let's say, 200 boys.

Random samples from populations display roughly the same characteristics as the parent population from which they were selected. Thus, we should expect the mean height for our sample to be approximately the same as the mean for the overall population. It will not be *exactly* the same, however. In fact, if we were to collect the heights for a second random sample of 200 boys, we would be likely to compute a slightly different mean than we had obtained for the first sample.

Different samples, even when each has been randomly selected from the same population, will almost certainly yield slightly different estimates of their parent population. The difference between the population mean and a sample mean constitutes an *error* in our estimation. Because we don't know what the exact population mean is, we also don't know how much error is in our estimate. We *do* know three things, however:

1. The means we might obtain from an infinite number of samples form a normal distribution.
2. The *mean of this distribution of sample means* is equal to the mean of the population from which the samples have been drawn (μ). In other words, the population mean equals the average, or mean, of all the sample means.
3. The standard deviation of this distribution of sample means is directly related to the standard deviation of the characteristic in question for the overall population.

This situation is depicted in Figure 11.11.

The third characteristic described, the standard deviation for the distribution of sample means, is known as the **standard error of the mean**. This index tells us how much the particular mean we calculate is likely to vary from one sample to another *when all samples are the same size and are drawn randomly from the same population*. Statistically, when all the samples are of a particular size (n), the standard error of the mean is represented as

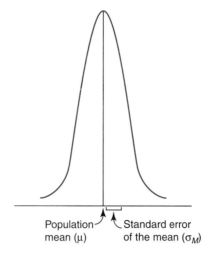

FIGURE 11.11

Distribution of sample means

Population mean (μ)   Standard error of the mean (σ_M)

$$\sigma_M = \frac{\sigma}{\sqrt{n}}$$

Here we are faced at once with a difficulty. The formula we just presented involves using the population standard deviation (σ), but the purpose of using the sample was to *avoid* having to measure the entire population. Fortunately, statisticians have devised a way to estimate the standard error of the mean from the standard deviation of a *sample* drawn from the population. This formula is

$$\sigma_M = \frac{s}{\sqrt{n-1}}$$

Notice how, in both formulas, the standard error of the mean is directly related to the standard deviation of the characteristic being measured: More variability in the population leads to a larger standard error of measurement—that is, to greater variability in the sample means that we might obtain. In addition, the standard error is *inversely* related to *n*, the size of the sample. As the sample size increases, the standard error of the mean decreases. Thus, a larger sample size will give us a sample mean that more closely approximates the population mean. This principle holds true for estimates of other population parameters as well. In general, *larger samples yield more accurate estimates of population parameters*.

Point Versus Interval Estimates

In making estimates of population parameters from sample statistics, we can make estimates of two types: point estimates and interval estimates.

A **point estimate** is a single statistic that is taken as a reasonable estimate of the corresponding population parameter; for instance, we might take a sample mean as a close approximation to the population mean. Although point estimates have the seeming benefit of being precise, in fact this precision is illusory. A point estimate will typically *not* correspond exactly with its true equivalent in the population. Let's return to our previous example of the connecting-rod pins. Perhaps the company has produced 500,000 pins, and Jan has selected a sample of 100 of them. When she measures the diameters of these pins, she finds that the mean diameter is 0.712 centimeters, and the standard deviation is 0.020 centimeters. She guesses that the mean and standard deviation of the diameters of *all* the pins are also 0.712 and 0.020, respectively. Her estimates will probably be close—and they are certainly better than nothing—but they won't necessary be dead-on.

So much for point estimation. A more accurate approach (although still not 100% dependable) is to identify **interval estimates** of parameters. In particular, we specify a range within whose limits a population parameter probably lies, and we state the probability that it actually lies there. Such an interval is often called a **confidence interval** because it attaches a certain level of probability to the estimate—a certain level of *confidence* that the estimated range is correct.

As an example, Jan might say that she is 95% certain that the mean of the 500,000 connecting-rod pin diameters her company has produced is somewhere between 0.708 and 0.716. What Jan has done is to determine that the standard error of the mean is 0.002 (see the previously presented formula for *estimated* σ_M). Jan knows that sample means fall in a normal distribution (Figure 11.11). She also knows that normal distributions have predictable proportions within each section of the curve (refer to Figure 11.6). In particular, Jan knows that about 68% (34.1% + 34.1%) of the sample means lie within one standard error of the population mean, and that about 95% (13.6% + 34.1% + 34.1% + 13.6%) lie within two standard errors of the population mean. What she has done, then, is to go two standard errors (2 × 0.002, or 0.004) to either side of her sample mean (0.712) to arrive at her 95% confidence interval of 0.708 to 0.716.

We have said enough about estimation for you to appreciate its importance. To venture further would get us involved in specific statistical procedures that are not the province of this text. For additional guidance, we urge you to consult statistics textbooks, such as those listed in the suggested readings at the end of the chapter.

Testing Hypotheses

The second major function of inferential statistics is the testing of hypotheses. At the outset, we should clarify our terminology. The term *hypothesis* can confuse you unless you understand that it has two different meanings in research literature. The first meaning relates to a *research hypothesis*; the second relates to a *statistical hypothesis*.

Most of our discussions of hypotheses in earlier chapters have involved the first meaning of the word *hypothesis* (e.g., recall Chapter 1's discussion of the homeowner who speculates about why a table lamp may have failed). A research hypothesis exists because the research problem or the subproblems issuing from it arouse curiosity in the researcher's mind; this arousal, in turn, leads to a *tentative guess* about how to resolve the problem situation. The research hypothesis is a reasonable conjecture, an educated guess. Its purpose is a practical one: It provides a temporary objective, an operational target, a logical framework that guides researchers as they collect and analyze data.

When we encounter the phrase "testing a hypothesis," however, the matter is entirely different. Here, the word *hypothesis* refers to a statistical hypothesis, usually a *null* hypothesis. A **null hypothesis** (often symbolized by the symbol H_0) postulates that any result observed is the result of chance alone. For instance, if we were to compare the means of two groups, our null hypothesis would be that both groups are parts of the same population and that any differences between them, including the difference we see between their means, are strictly the result of the fact that *any* two samples from the population will yield slightly different estimates of a population parameter.

Now let's say that we look at the *probability* that our result is due to chance alone. If, for example, we find that a difference between two group means would, if due entirely to chance, occur *only one time in a thousand*, then we could reasonably conclude that the difference is *not* due to chance, that, instead, something in the situation we are studying (perhaps an experimental treatment we have imposed) is systematically leading to a difference in the average performance of the two groups. This process of comparing observed data with the results that we would expect from chance alone is called *testing the null hypothesis*.

What Is Statistical Hypothesis Testing?

We can offer only a sketch here. The domain of statistical hypothesis testing is extensive, and we leave detailed discussion to statistics texts. Briefly, it involves comparing the distribution of data collected by a researcher with an ideal, or hypothetical distribution.

Nothing is perfect. Data will always show divergence when superimposed on the distribution we might expect in the ideal statistical world. We expect some variability between the two configurations, but we set limits on how far that variability may go.

At what point do researchers decide that a result has *not* occurred by chance alone? One common cutoff is a 1-in-20 probability: that any result that would occur by chance only 5% of the time probably is not due to chance but instead to another, systematic factor that is influencing the data. Other researchers use a more rigorous 1-in-100 criterion: The observed result would occur by chance only one time in 100. The probability that researchers use as their cutoff point, whether

.05, .01, or some other figure, is the **significance level**, or **alpha** (α). A result that, based on this criterion, we deem *not* to be due to chance is called **statistically significant**. In the process of deciding that a result is due to something other than chance, we *reject the null hypothesis*.

When we reject the null hypothesis, we must look to an alternative hypothesis (which may, in fact, be the *research hypothesis*) as being more probable. For instance, if our null hypothesis is that two groups are the same and we then obtain data that lead us to reject this hypothesis, we indirectly support the *opposite* hypothesis: that the two groups are *different*.

In brief, we permit a certain narrow margin of variation within our data, which we deem to be natural and the result of pure chance. Any variation within this statistically permissible range is not considered to be important enough to claim our attention. Whatever exceeds these limits, however, is considered to be the result of some determinative factor other than chance, and so the influence is considered to be an important one. The term *significant*, in the statistical sense in which we have been using it, is close to its etymological meaning—namely, "giving a signal" that something is operating below the surface of the statistic and merits further attention and investigation.

Making Errors in Hypothesis Testing

It is possible, of course, that we may make a mistake when we decide that a particular result is not the result of chance alone. In fact, *any* result could conceivably be due to chance; our sample, although selected randomly, may be a fluke that displays atypical characteristics simply through the luck of the draw. When we erroneously conclude that a result was not due to chance when in fact it *was* due to chance—when we incorrectly reject the null hypothesis—we are making a **Type I error** (also called an *alpha error*).

Yet in another situation, we might conclude that a result is due to chance when in fact it is *not*. In such a circumstance, we have failed to reject a null hypothesis that actually is false, something known as a **Type II error** (also called a *beta error*). For instance, imagine that we are testing the relative effects of a new medication versus the effects of a placebo in lowering blood cholesterol. Perhaps we find that people who have been taking the new medication have, on average, a lower cholesterol level than people taking the placebo, but the difference is a very small one. We might find that such a difference could occur 25 times out of 100 due to chance alone, and so we *retain the null hypothesis*. If, in actuality, the medication does reduce cholesterol more than a placebo does, we have made a Type II error.

Statistical hypothesis testing is all a matter of probabilities, and there is always the chance that we could make either a Type I or Type II error. We can decrease the odds of making a Type I error by lowering our level of significance, say, from .05 to .01, or perhaps even lower. In the process of doing so, however, we increase the likelihood that we will make a Type II error—that we will fail to reject a null hypothesis that is, in fact, incorrect. To decrease the probability of a Type II error, we would have to increase our level of significance, which, because it increases the odds of rejecting the null hypothesis, also increases the probability of a Type I error. Obviously, then, there is a trade-off between Type I and Type II errors: Whenever you decrease the risk of making one, you increase the risk of making the other.

Let's illustrate this trade-off by returning to our study of the potentially cholesterol-reducing medication. There are four possibilities:

1. We correctly conclude that the medication reduces cholesterol.
2. We correctly conclude that it does not reduce cholesterol.
3. We mistakenly conclude it's effective when it's not.
4. We mistakenly conclude that it's not effective when it is.

These four possibilities are illustrated in Figure 11.12. The three dotted vertical lines illustrate three hypothetical significance levels we might choose. Imagine that Line A represents a significance level of, say, .05. In this particular situation (such will not always be the case), we have a somewhat greater chance of making a Type I error (represented by the upper shaded area) than of making a Type II error (represented by the lower shaded area). But the significance level we choose is an arbitrary one. We could reduce our chance of a Type I error by decreasing our significance level to, say, .03. Line B in the figure represents such a change; notice how it would create a smaller box (lower probability) for Type I error but create a larger box (greater probability) for Type II error.

Alternatively, if we raise the significance level to, say, .06 (as might be represented by Line C in the figure), we decrease the probability of a Type II error but increase the probability of a Type I error.

There is perhaps nothing more frustrating for the novice researcher than obtaining insignificant results—those that, from a statistical standpoint, could have been due to chance alone. Following are three suggestions for decreasing the likelihood of making a Type II error and thus increasing the likelihood of correctly rejecting an incorrect null hypothesis. In other words, these are suggestions for increasing the **power** of a statistical test:

- *Use as large a sample size as is reasonably possible.* The larger the sample, the less the statistics you obtain will diverge from population parameters.
- *Maximize the validity and reliability of your measures.* No measure has "perfect" (100%) validity and reliability, but some measures are more valid and reliable than others. Research projects that use measures with high validity and reliability are more likely to yield statistically significant results. We refer you back to Chapters 2 and 5 for discussions of these two characteristics.
- *Use parametric rather than nonparametric statistics whenever possible.* As a general rule, nonparametric statistical procedures are less powerful than parametric techniques. By "less powerful," we mean that they typically require larger samples to yield results that enable the researcher to reject the null hypothesis.

Within this discussion, we must point out that *whenever we test more than one statistical hypothesis, we increase the probability of making at least one Type I error.* Let's say that, for a particular research project, we have set the significance level at .05, such that we will reject the null hypothesis whenever we obtain results that would be due to chance alone only 1 time in 20. And now let's say that as we analyze our data, we perform 20 different statistical tests, always setting α at .05. In this situation, although we won't necessarily make a Type I error, the odds are fairly high that we will.[2]

A Second Look at Research Hypotheses Versus Statistical Hypotheses

What often confuses the novice researcher is that testing the null hypothesis involves nothing more than a statistical comparison of the data from two situations—one hypothetical (a theoretical distribution) and one real (the data collected from a research sample). To the research data,

---

[2] When testing 20 hypotheses at a .05 significance level, the probability of making at least one Type I error is .642. More generally, the probability of making a Type I error when conducting multiple statistical tests is $1 - (1 - \alpha)^n$, where α is the significance level and n is the number of tests conducted.

we apply certain statistical procedures to determine whether calculated values sufficiently diverge from the statistical ideal to reject the null hypothesis.

It is frequently the case that the statistical hypothesis is the opposite of the research hypothesis. For example, we might, as our research hypothesis, propose that two groups are different from one another. As we begin our statistical analysis, we set out to test the statistical hypothesis that the two groups are the same. *By disconfirming the null hypothesis, we indirectly find support for our research hypothesis*. This is, to be sure, a backdoor approach to finding evidence for a research hypothesis, yet it is the approach that is typically taken. (The reasons for this approach are too complex to be dealt with in a text such as this one; suffice it to say that it is statistically much easier to test a hypothesis that an equivalence exists than a hypothesis that a difference exists.)

We should look at hypothesis testing from another point of view as well. Testing the null hypothesis, in and of itself, does not contribute much to the fulfillment of the basic aim of research: a systematic quest for undiscovered knowledge. Earlier, we described statistics as tools that enable us to find patterns in the data. Thus, they help us detect possible dynamics working within the data. These all-important dynamics are what the researcher seeks to identify and evaluate. To stop with a mere indication that *something* accounts for a significant difference between one data set and another is to settle for a ghost, and research is not a systematic quest for ghosts. It is a systematic search for knowledge.

Statistical hypothesis testing is of critical importance to researchers who must make decisions based on statistical characteristics of samples. All researchers must ultimately develop an intellectual acuity that looks with unprejudiced candor at their procedures and results. One must never stop at running data through a statistical formula and ending up with one or more numerical values. One must also *interpret* those values and give them meaning. The latter process includes the former, but the two should never be confused.

Examples of Statistical Techniques for Testing Hypotheses

Table 11.5 lists many commonly used parametric and nonparametric statistical techniques for testing hypotheses. We hope it will help you make decisions about the techniques that are most appropriate for your own research situation. We urge you to consult one or more statistics texts to learn as much as you can about whatever techniques you use, so that you apply them appropriately and thereby conduct accurate analyses of your data.

META-ANALYSIS

Occasionally researchers use inferential statistics not to analyze and draw conclusions from data they have collected but instead to analyze and draw conclusions about *other researchers' statistical analyses*. Such analysis of analyses is known as **meta-analysis**. A meta-analysis is most useful when many studies have already been conducted on a particular topic and another researcher wants to pull all the results together into a neat and mathematically concise package.

The traditional approach to synthesizing previous studies related to a particular research question is simply to describe them all, pointing out which studies yield which conclusions, which contradict others, and so on. In a meta-analysis, however, the researcher integrates the studies statistically rather than verbally. After pinning down the research problem, the researcher:

1. *Conducts a fairly extensive search for relevant studies.* The researcher does not choose willy-nilly among studies that have been reported about the research problem. Instead, he or she uses some systematic and far-reaching approach (e.g., searching through many professional journals, using online databases) to identify studies that have addressed the topic of interest.
2. *Identifies appropriate studies to include in the meta-analysis.* The researcher must certainly limit the studies to those that involve a particular experimental treatment (in experimental studies), preexisting condition (in ex post facto studies), or other factor that is the focus of the meta-analysis. He or she may further restrict the chosen studies to those that involve particular populations, settings, assessment instruments, or other factors that may impact a study's outcome.

TABLE 11.5

Examples of inferential statistical procedures and their purposes

Statistical Procedure	Purpose
Parametric Statistics	
Student's *t* test	To determine whether a statistically significant difference exists between two means.
Analysis of variance (ANOVA)	To look for differences among three or more means by comparing the variances (s^2) both within and across groups. If an ANOVA yields a significant result (i.e., a significant value for *F*), you should follow up by comparing various pairs of means using a *post hoc comparison of means*.
Analysis of covariance (ANCOVA)	To look for differences among means while controlling for the effects of a variable that is correlated with the dependent variable. This technique can be statistically more powerful (i.e., it decreases the probability of a Type II error) than ANOVA.
Regression	To examine how effectively one or more variables allow(s) you to predict the value of another (dependent) variable. A *simple linear regression* generates an equation in which a single independent variable yields a prediction for the dependent variable. A *multiple linear regression* yields an equation in which two or more independent variables are used to predict the dependent variable.
Factor analysis	To examine the correlations among a number of variables and identify clusters of highly interrelated variables that reflect underlying themes, or *factors*, within the data.
Structural equation modeling (SEM)	To examine the correlations among a number of variables in order to identify possible causal relationships (*paths*) among the variables. SEM encompasses such techniques as *path analysis* and *confirmatory analysis* and is typically used to test a previously hypothesized model of how variables are causally interrelated.
Nonparametric Statistics	
Sign test	To compare two correlated variables to determine if the values of one variable are significantly larger than the values of the other.
Mann-Whitney *U*	To compare two groups when the data are ordinal (e.g., ranked) rather than interval in nature. This procedure is the nonparametric counterpart of the *t* test in parametric statistics.
Kruskal-Wallis test	To compare three or more group means when the data are ordinal (e.g., ranked). This procedure is the nonparametric counterpart of ANOVA.
Wilcoxon matched-pair signed rank test	To determine whether two samples with ordinal data differ from each other when a relationship exists between the samples (i.e., when each data point in one sample is paired with a data point in the other sample).
Chi-square (χ^2) goodness-of-fit test	To determine how closely observed frequencies or probabilities match expected frequencies or probabilities. A chi-square can be computed for nominal, ordinal, interval, or ratio data.
Odds ratio	To determine whether two dichotomous nominal variables (e.g., smokers vs. nonsmokers and presence vs. absence of heart disease) are correlated.
Fisher's exact test	To determine whether two dichotomous variables (nominal or ordinal) are correlated when the sample sizes are quite small (e.g., $n < 30$).

3. *Converts each study's results to a common statistical index.* Previous researchers may very well have used different statistical procedures to analyze their data. For example, if each has compared two or more groups that received two or more different experimental interventions, one investigator may have used a *t*-test, another may have conducted an analysis of variance, and a third may have conducted a multiple regression. The meta-analytic researcher's job is to find a common denominator here. Typically, when an experimental intervention has been studied, an *effect size* is calculated for each study; that is, the researcher determines how much of a difference the intervention makes (in terms

of standard deviation units) in each study. The effect sizes of all the studies are then used to compute a more general effect size for that intervention.

The statistical procedures used in meta-analyses vary widely, depending, in part, on the research designs that the included studies reflect; for instance, correlational studies require different meta-analytic procedures than experimental studies. We must point out, too, that meta-analyses, while they can make an important contribution to the knowledge bases of many disciplines, are not for the mathematically fainthearted. If you are interested in conducting a meta-analysis, several of the resources listed in the "For Further Reading" section at the end of this chapter should prove helpful.

USING STATISTICAL SOFTWARE PACKAGES

Earlier in the chapter, we mentioned that general-purpose spreadsheet programs can be used to describe and analyze sets of quantitative data. However, many spreadsheets are limited in their statistical analysis capabilities. As an alternative, you may want to consider using one of the several statistical software packages (e.g., SPSS, SAS, SYSTAT, Minitab, StatView, Statistica) now widely available for use on personal computers. Such packages have several advantages:

- *Increased user-friendliness.* As statistical software programs have become more powerful, they have also become more accessible (thanks to personal computers) and user-friendly. In most cases, the programs are logical and easy to follow. All of the results are presented in easy-to-read table format. Selection of the proper statistic and interpretation of the results, however, are still left to the researcher.
- *Range of available statistics.* Many of these programs include a wide variety of statistical procedures, and they can easily handle large data sets, multiple variables, and missing data points.
- *Assumption testing.* A common feature of statistical software packages is to test for characteristics (e.g., skewness, kurtosis) that might violate the assumptions on which a parametric statistical procedure is based.
- *Speed of completion.* As always, a major benefit of using the computer is the speed with which it accomplishes tasks. Even relatively simple statistical procedures might take several hours if computed by hand; more complex analyses are, for all practical purposes, impossible for a researcher to conduct using only paper, pencil, and a hand-held calculator.
- *Graphics.* Many statistical programs allow the researcher to summarize and display data in tables, pie charts, bar graphs, or other graphics.

We show you some of the basics of one statistical software program, SPSS, in the Appendix.[3]

Yet we must caution you: *A computer cannot and should not do it all for you.* You may be able to perform sophisticated calculations related to dozens of statistical tests and present the results in a variety of ways, but if you do not understand how the results relate to your research problem, or if you cannot otherwise make logical, theoretical, or pragmatic sense of what your analyses have revealed, then all your efforts have been for naught. Powerful statistical software programs make it all too easy to conduct studies so large and complex that the researcher loses sight of the project. In the words of Krathwohl (1993), the researcher eventually behaves "like a worker in a laboratory handling radioactive material, . . . manipulating mechanical hands by remote control from a room outside a sealed data container. With no sense of the data, there is little basis for suspecting an absurd result, and we are at the mercy of the computer printout" (p. 608).

Ultimately you must be in control of your analyses; you must know what calculations are being performed and why. Only by having an intimate knowledge of the data can you derive true meaning from the statistics computed and use them to address your research problem.

---

[3] At the professor's request, this book can be packaged with either SPSS (Student Version 11.0 for Windows) or Macintosh Stat-pak (for PowerMac systems 7.0 or higher).

INTERPRETING THE DATA

At the beginning of the chapter, we presented a hypothetical data set for 11 school children and discovered that the 5 girls in the sample had higher reading achievement test scores than the 6 boys. Shortly thereafter, we presented actual data about growth marks on the shells of the chambered nautilus. Perhaps these examples piqued your curiosity. For instance, perhaps you wondered about questions such as these:

- Why were all the scores of the girls higher than those of the boys?
- Why were the intervals between each of the scores equidistant for both boys and girls?
- What caused the nautilus to record a growth mark each day of the lunar month?
- Is the relationship between the forming of the partitions and the lunar cycle singular to the nautilus, or are there other similar occurrences in nature?

Knowledge springs from questions like these. But we must be careful not to make snap judgments about the data we've collected. It is all too easy to draw hasty and unwarranted conclusions. Even the most thorough research effort can go astray at the point of drawing conclusions from the data.

For example, from our study of 11 children and their reading achievement scores, we might conclude that girls read better than boys. But we are not thinking carefully about the data. Reading is a complex and multifaceted skill. The data *do not* say that girls read better than boys. The data *do* say that, on a particular test given on a particular day to 11 children, the scores of the girls were, for this particular situation, higher than those of the boys and that each score was precisely equidistant from every other score for both boys and girls. Furthermore, the apparent excellence of the girls over the boys was limited to test performance in those reading skills that were specifically measured by the test. Honesty and precision dictate that all the conditions in the situation be considered and that we make generalizations only in strict accordance with the data. On the following day, the same test given to another 11 children might yield quite different data.

Interpreting the data means several things. In particular, it means:

1. *Relating the findings to the original research problem and to the specific research questions and hypotheses.*   Researchers must eventually come full circle to their starting point—why they conducted a research study in the first place and what they hoped to discover—and relate their results to their initial concerns and questions.

2. *Relating the findings to preexisting literature, concepts, theories, and research studies.*   To be useful, research findings must in some way be connected to the larger picture—to what people already know or believe about the topic in question. Perhaps the new findings confirm a current theoretical perspective, perhaps they cast doubt on common "knowledge," or perhaps they simply raise new questions that must be addressed before we can truly understand the phenomenon in question.

3. *Determining whether the findings have practical significance as well as statistical significance.*   Statistical significance is one thing; **practical significance**—whether findings are actually useful—is something else altogether. For example, let's return to that new medication for lowering blood cholesterol level. Perhaps we randomly assign a large sample of individuals to one of two groups; one is given the medication, and the other is given a placebo. At the end of the study, we measure cholesterol levels for the two groups and compare the group means using a *t*-test. If our sample size is quite large, the standard error of the mean will be very small, and so we may find that even a minor difference in the cholesterol levels of the two groups is statistically significant. Is the difference *practically* significant as well? That is, do the benefits of the medication outweigh its costs and any unpleasant side effects? A statistical test cannot answer this question. Only the human mind—the researcher, practitioners in the field of medicine, and so on—can answer it.

4. *Identifying limitations of the study.*   Finally, interpreting the data involves outlining the weaknesses of the study that yielded them. No research study can be perfect, and its imperfections inevitably cast at least a hint of doubt on its findings. Good researchers know—and they also report—the weaknesses along with the strengths of their research.

A Sample Dissertation

To illustrate this final step in the research process—interpretation of the data—we present excerpts from Kimberly Mitchell's doctoral dissertation in psychology conducted at the University of Rhode Island (Mitchell, 1998). The researcher was interested in identifying possible causal factors leading to eating disorders and substance abuse, and she hypothesized that family dynamics and child abuse might be among those factors. She drew on three theoretical perspectives that potentially had relevance to her research question: problem behavior theory, social cognitive theory, and the theory of cognitive adaptation. She administered several surveys to a large sample of undergraduate students and obtained a large body of correlational data about the students' childhoods, eating habits, drug use, and so on. She then used *structural equation modeling* (described briefly in Table 11.5) as a means of showing possible cause-and-effect relationships in her data set.

The dissertation refers to several psychological theories and concepts with which many of our readers may be unfamiliar. Nevertheless, as you read the excerpts, you should be able to see how the author frequently moves back and forth between her results and the broader theoretical framework. We pick up the dissertation at the point where she begins to summarize and interpret her results.

DISSERTATION ANALYSIS 8

DISCUSSION

Summary of Results and Integration

The purpose of this study was to integrate several theories that are beneficial for understanding health-risk behaviors. Problem Behavior Theory (Jessor, 1987), Social Cognitive Theory . . . (Bandura, 1977a), and the Theory of Cognitive Adaptation (Taylor, 1983) are similar in that they all pose a cognitive component within the individual that is crucial to overcome the potential negative consequences of life stressors. . . . This study supports these three theories, as well as previous research in the field. It extends the research by linking these theories into a single comprehensible framework for understanding the link between the childhood stressors of sexual abuse and negative family functioning and adult substance misuse of alcohol, illicit drugs, and eating.

A series of structural equation models revealed the powerful impact individuals' perceptions of their confidence and their interactions with their environment play on health-risk behavior. The first three models examined various ways childhood stressors (sexual abuse and family functioning) could predict current health-risk behaviors (alcohol use, illicit drug use, and binge eating). Examination of the first three models (Full, Direct, and Mediational) and chi-square difference tests revealed that the mediators (self-efficacy, life satisfaction, and coping) are extremely important in predicting health-risk behaviors. This [finding] supports Jessor's (1987) theory that problem behavior is the result of the interaction of the personality system, perceived environment, and the behavioral system. The personality system is measured by the cognitive mediator constructs; the perceived environment by the family functioning construct; and the behavioral system by the outcome constructs. . . . [T]he socialization an individual encounters throughout childhood through interactions with family members appears to influence both how the individual perceives the self and the environment around him/her. These factors seem to propel individuals to behave in ways that may or may not be risky for their health.

Comments

The author capitalizes the names of the three theories. More often, researchers use lowercase letters when referring to particular theoretical perspectives. Either approach is acceptable as long as the author is consistent.

Notice how the author begins with a "grand conclusion" of sorts, which she supports in subsequent paragraphs. She also explains how she has expanded on existing theories by integrating them to explain the phenomenon she has studied.

The "models" she refers to here are multivariable flowcharts that reflect how some variables may influence other variables, perhaps directly or perhaps indirectly through additional, mediator *variables.*

Self-efficacy refers to people's confidence in their ability to perform a task (e.g., resist the temptation to abuse alcohol) successfully. It is a central concept in Bandura's social cognitive theory, one the three theoretical frameworks on which the author bases her study.

Furthermore, Jessor (1987) suggests that problem behaviors in which adolescents engage are interrelated and co-vary. Donovan and Jessor (1985) suggest that diverse problem behavior, such as alcohol abuse, risky sexual behavior, and drug use constitute a single behavioral syndrome. The current study supports this notion. All of the structural models revealed a positive relationship between alcohol and drug use, as well as a positive relationship between drug use and binge eating. Although the relationship between alcohol use and binge eating was not found to be significant, they are indirectly related through drug use. Such relationships support the idea that these health-risk behaviors constitute a single behavioral syndrome. Future research with a longitudinal design is needed to see if there is a linear trend among these variables. . . .

Notice how the author continually connects her findings with the theoretical frameworks she is using.

Here the author points out both what she has found and what she has not *found.*

[The author continues with a discussion of more specific aspects of her findings and their relevance to the three theoretical frameworks. We pick up her discussion again when she summarizes her conclusions.]

Summary of Conclusions

There are several conclusions that can be drawn from this study. First, in support of Problem Behavior Theory (Jessor, 1987), health-risk behaviors may be part of a single behavioral syndrome. The consistent relationships found throughout the models between alcohol use and drug use, as well as [between] drug use and binge eating, reveal the presence of a higher order behavioral syndrome.

Second, there is a complex relationship between child sexual abuse and family functioning in terms of their ability to predict life satisfaction, coping, and self-efficacy. While child sexual abuse was found to significantly predict coping and life satisfaction, the inclusion of family functioning into the model made these paths disappear. The initial finding indicates a confounding of child sexual abuse and family functioning rather than sexual abuse itself. Furthermore, the constant relationship between child sexual abuse and family functioning shows that, although child sexual abuse does not directly predict the mediator constructs, it plays a role in the prediction indirectly.

Third, family functioning and cognitive mediators interact in specific and consistent ways to determine health-risk behaviors. Those students with high levels of family functioning are likely to have high life satisfaction, more effective coping strategies, and higher self-efficacy for alcohol use, drug use, and eating. In turn, these cognitive factors interact to predict health-risk behavior.

Although the author has previously presented each of her conclusions, she summarizes them all here. Such a summary is typical of lengthy research reports. It is quite helpful to readers, who might easily lose track of some important conclusions as they read earlier portions of a report.

The author makes the point that two of her independent (predictor) variables, child sexual abuse and family functioning, are highly interrelated. Their strong correlation is reflected in the models identified through her structural equation modeling procedures.

[The researcher continues with additional conclusions, and then turns to the limitations of her study.]

Study Limitations

The present study offers several important findings to the literature. Yet, there are some limitations to the study as well. First, the design was cross-sectional rather than longitudinal. Structural equation modeling is a multivariate technique that is well utilized with longitudinal data (Maruyama, 1998). By incorporating longitudinal data into the overall design, one can begin to establish causality in the results. The use of cross-sectional data with this sample does not allow the researcher to make causal statements about the findings. For example, the data cannot tell us whether self-efficacy for alcohol use comes before actual alcohol use or vice versa. Furthermore, the study asks the participant to answer a portion of the survey retrospectively, such as [is true for] the child sexual abuse and family functioning items. This

The author's use of the term cross-sectional *is somewhat different from our use of it in Chapter 9. She simply means that she collected all her data for her sample at one time, rather than following the sample over a lengthy period and collecting data at two or more times. As the author states, a longitudinal design would have better enabled her to identify important factors that preceded—and so may have had a causal effect on—other factors.*

brings up problems with how reliable the responses are due to the length of time that has passed between the incident(s) in question and the time of the study. . . .

A second limitation to this study is the nature of the sample itself. Although the sample size is excellent (n=469), there were disproportionate numbers of men and women (125 and 344, respectively). Furthermore, the sample was extremely homogeneous (87% White; 91% freshman or sophomore; 74% with family income over $35,000; and 73% Catholic or Protestant). This degree of similarity among participants limits the generalizability of the study results to other populations. Yet the results are still important because this is a population at high risk for alcohol use, drug use, and bulimia-related binge eating.

Another limitation to this study is the lack of response to the probing sexual abuse questions. Approximately one half of the 91 students who reported sexual abuse did not respond to the in-depth questions regarding the abuse experience(s) (e.g., degree of trust with perpetrator, frequency of abuse). This could be due to the nature of the survey itself or [to] the environment in which students filled out the survey. In terms of the nature of the survey, once students responded to the overall sexual abuse questions geared to determine whether they were abuse survivors or not, they were instructed to skip the next five questions if their responses to the previous seven questions were all "Never." It is possible that students who did not respond "Never" to the seven questions skipped the follow-up questions anyway in a desire to finish the survey quickly. The second possibility to the lack of response is the environment in which students took the survey. Students were asked to sign up for a designated one-hour time slot to participate in the study. It is highly likely that students signed up for the same time slots as their friends in class and subsequently sat next to each other while filling out the survey. Due to the close proximity and the sensitive nature of the questions, some sexual abuse survivors may not have wanted to fill out additional questions in fear that their friends might see. Better procedures in the future would be to have all students fill out all questions, whether they are abuse survivors or not, and/or to allow them to have more privacy while taking the survey. . . .

A final limitation of the study is the use of self-report data only. Self-report data may be fraught with problems derived from memory restrictions and perception differences. A more comprehensive design would include actual physical ways to measure the outcome variables. For example, the researcher could have strengthened the design by taking blood or urine samples to examine drug use. The problem here is that [the latter] method requires a great deal of time and money to undertake.

[The researcher concludes the discussion by talking about potential implications of her findings for clinical practice and social policy.]

The author points out a problem with using surveys to learn about people's prior life experiences: Human memory is not always accurate. Her use of the word reliable *here refers to accuracy and dependability (i.e., validity) of the results, rather than to reliability as we have previously defined the term.*

The author explains ways in which her sample was not completely representative of the overall population of older adolescents and young adults but also makes a good case for the value of studying this sample.

The author identifies "holes" in her survey data and suggests plausible explanations for them. At the end of the paragraph, she offers suggestions for how future research might minimize such holes.

By perception differences, *the author is presumably referring to how different participants may have interpreted their prior experiences and/or items on the survey. An additional weakness of self-report data is that some participants may have intentionally misrepresented their prior experiences and/or current behaviors.*

NOTE. From *Childhood Sexual Abuse and Family Functioning Linked with Eating and Substance Misuse: Mediated Structural Models* (pp. 92–94, 114–119) by K. J. Mitchell, 1998, unpublished doctoral dissertation, University of Rhode Island, Kingston. Reprinted with permission.

PRACTICAL APPLICATION Analyzing Data in a Quantitative Study

You can gain a clearer understanding of statistics and statistical procedures by reading about them in research reports and using them in actual practice. If your research project involves quantitative data, the following checklist can help you clarify which statistical analyses might be most appropriate for your situation.

✔ CHECKLIST

QUESTIONS TO CONSIDER WHEN CHOOSING A STATISTICAL PROCEDURE

CHARACTERISTICS OF THE DATA

_____   1. Are the data _____ continuous or _____ discrete?

_____   2. What scale do the data reflect? Are they _____ nominal, _____ ordinal, _____ interval, or _____ ratio?

_____   3. What do you want to do with the data?

        _____ Find a measure of central tendency? If so, which? _____

        _____ Find a measure of variability? If so, which? _____

        _____ Find a coefficient of correlation? If so, which? _____

        _____ Estimate population parameters? If so, which? _____

        _____

        _____ Test a null hypothesis? If so, at what confidence level? _____

        _____ Other? (specify) _____

_____   4. State your rationale for processing the data as you have just indicated you intend to do.

        _____

        _____

INTERPRETATION OF THE DATA

_____   5. After you have treated the data statistically to analyze their characteristics, what will you then have?

        _____

        _____

_____   6. From a research standpoint, what will your interpretation of the data consist of? How will the statistical analysis help you solve any part of your research problem?

        _____

        _____

_____   7. What remains to be done before your problem (or any one of its subproblems) can be resolved?

        _____

        _____

_____   8. What is your plan for carrying out this further interpretation of the data?

        _____

        _____

        _____

        _____

Now go to our Companion Website at http://www.prenhall.com/leedy to assess your understanding of chapter content and to complete the projects that will help you learn how to conduct research.

FOR FURTHER READING

Statistical Techniques for Analyzing Quantitative Data

Adèr, H. J., & Mellenbergh, G. J. (Eds.) (1999). *Research methodology in the life, behavioural, and social sciences*. Thousand Oaks, CA: Sage.

Agresti, A., & Finlay, B. (1997). *Statistical methods for the social sciences*. Upper Saddle River, NJ: Prentice Hall.

Arthur, W., Jr., Bennett, W., Jr., & Huffcutt, A. I. (2001). *Conducting meta-analysis using SAS*. Mahwah, NJ: Erlbaum.

Bechhofer, R. E., Santner, T. J., & Goldsman, D. (1995). *Design and analysis of experiments for statistical selection, screening, and multiple comparisons*. New York: Wiley.

Bruning, J. L., & Kintz, B. L. (1997). *Computational handbook of statistics* (4th ed.). Boston: Allyn & Bacon.

Clarke, G. M. (1994). *Statistics and experimental design: An introduction for biologists and biochemists* (3rd ed.). New York: Wiley.

Glass, G. V., & Hopkins, K. D. (1996). *Statistical methods in education and psychology* (3rd ed.). Boston: Allyn & Bacon.

Gravetter, F. J., & Wallnau, L. B. (2004). *Statistics for the behavioral sciences* (6th ed.). Belmont, CA: Wadsworth.

Haskins, L., & Jeffrey, K. (1990). *Understanding quantitative history*. New York: McGraw-Hill.

Heiman, G. W. (2003). *Basic statistics for the behavioral sciences* (4th ed.). Boston: Houghton Mifflin.

Hunter, J. E., Schmidt, F. L., & Jackson, G. B. (1982). *Meta-analysis: Cumulating research findings across studies*. Thousand Oaks, CA: Sage.

Journal of Experimental Education. (1993). 61(4). (Entire issue is devoted to the theme of statistical significance testing.)

Kirk, R. E. (1998). *Statistics: An introduction* (4th ed.). San Diego: Harcourt Brace.

Kranzler, J. H. (2003). *Statistics for the terrified* (3rd ed.). Upper Saddle River, NJ: Prentice Hall.

Lind, D. A., Mason, R. D., & Marchal, W. G. (2001). *Statistical techniques in business and economics* (11th ed.). New York: McGraw-Hill.

McCall, R. B. (2001). *Fundamental statistics for behavioral sciences* (8th ed.). Pacific Grove, CA: Brooks/Cole.

Myers, J. L., & Well, A. D. (1995). *Research design and statistical analysis*. Hillsdale, NJ: Erlbaum.

Phillemer, D. B. (1994). One- versus two-tailed hypothesis tests in contemporary educational research. *Educational Researcher*, 20(9), 13–17.

Phillips, J. L., Jr. (1999). *How to think about statistics* (6th ed.). New York: Freeman.

Rosner, B. (1999). *Fundamentals of biostatistics* (5th ed.). Belmont, CA: Duxbury.

Rowntree, D. (1981). *Statistics without tears: A primer for non-mathematicians*. New York: Scribner.

Wilkinson, L., & the Task Force on Statistic Inference. (1999). Statistical methods in psychology journals: Guidelines and explanations. *American Psychologist*, 54, 594–604.

Winer, B. J., Brown, D. R., & Michels, K. M. (1991). *Statistical principles in experimental design* (3rd ed.). New York: McGraw-Hill.

Wolf, F. M. (1986). *Meta-analysis: Quantitative methods for research synthesis*. Thousand Oaks, CA: Sage.

Wood, P. (2000). Meta-analysis. In G. M. Breakwell, S. Hammond, & C. Fife-Schaw (Eds.), *Research methods in psychology* (2nd ed., pp. 414–425). Thousand Oaks, CA: Sage.

Using Statistical Software for Data Analysis

Cramer, D. (1998). *Fundamental statistics for social research: Step-by-step calculations and computer techniques using SPSS for Windows*. New York: Routledge.

Field, A. (2000). *Discovering statistics using SPSS for Windows: Advanced techniques for the beginner*. Thousand Oaks, CA: Sage.

Spector, P. E. (2001). *SAS programming for researchers and social scientists* (2nd ed.). Thousand Oaks, CA: Sage.

Sweet, S. A. (1999). *Data analysis with SPSS*. Boston: Allyn & Bacon.

Part V

Preparing the Research Report

12

Technical Details: Style, Format, and Organization of the Research Report

The lexicographer Dr. Samuel Johnson once said to a young man who was seeking employment with him, "Boy, open thy mouth, that I may see thee!" Along a similar vein, one might say to every researcher, "Hand me thy written page—thy research report—that I may see thee." What you put on paper and how you put it there reveal your knowledge, the quality of your thinking, and your standards of excellence more eloquently than anything else you do.

Bringing a research effort to its rightful conclusion involves writing a report that is faithful to the data but also finds meaning in those data. The research report is a straightforward document that sets forth clearly and precisely what the researcher has done to resolve the research problem. In structure, it is factual and logical. Like the research proposal, it makes no pretense at being a work of fine literature. It must, however, be comprehensible, so that readers can easily grasp what the researcher has done and found. It must also be flawless in its sentence and paragraph structure, punctuation use, and spelling. The research document you write is a clear reflection of your scholarship as a researcher; this is why it is also often used as a culminating measure of a student's educational achievements.

GETTING STARTED

If you are writing a thesis or dissertation, be sure to check first with your university's graduate school office to ascertain whether it has a prescribed set of guidelines for writing theses. Check such matters as paper quality, width of margins, size and style of typeface, and heading format. What is permitted at one institution may be unacceptable at another. Ask whether your university has a style manual for writing research documents or whether it recommends that you adhere to a particular style manual.

University guidelines aside, different disciplines tend to adhere to different styles in research reports; for example, psychologists typically use APA style, whereas historians tend to use Chicago style. Differences among the styles are most noticeable in the formats used for citations and reference lists. For example, the sample proposal near the end of Chapter 4 includes citations within parentheses, consistent with American Psychological Association (APA) style. In contrast, the dis-

TABLE 12.1   Commonly used styles in research reports

Style	Manuals	Online Assistance
APA Style: American Psychological Association	American Psychological Association (APA). (2001). *Publication manual of the American Psychological Association* (5th ed.). Washington, DC: Author.	http://www.apastyle.org/ http://www.psychwww.com/resource/apacrib.htm http://www.wisc.edu/writing/ (click on "Writer's Handbook") http://www.dianahacker.com/resdoc/
CBE Style: Council of Biology Editors	Huth, E. J. (1994). *Scientific style and format: The CBE manual for authors, editors, and publishers* (6th ed.). New York: Cambridge University Press.	http://www.wisc.edu/writing/ (click on "Writer's Handbook") http://www.dianahacker.com/resdoc/
Chicago Style: University of Chicago	*Chicago manual of style* (15th ed.). (2003). Chicago: University of Chicago Press.	http://www.press.uchicago.edu/ (enter "Chicago Manual of Style" in the search box) http://www.wisc.edu/writing/ (click on "Writer's Handbook") http://www.dianahacker.com/resdoc/
MLA Style: Modern Language Association	Gibaldi, J. (1998). *MLA style manual and guide to scholarly publishing* (2nd ed.). New York: Modern Language Association.	http://www.mla.org/ http://www.wisc.edu/writing/ (click on "Writer's Handbook") http://www.dianahacker.com/resdoc/

sertation near the end of Chapter 8 uses footnotes, consistent with Chicago style. Table 12.1 lists four commonly used styles, along with sources of information about each one.

"Surfing" the Internet for Writing Assistance

USING TECHNOLOGY

Numerous sites on the World Wide Web offer assistance on the nitty-gritty details of different styles. In the rightmost column of Table 12.1 are several Web sites that are active as this book goes to press. Another strategy is to use a search engine (e.g., http://www.google.com) and type such keywords as "style manuals," "MLA style," and the like in the search box; doing so will lead you to many potentially useful sites at universities and elsewhere.

Some sites on the World Wide Web offer more general suggestions for writers. A good example is a Web site at Purdue University, in the Academic Services of the School of Liberal Arts. It is known as the Online Writing Lab (OWL) and is at the following Internet address:

http://owl.english.purdue.edu/

At this site, you can find dozens of documents on all types of writing problems and solutions. Discussions of such topics as "Strategies for Improving Sentence Clarity," "Verbs: Voice, and Mood," "Punctuation," and "Overcoming Writer's Block" are available for you to read and print out. From Purdue's OWL site, you can link to other online writing labs and additional helpful sites.

Learn by Looking

Perhaps the best way to understand and appreciate the nature of research reports (and to prepare yourself for writing one) is to look at some existing reports. Any university library should have a collection of theses and dissertations on its shelves. State and federal agencies issue research reports in many areas. Notable available reports include the U.S. Surgeon General's report on smoking and the numerous research reports issued by the National Institutes of Health, the American Medical Association, and other learned societies, professional associations, and occupational and trade groups. You may also want to look at the abstracts published in *Dissertation Abstracts International,* located in the reference section of any university library.

Most research reports use a somewhat formal and impersonal style and format. For instance, they sometimes use the passive voice to describe the procedures that the researcher followed (e.g., "Participants were instructed to . . ." rather than "I instructed the participants to . . ."). There are a few exceptions to this rule, however; for example, ethnographic studies are often described in a personal, literary, "storytelling" fashion (see Chapter 7), and historical researchers often tell a story as well (see Chapter 8). Perusing research reports in your own discipline can give you a good sense of the writing style that is most prevalent (and therefore most acceptable) in your field.

PLANNING A RESEARCH REPORT

A research report has a relatively simple format. In general, it should achieve four objectives:

- It should give readers a clear understanding of the research problem and why it merited an in-depth investigation.
- It should describe exactly how data were collected in an attempt to resolve the problem.
- It should present the data precisely and completely. The data presented in the report should substantiate all the interpretations and conclusions that the report contains.
- It should interpret the data for the reader and demonstrate exactly how the data resolve the research problem. A report that merely presents raw data and uninterpreted facts (in the form of tables, graphs, and other data-summary devices) is of little help to the reader in deriving meaning from those data.

In the following sections, we discuss each of these matters. We then address how best to conclude the report.

DESCRIPTION OF THE RESEARCH PROBLEM

The statement of the problem and any other information needed to understand it should comprise the first section or chapter of the final report. The reader should be able to comprehend *from the report alone* what the problem is and what its ramifications are. The reader should appreciate the setting in which the problem was conceived. In addition, the reader should learn why, from both an academic and practical standpoint, the study was an important one to conduct.

The first section of the research report should have but one purpose: to create a meeting of minds between the writer and the readers of the report. Many research reports begin badly because their writers have not reconstructed the problem for the readers and set it forth clearly and completely. Such omissions get readers off to a confused start, which will impose a cloudy haze over the rest of the report. The writer of a research report must keep in mind that readers are likely to know only those things that the writer has actually put on paper.

After a few introductory comments (perhaps a few paragraphs) that provide the background and a rationale for the study, the document should set forth clearly and unmistakably the problem that has been researched. Often, an appropriate subheading can draw the reader's attention to the research problem.

If the problem has been divided into subproblems, these should be presented following the statement of the problem and announced with proper subheadings. By presenting the problem and its subproblems, the writer gives the reader a clear and complete understanding of the *principal thrust* of the research effort. With this thrust in mind, the reader will then be in a better position to understand the interpretation of the data and to judge the merits of the research.

Terms that may be ambiguous or are used in a specialized sense must be defined. For a meeting of minds, it is imperative that reader and researcher have the same orientations to the problem, the same concepts, the same ideas. This is accomplished by careful definitions of any terms in either the problem or the subproblems that may be open to varied interpretation. In case you have forgotten what we said earlier about these matters, look once again at Chapter 3.

A research report provides no opportunity for imprecise thought or inexact expression. Readers should see explicitly what hypotheses have been tested; they should know exactly what assumptions the researcher made in testing them.

Any delimitations should also be clearly set forth. All who read the research report should know precisely how far the research effort extended and where the limits were set. Into what relevant areas did the research effort not inquire? What aspects of the problem have not been studied? Readers want answers to these questions, and they find those answers in the opening pages of the report.

The extent to which related literature is presented in the first section depends on the nature of the research report. In a journal article, the literature immediately relevant to the problem is summarized in the introductory paragraphs before the statement of the research problem. In a thesis or dissertation, only a few key works are identified in the first chapter, and the bulk of the literature is reserved for a separate, second chapter in the report.

DESCRIPTION OF THE METHOD

The method that was used to collect data—including the sample, assessment instruments, and procedures—should be described with the utmost precision. From this description, the reader should know exactly what was done, to the point where the reader could replicate the study and, presumably, get similar results.

More generally, the *design* of the study should be clear. In particular, the researcher should state whether qualitative or quantitative methods (or both) were used and what particular research traditions were followed—for example, whether the study was an ethnography, a grounded theory study, a longitudinal study, a survey, a single-group time-series study, or a 2-by-2 factorial experimental design—or perhaps some combination of approaches.

Qualitative researchers also engage in **reflexivity**: Because their data collection has inevitably been influenced by their own assumptions and values, they openly acknowledge their biases and speculate on how these may have affected what they did, what data they collected, and how they interpreted their results.

PRESENTATION OF THE DATA

After a reader fully understands just what the problem was and the manner in which it was investigated, the next question is, What is the evidence?

The data are presented *in terms of the problem*. You have gathered a mass of data. You have then codified, arranged, and separated the data into groups, each of which correspond to a particular part of the problem being studied. The problem has been expressed in subproblems to facilitate the management of the problem as a whole. There is, then, a one-to-one correspondence: Certain data relate to each subproblem. You describe these in a logical sequence within the report. As each subproblem and its attendant data are discussed, it is helpful to restate, at the beginning of such discussion, the subproblem, perhaps even in the exact wording in which it appeared both in the proposal and in the first section of the study. Doing so will keep your reader oriented to the progress of the research as it is being reported; it will, likewise, focus the reader's attention on the specific aspect of the research problem under discussion.

One logical approach is to devote a separate section (each announced with its own heading or subheading) to each subproblem and its pertinent data. Present the subproblem, present the data germane to it, analyze and interpret those data, and present conclusions warranted by the data. Each section might end with a brief summary in which the findings of that particular section are shown in relationship to the general problem and the previous subproblems.

So that the reader doesn't get lost in the data presentation, it is often helpful to begin the discussion of results with an *advance organizer* in which the researcher lays out the overall organization of how the results will be presented. We refer you back to Chapter 2's section on "Writing to Communicate" for a description of advance organizers.

The data should be presented thoroughly and, of course, accurately. In many cases, it is helpful to organize some of them into tables, figures, and other concise presentations. A **table** is usually an arrangement of words, numbers, signs, or combinations of them in a two-dimensional matrix for the purpose of exhibiting certain information in compact and comprehensive form. A **figure** is any kind of graphic illustration other than a table: a graph, chart, flowchart, photograph, drawing, sketch, or other device to convey an idea, often in a nonverbal fashion.

When the data have been subjected to statistical analysis, present your rationale for employing the particular statistical approach(es) you used. It is important to know not only that you used a particular technique but also *why* you used it. In fact, throughout the entire research process, you should keep in mind that, generally, the answer to the question "What?" is not nearly as important as the answer to the question "Why?" One of the weakest links in many research reports is the failure to substantiate what one has done with a solid rationale as to why one has done it.

In a strictly qualitative study, the data are typically not analyzed in any statistical manner. Rather, they must be presented in such a way that they speak for themselves. As mentioned in Chapters 5 and 7, qualitative researchers often engage in *thick description*, presenting the data in such detail that readers can see for themselves what is going on. One well-known ethnographer takes this approach:

> In striking the delicate balance between providing too much detail and too little, I would rather err on the side of too much; conversely, between overanalyzing and underanalyzing data, I would rather say too little. (Wolcott, 1994, p. 350)

Descriptions of data in quantitative studies are typically written in an objective, "scientific" style. Those in qualitative studies vary from the objective and aloof, on the one hand, to the more subjective and personal, on the other. Qualitative researchers frequently include dialogues and participants' statements to illustrate their findings. They may also use metaphors and analogies to make a point. We see a simple yet effective "anti-metaphor"—an example of what something was *not*—in Matthew McKenzie's (2003) dissertation about the Boston Marine Society (previously excerpted at length in Chapter 8):

> *No mere gentleman's club,* common work experiences defined the society as a community, set aside from the rest of the town. (McKenzie, 2003, p. 20; emphasis added)

Regardless of how you organize your presentation of the data, it is imperative that you present them as evidence for the conclusions that you draw from them. If the data are extensive and you choose to present them only in summary form in the body of the study, you should present them in their entirety in an appendix. In this way, anyone wishing to replicate the results of the research effort should be able to reach essentially the same conclusions.

Let's not forget that we are also testing a hypothesis. Somewhere—probably in the closing paragraphs of the chapter—you should indicate whether the data did or did not support the hypothesis being tested. Restate the hypothesis and say explicitly whether it was supported or not supported by the data.

INTERPRETATION OF THE DATA

All too frequently, researchers believe that, having once presented the facts and figures, they have done all that needs to be done. To display the data is certainly important, but as we have said so many times before, the *interpretation of the data* is the essence of research. Without inquiring into the intrinsic meaning of the data, no resolution of the research problem or its subproblems is possible.

One common error that many researchers make is to fail to exploit the data fully. One cannot turn over the facts too often, look at them from too many angles, or chart, graph, and arrange them in too many ways. Ask simple questions of those data. This is not to suggest that you should analyze the data to the point of virtually guaranteeing yourself a Type I error. But sometimes, simple questions, naive approaches, will afford you startling insights. Have you thought of plotting the data? What has caused the plotted data to peak? to reach a plateau? to dip or plummet? Do dynamics within the data have relevance to events that lie beyond them? Questions like these may sometimes crack the shell of the data and reveal the meaning within.

At the same time, a researcher must not go *too* far beyond the data. Beginning researchers often lose sight of what they have actually found; so enthusiastic are they about their topic that they make extravagant claims and unwarranted inferences. As an example, one of us authors once sat on a doctoral dissertation committee for a student who had been studying the use of regional dialects in children's literature. Although the student drew many appropriate conclusions from her data, one of her conclusions was that literature that incorporates a regional dialect can help children develop "an understanding and acceptance of sociocultural groups other than their own." The student had collected no data whatsoever about children who were reading such literature, let alone data specifically related to their understanding and acceptance of diverse sociocultural groups. The student's "conclusion" was, in reality, merely her strongly held conviction about the value of literature written in various dialects, and she should have presented it as such.

Research is indeed an exciting quest, but researchers must never let their enthusiasm influence their objectivity in interpreting and drawing conclusions from the data. The answer to the research question should rest solidly and completely on its own empirical foundation.

Look the data steadfastly in the face. Report honestly what those data reveal to you. Ferret out every conclusion you have drawn, underscore it in red, and then be sure that the data in the tables, graphs, and other exhibits solidly support what those words underlined in red declare. That is good research.

What if the data don't support your predictions? Does this mean your hypotheses were wrong? Not necessarily. Look once again at your methodology and statistical analyses to see if you can identify one or more weaknesses in what you have done. Perhaps one of your measurement instruments had lower validity or reliability than you had anticipated and so was not yielding accurate and dependable measures of a critical variable in your study. Perhaps you gave participants misleading instructions or asked them misleading questions. Perhaps your statistical analyses lacked power (maybe your sample was too small or your measures too unreliable) and so you made a Type II error. You should report any weaknesses and flaws in your study that may have influenced its outcome.

At the same time, maybe your hypotheses *were* wrong. In the interest of advancing the frontiers of knowledge, you must be sufficiently objective to admit when your thinking was flawed and offer reasonable explanations—perhaps in the form of alternative hypotheses that future research efforts might test—for the results that you obtained.

In the last analysis, *the data must speak for themselves*. The researcher is only the mouthpiece. You may not like what the data say. They may not confirm your fondest hopes or support your preconceived opinions, but the researcher is the servant of the scientific method. That method looks at evidence squarely and without prejudice; it reports candidly and precisely what the impersonal data affirm.

Defending one's research effort is an academic tradition. *Defend* in this sense means "to justify one's conclusions, to support one's statements with the backing of solid data that have been presented in the document." Nothing short of this will suffice.

CONCLUDING THE REPORT

Any research report should end by bringing closure to the interpretation of the data. In a thesis or dissertation, this discussion is often in a separate section or chapter entitled "Summary, Conclusions, and Recommendations."

In this section, all loose threads should be gathered together. This is the place for looking backward, for distilling into a few paragraphs precisely what has been accomplished in each phase of the research activity. One should be able to see the research endeavor as through the wrong end of a telescope: clearly, in miniature, with all significant aspects brought together in proper perspective. Here the researcher should clearly summarize the findings and conclusions pertaining to the problem and the subproblems. The conclusions should be entirely supported by the data presented. Then, the researcher is ready for three final steps: (a) stating whether the hypotheses have been supported or not, (b) identifying possible practical implications of the results, and (c) making recommendations for additional study, perhaps in those areas related to the problem that, during the research, the researcher recognized as worthy of further investigation.

A few words should be said about summaries. The whole research project—the problem, the data and their organization, the relationships and interrelationships—is so clear in the mind of the researcher that he or she may forget that the reader is not so intimately acquainted with the project. Through lengthy and intensive involvement in a study, the researcher has an acute awareness of the master plan, the relation of each component to the total study, the parts as they fit into the whole. Readers, however, are not so fortunate. As they proceed through the report, they need to stop occasionally to consider how the text fits into the total investigation.

To facilitate readers' "journey" through a research report, a good researcher provides regular guideposts in the form of headings, transitional words and paragraphs, and other means of helping readers follow the train of thought. But in addition, the researcher provides a summary at the close of each extended discussion. By pausing long enough to summarize what has been happening and what relevance such discussion has to the overall research effort, the researcher maintains the unity of the whole. Doing so is tantamount to helping readers keep their eyes on the goalpost when, in the frenzy of the game, they need orientation and reference points. Discussions that ramble on and on tend to produce psychological numbness, bewilderment, and confusion. Frequent summaries prevent such reader disorientation.

A GRAPHIC ORGANIZER FOR THE RESEARCH REPORT

One exercise that could prove valuable to the writer of a research report is to visualize the overall framework of the report. What is central can thus be distinguished from what is peripheral; what is basic, from what is ancillary. A good writer never leaves the reader in doubt as to what is happening during the discussion.

At the end of Chapter 1 is a figure showing the cyclical nature of research. We now incorporate this cyclical nature into a graphic organizer, depicted in Figure 12.1. Let's think of the research problem as metaphorically covering a certain "area" of investigation. The subproblems (we'll assume we have three) may each cover a significant portion of the area occupied by the problem. In the figure, the main dynamics of the research effort take place in a more or less vertical system of activity localized under the area that indicates the "spread" of the problem.

The dotted lines in the figure encompass things that are essential to any research activity. At the top is the area of the research problem; at the bottom is the realm of the data where the potential for solving the problem lies. In vertical paths that originate in the problem, but principally in the subproblem areas, is the research activity itself. This activity passes through and is focused in the direction of the data by the hypotheses. The activity loop contains two types of energy: *efferent,* the activity that originates in the researcher and in the problem area and that flows out toward the realm of the data in search of the evidence; and *afferent,* the return flow on the opposite side of the loop that is the data-bearing dynamic in the system. This flow returns to the

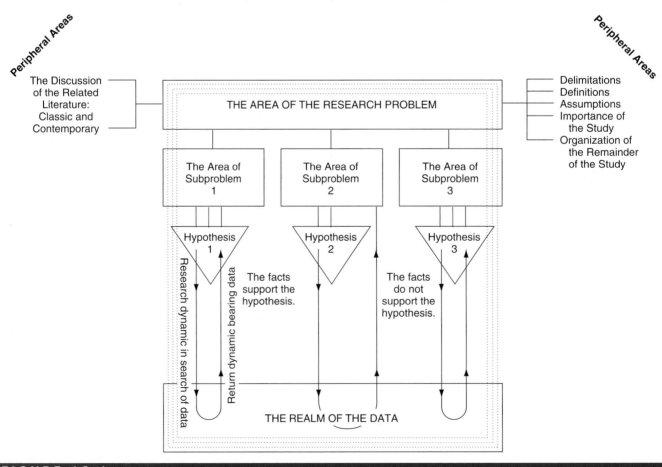

FIGURE 12.1

A framework for a research report

area of the subproblem. If the data have supported the hypothesis, they pass through the hypothesis itself. If they have not supported the hypothesis, they miss it entirely in returning to the subproblem. In the framework presented in Figure 12.1, the data support the hypotheses related to Subproblems 1 and 3; they do not support the hypothesis related to Subproblem 2.

Peripheral to the problem—and outside the dotted lines—lie other items whose principal function is to throw light on the problem by delimiting the extent of its boundaries, explaining the meaning of its terms, presenting the assumptions that the researcher has made, describing the importance and the relevance of the study, and outlining the remainder of the report organization. These matters help us understand the problem and research effort, but they are not an integral part of such matters.

The review of the related literature is one of these peripheral items that are in the problem *area* but are not an integral part of the problem. The literature discussion, though helpful in allowing us to see the problem under investigation in relation to previous studies, merely orients us within the total research environment. It does for us what a map does for the traveler.

FRONT MATTER AND END MATTER

In addition to the essential sections that we described earlier, many lengthy research reports, including theses and dissertations, also contain **front matter**—content that precedes the introductory first chapter—and **end matter**—content that follows the final chapter. We take a moment to describe this material briefly.

PRELIMINARY PAGES

The preliminary pages include all the introductory material that precedes the discussion of the research problem and study. The title page comes first; this also includes the author and, typically, a university affiliation and date. In a thesis or dissertation, the title page is followed by a page for signatures of the faculty advisor and research committee. Next are an abstract, a page for the dedication (if any), an acknowledgment of indebtedness to those who have assisted in the research, a table of contents, lists of any tables and figures, and, if desired, a preface.

In some instances, copyright information is included on the title page or the page immediately after it. **Copyright** is the protection given by law to the authors of literary, dramatic, musical, artistic, and other intellectual works. In the United States, this is U.S. Code, Title 17. Under the current U.S. law, which took effect in 1978, copyright protection lasts for 50 years following the author's death and is not renewable. A thesis or dissertation is protected by copyright law even if you do not register it with the United States Copyright Office. Nevertheless, registering it often provides reassurance and piece of mind. As of January 2003, the fee for filing a research report with the copyright office is $30. For more information, write to:

Copyright Office
Library of Congress
Washington, DC 20540

or go to the Copyright Office's Website at:

http://www.loc.gov/copyright/

An attorney working in the field of intellectual property, Benedict O'Mahoney, also provides a good overview of copyright basics at The Copyright Website:

http://www.benedict.com/

The **abstract** provides a summary of the entire research effort in a paragraph or two. For a journal article, the length of the abstract is usually 100 to 200 words, depending on the journal. For a dissertation, the abstract should be 350 words or less. The abstract should include sufficient information about the research problem, methodology, results, and interpretations to give potential readers an idea as to whether the study addresses a topic of concern to them and therefore merits their further attention. Remember, the abstract you write is likely to be included in one or more abstract collections (e.g., *Dissertation Abstracts International* or a published collection of abstracts specific to your academic discipline) that then become available at many research libraries around the world. It is essential, therefore, that you take seriously the task of writing the abstract and describe your project as clearly, precisely, and succinctly as you possibly can.

The **acknowledgments** page graciously recognizes the assistance of those through whose kindness the research effort has been possible. These people may include those who introduced the researcher to data sources that aided in completing the research or those who guided the study and gave counsel or support—perhaps an academic dissertation committee, a faithful typist and proofreader, and family members who encouraged and assisted in the research effort. The guild mark of education is to say thank you to those who have given their time and assistance to support your efforts and aspirations. The acknowledgments page is the proper place for the expression of such indebtedness.

The remainder of the front matter indicates the content and organization of the text. The most important of this material is the **table of contents.** The table of contents is a bird's-eye view of what the document contains, how it is organized, and where each part can be found. Following the main table of contents are often two more specific ones, one for the tables and another for the figures that appear throughout the report.

ENDNOTES AND FOOTNOTES

Generally, **endnotes** (appearing at the end of the text), which sometimes instead appear as **footnotes** at the bottom of relevant pages within the text itself, are used for three purposes. First, as seen in the sample dissertation at the end of Chapter 8, they are sometimes used to indicate sources of information and ideas; use of footnotes for this purpose depends on the style manual adhered to. Second, they may supplement information in the text of the report with additional information that strengthens the discussion. This type of note should be used sparingly and should not be used to explain complicated concepts. Keep such notes short and to the point. If you find your endnotes or footnotes becoming overly long and involved, sharpen your ideas and integrate them into the body of the report.

Third, endnotes and footnotes are occasionally used to acknowledge permission to quote or reproduce something from a copyrighted document. When you quote extensively or use a table or other graphic representation from a copyrighted work in a report you intend to publish or distribute widely, you must secure permission to reprint the material (in writing) from the owner of the copyright (the publisher or author). After you use the material, an endnote or footnote (rather than a citation) may be used to indicate the exact source from which the material was taken, followed by the words "Reprinted by permission of the publisher (or author)" or other wording stipulated by the copyright holder.

REFERENCE LIST

A reference list at the end of your report allows readers to locate and use the sources you have cited. For this reason, it is imperative that reference information be complete (e.g., it should include *all* of your citations) and accurate. Each reference entry should contain information about the author, year of publication, title of the work, and publication information.

To some extent, people in different academic disciplines format their reference lists differently, and you should follow the format that your institution or your discipline requires. Furthermore, you should apply that format consistently throughout your reference list.

One widely used style is that of the American Psychological Association (APA). APA style is described in detail in the association's *Publication Manual* (2001). We illustrate this format in Figure 12.2, which presents an excerpt from the reference list of Jackson's (1996) dissertation. Note, however, that Jackson <u>underlined</u> rather than *italicized* book titles and the names and volume numbers of journals. Underlining was widely used when research reports were typed on a typewriter rather than on a word processor. As use of word processing becomes almost universal, universities, publishing houses, and style manuals (including the 2001 edition of APA's

Jonassen, D. H., Beissner, K., & Yacci, M. (1993). Structural knowledge: Techniques for representing, conveying, and acquiring structural knowledge. Hillsdale, NJ: Erlbaum.

Kardash, C. M., & Amlund, J. T. (1991). Self-reported learning strategies and learning from expository text. Contemporary Educational Psychology, 16, 117–138.

Keppel, G. (1982). Design and analysis: A researcher's handbook (2nd ed.). Upper Saddle River, NJ: Prentice Hall.

Kiewra, K. A. (1985a). Learning from a lecture: An investigation of notetaking, review, and attendance at a lecture. Human Learning, 4, 73–77.

Kiewra, K. A. (1985b). Students' notetaking behaviors and the efficacy of providing the instructor's notes for review. Contemporary Educational Psychology, 10, 378–386.

Kiewra, K. A., Dennison, R. S., & Benton, S. L. (1995, April). How studying text supplements affects prose production. Paper presented at the annual meeting of the American Educational Research Association, San Francisco.

Kiewra, K. A., & Fletcher, H. J. (1984). The relationship between notetaking variables and achievement measures. Human Learning, 3, 273–280.

Publication Manual) are increasingly accepting italics in research report manuscripts. Before using italics, however, check with the institution or publisher to which you are submitting your report to be sure they are acceptable.

Let's briefly look at how entries in an APA-style reference list are formatted with respect to author, date, title, and publication information. We'll then consider additional information required for sources obtained on the Internet.

AUTHOR.   In an APA-style reference list, the author's name appears with the surname first, followed by the author's first and middle initials. When multiple authors are involved, the names are separated by commas. For example, the first and last references in Figure 12.2 have three and two authors, respectively. Commas are always used between the names (even between only two names), and an ampersand (&) is used before the last name in the list.

DATE OF PUBLICATION.   Following the author's name is the year of publication, in parentheses, followed by a period. Magazines, newsletters, newspapers, and presentations also include the month (and, when necessary to pin down the particular source, the day).

In Figure 12.2, notice that there are two articles written by Kiewra that were published in 1985. These have been listed alphabetically by article title, and the two articles are distinguished by designating the years as "1985a" and "1985b." Any citations in the text would then be either "Kiewra, 1985a" or "Kiewra, 1985b."

TITLE OF THE WORK.   In APA style, the title of the article, book, or other source follows the publication year. If you are referencing an article using APA style, the title of the article is *not* italicized or underlined, but the title of the journal in which it appears *is* (see, for example, the reference for Kardash and Amlund in Figure 12.2). The title of a book is always italicized or underlined. So, too, is the title of a paper presentation (see the reference for Kiewra, Dennison, and Benton) or doctoral dissertation.

Be sure to pay attention to the rules for capitalization in whatever style manual you are using. Can you determine what APA's rules are from the entries in the sample? Did you notice that the first word in a book, article, or presentation title is the only one capitalized (unless the word is a proper noun or proper adjective or it follows a colon) but that all the words of a journal title are capitalized?

PUBLICATION INFORMATION.   For journal articles, publication information usually includes the volume number (which is underlined or italicized), issue, and page numbers. (If separate issues within each volume begin with sequentially numbered pages—for example, if the first issue of a particular volume ends on page 96 and the second issue begins on page 97—then the issue number can be omitted.) Publication information for a book includes the city of publication and the publishing company. In the case of a paper presented at a conference, the name of the conference and its location are provided.

Notice how this information is formatted in the sample entries in Figure 12.2. All redundancy is eliminated; there are no extra words such as *volume*, *issue*, and *pages*. By their specific location in the citation, readers understand their meaning. This practice eliminates many extra words; such a reduction means fewer manuscript pages, which translates into lower printing costs.

Notice, too, that references to a publisher are short and succinct, excluding such words as *Publishing Company* and *Publishers, Inc.* These words add no new information and thus can be eliminated.

USING
TECHNOLOGY

REFERENCING SOURCES OBTAINED ON THE INTERNET.   Sources found on the Internet require additional information, typically including the Internet address (URL) and date on which the information was obtained. For example, in APA style, an article in an online journal would be referenced using the following format:

> Amrein, A. L., & Berliner, D. C. (2002, March 28). High-stakes testing, uncertainty, and student learning. Education Policy Analysis Archives, 10(18). Retrieved April 9, 2002, from http://epaa.asu.edu/epaa/v10n18/.

Information found on a public or private organization's Web site—in this case, one that has no specific date attached—would be referenced using this format:

> Autism Society of America (n.d.). What is autism? Retrieved May 28, 2003, from http://www. autism-society.org/site/PageServer.

The "n.d." in parentheses in the preceding reference means that the document cited has no date, year or otherwise, associated with it.

APPENDIX CONTENT

Following the main report may be supplementary **appendices** (also pluralized as *appendixes*) that may be helpful in understanding the research study more completely but are not absolutely essential to the comprehension of the body of the report. A rule of thumb is that *the material appearing in the appendix enables one to go further with the document, if that is so desired.* For instance, an appendix may include informed consent letters, questionnaires and other measurement instruments, response sheets, field notes, statistical computations, or extensive data tables.

In reporting research, nothing is hidden. All the data are laid before the reader. The researcher's integrity is thereby preserved, and the results and conclusions of the study can be readily verified.

ORGANIZING THE RESEARCH REPORT

Research reports for most quantitative studies are similar in their organizational format. After their preliminary pages (title page, acknowledgments, table of contents, etc.), they typically have five major sections: an introduction (which includes the statement of the problem, assumptions, definitions of terms, etc.), a review of the related literature, a description of the methodology, a discussion of results, and conclusions (including implications and suggestions for future research). They will, of course, also have a list of references and, sometimes, one or more appendices.

Reports of qualitative studies are less predictable, and their specific organization may be highly dependent on the nature and design of the studies themselves.

As illustrations, we present the outlines for two of the dissertations from which we've presented excerpts in previous chapters. The first is a traditional outline, used for a quantitative, quasi-experimental study; the second is less traditional, used for a qualitative, grounded theory study. In the interest of space, we omit any subheadings that appear under the major headings.

Effects of Training in Self-Generation on the Quality of Students' Questions, Class Notes and Examination Scores (Jackson, 1996)

Front Matter
Copyright Notice
Title Page
Signature Page
Abstract
Acknowledgments
Table of Contents
List of Tables
List of Figures

Body of the Report
Chapter I.   INTRODUCTION
                Statement of the Problem
                Purpose of the Study
                Research Questions and Hypotheses
                Limitations of the Study
                Definitions and Terms
Chapter II.   REVIEW OF THE LITERATURE
                Part I: Adjunct Questioning Research
                Part II: Self-Generated Questioning Theories and Models
                Part III: Note-Taking
                Summary
Chapter III.   METHOD
                Synopsis of the Pilot Study
                Comparison of the Pilot Study with the Present Study
                Subjects
                Materials and Procedures
                Examinations
                Maintaining Confidentiality
                Criteria for Coding Data
Chapter IV.   RESULTS
                Hypothesis One
                Hypothesis Two
                Hypothesis Three
                Hypothesis Four
                Hypothesis Five
                Summary
Chapter V.   DISCUSSION
                Study Design Based on Contemporary Literature
                Review of the Findings
                Other Findings
                Limitations
                Educational Implications
                Future Research
                Summary and Conclusions

End Matter
References
Appendix A: Sample Test Questions

Appendix B: Table of Specifications for Unit 2
Appendix C: Sample of Questions from Treatment Group
Appendix D: Sample of Questions from Control Group
Appendix E: Syllabus with Initial Training Handout
Appendix F: Mid-semester Training Handbook for Treatment Group
Appendix G: Mid-semester Training Handbook for Control Group
Appendix H: Question Coding Form
Appendix I: Sample Page of Notes from Treatment Group
Appendix J: Sample Page of Notes from Control Group
Appendix K: Note Coding Form

Uncovering the Conceptual Representations of Students with Reading Disabilities (Zambo, 2003)

Front Matter
Title Page
Signature Page
Abstract
Acknowledgements
Table of Contents
List of Tables
List of Figures

Body of the Report
Chapter I.   REVIEW OF THE LITERATURE
              Introduction [here the author presents the research problem]
              Conceptual Representations
              The Relationship Between Representation and Student Outcomes
              Evidence-Based Models of Reading
Chapter II.   METHODOLOGY
              Research Standards
              Pilot Study
              Design of the Study
              Data Analysis and Reporting of Data
Chapter III. TEXT, CONTEXT, AND METACOGNITION
              Introduction
              Reasons and Context for Reading
              The Reading Process
              The Knowledge of Memory Strategies
Chapter IV.   AFFECTIVE AND MOTIVATIONAL FACTORS OF THE READER
              Reflections, Present Situation, and Future Expectations
              Motivation
              Theory of Intelligence and Epistemological Views
              The Teacher's Views of the Students as Readers
Chapter V.   DYSLEXIA AND THE DYSLEXIC BRAIN
              Thinking About the Brain
Chapter VI.   CONCLUSIONS AND FUTURE DIRECTIONS
              Future Directions

End Matter
References
Appendix A: Teacher Interview Questions
Appendix B: Alignment Between Research Questions and Student Interview
              Questions
Appendix C: Sample of Student Questions and Activities
Appendix D: Sample Drawings Completed by the Students
Appendix E: Internal Review Board Approval Letter and Permission to Copy Ruddell and
              Unrau's Model from the International Reading Association

PREPARING THE REPORT

The research report is precisely that—*a report*. The researcher is reporting on what he or she has done over the course of the research effort. In the process, the researcher is acquainting the reader with the problem, the data brought to bear upon the resolution of the problem, the means employed in gathering those data, the processes of analysis to which they were submitted, and the conclusions reached.

STYLE OF PROSE

As noted earlier in the chapter, different academic disciplines and different style manuals have different standards with regard to style. For instance, the American Psychological Association (2001) prefers that authors write in *active voice* ("Smith interviewed the participants") rather than *passive voice* ("The participants were interviewed by Smith"). It also recommends that *past tense* be used for the literature review, the description of research methods, and the presentation of the results. When interpreting the results and presenting the conclusions, however, *present tense* is appropriate. If you are using a word processor, the grammar checker in your software may allow you to check for inconsistencies in your use of active versus passive voice or past versus present tense.

Although writing in the third person ("The researcher analyzed the data") was the preferred style only a few years ago, this practice has begun to change. For example, the APA *Publication Manual* (2001) describes the use of the third person as "ambiguous" and indicates that this usage may give the impression that you did not take part in your own study. Use of first person ("I analyzed the data") is thought to increase readability, and many journal editors now request that articles be written in this style. Whichever style you use, however, it is critical that your point of view remain consistent throughout the article. Check the "guidelines for authors" section of the journals in your discipline to determine the recommended approach.

Along these same lines, APA now recommends that any people in your study be referred to in a more personal manner than with the generic term *subjects*. Use such words as *participants*, *individuals*, *students*, or *respondents*. Again, active voice is recommended ("The participants completed the survey," as opposed to "The participants were given the survey").

PRINCIPLES OF WRITING

Remember that your report *is* you. It is also a powerful psychological weapon. Whether or not you intend it to do so, a report can say more about you to your reader than you can possibly imagine. It reveals the inner you and, from that standpoint, sends a message about what is vitally important to the acceptance of your research.

In preparing your report, therefore, three cardinal principles are requisite: (a) neatness and clarity, (b) precision, and (c) logical structure.

Neatness and Clarity

Your pages should be easy to read, with double-spaced lines and clean, crisp letters. In addition, whether you use a personal computer, word processor, or manual typewriter, you should format the text in a consistent manner, setting tabs for paragraph indents, bulleted lists, and the like, and setting the margins to control for line and page length. Word processing software also allows you to insert footnotes that will appear on the appropriate pages and create tables that present numbers and text in perfect columns.

The way you set your words onto paper, however, is much more than moving your fingers over the keyboard. Most important is that you express your thoughts clearly and logically. Show how your data resolve your subproblems and how the subproblems resolve the main problem. Such tactics provide evidence that you have approached the entire research endeavor in a thoughtful and systematic manner.

Such things—some little, some more consequential—leave lasting impressions.

Precision

In addition to neatness and clarity, a research report must be crisp with precision. There is no place in it for "sort-of's" and "I-guess-so's." This is not the time for ambiguous or foggy terms or half-stated conclusions. Your document should be clean-cut and present its ideas in a straightforward manner.

Every fact has its precise place within the research report structure. You may remember the weeks, the months, perhaps the years ago when you garnered a particular datum or cluster of data related to your study. You did not gather these as a child gathers wildflowers in a field—willy-nilly, without a guiding purpose. You gathered each datum because you envisioned it as a single building block that would support and advance the basic intent of all research: to enlighten a corner of the darkness related to a specific problem. We have come almost full circle, close to the place this book began. Everything you have done has been for a single purpose: to take one problem, one atom of darkness in human experience, and cause it to glow with the light of data and interpretation, crisply and precisely.

Logical Structure

A neat, clear, and precise report builds upon the basic structure of your original research proposal. You may have wondered why we have recommended that you be so fastidious and particular in drafting a research proposal. Our purpose has been to discipline your thinking and help you construct a logical plan upon which you could later build a clear, logical research report.

This construction of both a research plan and a report cannot be done haphazardly. The steps you take toward resolving a problem must be as ordered as the steps you would take emerging from a cave toward a blaze of clear sky and sunny landscape. Every step must progress logically toward cracking open the shell of the enigma you chose at the beginning as the goal of your quest. You may understand better now why we entitled Chapter 3 "The Problem: The Heart of the Research Process."

Thus, after you have written several pages of your research report, go back and read your headings and subheadings. Do they form a logical whole? Do the various levels of heads accurately depict how different sections of text are interrelated? For instance, do they appropriately show that some sections are smaller subparts of other, larger sections?

Are the headings as progressive as the steps of one who is emerging from a cave? They should be. Recall the *inverted pyramid* idea in Chapter 4, "Review of the Related Literature." There, we counseled you to "begin your discussion . . . from a comprehensive perspective, like an inverted pyramid—broad end first. Then, as you proceed, you can deal with more specific ideas and studies and focus in more and more on your own particular [central research] problem."

That is logic in practice. Logic comes from the Greek word *logos*, which means "reason, order, speech, word." Think of your research proposal as a skeleton that holds the body of the report together, the framework on which everything else depends. Now, adorn that skeleton with meat: clear, convincing data. March through each of your subproblems, laying datum upon datum, with as deliberate a precision as a mason cements masonry blocks in a skyscraper's wall. Reason, order, and data, carefully placed and cemented by the precise word, are the logic of the research report.

PRACTICAL APPLICATION DEVELOPING A WRITING SCHEDULE

Make no mistake about it, writing a research report, and especially writing one *well*, takes considerable time and effort. A research report is not something you can whip up in a few days' time. In the case of a lengthy report, such as a dissertation, you should plan on taking not several days, not several weeks, but several *months* to complete the report-writing process.

We know of too many sad cases in which aspiring doctoral students have completed all the required coursework for their doctoral degrees, passed their written and oral comprehensive exams with flying colors, gotten their dissertation proposals approved, collected and analyzed their data, and then become "stuck" indefinitely in the process of writing their final dissertations. Some never become unstuck: They never finish their dissertations and so never receive their doctoral degree. Such a waste, we think! And so unnecessary!

To help you start *and finish* a lengthy research report—to grease your wheels and keep them greased so that you don't get stuck somewhere along the way—we offer two pieces of advice. First, *develop a reasonable writing schedule for yourself.* Second, *stick to it!* The guidelines that follow can help you do both of these things.

GUIDELINES   DEVELOPING A WORKABLE SCHEDULE

At this point, we urge you to go back and review the Practical Application "Writing Your Proposal" in Chapter 6. Many of the guidelines in "Writing the First Draft" and "Revising Your Proposal" are equally relevant to writing a final research report.

We now offer several additional suggestions as well. These have emerged from our own experiences writing research reports (including our own doctoral dissertations) and other lengthy documents (including this textbook!).

1. *Identify small, easily accomplishable goals within the overall project.* A large research report, such as a dissertation, will seem less overwhelming if you break it down into small, manageable pieces. These pieces might have such labels as "revision of the methods section," "data analysis related to the first subproblem," "implications section," or "suggestions for future research." Make each piece small enough that you can complete it within a week's time or less.

2. *Set reasonable target dates for achieving each goal.* We strongly emphasize the word *reasonable* here. To get an idea of how much you can write in any given day or week, think about how long it has taken you to finish other lengthy writing projects. For instance, how long did it take you to complete your research proposal? How many pages could you write, and write *well*, in a day? (For instance, one of us authors has learned from experience that she can usually write, at most, about 8 to 10 double-spaced manuscript pages a day. After that, she's essentially "brain dead" until the following morning.)

Consider personal matters when you establish your schedule. Do you have a part-time or full-time job to consider? Do you have responsibilities to other family members that will take some of your time and energy? Have you built in adequate time for health and fitness, meals, shopping, home and car repairs, and occasional relaxation? You need to "get real" about how much you can accomplish, as well as how fast you can accomplish it, with respect to your writing project. Otherwise you will never stick to your schedule; you will be doomed to failure before you even start.

3. *Reward yourself each time you reach one of your goals.* Give yourself a "treat" of some sort after you successfully finish each piece of your report. Go to a movie, read a short novel, clean the house, surf the Internet—whatever you need to do to get refreshed and ready to tackle the next goal on your schedule.

4. *Seek regular feedback.* We've said it before and we'll say it again: Ask others to give you honest feedback about what you say and how clearly you say it. Honest feedback now may save you more serious criticism—and, we might add, it will save you considerable aggravation and heartache—later on.

5. *Build time into your schedule for at least two or three revisions.* Most research reports are reviewed by others before they ever see the light of day. A committee of university faculty looks closely at any thesis or dissertation. An editorial review board carefully scrutinizes any manuscript submitted to a professional journal. The review process ensures that all approved research reports meet basic standards of scholarship, accuracy, and scientific rigor.

In the case of dissertations, *we have yet to see a report that has not had to undergo at least two revisions.* In fact, a doctoral student often completes four or five rewrites before defending a dissertation before his or her doctoral committee. Let's face it: The researcher is very close to his or her research project and, at the end, is equally close to the report that he or she has written about the project. So close, sometimes, that omissions, errors, and logical inconsistencies that may be blatantly obvious to others are not at all obvious to the researcher. Furthermore, other people may have useful ideas about better ways to organize a discussion, suggestions about additional statistical analyses that may shed further light on the data, or new sources of literature that may be relevant to unexpected findings. The recommendations that others make, and the revisions that occur as a result of them, have one primary purpose: to make a research report the very best it can possibly be.

Furthermore, you must remember that any report bearing a stamp of approval from other individuals—whether that "stamp" takes the form of the signatures of a doctoral committee or the publication of a report in a scholarly journal—reflects not only on the author of the report but also on those who have approved the report. A poorly written research report makes a lot of people look bad.

The final stages of the writing project, especially the revisions, may seem to go on interminably. But persist! You have expended a great deal of time and effort in conducting your research project, and perhaps others have devoted considerable time and effort to it as well. It is only by completing your report that your project will ultimately contribute to the world's knowledge about the topic you have studied.

PRACTICAL APPLICATION   Critiquing a Research Report

Cheryl Beck (1990) has developed a list of insightful questions that every researcher should answer satisfactorily before submitting a final version of a research report. Although she created it for students and professional colleagues in the field of nursing, we have adapted her list of questions to apply to research report writers in general. The following checklist should both help you evaluate the reports you read and serve as a guide as you assess your own writing.

✔ CHECKLIST
CRITERIA FOR CRITIQUING A RESEARCH REPORT

STEP 1. THE PROBLEM

		YES	NO
_____	Is the problem clearly and concisely stated?	____	____
_____	Is the problem adequately narrowed down into a researchable problem?	____	____
_____	Is the problem significant enough to warrant a formal research effort?	____	____
_____	Is the relationship between the identified problem and previous research clearly described?	____	____

STEP 2. LITERATURE REVIEW

_____	Is the literature review logically organized?	____	____
_____	Does the review provide a critique of the relevant studies?	____	____
_____	Are gaps in knowledge about the research problem identified?	____	____
_____	Are important relevant references included?	____	____

STEP 3. THEORETICAL OR CONCEPTUAL FRAMEWORK

| _____ | Is the theoretical framework easily linked with the problem (or does it seem forced)? | ____ | ____ |
| _____ | If a conceptual framework is used, are the concepts adequately defined, and are the relationships among these concepts clearly identified? | ____ | ____ |

Step 4. Research Variables

_____   Are the independent and dependent variables operationally defined?   ____ ____

_____   Are any confounding variables present? If so, are they identified?   ____ ____

Step 5. Hypotheses

_____   Are the hypotheses clear, testable, and specific?   ____ ____

_____   Does each hypothesis describe a predicted relationship between
                two or more variables included in each hypothesis?   ____ ____

_____   Do the hypotheses logically flow from the theoretical or
                conceptual framework?   ____ ____

Step 6. Sampling

_____   Is the sample size adequate?   ____ ____

_____   Is the sample representative of the defined population?   ____ ____

_____   Is the method for selection of the sample appropriate?   ____ ____

_____   Is any sampling bias in the chosen method acknowledged?   ____ ____

_____   Are the criteria for selecting the sample clearly identified?   ____ ____

Step 7. Research Design

_____   Is the research design adequately described?   ____ ____

_____   Is the design appropriate for the research problem?   ____ ____

_____   Does the research design address issues related to the internal
                and external validity of the study?   ____ ____

Step 8. Data Collection Methods

_____   Are the data collection methods appropriate for the study?   ____ ____

_____   Are the data collection instruments described adequately?   ____ ____

_____   Do the measurement tools have reasonable validity and reliability?   ____ ____

Step 9. Data Analysis

_____   Is the results section clearly and logically organized?   ____ ____

_____   Is the type of analysis appropriate for the level of measurement
                for each variable?   ____ ____

_____   Are the tables and figures clear and understandable?   ____ ____

_____   Is the statistical test the correct one for answering the research question? ____ ____

Step 10. Interpretation and Discussion of the Findings

_____   Does the investigator clearly distinguish between actual findings
                and interpretations?   ____ ____

_____   Are the interpretations based on the data obtained?   ____ ____

_____   Are the findings discussed in relation to previous research and
                to the conceptual/theoretical framework?   ____ ____

_____   Are all generalizations warranted and defended?   ____ ____

	Are the limitations of the results identified?		
_____	Are the limitations of the results identified?	_____	_____
_____	Are implications of the results discussed?	_____	_____
_____	Are recommendations for future research identified?	_____	_____
_____	Are the conclusions justified?	_____	_____

BEYOND THE UNPUBLISHED RESEARCH REPORT: PRESENTING AND PUBLISHING

If you have completed an unpublished research report, such as a master's thesis or doctoral dissertation, consider this: In most cases, only a few people will ever read your report in its current form. If your research project has uncovered new information, new ideas, and new understandings that can make a significant contribution to the world's body of knowledge about a particular topic, then we urge you to seek a broader audience. Two excellent ways to do this are paper presentations and journal articles.

PAPER PRESENTATIONS

Many researchers present their research findings at regional, national, or international conferences. Some conferences are annual meetings sponsored by societies related to particular academic disciplines (e.g., American Sociological Association, Modern Language Association, American Educational Research Association). Others are more specific to particular interest areas (e.g., family violence, Piaget's theory of child development). The organizers of many of these conferences eagerly seek presentations (often called *papers*) from new researchers as well as from more experienced ones.

If you would like to present a paper at a professional conference, you will, in most cases, need to submit a *paper proposal* several months in advance to the association or institution sponsoring the conference. These proposals are usually much shorter than the research proposals described in Chapter 6. Furthermore, their purpose is different: You are submitting a proposal to present a research project that you either (a) have already completed or (b) are currently conducting but will definitely have completed before the conference.

Proposals for paper presentations are often only two or three pages in length. Their specific format varies considerably from one professional group to another, and we urge you to consult the *call for papers* that invites proposals for conference presentations. Regardless of the format, one thing is true for all paper proposals: They need to be written with the same clarity and academic rigor required for any research proposal or research report.

The paper presentations themselves may also be quite different from one another, depending on the conference; the many forms they may take are beyond the scope of this book. As you prepare for your first presentation, the best advice we can give you is to ask friends and colleagues who have previously presented papers at a particular conference for guidance and advice.

JOURNAL ARTICLES

An even more effective, and certainly more permanent, way to disseminate your findings and ideas is to submit a research report to an academic journal. The guidelines we have presented in this book should get you well on your way to writing a manuscript for submission to a research journal, but there is one further point to keep in mind: *Be concise.* As a rule, journal space is at a premium, so journal editors have little tolerance for researchers who say in 100 words what they could have said in 10.

Before you submit a manuscript to a particular journal, read several recent issues of the journal to make sure it is the right place for your article. Determine whether the journal includes research reports, including reports about your general topic, among its articles. Also look at the style of writing that is typical in the journal; you will want to use a similar style in any manuscript you submit. And (forgive us for saying this one more time), seek critical feedback from others about your manuscript, including from people who have published in that journal or similar ones, and use their suggestions to revise and strengthen what you have written.

SHARING AUTHORSHIP

Whether you are presenting a paper or submitting a manuscript to a research journal, you must, of course, determine whether you should be sole author or share authorship with one or more other individuals. For instance, in the case of master's theses and doctoral dissertations, students often share authorship with their major advisors and perhaps with one or two other faculty members as well.

A general rule of thumb is this: *Individuals who have made significant intellectual contributions to the work should share in its authorship.* Typically, any coauthors have been actively involved in the conceptualization, design, execution, and/or analysis of the research project. Multiple authors are typically listed in an order indicating which individuals have made the most substantial contributions.

People who have assisted with data collection, coding, computer programming, statistical analysis, typing, and so on, but who have not contributed *intellectually* to the work, usually do not warrant authorship (Elliott & Stern, 1997). Nor do people who have reviewed a paper or manuscript and given their suggestions for how the author(s) might improve it. Such minor contributions are more appropriately acknowledged in a footnote or endnote.

Sharing authorship with others who have contributed in important ways to your research project and listing coauthors in an order that acknowledges their relative contributions are twists on the "honesty with professional colleagues" issue that we mentioned in our discussion of ethics in Chapter 5. Not only must researchers be honest with their colleagues about what they have done and what they have found, but they must also be honest about who has helped them with their research endeavors.

A CLOSING THOUGHT

As you prepare to write your research report, you might do well, if you are not sure what makes writing readable, to study two books: *The Elements of Style* (Strunk & White, 1995) and *The Art of Readable Writing* (Flesch, 1974). Eschew the exaggerated expression; look sharply at your ill-advised and thoughtlessly chosen adjectives. Stick to the facts. Report them accurately but, in so doing, enliven your prose with variety in sentence structure, sentence length, and precision of verb and noun.

More do's and don'ts are probably unnecessary and unwarranted. We leave you with this last thought. Distilled into a brief stanza by an anonymous hand is a broad guideline for all your writing. Follow it.

Now go to our Companion Website at http://www.prenhall.com/leedy to assess your understanding of chapter content and to complete the projects that will help you learn how to conduct research.

The written word
Should be clean as bone:
Clear as light,
Firm as stone;
Two words are not
As good as one.

FOR FURTHER READING

American Psychological Association (APA). (2001). *Publication manual of the American Psychological Association* (5th ed.). Washington, DC: Author.

Balian, E. S. (1994). *The graduate research guidebook: A practical approach to doctoral-master's research.* Lanham, MD: University Press of America.

Barclay, W. R. (Ed.). (1981). *Manual for authors and editors: Editorial style and manuscript preparation.* East Norwalk, CT: Appleton & Lange.

Barzun, J. (1994). *Simple and direct: A rhetoric for writers.* Chicago: University of Chicago Press.

Boice, R. (1993). Writing blocks and tacit knowledge. *Journal of Higher Education, 64* (1), 19–54.

Boice, R. (1995). Writerly rules for teachers. *Journal of Higher Education,* 66 (1), 32–60.

Chicago Manual of Style (15th ed.). (2003). Chicago: University of Chicago Press.

Day, R. A. (1994). *How to write and publish a scientific paper* (4th ed.). Phoenix, AZ: Oryx.

Day, R. A. (1995). *Scientific English: A guide for scientists and other professionals* (2nd ed.). Phoenix, AZ: Oryx.

Elliott, D., & Stern, J. E. (Eds.) (1997). *Research ethics: A reader.* Hanover, NH: University Press of New England.

Evans, D. (1996). *How to write a better thesis or report.* Concord, NH: Paul & Co.

Flesch, R., & Lass, A. H. (1989). *A new guide to better writing.* New York: Warner Books.

Ford, J. E. (Ed.). (1995). *Teaching the research paper: From theory to practice, from research to writing.* Metuchen, NJ: Scarecrow.

Gebremedhin, T. G., & Tweeten, L. G. (1994). *Research methods and communication in the social sciences.* Westport, CT: Praeger.

Gopen, G. D., & Swan, J. A. (1990). The science of scientific writing. *American Scientist, 78,* 550–558.

Hacker, D. (1999). *A writer's reference* (4th ed.) New York: Bedford/St. Martin's.

Hacker, D. (2000). *A pocket style manual* (3rd ed.). New York: Bedford/St. Martin's.

Hacker, D. (2002). *Research and documentation online.* New York: Bedford/St. Martin's.

Hacker, D. (2004). *Rules for writers* (5th ed.). New York: Bedford/St. Martin's.

Haensly, P. A., Lupkowski, A. E., & McNamara, J. F. (1987). The chart essay: A strategy for communicating research findings to policymakers and practitioners. *Educational Evaluation and Policy Analysis, 9,* 63–75.

Hegde, M. N. (1993). *A coursebook on scientific and professional writing in speech-language pathology.* San Diego, CA: Singular.

Henson, K. T. (1995). *The art of writing for publication.* Boston: Allyn & Bacon.

Hult, C. A. (1995). *Researching and writing in sciences and technology.* Boston: Allyn & Bacon.

Huth, E. J. (1994). *Scientific style and format: The CBE manual for authors, editors, and publishers* (6th ed.). New York: Cambridge University Press.

Lane, M. K., Lindenfelser, L. F., & Powell, G. B., Jr. (1993). *Style manual for political science* (Rev. ed.). Washington, DC: American Political Science Association.

Levin, J. R., & Marshall, H. H. (1993). Publishing in the Journal of Educational Psychology: Reflections at midstream. *Journal of Educational Psychology, 85,* 3–6.

Li, X., & Crane, N. B. (1996). *Electronic styles: A handbook for citing electronic information* (Rev. ed.). Medford, NJ: Information Today.

Locke, D. (1992). *Science as writing.* New Haven, CT: Yale University Press.

Madigan, R., Johnson, S., & Linton, P. (1995). The language of style: APA style as epistemology. *American Psychologist, 50,* 428–436.

Matthews, J. R., Bowen, J. M., & Matthews, R. W. (1996). *Successful scientific writing: A step-by-step guide for the biological and medical sciences.* New York: Cambridge University Press.

McQuain, J. (1996). *Power of language: Getting the most out of your words.* Boston: Houghton Mifflin.

Meloy, J. (1994). *Writing the qualitative dissertation: Understanding by doing.* Hillsdale, NJ: Erlbaum.

Moore, G. E. (1986). Approved practices in reporting quantitative research. *Journal of Vocational Education Research, 11,* 1–24.

Morris, D. (1994). *Guidelines for writing a qualitative research report.* Chicago: American Marketing Association.

National Information Standards Organization Staff. (1995). *Scientific and technical reports: Elements, organization, and design.* Bethesda, MD: National Information Standards Organization Press.

Nicol, A. A. M., & Pexman, P. M. (1999). *Presenting your findings: A practical guide for creating tables.* Washington, DC: American Psychological Association.

Ogden, E. (1993). *Completing your doctoral dissertation or master's thesis: In two semesters or less.* Lancaster, PA: Technomic.

Passmore, D. L. (1987). There is nothing so practical as good research. *Journal of Industrial Teacher Education, 24*(2), 7–14.

Rehart, M. J. (1993). *Writing business research reports: A guide to scientific writing.* Los Angeles: Pyrczak.

Shank, G. D. (2002). *Qualitative research: A personal skills approach.* Upper Saddle River, NJ: Merrill/Prentice Hall. [See Chapter 10]

Stafford, N. E. (1991). *A writer's workbook: Style and grammar.* San Diego: Harcourt Brace.

Tuckman, B. W. (1990). A proposal for improving the quality of published educational research. *Educational Researcher, 19*(9), 22–25.

Turk, C., & Kirkman, J. (1989). *Effective writing: Improving scientific, technical, and business communication* (2nd ed.). New York: Routledge, Chapman, & Hall.

U.S. Government Printing Office. (2000). *Style manual.* Washington DC: U.S. Government Printing Office.

Westmeyer, P. M. (1994). *A guide for use in planning, conducting, and reporting research projects* (2nd ed.). Springfield, IL: Charles C Thomas.

Wilkinson, A. (1991). *A scientist's handbook for writing papers and dissertations.* Upper Saddle River, NJ: Prentice Hall.

Wilkinson, L., & the Task Force on Statistic Inference. (1999). Statistical methods in psychology journals: Guidelines and explanations. *American Psychologist, 54,* 594–604. [Offers suggestions for writing a clear research report]

Wolcott, H. F. (1990). *Writing up qualitative research.* Thousand Oaks, CA: Sage.

Using SPSS

A complete explanation of how to use SPSS (an acronym for Statistical Package for the Social Sciences) is well beyond the scope of a short appendix. However, a brief explanation of some of the basics can get you started. The version of SPSS we describe is Student Version 11.0 for Windows.

CREATING A DATA SET

Once you have loaded SPSS onto the hard drive of your computer (see the directions that come with the program for details), open the program. On your screen you will see a two-dimensional table that looks very much like a spreadsheet. Each row in the table designates a specific individual (subject) in your data set. Each column designates a specific variable in the data set. This is the table that, once you fill it in, will provide the basis for your data analyses.

As an example, we use data from a pilot study that Dinah Jackson conducted in preparation for her dissertation study (excerpts from her dissertation appear in Chapter 2 and Chapter 12). The data include the following information for 15 students in a college psychology class: (1) their scores on the three exams given during the semester; (2) the total of the three exam scores; (3) the quantity (number of pages) of class notes they took during the semester; (4) the proportion of discrete items in the notes that reflected integration of two or more ideas rather than a single, isolated fact (this proportion—which was the result of a content analysis of the notes—was assumed to be an index of the *quality* of the notes, with higher numbers indicating greater integration, and hence better quality); and (5) their gender.

When we enter the data for the 15 students, we get the table in Figure A.1. We have 15 rows, one for each student in our sample. We have seven columns, representing the three exam scores, the total of these scores, the number of pages of notes, the proportion of high-quality notes, and the gender of each student (1 = male, 2 = female).

Notice how the seven columns have short labels that tell us what each variable is. To insert such labels, we go down to the bottom of the screen, where there are two "tabs" called "Data View" and "Variable View." If we move the cursor down and click on "Variable View," we get another table, which looks like Figure A.2. In this table, we have entered information about each of the variables in the data set. Here the variables are the rows (rather than the columns, as they are in the "Data" table), and things we want to say about the variables are the columns. In the interest of brevity, we describe only some of these columns:

The "Data" table

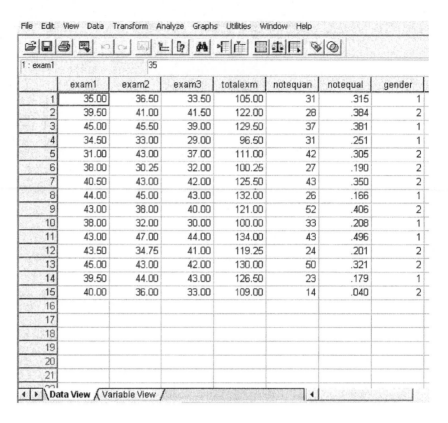

The "Variables" table

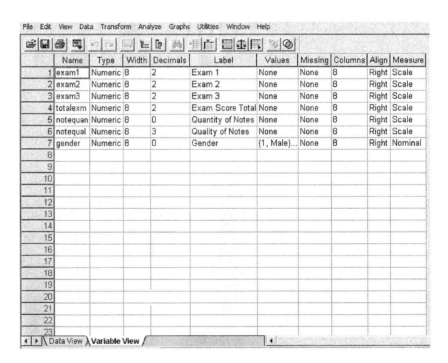

■ *Name:*   Indicates the label that will appear for the variable in the "Data View" table. This can be a maximum of eight characters, which may include lowercase letters and/or numbers.

■ *Type:*   Indicates the type of data the variable represents, perhaps a number (numeric data), a letter string, a dollar amount, a date, or something else altogether.

■ *Decimals:*   Indicates an upper limit on the number of digits that will appear to the right of a decimal point.

■ *Label:*   Indicates the labels that the variables will have when we create a table or graph.

■ *Values:*   Indicates labels that might be attached to particular values of a variable. For example, one of our variables is gender, a nominal scale. If we click on this cell, a little button appears at the right side of the cell. We click on the button, and a box appears that allows us to tell the computer that a value of 1 means "male" and a value of 2 means "female."

■ *Measure:*   Indicates whether the variable reflects a nominal scale ("nominal"), an ordinal scale ("ordinal"), or an interval or ratio scale ("scale").

As you can see in Figure A.2, our sample data set consists of six variables that are on an interval or ratio scale and a seventh that reflects a nominal scale.

COMPUTING BASIC DESCRIPTIVE STATISTICS

Now that we have our data set, let's conduct some simple analyses. First, let's compute basic descriptive statistics for the first six variables (computing a mean and standard deviation for the "gender" variable would, of course, be meaningless). We move the cursor to the word "Analyze" at the top of the screen and click on the mouse. A pull-down menu appears, and we move the mouse down until the word "Descriptive Statistics" is highlighted. Continuing to hold down the mouse button, we move the cursor toward the right, and another box appears. When we highlight the word "Descriptive," we release the mouse button. Yet another box appears in front of our data set. This box contains two smaller boxes, with all seven of our variables listed in the left box. To calculate descriptive statistics for the first six variables, we want to move them into the right box. We do this by highlighting each one and then clicking the right-arrow button between the two boxes. Figure A.3 shows how the screen will look after we've moved the appropriate six variables to the right-hand box.

Once we've moved these variables, we click on the "OK" button. At this point, a table appears that lists the number of observations (*N*), minimum and maximum values, mean, and standard deviation for each variable.

Now let's suppose that we want to see how exam performance, quantity of notes, and quality of notes are intercorrelated. To do this, we can calculate Pearson *r* correlation coefficients for each possible pairing of these three variables. Once again, we go up to "Analyze" at the top of the screen and click on the mouse. When the pull-down menu appears, we move the mouse down until the word "Correlate" is highlighted, move the mouse to the right until we highlight "Bivariate," and then release the mouse button. Once again, the two-box box appears, and we must move the three variables we want to analyze to the right box and then click on "OK." We now have a table that gives us the intercorrelations among these variables, which we can print out by going to "File" at the top of the screen, highlighting "Print," and then releasing the mouse button (see Figure A.4). The first number in each cell of the table tells us the Pearson *r* for a particular pair of variables (this number is 1 when a variable is correlated with itself), and the third

Identifying variables to be analyzed

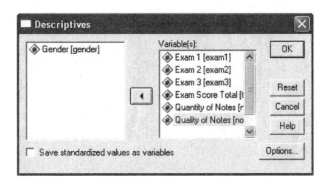

Correlations among
Exam Score Total,
Quantity of Notes, and
Quality of Notes

Correlations

		Exam Score Total	Quantity of Notes	Quality of Notes
Exam Score Total	Pearson Correlation	1	.323	.425
	Sig. (2-tailed)	.	.241	.114
	N	15	15	15
Quantity of Notes	Pearson Correlation	.323	1	.777**
	Sig. (2-tailed)	.241	.	.001
	N	15	15	15
Quality of Notes	Pearson Correlation	.425	.777**	1
	Sig. (2-tailed)	.114	.001	.
	N	15	15	15

** Correlation is significant at the 0.01 level (2-tailed).

number tells us the number of people for whom the r has been calculated. The middle number tells us the probability (p) that we would obtain an r that high if the two variables were *not* correlated in the overall population from which the sample has been drawn.

We'll use a significance level (α) of 0.05 for all of our analyses here (we'll ignore the 0.01 that appears in Figure A.4). Any p value that is *less* than this significance level indicates that the variables probably *are* correlated in the population from which our sample has been drawn. For example, the correlations between Exam Score Total and the Quantity and Quality of Notes are .323 and .425, respectively. Although these correlations are in the low-to-moderate range, the p values associated with them (.241 and .114) tell us that we might get correlations this high by chance when the two variables are actually unrelated in the overall population. (With a much larger sample size, such correlations would certainly be statistically significant. Our small sample size is probably leading us to make Type I errors here.) Now let's look at the correlation between Quantity of Notes and Quality of Notes. This correlation is .777, which has an associated probability of 0.001. This r is statistically significant: Students who take more notes also take better notes. We must be careful, however, that we don't conclude that there is a causal relationship here: Taking more notes does not necessarily cause a student to take better ones, nor does taking better ones cause a student to take more of them. Correlational data alone *never* allows us to draw clear-cut conclusions about cause-and-effect relationships.

COMPUTING INFERENTIAL STATISTICS

We have already ventured into inferential statistics. When we looked at the probabilities that our correlation coefficients occurred by chance for a set of possibly unrelated variables, we were drawing inferences. But now let's do so intentionally. Let's see if there are any gender differences in the test performance of males and females. To find out, we need to perform a t-test between the two groups. Once again, we go up to "Analyze," and this time we highlight "Compare Means" and then "Independent Samples T Test." A box similar to that shown in Figure A.3 appears, but this one has three boxes within it. We move our dependent variable (Exam Score Total) into the "Test Variable(s)" box and our independent variable (Gender) into the "Factor" box. Next, we click on the "Define Groups" button and tell the computer that a value of "1" puts a person in Group 1 (the males) and a value of "2" puts a person in Group 2 (the females). We click on the "Continue" button and then click on "OK." We get tables that provide descriptive statistics for the two groups, information about whether the variances of the two groups are equivalent, and results of t-tests. We can, of course, print out these tables (see Figure A.5). As you can see, the males are a significantly more variable group than the females, and so the computer has calculated two ts, one based on the assumption of equal variances and another based on the assumption of unequal variances. We will, of course, look at the second t, which is .055. This value indicates that the two groups are probably not different in their overall exam performance (the p value is .957). (You can find explanations for the other numbers in this table in most elementary statistics textbooks.)

We have room for one final statistical analysis. Let's say we want to know if the students performed differently on the three exams they took during the semester. To compare three means for

Group Statistics

	Gender	N	Mean	Std. Deviation	Std. Error Mean
Exam Score Total	Male	7	117.6429	16.38524	6.19304
	Female	8	117.2500	9.76418	3.45216

Independent Samples Test

		Levene's Test for Equality of Variances	
		F	Sig.
Exam Score Total	Equal variances assumed	8.335	.013
	Equal variances not assumed		

Independent Samples Test

		t-test for Equality of Means					95% Confidence Interval of the Difference	
		t	df	Sig. (2-tailed)	Mean Difference	Std. Error Difference	Lower	Upper
Exam Score Total	Equal variances assumed	.057	13	.955	.3929	6.85139	-14.40868	15.19439
	Equal variances not assumed	.055	9.520	.957	.3929	7.09022	-15.51373	16.29945

FIGURE A.5

Computing t to determine if males and females have different total exam scores

the same group of students, we would ideally want to conduct a repeated-measures analysis of variance. Unfortunately, the version of SPSS we are using here performs only between-subjects ANOVAs, so we will have to settle for three paired-samples t-tests.

To conduct our t-tests, we go back up to "Analyze," move the mouse down to highlight "Compare Means" and then move it to the right to highlight "Paired-Samples t Tests." We release the mouse button. Once again, we see our familiar two-box box. This time we simultaneously highlight Exam 1 and Exam 2 and then click on the right-arrow button. Next, we highlight Exam 1 and Exam 3 and then again click the right arrow. We do the same thing for the Exam 2 and Exam 3 pair. We now have three pairs of variables in the right-hand box. We click on "OK" and print out the three tables that the analysis generates (Figure A.6 on the next page). The first table gives us descriptive statistics; we've seen most of these before, but the column for standard error of the mean is new. We also see Pearson rs for the three pairs. We're most interested in the t values for three pairs of exam scores, which are shown in the seventh column in the bottom table. None of these ts is statistically significant at our significance level of .05 (see the rightmost column), although the Exam 1–Exam 3 pair comes close, with a p value of .087.

We have merely scratched the surface of what SPSS can offer. We have ignored some of the values in the statistical tables we've presented. And we haven't even touched on SPSS's graphing capabilities. We urge you to explore SPSS for yourself to discover the many analyses it can perform and the many graphical displays it can create.

Paired Samples Statistics

		Mean	N	Std. Deviation	Std. Error Mean
Pair 1	Exam 1	39.9667	15	4.15102	1.07179
	Exam 2	39.4667	15	5.42388	1.40044
Pair 2	Exam 1	39.9667	15	4.15102	1.07179
	Exam 3	38.0000	15	5.15128	1.33006
Pair 3	Exam 2	39.4667	15	5.42388	1.40044
	Exam 3	38.0000	15	5.15128	1.33006

Paired Samples Correlations

		N	Correlation	Sig.
Pair 1	Exam 1 & Exam 2	15	.388	.153
Pair 2	Exam 1 & Exam 3	15	.622	.013
Pair 3	Exam 2 & Exam 3	15	.814	.000

Paired Samples Test

		Paired Differences					t	df	Sig. (2-tailed)
		Mean	Std. Deviation	Std. Error Mean	95% Confidence Interval of the Difference				
					Lower	Upper			
Pair 1	Exam 1 - Exam 2	.5000	5.40089	1.39450	-2.4909	3.4909	.359	14	.725
Pair 2	Exam 1 - Exam 3	1.9667	4.14241	1.06956	-.3273	4.2607	1.839	14	.087
Pair 3	Exam 2 - Exam 3	1.4667	3.23329	.83483	-.3239	3.2572	1.757	14	.101

FIGURE A.6

Computing ts to determine if students performed differently on the three exams

REFERENCES

Abraham, E. P., Chain, E., Fletcher, C. M., Gardner, A. D., Heatley, N. G., Jennings, M. A., & Florey, H. W. (1941). Further observations on penicillin. *Lancet, 2,* 177–188.

Acheson, K. A., & Gall, M. D. (1992). *Techniques in the clinical supervision of teachers* (3rd ed.). New York: Longman.

Allen, E. M. (1960, November). Why are research grant applications disapproved? *Science, 132,* 1532–1534.

Altheide, D. L., & Johnson, J. M. (1994). Criteria for assessing interpretive validity in qualitative research. In N. K. Denzin & Y. S. Lincoln (Eds.), *Handbook of qualitative research* (pp. 485–499). Thousand Oaks, CA: Sage.

American Psychological Association (APA). (2001). *Publication manual of the American Psychological Association* (5th ed.). Washington, DC: Author.

Anderson, C. A., Lindsay, J. J., & Bushman, B. J. (1999). Research in the psychological laboratory: Truth or triviality? *Current Directions in Psychological Science, 8,* 3–9.

Barritt, L. (1986). Human science and the human image. *Phenomenology and Pedagogy, 4*(3), 14–21.

Bateman, W. L. (1990). *Open to question: The art of teaching and learning by inquiry.* San Francisco: Jossey-Bass.

Beck, C. T. (1990, January-February). The research critique: General criteria for evaluating a research report. *Journal of Gynecology and Neonatal Nursing, 19,* 18–22.

Benton, S. L. (1997). Psychological foundations of elementary writing instruction. In G. D. Phye (Ed.), *Handbook of academic learning: Construction of knowledge.* San Diego, CA: Academic Press.

Beyer, B. K. (1985). Critical thinking: What is it? *Social Education, 49,* 270–276.

Breisach, E. (1994). *Historiography: Ancient, medieval, and modern* (2nd ed.). Chicago: University of Chicago Press.

Campbell, D. T., & Fiske, D. W. (1959). Convergent and discriminant validation by the multitrait-multimethod matrix. *Psychological Bulletin, 56,* 81–105.

Campbell, D. T., & Stanley, J. C. (1963). Experimental and quasi-experimental designs for research on teaching. In N. L. Gage (Ed.), *Handbook of research on teaching* (pp. 171–246). Chicago: Rand McNally.

Chaatterjee, B. B., & Srivastava, A. K. (1982, April). A systematic method for drawing sociograms. *Perspectives in Psychological Research, 5,* 1–6.

Chain, E., Florey, H. W., Gardner, A. D., Heatley, N. G., Jennings, M. A., Orr-Ewing, J., & Sanders, A. G. (1940). Penicillin as a chemotherapeutic agent. *Lancet, 2,* 226.

Charmaz, K. (2000). Grounded theory: Objective and constructivist methods. In N. K. Denzin & Y. S. Lincoln (Eds.), *Handbook of qualitative research* (2nd ed., pp. 509–535). Thousand Oaks, CA: Sage.

Charmaz, K. (2002). Qualitative interviewing and grounded theory analysis. In J. F. Gubrium & J. A. Holstein (Eds.), *Handbook of interview research: Context and method.* Thousand Oaks, CA: Sage.

Chicago Manual of Style (15th ed.). (2003). Chicago: University of Chicago Press.

Coghill, R. D. (1944). Penicillin: Science's Cinderella. The background of penicillin production. *Chemical and Engineering News, 22,* 588–593.

Coghill, R. D., & Koch, R. S. (1945). Penicillin: A wartime accomplishment. *Chemical and Engineering News, 23,* 2310.

Cole, D. B., & Ormrod, J. E. (1995). Effectiveness of teaching pedagogical content knowledge through summer geography institutes. *Journal of Geography, 94,* 427–433

Creswell, J. W. (1998). *Qualitative inquiry and research design: Choosing among five traditions.* Thousand Oaks, CA: Sage.

Creswell, J. W. (2002). *Educational research: Planning, conducting, and evaluating quantitative and qualitative research.* Upper Saddle River, NJ: Merrill/Prentice Hall.

Cuca, J. M., & McLoughlin, W. J. (1987, May). Why clinical research grant applications fare poorly in review and how to recover. In *Preparing a research grant application to the National Institutes of Health: Selected articles* (a bulletin from the research branch of the Department of Health and Human Services). Washington, DC: Department of Health and Human Services. (Reprinted from *Clinical Investigation, 5,* pp. 55–58, 1987)

Deaver, C. M., Miltenberger, R. G., & Stricker, J. M. (2001). Functional analysis and treatment of hair twirling in a young child. *Journal of Applied Behavior Analysis, 34,* 535–538.

Delandshere, G., & Petrosky, A. R. (1998). Assessment of complex performances: Limitations of key measurement assumptions. *Educational Researcher, 27,* 14-24.

Dowson, M., & McInerney, D. M. (2001). Psychological parameters of students' social and work avoidance goals: A qualitative investigation. *Journal of Educational Psychology, 93,* 35–42.

Eaves, G. N. (1984, September). Preparation of the research-grant application: Opportunities and pitfalls. *Grants Magazine, 7,* 151.

Eisner, E. W. (1998). *The enlightened eye: Qualitative inquiry and the enhancement of educational practice.* Upper Saddle River, NJ: Merrill/Prentice Hall.

Elliott, D., & Stern, J. E. (Eds.). (1997). *Research ethics: A reader.* Hanover, NH: University Press of New England.

Ferguson, D. L., & Rosales-Ruiz, J. (2001). Loading the problem loader: The effects of target training and shaping on trailer-loading behavior of horses. *Journal of Applied Behavior Analysis, 34,* 409–424.

Fetterman, D. M. (1989). *Ethnography: Step by step.* Thousand Oaks, CA: Sage.

Fetterman, D. M. (1998). Webs of meaning: Computer and Internet resources for educational research and instruction. *Educational Researcher, 27*(3), 22–30.

Fleming, A. (1929). On the antibacterial action of cultures of a penicillium, with special reference to their use in the isolation of B. influenzae. *British Journal of Experimental Pathology, 10,* 226–236.

Flesch, R. (1974). *The art of readable writing.* New York: Harper & Row.

Forbes, M. L., Ormrod, J. E., Bernardi, J. D., Taylor, S. L., & Jackson, D. L. (1999). *Children's conceptions of space, as reflected in maps of their hometown.* Paper presented at the annual meeting of the American Educational Research Association, Montreal.

Gall, M. D., Borg, W. R., & Gall, J. P. (1996). *Educational research: An introduction* (6th ed.). White Plains, NY: Longman.

Gay, L. R., & Airasian, P. (2003). *Educational research: Competencies for analysis and application* (7th ed.). Upper Saddle River, NJ: Merrill/Prentice Hall.

Gibaldi, J. (1998). *MLA style manual and guide to scholarly publishing* (2nd ed.). New York: Modern Language Association.

Glaser, B. G. (1992). *Basics of grounded theory analysis.* Mill Valley, CA: Sociology Press.

Glaser, B. G., & Strauss, A. (1967). *The discovery of grounded theory.* Chicago: Aldine.

Glesne, C., & Peshkin, A. (1992). *Becoming qualitative researchers: An introduction.* White Plains, NY: Longman.

Good, R. (1993). More guidelines for reviewing research. *Journal of Research in Science Teaching, 30*(1), 1–2.

Greene, S., & Ackerman, J. M. (1995). Expanding the constructivist metaphor: A rhetorical perspective on literacy research and practice. *Review of Educational Research, 65,* 383–420.

Guba, E., & Lincoln, Y. S. (1988). Do inquiry paradigms imply inquiry methodologies? In D. M. Fetterman (Ed.), *Qualitative approaches to evaluation in education* (pp. 89-115). New York: Praeger.

Halpern, D. F. (1998). Teaching critical thinking for transfer across domains. *American Psychologist, 53,* 449–455.

Harwell, M. R., & Gatti, G. G. (2001). Rescaling ordinal data to interval data in educational research. *Review of Educational Research, 71,* 105–131.

Haskins, L., & Jeffrey, K. (1990). *Understanding quantitative history.* New York: McGraw-Hill.

Heck, A., Collins, J., & Peterson, L. (2001). Decreasing children's risk taking on the playground. *Journal of Applied Behavior Analysis, 34,* 349–352.

Historical statistics of the United States: Colonial times to 1970 (Part 1, bicentennial edition). (1975). Washington, DC: U.S. Department of Commerce.

Howe, K., & Eisenhardt, M. (1990). Standards for qualitative (and quantitative) research: A prolegomenon. *Educational Researcher, 19*(4), 2–9.

Huth, E. J. (1994). *Scientific style and format: The CBE manual for authors, editors, and publishers* (6th ed.). New York: Cambridge University Press.

Jackson, D. L. (1996). *Effects of training in self-generation on the quality of students' questions, class notes and examination scores.* Unpublished doctoral dissertation, University of Northern Colorado, Greeley.

Janos, P. M., & Robinson, N. M. (1985). Psychosocial development in intellectually gifted children. In F. D. Horowitz & M. O'Brien (Eds.), *The gifted and talented: Developmental perspectives.* Washington, DC: American Psychological Association.

Johnson, B. (2001). Toward a new classification of nonexperimental quantitative research. *Educational Researcher, 30*(2), 3–13.

Kahn, P. G. K., & Pompea, S. (1978, October 19). Nautiloid growth rhythms and dynamical evolution of the earth-moon system. *Nature, 275,* 606–611.

Kearns, K. C. (1994). *Dublin tenement life.* Dublin, Ireland: Gill & MacMillan.

Kellogg, R. T. (1994). *The psychology of writing.* New York: Oxford University Press.

Kinnick, V. (1989). *Learning fetal monitoring under three conditions of concept teaching.* Unpublished doctoral dissertation, University of Colorado, Boulder.

Kontos, S. (1999). Preschool teachers' talk, roles, and activity settings during free play. *Early Childhood Research Quarterly, 14*(3), 363–382.

Krathwohl, D. R. (1993). *Methods of educational and social science research: An integrated approach.* White Plains, NY: Longman.

Kvale, S. (1996). *InterViews: An introduction to qualitative research interviewing.* Thousand Oaks, CA: Sage.

Lather, P. (1991). *Getting smart: Feminist research and pedagogy with/in the postmodern.* New York: Routledge.

Lauer, J. M., & Asher, J. W. (1988). *Composition research: Empirical designs.* New York: Oxford University Press.

Leavenworth, P. S. (1998). "*The best title that Indians can claime . . .": Native agency and consent in the transferral of Penacook-Pawtucket land in the seventeenth century.* Unpublished master's thesis, University of New Hampshire, Durham.

Lewis, D. W. (1988, July). Inventing the electronic university. *College & Research Libraries, 49,* 291–304.

Lincoln, Y. S., & Guba, E. G. (1985). *Naturalistic inquiry.* Thousand Oaks, CA: Sage.

Locke, L. F., Spirduso, W. W., & Silverman, S. J. (1993). *Proposals that work: A guide for planning dissertations and grant proposals.* Thousand Oaks, CA: Sage.

Loftus, E. F., & Palmer, J. C. (1974). Reconstruction of automobile destruction: An example of the interaction between language and memory. *Journal of Verbal Learning and Verbal Behavior, 13,* 585–589.

Lowes, J. L. (1927). *The road to Xanadu.* Boston: Houghton Mifflin.

Lowes, J. L. (1955). *The road to Xanadu: A study in the ways of the imagination* (Rev. ed.). Boston: Houghton Mifflin.

Marius, R. (1989). *A short guide to writing about history.* New York: HarperCollins.

Marsh, H. W. (1990). Causal ordering of academic self-concept and academic achievement: A multiwave, longitudinal panel analysis. *Journal of Educational Psychology, 82,* 646–656.

Mason, R. D., & Lind, D. A. (1990). *Statistical techniques in business and economics* (7th ed.). Homewood, IL: Irwin.

Maurois, A. (1959). *The life of Alexander Fleming: Discoverer of penicillin.* New York: E. P. Dutton.

McCallin, R. C. (1988). *Knowledge application orientation, cognitive structure, and achievement.* Unpublished doctoral dissertation, University of Northern Colorado, Greeley.

McGraw, K. O., Tew, M. D., & Williams, J. E. (2000). The integrity of Web-delivered experiments: Can you trust the data? *Psychological Science, 11,* 502–506.

McGrew, K. S., Flanagan, D. P., Zeith, T. Z., & Vanderwood, M. (1997). Beyond *g*: The impact of *Gf-Gc* specific cognitive abilities research on the future use and interpretation of intelligence tests in the schools. *School Psychology Review, 26,* 189–210.

McKenzie, M. G. (2003). *Vocational science and the politics of independence: The Boston Marine Society, 1754–1812.* Unpublished doctoral dissertation, University of New Hampshire, Durham.

Medawar, P. B. (1979). *Advice to a young scientist.* New York: Harper & Row.

Miksa, F. L. (1987). *Research patterns and research libraries.* Dublin, OH: OCLC.

Milch-Reich, S., Campbell, S. B., Pelham, W. E., Jr., Connelly, L. M., & Geva, D. (1999). Developmental and individual differences in children's on-line representations of dynamic social events. *Child Development, 70,* 413–431.

Miller, S. M., Nelson, M. W., & Moore, M. T. (1998). Caught in the paradigm gap:

Qualitative researchers' lived experience and the politics of epistemology. *American Educational Research Journal, 35,* 377–416.

Mills, G. E. (2003). *Action research: A guide for the teacher researcher* (2nd ed.). Upper Saddle River, NJ: Merrill/Prentice Hall.

Mitchell, K. J. (1998). *Childhood sexual abuse and family functioning linked with eating and substance misuse: Mediated structural models.* Unpublished doctoral dissertation, University of Rhode Island, Kingston.

Moss, P. A. (1996). Enlarging the dialogue in educational measurement: Voices from interpretive research traditions. *Educational Researcher, 27*(1), 20–28, 43.

Neuman, W. L. (1994). *Social research methods: Qualitative and quantitative approaches* (2nd ed.). Boston: Allyn & Bacon.

Nichols, J. D. (1998). Multiple perspectives of collaborative research. *International Journal of Educational Reform, 7,* 150–157.

Novick, P. (1988). *That noble dream: The "objectivity question" and the American historical profession.* Cambridge, England: Cambridge University Press.

Ormrod, J. E. (2004). *Human learning* (4th ed.). Upper Saddle River, NJ: Merrill/Prentice Hall.

Ormrod, J. E., Jackson, D. L., Kirby, B., Davis, J., & Benson, C. (1999, April). *Cognitive development as reflected in children's conceptions of early American history.* Paper presented at the American Educational Research Association, Montreal.

Ormrod, J. E., Ormrod, R. K., Wagner, E. D., & McCallin, R. C. (1988). Reconceptualizing map learning. *American Journal of Psychology, 101,* 425–433.

Ormrod, R. K. (1974). *Adaptation in cultural ecosystems: Early 19th century Jamaica.* Unpublished doctoral dissertation, The Pennsylvania State University, University Park.

Ormrod, R. K., & Trahan, R. G. (1982). Can signs help visitors control their own behavior? *Trends, 19*(4), 25-27.

Ott, R. L., Larson, R., Rexroat, C., & Mendelhall, W. (1991). *Statistics: A tool for the social sciences* (5th ed.). Belmont, CA: Duxbury.

Peshkin, A. (1993). The goodness of qualitative research. *Educational Researcher, 22*(2), 23–29.

Polkinghorne, D. E. (1989). Phenomenological research methods. In R. S. Valle & S. Halling (Eds.), *Existential-phenomenological perspectives in psychology* (pp. 41–60). New York: Plenum.

Ramirez, I. L. (2001). *The relation of acculturation, criminal history, and social integration of Mexican American and non-Mexican students to assaults on intimate partners.* Unpublished doctoral dissertation, University of New Hampshire, Durham.

Rogelberg, S. G., & Luong, A. (1998). Nonresponse to mailed surveys: A review and guide. *Current Directions in Psychological Science, 7,* 60–65.

Schacter, D. L. (1999). The seven sins of memory: Insights from psychology and neuroscience. *American Psychologist, 54,* 182–203.

Schram, T. H. (2003). *Conceptualizing qualitative inquiry: Mindwork for fieldwork in education and the social sciences.* Upper Saddle River, NJ: Merrill/Prentice Hall.

Schwarz, N. (1999). Self-reports: How the questions shape the answers. *American Psychologist, 54,* 93–105.

Senders, V. L. (1958). *Measurement and statistics: A basic text emphasizing behavioral science.* New York: Oxford University Press.

Shaklee, J. M. (1998). *Elementary children's epistemological beliefs and understandings of science in the context of computer-mediated video conferencing with scientists.* Unpublished doctoral dissertation, University of Northern Colorado.

Shank, G. D. (2002). *Qualitative research: A personal skills approach.* Upper Saddle River, NJ: Merrill/Prentice Hall.

Shipman, S., & Shipman, V. C. (1985). Cognitive styles: Some conceptual, methodological, and applied issues. In E. W. Gordon (Ed.), *Review of research in education* (Vol. 12). Washington, DC: American Educational Research Association.

Silverman, D. (1993). *Interpreting qualitative data: Methods for analysing talk, text and interaction.* London: Sage.

Silverman, D., Masland, R., Saunders, M. G., & Schwab, R. S. (1970, June). Irreversible coma associated with electrocerebral silence. *Neurology, 20,* 525–533.

Smith, R. M. (1999). *Academic engagement of high school students with significant disabilities: A competence-oriented interpretation.* Unpublished doctoral dissertation, Syracuse University, Syracuse, New York.

Sobel, D. (2000). *Galileo's daughter.* New York: Penguin Books.

Solomon, R. I. (1949). An extension of control group design. *Psychological Bulletin, 46,* 137–150.

Stake, R. (1995). *The art of case study research.* Thousand Oaks, CA: Sage.

Stevens, S. S. (1946, June 7). On the theory of scales of measurement. *Science, 103,* 677–680.

Strauss, A., & Corbin, J. (1990). *Basics of qualitative research: Grounded theory procedures and techniques.* Thousand Oaks, CA: Sage.

Strauss, A., & Corbin, J. (1994). Grounded theory methodology: An overview. In N. K. Denzin & Y. S. Lincoln (Eds.), *Handbook of qualitative research* (pp. 273–285). Thousand Oaks, CA: Sage.

Strauss, A., & Corbin, J. (1998). *Basics of qualitative research: Techniques and procedures for developing grounded theory* (2nd ed.). Thousand Oaks, CA: Sage.

Strunk, W., & White, E. B. (1995). *The elements of style.* Needham Heights, MA: Allyn & Bacon.

Survey Research Center, Institute for Social Research at the University of Michigan. (1976). *Interviewer's manual* (Rev. ed.). Ann Arbor: Author.

Tennyson, R. D., & Cocchiarella, M. J. (1986). An empirically based instructional design theory for teaching concepts. *Review of Educational Research, 56,* 40–71.

Tesch, R. (1994). The contribution of a qualitative method: Phenomenological research. In M. Langenbach, C. Vaughn, & L. Aagaard (Eds.), *An introduction to educational research* (pp. 143–157). Needham Heights, MA: Allyn & Bacon.

Thrailkill, N. J. (1996). *Imagery-evoking and attention-attracting material as facilitators of learning from a lecture.* Unpublished doctoral dissertation, University of Northern Colorado, Greeley.

Toynbee, A. (1939–1961). *A study of history* (12 vols.). London: Oxford University Press, Royal Institute of International Affairs.

Trahan, R. G. (1978). *Social science research: Rocky Mountain National Park* (Contract agreement PX 1520-8-A529). Greeley, CO: Author.

Use of elegant statistics. (1987). *Research in Nursing and Health, 10,* iii.

Wolcott, H. F. (1994). *Transforming qualitative data: Description, analysis, and interpretation.* Thousand Oaks, CA: Sage.

Zambo, D. (2003). *Uncovering the conceptual representations of students with learning disabilities.* Unpublished doctoral dissertation, Arizona State University, Tempe.

INDEX